The Research Process

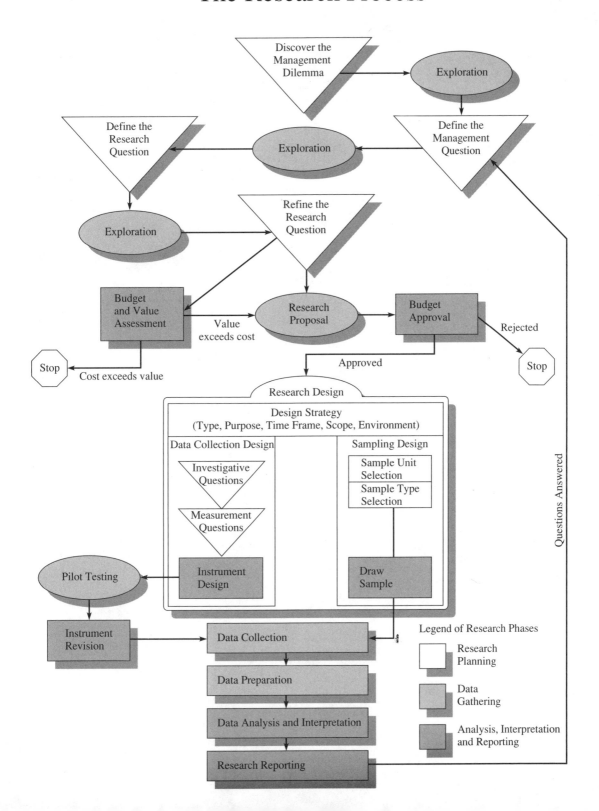

SIXTH EDITION

BUSINESS RESEARCH METHODS

THE IRWIN/MCGRAW-HILL SERIES

Operations And Decision Sciences

BUSINESS STATISTICS

Aczel, *Complete Business Statistics, Third Edition*

Bowerman and O'Connell, *Applied Statistics: Improving Business Processes, First Edition*

Bryant and Smith, *Practical Data Analysis: Case Studies in Business Statistics, Volumes I and II, First Edition*

Cooper and Schindler, *Business Research Methods, Sixth Edition*

Delurgio, *Forecasting Principles and Applications, First Edition*

Doane, Mathieson, and Tracy, *Visual Statistics, First Edition*

Duncan, *Quality Control & Industrial Statistics, Fifth Edition*

Gitlow, Oppenheim, and Oppenheim, *Quality Management: Tools and Methods for Improvement, Second Edition*

Hall, *Computerized Business Statistics, Fourth Edition*

Hanke and Reitsch, *Understanding Business Statistics, Second Edition*

Lind and Mason, *Basic Statistics for Business and Economics, Second Edition*

Mason and Lind, *Statistical Techniques in Business and Economics, Ninth Edition*

Merchant, Goffinet, Koehler, *Basic Statistics Using Excel, First Edition*

Neter, Kutner, Nachtsheim, and Wasserman, *Applied Linear Statistical Models, Fourth Edition*

Neter, Kutner, Nachtsheim, and Wasserman, *Applied Linear Regression Models, Third Edition*

Shin, *The Irwin Statistical Software Series: Minitab, SAS, SPSS Guides, Second Editions; Statgraphics, First Edition*

Siegel, *Practical Business Statistics, Third Edition*

Webster, *Applied Statistics for Business and Economics: An Essentials Version, Third Edition*

Wilson and Keating, *Business Forecasting, Third Edition*

QUANTITATIVE METHODS AND MANAGEMENT SCIENCE

Bodily, Carraway, Frey, Pfeifer, *Quantitative Business Analysis: Casebook, First Edition*

Bodily, Carraway, Frey, Pfeifer, *Quantitative Business Analysis: Text and Cases, First Edition*

Bonini, Hausman, and Bierman, *Quantitative Analysis for Business Decisions, Ninth Edition*

Hesse, *Managerial Spreadsheet Modeling and Analysis, First Edition*

Lofti and Pegels, *Decision Support Systems for Operations and Management Science, Third Edition*

Stevenson, *Introduction to Management Science, Second Edition*

Turban and Meredith, *Fundamentals of Management Science, Sixth Edition*

SIXTH EDITION

BUSINESS RESEARCH METHODS

Donald R. Cooper
Florida Atlantic University

Pamela S. Schindler
Wittenberg University

Boston   Burr Ridge, IL   Dubuque, IA   Madison, WI   New York   San Francisco   St. Louis
Bangkok   Bogotá   Caracas   Lisbon   London   Madrid
Mexico City   Milan   New Delhi   Seoul   Singapore   Sydney   Taipei   Toronto

Irwin/McGraw-Hill

A Division of The McGraw·Hill Companies

BUSINESS RESEARCH METHODS

This book is printed on acid-free paper.

1 2 3 4 5 6 7 8 9 0 DOC/DOC 90987

ISBN 0-256-23952-5

Vice president and editorial director: *Michael W. Junior*
Publisher: *Jeffrey J. Shelstad*
Senior sponsoring editor: *Scott Isenberg*
Senior developmental editor: *Gail Korosa*
Marketing manager: *Nelson Black*
Project manager: *Jim Labeots*
Production supervisor: *Michael McCormick*
Senior designer: *Crispin Prebys*
Compositor: *Precision Graphics*
Typeface: *10/12 Times Roman*
Printer: *R. R. Donnelley & Sons Company*

Library of Congress Cataloging-in-Publication Data

Cooper, Donald R.
    Business research methods / Donald R. Cooper, Pamela S. Schindler. —
  6th ed.
        p.   cm.
    Includes bibliographical references and index.
    ISBN 0-256-23952-5
    1. Industrial management—Research. I. Schindler, Pamela S.
  II. Title.
  HD30.4.E47 1998
  658'.0072—dc21   97-30873

http://www.mhhe.com

In loving memory

Chrissy Cooper
1973–1995

PREFACE

Business Research Methods has evolved often since its introduction in 1976. Technology has continued to transform information processing and managerial problem solving. And, as the field of research in organizations grew dramatically during the late 1970s and 1980s then matured during the 1990s, our textbook kept pace with industry changes and stayed on the leading edge of teaching pedagogy. We continue to deliver on those same promises in the sixth edition where *Business Research Methods* truly comes of age by again responding aggressively to adopter and reviewer suggestions.

We listen to you carefully. The result is greater relevancy for practicing managers, improved coverage of the research process in the business setting, and a textbook that spans the disciplines of business, providing breadth, depth, and serving as a valuable reference for post-course use.

As the leading text in this market, we wanted the sixth edition to exceed instructor expectations and student needs without altering the features you valued in the fifth edition. You'll still find:

- A balanced presentation of practical application and fundamental concepts.

- Timely coverage of news-making issues and concepts—in the cases, Bringing Research to Life vignettes, Close-Ups, and Key Terms.

- An indepth treatment of concepts, not cursory reviews.

- A comprehensive coverage of the field organized to optimize the flow of information to students.

- Appendices that offer extensive reference materials and specialized information for advanced students.

- Compatibility with the Irwin/McGraw-Hill software series.

In this edition, Pamela S. Schindler joins the team. She is a veteran of twenty-three years in the undergraduate classroom and more than two decades of supervising and conducting research for nonprofit, profit-driven, and governmental organizations. She brings a fresh perspective to the topics and a keen understanding of the visual and verbal learning styles of students. As a trusted user and reviewer of this text for the last three editions, I could not have chosen a more compatible partner—one who shares my strong interest in student learning and passion for research methods. Welcome, Pam.

Target Audience

Over the years, we have taught research and data analysis for MBAs, executive MBAs, doctoral students, and public managers. *Business Research Methods* is appropriate for MBA programs, MPA programs, programs with a cross-functional research emphasis, and undergraduate programs where students have a foundation in elementary statistics. The chapter-to-chapter readability consistently accommodates learners at all levels.

Features of the Sixth Edition

As you've come to expect with our revised editions, you'll also find numerous enrichments that enhance the learning experience for the student and the teaching experience for the classroom-focused teacher:

A stronger decision making emphasis

- Cases throughout the text and chapter examples emphasize a variety of management-related scenarios.
- Case discussions integrated into the body of the chapter cement key concepts early.
- Nineteen optional cases can be packaged with the text to assist with quantitative concepts and are identified at the end of appropriate chapters. The Bryant & Smith cases reference a data disk that instructor's may order (ISBN 0-256-15829-0).
- Bringing Research to Life (BRL) vignettes now appear in all chapters with a fuller integration of BRL concepts and issues in the body of each chapter.
- A continuing character in the BRL series has joined MindWriter as a manager who must juggle three different research-related roles: research provider, out-source research coordinator, and client.
- Case and BRL discussion continually emphasize the integrated nature of research methodology—critical for the execution of quality research projects.
- End-of-chapter questions directly address the BRL vignettes providing the professor and student with a lively discussion platform—similar to a mini-case but much richer in detail—as the vignette's characters and the MindWriter body of knowledge builds from chapter to chapter.
- A significantly revised *Instructor's Manual* offers enriched course design ideas, student projects, in-depth discussion of end-of-chapter exercises, new review questions, and PowerPoint slides.
- Ethical considerations for managers receive early introduction and chapter-level emphasis (Chapter 5) with additional integration within chapters and throughout the BRL vignettes.

Graphically enhanced and fully integrated Research Process Model

- The Research Process Model, along with accompanying tables, provides a practical guide to course and post-course use by students and managers conducting or supervising research. As such, it has received more emphasis as the foundation model of the text (Chapter 3).
- The Research Process Model is revisited throughout the book with newly introduced concepts tied to it both verbally and graphically.
- The Management-Research Question Hierarchy is more fully integrated into the model making the transition from theory to research instrument more understandable (Chapter 3).
- New model-related figures have been added along with improvements to the figures retained from the fifth edition.

Enhanced topical coverage

- Exploratory study applications are expanded in the discussion of research design (Chapter 6).
- Numerous graphical examples appear in the streamlined treatment of measurement (Chapter 7) and scaling (Chapter 8).
- Sampling examples and notation are updated (Chapter 9).
- An exciting new chapter on Secondary Data Sources (Chapter 10) boasts a powerful elec-

tronic search orientation and timely examples in the chapter Close-Up.

- Appendix A provides alternative search strategies and is duplicated on the text's WWW site with hot links.
- The WWW site offers updated sources and URLs for rapidly changing Internet material.
- A reorganized chapter on Survey Methods (Chapter 11) introduces a graphical model for the selection of data collection approaches so choices are more apparent and this step is more distinctly tied to the Research Process Model.
- A major reorganization of Instruments for Respondent Communication (Chapter 12) helps students recognize and follow a clearly defined instrument design process linking design decisions with issues in prior and subsequent chapters.
- Data warehousing and data mining update the chapter on Data Preparation and Preliminary Analysis (Chapter 15).
- Tables and figures for exploratory data analysis techniques receive new graphics, more cogent explanation, and current data examples (Chapter 15).
- New sections on the graphical techniques for quality control and improvement appear in an expanded chapter on Presenting Results: Written and Oral Reports (Chapter 19).

Acknowledgments

We are grateful to reviewers who helped us prepare the sixth edition. They were: Hamid Falatoon, University of Redlands; Frederick A. Grodecki, Lake Forrest Graduate School of Management; John Hanke, Eastern Washington University; Elizabeth E. Regimbal, Cardinal Stritch College; Randi L. Sims, Nova Southeastern University; and Craig Swenson, University of Phoenix (Utah). Thank you for your insightful contributions.

A few people deserve special thanks. Jay S. Mendell, Florida Atlantic University, continued as the creator of our distinctive BRL vignettes, and contributed Chapter 10 and Appendix A. Many adopters noted the humor and vitality that the vignettes add by breathing "real" life into research. John Hanke, Eastern Washington University, assisted with statistical revisions in several chapters. Paul D. Cooper, a graphic designer from Arizona State University, created a contemporary cover design that reflects the book's direction and focus. C. William Emory leaves with us a legacy of knowledge and dedication to research methods. We will miss you, Bill.

We have the utmost respect for Gail Korosa at Irwin/McGraw-Hill. As Senior Developmental Editor, her knowledge of the market, keen insight into packaging options and features, and coordination skills were essential for keeping this edition on target. She was always there with an uncanny ability to fix things and a word of encouragement. We thank Scott Isenberg, our Editor, for his valor in fighting unwinnable bureaucratic battles and remaining dignified in defeat. We appreciate the work of the production team in bringing this effort to culmination but particularly Pat Herbst, our copy editor, who brought a new level of clarity to the exposition.

We remain indebted to those who helped with the first five editions of the book: J. K. Bandyopedyay, Phillip Beukema, Alan D. Carey, Francis Connelly, Thomas J. Dudley, William J. Evans, Hamid Falatoon, Robert Fetter, Stewart E. Fleige, Claude McMillan, Ralph J. Melaragno, Hamid Noori, Walter Nord, J. Paul Peter, Harold F. Rahmlow, Elizabeth E. Regimbal, Pamela S. Schindler, Perri J. Stinson, Alexander Voloatta, and Richard A. Wald.

Donald R. Cooper

BRIEF CONTENTS

CONTENTS

PART IV

ANALYSIS AND PRESENTATION OF DATA

PART I
INTRODUCTION TO BUSINESS RESEARCH

CHAPTER 1 RESEARCH IN BUSINESS

 CHAPTER NAVIGATION

BRINGING RESEARCH TO LIFE

WHY STUDY RESEARCH?

THE VALUE OF ACQUIRING SKILLS

WHAT IS RESEARCH?

WHAT IS GOOD RESEARCH?

THE MANAGER-RESEARCHER RELATIONSHIP

SUMMARY

KEY TERMS

DISCUSSION QUESTIONS

REFERENCE NOTES

SUGGESTED READINGS

BRINGING RESEARCH TO LIFE

"Jason Henry? I'm Myra Wines."

"Yes, come in, Ms. Wines. We'll meet here in the conference/living room. Watch your step around the cables, though."

The stylish, middle-aged woman found her way among several crates of partially unpacked computer systems, stepped over a strip of duct tape that held several cables securely in place on the carpet, pushed aside a pile of accounting books and tax manuals that had been stacked on the sofa, seated herself as gracefully as she could among the heap of books, electronic gear, and unopened paper boxes, then snapped open a briefcase to produce a miniature cassette recorder, which she clicked on. "If this makes you nervous, I'll turn it off," she said. "I was a TV investigative reporter for fifteen years, and my rule was to run a recording until they told me to turn it off. Old habits die hard . . . especially ones that have gotten you out of a dozen jams."

"Turn it off then," said the younger man, curtly. "It doesn't make me nervous, but I fail to see the need of it. How long have you been out of TV? Were you in TV down here? You must have been on local, not network, because I don't recognize you. As I told you when you called, we're just establishing our Florida office. Of course, you can see that." All this came out in one breath.

Myra picked up the thread of the monologue. "You moved here from Ottawa where you and your wife were employed by the United Nations. Your wife is a doctor in public health. You are an accountant turned business economist and consultant. You both graduated from college in California. You have opened several corporations here in Florida—to do auditing, economic analysis, epidemiological consulting, and diversified business research. I don't know why you need four separate corporations, but that's your business. . . . What have I missed?"

"My wife did a weekly public service TV program for distribution by the United Nations. She speaks four languages."

"I knew that. A TV producer in Toronto who works for United Nations TV alerted me to your move to Florida."

"Then that covers everything, doesn't it," he said with asperity, "except a birthmark above my knee."

"Your right knee," she said positively. Panic flickered in his eyes, and quickly she added, "Just a guess. Fifty-fifty chance of being right, you know."

That broke the tension. He chuckled. "I have a gold filling in one of my teeth. Can you tell me which one?"

Now she laughed. "I never bluff against such high odds as 32-to-1."

They both smiled. Then he killed the merriment by adding, "The odds would be 31-to-1, by the way, not 32-to-1. There would be one right answer and thirty-one wrong. Obviously, that makes the odds 31-to-1."

"How many computers do you have?" she asked, changing the subject.

"Counting the portables, five, plus several dumb terminals. Plus three printers and one fax for incoming and one for outgoing. And a voice-mail system and a pager. I am networking all of this together, as you can see. I have had six phone lines run in here, though I need only four right now. I took two extra, because I don't want the phone company coming in once I am all set up. We don't want the hassle of separate office space so we're locating the office on the main floor of our residence. Most of my clients will never see the office, so you'll have to excuse the mess. As far as my clients in Phoenix, Butte, and Ottawa know, I am working out of the classiest suite in this city's best office building, because faxes and phone calls and electronic mail are all the contact they have with me. I'll rethink the office if we add teleconferencing."

"Well. . . ," she said doubtfully.

"Yes, it's quite a few computers. But I'm your basic unapologetic computer jockey. I believe that you find the truth by crunching the numbers. I believe that. I really do."

"I don't agree. I'm your basic ex-TV reporter turned PR manager. I believe you get the truth by

(continued)

staying in touch with people, watching world events, seeing the big picture, and digging for revealing details. I have four phone lines—one each for a fax and an answering machine, one for a computer that I use to dial into commercial online databases, and two additional phones so I can talk to two people at the same time. I have my own domestic incoming/outgoing 800 number, and if I don't run up a thousand dollar a month long-distance bill for international calls, I know I'm not living right."

"Really? I find it difficult to believe that being an ex-reporter is so very lucrative?"

"No, it isn't," she admitted with a chuckle. "After fifteen years the station told me I needed a face-lift, and when I said no, they canned me. Just like that. I got the scariest lawyer in town—someone so vicious I had once run a week-long exposé of him—and he got me a terrific settlement. I picked up a few thousand a month by giving lectures to conventioneers. One of my best talks was 'The Angry Consumer.' I always included lots of facts that were absolutely up-to-date, because I was— and am—in daily touch with consumer advocates in every state capital, plus D.C., Ottawa, and even Tokyo and London."

"Is it all opinion and anecdote, or do you have some substantiating statistics?"

"My phone bill is astronomic."

"So it's anecdotal; that's what you're saying."

"If that's what you want to call it," she declared with a tinge of crankiness. "Anyway, to turn a long story into a brief audio bite, after one of my particularly hard-hitting talks, one member of the audience approached me, asked a lot of questions about my laptop computer, which I used to control my slide show. It turns out she was a headhunter looking for a consumer affairs manager of the company whose computer I use, MindWriter. Ultimately, after several interviews, they made me an offer I couldn't refuse."

"I know the brand. It's good equipment at a good price, but if it breaks down, you're in trouble according to the computer magazines. However, I have no firsthand evidence the magazines are accurate."

"We do have some concerns about customer satisfaction especially in product service. The corporate higher-ups have assigned me my first task— assessing customer satisfaction, or dissatisfaction, as it may be. There is a meeting next week in Austin, Texas, to discuss the background and preliminaries. I've been told to bring my ideas and my 'number cruncher.'"

"And who would that be?" inquired Jason.

"You, I hope. I'll level with you. I am not a numbers person."

"I know that. You miscounted your telephone lines a minute ago. Fax. Answering machine. Dial-up databases. Two for personal calls. That makes five. You said four."

She flushed and counted silently to ten. This young man may have lots of numbers knowledge, she thought, but he certainly had not learned to be tactful. "Then you know what I'm talking about," she said a little too sharply. "Well, I would really like to impress the folks in Texas, this being my first project, but not a soul in my office can be counted as a number cruncher and I can't show up at the meeting without one."

"I know something about customer research, and you're right to be nervous. . . ."

"Not nervous. Properly concerned."

"Concerned then. Have it your way. You are right to be concerned. The first step will be to listen carefully and discover exactly what facts management has gathered, what they are concerned about, what the problem is from their point of view, what the problem really is at various levels of abstraction. . . ."

"Listening to people. Discussing. Looking at things from different viewpoints. The kind of thing I am very good at. . . ."

"Right. And after we hear them out, we come to what I am good at: Measurement. Scaling. Survey design. Sampling the customers. Finally we would have to collaborate on the report of results. . . ."

"To which we would each contribute. Right?"

"Right, that's what collaborate means."

"I have two tickets to Austin for next Wednesday. Can you break away from all of this unpacking and cabling and fly over with me?"

"Sure. We'll work out the money details later. OK?"

"OK. My source in Toronto says you are intelligent, prickly, and pigheaded, inclined to be overly left-brained and intolerant, but dependable, reasonably priced, and respectful of your elders. I think we'll get along OK."

"I am willing to proceed on that hypothesis. We'll certainly know if we can work together by the time we return from Texas."

WHY STUDY RESEARCH?

Assume for the moment that you are the chairperson of the academic department in which you are majoring. As the head of this department you are responsible for chairing the committee that selects the textbook for the course in business research methodology. What will you do? Where will you start? Try another decision-making scenario: You are the manager chef of your favorite full-service restaurant. (Taco Bell doesn't qualify here; think of something else.) You are experiencing significant turnover in your waiter/waitress pool, and long time customers have been commenting that the friendly atmosphere that has historically drawn them to your door is changing. Where will you start to solve this problem?

The study of research methods provides you with the knowledge and skills you need to solve the problems and meet the challenges of a fast-paced decision-making environment. Business research courses are a recognition that students preparing to manage business, not-for-profit, and public organizations—in all functional areas— need training in a disciplined process for conducting an inquiry related to a management dilemma. Three factors stimulate an interest in a scientific approach to decision making: (1) the manager's increased need for more and better information, (2) the availability of improved techniques and tools to meet this need, and (3) the resulting information overload if discipline is not employed in the process.

During the last two decades, we have witnessed dramatic changes in the business environment. Emerging from a historically economic role, the business organization has evolved in response to the social and political mandates of national public policy, explosive technology growth, and continuing innovations in global communications. These changes have created new knowledge needs for the manager and new publics to consider when evaluating any decision. Other knowledge demands have arisen from problems with mergers, trade policies, protected markets, technology transfers, and macroeconomic savings-investment issues.

The trend toward complexity has increased the risk associated with business decisions, making it more important to have a sound information base. Each of the factors listed below, which characterize the complex business decision-making environment, demands that managers have more and better information on which to base decisions:

- There are more variables to consider in every decision.
- More knowledge exists in every field of management.
- Global and domestic competition is more vigorous, with many businesses downsizing to refocus on primary competencies, reduce costs, and make competitive gains.

- The quality of theories and models to explain tactical and strategic results is improving.
- Government continues to show concern with all aspects of society, becoming increasingly aggressive in protecting these various publics.
- The explosive growth of company sites on the World Wide Web and company publications via desktop and electronic publishing have brought the prospect of extensive new arrays of information—but information quality is increasingly suspect.
- Workers, shareholders, customers, and the general public are demanding to be included in company decision making; they are better informed and more sensitive to their own self-interests than ever before.
- Organizations are increasingly practicing **data mining**, learning to extract meaningful knowledge from volumes of data contained within **internal databases**.
- Computer advances have allowed businesses to create the architecture for **data warehousing**, electronic storehouses where vast arrays of collected, integrated data are ready for mining.
- The power and ease of use of today's computer have given us the capability to analyze data to deal with today's complex managerial problems.
- Techniques of quantitative analysis take advantage of increasingly powerful computing capabilities.
- The number and power of the tools used to conduct research have increased, commensurate with the growing complexity of business decisions.
- Communication and measurement techniques within research have been enhanced.

To do well in such an environment, you will need to understand how to identify quality information and to recognize the solid, reliable research on which your high-risk decisions as a manager can be based. You also will need to know how to conduct such research. Developing these skills requires understanding of scientific method as it applies to the managerial decision-making environment. This book addresses your needs as an information processor.

THE VALUE OF ACQUIRING SKILLS

You can profit by having research skills in at least five situations.

1. As a decision maker you'll often feel the need for more information before selecting a course of action (see Case 1). Your options are limited if there is no one to whom you can delegate this task. You either make an intuitive judgment without gathering additional information, or you gather the data yourself with some reasonable level of skill. Gathering information may involve data mining existing databases and information sources or collecting new information. At the early levels of your career in management, when your experience is limited and your intuitive judgment less reliable, it should be obvious which option is better.

2. In a second instance, you may be called on to do a research study for a higher-level executive. Such a task, often coming early in your career, can be seen as a career-boosting opportunity; it can be the chance to make a favorable impression on that executive (see Cases 1, 2, and 3).

3. The third scenario has you buying research services from others or evaluating proposals for research prepared by others. If you can understand the research design proposed and adequately judge the quality of the planned activities and the likelihood that such activities will assist you in making a decision, you can save your organization both time and money (see "Bringing Research to Life" at the beginning of this chapter).

4. Because much decision making relies on using information collected during prior research projects, with research skills you will be able to deal professionally with the fourth scenario: evaluating the applicability of prior research to assist in resolving a current management dilemma (see "Bringing Research to Life" and Case 4).

5. A fifth reason to study research methods is so that you may establish a career as a research specialist. As a specialized function, research offers attractive career opportunities, especially in financial analysis, marketing research, operations research, public relations, and human resources management. Job opportunities for research specialists exist in all fields of management and in all industries (see "Bringing Research to Life").

WHAT IS RESEARCH?

Rather than give you a template-like definition of research in the managerial setting, we'll begin with a few examples of management problems involving decision making based on information gathering. From each of these illustrations, we can abstract the essence of research. How is it carried out? What can it do? And what should it not be expected to do? As you read the four cases, be thinking about the possible range of situations for conducting business research, and try answering the following questions:

- What is the decision-making dilemma facing the manager?
- What must the researcher accomplish?

CASE 1

You work for a corporation that is considering the acquisition of a toy manufacturer. The senior vice president for development asks you to head a task force to investigate six companies that are potential candidates. You assemble a team composed of representatives from the relevant functional areas. Pertinent data are collected from public sources because of the sensitive nature of the project. You examine all of the following: company annual reports, articles in business journals, trade magazines, newspapers, financial analysts' assessments, and company advertisements. The team members then develop summary profiles of the candidate firms based on the characteristics gleaned from the sources. The final report highlights the opportunities and problems that acquisition of the target firm would bring to all areas of the business.

CASE 2

You are the business manager for a large group of physicians specializing in nuclear medicine and imaging. A prominent health insurance organization has contacted you to promote a new cost containment program. The doctors' committee to whom you will make a recommendation will have a narrow enrollment window for their decision. If they choose to join, they will agree to a reduced fee schedule in exchange for easier filing procedures, quicker reimbursement, and listing on a physicians' referral network. If they decline, they will continue to deal with their patients and the insurance carrier in the current manner. You begin your investigation by mining data from patient files to learn how many are using this carrier, frequency of care visits, complexity of filings, and so on. You then consult insurance industry data to discover how many potential patients in your area use this care plan or similar care plans with alternative insurance carriers, and the likelihood of a patient choosing or switching doctors to find one that subscribes to the proposed program. You attempt to confirm your data with information from professional and association journals. Based on this information, you develop a profile that details the number of patients, overhead, and potential revenue realized by choosing to join the plan.

CASE 3

A paint manufacturer is having trouble maintaining profits. The owner believes inventory management is a weak area of the company's operations. In this industry, the many paint colors, types of paint, and container sizes make it easy for a firm to accumulate large inventories and still be unable to fill customer orders. The owner asks you to make recommendations. You look into the present warehousing and shipping operations and find excessive sales losses and delivery delays because of out-of-stock conditions. An informal poll of customers confirms your impression. You suspect the present inventory database and reporting system do not provide the prompt, usable information needed for appropriate production decisions.

Based on this supposition, you familiarize yourself with the latest inventory management techniques in a local college library. You ask the warehouse manager to take an accurate inventory, and you review the incoming orders for the last year. In addition, the owner shows you the production runs of the last year and his method for assessing the need for a particular color or paint type.

Modeling the last year of business using production, order, and inventory management techniques, you choose the method that provides the best theoretical profit. You run a pilot line using the new control methodology. After two months, the data show a much lower inventory and a higher order fulfillment rate. You recommend that the owner adopt the new inventory method.

CASE 4

You work for the alumni association of a private university. The university is eager to develop closer ties with its aging alumni, to provide strong stimuli to encourage increased donations, and to induce older, nontraditional students to

(continued)

return to the university to supplement enrollment. The president's office is considering starting a retirement community geared toward university alumni and asks your association to assess the attractiveness of the proposal from an alumni viewpoint. Your director asks you to divide the study into four parts.

Phase 1. First you are to report on the number of alumni who are in the appropriate age bracket, the rate of new entries per year, and the actuarial statistics for the group. This information allows the director to assess whether the project is worth continuing.

Phase 2. Your early results reveal there are sufficient alumni to make the project feasible. The next step in the study is to describe the social and economic characteristics of the target alumni group. You review gift statistics, analyze job titles, and assess home location and values. In addition, you review files from the last five years to see how alumni responded when they were asked about their income bracket. You are able to describe the alumni group for your director when you finish.

Phase 3. It is evident that the target alumni can easily afford a retirement community as proposed. The third phase of the study is to explain the characteristics of alumni who would be interested in a university-related retirement community. For this phase, you engage the American Association of Retired Persons (AARP) and a retirement community developer. In addition, you search for information on senior citizens from the federal government. From the developer you learn what characteristics of retirement community planning and construction are most attractive to retirees. From AARP you learn the main service and features that potential retirees look for in a retirement community. From the government publications you learn regulations and recommendations for operating retirement communities and a full range of descriptive information on the typical retirement community dweller. You make an extensive report to both the alumni director and the university president. The report covers the number of eligible alumni, their social and economic standings, and the characteristics of those who would be attracted by the retirement community.

Phase 4. The report excites the university president. She asks for one additional phase to be completed. She needs to predict the number of alumni who would be attracted to the project so she can adequately plan the size of the community. At this point, you call on the business college's research methods class for help in designing a questionnaire for the alumni. By providing telephones and funding, you arrange for the class to conduct a survey among a random sample of the eligible alumni population. In addition, you have the class devise a second questionnaire for alumni who will become eligible in the next 10 years. Using the data collected, you can predict the initial demand for the community and estimate the growth in demand over the next 10 years. You submit your final report to the director and the president.

What Is the Dilemma Facing the Manager?

The dilemma facing the manager is fairly well defined in the four cases. Let's see how carefully you read and understood them. In Case 1 the manager, the senior vice president for development, must make a proposal to the president or possibly the board of directors about whether to acquire a toy manufacturer, and if one is to be acquired, which one of the six which were studied is the best candidate. In Case 2 the physicians in the group must decide whether to join the proposed managed health care plan of one of their primary insurers. In Case 3 the owner of the paint manufacturer must decide on whether to implement a new inventory management system. In Case 4 the president must propose to the university's board of directors whether to fund the development of a retirement community. How did you do? If you didn't come to the same conclusion about the dilemma, reread the cases before proceeding, to catch what you missed.

In real life, management dilemmas are not always so clearly defined. In the case of MindWriter (the "Bringing Research to Life" vignette), Myra Wines knows there is concern about customer satisfaction, but her personal positive experience gives her no clues about what is causing management's concern. Jason Henry has read an article in the business press that implied after-purchase service might be to blame. In Case 3, rather than pinpointing the problem as one of inventory management, the paint manufacturer's owner could have faced several interactive phenomena: (1) a strike by the teamsters impacting inventory delivery to retail and wholesale customers, (2) the development of a new paint formula offering superior coverage but requiring a relatively scarce ingredient to manufacture thereby affecting production rates, (3) a fire that destroyed the primary loading dock of the main shipping warehouse in the Midwest, or (4) the simultaneous occurrence of all three events. As the research process starts with a manager's decision-making task, accurately defining the dilemma is paramount but often difficult. We address this issue in Chapter 3.

What Must the Researcher Accomplish?

The types of study the four cases represent can be classified as reporting, descriptive, explanatory, or predictive.

Reporting   Case 1 and the first phase of Case 4 illustrate a **reporting study**. At the most elementary level, an inquiry may be made only to provide an account or summation of some data, perhaps the generation of some statistics. The task may be quite simple and the data readily available. At other times, the information may be difficult to find. A reporting study calls for knowledge and skill with information sources and gatekeepers of information sources. Such a study usually requires little inference or conclusion drawing. In Case 1 the researcher needs to know what information should be evaluated to value a company. In the study of management, this knowledge would be acquired primarily in courses in financial management, accounting, and marketing. Knowing the type of information needed, the researcher in Case 1 identifies sources of information, like trade press articles and annual reports. Because of the possible effect of the toy manufacturer evaluation on the stock prices of the conglomerate instigating the study and each toy company, only public sources are used. Other reporting studies of a less sensitive nature might have the researcher interviewing source gatekeepers. In Case 4, for example, interviewing the director of local retirement facilities might have revealed other sources to include in the search. Such an expert is considered a gatekeeper. Early in your career, identifying gate-keepers for your firm and industry is critical to success as a manager.

Purists claim that reporting studies do not qualify as research, although carefully gathered data can have great value. Others argue that at least one form, investigative reporting, has a great deal in common with widely accepted qualitative and clinical research.[1] A research design does not have to be complex and require inferences for a project to be called research. In the early part of your career, you will likely be asked to perform a number of reporting studies. Many managers consider execution of such studies an excellent way for new employees to become familiar with their employer and its industry.

Descriptive　　Case 2 and the second phase of Case 4 illustrate a **descriptive study**. Descriptive studies try to discover answers to the questions *who*, *what*, *when*, *where*, and sometimes *how*. The researcher attempts to describe or define a subject, often by creating a profile of a group of problems, people, or events. Such studies may involve the collection of data and the creation of a distribution of the number of times the re-searcher observes a single event or characteristic (known as a **research variable**), or they may involve relating the interaction of two or more variables. In Case 2, the re-searcher must present data that reveals who is affiliated with the insurer, who uses managed health care programs (both doctors and patients), the general trends in use of imaging technology in diagnosing illness or injury severity; and the relationship of patient characteristics, doctor referrals, and technology use patterns.

Descriptive studies may or may not have the potential for drawing powerful in-ferences. Organizations that maintain databases of their employees, customers, and suppliers already have significant data to conduct descriptive studies using internal information. Yet many firms that have such data files do not mine them regularly for the decision-making insight they might provide. In the MindWriter vignette, Myra Wines could mine numerous company databases for insight into the nature and num-ber of service-related problems arising after purchase and, similarly, for information about product use inquiries. A database generated by warranty registration cards could reveal significant data concerning purchaser characteristics, as well as pur-chase location and product use behavior. A descriptive study, however, does not ex-plain why an event occurred or why the variables interact the way they do.

The descriptive study is popular in business research because of its versatility across disciplines. In not-for-profit corporations and other organizations, descriptive investigations have a broad appeal to the administrator and policy analyst for plan-ning, monitoring, and evaluating. In this context, *how* questions address issues such as quantity, cost, efficiency, effectiveness, and adequacy.[2]

Explanatory　　Academics have debated the relationship between the next two types of studies, explanatory and predictive, in terms of which precedes the other. Both types of research are grounded in theory, and theory is created to answer *why* and *how* questions. For our purposes, an **explanatory study** goes beyond description and at-tempts to explain the reasons for the phenomenon that the descriptive study only observed. Case 3 and the third phase of Case 4 represent explanatory studies. The researcher uses theories or at least hypotheses to account for the forces that caused a certain phenomenon to occur. In Case 3, believing the problem with paint stockouts is the result of inventory management, the owner asks the researcher to detail warehousing and shipping processes. This would be a descriptive study if it had stopped here. But if problems in the processes could be linked with sales losses due to an inability to make timely deliveries to retail or wholesale customers, then an explanatory study would emerge. The researcher tests this hypothesis by modeling the last year of business using the relationships between processes and results.

Predictive   If we can provide a plausible explanation for an event after it has occurred, it is desirable to be able to predict when and in what situations the event will occur. A **predictive study**, the fourth type, is just as rooted in theory as explanation. The aviation industry may be interested in explaining the radiation risks for flight crews and passengers from the sun and stars. The variables might include altitude, proximity of air routes to the poles, time of year, and aircraft shielding. Perhaps the relations among the four variables explain the radiation risk variable. This type of study often calls for a high order of inference making. Why, for example, would a flight at a specified altitude at one time of year not produce so great a radiation risk to the airliner's occupants as the same flight in another season? The answer to such a question would be valuable in planning air routes. It also would contribute to the development of a better theory of the phenomenon. In business research, prediction is found in studies conducted to evaluate specific courses of action or to forecast current and future values.

The final phase of Case 4 is example of prediction. The researcher is asked to predict for the president the success of the proposed retirement facility for alumni based on the number of applicants for residency the project will attract. This prediction will be based on the explanatory hypothesis that alumni frequent programs and projects sponsored by the university because of an association they maintain between images of youthfulness and mental and physical stimulation with their university experience.

Finally, we would like to be able to control a phenomenon once we can explain and predict it. Being able to replicate a scenario and dictate a particular outcome is the objective of **control**. In Case 4, if we assume that the university proceeds with its retirement community and enjoys the predicted success, the president will find it attractive to be able to build a similar facility to serve another group of alumni and duplicate that success.

Control is a logical outcome of prediction. The complexity of the phenomenon and the adequacy of the prediction theory, however, largely decide success in a control study. In Case 4, if a control study were done of the various promotional approaches used with alumni to stimulate images of youthfulness, the promotional tactics that drew the largest number of alumni applications for residency could be identified. Once known, this knowledge could be used successfully with different groups of alumni *only if* the researcher could account for and control all other variables influencing applications.

Is Research Always Problem-Solving Based?

In the four cases, researchers were asked to respond to "problems" that managers needed to solve. **Applied research** has a practical problem-solving emphasis, although the problem solving is not always generated by a negative circumstance. Applied research is often used to evaluate opportunities as in Case 1 and Case 4. Whether the "problem" is negative, like rectifying an inventory system that is resulting in lost sales (Case 3), or an opportunity to increase stockholder wealth through acquiring another firm (Case 1), problem solving is prevalent in business research.

The problem-solving nature of applied research means it is conducted to reveal answers to specific questions related to action, performance, or policy needs. In this respect, all four examples appear to qualify as applied research. Pure, or basic, research is also problem-solving based, but in a different sense. It aims to solve perplexing questions (that is, problems) of a theoretical nature that have little direct impact on action, performance, or policy decisions. **Pure research or basic research** in the business arena might involve a researcher for an advertising agency who is studying the results of the use of coupons versus rebates as demand stimulation tactics, but not in a specific instance or in relation to a specific client's product. Thus, both applied and pure research are problem-solving based, but applied research is directed much more to making immediate managerial decisions.

Some authorities equate research with basic or scientific investigations and would reject all four examples. History shows, however, that science typically has its beginnings in pragmatic problems of real life. Interest in basic research comes much later, after development of a field's knowledge. Research is too narrowly defined if it is restricted to the basic research variety.

One respected author defines scientific research as a "systematic, controlled, empirical, and critical investigation of natural phenomena guided by theory and hypotheses about the presumed relations among such phenomena."[3] The terms *systematic* and *controlled* in this definition refer to the degree to which the observations are controlled and alternative explanations of the outcome are ruled out. The terms *empirical* and *critical* point to the requirements for the researcher to test subjective beliefs against objective reality and have the findings open to further scrutiny and testing. These qualities are what this author means by "scientific." Whether all business research needs to be this stringent or should be "guided by theory and hypotheses about presumed relations" is debatable.

The classical concept of basic research does call for a hypothesis,[4] but in applied research such a narrow definition omits at least two types of investigation that are highly valued. First is the exploratory study in which the investigator knows so little about the area of study that hypotheses have not yet emerged.[5] An equally important area of study is that which purists call merely descriptive. The importance of descriptive research to business should be reinforced:

> There is no more devastating condemnation that the self-designated theorist makes of the researcher than to label his work purely descriptive. There is an implication that associates "purely descriptive" research with empty-headedness; the label also implies that as a bare minimum every healthy researcher has at least one hypothesis to test, and preferably a whole model. This is nonsense.

In every discipline, but particularly in its early stages of development, purely descriptive research is indispensable. Descriptive research is the stuff out of which the mind of man, the theorist, develops the units that compose his theories. The very essence of description is to name the properties of things: you may do more, but you cannot do less and still have description. The more adequate the description, the greater is the likelihood that the units derived from the description will be useful in subsequent theory building.[6]

In answer to the question posed at the beginning of this section, "Is research always problem-solving based?" the answer is yes. Whether basic or applied, simple or complex, all research should provide an answer to some question. If managers always knew what was causing problems or offering opportunities in their realm of responsibility, there would be little need for applied research, pure research, or basic research; intuition would be all that was necessary to make quality decisions.

Business Research Defined

Any of the four types of studies—reporting, descriptive, explanatory, or predictive—can properly be called research. We also can conclude from the various examples that research is a systematic inquiry aimed at providing information to solve managerial problems. This defines the bare minimum that any effort must meet to be called research. Thus, we define **business research** as a systematic inquiry that provides information to guide business decisions.

All four cases presented meet this definition, but they suggest different stages of scientific development. A rough measure of the development of science in any field is the degree to which explanation and prediction have replaced reporting and description as research objectives. By this standard, the development of business research is in a comparatively formative stage.

How Scientific Is Business Research?

The development of scientific method in business research lags behind similar developments in the physical sciences. Physical scientists have been more rigorous in their concepts and research procedures. They are much more advanced in their theory development than are business scientists. The public domain has sponsored much physical research, some of it for hundreds of years. Governments have allocated billions of dollars to support such research, driven by the motivation to overcome disease or to improve the human condition. Nations driven by threat of war and national pride have also played a major role in the advance of physical science. Much of the findings of their research is in the public domain.

Business research is of much more recent origin and is largely supported by business organizations that hope to achieve a competitive advantage. Research methods and findings cannot be patented, and sharing findings often results in a loss of competitive advantage. The more valuable the research result is, the greater the value in keeping it secret. Under such conditions, access to findings is obviously restricted. Even though there is a growing amount of academic business research, it receives meager support when compared to research in the physical sciences.

Business research operates in a less favorable environment in other ways too. Physical research is normally conducted under controlled laboratory conditions; business research seldom is. Business research normally deals with topics such as human attitudes, behavior, and performance. People think they already know a lot about these topics and do not easily accept research findings that differ from their opinions.

Even with these hindrances, business researchers are making great strides in the scientific arena. New techniques are being developed, and rigorous research procedures are advancing rapidly. Computers and powerful analytical methods have contributed to this movement, but a greater understanding of the basic principles of sound research is more important.

One outcome of these trends is that research-based decision making will be more widely used in the future than it has been in the past. Managers who are not prepared for this change will be at a severe disadvantage.

WHAT IS GOOD RESEARCH?

Good research generates dependable data, being derived by practices that are conducted professionally, that can be used reliably for managerial decision making. Good research differs from poor research that is carelessly planned and conducted, resulting in data that a manager can't use to reduce his or her decision-making risks. Good research follows the standards of the scientific method. We list several defining characteristics of the **scientific method** below, discussing the managerial dimensions of each. A more thorough discussion occurs in Chapter 2.

1. *Purpose clearly defined.* The purpose of the research—the problem involved or the decision to be made—should be clearly defined and sharply delineated in terms as unambiguous as possible. Getting this in writing is valuable even in instances where the decision maker and researcher are the same person. The statement of the decision problem should include its scope, limitations, and precise specifications of the meanings of all words and terms significant to the research. Failure of the researcher to do this adequately may raise legitimate doubts in the minds of research report readers as to whether the researcher has sufficient understanding of the problem to make a sound proposal to attack it. This characteristic is comparable to developing a strategic plan before developing a tactical plan or an action map for achieving an objective.

2. *Research process detailed.* The research procedures used should be described in sufficient detail to permit another researcher to repeat the research. Except when secrecy is imposed, research reports should reveal with candor the sources of data and the means by which they were obtained. Omission of significant procedural details makes it difficult or impossible to estimate the validity and reliability of the data and justifiably weakens the confidence of the reader in the research and any recommendations based on the research. This characteristic is comparable to developing a tactical plan.

3. *Research design thoroughly planned.* The procedural design of the research should be carefully planned to yield results that are as objective as possible. When a sampling of the population is involved, the report should include evidence concerning the degree of representativeness of the sample. A survey of opinions or recollections ought not to be used when more reliable evidence is available from documentary sources or by direct observation. Bibliographic searches should be as thorough and

complete as possible. Experiments should have satisfactory controls. Direct observations should be recorded in writing as soon as possible after the event. Efforts should be made to minimize the influence of personal bias in selecting and recording data. This characteristic is comparable to developing detailed action plans for each tactic.

4. *High ethical standards applied.* Researchers often work independently and have significant latitude in designing and executing research projects. A research design that includes safeguards against causing mental or physical harm to participants, and makes data integrity a first priority, should be highly valued. Ethical issues in research reflect important moral concerns about the practice of responsible behavior in society. Researchers frequently find themselves precariously balancing the rights of their subjects against the scientific dictates of their chosen method. When this occurs, they have a responsibility to guard the welfare of the participants in the studies, and also the organizations to which they belong, their clients, colleagues, and themselves. Careful consideration must be given to research situations when there is a possibility for physical or psychological harm, exploitation, invasion of privacy, and loss of dignity. The research need must be weighed against the potential for adverse effects. Typically, you can redesign a study, but sometimes you cannot. The researcher should be prepared for this dilemma. As part of that preparation we will address this topic in Chapter 5.

5. *Limitations frankly revealed.* The researcher should report, with complete frankness, flaws in procedural design and estimate their effect on the findings. There are very few perfect research designs. Some of the imperfections may have little effect on the validity and reliability of the data; others may invalidate them entirely. A competent researcher should be sensitive to the effects of imperfect design, and his or her experience in analyzing the data should provide a basis for estimating their influence. As a decision maker, you should question the value of research where no limitations are reported.

6. *Adequate analysis for decision maker's needs.* Analysis of the data should be sufficiently adequate to reveal its significance, and the methods of analysis used should be appropriate. The extent to which this criterion is met is frequently a good measure of the competence of the researcher. Adequate analysis of the data is the most difficult phase of research for the novice. The validity and reliability of data should be checked carefully. The data should be classified in ways that assist the researcher to reach pertinent conclusions and clearly reveal the findings that lead to those conclusions. When statistical methods are used, the probability of error should be estimated and the criteria of statistical significance applied.

7. *Findings presented unambiguously.* Some evidence pertinent to estimates of the competence and integrity of the researcher may be found in the report itself. Language that is restrained, clear, and precise; assertions that are carefully drawn and hedged with appropriate reservations; and an apparent effort to achieve maximum objectivity tend to leave a favorable impression of the researcher with the decision maker. Generalizations that outrun the evidence on which they are based, exaggerations, and unnecessary verbiage tend to leave an unfavorable impression.[7] Such reports are not valuable to managers wading through the minefields of business decision making. Presentation of data should be comprehensive, easily understood by the decision maker, and organized so that the decision maker can readily locate critical findings.

8. *Conclusions justified.* Conclusions should be confined to those justified by the data of the research and limited to those for which the data provide an adequate basis. Researchers are often tempted to broaden the basis of induction by including personal experiences and their interpretations—data not subject to the controls under which the research data were gathered. Equally undesirable is the all-too-frequent practice of drawing conclusions from a study of a limited population and applying them universally. Researchers may also be tempted to rely too heavily on data collected in a prior study and use it in the interpretation of a new study. Such a practice is sometimes prevalent among research specialists who confine their work to clients in a small industry. These actions tend to decrease the objectivity of the research and weaken confidence in the findings. Good researchers always specify the conditions under which their conclusions seem to be valid.

9. *Researcher's experience reflected.* Greater confidence in the research is warranted if the researcher is experienced, has a good reputation in research, and is a person of integrity. Were it possible for the reader of a research report to obtain sufficient information about the researcher, this criterion perhaps would be one of the best bases for judging the degree of confidence a piece of research warrants and the value of any decision on which it rests. For this reason, the research report should contain information about the qualifications of the researcher.

These nine criteria provide an excellent summary of what is desirable in decision-oriented research (see Figure 1–1). They are especially appropriate to guide research done by managers themselves, for they create barriers to adjusting research findings to meet desired ends rather than to reflect reality.

Criterion 2 calls for a detailed proposal specifying what will be done, but in many exploratory studies it is not possible to be that precise prior to starting the study. It is even more important, therefore, when researcher and manager are separated by organizational boundaries, to state the nature of the decision problem clearly and unambiguously (criterion 1).

The threat of bias is mentioned under criterion 2, but it should be given more emphasis. The business researcher often knows from the beginning what results the sponsor would like to have. To combat this potentially biasing influence, it may be necessary to secure an understanding between manager and researcher before starting that the objective is to uncover reality— wherever that leads.

Criterion 3 calls for complete disclosure of methods and procedures used in the research study. This also is highly desirable, because it enables others to test findings through replication. Such openness to scrutiny has a positive effect on the quality of research. However, competitive advantage often mitigates against methodology disclosure in business research. Sometimes even the acknowledgment of a study's existence is considered unwise. For example, firms like J. D. Power and Associates will not provide enough information on their methodology to repeat an automotive market study. Similarly, neither Compaq nor IBM knew of the extensive research the other was engaged in at the time each developed its low-cost line of desktop computers. In the current litigation by states attorneys general against cigarette companies, it could prove disastrous if evidence is revealed that cigarette companies performed studies manipulating nicotine levels to enhance the addictive power of tobacco products.

FIGURE   1–1   What Actions Guarantee Good Research?

Characteristics of Good Research	*What a Manager Should Look for in Research Done by Others or Include in Self-Directed Research*	*Chapter*
Purpose clearly defined	• Researcher distinguishes between symptom of organization's problem, the manager's perception of the problem, and the research problem	Chapter 3
Research process detailed	• Researcher provides complete research proposal	Chapter 4
Research design thoroughly planned	• Exploratory procedures are outlined with constructs defined • Sample unit is clearly described along with sampling methodology • Data collection procedures are selected and designed	Chapters 2, 3
Limitations frankly revealed	• Desired procedure is compared with actual procedure in report • Desired sample is compared with actual sample in report • Impact on findings and conclusions are detailed	Chapters 6, 9, 15, 19
High ethical standards applied	• Safeguards are in place to protect study participants, organizations, clients, and researchers • Recommendations do not exceed the scope of the study • The study's methodology and limitations sections reflect researcher restraint and concern for accuracy	Chapter 5
Adequate analysis for decision maker's needs	• Sufficiently detailed findings are tied to collection instruments	Chapters 15–18
Findings presented unambiguously	• Findings are clearly presented in words, tables, and graphs • Findings are logically organized to facilitate reaching a decision about the manager's problem • Executive summary of conclusions is outlined • Detailed table of contents is tied to the conclusions and findings presentation	Chapters 15–19
Conclusions justified	• Decision-based conclusions are matched with detailed findings	Chapters 15–19
Researcher's experience reflected	• Researcher provides experience/credentials with report	Chapter 19

Criteria 1 through 9 should guide all research studies. Although these criteria use phraseology such as "unambiguous as possible," this only recognizes the reality of research work. The aim is always to be objective, yet we are all subjective. We also must recognize that research designs have flaws, even though calling attention to them in our work may be painful (criterion 5).

THE MANAGER-RESEARCHER RELATIONSHIP

Information gathering is an integral part of any manager's job. So it is not surprising that many managers do their own research, at least part of the time. The lower a manager is in the decision-making hierarchy, the more likely he or she is to do most of his or her own research. When managers lack either research time or talent, they may delegate the task to a staff assistant or a research specialist. This delegation of responsibility can result in greater synergy, especially if the research is decision driven and each party makes a full contribution to the joint venture. However, the separation of research user from research conductor can pose problems in data analysis, interpretation, conclusion finding, and recommendations. This is why businesses that regularly use outside research specialists often use the same firm repeatedly: Knowledge of the company, its people, and its processes is as critical as knowledge of the decision-making dilemma.

In an organizational setting, the researcher should look on the manager as a client. An effective working relationship between researcher and manager is not achieved unless both fulfill their respective obligations and several critical barriers are overcome.

Manager-Researcher Contributions

The obligations of managers are to specify their problems and provide researchers with adequate background information and access to company information gatekeepers. It is usually more effective if managers state their problems in terms of the decision choices they must make rather than specify the information they think they need. If this is done, both manager and researcher can jointly decide what information is needed.

MindWriter's customer affairs manager Myra Wines, as a staff rather than a line manager, may need assistance from managers with line responsibilities to define that plausible actions that could affect postpurchase service. She has clearly been charged with the responsibility to execute the customer satisfaction study, but she does not have authority to implement conclusions affecting, for example, product engineering, product manufacture, or distributor relationships. Thus she needs to clarify with those line managers what courses of action might be taken to correct identified problems. If, however, dissatisfaction is arising because of how customers with questions are treated when interacting with the customer affairs staff, Myra has direct line authority to determine plausible actions to correct such problems within her own domain.

Researchers also have obligations. Organizations expect them to develop a creative research design that will provide answers to important business questions. Not only should researchers provide data analyzed in terms of the problem specified, but they also should point out the implications that flow from the results. In the process, conflict may arise between what the decision maker wants and what the researcher can provide or thinks should be provided. The decision maker wants certainty and simple, explicit recommendations, while the researcher often can offer only probabilities and hedged interpretations. This conflict is inherent in their respective roles and has no simple resolution. However, a workable balance can usually be found if each person is sensitive to the demands and restrictions imposed on the other.

Manager-Researcher Conflicts

Some conflicts between decision makers and researchers are traced to management's limited exposure to research. Managers seldom have either formal training in research methodology or research expertise gained through experience. And, due to the explosive growth of research technology in recent years, a knowledge gap has developed between managers and research specialists as model building and more sophisticated investigative techniques have come into use. Thus the research specialist removes the manager from his or her comfort zone: The manager must now put his or her faith, and sometimes his or her career, in the hands of the research specialist and hope for the best.

In addition, managers often see research people as threats to their personal status. Managers still view management as the domain of the "intuitive artist" who is the master in this area. They may believe a request for research assistance implies they are inadequate to the task. These fears are often justified. The researcher's function is to test old ideas as well as new ones. To the insecure manager, the researcher is a potential rival.

The researcher will inevitably have to consider the corporate culture and political situations that develop in any organization. Members strive to maintain their niches and may seek ascendancy over their colleagues. Coalitions form and people engage in various self-serving activities, both overt and covert. As a result, research is blocked, or the findings or objectives of the research are distorted for an individual's self-serving purposes. To allow one's operations to be probed with a critical eye may be to invite trouble from others competing for promotion, resources, or other forms of organizational power.

A fourth source of stress for researchers is their frequent isolation from managers. Researchers draw back into their specialty and talk among themselves. Management's lack of understanding of research techniques compounds this problem. The research department can become isolated, reducing the effectiveness of conclusions a researcher may draw from research findings.

These problems have caused some people to advocate the use of a "research generalist." Such a person would head the research activity, help managers detail their research needs, and translate these needs into research problems. He or she also would facilitate the flow of information between manager and researcher that is so important for bringing the researcher into the decision-making process.

Decision-Driven Research

Business research has an inherent value to the extent that it helps management make better decisions. Interesting information about consumers, employees, or competitors might be pleasant to have, but its value is limited if the information cannot be applied to a critical decision. If a study does not help management select more efficient, less risky, or more profitable alternatives than otherwise would be the case, its use should be questioned. The important point is that applied research in a business environment finds its justification in the contribution it makes to the decision maker's task and to the bottom line.

One objective of this text is to provide you with plausible solutions to potential sources of manager-researcher conflicts. In the chapters that follow, we discuss scientific research procedures and show their application to pragmatic problems of the organization manager. At a minimum, our objective is to make you a more intelligent consumer of research products prepared by others, as well as able to do quality research for your own decisions and those of others to whom you report.

Summary

The managers of tomorrow will need to know more than any managers in history. Research will be a major contributor to that knowledge. Managers will find knowledge of research methods to be of value in many situations. They may need to conduct research either for themselves or for others. As buyers of research services they will need to be able to judge research quality. Finally, they may become research specialists themselves.

Research is any organized inquiry carried out to provide information for solving problems. Business research is a systematic inquiry that provides information to guide business decisions. This includes reporting, descriptive, explanatory, and predictive studies. We emphasize the last three in this book.

What characterizes good research? Generally, one expects good research to be purposeful, with a clearly defined focus and plausible goals, with defensible, ethical, and repeatable procedures, and with evidence of objectivity. The reporting of procedures—their strengths and weaknesses—should be complete and honest. Appropriate analytical techniques should be used; conclusions drawn should be limited to those clearly justified by the findings; and reports of findings and conclusions should be clearly presented and professional in tone, language, and appearance. If the investigator has an established reputation for quality work, so much the better. The research objective and its benefits should be weighed against potentially ad verse effects.

The relationship between manager and researcher is an important one. Both share the obligation of making a project meaningful. Several factors complicate this relationship. Among these are ethical considerations and the political environment.

Key Terms

applied research	explanatory studies
basic research	internal databases
business research	predictive studies
control	pure research
data mining	reporting studies
data warehousing	research variable
descriptive studies	scientific method

Discussion Questions

1. What is research? Why should there be any question about the definition of research?

2. Managers who wish to have information on which to base a decision face a make-or-buy situation. What are the problems they face in selecting either of these alternatives?

3. You are manager of the midwestern division of a major corporation, supervising five animal-feed plants scattered over four states. Corporate headquarters asks you to conduct an investigation to determine whether any of these plants should be closed, expanded, moved, or reduced. Is there a possible conflict between your roles as researcher and manager? Explain.

4. Advise each of the following persons on a specific research study that he or she might find useful. Classify each proposed study as reporting, descriptive, explanatory, or predictive.

    a. When the management decision problem is known:

      (1) Manager chef of a full-service restaurant with high employee turnover

      (2) Head of an academic department committee charged with selecting a research methods textbook

    b. When the management decision problem has not yet been specified:

      (1) Manager of the men's furnishings department at a national chain

      (2) Plant manager at a Ford auto assembly plant

      (3) Director of admissions at a large state university

      (4) Investment analyst at an investment firm

      (5) Director of personnel at a large metropolitan hospital

      (6) Product manager for Crest toothpaste at Procter & Gamble

      (7) Housing programs officer for a city

      (8) Office manager for a dentist

5. The new president of an old, established company is facing a problem. The company is currently unprofitable and is, in the president's opinion, operating inefficiently. The company sells a wide line of equipment and supplies to the dairy industry. Some items it manufactures, and many it wholesales to dairies, creameries, and similar plants. Because the industry is changing in several ways, survival will be more difficult in the future. In particular, many equipment companies are bypassing the wholesalers and selling directly to dairies. In addition, many of the independent dairies are being taken over by large food chains. How might research help the new president make the right decisions? In answering this question, consider the areas of marketing and finance as well as the whole company.

6. You have received a research report done by a consultant for your firm, a life insurance company. The study is a survey of morale in the home office and covers the opinions of about 500 secretaries and clerks plus about 100 executives and actuaries. You are asked to comment on its quality. What will you look for?

7. As area sales manager for a company manufacturing and marketing outboard engines, you have been assigned the responsibility of conducting a research study to estimate the sales potential of your products in the domestic (U.S. or Canadian) market. Discuss key issues and concerns arising from the fact that you, the manager, are also the researcher.

Reference Notes

1. See, for example, Murray Levine, "Investigative Reporting as a Research Method: Analysis of Bernstein and Woodward's *All the President's Men*," *American Psychologist* 35 (1980), pp. 626–38.

2. See, for example, Elizabethann O'Sullivan and Gary R. Rassel, *Research Methods for Public Administrators* (New York: Longman, 1989), pp. 19–39.

3. Fred N. Kerlinger, *Foundations of Behavioral Research*, 3rd ed. (New York: Holt, Rinehart & Winston, 1986), p. 10.
4. A hypothesis is a statement that is advanced for the purpose of testing its truth or falsity.
5. An exploratory study describes an investigation when the final research problem has not yet been clearly fixed. Its aim is to provide the insights needed by the researcher to develop a more formal research design.
6. Reprinted with permission of Macmillan Publishing Co., Inc., from *Theory Building*, rev. ed. 1978, by Robert Dubin. Copyright © 1969 by The Free Press, a division of Macmillan Co.
7. James Harold Fox, "Criteria of Good Research," *Phi Delta Kappan* 39 (March 1958), pp. 285–86.

Suggested Readings

1. Brachman, R. J., T. Khabaza, W. Kloesgen, G. Piatentsky-Shapiro, and E. Simoudis. "Mining Business Databases." *Communications of the ACM*, Vol. 39, No. 11, November 1996, pp. 42–48. Describes, with examples, tools used in data mining.
2. Colon, Ginger. "What the !@#!*?!! Is a Data Warehouse?" *Sales and Marketing Management*, April 1997, pp. 41–46. Defines a data warehouse and provides examples of companies using them.
3. Foreman, Howard E., and Clarence C. Sherwood. *Social Research and Social Policy*. Englewood Cliffs, NJ: Prentice Hall, 1970. Chapter 2 discusses the contribution of research to social policy.
4. Random, Matthew. *The Social Scientist in American Industry*. New Brunswick, NJ: Rutgers University Press, 1970. A research report of experiences of social scientists employed in industry. Chapter 9 presents a summary of findings.
5. Richie, J. R. Brent. "Roles of Research in the Management Process." *MSU Business Topics*, Summer 1976, pp. 13–22. A description of the relationship between research methodology and the management process with a classification scheme.

2 SCIENTIFIC THINKING

CHAPTER NAVIGATION

BRINGING RESEARCH TO LIFE

"Every summer," said Myra, "I was called up for Army Reserve. They never knew what to do with me, a woman, a captain, and a TV journalist. I think they feared my snoopiness would break out of control.

"One summer I was sent to a firing range to test a cannon.

"The range was several hundred acres that had been strip-mined until it was worse than a moonscape. Nothing in there lived or moved; nothing but craters and trenches existed there. And the nearest town—it was so severely depressed that, for the pitifully few jobs we provided, the folks welcomed us in, to bomb their backyard to flinders. Mining was totally played out. Dead. Yet this had been, in its day, one of the most prosperous mining regions, where the people were known for fearlessly and proudly going out to dig and produce.

"The cannon was impressive. We armed it with three-inch shells, put on ear protectors and goggles and lobbed shells into the range. There would be a tremendous flash and boom, and the shells would go roaring and soaring out of sight, and then we would hear a tremendous boom coming back to us, and then see dust and ash kicked up several hundred feet. We were all very happy not to be down range, I can tell you. We went down range later. There would be a huge crater and a fused puddle of iron, but nothing recognizable except slag and molten rocks, if you call them recognizable.

"There was this one problem. About every 20th shell would be a dud. It would fly off and land, and maybe kick up some dust, but explode it would not.

"On paper, this was not supposed to be a problem. The duds were supposed to be quite safe. The arsenal sent down an officious second lieutenant, and he showed us reports that the Army had dropped such duds from hundred-foot platforms, from helicopters, had applied torches to them—everything—and had discovered them to be completely inert. The only thing to ignite one of these duds would be to drop another, live bomb on it.

"Regrettably, this proved not to be the case, because often in the middle of the night we would hear one of these so-called 'duds' explode. We would rush out at dawn, and sure enough, find a new crater, molten slag, molten rock, and so forth. It was quite a mystery.

"So I did what I am supposed to be good at and nosed around. I sat up one night on a hill overlooking the range, and, sure enough, I saw people with flashlights moving around in there.

"Locals were coming in at night, intending to crack open the bombs and scavenge for copper wire or anything they thought was salvageable. Except, of course, this ignited one of the beauties, in a crime that erased any evidence of its perpetration, so to speak, as the perpetrators were vaporized on the spot.

"I hung around town and mixed with the folks, saw how they occupied themselves. They were involved in auto racing, demolition derbies, every kind of thrill sport. It was not unusual to see a fifty-mile race with four ambulances on hand on the edge of the oval, to cart off the carnage to the surgical hospital in the next county. I saw men leap into cars with threadbare tires, loose wheels, malfunctioning brakes, brake fluid and transmission fluid drooling all over the track. Nobody thought anything of this. If I asked, their answer was, 'I'll go when my number is up,' or 'It's not in my hands.'

"These good folk had lost all sense of cause and effect. They could wheel their cars out onto the track on a tire they knew was thin as tissue, and if it blew out and put them in the hospital, their reaction was, 'My time came,' or 'Some days you can't win for losin'.'

"It made sense, from a cultural-economic view. That very nonscientific attitude was what has let their men go down in the mines year after year. Was the fire detection and control system out of commission? 'No big deal, 'cause if your number is not up, you have nothing to worry about, and if it's up, nothing you can do 'bout it, brother.'

"I begged the sheriff to warn them away from our range. 'What's the big problem, Captain *(continued)*

Wines?' he asked. 'They are going to kill them-selves,' I said. 'They are going to die anyway,' he said. 'We all are going to die. People die every month who never went out on the range.'

"There is no way to deal with such nonscientific thinking by applying logic. We changed our proce-dure. We would fire the shells in the morning and spend the afternoon finding the duds, to which we would attach kerosene lanterns. At dusk, a fighter-bomber would fly over the area and bomb the lanterns—and the 'dud'—to a molecular state. It was neat and it worked."

STYLES OF THINKING

At the heart of every research course is the question of perspective. How one sees the world affects the kind of questions asked and what can be accepted as explanations. Of the hundreds of questions about organizations or finance or marketing that could be asked, each would presuppose a normative perspective for that particular ques-tion, and some would be more productive for obtaining answers.

We open this chapter with a discussion of the ways people think about prob-lems. The method of scientific inquiry is one of them, and, as a preferred form, its features are contrasted with other styles of thinking. Next covered are the tools of in-duction and deduction that are necessary for reasoning throughout the research process. Their relation to scientific problem solving is illustrated. Also explored is the role of the scientific attitude in energizing the conduct of research. Finally, we turn to the terminology of science that has been adopted as a specialized language of research. In that section, the building blocks for constructing theory and designing research studies are defined and explained.

Sources of Knowledge

Sources of knowledge range from untested opinion to highly systematic styles of thinking. We rarely think about how we know something or where this knowledge originated as we go about our daily lives, but this is a significant subject for re-searchers. From ancient times to the present, there has been a persistent interest in dis-covering how we know. Researchers depend on an ability to discriminate among knowledge sources to identify those that produce the best results for a given situation.

The philosophy of science provides the classifications that help us with this task. Over the years, there has been considerable discussion about the effectiveness of var-ious sources of knowledge. Thinking styles associated with the scientific method are generally regarded as the preeminent means for securing truth, though that truth may not be permanent. But the scientific method is not the only source of our knowledge, as this section will attempt to explain.

Figure 2–1 classifies some of the styles of thinking and locates them from the standpoint of logic.[1] The axes orient us. The horizontal axis ranges from a highly idealistic interpretation on one end to empiricism on the other. **Empiricism** is said "to denote observations and propositions based on sense experience and/or derived from such experience by methods of inductive logic, including mathematics and sta-tistics."[2] Empiricists attempt to describe, explain, and make predictions through ob-servation. *This book is concerned with empiricism—with the design of procedures to collect factual information about hypothesized relationships that can be used to de-cide if a particular image of a problem is correct.*

FIGURE   2–1   Styles of Thinking

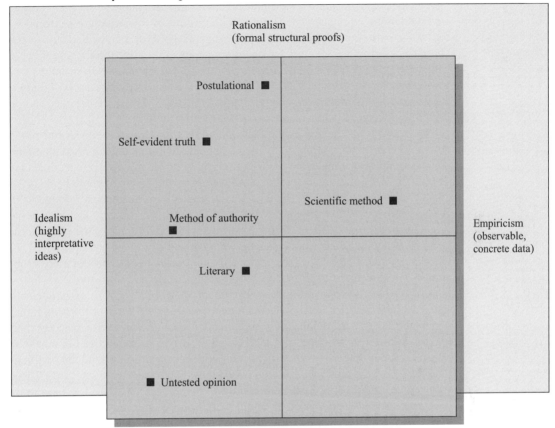

Scientific knowledge is obtained through inductive, empirical approaches. It is also secured through theoretical means that are based in deductive reasoning. The vertical axis is used to represent this orientation in Figure 2–1. The rationalism end of the continuum is of interest. By **rationalism** we mean that reason is a primary source of knowledge. Rationalism differs from empiricism in that rationalists believe all knowledge can be deduced from known laws or basic truths of nature. This is claimed to be possible because underlying laws structure the world logically. From the time of Sir Frances Bacon to the present, adherents of this view maintain that problems are best understood and resolved through formal logic or mathematics. Such efforts, of course, operate independently of observation and data collection.

Untested opinion is a form of knowing that people cling to despite contrary evidence. In the indoctrination programs of less enlightened organizations, it is not unusual for new employees to hear, "That's the way we've always done it here," a remark that confuses entrenchment and habit with efficiency. Most families have an old relative who maintains a conspiracy theory for a memorable world event despite overwhelming evidence. The illogical conclusions of this style are captured by Myra's experience with the locals on the firing range. Myth, superstition, and hunch have been serious competitors for scientific thinking down through time because, as one writer notes, "they have the reassuring feel of certainty before the event they try to predict or control, though seldom afterwards."[3] Business researchers will find little to improve their understanding of reality from this position, though they should be prepared to cope with it on occasion.

A way of knowing often called the method of *self-evident truth* was illustrated by the sheriff in our example. It was self-evident to him that people would die no matter what precautions were taken. If they didn't die on the firing range, then they would die as a result of something else. Death was inevitable; it could be deduced from known laws of nature. But what about propositions that appear reasonable to one person or even to many but are not true? For example, "Everyone drives on the right side of the road." This "truth" is self-evident to only *some* of the world's drivers. "Women make inferior managers," "men of noble birth are natural leaders," or "Japanese quality practices are universally applicable to U.S. productivity problems." These were once self-evident propositions that are now dismissed.

Since not all propositions are self-evident, we rely on *persons of authority* to improve our confidence. Too often authority depends on status or position rather than on true expertise. Such authorities are often wrong, so it is wise to accept their views cautiously. Authorities serve as important sources of knowledge but should be judged by their integrity, the quality of the evidence they present, and their willingness to present an open and balanced case. Many do not meet these standards. Those who do are often misapplied: Henry Ford on international relations, Lee Iacocca on protected markets, Jack Welch on small business, or John Sculley on brand management.

The *literary style of thought* occupies a viewpoint toward the center of Figure 2–1. The literary style of thinking is responsible for many classic case studies in the social sciences. Case studies have played a prominent role in the development of business knowledge. Portions of anthropology, psychiatry, and clinical sociology can also trace their roots to this origin. Maslow's theory of motivation is one example from psychology that is well known in business. Business case studies are a preferred method of teaching in many programs. The literary perspective is one where "a person, a movement, or a whole culture is interpreted, but largely in terms of the specific purposes and perspectives of the actors, rather than in terms of the abstract and general categories of the scientist's own explanatory scheme."[4] Because it is difficult to generalize from individual case studies, our ability to derive principles is restricted.

Figure 2–1 positions the *scientific method* close to the empirical end of the horizontal axis. The essential tenets of science are (1) direct observation of phenomena, (2) clearly defined variables, methods, and procedures, (3) empirically testable hypotheses, (4) the ability to rule out rival hypotheses, (5) the statistical rather than linguistic justification of conclusions, and (6) the self-correcting process. One author has noted, "Current scientific methods wed the best aspects of the logic of the rational approach with the observational aspects of the empirical orientation into a cohesive, systematic perspective."[5] The application of previously tested and verifiable procedures solved Myra's dilemma with the unexploded bombs. Case 4 in Chapter 1 is an example of business research that uses the scientific method.

Competing styles of thinking influence research directions in business just as they do throughout the social and behavioral sciences. The *postulational style* can be found in the upper portion of the diagram. Studies in operations research, management science, mathematical modeling, and simulation are postulational. For example, many firms run simulations of their market before a product announcement. These might examine different pricing levels and manufacturing output to optimize profitability. One goal of this perspective is to reduce the object of study to mathematical, formal terms. These terms, called postulates, are used to devise theorems that represent logical proofs. The objective is to deduce a structure that may account for any phenomenon having similar form.

There is no single best perspective from which to view reality or to do science, only preferred perspectives. The range of available styles of thinking offers many frameworks to confront the diverse problems of business. Some perspectives, such as the postulational style, rely on deductive logical processes. In contrast, the scientific method uses induction; inferences are made about the characteristics of populations based on the observed characteristics of samples. We have also mentioned less desirable ways of thinking that lack a logical foundation and rely on feeling and intuition to understand reality. Useful knowledge abounds; one should simply be aware of the vantage point selected to find it and the strengths and weaknesses of that position.

THE THOUGHT PROCESS: REASONING

Scientific inquiry has been described as a puzzle-solving activity.[6] For the researcher, puzzles are solvable problems that may be clarified or resolved through reasoning. In the opening scene of *The Sign of the Four*, Sir Arthur Conan Doyle uses a conversation between Sherlock Holmes and Dr. Watson to demonstrate the importance of precise reasoning and careful observation in the solving of puzzles and unraveling of mysteries. Watson provides the test by handing Holmes a watch and asking him to venture an opinion on the character or habits of the late owner. Sherlock Holmes's fans are not disappointed in the outcome. After a few moments' examination, Holmes correctly infers the watch belonged to Watson's careless and untidy elder brother, a man who inherited wealth, treated his prospects foolishly, and died a drunkard. The speed of the conclusion is startling, but the trail of his reasoning process from small facts to inductions and on to conclusions, which he confirms with Watson, is a common thought process for detectives, scientists, and puzzle solvers.

Every day we reason with varying degrees of success and communicate our message, called meaning, in ordinary language or, in special cases, in symbolic, logical form. Our meanings are conveyed through one of two types of discourse: exposition or argument. *Exposition* consists of descriptive statements that merely state and do not give reasons. *Argument* allows us to explain, interpret, defend, challenge, and explore meaning. Two types of argument of great importance to research are deduction and induction.

Deduction

Deduction is a form of inference that purports to be conclusive—the conclusion must necessarily follow from the reasons given. These reasons are *said to imply the conclusion and to represent a proof*. This is a much stronger and different bond between reasons and conclusions than is found with induction.

For a deduction to be correct, it must be *both true and valid*—that is, the premises (reasons) given for the conclusion must agree with the real world (be true). In addition, the premises must be arranged in a form such that the *conclusion must necessarily follow from the premises*. A deduction is valid if it is impossible for the conclusion to be false if the premises are true. Logicians have established rules by which one can judge whether a deduction is valid. Conclusions are not logically justified if (1) one or more premises are untrue or (2) the argument form is invalid. Yet a conclusion may still be a true statement, but for reasons other than those given. For example, consider the following simple deduction:

(Premise 1)—All regular employees can be trusted not to steal.

(Premise 2)—John is a regular employee.

(Conclusion)—John can be trusted not to steal.

If we believe that John can be trusted, we might think this is a sound deduction. But this conclusion cannot be accepted as a sound deduction unless the argument form is valid and the premises are true. In this case, the form is valid, and premise 2 can be easily confirmed. However, many may challenge the sweeping premise that "All regular employees can be trusted not to steal." While we may believe John will not steal, such a conclusion is a sound deduction only if both premises are accepted as true. If one premise fails the acceptance test, then the conclusion is not a sound deduction. This is so even if we still have great confidence in John's honesty. Our conclusion, in this case, must be based on our confidence in John as an individual rather than on a general premise that all regular employees are honest.

We may not recognize how much we use deduction to reason out the implications of various acts and conditions. For example, in planning a survey, we might reason as follows:

(Premise 1)—Inner-city household interviewing is especially difficult and expensive.

(Premise 2)—This survey involves substantial inner-city household interviewing.

(Conclusion)—The interviewing in this survey will be especially difficult and expensive.

On reflection, it should be apparent that a conclusion that results from deduction is, in a sense, already "contained in" its premises.[7]

Induction

Inductive argument is radically different. There is no such strength of relationship between reasons and conclusions in **induction**. *To induce is to draw a conclusion from one or more particular facts or pieces of evidence.* The conclusion explains the facts, and the facts support the conclusion. To illustrate, suppose you push the light switch in your room and the light fails to go on. This is a fact—the light does not go on when you push the switch. Under such circumstances, we ask, "Why?"

One likely answer to this question is a conclusion that the light bulb has burned out. This conclusion is an induction because we know from experience that (1) the light should go on when you push the switch and (2) if the bulb is burned out, the light will not function. The nature of induction, however, is that the conclusion is only a hypothesis. It is one explanation, but there are others that fit the fact just as well. It could be that the electrical power is off in the neighborhood, or the switch might be malfunctioning.

In this example, we see the essential nature of inductive reasoning. The inductive conclusion is an inferential jump beyond the evidence presented—that is, although one conclusion explains the fact of no light, other conclusions also can explain the fact. It may even be that none of the three conclusions we have advanced correctly explains the failure of the light to go on. Myra Wines wasn't convinced that the unexploded "dud" shells were harmless. While this is one conclusion, certainly at least one other was as valid before confirmation—that the unexploded shell experienced a delayed reaction and would explode upon future handling.

For another example, let's consider the situation of Tracy Nelson, a salesperson at the Square Box Company. Tracy has one of the poorest sales records in the company. Her unsatisfactory performance prompts us to ask the question, "Why is she doing so badly?" From our knowledge of Tracy's sales practices, the nature of box selling, and the market, we might conclude (hypothesize) that her problem is that she makes too few sales calls per day to build a good sales record. Other hypotheses might also occur to us on the basis of available evidence. Among them are the following:

1. Tracy's territory does not have the market potential of other territories.
2. Tracy's sales-making skills are so poorly developed that she is not able to close sales effectively.
3. Tracy's territory has been the scene of intense price-cutting by local manufacturers, and this has caused her to lose many sales.
4. Some types of people just cannot sell boxes, and Tracy is one of these people.

All of the above hypotheses are inductions we might base on the evidence of Tracy's poor sales record, plus some assumptions or beliefs we hold about her and the selling of boxes. All of them have some chance of being true, but we would probably have more confidence in some than in others. All must be subject to further confirmation before we could hold any of them with much confidence. Confirmation comes with more evidence. The task of research is largely to determine the nature of the evidence needed and to design methods by which to discover and measure this other evidence.

Combining Induction and Deduction

Induction and deduction are used in research reasoning in a sequential manner. John Dewey described this process as the **double movement of reflective thought**.[8] Induction occurs when we observe a fact and ask, "Why is this?" In answer to this question, we advance a tentative explanation (hypothesis). The hypothesis is plausible if it explains the event or condition (fact) that prompted the question. Deduction is the process by which we test whether the hypothesis is capable of explaining the fact. The process is illustrated in Figure 2–2:

1. You push the light switch and find no light. ($Fact_1$)
2. You ask the question, "Why no light?" (Induction)
3. You infer a conclusion (hypothesis) to answer the question: The bulb is burned out. (Hypothesis)
4. You use this hypothesis to conclude (deduce) that the light will not go on when you push the switch. You know from experience that a burned-out bulb will not light. ($Deduction_1$)

This example, an exercise in circular reasoning, does point out that one must be able to deduce the initiating fact from the hypothesis advanced to explain that fact. A second critical point is also illustrated in this figure: To test a hypothesis, one must be able to deduce from it other facts that can then be investigated. This is what classical research is all about. We must deduce other specific facts or events from the hypothesis and then gather information to see if the deductions are true. In the light example, we deduce:

FIGURE   2–2   Why Doesn't the Light Go On?

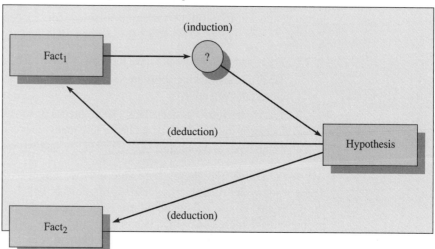

$Fact_1$ = Pushing the light switch results in no light
$Fact_2$ = Inserting a new bulb brings light when switch is pushed

5. A new bulb put in the lamp will result in light when the switch is pushed. (Deduction$_2$)

6. We put in the new bulb and push the switch. The light goes on. (Fact$_2$)

How would the double movement of reflective thought work when applied to Tracy Nelson's problem? The process is illustrated in Figure 2–3. The initial observation (fact$_1$) leads to hypothesis$_1$ that Tracy is lazy. We deduce several other facts from the hypothesis. These are shown as fact$_2$ and fact$_3$. We use research to find out if fact$_2$ and fact$_3$ are true. If they are found to be true, they confirm our hypothesis. If they are not, our hypothesis is not confirmed, and we must look for another explanation.

In most research, the process is more complicated than these simple examples suggest. For instance, we often develop multiple hypotheses by which to explain the phenomenon in question. Then we design a study to test all the hypotheses at once. Not only is this more efficient, but it is also a good way to reduce the attachment (and potential bias) of the researcher for any given hypothesis.

Reflective Thinking and the Scientific Method

Induction and deduction, observation, and hypothesis testing can be combined in a systematic way to illustrate the scientific method. The ideas that follow, originally suggested by Dewey and others for problem-solving analysis, represent one approach to assessing the validity of conclusions about observable events; and they are

FIGURE   2–3   Why Is Tracy Nelson's Performance So Poor?

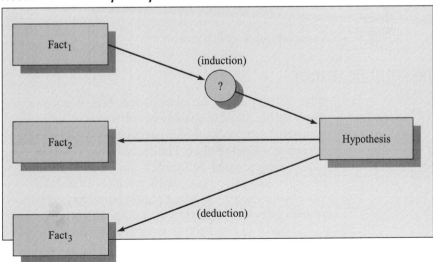

Fact$_1$ = Poor performance record
Fact$_2$ = Late to work regularly
Fact$_3$ = Fewer calls per day than average performance

particularly appropriate for researchers whose conclusions depend on empirical data.[9] The researcher

- Encounters a curiosity, doubt, barrier, suspicion, or obstacle
- Struggles to state the problem: asks questions, contemplates existing knowledge, gathers facts, and moves from an emotional to an intellectual confrontation with the problem
- Proposes hypotheses to explain the facts that are believed to be logically related to the problem
- Deduces outcomes or consequences of the hypotheses: attempts to discover what happens if the results are in the opposite direction of that predicted or if the results support the expectations
- Formulates several rival hypotheses
- Devises and conducts a crucial empirical test with various possible outcomes, each of which selectively excludes one or more hypotheses
- Draws a conclusion, an inductive inference, based on acceptance or rejection of the hypotheses
- Feeds information back into the original problem, modifying it according to the strength of the evidence

Eminent scientists who claim there is no such thing as the scientific method, or if it exists, it is not revealed by what they write, caution researchers about using template-like approaches. Their admonitions are well taken, and we would add that the ideas presented here are highly interdependent, are not sequentially fixed, and may be expanded or eliminated based on the nature of the problem and the perspective one has chosen to view it from.[10] Nevertheless, beginning researchers should understand that research, when conducted scientifically, is a process. Chapter 3 is devoted to an elaboration of that process.

THE SCIENTIFIC ATTITUDE

If the tools of thinking are the mind of science, then the scientific attitude is the spirit. The scientific attitude unleashes the creative drive that makes discovery possible. The portraits of scientists involved in some of the most spectacular discoveries of the twentieth century—Crick, Watson, Pauling, and others— are the stories of imagination, intuition, curiosity, suspicion, anguish, the rage to know, and self-doubt.[11] But these predispositions are not the exclusive province of the natural scientist. All researchers exercise imagination in the discovery process, in capturing the most essential aspect of the problem, or in selecting a technique that reveals a phenomenon in its most natural state.

Curiosity in its many forms characterized the persistent efforts to understand the relationship between productivity and worker satisfaction. Starting first with the Hawthorne studies, it was thought that employee satisfaction improved productivity.[12] Later research did not bear this out, and the second general conclusion was that satisfaction and productivity were not directly connected since the relationship was affected by a number of other variables. Currently, we believe that satisfaction is sought for reasons not consistently related to work, and productivity varies from simple to challenging tasks. Many contextual variables are now viewed as essential for understanding the original relationship.[13] Over 30 years elapsed while this research was being sorted out. The curiosity to ask questions compounded by the passion not to let go and the discomfort with existing answers sustained these researchers through periods of failure and self-doubt.

Thomas Kuhn, writing in *The Structure of Scientific Revolutions,* has also addressed the question of why scientists attack their problems with such passion and devotion. Scientific inquiry, he says, attracts people for a variety of motives. "Among them are the desire to be useful, the excitement of exploring new territory, the hope of finding order, and the drive to test established knowledge."[14] From applied researchers addressing a manager's need to academicians fascinated with the construction of grand theories, the attitude of science is the enabling spirit of discovery.

UNDERSTANDING THEORY: COMPONENTS AND CONNECTIONS

When we do research, we seek to know *what is* in order to understand, explain, and predict phenomena. We might want to answer the question, "What will be the employee reaction to the new flexible work schedule?" or "Why did the stock market price surge higher when all normal indicators suggested the market would go down?" When dealing with such questions, we must agree on definitions. Which employees? What kind of reaction? What are the major indicators? These questions require the use of concepts, constructs, and definitions. Later we will use variables and hypotheses to make statements and propose tests for the relationships that our questions express. These components, or building blocks, of theory are reviewed in the next few sections.

Concepts

If one is to understand and communicate information about objects and events, there must be a common ground on which to do it. Concepts are used for this purpose. A **concept** is a bundle of meanings or characteristics associated with certain events, objects, conditions, situations, and the like. Classifying and categorizing objects or events that have common characteristics beyond the single observation create concepts. When you think of a spreadsheet or a warranty card, what comes to mind is not a single instance but collected memories of all spreadsheets and warranty cards abstracted to a set of specific and definable characteristics.

We abstract such meanings from reality and use words as labels to designate them. For example, we see a man passing and think he is running, walking, skipping, crawling, or hopping. These movements all represent concepts. We also have abstracted certain visual elements by which we identified that the moving object was a he not a she or a truck or a horse. We obviously use large numbers of concepts daily in our thinking, conversing, and other activities.

Sources of Concepts   Concepts that are in frequent and general use have been developed over time through shared usage. We have acquired them through personal experience. If we lived in another society, we would hold many of the same concepts (though in a different language). Some concepts, however, are unique to a particular culture and are not readily translated into another language.

Ordinary concepts make up the bulk of communication even in research, but we can often run into difficulty trying to deal with an uncommon concept or a newly advanced idea. One way to handle this problem is to borrow from other languages (for example, *gestalt*) or to borrow from other fields. The concept of gravitation is borrowed from physics and used in marketing in an attempt to explain why people shop where they do. The concept of distance is used in attitude measurement to describe degrees of difference between the attitudes of two or more persons. Threshold is used effectively to describe a concept in perception studies; velocity is a term borrowed by the economist from the physicist.

Borrowing is not always practical, so we need to (1) adopt new meanings for words (make a word cover a different concept) or (2) develop new labels (words) for concepts. The recent broadening of the meaning of *model* is an example of the first instance; the development of concepts such as sibling and status stress are examples of the second. When we adopt new meanings or develop new labels, we begin to develop a specialized jargon or terminology. Researchers in medicine, the physical sciences, and related fields frequently use terms that are unintelligible to outsiders. Jargon no doubt contributes to efficiency of communication among specialists, but it excludes everyone else.

Importance to Research   Concepts are basic to all thought and communication, yet we pay little attention to what they are and the problems encountered in their use. In research, special problems grow out of the need for concept precision and inventiveness. We design hypotheses using concepts. We devise measurement concepts by which to test these hypothetical statements. We gather data using these measurement concepts. We may even invent new concepts to express ideas. The success of research hinges on (1) how clearly we conceptualize and (2) how well others understand the concepts we use. For example, when we survey people on the question of tax equity, the questions we use need to tap faithfully the attitudes of the respondents. Attitudes are abstract, yet we must attempt to measure them using carefully selected concepts.

The challenge is to develop concepts that others will clearly understand. We might, for example, ask respondents for an estimate of their family's total income. This may seem to be a simple, unambiguous concept, but we will receive varying and confusing answers unless we restrict or narrow the concept by specifying (1) time period, such as weekly, monthly, or annually; (2) before or after income taxes; (3) for head of family only or for all family members; and (4) for salary and wages only or also for dividends, interest, and capital gains. (And how about income in kind such as free rent, employee discounts, or food stamps?)

Problems in Concept Use   The use of concepts presents difficulties that are accentuated in a research setting. First, people differ in the meanings they include under the particular label. This problem is so great in normal human communication that we often see cases where people use the same language but do not understand each other. We might all agree to the meaning of such concepts as dog, table, electric light, money, employee, and wife. We may encounter more difficulties, however, when we communicate concepts such as household, retail transaction, dwelling unit, regular user, debit, and wash sale. Still more challenging are concepts that are familiar but not well understood, such as leadership, motivation, personality, social class, and fiscal policy. For example, personality has been defined in the research literature in more than 400 ways.[15] Although this may seem extreme, writers are not able to express the complexity of the determinants of personality and its attributes (e.g., authoritarianism, risk taking, locus of control, achievement orientation, and dogmatism) in a fashion that produces agreement.

The concepts described represent progressive levels of abstraction—that is, the degree to which the concept does or does not have objective referents. Table is an objective concept in that we can point to tables and we can conjure up in our mind images of tables. An abstraction like personality is much more difficult to visualize. Such abstract concepts are often called constructs.

Constructs
As used in research in the social sciences, a **construct** is an image or idea specifically invented for a given research and/or theory-building purpose. We build constructs by combining the simpler concepts, especially when the idea or image we intend to convey is not directly subject to observation. When Jason and Myra tackle MindWriter's research study, they will struggle with the construct of a satisfied service customer.

Concepts and constructs are easily confused. Here's an example to clarify the differences. A human resource analyst in a software company that employs technical writers is analyzing task attributes of a job in need of redesign. She knows the job description for technical writers consists of three components: presentation quality, language skill, and job interest. Her job analysis reveals more specific characteristics.

Figure 2–4 illustrates some of the concepts and constructs she is dealing with. The concepts at the bottom of the figure (format accuracy, manuscript errors, and typing speed) are the most concrete and easily measured. We can observe typing speed, for example, and even with crude measures agree on what constitutes slow and fast typists. Typing speed is one concept in the group that defines a construct that the human resource analyst called "presentation quality." Presentation quality is a nonexistent entity, a "constructed type." It is used to communicate the combination of meanings of the three concepts. The analyst uses it as a label for the concepts she has found empirically to be related.

Concepts in the next level in Figure 2–4 are vocabulary, syntax, and spelling. The analyst also found them to be related. They form a construct that she called "language skill." She chose this term because these three concepts together defined the language requirement in the job description. Language skill is placed at a higher level of abstraction in the figure because the concepts that comprise it are more difficult to observe and their measures are more complex.

The analyst has not yet measured the last construct, "job interest." It is the least observable and most difficult to measure. It will likely be composed of numerous

FIGURE   2–4   Constructs Composed of Concepts in a Job Redesign Example

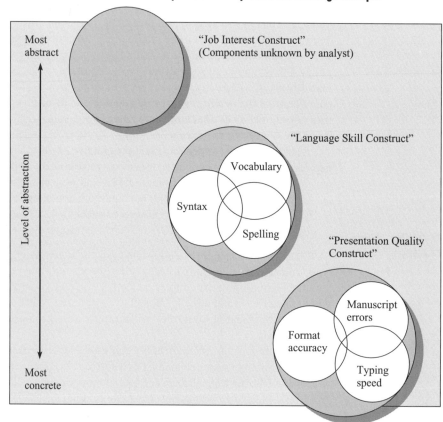

concepts—many of which will be quite abstract. Researchers sometimes refer to such entities as *hypothetical constructs* because they can be inferred only from the data; thus, they are presumed to exist but must await further testing. If research ultimately shows the concepts and constructs in this example to be interrelated, and if the propositions that specify the connections can be supported, the researcher will have the beginning of a **conceptual scheme.** In graphic form it would depict the relationships among the knowledge and skill requirements necessary to clarify the job redesign effort.

Definitions

Confusion about the meaning of the concepts can destroy a research study's value without the researcher or client even knowing it. If words have different meanings to the parties involved, then they are not communicating on the same wavelength. Definitions are one way to reduce this danger.

While there are various types of definitions, the most familiar are dictionary definitions. In these, a concept is defined with a synonym. For example, a customer is defined as a patron; a patron, in turn, is defined as a customer or client of an establishment; a client is defined as one who employs the services of any professional. . . , also, loosely, a patron of any shop.[16] Circular definitions such as these may be adequate for general communication but not for research. Here we must measure concepts, and this requires a more rigorous definition.

Operational Definitions   An **operational definition** is a definition stated in terms of specific testing criteria or operations. These terms must have empirical referents (that is, we must be able to count, measure, or in some other way gather the information through our senses). Whether the object to be defined is physical (e.g., a machine tool) or highly abstract (e.g., achievement motivation), the definition must specify the characteristics to study and how they are to be observed. The specifications and procedures must be so clear that any competent person using them would classify the objects in the same way.

During her military service, Myra observed numerous shells that when fired did not explode on impact. She knew the army applied the operational definition of *dud* to each such shell. But if asked, Myra would have applied the operational term *dud* only to a shell that, once fired from a cannon, could not be made to explode by any amount of manipulation, human or mechanical. Based on her definition, the town's residents rarely encountered "duds" during their excursions onto the firing range.

For another example, suppose college undergraduates are to be classified by class. No one has much trouble understanding such terms as *freshman, sophomore,* and so forth. But the task may not be that simple if you must determine which students fall in each class. To do this, you need operational definitions.

Operational definitions may vary, depending on your purpose and the way you choose to measure them. Here are two different situations requiring different definitions of the same concepts.

1. You conduct a survey among students and wish to classify their answers by their class levels. You merely ask them to report their class status, and you record it. In this case, class is freshman, sophomore, junior, or senior, and you accept the answer each respondent gives as correct. This is a rather casual definition process but nonetheless an operational definition. It is probably adequate in this case even though some of the respondents report inaccurately.

2. You make a tabulation of the class level of students for the university registrar's annual report. The measurement task here is more critical so your operational definition needs to be more precise. You decide to define class levels in terms of semester hours of credit completed and recorded in each student's record in the registrar's office:

Freshman   less than 30 hours' credit

Sophomore   30 to 59 hours' credit

Junior   60 to 89 hours' credit

Senior   over 90 hours' credit

Those examples deal with relatively concrete concepts, but operational definitions are even more critical for treating abstract ideas. Suppose one tries to measure a construct called "organizational commitment." We may intuitively understand what this means, but to attempt to measure it among workers is difficult. We would probably develop a commitment scale, or we may use a scale that has already been developed and validated by someone else. The scale then operationally defines the construct.

While operational definitions are needed in research, they also present some problems. There is the ever-present danger of thinking that a concept and the operational definition are the same thing. We forget that our definitions provide only limited insight into what a concept or construct really is. In fact, the operational definition may be quite narrow and not at all similar to what someone else would use when researching the same topic. When measurements by two different definitions correlate well, the correlation supports the view that each definition adequately measures the same concept.

The problems of operational definitions are particularly difficult when dealing with constructs. In this case, there are few empirical referents by which to confirm that an operational definition really measures what we hope it does. The correlation between two different definition formulations strengthens the belief that we are measuring the same thing. On the other hand, if there is little or no correlation, it may mean we are tapping several different partial meanings of a construct. It may also mean one or both of the definitions are not true labels.

Whatever the form of definition, its purpose in research is basically the same—to provide an understanding and measurement of concepts. We may need to provide operational definitions for only a few critical concepts, but these will almost always be the definitions used to develop the relationships found in hypotheses and theories.

Variables

Scientists operate at both theoretical and empirical levels. At the theoretical level, there is a preoccupation with identifying constructs and their relations to propositions and theory. At this level, constructs cannot, as we've said before, be observed. At the empirical level where the propositions are converted to hypotheses and testing occurs, the scientist is likely to be dealing with variables. In practice, the term **variable** is used as a synonym for *construct* or the property being studied. In this context, a variable "is a symbol to which numerals or values are assigned."[17]

The numerical value assigned to a variable is based on the variable's properties. For example, some variables, said to be *dichotomous*, have only two values reflecting the presence or absence of a property: employed-unemployed or male-female have two values, generally 0 and 1. When Myra Wines observed the cannon shells, they were exploded or unexploded. Variables also take on values representing added categories such as the demographic variables of race or religion. All such variables that produce data that fit into categories are said to be *discrete* since only certain values are possible. An automotive variable, for example, where "Chevrolet" is assigned a 5 and "Honda" is assigned a 6, provides no option for a 5.5.

Income, temperature, age, or a test score are examples of *continuous* variables. These variables may take on values within a given range or, in some cases, an infinite set. Your test score may range from 0 to 100, your age may be 23.5, and your present income could be $35,000.

FIGURE   2–5   Defining Independent and Dependent Variables

Independent Variable	*Dependent Variable*
Presumed cause	Presumed effect
Stimulus	Response
Predicted from . . .	Predicted to . . .
Antecedent	Consequence
Manipulated	Measured outcome

Independent and Dependent Variables   Researchers are most interested in relationships among variables. For example, does a participative leadership style (independent variable) influence job satisfaction or performance (dependent variables) or can a superior's modeling of ethical behavior influence the behavior of the subordinate? Figure 2–5 lists some terms that have become synonyms for **independent variable** and **dependent variable**. It is important to remember there are no preordained variables waiting to be discovered "out there" that are automatically assigned to one category or the other. As one writer notes:

> There's nothing very tricky about the notion of independence and dependence. But there is something tricky about the fact that the relationship of independence and dependence is a figment of the researcher's imagination until demonstrated convincingly. Researchers *hypothesize* relationships of independence and dependence: they invent them, and then they try by reality testing to see if the relationships actually work out that way.[18]

Moderating Variables   In each relationship, there is at least one independent variable (IV) and a dependent variable (DV). It is normally hypothesized that in some way the IV "causes" the DV to occur. For simple relationships, all other variables are considered extraneous and are ignored. Myra sets out to discover why the locals are scavenging salvageable materials from the unexploded cannon shells. She hypothesizes that their conviction that predetermined fate dictates time and place of death (IV) has lead them to undertake life-threatening behaviors—scavenging on the firing range (DV). She further hypothesizes that if they could be warned of the danger (IV) of their actions, they would change their nocturnal behavior (DV). The sheriff ultimately convinces her that only a change in army procedure would bring about the decline in shell-induced deaths caused by the nocturnal scavenging.

In a typical office, we might be interested in a study of the effect of the four-day workweek on office productivity and hypothesize the following:

> The introduction of the four-day workweek (IV) will lead to increased office productivity per worker-hour (DV).

In actual study situations, however, such a simple one-on-one relationship needs to be conditioned or revised to take other variables into account. Often one uses another type of explanatory variable of value here—the moderating variable (MV). A **moderating variable** is a second independent variable that is included because it is believed to have a significant contributory or contingent effect on the originally stated IV-DV relationship. For example, one might hypothesize that

> The introduction of the four-day workweek (IV) will lead to higher productivity (DV), especially among younger workers (MV).

In this case, there is a differential pattern of relationship between the four-day week and productivity that is the result of age differences among the workers.

Whether a given variable is treated as an independent or as a moderating variable depends on the hypothesis. If you are interested in studying the impact of length of workweek, you would make the length of week the IV. If you were focusing on the relationship of age of worker and productivity, you might use workweek length as a moderating variable. If Myra had been a reporter (rather than an Army Reserve Captain), viewing the local death and injury statistics she might have arrived at a different hypothesis:

> The loss of mining jobs (IV) leads to acceptance of higher-risk behaviors to earn a family-supporting income—race-car driving or nocturnal scavenging (DV) especially due to the proximity of the firing range (MV) and limited education (MV) of the residents.

Extraneous Variables   An almost infinite number of **extraneous variables** (EV) exists that might conceivably affect a given relationship. Some can be treated as independent or moderating variables, but most must either be assumed or excluded from the study. Fortunately, the infinite number of variables has little or no effect on a given situation. Most can be safely ignored. Others may be important, but their impact occurs in such a random fashion as to have little effect. Using the example of the effect of the four-day workweek, one would normally think the imposition of a local sales tax, the election of a new mayor, a three-day rainy spell, and thousands of similar events and conditions would have little effect on workweek and office productivity.

However, there may be other extraneous variables to consider as possible confounding variables to our hypothesized IV-DV relationship. For example, Myra might think that level of education as it impacts job skills might have an impact on income-producing activity. This notion might lead to our introducing an extraneous variable as the **control**:

> Among residents with less than a high school education (EV-control), the loss of high income mining jobs (IV) leads to acceptance of higher-risk behaviors to earn a family-supporting income—race-car driving or nocturnal scavenging (DV) especially due to the proximity of the firing range (MV).

Alternatively, one might think that the *kind of work being done* would have an effect on any workweek length impact on office productivity. This might lead to our introducing a control as follows:

> In routine office work (EV-control), the introduction of a four-day workweek (IV) will lead to higher productivity (DV), especially among younger workers (MV).

In our office example, we would attempt to control for type of work by studying the effects of the four-day week within groups performing different types of work, just as Myra would attempt to control for employable job skills by studying education patterns of the scavengers.

Intervening Variables The variables mentioned with regard to causal relationships are concrete and clearly measurable; they can be seen, counted, or observed in some way. Sometimes, however, one may not be completely satisfied by the explanations they give. Thus, while we may recognize that a four-day workweek results in higher productivity, we might think this is not the full explanation— that workweek length affects some intervening variable, which, in turn, results in higher productivity. An intervening variable is a conceptual mechanism through which the IV and MV might affect the DV. The **intervening variable** (IVV) may be defined as "that factor which theoretically affects the observed phenomenon but cannot be seen, measured, or manipulated; its effect must be inferred from the effects of the independent and moderator variables on the observed phenomenon."[19]

In the case of the workweek hypothesis, one might view the intervening variable (IVV) to be job satisfaction, giving a hypothesis such as:

> The introduction of a four-day workweek will lead to higher productivity by increasing job satisfaction (IVV).

Here are additional examples illustrating the relationships involving independent, moderating, controlled extraneous, and dependent variables. The management of a bank wishes to study the effect of promotion on savings. It might advance the following hypothesis:

> A promotion campaign (IV) will increase savings activity (DV), especially when free prizes are offered (MV), but chiefly among smaller savers (EV-control). The results come from enhancing the motivation to save (IVV).

Or suppose you are studying a situation involving the causes of defective parts production. You might hypothesize the following:

> Changing to worker self-inspection (IV) will reduce the number of defective parts (DV), when the part can be identified with its producer (MV), in electronic assembly work (EV-control), by stimulating the worker's sense of responsibility (IVV).

And, finally, Myra's proposal to the Army hypothesized that

> Marking "dud" shells with kerosene lanterns for same-evening detonation (IV) will reduce nocturnal scavenging (DV) by poorly educated local residents (MV) by eliminating the profit motive for such behavior (IVV).

Propositions and Hypotheses

The research literature disagrees about the meanings of the terms *proposition* and *hypothesis*. We define a **proposition** as a statement about concepts that may be judged as true or false if it refers to observable phenomena. When a proposition is formulated for empirical testing, we call it a **hypothesis.** As a declarative statement, a hypothesis is of a tentative and conjectural nature.

Hypotheses have also been described as statements in which we assign variables to cases. A **case** is defined in this sense as the entity or thing the hypothesis talks about. The variable is the characteristic, trait, or attribute that, in the hypothesis, is imputed to the case.[20] For example, we might form the hypothesis, "Executive Jones (case) has a higher-than-average achievement motivation (variable)." If our hypothesis were based on more than one case, it would be a *generalization*. For example, "Executives in Company Z (cases) have a higher-than-average achievement motivation (variable)." Both of these hypotheses are examples of **descriptive hypotheses**.

Descriptive Hypotheses   *These are propositions that typically state the existence, size, form, or distribution of some variable.* For example, "The current unemployment rate in Detroit exceeds 6 percent of the labor force." In this example, the case is Detroit and the variable is the unemployment rate. Examples of other simple descriptive hypotheses are: "American cities are experiencing budget difficulties," and "Eighty percent of Company Z stockholders favor increasing the company's cash dividend." In the first illustration, "city" is the case and "budget difficulties" is the variable. In the second example, "Company Z stockholders" is the case and "stockholder attitude toward increased cash dividends" is the variable. Or "Seventy percent of the high school–educated males (case) scavenge in the Army firing range for salvageable metals" (variable).

Researchers often use a research question rather than a descriptive hypothesis. Thus, in place of the above hypotheses, we might use the following questions: "What is the unemployment rate in Detroit?" "Are American cities experiencing budget difficulties?" "Do stockholders of Company Z favor an increased cash dividend?" "Do a majority of male residents scavenge in the Army firing range for salvageable metals?" Either format is acceptable, but the hypothesis has several advantages. It encourages researchers to crystallize their thinking about the likely relationships to be found; it further encourages them to think about the implications of a supported or rejected finding. Finally, hypotheses are especially useful for testing statistical significance. Research questions are less frequently used with the next type of situation—one calling for **relational hypotheses**.

Relational Hypotheses   *These are statements that describe a relationship between two variables with respect to some case.* For example, "Foreign cars are perceived by American consumers to be of better quality than domestic cars." In this instance, the case is "American consumers" and the variables are "country of origin" and "perceived quality." The nature of the relationship between the two variables is not specified. Is there only an implication that the variables occur in some predictable relationship, or is one variable somehow responsible for the other? The first interpretation (unspecified relationship) indicates a *correlational* relationship; the second (predictable relationship) indicates an *explanatory*, or *causal*, relationship.

Correlational relationships state merely that the variables occur together in some specified manner without implying that one causes the other. Such weak claims are often made when we believe there are more basic causal forces that affect both variables or when we have not developed enough evidence to claim a stronger linkage. Here are three sample correlational hypotheses: (1) Young machinists (under 35 years of age) are less productive than those who are 35 years or older. (2) The height of women's hemlines varies directly with the level of the business cycle. (3) People in Atlanta give the president a more favorable rating than do people in St.

Louis. By labeling these as **correlational hypotheses**, we make no claim that one variable causes the other to change or take on different values. Other persons, however, may view one or more of these hypotheses as reflecting cause-and-effect relationships.

With **explanatory, (causal), hypotheses**, there is an implication that the existence of, or a change in, one variable causes or leads to an effect on the other variable. As we noted previously, the causal variable is typically called the independent variable (IV) and the other the dependent variable (DV). *Cause* means roughly to "help make happen." So, the IV need not be the sole reason for the existence of, or change in, the DV. Here are four examples of explanatory hypotheses:

1. An increase in family income leads to an increase in the percentage of income saved.
2. Exposure to the company's messages concerning industry problems leads to more favorable attitudes by production workers toward the company.
3. Loyalty to a particular grocery store increases the probability of purchasing the private brands sponsored by that store.
4. An increase in the price of salvaged copper wire leads to an increase in scavenging on the Army firing range.

In proposing or interpreting causal hypotheses, the researcher must consider the direction of influence. In many cases, the direction is obvious from the nature of the variables. Thus, in example 1, one would assume that family income influences savings rate rather than the reverse case. This also holds true for example 4. In example 2, our ability to identify the direction of influence depends on the research design. If the message clearly precedes the attitude measurement, then the direction of exposure to attitude seems clear; if information about both exposure and attitude were collected at the same time, there might be justification for saying that different attitudes led to selective message exposure or nonexposure. In example 3, the variables appear to be interdependent. Loyalty to a store may increase the probability of buying the store's private brands, but the use of private brands may also lead to greater store loyalty.

The Role of the Hypothesis   In research, a hypothesis serves several important functions. The most important is that it guides the direction of the study. A frequent problem in research is the proliferation of interesting information. Unless the researcher curbs the urge to include additional elements, a study can be diluted by trivial concerns that do not answer the basic questions posed. The virtue of the hypothesis is that, if taken seriously, it limits what shall be studied and what shall not. It identifies facts that are relevant and those that are not; in so doing, it suggests which form of research design is likely to be most appropriate. A final role of the hypothesis is to provide a framework for organizing the conclusions that result.

To consider specifically the role of the hypothesis in determining the direction of the research, suppose we use this:

Husbands and wives agree in their perceptions of their respective roles in purchase decisions.

The hypothesis specifies who shall be studied (married couples), in what context they shall be studied (their consumer decision making), and what shall be studied (their individual perceptions of their roles).

The nature of this hypothesis and the implications of the statement suggest that the best research design is probably a survey or an interview. We have at this time no other practical means to ascertain perceptions of people except to ask about them in one way or another. In addition, we are interested only in the roles that are assumed in the purchase or consumer decision-making situation. The study should not, therefore, involve itself in seeking information about other types of roles husband and wife might play. Reflection upon this hypothesis might also reveal that husbands and wives disagree on their perceptions of roles but these differences may be explained in terms of additional variables, such as age, social class, background, personality differences, and other factors not associated with their differences of gender.

What Is a Good Hypothesis?   A good hypothesis should fulfill three conditions. The most elementary requirement is that it be *adequate for its purpose*. For a descriptive hypothesis, this means it clearly states the condition, size, or distribution of some variable in terms of values meaningful to the research task. If it is an explanatory hypothesis, it must explain the facts that gave rise to the need for explanation. Using the hypothesis, plus other known and accepted generalizations, one should be able to deduce the original problem condition.

A second major condition is that the hypothesis must be *testable*. A hypothesis is not testable if it calls for techniques that are not available with the present state of the art. A hypothesis is also untestable if it calls for an explanation that defies known physical or psychological laws. Explanatory hypotheses are also untestable if there are no consequences or derivatives that can be deduced for testing purposes.

For explanatory hypotheses, there is another major condition: The hypothesis must be *better than its rivals*. Generally, the better hypothesis has a greater range than its rivals; it explains more facts and a greater variety of facts than do others. The better hypothesis is also the one that informed judges accept as being the most likely. Their opinions can be highly subjective but depend chiefly on their judgment of which hypothesis fits best with other information. Finally, the better hypothesis is the simple one requiring few conditions or assumptions.

Hypotheses play an important role in the development of theory. While theory development has not historically been an important aspect of business research, it is becoming more so.

Theory

A person not familiar with research uses the term *theory* to express the opposite of *fact*. In this sense, theory is viewed as being speculative or ivory tower. One hears that Professor X is too theoretical, that managers need to be practical, or that some idea will not work because it is too theoretical. This is an incorrect picture of the relationship between fact and theory.

When you are too theoretical, your basis of explanation or decision is not sufficiently attuned to specific empirical conditions. This may be so, but it does not prove that theory and fact are opposites. The truth is that fact and theory are each necessary for the other to be of value. Our ability to make rational decisions, as well as to develop scientific knowledge, is measured by the degree to which we combine fact and theory.

We all operate on the basis of theories we hold. In one sense, theories are the generalizations we make about variables and the relationships among them. We use these generalizations to make decisions and predict outcomes. For example, it is midday and you note that the outside natural light is dimming, dark clouds are moving rapidly in from the west, the breeze is freshening, and the air temperature is cooling. Would your understanding of the relationship among these variables (your weather theory) lead you to a prediction that something undesirable will probably occur in a short time?

Consider a situation where you are called on to interview two persons for possible promotion to the position of department manager. Do you have a theory about what characteristics such a person should have? Suppose you interview Ms. A and observe that she answers your questions well, openly, and apparently sincerely. She also expresses thoughtful ideas about how to improve departmental functioning and is articulate in stating her views. Ms. B, on the other hand, is guarded in her comments and reluctant to advance ideas for improvements. She answers questions by saying what "Mr. General Manager wants." She is also less articulate and seems less sincere than Ms. A. You would probably choose A, based on the way you combine the concepts, definitions, and propositions mentioned into a theory of managerial effectiveness. It may not be a good theory because of the variables we have ignored, but it illustrates that we all use theory to guide our decisions, predictions, and explanations.

A **theory** is a set of systematically interrelated concepts, definitions, and propositions that are advanced to explain and predict phenomena (facts). In this sense, we have many theories and use them continually to explain or predict what goes on around us. To the degree that our theories are sound, and fit the situation, we are successful in our explanations and predictions. Thus, while a given theory and a set of facts may not fit, they are not opposites. Our challenge is to build a better theory and to be more skillful in fitting theory and fact together.

A point that may also cause some confusion is that of how theory differs from hypothesis. One person may advance an explanation and call it a theory, while another may call it a hypothesis. It may be difficult to distinguish one from the other since both involve concepts, definitions, and relationships among variables. The basic differences are in the level of complexity and abstraction. Theories tend to be abstract and involve multiple variables; hypotheses tend to be simple, two-variable propositions involving concrete instances. *In this book, we make the general distinction that the difference between theory and hypothesis is one of degree of complexity and abstraction.* At times theory and hypotheses are used synonomously but doing so should not make much practical research difference.

Theory and Research   It is important for researchers to recognize the pervasiveness and value of theory. Theory serves us in many useful ways. First, as orientation, it narrows the range of facts we need to study. Any problem may be studied in a number of different ways, and theory suggests which ways are likely to yield the greatest meaning. Theory may also suggest a system for the researcher to impose on data in order to classify them in the most meaningful way. Theory also summarizes what is known about an object of study and states the uniformities that lie beyond the immediate observation; when it does so, theory can also be used to predict further facts that should be found.

Models

The term *model* is used throughout the various fields of business and allied disciplines with little agreement as to its definition. This may be because of the numerous functions, structures, and types of models. However, most definitions agree that models represent phenomena through the use of analogy. A **model** is defined here as a representation of a system that is constructed to study some aspect of that system or the system as a whole. Models differ from theories in that a theory's role is explanation whereas a model's role is representation:

> A model is not an explanation; it is only the structure and/or function of a second object or process. A model is the result of taking the structure or function of one object or process and using that as a model for the second. When the substance, either physical or conceptual, of the second object or process has been projected onto the first, a model has been constructed.[21]

Many ideas about new product adoption, for example, can be traced to rural sociology models that described how information and innovations spread throughout communities or cultures. Those models were constructed using the analogues of more established medical theories of epidemiology because of the inadequacy of social science theories at the time.

Models may be used for applied or highly theoretical purposes. Almost everyone is familiar with queuing models of services: banks, post offices, telephone switchboards, or airport security stations. Other models that consider assembly lines, transportation, and inventory also attempt to solve immediate practical needs. A model to advance a theory of quality of work life, for example, could target employee behavior under conditions of flextime, permanent part-time, job sharing, and compressed workweek.

Description, explication, and simulation are the three major functions of modeling. Each of these functions is appropriate for applied research or theory building. Descriptive models seek to describe the behavior of elements in a system where theory is inadequate or nonexistent. Explicative models are used to extend the application of well-developed theories or improve our understanding of their key concepts. Simulation models go beyond the goal of clarifying the structural relations of concepts and attempt to reveal the process relations among them.[22] Monte Carlo simulation models are examples of static simulations that represent a system at one point in time. They simulate probabilistic processes using random numbers. Simulations that represent the evolution of a system over time are called dynamic. Redistribution of market share, brand switching, and prediction of future values are examples that benefit from dynamic modeling.

Summary

Styles of thinking are perspectives or filters for determining how we view and understand reality. They affect what we accept as truth and specify how rigorously we test the information we receive before endorsing it. Although the scientific method is the preeminent means by which we secure empirical information, it is not the only source of truth. Other styles of thinking also have an apparent and often useful influence on business disciplines and place their imprimatur on the theory-building and problem-solving approaches of those fields.

Scientific inquiry is grounded in the inference process. This process is used for the development and testing of various propositions largely through the double movement of reflective thinking. Reflective thinking consists of sequencing induction and deduction in order to explain inductively (by hypothesis) a puzzling condition. In turn, the hypothesis is used in a deduction of further facts that can be sought to confirm or deny the truth of the hypothesis.

Researchers think of the doing of science (rather than the inspiration for discovery or the scientific attitude) as an orderly process that combines induction, deduction, observation, and hypothesis testing into a set of reflective thinking activities. Although the scientific method consists of neither sequential nor independent stages, the problem-solving process that it reveals provides insight into the way research is conducted.

Scientific methods and scientific thinking are based on concepts, the symbols we attach to bundles of meaning that we hold and share with others. We invent concepts to think about and communicate abstractions. We also use higher-level concepts—constructs—for specialized scientific explanatory purposes that are not directly observable. Concepts, constructs, and variables may be defined descriptively or operationally. Operational definitions, which are essential in research, must specify adequately the empirical information needed and how it will be collected. In addition, they must have the proper scope or fit for the research problem at hand.

Concepts and constructs are used at the theoretical levels; variables are used at the empirical level. Variables accept numerals or values for the purpose of testing and measurement. They may be classified as explanatory (independent, dependent, or moderating), extraneous, and intervening.

Propositions are of great interest in research because they may be used to assess the truth or falsity of relationships among observable phenomena. When we advance a proposition for testing, we are hypothesizing. A hypothesis describes the relationships between or among variables. A good hypothesis is one that can explain what it claims to explain, is testable, and has greater range, probability, and simplicity than its rivals.

Sets of interrelated concepts, definitions, and propositions that are advanced to explain and predict phenomena are theories. Models differ from theories in that models are analogies or representations of some aspect of a system or of the system as a whole. Models are used for description, explication, and simulation.

Key Terms

case(s)	model
concept	operational definition
conceptual scheme	proposition
construct	rationalism
deduction	theory
double movement of reflective thought	variable(s)
empiricism	control
hypothesis	dependent
correlational	extraneous
descriptive	extraneous (control)
explanatory (causal)	independent
relational	intervening
induction	moderating

Discussion Questions

1. Distinguish among the following sets of items, and suggest the significance of each in a research context.

    a. Concept and construct

    b. Deduction and induction

    c. Operational definition and dictionary definition

    d. Concept and variable

    e. Hypothesis and proposition

    f. Theory and model

    g. Scientific method and scientific attitude

2. Describe the characteristics of the scientific method.

3. Find the inductions and deductions in the following statements. If there are gaps, supply what is needed to make them complete arguments.

    a. Repeated studies indicate that economic conditions vary with—and lag 6 to 12 months behind—the changes in the national money supply. Therefore, we may conclude the money supply is the basic economic variable.

    b. Research studies show that heavy smokers have a higher rate of lung cancer than do nonsmokers; therefore, heavy smoking causes lung cancer.

    c. Show me a person who goes to church regularly, and I will show you a reliable worker.

4. What are the differences among the research approaches (and thinking styles) that guide the predominant kinds of studies done in operations research, marketing, finance, or organizational behavior?

5. Here are some terms commonly found in a management setting. Are they concepts or constructs? Give two different operational definitions for each.

    a. first-line supervisor   *c.* assembly line

    b. employee morale   *d.* overdue account

    e. line management   *h.* union democracy

    f. leadership   *i.* ethical standards

    g. price-earnings ratio

6. In your company's management development program, there was a heated discussion between some people who claimed, "Theory is impractical and thus no good," and others who claimed, "Good theory is the most practical approach to problems." What position would you take and why?

7. You wish to study a condition that you have observed: "Some workers seem to be much more diligent than others."

    a. Propose at least three concepts and three constructs you might use in such a study.

    b. How might any of these concepts and/or constructs be related to explanatory hypotheses?

8. In a metal-stamping plant, the production manager is facing a quality problem. The production process forms large sheets of metal into auto fenders using large stamping machines. Suddenly, yesterday, the quality of the stamped fenders deteriorated. This problem began in department A but quickly spread to the other departments. At a meeting to deal with this problem, the assistant plant manager reported that yesterday, on the first shift, the foreman in department A caught a worker drinking on the job and summarily fired him. This man had been a problem in the past, and it was reported that he and the foreman had often argued. The workers in department A were angered by this treatment of one of their popular co-workers. The shop steward claimed the firing was unfair and violated the union contract. As a result of the firing, there was considerable negative reaction among the workers.

    a. Propose several hypotheses that might account for the sudden surge in poor-quality output.

    b. Using the double movement of reflective thought, show how you would test these hypotheses.

9. An automobile manufacturer observes the demand for its brand increasing as per capita income increases. Sales increases also follow low interest rates, which ease credit conditions. Buyer purchase behavior is seen to be dependent on age and gender. Other factors influencing sales appear to fluctuate almost randomly (competitor advertising, competitor dealer discounts, introductions of competitive new models).

    a. If sales and per capita income are positively related, classify all variables as dependent, independent, moderating, extraneous, or intervening.

    b. Comment on the utility of a model based on the hypothesis.

Reference Notes   1. The title of Figure 2–1, and the section, "Styles of Thinking," are borrowed from Abraham Kaplan, *The Conduct of Inquiry* (San Francisco: Chandler, 1964), pp. 259–62. The axes and the positions of C. W. Churchman's inquiring systems are based on the work of I. I.

Mitroff and R. O. Mason, "Business Policy and Metaphysics: Some Philosophical Considerations," *Academy of Management Review 7* (1982), pp. 361–71. The locations of the other philosophical viewpoints in the figure are approximations.

2. P. McC. Miller and M. J. Wilson, eds., *A Dictionary of Social Sciences Methods* (New York: Wiley, 1983), p. 27. Also see Benjamin B. Wolman, ed., *Dictionary of Behavioral Science,* 2nd ed. (New York: Academic Press, 1989).

3. Kenneth R. Hoover, *The Elements of Social Scientific Thinking,* 5th ed. (New York: St. Martin's Press, 1991), p. 5.

4. Kaplan, *The Conduct of Inquiry.*

5. George S. Howard, *Methods in the Social Sciences* (Glenview, IL: Scott, Foresman, 1985), p. 7.

6. Thomas S. Kuhn, *The Structure of Scientific Revolutions* (Chicago: University of Chicago Press, 1970).

7. Howard Kahane, *Logic and Philosophy*, 2nd ed. (Belmont, CA: Wadsworth, 1973), p. 3.

8. John Dewey, *How We Think* (Boston: Heath, 1910), p. 79.

9. This section is based on Dewey, *How We Think*; Robert J. Kibler, "Basic Communication Research Considerations," in *Methods of Research in Communication*, eds. Philip Emmert and William D. Brooks (Boston: Houghton Mifflin, 1970); and John R. Platt, "Strong Inference," *Science*, October 16, 1964, pp. 347–53.

10. See, for example, C. Wright Mills, *The Sociological Imagination* (London: Oxford University Press, 1959); and Peter B. Medawar, *The Art of the Soluable* (London: Methuen, 1967).

11. See, for example, Horace F. Judson, *The Eighth Day of Creation: Makers of the Revolution in Biology* (New York: Simon & Schuster, 1979).

12. F. J. Roethlisberger and W. J. Dickson, *Management and the Worker* (Cambridge, MA: Harvard University Press, 1939).

13. Paul R. Lawrence, "Historical Development of Organizational Behavior," in *Handbook of Organizational Behavior*, ed. Jay W. Lorsch (Englewood Cliffs, NJ: Prentice-Hall, 1987), p. 6.

14. Kuhn, *The Structure of Scientific Revolutions*, p. 37.

15. Hoover, *The Elements of Social Scientific Thinking*, p. 21.

16. *Webster's New Collegiate Dictionary* (Springfield, MA: G & C Merriam, 1961), pp. 205, 617, and 154.

17. Fred N. Kerlinger, *Foundations of Behavioral Research*, 3rd ed. (New York: Holt, Rinehart & Winston, 1986), p. 27.

18. Hoover, *The Elements of Social Scientific Thinking*, p. 71.

19. Bruce Tuckman, *Conducting Educational Research* (New York: Harcourt Brace Jovanovich, 1972), p. 45.

20. William N. Stephens, *Hypotheses and Evidence* (New York: Thomas Y. Crowell, 1968), p. 5.

21. Leonard C. Hawes, *Pragmatics of Analoguing: Theory and Model Construction in Communication* (Reading, MA: Addison-Wesley, 1975), p. 111.

22. Ibid., pp. 116–22.

Suggested Readings

1. Beardsley, Monroe. *Practical Logic*. Englewood Cliffs, NJ: Prentice-Hall, 1969. A lucid discussion of deduction and induction as well as an excellent coverage of argument analysis.

2. Churchman, C. W. *The Design of Inquiring Systems*. New York: Basic Books, 1971. An essential work for understanding the connections between philosophy, science, and the nature of inquiry.

3. Hawes, Leonard C. *Pragmatics of Analoguing: Theory and Model Construction in Communication*. Reading, MA: Addison-Wesley, 1975. A splendid discussion on theory and model building with behavioral science examples.

4. Hoover, Kenneth R., and Todd Donovan. *The Elements of Social Scientific Thinking,* 6th ed. New York: St. Martin's Press, 1995. A brief but highly readable treatise on the elements of science and scientific thinking.

5. Kaplan, Abraham. *The Conduct of Inquiry*. San Francisco: Chandler, 1964. A classic source for the philosophy of science and logical reasoning.

6. Kerlinger, Fred N. *Foundations of Behavioral Research*, 3rd ed. New York: Holt, Rinehart & Winston, 1986. Comprehensive coverage of the scientific concepts and ways of knowing.

THE RESEARCH PROCESS

 CHAPTER NAVIGATION

BRINGING RESEARCH TO LIFE

On the return flight from Austin, Jason and Myra were euphoric. "That went really well," he said. "Better even than I hoped for."

"Yes. Terrific," she said. "Just fine. You handled yourself very well, Jason. You were so patient. Of course, we are not home free. We have lots of work ahead before we satisfy the big bosses at Mind-Writer. But it was a good start. Definitely."

"Definitely."

They toasted each other and their visit with the MindWriter product people, especially Gracie Uhura, the product manager. They sat and sipped their drinks, enjoying a feeling of accomplishment.

"On the other hand," said Jason, by and by, "there are going to be a few problems."

"Aren't there always?"

"Gracie wants the sun, the sky, and the moon. She wants everything. Wants to know the demographic characteristics of her users . . . their job descriptions . . . their salaries . . . their ethnicities . . . their educations. Wants to know their perception of your company . . . of the quality of MindWriter's specific models. Wants to know their satisfaction with the purchase channel and with the service department, too."

"What's wrong with wanting all that, if Mind-Writer is willing to pay?"

"I may perceive the company as hugely profitable and a bottomless source of research dollars, but you and she need to keep your eye on the bottom line. You can bet there is a bean counter somewhere who will want to know how you and Gracie can justify asking all these questions. What is going to be the payoff in knowing the ethnicity of customers, they will ask? And if you or Gracie can't explain the justification for needing the information, if one of you can't establish that the dollar benefit of knowing is at least as great as the dollar cost of finding out, Mr. Bean Counter is going to strike the question off the list and reduce what MindWriter is willing to pay for."

"Is there no way we can justify knowing everything Gracie wants to know? After all, this is my first project with her. It certainly wouldn't hurt my reputation within MindWriter by showing how well I can deliver what my top executives want."

"Sure there is. Or at least there may be. We can do a pilot study for her of a few hundred customers and see if the ethnic background, or the salary level, or any other nonattitudinal item that Gracie cares about, is a good indicator of satisfaction, willingness to make a repeat purchase, postpurchase service satisfaction, and so forth. If it is, maybe more extensive measurement can be justified."

"Clever!"

"Well, that's why you came to me; we do exemplary research."

"So, am I right in believing you feel we need to propose an exploratory study for that problem first, and propose a larger study later?"

"That would be standard practice. There are questions that have to be resolved before each side can commit to a major study. We want to minimize the risks to both sides. For example, Gracie wants to know the customers' perception of MindWriter's overall quality. But we have to ask ourselves, 'Are these customers really qualified to form independent opinions, or will they simply be parroting what they have read in the computer magazines or what a dealer told them?' We will have to do a pilot study of a few hundred users to determine if it is really useful to ask them their overall impression of the product."

"I follow you!"

"On the other hand, the repair problem really interests me. We can be reasonably sure that the customers know their own minds when it comes to evaluating their firsthand experience with Mind-Writer's service department. This business of returning a computer for service is something you experience firsthand, not something in a magazine, and it's worth studying. I had a chance last night to look over the letters you gave me."

He dug into his briefcase and extracted a sheaf of photocopies. "These are the letters the service department received about MindWriter. And here are notes on phone conversations that Gracie gave *(continued)* me. One person writes, 'My MindWriter was badly damaged on arrival. I could not believe its condition when I unpacked it.' And here is 'The service technicians seemed to be unable to understand my complaint, but once they understood it, they performed immediate repairs.' You and I will boil these down—and possibly dozens more like them—to a couple of representative questions that can be pilot-tested for clarity, reliability, and validity. . . . I'll explain these terms later. The point is, MindWriter has

to pay for everything Gracie says she wants, what she wants that has a payoff, what she wants that has a payoff and is researchable. . . . We are going to be very busy in the next few weeks."

"I understand what you are saying, believe it or not. Yes, you are starting to make good sense. I think we are going to get along."

"You know what, Myra? I'm starting to think you're right."

THE RESEARCH PROCESS

Writers usually treat the research task as a sequential process involving several clearly defined steps. Variations are suggested for different situations, but there is much similarity among the sequences proposed. No one claims that research requires completion of each step before going to the next. Recycling, circumventing, and skipping occur. Some steps are begun out of sequence, some are carried out simultaneously, and some may be omitted. Despite these variations, the idea of a sequence is useful for developing a project and for keeping the project orderly as it unfolds.

Figure 3–1 models the sequence of the **research process.** We refer to it often as we discuss each step in subsequent chapters. Our discussion of the questions that guide project planning and data gathering is incorporated into the model (see the inverted pyramids in Figure 3–1 and compare them with Figure 3–2). Figure 3–1 also organizes this chapter and introduces the remainder of the book.

The research process begins much as the vignette suggests. A management dilemma triggers the need for a decision. For MindWriter, a growing number of complaints about postpurchase service started the process. In other situations, a controversy arises, a major commitment of resources is called for, or conditions in the environment signal the need for a decision. For MindWriter, the critical event could have been the introduction by a competitor of new technology that would revolutionize the processing speed of laptops. Such events cause managers to reconsider their purposes or objectives, define a problem for solution, or develop strategies for solutions they have identified.

In our view of the research process, the management question—its origin, selection, statement, exploration, and refinement—is the critical activity in the sequence. Throughout the chapter we emphasize problem-related steps. A familiar quotation from Albert Einstein, no less apt today than when it was written, supports this view:

> The formulation of a problem is far more often essential than its solution, which may be merely a matter of mathematical or experimental skill. To raise new questions, new possibilities, to regard old problems from a new angle requires creative imagination and marks real advance in science.[1]

FIGURE 3–1 **The Research Process**

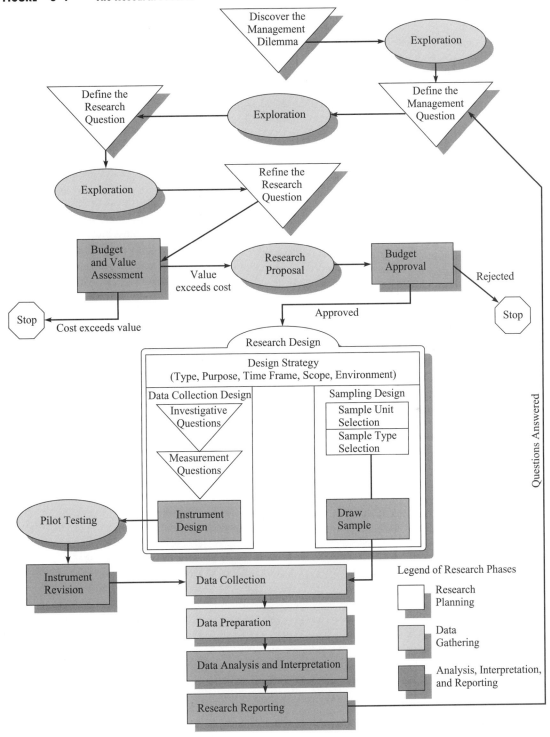

Whether the researcher is involved in basic or applied research, a thorough understanding of the management question is fundamental to success in the research enterprise.

THE MANAGEMENT-RESEARCH QUESTION HIERARCHY

A useful way to approach the research process is to state the basic dilemma that prompts the research, and then try to develop other questions by progressively breaking down the original question into more specific ones. You can think of the outcome of this process as the **management-research question hierarchy** (see Figure 3–2). Figure 3–4 provides an example of the kinds of questions asked at each level of the hierarchy.

The process begins at the most general level with the **management dilemma.** This is a symptom of an actual problem. It might be rising costs, the discovery of an expensive chemical compound that would increase the efficacy of a drug, increasing tenant moveouts from an apartment complex, declining sales, increasing employee turnover in a restaurant, a larger number of product defects during manufacture of an automobile, or as in MindWriter, an increasing number of letters and phone complaints about postpurchase service. (You can follow the research process as it develops for MindWriter in Figure 3–3.)

Identifying management dilemmas is rarely difficult (unless the organization fails to track its performance factors—like sales, profits, employee turnover, manufacturing output and defects, on-time deliveries, customer satisfaction, etc.). However, choosing one dilemma on which to focus may be difficult. Choosing incorrectly will direct valuable resources (time, manpower, money, equipment) on a path that may not provide critical decision-making information (the purpose of good research). The choice is like learning to balance a pencil on its point on your finger, a

FIGURE   3–2   Management-Research Question Hierarchy

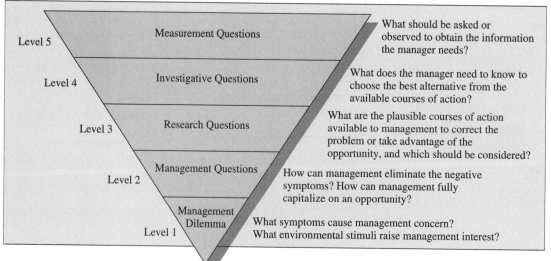

coin on its edge, or a pyramid on its pinnacle: only practice as a manager makes you proficient. For new managers, or established managers facing new responsibilities, developing several management-research question hierarchies, each starting with a different dilemma, will assist in the choice process. In all figures related to the research process model, in this and subsequent chapters, we use an inverted pyramid to represent the management-research question hierarchy to reinforce the precarious nature of the foundation decisions in the research process.

The Management Question

The manager must move from the management dilemma to the **management question** to proceed with the research process. The management question restates the dilemma in question form. What should be done to reduce employee turnover? What should be done to increase tenant residency and reduce moveouts? What should be done to reduce costs?

Management Question Categories   Management questions are too numerous to list, but we can categorize them. The first type concerns the *choice of purposes or objectives*. The general question is, "What do we want to achieve?" At the company level the question might be, "Should we at XYZ Corporation reconsider our basic corporate objectives as they concern our public image?" More narrowly, a management question on objectives might ask, "What goals should XYZ try to achieve in our next labor negotiations?"

A second category of management questions concerns the *generation and evaluation of solutions*. The general question is, "How can we achieve the ends we seek?" Research projects in this group usually deal with concrete problems that managers quickly recognize as useful. Projects can involve such questions as, "How can we achieve our five-year goal of doubled sales and net profits?" Mind-Writer's management question might be, "What should be done to improve the CompleteCare program for MindWriter product repairs and servicing?" or "What should be done to reduce postpurchase service complaints?"

A third class of management questions concerns the *troubleshooting or control situation*. The problem usually involves monitoring or diagnosing various ways in which an organization is failing to achieve its established goals. This group includes such questions as, "Why does our department incur the highest costs?" and "How well is our program meeting its goals?"

Since the definition of the management question sets the research task, a poorly defined management question will misdirect research efforts. No matter how the management question is defined, many research directions can be taken. A specific question can lead to many studies. Concern for the XYZ's company image might lead to a survey among various groups to discover their attitudes toward the company. This question might suggest research into what other companies are doing to polish their images. Another question might call for a forecast of expected changes in social attitudes. The question concerning XYZ's labor negotiation objectives might prompt research into what recent settlements in the industry have been. Alternatively, it might involve a survey among workers to find out how well management has met their concerns about the quality of work life. It is the joint responsibility of the researcher and the manager to choose the most productive project.

The Nature of the Management Question   Assume, for example, a researcher is asked to help the new management of a bank. The president is concerned about erosion of the bank's profitability (the management dilemma) and wants to turn this situation around. Center City Bank is the oldest and largest of three banks in a city of about 50,000 population. Profits have stagnated in recent years. The president and the consultant discuss the problem facing the organization and settle on this management question: "How can we improve our profit picture?"

The management question does not specify what kind of research is to be done. This question is strictly managerial in thrust. It implies that the bank's management faces the task of developing a strategy for increasing profits. The question is broad. Notice that it doesn't indicate whether management should increase profits via increased deposits, downsizing personnel, outsourcing of the payroll function, or some other means.

Further discussion between the bank president and the researcher shows there are really two questions to be answered. The problem of low deposit growth is linked to concerns of a competitive nature. While lowered deposits directly affect profits, another part of the profit weakness is associated with negative factors within the organization that are increasing costs of operation. A qualified researcher knows that the management question as stated is too broad to guide a definitive research project. As a starting point, the broadly worded question is fine, but Center City Bank will want to refine its management question into more specific subquestions: "How can we improve deposits?" and "How can we reduce costs?" This separation of the management question into two subquestions may not have occurred without a discussion between the researcher and the manager.

Exploration

Center City Bank had done no formal research in the past. It has little specific information about competitors or customers and has not analyzed its internal operations. To move forward in the management-research question hierarchy (to define the research question), the client needs to collect some exploratory information on (1) what factors contribute to the bank's failure to achieve a stronger growth rate in deposits and (2) how well the bank is doing regarding work climate, efficiency of operations compared to industry norms, and financial condition compared to industry norms and competitors. A small focus group is conducted among employees, and trade association data is acquired to compare financial and operating statistics from company annual reports and end-of-year division reports. From the results of these two exploratory activities, it is obvious that the bank's operations are not as progressive as its competitors' but it has its costs well in line. So the revised management question becomes: "What should be done to make the bank more competitive?"

Exploration has an opportunity to surface within the research process in several locations (see Figure 3–1). An **exploration** typically begins with a search of published data. In addition, the researchers often seek out people well-informed on the topic, especially those who have clearly stated positions on controversial aspects of the problem. Take the case of a company interested in enhancing its position in a given technology that appears to hold potential for future growth. This interest or need might quickly elicit a number of questions:

1. How fast might this technology develop?
2. What are the likely applications of this technology?
3. What companies now possess it, and which ones are likely to make a major effort to get it?
4. How much will it take in resources?
5. What are the likely payoffs?

In the above investigation of opportunities, the researchers would probably begin with specific books and periodicals. They would be looking for only certain aspects in this literature, such as (1) recent developments, (2) predictions by informed figures about the prospects of the technology, (3) identification of those involved in the area, and (4) accounts of successful ventures and failures by others in the field. After becoming familiar with the literature, researchers might seek interviews with scientists, engineers, and product developers who are well known in the field. They would give special attention to those who stand at the extremes of opinion about the prospects of the technology. If possible, they would talk with persons having information on particularly thorny problems in development and application. Of course, much of the information will be confidential and competitive. However, skillful investigation can uncover many useful indicators.

For MindWriter, Myra searched her local library and company archives to discover PC industry studies on service and technical support (see Figure 3–3), as well as published customer satisfaction comparisons among companies and products. Then in the meeting in Austin, both Myra and Jason delved deeply for Gracie's knowledge and perceptions of the CompleteCare program. They also developed a more thorough understanding of production and distribution. Shortly after returning from Austin, Myra and Jason both realize from studying customer correspondence that they need more knowledge on product design, CompleteCare, and product handling, so they plan a second exploratory venture to include expert interviews.

An unstructured exploration allows the researcher to develop and revise the management question and determine what is needed to secure answers to the proposed question. The usefulness of a literature search, experience survey, and focus groups in exploration is discussed in Chapter 6.

The Research Question   Once the researcher has a clear statement of the management question, she and the manager must translate it into a research question. Consider the research question to be a fact-oriented, information-gathering question. There are many different ways to address most management dilemmas. It is at this point of formulating research questions where the insight and expertise of the manager come into play. Only reasonable alternatives should be considered. If the researcher is not

FIGURE   3–3   Research Process for MindWriter

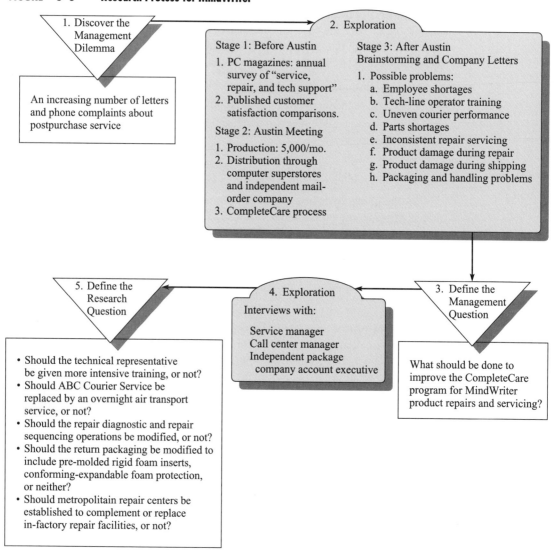

1. Discover the Management Dilemma

An increasing number of letters and phone complaints about postpurchase service

2. Exploration

Stage 1: Before Austin
1. PC magazines: annual survey of "service, repair, and tech support"
2. Published customer satisfaction comparisons.

Stage 2: Austin Meeting
1. Production: 5,000/mo.
2. Distribution through computer superstores and independent mail-order company
3. CompleteCare process

Stage 3: After Austin
Brainstorming and Company Letters
1. Possible problems:
   a. Employee shortages
   b. Tech-line operator training
   c. Uneven courier performance
   d. Parts shortages
   e. Inconsistent repair servicing
   f. Product damage during repair
   g. Product damage during shipping
   h. Packaging and handling problems

3. Define the Management Question

What should be done to improve the CompleteCare program for MindWriter product repairs and servicing?

4. Exploration

Interviews with:

Service manager
Call center manager
Independent package company account executive

5. Define the Research Question

- Should the technical representative be given more intensive training, or not?
- Should ABC Courier Service be replaced by an overnight air transport service, or not?
- Should the repair diagnostic and repair sequencing operations be modified, or not?
- Should the return packaging be modified to include pre-molded rigid foam inserts, conforming-expandable foam protection, or neither?
- Should metropolitain repair centers be established to complement or replace in-factory repair facilities, or not?

part of the manager's decision-making environment, the researcher can be of minimal help in this translation. The manager's direction to the researcher is most important. If however, the researcher is an integral part of the decision-making environment, she may assist the manager in evaluating which courses of action should and can be researched.

In their post-Austin brainstorming session (see Figure 3–3), Jason and Myra hypothesized several possible problems that could have resulted from the complaints in customer letters. Some problems are not as correctable as others (e.g., correcting parts shortages might not be within MindWriter's immediate control, but improving tech-line operator training clearly is). Focusing too early on correcting one problem versus another, could misdirect the research, wasting valuable resources. If Mind-Writer does not maintain a database of complaints, an exploratory study might have to be undertaken to determine which category of complaints is most troublesome. Incorrectly defining the research question is a fundamental weakness in the research process. Time and money can be spent studying an alternative that won't help the manager rectify the dilemma.

The researcher's task is to assist the manager to formulate a research question that fits the need to resolve the management dilemma. A **research question** is the choice hypothesis that best states the objective of the research study. It is a more specific management question, which must be answered. It may be more than one question, or just one. A research process that answers this more specific question provides the manager with the desired information necessary to make the decision he or she is facing.

One of the letters Jason reads on the flight back to Florida from the MindWriter meeting in Austin describes the deplorable condition of a MindWriter laptop upon delivery to the customer. After consulting Gracie, Jason and Myra identify one credible option: to reinforce the shipping carton with rigid foam inserts (in place of the current foam pellets) to prevent damage to the laptop case during shipping. Another option is to use conforming-expanding foam insulation in the shipping carton. A third option is to leave the shipping carton specification as is but ship via an overnight air delivery service rather than using the current ground transportation courier service. Yet another option is to establish authorized repair facilities in major cities, so that a customer could deliver a MindWriter for repair, eliminating shipping altogether.

These choices lead to several research questions: Should MindWriter change the laptop shipping specifications to include rigid foam or conforming-expanding foam or stay with the current foam pellets? Should MindWriter change its shipping carrier from ABC Courier Service to an air transportation service? Should MindWriter establish metropolitan repair centers to complement or replace its existing in-factory repair facilities?

Meanwhile at Center City Bank, the president has agreed to research guided by this research question: Should the Center City Bank position itself as a modern, progressive institution (with appropriate changes in services and policies) or maintain its image as the oldest, most reliable institution in town?

Fine-Tuning the Research Question   The term *fine-tuning* might seem to be an odd usage for research, but it creates an image that most researchers come to recognize. Fine-tuning the question is precisely what a skillful practitioner must do after the exploration is complete. At this point, a clearer picture of the management and research questions begins to emerge. After a preliminary review of the literature, a brief exploratory study, or both, the project begins to crystallize in one of two ways: (1) It is apparent the question has been answered and the process is finished, or (2) a question different from the one originally addressed has appeared. The research question does not have to be materially different, but it will have evolved in some fashion. This is not cause for discouragement. The refined research question(s) will have better focus and move the research forward with more clarity than the initially formulated question(s).

In addition to fine-tuning the original question, other research question-related activities should be addressed in this phase to enhance the direction of the project:

1. Examine the concepts and constructs to be used in the study. Are they satisfactorily defined? Have operational definitions been employed where appropriate?
2. Review the research questions with the intent of breaking them down into specific second- and third-level questions.
3. If hypotheses are used, be certain they meet the quality tests mentioned in the last chapter.
4. Determine what evidence must be collected to answer the various questions and hypotheses.
5. Set the scope of your study by stating what is not a part of the research question. This will establish a boundary to separate contiguous problems from your primary objective.

Investigative Questions   Once the general research question(s) has been selected, researcher thinking moves to a more specific level, that of investigative questions (see Figure 3–4). These questions reflect what the manager feels he or she needs to know to answer the research question. When the characteristics of the problem are well defined and the research question is clearly stated, it is possible to deduce the essential subquestions that will guide the project-planning stages of the research process. However, if the research question is not well defined, or even somewhat ill defined, the research will need to enter the exploration and question revision stages to refine the original question and generate the material for constructing investigative questions.

Investigative questions are questions the researcher must answer to satisfactorily arrive at a conclusion about the research question. To formulate them, the researcher takes a general research question and breaks it into more specific questions about which to gather data. This fractionating process can continue down through several levels of increasingly specific questions. Investigative questions should be included in the research proposal, for they guide the development of the research design. They are the foundation for creating the research data collection instrument.

The researcher working on the Center City Bank project develops two major investigative questions for studying the market with several subquestions under each. The questions provide insight into the lack of deposit growth:

1. What is the public's position regarding financial services and their use?
   a. What specific financial services are used?
   b. How attractive are various services?
   c. What bank-specific and environmental factors influence a person's use of a particular service?

FIGURE 3-4 **Sample Management-Research Question Hierarchy**

Please rate your level of concern for each of the following outcomes if management were to change your compensation to a commission-based system compared to the current salary system. For each outcome, indicate a number between 1 and 7, where 7 = extreme concern, 4 = neither concerned nor unconcerned, 1 = no concern at all.

_____ lack of predictability of monthly pay

_____ increased internal competition for sales prospects

_____ reduced time for postsale servicing of customer needs

What is the likelihood that we will lose excellent salespeople in the South and Northeast if we implement the compensation change? What is the likelihood that current customer satisfaction in these regions will decrease? What is the likelihood that future sales to existing customers will be lost?

Should we introduce a 2% incentive commision-based compensation system on all sales over quota for salespeople in the South and Northeast or a 5% of profit regional bonus to the region that increases sales by 10% over quota (and to be shared proportionately by salespeople in the region)? Should we modify the product formula for distribution in the South and Northeast? Should we increase the level of advertising via trade publications in South and Northeast editions?

How can we improve sales in the South and Northeast?

Why are our sales declining in the South and Northeast, while sales are booming in the Southwest, West, and Midwest regions?

2. What is the bank's competitive position?

   a. What are the geographic patterns of our customers and of our competitors' customers?

   b. What demographic differences are revealed among our customers and those of our competitors?

   c. What words or phrases does the public (both customers and noncustomers) associate with CCB? With CCB's competitors?

   d. How aware is the public of the bank's promotional efforts?

   e. What opinion does the public hold of the bank and our competitors?

   f. How does growth in services compare among competing institutions?

Return again to the MindWriter situation. What does management need to know to choose among differing packaging specifications? As you develop your information needs, think broadly. In developing your list of investigative questions, try to include performance considerations (like the relative costs of the options, speed of packing serviced laptops, condition of test laptops packaged with different materials), attitudinal issues (like perceived service quality), as well as behavioral issues (like employee's ease of use in packing with the considered materials).

Measurement Questions   Measurement questions should be outlined by completion of the project-planning activities but usually await pilot testing for refinement. Some studies lend themselves to predesigned, readily available measurement devices. In such cases, measurement questions have been formulated and tested by previous researchers, are recorded in the literature, and may be applied literally or be adapted for the project at hand. More often, the measurement questions should be devised and tailored to parallel the investigative questions. The resources for this task will be the collective insights from all the activities in the research process completed to this point, particularly insights from exploration and pilot testing of the data collection instrument(s).

Measurement questions constitute the fifth and final level of the hierarchy (see Figure 3–4). In surveys, **measurement questions** are the questions we actually ask the respondents. They appear on the questionnaire. In an observation study, measurement questions are the observations researchers must record about each subject studied.

Center City Bank conducts a survey of local residents. The questionnaire contains many measurement questions seeking information that will provide answers to the investigative questions. Two hundred residents complete questionnaires, and the information collected is used to guide a reorientation of the bank's image.

The assumptions and facts used to structure the management-research question hierarchy set the direction of the project. Using the hierarchy is a good way to methodically think through the various issues. Think of the hierarchy as five sequential levels moving from the general to the specific. While our approach suggests five discrete levels, the hierarchy is actually more of a continuum. The investigative question stage, in particular, may involve several levels of questioning before it is possible to develop satisfactory measurement questions.

CLOSE-UP

The next morning, at 7 A.M. sharp, Myra appears at Jason's home/office. As she presses the doorbell, she hears furniture being wrestled across the floor.

"It's open," hollers Jason.

Inside, Jason has cleared furniture and pictures from the south wall and has leaned a sheet of plywood against that wall. "There's coffee and doughnuts," he says. "But first give me a hand with this."

"This" is a roll of brown wrapping paper. The two of them work together and unroll the hard-to-handle paper left to right across the top two feet of plywood, cut it, and tack down its corners so it covers the top half of the plywood. Then they start on the lower left side of the plywood and repeat the process until the board is fully covered.

They now have a 4- by 8-foot chartboard.

Across the top of the first sheet, Myra writes, "Satisfaction with the Service Department." Today they focus on the easiest task and leave the customer profile pilot study for later. Besides, Gracie is pressed for answers on how the CompleteCare repair program is being received. If she is responsive on the smaller project, they are sure they'd get the OK for the more ambitious one.

They help themselves to coffee and doughnuts, pull two chairs in front of the chartboard, and for five minutes stare in silence at its awful blankness.

Jason has learned a lot about MindWriter. First with a visit to the Internet and an intense search through MindWriter's archives before their Austin trip, and then the meetings in Austin, they know the product is sold through computer superstores and independent mail-order companies. They also learned that MindWriter ships about 5,000 portable/laptop computers per month. The product is successful yet constrained by the same supply shortages as the rest of the industry. Personal computer magazines were consulted for their annual surveys on service, repair, and technical support. Overall customer satisfaction comparisons were obtained from published sources.

The exploratory sessions in Austin revealed much about the CompleteCare process. Myra summarizes the information under the label "CC Process."

When customers experience a malfunction, they call an 800 number. The call center answers service, support, and ordering questions. Technical representatives are trained to

- Take the name, phone, address, and MindWriter model number
- Listen to the customer and ask questions to detect the nature of the problem
- Attempt to resolve the problem if they can walk the customer through corrective steps

If not, the representative provides a return authorization code and dispatches a package courier to pick up the unit before 5 P.M. The unit is delivered to Austin for service the next morning. The CompleteCare repair facility calls the customer if the repair information is incomplete. The unit is repaired by the end of that day and picked up by the courier. The call center then updates its database with service record information. If all goes well, the customer receives the repaired unit by 10 A.M. the following morning, 48 hours after MindWriter received the customer's original problem call.

When Myra finishes, Jason begins to rough out the known "problems." There are employee shortages at the call center and difficulties getting the new technical representatives trained. The courier is uneven in executing its pickup and delivery contract. MindWriter is experiencing parts availability problems for some models. And, occasionally, units are returned to the customer either not fixed or damaged in some way. Jason believes this means the service area is not doing an adequate job. But Myra asserts that problems could be in the original packing, in handling, or even from activities related to taking the boxes on and off the shipping pallets.

Because of their brainstorming, they are able to restate management's question: "What should be done to improve the CompleteCare program for MindWriter product repairs and servicing?" After exploration Myra and Jason brainstormed research and investigative questions as follows:

RESEARCH QUESTIONS

1. Should the technical representative be given more intensive training, or not?
2. Should ABC Courier Service be replaced with an overnight air transport service, or not?
3. Should the repair diagnostic and repair-sequencing operations be modified, or not?

(continued)

4. Should the return packaging be modified to include premolded rigid foam inserts, conforming-expandable foam protection, or neither?

5. Should metropolitan repair centers be established to complement or replace in-factory repair facilities, or not?

INVESTIGATIVE QUESTIONS

1. How well is the call center helping the customers? Are they helping the customer with instructions? What percentage of customers' technical problems are they solving without callbacks? How long do customers wait on the phone?

2. How good is the transportation company? Did they pick up and deliver the laptop responsively? How long do customers wait for them? Was the laptop damaged due to package handling? What available packaging alternatives are cost-effective?

3. How good is the repair group? What is the sequencing of the repair program, diagnostic through completion? Is the repair complete? Are customers' problems resolved? Are new repair problems emerging? Are customers' repair-time expectations being met?

4. (Do this set of questions on your own. See Discussion Question 4 at the end of this chapter.)

5. What is the overall satisfaction with CompleteCare, and with the MindWriter product?

Myra now has enough information to go back to Gracie at MindWriter. In particular, Myra wants to know whether she and Jason have translated Gracie's management question in a way that will adequately fulfill Gracie's need for information. They also want to do in-depth interviews with the service manager, the call center manager, and the independent package company's account executive to determine if they are on the right track with their investigative questions. These people will be able to answer some investigative questions. The rest of the investigative questions will need to be translated into measurement questions to ask customers. If Myra and Jason are comfortable with the additional insight from their interviews (and any additional customer letters), they can then develop a questionnaire for CompleteCare customers.

Jason plans to pilot-test the questionnaire with a limited number of customers, revise the questions, set up the logistics, and then roll out the research program. Sampling will be a critical matter. If Gracie's budget is large, they can use a probability sample from the customer list that MindWriter generates every week. This will make telephone interviews possible. If a less expensive alternative is needed, however, they can propose a questionnaire postcard survey be included with every laptop as it is returned to the customer. They also will do random sampling from the list of customers who do not respond. Nonresponders will be interviewed on the telephone. This way Myra and Jason can be assured of a cost-effective questionnaire with correction for nonresponse bias.

Myra and Jason devise a tentative schedule before calling to arrange the follow-up interviews (see Figure 3–5). They want to give Gracie target dates for completion of the exploratory phase, completion of the instrument and pilot test, and a deadline for the first month's results.

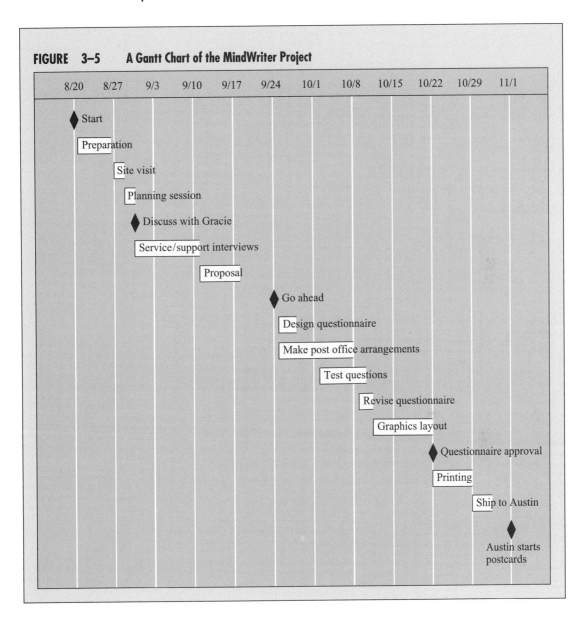

FIGURE   3–5   A Gantt Chart of the MindWriter Project

RESEARCH PROCESS PROBLEMS

Although it is desirable for research to be thoroughly grounded in management decision priorities, studies can wander off target or be less effective than they should be. Several major causes are detailed here.

The Favored Technique Syndrome

Some researchers are method-bound. They recast the management question so it is amenable to their favorite methodology—a survey, for example. Others might prefer to emphasize the case study, while still others wouldn't consider such an approach.

Not all researchers are comfortable with experimental designs. The past reluctance of most social scientists to use experimental designs is believed to have retarded the development of scientific research in the social science arena.

The availability of technique is an important factor determining how research will be done or whether a given study can be done. Persons skilled in given techniques are too often blinded by their special competencies. Their concern for technique dominates the decisions concerning what will be studied (both investigative and measurement questions) and how (research design). It is the role of the manager in the research process to spot a technique-driven research proposal that is not the optimal choice for answering the management question.

Since the advent of Total Quality Management (TQM), numerous, standardized customer satisfaction questionnaires have been developed. Jason may have done studies using these instruments for any number of his clients. Myra should be cautious. She must not let Jason steamroller her into the use of an instrument he has developed for another client, even though he might be very persuasive about its success in the past. Such a technique might not be appropriate for MindWriter's search to resolve postpurchase service dissatisfaction.

Company Database Strip-Mining

The existence of a pool of information or a database can distract a manager, seemingly reducing the need for other research. Modern management information systems are capable of providing massive volumes of data. One frequently hears, "We should use the information we already have before collecting more."

Each field in a database was originally created for a specific reason, a reason that may or may not be compatible with the management question facing the organization. The MindWriter service department's database, for example, probably contains several fields about the type of problem, the location of the problem, the remedy used to correct the problem, and so forth. Jason and Myra can accumulate facts concerning the service, and they can match each service problem with a particular MindWriter model and production sequence (from a production database), and, using yet another database (generated from warranty registration), they can match each problem to a name and address of an owner. But, having done all that, they still aren't likely to know how a particular owner uses his or her laptop or how satisfied an owner was with MindWriter's postpurchase service policies and practices.

While mining management information databases is fashionable and often a starting point in decision-based research, rarely will such activity answer all management questions. Our emphasis in this text is on information projects that tend to be nonroutine, nonrecurring, and complex, rather than on database management.

Unresearchable Questions

Not all questions are researchable, and not all research questions are answerable. To be researchable, a question must be one for which observation or other data collection can provide the answer. Many questions cannot be answered on the basis of information alone.

Questions of value and policy must often be weighed in management decisions. Management may be asking, "Should we hold out for a liberalization of the seniority rules in our new labor negotiations?" While information can be brought to bear on this question, such additional considerations as "fairness to the workers" or "management's right to manage" may be important to the decision. It may be possible for many of these questions of value to be transformed into questions of fact. Concerning "fairness to the workers," one might first gather information from which to estimate the extent and degree to which workers will be affected by a rule change; then one could gather opinion statements by the workers about the fairness of seniority rules. Even so, substantial value elements remain. Left unanswered are such questions as, "Should we argue for a policy that will adversely affect the security and well-being of older workers who are least well equipped to cope with this adversity?" Even if a question can be answered by facts alone, it might not be researchable because procedures or techniques are inadequate.

Ill-Defined Management Problems

Some categories of problems are so complex, value-laden, and bound by constraints that they prove to be intractable to traditional forms of analysis. These ill-defined or ill-structured research questions have characteristics that are virtually the opposite of those of well-defined problems. One author describes the differences like this:

> To the extent that a problem situation evokes a high level of agreement over a specified community of problem solvers regarding the referents of the attributes in which it is given, the operations that are permitted, and the consequences of those operations, it may be termed unambiguous or well defined with respect to that community. On the other hand, to the extent that a problem evokes a highly variable set of responses concerning referents of attributes, permissible operations, and their consequences, it may be considered ill-defined or ambiguous with respect to that community.[2]

Another author points out that ill-defined research questions are least susceptible to attack from quantitative research methods because such problems have too many interrelated facets for measurement to handle with accuracy.[3] Yet another authority suggests there are some research questions of this type for which methods do not presently exist or, if the methods were to be invented, they might still not provide the data necessary to solve them.[4] Novice researchers should avoid ill-defined problems. Even seasoned researchers will want to conduct a thorough exploratory study before proceeding and consider the latest approaches.

Politically Motivated Research

It is important to remember that a manager's motivations for seeking research are not always obvious. Managers might express a genuine need for specific information on which to base a decision. This is the ideal scenario for quality research. Sometimes, however, a research study may not really be desirable but is authorized anyway, chiefly because its presence may win approval for a certain manager's pet idea. At other times, research may be authorized as a measure of personal protection for a decision maker in case he or she is criticized later. In these less-than-ideal cases, the researcher may find it more difficult to win the manager's support for a sound research design.

DESIGNING THE STUDY

The **research design** is the blueprint for fulfilling objectives and answering questions. Selecting a design may be complicated by the availability of a large variety of methods, techniques, procedures, protocols, and sampling plans. For example, you may decide on a secondary data study,[5] case study, survey, experiment, or simulation. If a survey is selected, should it be administered by mail, computer, telephone, or personal interview? Should all relevant data be collected at one time or at regular intervals? What kind of structure will the questionnaire or interview guide possess? What question wording should be employed? Should the responses be scaled or open-ended? How will reliability and validity be achieved? Will characteristics of the interviewer influence responses to the measurement questions? What kind of training should the data collectors receive? Is a sample or a census to be taken? What types of sampling should be considered? These questions represent only a few of the decisions that have to be made when just one method is chosen.

The creative researcher can benefit from this confusing array of options. The numerous combinations spawned by the abundance of tools may be used to construct alternative perspectives on the same problem. By creating a design using diverse methodologies, researchers are able to achieve greater insight than if they followed the most frequent method encountered in the literature or suggested by a disciplinary bias. Although it must be conceded that students or managers rarely have the resources to pursue a single problem from a multimethod, multistudy strategy, the advantages of several competing designs should be considered before settling on a final one. Chapter 6 discusses the ways in which various research designs may be identified and classified, and Part III of the book provides information on specific methodologies.

Jason's preference for MindWriter is to collect as much information as possible from exploration of company records, from company managers of various departments, and then from multiple phone surveys. Financial constraints, however, might force the substitution of a less expensive methodology: a self-administered study in the form of a postcard sent to each CompleteCare program user with his or her returned laptop, followed by phone contact with nonresponders.

SAMPLING DESIGN

Another step in planning the design is to identify the target population and select the sample if a census is not desired. The researcher must determine how many people to interview and who they will be; what and how many events to observe; or how many records to inspect and which ones. A **sample** is a part of the target population, carefully selected to represent that population. When researchers undertake sampling studies, they are interested in estimating one or more population values and/or testing one or more statistical hypotheses.

If a study's objective is to examine the attitudes of U.S. automobile assemblers about quality improvement, the population may be defined as the entire adult population of auto assemblers employed by the auto industry in the United States. Definition of the terms *adult* and *assembler* and the relevant job descriptions included under "assembly" and "auto industry" may further limit the population under study.

The investigator may also want to restrict the research to readily identifiable companies in the market, vehicle types, or assembly processes.

The sampling process must then give every person within the target population a known nonzero chance of selection if probability sampling is used. If there is no feasible alternative, a nonprobability approach may be used. Jason knows that his target population comprises MindWriter customers who have firsthand experience with the CompleteCare program. Given that a sample frame of program users is readily available each month, a probability sample is feasible. Chapter 9 describes both types of samples and the determination of sample size.

RESOURCE ALLOCATION AND BUDGETS

General notions about research budgets have a tendency to single out data collection as the most costly activity. Data collection requires substantial resources but perhaps less of the budget than clients will expect. Employees must be paid, training and travel must be provided, and other expenses are incurred; but this phase of the project often takes no more than one-third of the total research budget. The geographic scope and the number of observations required do affect the cost, but much of the cost is relatively independent of the size of the data-gathering effort. Thus, a guide might be that (1) project planning, (2) data gathering, and (3) analysis, interpretation, and reporting each share about equally in the budget.

Without budgetary approval, many research efforts are terminated for lack of resources (see Figure 3–1). A budget may require significant development and documentation as in grant and contract research, or it may require less attention as in some in-house projects or investigations funded out of the researcher's own resources. The researcher who seeks funding must be able not only to persuasively justify the costs of the project but also to identify the sources and methods of funding. One author identifies three types of budgets in organizations where research is purchased and cost containment is crucial: (1) *Rule-of-thumb budgeting* involves taking a fixed percentage of some criterion. For example, a percentage of the prior year's sales revenues may be the basis for determining the marketing research budget for a manufacturer. (2) *Departmental or functional area budgeting* allocates a portion of total expenditures in the unit to research activities. Government agencies, not-for-profits, and the private sector alike will frequently manage research activities out of functional budgets. Units such as human resources, marketing, or engineering then have the authority to approve their own projects. (3) *Task budgeting* selects specific research projects to support on an ad hoc basis. This type is the least proactive but does permit definitive cost-benefit analysis.[6]

VALUING RESEARCH INFORMATION

There is a great deal of interplay between budgeting and value assessment in any management decision to conduct research. An appropriate research study can help managers avoid losses and increase profits; otherwise, research can be wasteful. The decision makers usually must face this evaluation question. Typically, they want a firm cost estimate for a project and an equally precise assurance that useful information will result from the study. Even if the researcher can give good cost and information estimates, the managers still must judge whether the benefits outweigh the costs.

Conceptually, the value of applied research is not difficult to determine. In a business situation, the research should produce added revenues or reduce expenses in much the same way as any other investment of resources. One source suggests that the value of research information may be judged in terms of "the difference between the result of decisions made with the information and the result that would be made without it."[7] While such a criterion is simple to state, its actual use presents difficult measurement problems.

Evaluation Methods

Ex Post Facto Evaluation

If there is any measurement of the value of research, it is usually an after-the-fact event. Twedt reports on one such effort, an evaluation of marketing research done at a major corporation.[8] He secured "an objective estimate of the contribution of each project to corporate profitability." He reports that most studies were intended to help management determine which one of two (or more) alternatives was preferable. He guesses that in 60 percent of the decision situations, the correct decision would have been made *without* the benefit of the research information. In the remaining 40 percent of the cases, the research leads to the correct decision. Using these data, he estimates that the return on investment in marketing research in this company was 351 percent for the year studied. However, he acknowledges the return-on-investment figure was inflated because only the direct research costs were included.

This effort at cost-benefit analysis is commendable even though the results come too late to guide a current research decision. Such analysis may sharpen the manager's ability to make judgments about future research proposals. However, the critical problem remains, that of project evaluation *before the study is done*.

Prior Evaluation

A proposal to conduct a thorough management audit of operations in a company may be a worthy one, but neither its costs nor its benefits are easily estimated in advance. Such projects are sufficiently unique that managerial experience seldom provides much aid in evaluating such a proposal. But even in these situations, managers can make some useful judgments. They may determine that a management audit is needed because the company is in dire straits and management does not understand the scope of its problems. The management information need may be so great as to ensure that the research is approved. In such cases, managers may decide to control the research expenditure risk by doing a study in stages. They can then review costs and benefits at the end of each stage and give or withhold further authorization. Typical of this approach is the two-stage study discussed in Chapter 6.

Option Analysis

Some progress has been made in the development of methods for assessing the value of research when management has a choice between well-defined options. Each alternative can be judged in terms of estimated costs and benefits associated with it, and a formal analysis can be conducted; but managerial judgment still plays a major role.

While both costs and benefits present major estimating problems, the development of the cost side of the equation is normally the easiest. If the research design can be stated clearly, one can estimate an approximate cost. The critical task is to quantify the benefits from the research. At best, estimates of benefits are crude and largely reflect a more orderly way to estimate outcomes under uncertain conditions. To illustrate how the contribution of research is evaluated in such a decision situation, we must digress briefly into the rudiments of decision theory.

Decision Theory   To compare two or more alternatives, a manager must estimate the expected outcome of each alternative. The case of two choices will be discussed here, although the same approach can be used with more than two choices. Two possible actions (A_1 and A_2) may represent two different ways to organize a company, to provide financing, to produce a product, and so forth. We need not specify the nature of the alternatives in order to describe the approach.

When there are alternatives from which to choose, a rational way to approach the decision is to try to assess the outcomes of each action; then one can choose the outcome that best meets the criterion established for judging alternatives. This criterion is a combination of a **decision rule** and a **decision variable.** The decision variable might be "direct dollar savings," "contribution to overhead and profits," "time required for completion of the project," and so forth. For MindWriter, the decision variable might be number of postservice complaints or the level of postservice satisfaction. Usually the decision variable is expressed in dollars, representing sales, costs, or some form of profits or contribution. The decision rule may be "choose the course of action with the lowest loss possibility" or perhaps "choose the alternative that provides the greatest annual net profit." For MindWriter, the decision rule might be "choose the alternative that provides the highest level of postservice satisfaction."

The alternative selected (A_1 versus A_2) depends on the decision variable chosen and the decision rule used. The evaluation of alternatives requires that (1) each alternative is explicitly stated, (2) a decision variable is defined by the outcome that may be measured, and (3) a decision rule is determined by which outcomes might be compared. For readers who have not been exposed to this approach, an example is provided in Appendix B.

THE RESEARCH PROPOSAL

Figure 3–1 depicts the research proposal as an activity that incorporates decisions made during early research-project planning phases of the study including the management-research question hierarchy and exploration. The proposal thus incorporates the choices the investigator makes in the preliminary steps.

A written proposal is often required when a study is being suggested. It ensures that the parties concur on the project's purpose and on the proposed methods of investigation. Time and budgets are often spelled out, as are other responsibilities and obligations. Depending on the needs and desires of the manager, substantial background detail and elaboration of proposed techniques may be included.

The length and complexity of research proposals range widely. Business research proposals normally range from one to ten pages. Applicants for foundation or government research grants typically file a proposal request of a few pages, often in a standardized format specified by the granting agency. A research proposal may also be oral, where all aspects of the research are discussed but not codified in writing. This is more likely when a manager directs her or his own research.

Proposal Content   Every proposal, regardless of length, should include two basic sections: a statement of the research question and a brief description of research methodology.

In a brief memo-type proposal, the research question may be incorporated into a paragraph that also sets out the management dilemma and management question and categories of investigative questions. The following statements give the management question facing the respective managements and point out the nature of the research that will be undertaken:

1. The Center City Bank, currently the leading bank in the city, has not been growing as fast as its major competitors. Before developing a long-range plan to enhance the bank's competitive position, it is important to determine the bank's present competitive status, its advantages and opportunities, and its major deficiencies. The primary objective of this proposed research is to develop a body of benchmark information about the Center City Bank, its major competitors, and the Center City metropolitan area as a market for banking services.

2. Management is faced with a problem of locating a new plant to serve eastern markets. Before this location decision is made, it is proposed that a feasibility study be conducted to determine, for each of five sites, the estimated

    a. Costs of serving existing customers

    b. Building, relocation, tax, and operating costs

    c. Availability of local labor in the six major crafts used in production

    d. Attractiveness of the living environment for professional and management personnel

A second section includes a statement of what will be done: the bare bones of the research design. For Center City Bank, the researcher might propose:

Personal interviews will be conducted with a minimum of 200 residents to determine their knowledge of, use of, and attitudes toward local banks. In addition, information will be gathered about their banking and financing practices and preferences. Other information of an economic or demographic nature will also be gathered from published sources and public agencies.

Often research proposals are much more detailed and describe specific measurement devices that will be used, time and cost budgets, sampling plans, and many other details. Chapter 4 describes the construction of these more detailed research proposals.

PILOT TESTING

The data-gathering phase of the research process typically begins with pilot testing. Pilot testing may be skipped when the researcher tries to condense the project time frame.

A **pilot test** is conducted to detect weaknesses in design and instrumentation and provide proxy data for selection of a probability sample. It should therefore draw subjects from the target population and simulate the procedures and protocols that have been designated for data collection. If the study is a survey to be executed by mail, the pilot questionnaire should be mailed. If the design calls for observation by an unobtrusive researcher, this behavior should be practiced. The size of the pilot group may range from 25 to 100 subjects, depending on the method to be tested, but the respondents do not have to be statistically selected. In very small populations or special applications, pilot testing runs the risk of exhausting the supply of respondents and sensitizing them to the purpose of the study. This risk is generally overshadowed by the improvements made to the design by a trial run.

There are a number of variations on pilot testing. Some of them are intentionally restricted to data collection activities. One form, *pretesting,* may rely on colleagues, respondent surrogates, or actual respondents for the purpose of refining a measuring instrument. This important activity has saved countless survey studies from disaster by using the suggestions of the respondents to identify and change confusing, awkward, or offensive questions and techniques. One interview study in which one of the authors participated was designed by a group of college professors for an educational television consortium. In the pilot test, we discovered that the wording of nearly two-thirds of the questions was unintelligible to the target group, later found to have a median eighth-grade education. The revised instrument used the respondents' language and was successful. Pretesting may be repeated several times to refine instruments and procedures.

DATA COLLECTION

The gathering of data may range from a simple observation at one location to a grandiose survey of multinational corporations at sites in different parts of the world. The method selected will largely determine how the data are collected. Questionnaires, standardized tests, observational forms, laboratory notes, and instrument calibration logs are among the devices used to record raw data.

But what are data? One writer defines **data** as the facts presented to the researcher from the study's environment. Data may be further characterized by their (1) abstractness, (2) verifiability, (3) elusiveness, and (4) closeness to the phenomenon.[9] As abstractions, data are more metaphorical than real. For example, the growth in GNP cannot be observed directly; only the effects of it may be recorded. Second, data are processed by our senses—often limited in comparison to the senses of other living organisms. When sensory experiences consistently produce the same result, our data are said to be trustworthy because they may be verified. Third, capturing data is complicated by the speed at which events occur and the time-bound nature of observation. Opinions, preferences, and attitudes vary from one milieu to another and with the passage of time. For example, attitudes about spending during the 1980s differ dramatically one decade later in the same population. Finally, data classify their verity by closeness to the phenomena. *Secondary data* have had at least one level of interpretation inserted between the event and its recording. *Primary data* are sought for their proximity to the truth and control over error. These cautions remind us to use care in designing data collection procedures and generalizing from results.

Data are edited to ensure consistency across respondents and to locate omissions. In the case of survey methods, editing reduces errors in the recording, improves legibility, and clarifies unclear and inappropriate responses. Edited data are then put into a form that makes analysis possible. Because it is impractical to place raw data into a report, alphanumeric codes are used to reduce the responses to a more manageable system for storage and future processing. The codes follow various decision rules that the researcher has devised to assist with sorting, tabulating, and analyzing. Personal computers have made it possible to merge editing, coding, and data entry into fewer steps even when the final analysis may be run on a mainframe. Data collection is addressed in detail in Part III of this book.

ANALYSIS AND INTERPRETATION

Raw data are rarely useful in management decision making. Managers need information. Researchers generate information by analyzing data after its collection. **Data analysis** usually involves reducing accumulated data to a manageable size, developing summaries, looking for patterns, and applying statistical techniques. Scaled responses on questionnaires and experimental instruments often require the analyst to derive various functions, and relationships among variables are frequently explored after that. Further, researchers must interpret these findings in light of the client's research question or determine if the results are consistent with their hypotheses and theories.

A modest example involves a market research firm that polls 2,000 people from its target population for a new generation of wallet-sized portable telephones. Each respondent will be asked four questions: (1)"Do you prefer the convenience of Pocket-Phone over existing cellular telephones?" (2)"Are there transmission problems with Pocket-Phone?" (3)"Is Pocket-Phone better suited to transmission from your car than a cellular phone?" (4)"Would cost alone persuade you to purchase Pocket-Phone?" The answers will produce 8,000 pieces of data. Reducing the data to a workable size will yield eight statistics: the percentage of yes and no answers to each question. If a half-dozen demographic questions about the respondents were added, the total amount of data could easily triple. And if the questions were scaled, the analysis would likely require more powerful statistical analysis. Chapters 15 through 18 deal with these topics in-depth.

REPORTING THE RESULTS

Finally, it is necessary to prepare a report and transmit the findings and recommendations to the manager for the intended purpose of decision making. The style and organization of the report will differ according to the target audience, the occasion, and the purpose of the research. The results of applied research may be communicated in a conference call, a letter, a written report, or an oral presentation—and sometimes all of them. Reports should be developed from the client's perspective. The sophistication of the design and sampling plan or the software used to analyze the data may help to establish the researcher's credibility, but in the end, solving the problem is foremost on the manager's mind. Thus, the researcher must accurately assess the manager's needs throughout the research process and incorporate this understanding into the final product, the research report.

Research reports are occasionally shelved without action. Inferior communication of results is a primary reason for this outcome. Insightful adaptation to the client's needs and carefully executed work are the prescribed remedies. Occasionally, organizational and environmental forces beyond the researcher's control auger against the implementation of results. Such was the case in a study conducted for the Association of American Publishers, which needed an ad campaign to encourage people to read more books. The project, costing $125,000, found that only 13 percent of Americans buy general-interest books in stores. When the time came to commit $14 million to the campaign to raise book sales, the membership's interest had faded and the project died.[10]

At a minimum, a research report should contain these sections:

- An *executive summary* consisting of a synopsis of the problem, findings, and recommendations
- An *overview of the research:* the problem's background, literature summary, methods and procedures, conclusions
- A section on implementation strategies for the recommendations
- A *technical appendix* with all the materials necessary to replicate the project

Chapter 19 covers this topic in detail.

Summary

Research originates in the decision process. A manager needs specific information for setting objectives, defining tasks, finding the best strategy by which to carry out the tasks, or judging how well the strategy is being implemented.

A dilemma-centered emphasis—the problem's origin, selection, statement, exploration, and refinement—dominates the sequence of the research process. A management dilemma can originate in any aspect of an organization. A decision to do research can be inappropriately driven by the availability of coveted tools and databases. To be researchable, a problem must be subject to observation or other forms of empirical data collection.

How one structures the research question sets the direction for the project. A management problem or opportunity can be formulated as a hierarchical sequence of questions. At the most general level is the management dilemma. This is translated into a management question and then into a research question—the major objective of the study. In turn, the research question is further expanded into investigative questions. These questions represent the various facets of the problem to be solved, and they influence research design, including design strategy, data collection planning, and sampling. At the most specific level are measurement questions that are answered by respondents in a survey or answered about each subject in an observational study.

Exploration of the problem is accomplished through familiarization with the available literature, interviews with experts, focus groups, or some combination. Revision of the management or research questions is a desirable outcome of exploration and enhances the researcher's understanding of the options available for developing a successful design.

Decisions concerning the type of study, the means of data collection, measurement, and sampling plans must be made when planning the design. Most researchers undertake sampling studies because of an interest in estimating population values or testing a statistical hypothesis. Carefully constructed delimitations are essential for specifying an appropriate probability sample. Nonprobability samples are also used.

Budgets and value assessments determine whether most projects receive necessary funding. Their thorough documentation is an integral part of the research proposal. Proposals are required for many research projects and should, at a minimum, describe the research question and the specific task the research will undertake.

Pilot tests are conducted to detect weaknesses in the study's design, data collection instruments, and procedures. Once the researcher is satisfied that the plan is sound, data collection begins. Data are collected, edited, coded, and prepared for analysis.

Data analysis involves reduction, summarization, pattern examination, and statistical evaluation of hypotheses. A written report describing the study's findings is used to transmit the results and recommendations to the intended decision maker. By cycling the conclusions back into the original problem, a new research iteration may begin, and findings may be applied.

Key Terms	data data analysis decision rule decision variable exploration investigative questions management dilemma management question	management-research question hierarchy measurement questions research design research process research question(s) pilot test sample

Discussion Questions

1. Describe the management-research question hierarchy, citing management dilemma, management question, and research question(s) for each of the following.

   a. The production manager of a shoe factory

   b. The president of a home healthcare services firm

   c. The vice president of labor relations for an auto manufacturer *d.* The retail advertising manager of a major metropolitan newspaper

      e. The chief of police in a major city

2. Take one of the alternative MindWriter possible problems causing the management dilemma (see "Close-Up" and Figure 3–3), and develop plausible management and research questions.

3. Using the "uneven courier performance" problem or the "product damaged during repair" problem (see "Close-Up" and Figure 3–3), develop some exploration activities that would let Jason or Myra proceed to develop a more refined research question dealing with this problem.

4. Using the MindWriter post-servicing packaging alternative as the research question, develop appropriate investigative questions within the management-research question hierarchy by preparing a figure similar to Figure 3–4.

5. Confronted by low productivity, the president of Oaks International Inc. asks a research company to study job satisfaction in the corporation. What are some of the important reasons that this research project may fail to make an adequate contribution to the solution of management problems?

6. The vice president of administration calls you into her office and states that the computer programming department is not functioning well because there is excessive turnover among the programmers. She suggests you conduct a survey among other major companies in the region to learn how they handle the problem of high programmer turnover.

      a. What do you think of this research suggestion?

      b. How, if at all, could you improve on the vice president's formulation of the research question?

7. A company is experiencing a poor inventory management situation and receives alternative research proposals. Proposal 1 is to use an audit of last year's transactions as a basis for recommendations. Proposal 2 is to study and recommend changes to the procedures and systems used by the materials department. Discuss issues of evaluation in terms of

      a. Ex post facto versus prior evaluation

      b. Evaluation using option analysis and decision theory

8. Some questions are answerable by research and others are not. Using some management problems of your choosing, distinguish between them.

9. You have been approached by the editor of *Gentlemen's Magazine* to carry out a research study. The magazine has been unsuccessful in attracting shoe manufacturers as advertisers. When the sales force tried to secure advertising from shoe manufacturers, they were told men's clothing stores are a small and dying segment of their business. Since *Gentlemen's Magazine* goes chiefly to men's clothing stores, the manufacturers reasoned that it was, therefore, not a good vehicle for their advertising.

The editor believes that a survey (via mail questionnaire) of men's clothing stores in the United States will probably show that these stores are important outlets for men's shoes and are not declining in importance as shoe outlets. He asks you to develop a proposal for the study and submit it to him. Develop the management-research question hierarchy that will help you to develop a specific proposal.

10. Discuss the problems of trading off exploration and pilot testing under tight budgetary constraints. What are the immediate and long-term effects?

Reference Notes

1. Albert Einstein and L. Infeld, *The Evolution of Physics* (New York: Simon & Schuster, 1938), p. 95.
2. Walter B. Reitman, "Heuristic Decision Procedures, Open Constraints, and the Structure of Ill-Defined Problems," in *Human Judgments and Optimality*, eds. Maynard W. Shelly II and Glenn L. Bryan (New York: Wiley, 1964), p. 285.
3. Carl M. Moore, *Group Techniques for Idea Building*, 2nd ed. (Thousand Oaks, CA: Sage Publications, 1994).
4. Fred N. Kerlinger, *Foundations of Behavioral Research*, 3rd ed. (New York: Holt, Rinehart & Winston, 1986), pp. 436–37.
5. We have discussed literature review or secondary data studies previously under the heading "Exploration." The option to select secondary data collection as a principal methodology—as an in-depth, critical examination—should be distinguished from the use of published data to enhance one's preliminary knowledge of the problem in the initial stages of research.
6. Walter B. Wentz, *Marketing Research: Management, Method, and Cases* (New York: Harper & Row, 1979), p. 35.
7. Robert D. Buzzell, Donald F. Cox, and Rex V. Brown, *Marketing Research and Information Systems* (New York: McGraw-Hill, 1969), p. 595.
8. Dik Warren Twedt, "What Is the 'Return on Investment' in Marketing Research?" *Journal of Marketing* 30 (January 1966), pp. 62–63.
9. Paul D. Leedy, *How to Read Research and Understand It* (New York: Macmillan, 1981), pp. 67–70.
10. Roger Cohen, "For U.S. Publishers, Awash in Red Ink, the Moment of Truth Looms," *International Herald Tribune,* March 6, 1990, p. 6.

Suggested Readings

1. Fox, David J. *The Research Process in Education.* New York: Holt, Rinehart & Winston, 1969. Chapter 2 includes a research process model to compare with the one in this chapter.
2. Leedy, Paul D. *Practical Research: Planning & Design,* 6th ed. Englewood Cliffs, NJ: Prentice-Hall, 1996. Practical and readable sections guide students through the research process.
3. Murdick, Robert G., and Donald R. Cooper. *Business Research: Concepts and Guides.* Columbus, OH: Grid, 1982. A supplementary text with a strong emphasis on problem identification and formulation.

4. Selltiz, Claire, Lawrence S. Wrightsman, and Stuart M. Cook. *Research Methods in Social Relations,* 3rd ed. New York: Holt, Rinehart & Winston, 1976. Chapters 1 and 2 present a good research process example and discussion of formulating a research problem.

5. Tull, Donald S., and Del I. Hawkins. *Marketing Research: Meaning, Measurement, and Method,* 6th ed. New York: Macmillan, 1992. The authors provide good coverage of the valuation of research information through a Bayesian decision theory approach.

THE RESEARCH PROPOSAL

CHAPTER NAVIGATION

BRINGING
RESEARCH TO LIFE

"**C**ome on over here and meet Robert Buffet." The president of the Economic Development Council seized Myra Wines by the elbow and propelled her across the dining room to meet a tall young man suited in navy-blue pinstripes. She recognized his name: He was local manager of a national accounting firm.

"Robert Buffet, this is Myra Wines, consumer affairs manager for MindWriter."

"Hello, Robert," she said. She studied him carefully, sweeping her eyes from his brightly shined black shoes to his razor cut hair. He was about the same age as her new consultant, Jason Henry, but something in the way he held himself suggested a self-assurance that Jason had not yet developed. This young man dressed like a banker, while Jason suggested a librarian, a sincere yet somehow impatient librarian.

"And what a pleasure it is to meet you," he said in a ripe baritone voice, smiling with his lips but not his eyes, which had wandered to a prominent banker who was chatting with a competing CPA.

"Here's the situation, Myra," said the president. "The state commerce secretary has been concerned for some time about the extent to which entrepreneurial companies, which are popping up all over the state, are actually investing in job-building technology. They have contracted with Robert's firm to study the situation in five counties, to assess job creation and the like, and report this back to Tallahassee."

Myra asked, "Am I right in suspecting that the governor is worried that these start-up companies are investing in robotics and computers and not creating new manufacturing jobs?"

"Basically, that is the concern, Ms. Wines," said the tall young man. "We have already cut the contract, you see, in Tallahassee, and so we have the green light to select our five sites and commence the interviewing."

"The thing is, Myra," said the president, "before their task force can come into a county and start interviewing and collecting data, they have got to have the auspices, the sponsorship, so to speak, of a business group. In this county, it is our council that has to look over their proposal and assure the business community it is in their best interests to cooperate."

"And you want me to critically examine their proposal and let you know what I think."

"By two weeks from Friday, please," said the president, "as a favor."

"Here is a copy of our proposal," said the tall young man. "How awfully nice chatting with you." He grasped her hand, gave it one shake, patted the council president on the shoulder, and headed for the refreshment table, where a local auto dealer presented an easy target for a sales pitch.

THE PURPOSE OF THE RESEARCH PROPOSAL

A proposal is an individual's or company's offer to produce a product or render a service to a potential buyer or sponsor. The purpose of the research proposal is

1. To present the management question to be researched and its importance
2. To discuss the research efforts of others who have worked on related management questions
3. To suggest the data necessary for solving the management question and how the data will be gathered, treated, and interpreted (Reference: investigative questions)

In addition, the proposal of a contract researcher must present its plan, services, and credentials in the best possible way to encourage its selection over competitors. In contract research, the survival of companies depends on their ability to develop winning proposals.[1] A **proposal** is also known as a work plan, prospectus, outline, statement of intent, or draft plan.[2] The proposal tells us what, why, how, where, and to whom it will be done. It must also show the benefit of doing it.[3]

Many students and beginning researchers view the proposal as unnecessary work. In actuality, the more inexperienced a researcher is, the more important it is to have a well-planned and adequately documented proposal. The research proposal is essentially a road map, showing clearly the location from which a journey begins, the destination to be reached, and the method of getting there. Well-prepared proposals include potential problems that may be encountered along the way and methods for avoiding or working around them, much as a road map indicates alternate routes for a detour.

SPONSOR USES

All research has a sponsor in one form or another. The student researcher is responsible to the class instructor. In a corporate setting, whether the research is being done in-house by a research department or under contract to an external research firm, management sponsors the research. University, government, or corporate-sponsored (grant) research uses grant committees to evaluate the work.

A research proposal allows the sponsor to assess the sincerity of your purpose, the clarity of your design, the extent of your background material, and your fitness for undertaking the project. The proposal displays your discipline, organization, and logic. A poorly planned, poorly written, or poorly organized proposal damages your reputation more than the decision not to submit one. Depending on the type of research and the sponsor you have, various aspects of a standard proposal design are emphasized. The proposal, then, provides a document the sponsor can evaluate based on current organizational, scholastic, or scientific needs. It allows the research sponsor to assess both the researcher and the proposed design, to compare them against competing proposals, and to make the best selection for the project.

Comparison of the results with the proposal is the first step in the evaluation process. It provides a basis for the sponsor to evaluate the results of a project. By comparing the final product with the stated objectives, it is easy for the sponsor to decide if the research goals have been achieved.

Another benefit of the proposal is the discipline it brings to the sponsor. Many managers, requesting an in-house, departmental research project, do not adequately define the problem they are addressing. The research proposal acts as a catalyst for discussion between the person conducting the research and the manager. The researcher translates the management question, as described by the manager, into the research question and outlines the objectives of the study. Upon review, the manager may discover that the interpretation of the problem does not encompass all the original symptoms. The proposal, then, serves as the basis for additional discussion between the manager and the researcher until all aspects of the management question are understood. Parts of the problem may not be researchable, or at least not subject to empirical study. An alternate design, such as a qualitative or policy analytic study may need to be proposed. Upon completion of the discussions, a carefully worded research question should emerge. As Figure 4–1 reveals, proposal development can work in an iterative fashion until authorization to proceed is granted.

For an outside contract, the process is different. Proposals are usually submitted in response to a request for bid, or **request for proposal (RFP)**. The researchers

FIGURE   4–1   Proposal Development

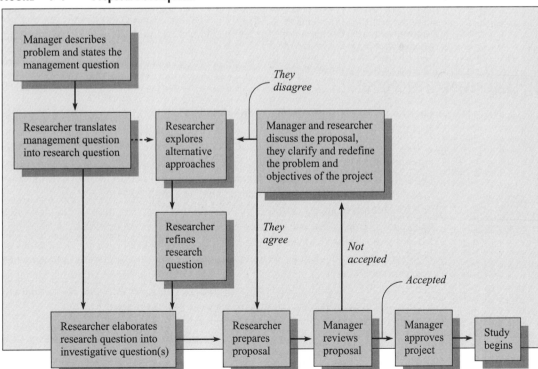

may wish to convince the sponsor that their approach to the research question differs from the problem (management question) specified in the initial RFP. In this way, the researchers can show superior understanding of the problem over competing proposals. Appendix C provides further information on RFPs.

RESEARCHER BENEFITS

A proposal is more beneficial for the beginning researcher than for the sponsor. This does not diminish its relevance to the sponsor. But it is imperative for the new researcher to have a tentative work plan that charts the logical steps needed to accomplish the stated goals.

The process of writing a proposal allows the researcher to plan and review the project's steps. Related literature should be examined, thus prompting the researcher to assess previous approaches to the problem and revise the plan accordingly. Additionally, there is the opportunity to spot flaws in the logic, errors in assumptions, or even problems that are not adequately addressed by the objectives and design.

After acceptance of the proposal, the document serves as a guide for the researcher throughout the investigation. Progress can be monitored and milestones noted. At completion, the proposal contains everything needed, outlining the final research report.[4]

A final benefit, especially for the beginning researcher, is that the proposal forces time and budget estimates. These estimates allow researchers to plan the project so work progresses steadily toward the deadline. Since many people are inclined to procrastinate, having a schedule helps them work methodically toward the completion of the project.

TYPES OF RESEARCH PROPOSALS

Depending on the type of project, the sponsoring individual or institution, and the cost of the project, different levels of complexity are required for a proposal to be judged complete. As shown in Figure 4–2, government agencies demand the most complex proposals for their funding analyses. On the other extreme, an exploratory study done within a manager's department may need merely a one- to three-page memo outlining the objectives, approach, and time allotted to the project.

In general, business proposals can be divided between those generated internally and externally. An internal proposal is done for the corporation by staff specialists or by the research department of the firm. External proposals are either solicited or unsolicited. Sponsors can be university grant committees, government agencies, government contractors, corporations, and so forth. With few exceptions, the larger the project, the more complex is the proposal. In public sector work, the complexity is generally greater than in a comparable private sector proposal.

There are three general levels of complexity. The exploratory study is the first, most simple business proposal. More complex and common in business is the small-scale study—either an internal study or an external contract research project. The large-scale professional study, worth up to several million dollars, is the

FIGURE   4–2   Proposal Complexity

	Complexity			
Type	*Least*			*Most*
Management proposals				
Internal	Exploratory study	Small-scale study	Large-scale study	
External	Exploratory contract research	Small-scale contract research	Large-scale contract research	Government sponsored
Student proposals	Term paper	Master's thesis	Doctoral thesis	

most complex proposal we deal with here. Government agency proposals, running several hundred pages, use the same modules that we discuss below. However, each agency has unique requirements, making generalized coverage beyond the scope of this text.

Figure 4–3 displays a set of modules for building a proposal. Based on the type of proposal you are writing, you may choose the appropriate modules for inclusion. This is a general guide, and sometimes more or less than what is shown here is appropriate for a specific purpose. For example, most small-scale studies do not require a glossary of terms. Terms are defined within the body of the proposal. However, if the proposal deals with an esoteric subject that is not familiar to management, it is appropriate to add a glossary. Notice the differences between the proposal types in Figure 4–3.

Internal Proposals

Internal proposals are more succinct than external ones. At the least complex end of the continuum, a memo from the researcher to management outlining the problem statement, study objectives, research design, and schedule is enough to start an exploratory study. Privately and publicly held firms are concerned with how to solve a particular problem, make a decision, or improve an aspect of their business. Seldom do businesses begin research studies for other reasons. In the small-scale proposal, the literature review and bibliography are consequently not stressed and can often be stated briefly in the research design. Since management insists on brevity, an executive summary is mandatory for all but the most simple of proposals (projects that can be proposed in a two-page memo do not need an executive summary). Schedules and budgets are necessary for funds to be committed. For the smaller-scale projects, descriptions are not required for facilities and special resources, nor is there a need for a glossary. Since small projects are sponsored by managers familiar with the problem, the associated jargon, requirements, and definitions should be included directly in the text. Also, the measuring instrument and project management modules are not required. Managers will typically leave this detail for others.

FIGURE 4–3   Modules to Include in Proposals: A Comparison of Management-Oriented Proposals and Student Proposals

Proposal Types / *Proposal Modules*	Management							Student		
	Internal			External						
	Exploratory Study	*Small-Scale Study*	*Large-Scale Study*	*Exploratory Study*	*Small-Scale Contract*	*Large-Scale Contract*	*Government Grant or Contract*	*Term Paper*	*Master's Thesis*	*Doctoral Thesis*
Executive summary		✔	✔	✔	✔	✔	✔			
Problem statement	✔	✔	✔	✔	✔	✔	✔	✔	✔	✔
Research objectives	✔	✔	✔	✔	✔	✔	✔	✔	✔	✔
Literature review			✔			✔	✔		✔	✔
Importance/ benefits of study			✔	✔	✔	✔	✔			✔
Research design	✔	✔	✔	✔	✔	✔	✔		✔	✔
Data analysis						✔	✔			✔
Nature and form of results		✔	✔		✔	✔	✔		✔	✔
Qualification of researchers				✔	✔	✔	✔			
Budget		✔	✔	✔	✔	✔	✔			
Schedule	✔	✔	✔	✔	✔	✔	✔			✔
Facilities and special resources			✔	✔	✔	✔	✔		✔	✔
Project management			✔			✔	✔			
Bibliography			✔			✔	✔	✔	✔	✔
Appendices Glossary of terms			✔			✔	✔		✔	✔
Measurement instrument			✔			✔	✔			✔

External Proposals   An external proposal is either solicited or unsolicited. A solicited proposal is often in response to an RFP. The proposal is likely competing against several others for a contract or grant. An unsolicited proposal has the advantage of not competing against others but the disadvantage of having to speculate on the ramifications of a problem facing the firm's management. Even more difficult, the writer of an unsolicited proposal must decide to whom the document should be sent.

The most important sections of the external proposal are the objectives, design, qualifications, schedule, and budget. The executive summary of an external proposal may be included within the letter of transmittal. As the complexity of the project increases, more information is required about project management and the facilities and special resources. In contract research, the results and objectives sections are the standards against which the completed project is measured. As we move toward government-sponsored research, particular attention must be paid to each specification in the RFP. To ignore or not meet any specification is to automatically disqualify your proposal as "nonresponsive."[5]

STRUCTURING THE RESEARCH PROPOSAL

Consider again Figure 4–3. Using this reference, you can put together a set of modules that tailor your proposal to the intended audience. Each of the following modules is flexible, so its content and length may be adapted to specific needs.

Executive Summary   The **executive summary** allows a busy manager or sponsor to understand quickly the thrust of the proposal. It is essentially an informative abstract, giving executives the chance to grasp the essentials of the proposal without having to read the details.[6] The goal of the summary is to secure a positive evaluation by the executive who will pass the proposal on to the staff for a full evaluation. As such, the executive summary should include brief statements of the management dilemma and management question, the research objectives/research questions(s), and the benefits of your approach. If the proposal is unsolicited, a brief description of your qualifications is also appropriate.

Problem Statement   This section needs to convince the sponsor to continue reading the proposal. You should capture the reader's attention by stating the management dilemma, its background, and consequences, and the resulting management question. As discussed in Chapter 3, the management question starts the research task. The importance of researching the management question should be emphasized here if a separate module on the importance/benefits of study is not included later in the proposal. In addition, this section should include any restrictions or areas of the management question that will not be addressed.

Problem statements too broadly defined cannot be addressed adequately in one study. It is important that the management question be distinct from related problems and that the sponsor see the delimitations clearly. Be sure your problem statement is clear without the use of idioms or clichés. After reading this section, the potential sponsor should know the management dilemma and the question, its significance, and why something should be done to change the status quo.[7]

Research Objectives

This module addresses the purpose of the investigation. It is here that you lay out exactly what is being planned by the proposed research. In a descriptive study, the objectives can be stated as the research question. Recall that the research question can be further broken down into investigative questions. If the proposal is for a causal study, then the objectives can be restated as a hypothesis.

The objectives module flows naturally from the problem statement, giving the sponsor specific, concrete, and achievable goals. It is best to list the objectives either in order of importance or in general terms first, moving to specific terms (i.e., research question followed by underlying investigative questions). The research questions (or hypotheses, if appropriate) should be set off from the flow of the text so they can be found easily.

The research objectives section is the basis for judging the remainder of the proposal and, ultimately, the final report. Verify the consistency of the proposal by checking to see that each objective is discussed in the research design, data analysis, and results sections.

Literature Review

The **literature review** section examines recent (or historically significant) research studies, company data, or industry reports that act as a basis for the proposed study. Begin your discussion of the related literature and relevant secondary data from a comprehensive perspective, moving to more specific studies that are associated with your problem. If the problem has a historical background, begin with the earliest references.

Avoid the extraneous details of the literature; do a brief review of the information, not a comprehensive report. Always refer to the original source. If you find something of interest in a quotation, find the original publication and ensure you understand it. In this way, you will avoid any errors of interpretation or transcription. Emphasize the important results and conclusions of other studies, the relevant data and trends from previous research, and particular methods or designs that could be duplicated or should be avoided. Discuss how the literature applies to the study you are proposing; show the weaknesses or faults in the design, discussing how you would avoid similar problems. If your proposal deals solely with secondary data, discuss the relevance of the data and the bias or lack of bias inherent in it.

The literature review may also explain the need for the proposed work to appraise the shortcomings and informational gaps in secondary data sources. This analysis may go beyond scrutinizing the availability or conclusions of past studies and their data, to examining the accuracy of secondary sources, the credibility of these sources, and the appropriateness of earlier studies. A choice often revealed by this exercise is that of using a secondary data approach instead of collecting primary data. (See Figure 3–1 in Chapter 3.) A comprehensive review lays the basis for this choice.

Close the literature review section by summarizing the important aspects of the literature and interpreting them in terms of your problem. Refine the problem as necessary in light of your findings. For more on the literature review, see Chapter 10, "Secondary Data Sources."

Importance/ Benefits of the Study

This section allows you to describe explicit benefits that will accrue from your study. The importance of "doing the study now" should be emphasized. Usually, this section is not more than a few paragraphs. If you find it difficult to write, then you have probably not understood the problem adequately. Return to the analysis of the problem and ensure, through additional discussions with your sponsor or your research team, or by a reexamination of the literature, that you have captured the essence of the problem.

This section also requires you to understand what is most troubling to your sponsor. If it is a potential union activity, you cannot promise that an employee survey will prevent unionization. You can, however, show the importance of this information and its implications. This benefit may allow management to respond to employee concerns and forge a linkage between those concerns and unionization.

The importance/benefits section is particularly important to the unsolicited external proposal. You must convince the sponsoring organization that your plan will meet its needs.

Research Design

Up to now, you have told the sponsor what the problem is, what your study goals are, and why it is important for you to do the study. The proposal has presented the study's value and benefits. The design module describes what you are going to do in technical terms. This section should include as many subsections as needed to show the phases of the project. Provide information on your proposed design for tasks such as sample selection and size, data collection method, instrumentation, procedures, and ethical requirements. When more than one way exists to approach the design, discuss the methods you rejected and why your selected approach is superior.

Refer to Chapter 6, "Design Strategies," for additional information on research design.

Data Analysis

A brief section on the methods used for analyzing the data is appropriate for large-scale contract research projects and doctoral theses. With smaller projects, the proposed data analysis would be included within the research design section. Describe your proposed treatment and the theoretical basis for using the selected techniques. The object of this section is to assure the sponsor you are following correct assumptions and using theoretically sound data analysis procedures.

This is often an arduous section to write. By use of sample charts and dummy tables, you can make it easier to understand your data analysis. This will make the section easier to write and easier to read. The data analysis section is important enough to contract research that you should contact an expert to review the latest techniques available for your use. If there is no statistical or analytical expertise within your company, be prepared to hire a professional to help with this activity.

Nature and Form of Results

Upon finishing this section, the sponsor should be able to go back to the problem statement and research objectives and discover that each goal of the study has been covered. One should also specify the types of data to be obtained and the interpretations that will be made in the analysis. If the data are to be turned over to the sponsor for proprietary reasons, make sure this is reflected. Alternatively, if the report will go to more than one sponsor, that should be noted.

This section also contains the contractual statement telling the sponsor exactly what types of information will be received. Statistical conclusions, applied findings, recommendations, action plans, models, strategic plans, and so forth are examples of the forms of results.

Qualifications of Researchers

This section should begin with the principal investigator. It is also customary to begin qualifications with the highest academic degree held. Experience in carrying out previous research is important, especially in the corporate marketplace, so a concise description of similar projects should be included. Also important to business sponsors is experience as an executive or employee of an organization involved in a related field. Often businesses are reluctant to hire individuals to solve operational problems if they do not have practical experience. Finally, relevant business and technical societies to which the researcher belongs can be included where this information is particularly relevant to the research project.[8]

The entire curriculum vitae of each researcher should not be included unless required by the RFP. Instead, refer to the relevant areas of experience and expertise that make the researchers the best selection for the task. Complete vitae information is often placed in an appendix for review by interested sponsors.

Budget

The budget should be presented in the form the sponsor requests. For example, some organizations require secretarial assistance to be individually budgeted, whereas others insist it be included in the research director's fees or the overhead of the operation. In addition, limitations on travel, per diem rates, and capital equipment purchases can change the way in which you prepare a budget.

Typically, the budget should be no more than one to two pages. Figure 4–4 shows a format that can be used for small contract research projects. Additional information, backup details, quotes from vendors, and hourly time and payment calculations should be put into an appendix if required or kept in the researcher's file for future reference.

The budget statement in an internal research proposal is based on employee and overhead costs. The budget presented by an external research organization is not just the wages or salaries of their employees but the person-hour price that the contracting firm charges.

The detail presented may vary depending on both the sponsors' requirements and the contracting research company's policy. Some research companies, particu-

FIGURE 4–4   Budget Example

Research Program Budget

Budget Items	Rate	Total Days	Charge
A. Salaries			
1. Research director, Jason Henry	$200/hr	20 hours	$ 4,000
2. Associate	$100/hr	10 hours	$ 1,000
3. Research assistants (2)	$20/hr	300 hours	$ 6,000
4. Secretarial (1)	$12/hr	100 hours	$ 1,200
Subtotal			$12,200
B. Other costs			
5. Employee services and benefits			
6. Travel			$ 2,500
7. Office supplies			$ 100
8. Telephone			$ 800
9. Rent			
10. Other equipment			
11. Publication and storage costs			$ 100
Subtotal			$ 3,500
C. Total of direct costs			$15,700
D. Overhead support			$ 5,480
E. Total funding requested			$21,180

larly in database and computerized analysis areas, quote on the basis of "man-machine hours" involved in a project. The man-machine hour is the hourly fee charged for a person with computer hardware and organizational resources. Here, rather than disaggregating the "other costs" of Figure 4–4, these costs are embedded in a combined rate. One reason why external research agencies avoid giving detailed budgets is the possibility that disclosures of their costing practices will make their calculations public knowledge, reducing their negotiating flexibility. Since budget statements embody a financial work strategy that could be used by the recipient of the bid to develop an independent work plan, vendors are often doubly careful.

The budget section of an external agency's proposal states the total fee payable for the assignment. When it is accompanied by a proposed schedule of payment, this is frequently detailed in a purchase order. Unlike most product sale environments, research payments can be divided and paid at stages of completion. Sometimes a retainer is scheduled for the beginning of the contract, then a percentage at an intermediate stage, and the balance on completion of the project.

It is extremely important that you retain all information you use to generate your budget. If you use quotes from external contractors, get the quotation in writing for your file. If you estimate time for interviews, keep explicit notes on how you made the estimate. When the time comes to do the work, you should know exactly how much money is budgeted for each particular task.[9]

Some costs are more elusive than others. Do not forget to build the cost of proposal writing into your fee. Publication and delivery of final reports can be a last-minute expense that can easily be overlooked in preliminary budgets.

Schedule

Your schedule should include the major phases of the project, their timetables, and the milestones that signify completion of a phase. For example, major phases may be (1) exploratory interviews, (2) final research proposal, (3) questionnaire revision, (4) field interviews, (5) editing and coding, (6) data analysis, and (7) report generation. Each of these phases should have an estimated time schedule and people assigned to the work.

It may be helpful to you and your sponsor if you chart your schedule. You can use a Gantt chart, shown in Chapter 3, Figure 3–5. Alternatively, if the project is large and complex, a **critical path method** (CPM) of scheduling may be included.[10] In a CPM chart, the nodes represent major milestones, and the arrows suggest the work needed to get to the milestone. More than one arrow pointing to a node indicates all those tasks must be completed before the milestone has been met. Usually a number is placed along the arrow showing the number of days or weeks required for that task to be completed. The pathway from start to end that takes the longest time to complete is called the critical path, because any delay in an activity along that path will delay the end of the entire project. An example of a CPM chart is shown in Figure 4–5.[11] Software programs designed for project management will simplify scheduling and charting the schedule. Most are available for personal computers.

Facilities and Special Resources

Often, projects will require special facilities or resources that should be described in detail. For example, a contract exploratory study may need specialized facilities for focus group sessions. Computer-assisted telephone or other interviewing facilities may be required. Alternatively, your proposed data analysis may require sophisti-

FIGURE   4–5   CPM Schedule

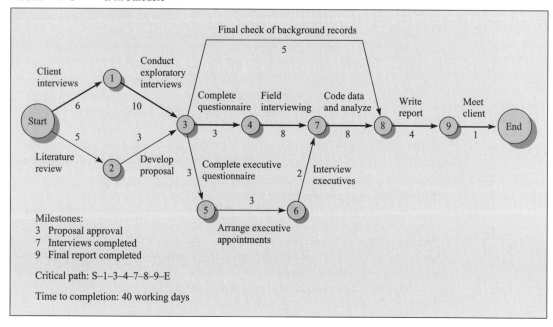

cated computer algorithms, and therefore, you need access to an adequate system. These requirements will vary from study to study. The proposal should carefully list the relevant facilities and resources that will be used.

Project Management

The purpose of the **project management** section is to show the sponsor that the research team is organized in a way to do the project efficiently. A master plan is required for complex projects to show how the phases will all be brought together. The plan includes

- The research team's organization
- Management procedures and controls for executing the research plan
- Examples of management and technical reports
- Research team relationship with the sponsor
- Financial and legal responsibility
- Management competence

Tables and charts are most helpful in presenting the master plan. The relationships between researchers and assistants need to be shown when several researchers are part of the team. Sponsors must know that the director is an individual capable of leading the team and being a useful liaison to the sponsor. In addition, procedures for information processing, record control, and expense control are critical to large operations and should be shown as part of the management procedures.

The type and frequency of progress reports should be recorded so the sponsor can expect to be kept up-to-date and the researchers can expect to be left alone to do research. The sponsor's limits on control during the process should be delineated.

Details such as printing facilities, clerical help, or information-processing capabilities that are to be provided by the sponsor are discussed. In addition, rights to the data, the results, and authority to speak for the researcher and for the sponsor are included.

Payment frequency and timing are also covered in the master plan. Finally, proof of financial responsibility and overall management competence are provided.[12]

Bibliography

For all projects that require literature review, a bibliography is necessary. Use the bibliographic format required by the sponsor. If none is specified, a standard style manual (e.g., Kate L. Turabian, *A Manual for Writers of Term Papers, Theses, and Dissertations;* Joseph Gibaldi and Walter S. Achtert, *MLA Handbook for Writers of Research Papers;* or the *Publication Manual of the American Psychological Association*) will provide the details necessary to prepare the bibliography. Many of these sources also make suggestions for successful proposal writing.

Appendices

Glossary   A glossary of terms should be included whenever there are many words unique to the research topic and not understood by the general management community. This is a simple section consisting of terms and definitions. Also, define any acronyms that you use, even if they are defined within the text.

Measurement Instrument   For large projects, it is appropriate to include samples of the measurement instruments if they are available when you assemble the proposal. This allows the sponsor to discuss particular changes in one or more of the instruments. If exploratory work precedes the selection of the measurement instruments, you will not use this appendix section.

Other   Any detail that reinforces the body of the proposal can be included in an appendix. This includes researcher vitae, budget details, and lengthy descriptions of special facilities or resources.

EVALUATING THE RESEARCH PROPOSAL

Proposals are subjected to formal and informal reviews. The formal method has some variations, but its essence is described as follows. Before the proposal is received, criteria are established and each is given weights or points. The proposal is evaluated with a checklist of criteria in hand. Points are recorded for each category reflecting the sponsor's assessment of how well the proposal meets the category's established criteria. Several people, each of whom is assigned to a particular section, typically review long and complex proposals. After the review, the category scores are added to provide a cumulative total. The proposal with the highest number of points will win the contract. The formal method is most likely to be used for competitive government, university, or public sector grants and also for large-scale contracts.

Small-scale contracts are more prone to informal evaluation. With informal evaluation, the project needs, and thus the criteria, are well understood but not usually well documented. In contrast to the formal method, a system of points is not used and the criteria are not ranked. The process is more qualitative and impressionistic. Figure 4–6 shows Myra Wines's informal review of the proposal discussed in the opening vignette.

In practice, many items contribute to a proposal's acceptance and funding. Primarily, the content discussed above must be included to the level of detail required by the sponsor. Beyond the required modules, there are factors that can quickly eliminate a proposal from consideration and factors that improve the sponsor's reception of the proposal.

First, the proposal must be neatly presented. Although a proposal produced on a word processor and bound with an expensive cover will not overcome design or analysis deficiencies, a poorly presented, unclear, or disorganized proposal will not get serious attention from the reviewing sponsors. Second, the proposal's major topics should be easily found and logically organized. The reviewer should be able to page through the proposal to any section of interest. The proposal also must meet specific guidelines set by the sponsoring company or agency. These include budgetary restrictions and schedule deadlines.[13]

A fourth important aspect is the technical writing style of the proposal. The problem statement must be easily understood. The research design should be clearly outlined and the methodology explained. The importance/benefits of the study must allow the sponsor to see why the research should be funded. The objectives and results sec-

FIGURE   4–6   Informal Proposal Review

Myra Wines
200 ShellPoint Tower
Palm Beach, Florida 33480

The President
Economic Development Council
1800 ShellPoint Tower
Palm Beach, Florida 33480

Dear Harry,

I have reviewed Robert Buffet's proposal for an investigation of the job creation practices of local companies and, in short, I am very much concerned with several aspects of the "proposal." It is not really a proposal at all, as it lacks sufficient detail.

First let me mention that I shared Buffet's proposal with Mr. Jason Henry, an independent research consultant working with me on a MindWriter project. Mr. Buffet and his organization may one day represent competition for Mr. Henry, and you must therefore be aware of a potential conflict of interest and perhaps discount the opinions stated here. Since I am delivering this letter to you in two days rather than the two weeks you requested, you may wish to discuss my comments with others.

What you and Mr. Buffet gave me is an abbreviated research plan for our county, but since it lacks many features found in a comprehensive proposal, I immediately saw it was not the full proposal that had been funded by the state Commerce Secretary. I called Tallahassee and reached a young woman who hemmed and hawed and refused to say if she was authorized to mail me the full proposal. Finally, I gave up arguing and gave her your address and told her she could mail it you if she experienced an outbreak of belief in government-in-the-sunshine.

I then made several calls to people in Tallahassee whom I know from my days in TV. Did you know that this research idea is being floated by our senior U.S. senator, who is eager to throw a monkey wrench into the president's tax incentives plan? The senator whispered it to the governor and the governor whispered it to her commerce secretary, and here we are.

The problem statement is rather long and convoluted, but, in short, it poses the questions, "Are new high-tech companies creating jobs for residents of our county? Or are they bringing technical and manufacturing workers from outside the state and by-passing the local work force? Or are they doing research in these companies with a low level of manufacturing job creation? Or are they investing in 'smart' capital equipment that does not create jobs?" If you cut through the verbiage, I think you can see the project is right dead on the mark with its questions.

The research objectives section is fairly straightforward. Buffet's people are going to identify all the companies in this county in the SIC code groups associated with "high tech," and collect information on the number of locally hired employees in various job categories, chiefly in production, and also collect data on capital investments, debt, and other financial data, which Mr. Henry says makes good sense to collect and ought to be easy to do.

There is a section call Importance of the Study, which is full of platitudes and does not get around to mentioning the pending tax legislation. But at least the platitudes are brief.

I become nervous in the Design section. It calls for Mr. Buffet's group to go on site with a "team" and conduct in-depth interviews of the chief operating officer (COO), treasurer, and comptroller of each company, and enter the data into a spreadsheet. I have double-checked this with Mr. Henry and also with a banker friend, and both of them assure me that a simple questionnaire might be mailed to the COO. There is no need whatever to send in a team to conduct open-ended interviews. While there might be a noncompliance problem associated with filling out a form, this might appropriately be attended to by pointing out the auspices—the state Commerce Secretary and your Economic Development Council—with an interview request as a last resort.

The proposal contains no budget and no specific list of researchers who will comprise the team. The firm would have carte blanche to go in with anyone on their payroll and try to induce the subjects to stray beyond the stated research objectives to talk about anything at all. Obviously such license would be a marketing tool and might allow the researchers to collect a list of researchable problems not related to the Secretary's needs, as stated in the problem section.

I strongly advise you to tell Mr. Buffet to collect the information through a simple mail survey. Offer to send it out under your Council's letterhead, or see if you can get the Commerce office or even the Governor's office to send it out. But do not subject your local business community to unstructured, free-ranging visits, which are clearly not justified by the research objectives.

Sincerely,

Myra Wines

tions should communicate exactly the goals and concrete results that will come from the study. Finally, budget and schedule considerations must be kept in mind. A late proposal will not be reviewed. A schedule that does not meet the expected deadlines will disqualify the proposal. A budget that is too high for the allocated funds will be rejected. Conversely, a low budget compared to competing proposals suggests that something is missing or there is something wrong with the researchers.

CLOSE-UP

When last we checked Myra and Jason were preparing a proposal for Gracie Uhura, product manager at MindWriter Corporation.

Myra decided to exclude the "executive summary" for two reasons: The proposal is short and the essentials will be contained in the cover letter. The proposal follows the components discussed in this chapter. It is an appropriate adaptation for an internal, small-scale study. The module "qualification of researcher" was not needed because MindWriter's employee solicited the proposal; Myra had prejudged the researcher's qualifications.

REPAIR PROCESS SATISFACTION PROPOSAL MINDWRITER CORPORATION COMPLETECARE PROGRAM

Problem Statement

MindWriter Corporation has recently created a service and repair program, CompleteCare, for its portable/laptop/notebook computers. This program promises to provide a rapid response to customers' service problems.

MindWriter is currently experiencing a shortage of trained technical operators in its telephone center. The package courier, contracted to pick up and deliver customers' machines to Complete-Care, has provided irregular execution. Mind-Writer has also experienced parts availability problems for some machine types.

Recent phone logs at the call center show complaints about CompleteCare; it is unknown how representative these complaints are and what implications they may have for satisfaction with MindWriter products.

Management desires information on the program's effectiveness and its impact on customer satisfaction to determine what should be done to improve the CompleteCare program for Mind-Writer product repair and servicing.

Research Objectives

The purpose of this research is to discover the level of satisfaction with the CompleteCare service program. Specifically, we intend to identify the component and overall levels of satisfaction with CompleteCare. Components of the repair process are important targets for investigation because they reveal: (1) how customer tolerance levels for repair performance affect overall satisfaction and (2) which process components should be immediately improved to elevate overall satisfaction of MindWriter customers experiencing product failures.

We will also discover the importance of types of product failure on customer satisfaction levels.

Importance/Benefits

High levels of user satisfaction translate into positive word-of-mouth product endorsements. These endorsements influence the purchase outcomes for (1) friends and relatives and (2) business associates.

Critical incidents, such as product failures, have the potential to either undermine existing satisfaction levels or preserve and even increase the resulting levels of product satisfaction. The outcome of the episode depends on the quality of the manufacturer's response.

An extraordinary response by the manufacturer to such incidents will preserve and enhance user satisfaction levels to the point that direct and indirect benefits derived from such programs will justify their costs.

This research has the potential for connecting to ongoing MindWriter customer satisfaction programs and measuring the long-term effects of CompleteCare (and product failure incidents) on customer satisfaction.

Research Design

Exploration: Qualitative We will augment our knowledge of CompleteCare by interviewing the service manager, the call center manager, and the independent package company's account executive. Based on a thorough inventory of CompleteCare's internal and external processes, we propose to develop a mail survey.

Questionnaire Design A self-administered questionnaire (postcard size) offers the most cost-effective method for securing feedback on the effectiveness of CompleteCare. The introduction on the postcard will be a variation of MindWriter's current advertising campaign.

Some questions for this instrument will be based on the investigative questions we presented to you previously, and others will be drawn from the executive interviews. We anticipate a maximum of 10 questions. A new five-point expectation scale, compatible with your existing customer satisfaction scales, is being designed.

Although we are not convinced that open-ended questions are appropriate for postcard questionnaires, we understand that you and Mr. Malraison like them. A comments/suggestions question will be included. In addition, we will work out a code block that captures the call center's reference number, model, and item(s) serviced.

Logistics The postal arrangements are: box rental, permit, and "business reply" privileges to be arranged in a few days. The approval for a reduced postage rate will take one to two weeks. The budget section itemizes these costs.

Pilot Test We will test the questionnaire with a small sample of customers using your tech-line operators. This will contain your costs. We will then revise the questions and forward them to our graphics designer for layout. The instrument will then be submitted to you for final approval.

Evaluation of Nonresponse Bias A random sample of 100 from the list of customers who do not return the questionnaire will be secured. Call center records will be used for establishing the sampling frame. Nonresponders will be interviewed on the telephone and their responses compared statistically to responders'.

Data Analysis

We will review the postcards that are returned and send you a weekly report listing customers who either are dissatisfied (score a "1" or "2") with any item of the questionnaire or submit a negative comment. This will improve your timeliness in resolving customer complaints. Each month, we will provide you with a report consisting of frequencies and category percentages for each question. Visual displays of the data will be in bar chart/histogram form. We propose to include at least one question dealing with overall satisfaction (of CompleteCare and/or MindWriter). This overall question would be regressed on the individual items to determine each item's importance. A performance grid will identify items needing improvement with an evaluation of priority. Other analyses can be prepared on a time and materials basis.

The open-ended questions will be summarized and reported by model code. If you wish, we also can provide content analysis of these questions.

Results: Deliverables

1. Development and production of a postcard survey. MindWriter employees will package the questionnaire with the returned merchandise.
2. Weekly exception reports (transmitted electronically) listing customers who meet the dissatisfied customer criteria.
3. Monthly reports as described in the data analysis section.
4. An ASCII diskette with each month's data shipped to Austin by the fifth working day of each month.

Budget

Card Layout and Printing Based on your card estimate, our designer will lay out and print 2,000 cards in the first run ($500.00). The specifications are as follows: 7-point Williamsburg offset hi-bulk

with one-over-one black ink. A gray-scale layer with a MindWriter logo or CompleteCare can be positioned under the printed material at a nominal charge. The two-sided cards are 4 1/4 by 5 1/2.

This allows us to print four cards per page. The opposite side will have the business reply logo, postage paid symbol, and address.

Cost Summary

Interviews	$1,550.00
Travel costs	$2,500.00
Questionnaire development	$1,850.00
Equipment/supplies	$1,325.00
Graphics design	$800.00
Permit fee (annual)	$75.00
Business reply fee (annual)	$185.00
Box rental (annual)	$35.00
Printing costs	$500.00
Data entry (monthly)	$130.00
Monthly data files (each)	$50.00
Monthly reports (each)	$850.00
Total start-up costs	$8,820.00
Monthly run costs	$1,030.00*

*An additional fee of $0.21 per card will be assessed by the post office for business reply mail. At approximately a 30% return rate, we estimate the monthly cost to be less than $50.

Summary

A proposal is an offer to produce a product or render a service to the potential buyer or sponsor. The research proposal presents a problem, discusses related research efforts, outlines the data needed for solving the problem, and shows the design used to gather and analyze the data.

Proposals are valuable to both the research sponsor and the researcher. The sponsor uses the proposal to evaluate a research idea. The proposal is also a useful tool to ensure the sponsor and investigator agree on the research question. For the beginning researcher, the proposal enables learning from other researchers. In addition, the completed proposal provides a logical guide for the investigation.

We discuss two types of proposals: internal and external. Internal and external proposals have a problem-solving orientation. The staff of a company generates internal proposals. External proposals are prepared by an outside firm to obtain contract research. External proposals emphasize qualifications of the researcher, special facilities and resources, and project management aspects such as budgets and schedules. Within each type of proposal there are varying degrees of complexity; a proposal can vary in length from a 2-page memo to more than 100 pages, from a telephone conversation to a multimedia presentation.

Proposals can be written with a set of sections or modules. The difference in the type of proposal and the level of complexity of the project determines what modules should be included.

Proposals can be evaluated formally or informally. The formal process uses a list of criteria and an associated point scale. The informal process is more qualitative. Important aspects beyond content include presentation style, timeliness, and credibility.

Key Terms

critical path method
executive summary
literature review
project management
proposal
request for proposal (RFP)

Discussion Questions

1. What, if any, are the differences between solicited and unsolicited proposals?

2. Select a research report from a management journal. Outline a proposal for the research as if it had not yet been performed. Make estimates of time and costs.

3. You are the new manager of market intelligence in a rapidly expanding software firm. Many product managers and corporate officers have requested market surveys from you on various products. Design a form for a research proposal that can be completed easily by your research staff and the sponsoring manager. Discuss how your form improves communication of the research objectives between the manager and the researcher.

4. What modules would you suggest be included in a proposal for each of the following cases?

   a. The president of your company has asked for a study of the company's health benefits plan and for a comparison of it to other firms' plans.

   b. You are competing for a university-sponsored student research grant, awarded to seniors and graduate students.

   c. A bank is interested in understanding the population trends by location so that it can plan its new branch locations for the next five years. They contacted you for a proposal.

    d. You are interested in starting a new research service, providing monthly information about the use of recyclable items in your state. The proposal will go to several city and county planning agencies, independent waste service providers, and independent and government landfill providers.

5. Consider the new trends in desktop publishing, multimedia computer authoring and display capabilities, and inexpensive video taping and playback possibilities. How might these be used to enhance research proposals? Give several examples of appropriate use.

6. You are the manager of a research department in a large department store chain. Develop a list of criteria for evaluating the types of research activities listed below. Include a point scale and weighting algorithm.

    a. Market research

    b. Advertising effectiveness

    c. Employee opinion surveys

    d. Credit card operations

    e. Computer service effectiveness at the individual store level

---

Reference Notes

1. Charles T. Brusaw, Gerald J. Alred, and Walter E. Oliu, *Handbook of Technical Writing,* 4th ed. (New York: St. Martin's Press, 1992), p. 375.

2. Paul D. Leedy, *Practical Research: Planning and Design*, 2nd ed. (New York: Macmillan, 1980), p. 79.

3. R. Lesikar and John Pettit, *Report Writing for Business*, 9th ed. (Burr Ridge, IL: Irwin, 1995).

4. Ibid., p. 51.

5. William J. Roetzheim, *Proposal Writing for the Data Processing Consultant* (Englewood Cliffs, NJ: Prentice-Hall, 1986), p. 106.

6. Brusaw, Alred, and Oliu, *Handbook,* p. 11.

7. Philip V. Lewis and William H. Baker, *Business Report Writing* (Columbus, OH: Grid, 1978), p. 58.

8. Robert G. Murdick and Donald R. Cooper, *Business Research: Concepts and Guides* (Columbus, OH: Grid, 1982), p. 112.

9. Roetzheim, *Proposal Writing,* pp. 67–68.

10. Many texts cover project management and network analysis. These include details of scheduling and charting techniques such as Gantt charts and CPM charts, which are beyond the scope of this text. See, for example, Chapter 3, "Network Analysis," in Don T. Philips, A. Ravindran, and James J. Solberg, *Operations Research: Principles and Practice* (New York: Wiley, 1976); or Chapter 6, "Network Models," in K. Roscoe Davis and Patrick G. McKeon, *Quantitative Models for Management* (Boston: Kent, 1981).

11. Murdick and Cooper, *Business Research,* p. 114.

12. Ibid., pp. 114–16.

13. Ibid., p. 117.

Suggested Readings

1. Krathwohl, David R. *How to Prepare a Research Proposal,* 3rd ed. Syracuse, NY: Syracuse University Press, 1988. A practical guide and framework for student projects.
2. Leedy, Paul D. *Practical Research: Planning and Design,* 6th ed. Englewood Cliffs, NJ: Prentice-Hall, 1996. Practical and readable sections guide students through the research process.
3. Locke, Lawrence F., Waneen Wyrick Spiduso, and Stephen J. Silverman. *Proposals That Work: A Guide to Planning Dissertations and Grant Proposals,* 3rd ed. Thousand Oaks, CA: Sage Publications, 1993. An excellent guide for students and faculty advisers.

CHAPTER
5

ETHICS IN BUSINESS RESEARCH

 CHAPTER NAVIGATION

BRINGING RESEARCH TO LIFE

WHAT ARE RESEARCH ETHICS?

ETHICAL TREATMENT OF RESPONDENTS AND SUBJECTS

ETHICS AND THE CLIENT

RESEARCHERS AND TEAM MEMBERS

CLOSE-UP

PROFESSIONAL STANDARDS

RESOURCES FOR ETHICAL AWARENESS

SUMMARY

KEY TERMS

CASES

REFERENCE NOTES

SUGGESTED READINGS

106

BRINGING
RESEARCH TO LIFE

"**M**y brother-in-law, 'Slick Billy' Henderson, has been in and out of trouble all his life," said Myra, "but hasn't spent a night in jail. He knows the difference between what is unethical and what is actually illegal."

"Have they ever prosecuted the guy?" asked Jason.

"No, but he may soon be broke. He is in computer peripherals in Silicon Valley and has taken a near-lead position in peripherals for laptop computing. Well, laptop peripherals are volatile. Do I have to tell you? They grow smaller every month and have to be sold more cheaply. According to my sister, Janet, a detailed market report was needed, which Bill could very well afford to pay for, but decided to get it through one of his notorious fiddles. So he went to a hungry headhunter—a management placement specialist—and said he wanted to interview six candidates for Senior Diversification Manager.

"His security chief, who Jan swears is an ex-secret police Eastern Bloc immigrant, rigged Bill's office and conference room with listening devices and recorded every interview. Bill even wore a 'wire' so he could record conversations in the men's room and over lunch. The first few interviews added greatly to Bill's understanding of the competition, but when the headhunter brought in an exec from ConToCon, the company that was Bill's number one competitor, he knew he had struck pay dirt.

"On the basis of the interview with Mr. Smithson from ConToCon, Bill decided to shut down the California production line for a certain peripheral and open production in Mexico for a smaller, faster, cheaper version. Bill summoned his vice presidents to announce his decision and provide transcripts of his interview with Smithson. Immediately, without actually reading the transcripts, Bill's chief attorney scrawled her resignation on a notepad and walked out, without even stopping to empty her office. The human resource VP caved in, however, and soon announced a layoff of their California factory employees, and the production VP flew to Mexico to ink a contract to expand a plant there."

"Did your brother actually make any of the candidates a job offer?"

"Please, Jason. He is my *brother-in-law* not my brother, and no, he saw no need to make any offers. He told Jan that the 'tricky s.o.b.'s,' as he called them, probably never intended to work for him. He insisted that the interviewees were wasting his time and money and they only wanted job offers to extract a raise from their current employers.

"Slippery folks believe the world is populated by even slipperier folks," said Jason, philosophically.

"Well, no sooner had Bill laid off his California workers and flown to Mexico to make a down payment on a plant there, when ConToCon announced that it was expanding in California, exactly contrary to what Smithson had said. In fact, according to the trade press, Smithson was given the boot; no one ever knew why, although there was no shortage of rumors.

"So Bill has sunk his own ship and cannot bail it out now. Nevertheless, he remains unrepentant and blames the lawyer who quit, the headhunter, the interviewees, Smithson most of all, and his production VP. Bill maintains he is the victim of an innocent mistake.

"Jan filed for divorce yesterday. She has 8 by 10 glossy pictures of him frolicking on a private beach in Acapulco with a local *señorita*."

"And how is Bill taking this?"

"Bill is incensed, of course, and demands to know what sort of woman hires a detective to spy on her husband."

WHAT ARE RESEARCH ETHICS?

Like other aspects of business, research demands ethical behavior from its participants. **Ethics** are norms or standards of behavior that guide moral choices about our behavior and our relationships with others. The goal of ethics in research is to ensure that no one is harmed or suffers adverse consequences from research activities. This objective is usually achieved. However, unethical activities are pervasive and include violating nondisclosure agreements, breaking respondent confidentiality, misrepresenting results, deceiving people, invoicing irregularities, avoiding legal liability, and more.

The recognition of ethics as a problem for economic organizations was shown in a survey where 80 percent of organizations reported the adoption of an ethical code. Surprisingly, the evidence that this effort has improved ethical practices is questionable. The same study reports limited success for codes of conduct that attempt to restrain improper behavior.[1]

There is no single approach to ethics. Advocating strict adherence to a set of laws is difficult because of the unforeseen constraint put on researchers. Because of Germany's war history, for example, the government forbids many types of medical research. Consequently, the German people do not benefit from many advances in biotechnology and may be unable to use genetically altered drugs in the future. Alternatively, relying on each individual's personal sense of morality is equally problematic. Consider the clash between those who believe death is deliverance from a life of suffering and those who value life to the point of preserving it indefinitely through mechanical means. Each value system claims superior knowledge of moral correctness.

Clearly, a middle ground between being completely code governed and ethical relativism is necessary. The foundation for that middle ground is an emerging consensus on ethical standards for researchers. Codes and regulations guide researchers and sponsors. Review boards and peer groups help researchers examine their research proposals for ethical dilemmas. Many design-based ethical problems can be eliminated by careful planning and constant vigilance. In the end, responsible research anticipates ethical dilemmas and attempts to adjust the design, procedures, and protocols during the planning process rather than treating them as an afterthought. Ethical research requires personal integrity from the researcher, project manager, and the client.

Because integrity in research is vital, we are discussing its components early in this book and emphasizing ethical behavior throughout our coverage. Our objective is to stimulate an ongoing exchange about values and practical research constraints in the chapters that follow. This chapter is organized around the theme of ethical treatment of respondents, clients, research sponsors, and other researchers. We also highlight appropriate laws and codes, resources for ethical awareness, and cases for application.

ETHICAL TREATMENT OF RESPONDENTS AND SUBJECTS

When ethics are discussed in research design, we often think first about protecting the rights of the respondent or subject. Whether data are gathered in an experiment, interview, observation, or survey, the respondent has many rights to be safeguarded.

In general, research must be designed so a respondent does not suffer physical harm, discomfort, pain, embarrassment, or loss of privacy. To safeguard these, the researcher should follow three guidelines:[2]

1. Begin data collection by explaining to the respondents the benefits expected from the research. Neither overstate nor understate the benefits so the respondents are not inclined to exaggerate answers.

2. Explain to the respondents that their rights and well-being will be adequately protected, and say how that will be done. This may be accomplished by maintaining confidentiality of the responses or by destroying the names and addresses of the respondents.

3. Be certain that interviewers obtain the informed consent of the respondents. Also, require that the method of getting the consent be appropriate and adequate. When questionnaires contain sensitive questions about family income, it is inadequate to obtain a blanket consent for the questionnaire. Instead, the researcher should explain that the questionnaire contains some sensitive questions and the respondents are free not to answer any question that makes them uncomfortable.

Benefits

Whenever direct contact is made with a respondent, the research benefits should be discussed. An interviewer should begin an introduction with his or her name, the name of the research organization, and a brief description of the purpose and benefit of the research. This puts respondents at ease, they know to whom they are speaking, and it motivates them to answer questions truthfully. In short, knowing why one is being asked questions improves cooperation through honest disclosure of purpose. Inducements to participate, financial or otherwise, should not be disproportionate to the task or presented in a fashion that results in coercion.

Sometimes the actual purpose and benefits of your study or experiment must be concealed from the respondents to avoid introducing bias. The need for concealing objectives leads directly to the problem of deception.

Deception

Deception occurs when the respondents are told only part of the truth or when the truth is fully compromised. Some believe this should never occur. Others suggest two reasons for deception: (1) to prevent biasing the respondents before the survey or experiment and (2) to protect the confidentiality of a third party (e.g., the client). Deception should not be used in an attempt to improve response rates.

The benefits to be gained by deception should be balanced against the risks to the respondents. When possible, an experiment or interview should be redesigned to reduce reliance on deception. In addition, the respondents' rights and well-being must be adequately protected. In instances where deception in an experiment could produce anxiety, a subject's medical condition should be checked to ensure that no adverse physical harm follows. The American Psychological Association's Ethics Code states that the use of deception is inappropriate unless deceptive techniques are justified by the study's expected scientific, educational, or applied value, and equally effective alternatives that do not use deception are not feasible.[3] And finally, the respondents must have given their informed consent before participating in the research.

Informed Consent

Securing **informed consent** from respondents is a matter of fully disclosing the procedures of the proposed survey or other research design before requesting permission to proceed with the study. There are exceptions that argue for a signed consent form. When dealing with children, it is wise to have a parent or other person with legal standing sign a consent form. When doing research with medical or psychological ramifications, it is also wise to have a consent form. If there is a chance the data could harm the respondent or if the researchers offer only limited protection of confidentiality, a signed form detailing the types of limits should be obtained. For most business research, oral consent is sufficient. An example of how informed consent procedures are implemented is shown in Figure 5–1. In this example, a university research center demonstrates how they adhere to the highest ethical standards for survey procedures.[4]

In situations where respondents are intentionally or accidentally deceived, they should be debriefed once the research is complete.

Debriefing Respondents

Debriefing explains the truth to the participants and describes the major goals of the study and the reasons for using deception. In cases where severe reactions occur,

FIGURE   5–1   Informed Consent Procedures for Surveys

Surveys conducted by the Indiana University Center for Survey Research contain the following informed consent components in their introductions:

1. Introduce ourselves—interviewer's name and Indiana University Center for Survey Research
2. Briefly describe the survey topic (e.g., barriers to health insurance)
3. Describe the geographic area we are interviewing (e.g., people in Indiana) or target sample (e.g., aerospace engineers)
4. Tell who the sponsor is (e.g., National Endowment for the Humanities)
5. Describe the purpose(s) of the research (e.g., satisfaction with services received provided by a local agency)
6. Give a "good-faith" estimate of the time required to complete the interview
7. Promise anonymity and confidentiality (when appropriate)
8. Tell the respondent the participation is voluntary
9. Tell the respondent that item-nonresponse is acceptable
10. Ask permission to begin

Sample Introduction.   Hello, I'm [fill NAME] from the Center for Survey Research at Indiana University. We're surveying Indianapolis area residents to ask their opinions about some health issues. This study is sponsored by the National Institutes of Health and its results will be used to research the effect of community ties on attitudes toward medical practices.

The survey takes about 40 minutes. Your participation is anonymous and voluntary, and all your answers will be kept completely confidential. If there are any questions that you don't feel you can answer, please let me know and we'll move to the next one. So, if I have your permission, I'll continue.

Sample Conclusion.   The respondent is given information on how to contact the principal investigator. For example: John Kennedy is the Principal Investigator for this study. Would you like Dr. Kennedy's address or telephone number in case you want to contact him about the study at any time?

follow-up medical or psychological attention should be provided to continue to ensure the participants remain unharmed by the research.

Even when research does not deceive the respondents, it is a good practice to offer them follow-up information. For surveys and interviews, respondents can be offered a report of the findings. Usually, they will not request additional information. Occasionally, however, the research will be of particular interest to a respondent. A simple set of descriptive charts can be generated for such an individual. This retains the goodwill of the respondent, providing an incentive to participate in future research projects.

For experiments, all subjects should be debriefed. As mentioned previously, this corrects any deception that occurred and it allows subjects to put the experiment into context. Debriefing usually includes a description of the hypothesis being tested and the purpose of the study. Subjects who were not deceived still benefit from the debriefing session. They will be able to understand why the experiment was created. The researchers also gain important insight into what the subjects thought about during and after the experiment. This may lead to modifications in future research designs. Like survey and interview respondents, subjects in experiments and observational studies should be offered a report of the findings.

To what extent do debriefing and informed consent reduce the effects of deception? Research suggests that the majority of subjects do not resent temporary deception and may have more positive feelings about the value of the research after debriefing than those who didn't participate in the study.[5] Nevertheless, this is an ethically thorny issue and should be addressed with sensitivity and concern for research participants.

Rights to Privacy

Privacy laws in the United States are taken seriously. All individuals have a right to privacy, and researchers must respect that right. The importance of the right to privacy is illustrated with an example.

An employee of a large video rental company is also a student at the local university. For a research project, this student and his team members decide to compare the video-viewing habits of a sample of customers. Using telephone interviews, the students begin their research. After inquiring about people's viewing habits and the frequency of rentals versus purchases, the students move on to the types of films people watch. They find that most respondents answer questions about their preferences for children's shows, classics, bestsellers, mysteries, and science fiction. But the cooperation ceases when the students question the viewing frequency of pornographic movies. Without the guarantee of privacy, most people will not answer these kinds of questions truthfully, if at all. The study then loses key data.

The privacy guarantee is important not only to retain validity of the research but also to protect respondents. In the previous example, imagine the harm that could be caused by releasing information on the viewing habits of certain citizens. Clearly, the confidentiality of survey answers is an important aspect of the respondents' right to privacy.

Once the guarantee of **confidentiality** is given, protecting that confidentiality is essential. Researchers should restrict access to information that reveals names, telephone numbers, addresses, or other identifying features. Only researchers who have signed nondisclosure, confidentiality forms should be allowed access to the data. Links between the data or database and the identifying information file should be weakened. Individual interview response sheets should be inaccessible to everyone except the editors and data entry personnel. Occasionally, data collection instruments should be destroyed once the data are in a data file. Data files that make it easy to reconstruct the profiles or identification of individual respondents should be carefully controlled. For very small groups, data should not be made available because it is often easy to pinpoint a person within the group. Employee-satisfaction survey feedback in small units can be easily used to identify an individual through descriptive statistics alone. These last two protections are particularly important in personnel research.[6]

But privacy is more than confidentiality. A **right to privacy** means one has the right to refuse to be interviewed or to refuse to answer any question in an interview. Potential participants have a right to privacy in their own homes, including not admitting researchers and not answering telephones. And they have the right to engage in private behavior in private places without fear of observation. To address these rights, ethical researchers ask permission to interview respondents. They inform respondents of their right to refuse to answer any question. They schedule field interviews only during daylight (and not at mealtime), or they call in advance to set an appointment for an interview. Telephone interviews are limited in time and occur only during reasonable hours. Observation is restricted to public behavior.

Data Collection in Cyberspace

Some ethicists argue that the very conduct that results in resistance from respondents—interference, invasiveness in their lives, denial of privacy rights—has encouraged researchers to investigate topics online that have long been the principal commodity of offline investigation. The novelty and convenience of communicating by computer has led researchers to cyberspace in search of abundant sources of data. Whether we call it the "wired society," "digital life," "computer-mediated communication," or "cyberculture," the growth of cyber studies causes us to question how we gather data online, deal with subjects, and present results.

In a special ethics issue of *Information Society*, scholars involved in cyberspace research concluded

> all participants agree that research in cyberspace provides no special dispensation to ignore ethical precepts. Researchers are obligated to protect human subjects and "do right" in electronic venues as in more conventional ones. Second, each participant recognizes that cyberspace poses complex ethical issues that may lack exact analogs in other types of inquiry. The ease of covert observation, the occasional blurry distinction between public and private venues, and the difficulty of obtaining the informed consent of subjects make cyberresearch particularly vulnerable to ethical breaches by even the most scrupulous scholars. Third, all recognize that because research procedures or activities may be permissible or not precluded by law or policy, it does not follow that they are necessarily ethical or allowable. Foruth, all agree that the individual researcher has the ultimate responsiblity for assuring that inquiry is not only done honestly, but done with ethical integrity.[7]

Yet questions remain on defining specific ethical behaviors for cyber research, the sufficiency of existing professional guidelines, and the question of ultimate responsibility for respondents. If researchers are responsible for the ethical conduct of their research, are they solely responsible for the burden of protecting subjects from every conceivable harm?

ETHICS AND THE CLIENT

There are also ethical considerations to keep in mind when dealing with the research client. Whether undertaking product, market, personnel, financial, or other research, a client has the right to receive ethically conducted research.

Confidentiality

Some clients require confidentiality for various reasons. Many clients wish to undertake research without revealing themselves. This is one reason for hiring outside consulting firms to complete research projects. When a company is testing a new product idea, it may not want consumers to be influenced by the company image. If a company is contemplating entering a new market, it may not wish to have competitors aware of its plans. For these and other reasons, corporations have a right to dissociate themselves from the sponsorship of the project. This type of confidentiality is called **sponsor nondisclosure.** It is the responsibility of the research firm to respect that desire and devise a plan that safeguards the identity of the client.

The second reason for confidentiality involves the purpose of the study or its details. A client may be testing a new idea that is not yet patented and does not want the competition to know of its plans. It may be investigating employee complaints and does not want to spark union activity. Or a new public offering might be contemplated. For whatever reason, clients have the right to demand and receive **purpose nondisclosure** and **findings nondisclosure** between themselves and the researchers.

Right to Quality Research

An important ethical consideration for the researcher and the (internal and external) client is the client's right to quality research. From the proposal through the design to data analysis and final reporting, the researcher guides the client on the proper techniques and interpretations. Ethical researchers provide the client with the type of study he or she needs to solve the management question. Often clients will have heard about a sophisticated data-handling technique and will want it used even when it is inappropriate for the problem at hand. The researcher should guide the client so this does not occur. The design of the project should be suitable for the problem; research techniques should not be chosen so maximum researcher revenue or minimum researcher effort is achieved at the sponsor's expense.

The second aspect of quality research lies in the reporting techniques. We have all heard the remark, "You can lie with statistics." It is the researcher's responsibility to prevent that from occurring. As you learn about research design, sampling, statistics, and reporting techniques, you'll see that various conditions must be met for results to be valid. The ethical researcher always follows the rules and meets these conditions. The ethical researcher reports findings in ways that minimize the drawing of false conclusions. The ethical researcher also uses charts, graphs, and tables to show the data objectively, despite the sponsor's preferred outcomes.

Client's Ethics

Occasionally, researchers may be asked by clients to identify respondents or their groups, change the data, interpret the data in a favorable light, omit sections of data analysis and conclusions, or change the research findings. Each of these is an example of unethical client behavior. Compliance by the researcher would be a breach of ethical standards.

Let's examine the types of coercion that may occur. A sponsor may offer a promotion, future contracts, or a larger payment for the existing research contract; or the client may threaten to fire the researcher or tarnish the researcher's reputation. For some, the request may seem trivial and the reward high. But imagine, for a moment, what will happen to the researcher who changes research results. Although there is a promise of future research, the client can never trust that researcher again. If ethics are for sale, who might be the highest bidder next time? Although the promise of future contracts is enticing, it is unlikely to be kept. Each type of coercive reward or punishment has an equally poor outcome. The "greater than" contracted payment is a payoff. The threats to one's professional reputation cannot be carried out effectively by a client who has tried to purchase you. So the rewards for behaving unethically are illusory.

What's the ethical course? Often, it requires confronting the client's demand. Educate the sponsor to the purpose of research and the researcher's role in fact finding versus the sponsor's role in decision making. Explain how distorting the truth or breaking faith with respondents leads to future problems. Failing moral suasion, terminate the relationship with the client.

RESEARCHERS AND TEAM MEMBERS

Another ethical responsibility of researchers is their team's safety and their own. In addition, the responsibility for ethical behavior rests with the researcher who, along with assistants, is charged with protecting the anonymity of both the client and the respondent.

Safety

It is the researcher's responsibility to design a project so the safety of all interviewers, surveyors, experimenters, or observers is protected. Several factors may be important in these situations. Some urban areas and undeveloped rural areas may be unsafe for research assistants. If, for example, the researcher must personally interview people in a high-crime district, it is reasonable to provide a second team member to protect the researcher. Alternatively, if an assistant feels unsafe after visiting a neighborhood by car, an alternate researcher should be assigned to the destination.[8] It is unethical to require staff members to enter an environment where they feel physically threatened. Researchers who are insensitive to these concerns face both research and legal risks—the least of which involves having interviewers falsify instruments.

Ethical Behavior of Assistants

Researchers should require ethical compliance from team members just as sponsors expect ethical behavior from the researcher. Assistants are expected to carry out the sampling plan, to interview or observe respondents without bias, and to accurately record all necessary data. Unethical behavior, such as filling in an interview sheet without having asked the respondent the questions, cannot be tolerated. The behavior of the assistants is under the direct control of the responsible researcher or field supervisor. If an assistant behaves improperly in an interview or shares a respondent's interview sheet with an unauthorized person, it is the researcher's responsibility. Consequently, all assistants should be well trained and supervised.

Protection of Anonymity

As discussed previously, researchers and assistants protect the confidentiality of the client's information and the anonymity of the respondents. Each researcher handling data should have signed a confidentiality and nondisclosure statement.

CLOSE-UP

Do Data Warehouses Challenge Fair Play?
H. Jefferson Smith

One of the most popular concepts in information technology these days is data warehousing, which stores a company's data in a central repository. The information in the database is updated frequently, and is make available to the firm's managers and employees for planning, marketing and decision making.

Data warehouses are designed to support on-line analytical processing and data mining. These technologies have been described as akin to turning 100 statisticians loose on your data at the same time.

Many kinds of business questions can be answered through these technologies. You can find and track customers, analyze their behavior, segment a customer base, customize products, model past attrition behavior (thus reducing past customer defections), and refine a business strategy by massaging the warehouse data.

For example, one consumer credit company has a data warehouse that contains almost 1,000 attributes per customer. The database is so large that updates take more than 48 hours and rely on 50 different feeder files. But the payback is also large: Analysts are making more than 200 queries per day, and in-depth reports on spending patterns and demographics are available to the company's marketers. The analysts and marketers have also used the warehouse to generate targeted mailings to customers.

Nevertheless, along with the potential benefits of data warehousing come some serious considerations about fair play in the use of customer data. The various issues that arise depend on whether an organization's customers are other businesses or individual consumers.

IT'S JUST BUSINESS

Almost every company has relationships with other firms. Some are suppliers that provide the company with products or services, while others distribute or purchase its products and services. In addition, a company has relationships with individual consumers who buy its products—either directly or through a distributor or retailer. Thus, when an enterprise warehouses data about its customers in business-to-business transactions, a corporation should think about what constitutes fair play from the perspective of several different players: the company that is its direct customer, the firms supplying that customer, and the firms or individual consumers buying that customer's products.

In general, the company with the data warehouse should follow a two-edged principle. It is *fair* to use the customer data to deduce ways in which the relationship with this business customer (or other potential customers of this type) could be strengthened.

It would be fair, for example, to create statistical profiles of current customers based on the warehouse data and to use those profiles to deduce which market segments might be most appropriate for future targeting. It would also be acceptable to conclude which additional products or services would be most appropriate for current customers, and to focus special attention on creating and marketing those products or services to those customers.

On the other hand, it is *unfair* to use the customer data in any of the following three ways: First, it is unfair to do anything that might harm the customer's relationships with any of *its* suppliers or customers. Suppose, for example, that company B, after careful scrutiny of its warehouse data, realized that most of the purchases customer C made were being resold to one of C's clients, D. Obviously, both B and D could benefit if D bought its products directly from B and bypassed C. B could charge D a price that was higher than what it charged C but lower than what D paid C.

Though this scenario appears economically efficient, B's contacting D to suggest such a deal would constitute gross unfairness to C. B would be using data about its relationship with C to undercut C's position with D.

Second, it is unfair to use customer data in any way that intrudes on the customer's proprietary know-how. Suppose that its data warehouse gave company E knowledge about the specific methods and techniques that one of its customers, F,

was using to design and produce its products. It would be unfair for E to reveal this information to others or to use this knowledge to take advantage of F in future negotiations.

Third, it is unfair to use customer data to change an industry structure if that change is detrimental to any of the firm's customers. Suppose, for example, that company G was a supplier to a number of firms in an industry. This industry has a value system of suppliers, manufacturers, distributors, and consumers. Several companies are involved in the manufacturing process—from raw materials to the final product—with each firm adding some value to the product.

By carefully massaging its data warehouse, G might discover a new scheme for manufacturing and distributing products that would increase the overall efficiency of the system, reduce the cost of production (leading to greater industry profits and more sales for G), and lead to greater sales and profits for *some* of the manufacturers (G's customers).

On the other hand, the scheme would hurt the sales and profits of other firms that are also G's customers. Although some people might disagree, I would argue that G had an obligation to protect the interests of *all* its customers and to take no action that would harm any of them. Since G had the data in its warehouse only because of its relationship with its customers, it would be a betrayal to use that data in a manner that would harm any of them.

MAKING IT PERSONAL

When a company's customers are individual consumers instead of other businesses, different rules of fairness apply because concepts of fair information use at this level are often viewed as a human rights issue. Therefore, issues related to consumer privacy—a concept quite distinct from that of corporations' right to proprietary trade knowledge—quickly come into play.

The general rules of fairness in warehousing consumer data should be the same as those that are becoming generally accepted for other applications that involve personal data:

• Consumers should be fully informed of the intended uses of data before the data are collected.

• Consumers should be allowed to opt out of any uses they find offensive.

• Data collected from consumers for one purpose should not be used for another purpose without the consumer's permission.

The rules suggest that it will be difficult to begin warehousing consumer data *unless* some up-front work has been done to ensure that the consumers were fully informed of the intended uses ahead of time and were given an opportunity to opt out.

For example, unless consumers are told in advance that transaction data will be used to assess their spending patterns and create psychographic profiles of their activities, such analysis should not be done. Fortunately, the consumer credit company discussed earlier has engaged in just such a notification program.

Assuming that the analysts have access to a set of "clean" consumer data (data gathered under the policies outlined above), they can proceed to mine the data, classifying consumers as appropriate, targeting specific customers for certain offers and developing plans for soliciting new customers.

However, a word of warning is in order, based on experiences in the database marketing industry: The results of the mining activities should be carefully evaluated to ensure that they produce no socially negative outcomes or, at least, that the outcomes are grounded in business decisions rather than in unintended discrimination. For example, the targeting of special purchase offers were sent to specific residents in one urban area has been called discriminatory because the offers were sent disproportionally to one racial group and excluded members of other groups.

It seems obvious that the use of data warehousing introduces new ethical challenges into both business-to-business and business-to-consumer relationships. However, the lines are not drawn clearly in all areas, and there is still room for judgment calls on many issues. Therefore, in the interest of fair play, corporate and IT executives who want to take advantage of this technology should pay serious attention to *all* the issues involved.

PROFESSIONAL STANDARDS

Various standards of ethics exist for the professional researcher. Many corporations, professional associations, and universities have a **code of ethics.** The impetus for these policies and standards can be traced to two documents, the Belmont Report of 1979 and the *Federal Register* of 1991.[9] Society or association guidelines include ethichal standards for the conduct of research. One comprehensive source contains 51 official codes of ethics issued by 45 associations in business, health, and law.[10] The business section of this source consists of ethics standards for

Accounting—American Institute of Certified Public Accountants

Advertising—American Association of Advertising Agencies; Direct Marketing Association

Banking—American Bankers Association

Engineering—American Association of Engineering Societies; National Society of Professional Engineers

Financial planning—Association for Investment Management and Research; Certified Financial Planner Board of Standards/Institute of Certified Financial Planners; International Association for Financial Planning

Human resources—American Society for Public Adminstration; Society for Human Resource Management.

Insurance—American Institute for Chartered Property Casualty Underwriters; American Society of Chartered Life Underwriters and Chartered Financial Consultants

Management—Academy of Management; The Business Roundtable

Real estate—National Association of Realtors

Other professional associations' codes have detailed research sections: the American Marketing Association, the American Association for Public Opinion Research, the American Psychological Association, the American Political Science Association, and the American Sociological Association. These associations update their codes frequently.

We commend professional societies and business organizations for developing standards. However, without enforcement, standards are ineffectual. Effective codes (1) are regulative, (2) protect the public interest and the interests of the profession served by the code, (3) are behavior specific, and (4) *are enforceable*. A study that assessed the effects of personal and professional values on ethical consulting behavior concluded:

> The findings of this study cast some doubt on the effectiveness of professional codes of ethics and corporate policies that attempt to deal with ethical dilemmas faced by business consultants. A mere codification of ethical values of the profession or organization may not counteract ethical ambivalence created and maintained through reward systems. The results suggest that unless ethical codes and policies are consistently reinforced with a significant reward and punishment structure and truly integrated into the business culture, these mechanisms would be of limited value in actually regulating unethical conduct.[11]

Federal, state, and local governments also have laws, policies, and procedures in place to regulate research on human beings. The U.S. government began a process that covers all research having federal support. Initially implemented in 1966, the Institutional Review Boards (IRBs) engage in a risk assessment and benefit analysis review of proposed research. The federal regulations were developed into policy by the Department of Health and Human Services (HHS). Most other federal and state agencies follow the HHS-developed guidelines.

Since 1981, the review requirement has been relaxed so research that is routine no longer needs to go through the complete process.[12] Each institution receiving funding from HHS or doing research for HHS is required to have its own IRB

FIGURE   5–2   Resources for Ethical Awareness

Journals and Magazines

Business Ethics
Business Ethics Quarterly
Ethikos
Journal of Business Ethics

Research, Training, and Conferences

Business ethics conferences, The Conference Board, New York, NY (212-759-0900)
Center for Professional Ethics, Manhattan College, Riverdale, NY (718-862-7442)
Center for the Study of Ethics in the Professions, Illinois Institute of Technology, Chicago, IL
    (312-567-3017)
Ethics Corps Training for Business Leaders, Josephson Institute of Ethics, Los Angeles, CA
    (310-306-1868)
Ethics Resource Center, Washington, DC (202-737-2258)
European Business Ethics Network, Breukelen, The Netherlands
Graduate Research Ethics Education Workshop, Association of Practical and Professional Ethics,
    Indiana University, Bloomington, IN (812-855-6450)
Institute for Business and Professional Ethics, DePaul University, Chicago, IL (312-362-6569)
International Conference on Business Ethics, The World Center for Business Ethics/The Management
    Roundtable International, Inc., Denver, CO (303-759-8845)
Teaching Research Ethics, Poynter Center, Indiana University, Bloomington, IN (812-855-0261)
The Beard Center for Leadership in Ethics, A. J. Palumbo School of Business Administration,
    Duquesne University, Pittsburgh, PA (412-396-5475)
The Center for Business Ethics, Bentley College, Waltham, MA (617-891-2000)
The Center for Professional and Applied Ethics, University of North Carolina, Charlotte, NC
    (704-547-3542)
The Institute for the Study of Applied and Professional Ethics, Dartmouth College, Hanover, NH
    (603-646-1263)
The Program in Ethics and the Professions, Harvard University, Cambridge, MA
    (617-495-1336/3990)
The Wharton Ethics Program, University of Pennsylvania, Philadelphia, PA (215) 898-1166

---

to review research proposals. Many institutions require all research, funded and unfunded, to undergo review by the local IRB. The IRBs concentrate on two areas. First is the guarantee of obtaining complete, informed consent from participants. This can be traced to the first of 10 points in the Nuremberg Code.[13] Complete informed consent has four characteristics:

1. The respondent must be competent to give consent.
2. Consent must be voluntary, free from coercion, force, requirements, and so forth.
3. Respondents must be adequately informed to make a decision.
4. Respondents should know the possible risks or outcomes associated with the research.

The second item of interest to the IRB is the risk assessment and benefit analysis review. In the review, risks are considered when they add to the normal risk of daily life. Significantly, the only benefit considered is the immediate importance of the knowledge to be gained. Possible long-term benefits from applying the knowledge that may be gained in the research are not considered.[14]

Other federal legislation that governs, or influences, the ways in which research is carried out are the Right to Privacy laws. Public Law 95-38 is the Privacy Act of 1974. This was the first law guaranteeing Americans the right to privacy. Public Law 96-440, the Privacy Protection Act of 1980, carries the right to privacy further. These two laws are the basis for protecting the privacy and confidentiality of the respondents and the data.

RESOURCES FOR ETHICAL AWARENESS

There is optimism for improving ethical awareness. According to the Center for Business Ethics at Bentley College, a third of the Fortune 500 have ethics officers, a substantial rise since the late 1980s. Almost 90 percent of business schools have ethics programs, up from a handful several years ago.[15] Figure 5–2 provides a list of recommended resources for business students, researchers, and managers.

Summary

Ethics are norms or standards of behavior that guide moral choices about our behavior and our relationships with others. The goal of ethics in research is to ensure that no one is harmed or suffers adverse consequences from research activities.

As research is designed, several ethical considerations must be balanced:

- Protect the rights of the *respondent* or subject.
- Ensure the *client* receives ethically conducted and reported research.
- Follow ethical standards when *designing research*.
- Protect the *safety* of the researcher and team.
- Ensure the *research team* follows the design.

In general, research must be designed so a *respondent* does not suffer physical harm, discomfort, pain, embarrassment, or loss of privacy. Begin data collection by explaining to respondents the benefits expected from the research. Explain that their rights and well-being will be adequately protected and say how that will be done. Be certain that interviewers obtain the informed consent of the respondent. The use of deception is questionable; when it is used, debrief any respondent who has been deceived.

Many *clients* wish to undertake research without revealing themselves. Clients have the right to demand and receive confidentiality between themselves and the researchers. Ethical researchers provide clients with the research design needed to solve the managerial question. The ethical researcher shows the data objectively, despite the client's preferred outcomes.

The research team's safety is the responsibility of the researcher. Researchers should require ethical compliance from team members in following the research design, just as clients expect ethical behavior from the researcher.

Many corporations and research firms have adopted a code of ethics. Several professional associations have detailed research provisions. Of interest are the American

Association for Public Opinion Research, the American Marketing Association, the American Political Science Association, the American Psychological Association, and the American Sociological Association. Federal, state, and local governments have laws, policies, and procedures in place to regulate research on human beings.

Key Terms

code of ethics	nondisclosure
confidentiality	findings
debriefing	purpose
deception	sponsor
ethics	right to privacy
informed consent	

Cases

The cases below cover a broad range of ethical decisions. You may have experienced similar circumstances or expect to encounter research situations like these. Consider the material in this section and your own standards of conduct as you offer advice to the individuals in these cases.

- What are the most prudent decisions they can make about their responsibilities to themselves and others?
- What are the implications of those decisions even if there is no violation of law or regulation?

CASE 1

A COMPETITIVE COUP IN THE IN-FLIGHT MAGAZINE

When the manager for market intelligence of a major automotive manufacturer boarded the plane in Chicago, her mind was on shrinking market share and late product announcements. As she settled back to enjoy the remains of a hectic day, she reached for the in-flight magazine. It was jammed into the seat pocket in front of her.

Crammed into this already tiny space was a report with a competitor's logo, marked "Confidential-Restricted Circulation." It contained a description of new product announcements for the next two years. Not only was it intended for a small circle of senior executives but it also answered the questions she had recently proposed to an external research firm.

The proposal for the solicited research could be canceled. Her research budget, already savaged, could be saved. She was home free, legally and career-wise.

She foresaw only one problem. In the last few months, the company's newly hired ethicist had revised the Business Conduct Guidelines. They now required company employees in possession of a competitor's information to return it or face dismissal. But it was still a draft and not formally approved. She had the rest of the flight to decide whether to return the document to the airline or slip it into her briefcase.

FREE WATERS IN MIRO BEACH: BOATERS INC. VERSUS CITY GOVERNMENT[16]

CASE 2

In 1989, the city commissioners of Miro Beach proposed limits on boaters who anchor offshore in waterfront areas of the St. Lucinda River adjoining the city. Residents had complained of pollution from the live-aboarders and of a boat parking lot from absentee boaters.

The city based its proposed ordinance on research done by the staff. The staff did not hold graduate degrees in either public or business administration, and it was not known if staff members were competent to conduct research. The staff requested a proposal from a team of local university professors who had conducted similar work in the past. The research cost was $10,000. After receiving the proposal, the staff chose to do the work itself and not expend resources for the project. Through an unidentified source, the professors later learned their proposal contained enough information to guide the city's staff and suggested data collection areas that might provide information that could justify the boaters' claims.

Based on the staff's one-time survey of waterfront litter, "pump-out" samples, and a weekly frequency count of boats, an ordinance was drafted and a public workshop was held. Shortly after, a group of concerned boat owners formed Boaters Inc., an association to promote boating, raise funds, and lobby the commission. The group's claims were that the boaters spent thousands of dollars on community goods and services, did not create the litter, and the commission's fact finding was flawed.

With the last claim in mind, the boaters flooded the city with public record requests. The clerks reported that some weeks the requests were one per day. Under continued pressure, the city attorney hired a private investigator (PI) to infiltrate Boaters Inc. to collect information. He rationalized this on the grounds that the boaters had challenged the city's grant applications in order to "blackmail the city into dropping plans to regulate the boaters."

The PI posed as a college student and worked for a time in the home of the boater organization's sponsor while helping with mailings. Despite the PI's inability to corroborate the city attorney's theory, he recommended conducting a background investigation on the organization's principal, an employee of a tabloid newspaper. (The FBI on request of city or county police organizations generally performs background investigations.)

The PI was not a boating enthusiast and soon drew suspicion. Simultaneously, the organization turned up the heat on the city by requesting what amounted to 5,000 pages of information—"studies and all related documents containing the word 'boat.'" Failing to get a response from Miro Beach, the boaters filed suit under the Florida Public Records Act. By this time, the city had spent $20,000.

The case stalled, went to appeal, and was settled in favor of the boaters. A year later, the organization's principal filed an invasion of privacy and slander suit against the city attorney, the PI, and the PI's firm. After six months, the suit was amended to include the city itself and sought $1 million in punitive damages.

THE HIGH COST OF ORGANIZATIONAL CHANGE

CASE 3

It was his first year of college teaching, and there were no summer teaching assignments for new hires. But the university was kind enough to steer him to an aviation firm that needed help creating an organizational assessment survey. The assignment was to last five weeks, but it paid about the same as teaching all summer. The work was just about as perfect as it gets for an organizational behavior specialist. The vice president who met him the first day was cordial and smooth. The researcher would report to a senior manager who was coordinating the project with the personnel and legal departments.

It was soon apparent that in the 25-year history of the organization, there had never been an employee survey. This was understandable given management's lack of concern for employee complaints. Working conditions had deteriorated without management intervention, and government inspectors counted the number of heads down at desks as an index of performance. To make matters worse, the engineers were so disgruntled that word of unionization had spread like wildfire. A serious organizing effort was planned before the VP could approve the survey.

Headquarters dispatched nervous staffers to monitor the situation and generally involve themselves with every aspect of the questionnaire. Shadowed, the young researcher began to feel apprehension turn to paranoia. He consoled himself, however, with the goodwill of 500 enthusiastic, cooperative employees who had pinned their hopes for a better working environment to the results of this project.

The data collection was textbook perfect. No one had asked to preview the findings or had shown any particular interest. In the fifth week, he boarded the corporate jet with the VP and senior manager to make a presentation at headquarters. Respondents at the headquarters location were invited to attend. Management was intent on heading off unionization by showing their confidence in the isolated nature of "a few engineers' complaints." They had also promised to engage the participants in action planning over the next few days.

An hour into the flight, the VP turned from his reading to the young researcher and said, "We have seen your results, you know. And we would like you to change two key findings. They are not all that critical to this round of fixing the 'bone orchard,' and you'll have another crack at it as a real consultant in the fall."

"But that would mean breaking faith with your employees, people who trusted me to present the results objectively. It's what I thought you wanted . . ."

"Yes, well, look at it this way," replied the VP. "All of your findings we can live with except these two. They're an embarrassment to senior management. Let me put it plainly. We have government contracts into the foreseeable future. You could retire early with consulting income from this place. Someone will meet us on the runway with new slides. What do you say?"

DATA MINING ETHICS AND COMPANY GROWTH SQUARE-OFF

CASE 4

XYZ Corporation Inc. is a supplier to a number of firms in an industry. This industry has a structure that includes suppliers, manufacturers, distributors, and consumers. Several companies are involved in the manufacturing process—from processed parts to the creation of final product—with each firm adding some value to the product.

By carefully mining its customer data warehouse, XYZ Corp. reveals a plausible new model for manufacturing and distributing industry products that would increase the overall efficiency of the industry system, reduce costs of production (leading to greater industry profits and more sales for XYZ Corp.), and greater sales and profits for *some* of the industry's manufacturers (XYZ Corp.'s customers).

On the other hand, implementing the model would hurt the sales and profits of other firms that are also XYZ Corp.'s customers but which are not in a position (due to manpower, plant, or equipment) to benefit from the new manufacturing/distribution model. These firms would lose sales, profits, and market share and potentially go out of business.

Does XYZ Corp. have an obligation to protect the interests of *all* its customers and take no action that would harm any of them, since XYZ Corp. had the data within its warehouse only because of its relationship with its customers? (It would betray some of its customers if it uses the data in a manner that would cause these customers harm.) Or does it have a more powerful obligation to its stockholders and employees to aggressively pursue the new model that research reveals would substantially increase its sales, profits, and market share against competitors?

Reference Notes

1. C. S. Benson, "Codes of Ethics," *Journal of Business Ethics* (1989), pp. 305–9.
2. Elizabethann O'Sullivan and Gary R. Rassel, *Research Methods for Public Administrators* (New York: Longman, 1989), pp. 209–10
3. American Psychological Association, *Ethical Principles of Psychologists and Code of Conduct* (Washington, D.C.: Author, 1997).
4. This figure shows the standard procedures used for informed consent in surveys conducted by the Center for Survey Research, Indiana University. Wording and protocol by CSR IU.
5. Robert A. Baron and Donn Byrne, *Social Psychology: Understanding Human Interaction* (Boston: Allyn and Bacon, 1991), p. 36.

6. Floyd J. Fowler, Jr., *Survey Research Methods,* rev. ed. (Beverly Hills, CA: Sage Publications, 1988), p. 138.

7. Jim Thomas, "Introduction: A Debate About the Ethics of Fair Practices for Collecting Social Science Data in Cyberspace," *Information Society* 12, no. 2 (1996).

8. Fowler, *Survey Research Methods,* p. 139.

9. See Thomas, *Information Society.* The Belmont Report was produced by the National Commission for the Protection of Human Subjects of Biomedical and Behavioral Research under the title *Ethical Principles and Guidelines for the Protection of Human Subjects of Research* (Washington, D.C.: Department of Health, Education, and Welfare, 1979). The other source of ethical standards was the *Federal Register,* Part II, "Federal Policy for the Protection of Human Subjects: Notices and Rules" (Washington, D.C.: U.S. Government Printing Office, 1991).

10. *Codes of Professional Responsibility,* 3rd ed., ed. R. Gorlin (Washington, D.C.: BNA Books, 1994).

11. Jeff Allen and Duane Davis, "Assessing Some Determinant Effects of Ethical Consulting Behavior: The Case of Personal and Professional Values," *Journal of Business Ethics* (1993), p. 449.

12. Paul Davidson Reynolds, *Ethics and Social Science Research* (Englewood Cliffs, NJ: Prentice-Hall, 1982), pp. 103–8.

13. The Nuremberg Code is a set of 10 moral, ethical, and legal principles for medical experimentation on humans. It comes from the judgment of the Nuremberg Military Tribunal against doctors and scientists who committed World War II Nazi atrocities. For a full listing of the Nuremberg Code, see Jay Katz, *Experimentation with Human Beings* (New York: Russell Sage Foundation, 1972), pp. 305–6. See also Allan J. Kimmel, *Ethics and Values in Applied Social Research* (Newbury Park, CA: Sage Publications, 1988), pp. 54–56.

14. Reynolds, *Ethics,* pp. 103–8.

15. The Center for Business Ethics, Bentley College (Waltham, MA); syndicated news release: Daniel Fisher, *Bloomberg Financial News,* November 2, 1993.

16. Adapted from stories in the *Palm Beach Post* during September 1992.

Suggested Readings

1. National Academy of Sciences. *On Being a Scientist: Responsible Conduct in Research,* 2nd ed. Washington, D.C.: National Academy Press, 1995. Written for beginning researchers, it describes the ethical foundations of scientific practices, personal and professional issues, and research applications for industrial, governmental, and academic settings.

2. Rosnow, Ralph L., and Robert Rosenthal. *People Studying People: Artifacts and Ethics in Behavioral Research.* New York: Freeman, 1997. A potent source of analysis and advice particularly appropriate for Chapters 13 and 14 on observation and experimentation.

3. Stanley, Barbara H., et al., eds. *Research Ethics: A Psychological Approach.* Lincoln: University of Nebraska Press, 1996. Addresses important issues such as the discovery and neutralization of bias, sensitivity to the interests of experimental subjects, and the counterweighing factors in rules, regulations, and enforcement.

4. Stern, Judy E., and Deni Elliott, eds. *Research Ethics: A Reader.* Hanover, NH: University Press of New England, 1997. An insightful review of ethical issues for managers and researchers.

THE DESIGN OF RESEARCH

CHAPTER

6   DESIGN STRATEGIES

 CHAPTER NAVIGATION

BRINGING
RESEARCH TO LIFE

"**A**rghh!"

Jason Henry leaped up and tossed a paper cup full of coffee at his TV. It hit the set and bounced off, leaving coffee dripping down the screen.

"What's wrong? Is one of you hurt? I'M A DOCTOR!" hollered Dorrie from the bedroom. "And what time is it anyway?"

"Go back to sleep, Dorrie," replied Myra. "It's 2:30 A.M., and your husband just chose to throw his coffee at the TV, rather than drink it, because he doesn't care for the anchor on cable news."

"She's totally unscientific, you know," grumped Jason.

"She's an inexperienced kid getting her first break on the network," stated Myra, "at an hour when no sane person is watching TV anyway, let alone subjecting it to scientific criticism. So chill out, lad."

To Dorrie she shouted, "We are almost finished here, and soon you will have your husband back."

"It is terrifically unscientific," he said, "to make unsubstantiated conclusions as she did."

"I thought she did a fine job interviewing that psychiatrist—terribly amusing" said Myra. "He was a beautiful choice, with his accent and a beard that reminded me of Freud himself."

"That's not the issue, Myra, and you know it. The fact is, she should not have claimed that when the recent hurricane brushed Galveston, it caused a rash of complaints against auto dealerships."

"I thought she did a moderately good job in the interviews. That was an adorable young couple she found picketing the Mercedes dealership—the girl in a mink jacket and her husband in Gucci loafers, and both of them complaining they were powerless against big business—and you already know how effective I thought the shrink was in presenting his theory of hurricane-induced anger causing people to lash out at business."

"Not the point, again. As entertainment it was admirable. But it was rotten science. She had no before-after comparison. I want to know how many people had complaints against dealerships before the hurricane hit. Pretty clearly, she not only had no file footage of before the hurricane, but she also had no statistics. For all I know the complaint behavior has not changed."

"Do you really believe, Jason, that anyone would have the foresight to collect such information?"

"Why not? The newspapers and TV stations on the Gulf are continually hyping the threat of hurricanes. They must make a fortune selling commercial time at inflated rates during hurricane season. So, yes, they knew a hurricane was due sometime in the near future, or at least possible, and if they were responsible they would have done baseline measurements. . . ."

"Not really feasible. . . ."

". . . or at least refrain from such pseudoscientific bunkum."

"Is that it? Is that your complaint?"

"That's part of it. The other part is that the hurricane brushed Galveston then skittered out into the Gulf. Forty miles away, Houston was barely touched. Did she bother to check if complaint behavior in Houston was also elevated? Because if it was, that would debunk her theory that the hurricane caused the complaint behavior. You can't blame something that occurred in one location and not in the other for causing behavior seen in both locations. Can you?"

"I guess not."

"So, what did you learn, Myra?" he asked with a touch of condescension.

She laughed heartily. "I learned not to pick a fight with you after hours of steady proposal writing. I learned that after thirteen cups of coffee you become humorless, pedantic, and compulsively left-brained. I learned it is time for you to join your infinitely patient wife. See you for breakfast."

WHAT IS RESEARCH DESIGN?

There are many definitions of research design, but no one definition imparts the full range of important aspects. Several examples from leading authors can be cited:

> The research design constitutes the blueprint for the collection, measurement, and analysis of data. It aids the scientist in the allocation of his limited resources by posing crucial choices: Is the blueprint to include experiments, interviews, observation, the analysis of records, simulation, or some combination of these? Are the methods of data collection and the research situation to be highly structured? Is an intensive study of a small sample more effective than a less intensive study of a large sample? Should the analysis be primarily quantitative or qualitative?[1]
>
> Research design is the plan and structure of investigation so conceived as to obtain answers to research questions. The plan is the overall scheme or program of the research. It includes an outline of what the investigator will do from writing hypotheses and their operational implications to the final analysis of data. A structure is the framework, organization, or configuration of . . . the relations among variables of a study. A research design expresses both the structure of the research problem and the plan of investigation used to obtain empirical evidence on relations of the problem.[2]

These definitions differ in detail, but together they give the essentials of **research design.** First, the design is a plan for selecting the sources and types of information used to answer the research question. Second, it is a framework for specifying the relationships among the study's variables. Third, it is a blueprint that outlines each procedure from the hypotheses to the analysis of data. The design provides answers for such questions as these: What techniques will be used to gather data? What kind of sampling will be used? How will time and cost constraints be dealt with?

Classification of Designs

Early in any research study, one faces the task of selecting the specific design to use. A number of different design approaches exist, but unfortunately no simple classification system defines all the variations that must be considered. We can classify research design using at least eight different descriptors.[3]

1. The degree to which the research question has been crystallized (the study may be either exploratory or formal)
2. The method of data collection (studies may be observational or communication based)
3. The power of the researcher to produce effects in the variables under study (the two major types of research are experimental and ex post facto)
4. The purpose of the study (research studies may be descriptive or causal)
5. The time dimension (research may be cross-sectional or longitudinal)
6. The topical scope—breadth and depth—of the study (a case or statistical study)
7. The research environment (most business research is conducted in a field setting, although laboratory research is not unusual; simulation is another option)
8. The subjects' perceptions of the research (do they perceive deviations from their everyday routines)

A brief discussion of these descriptors illustrates their nature and contribution to research.

Degree of Research Question Crystallization   A study may be viewed as exploratory or formal. The essential distinction between these two is the degree of structure and the immediate objective of the study. **Exploratory studies** tend toward loose structures with the objective of discovering future research tasks. The immediate purpose of exploration is usually *to develop hypotheses or questions for further research.* The **formal study** begins where the exploration leaves off—it begins with a hypothesis or research question and involves precise procedures and data source specifications. The goal of a formal research design is *to test the hypotheses or answer the research questions posed.*

The exploratory-formalized dichotomy is less precise than some other classifications. All studies have elements of exploration in them, and few studies are completely uncharted. Recall the sequence discussed in Chapter 3 suggests that more formalized studies contain at least an element of exploration before the final choice of design. More detailed consideration of exploratory research is found later in this chapter.

Method of Data Collection   This classification distinguishes between monitoring and interrogation/communication processes. The former includes **observational studies,** in which the researcher inspects the activities of a subject or the nature of some material without attempting to elicit responses from anyone. Traffic counts at an intersection, a search of the library collection, an observation of the actions of a group of decision makers—all are examples of monitoring. In each case the researcher notes and records the information available from observations. Observation for Mind-Writer might include "following" a computer through the repair process, documenting each activity or interaction between CompleteCare and call center employees and the damaged laptop.

In the **interrogation/communication mode,** the researcher questions the subjects and collects their responses by personal or impersonal means. The collected data may result from (1) interview or telephone conversations, (2) self-administered or self-report instruments sent through the mail, left in convenient locations, or transmitted electronically or by another means, or (3) instruments presented before and/or after a treatment or stimulus condition in an *experiment.* (We use the term *communication* to contrast with *observational* because collecting data by questioning encompasses more than the "survey method.") Myra and Jason propose a communication study, using a response card inserted in the packaging of laptops returned after CompleteCare servicing.

Researcher Control of Variables   In terms of the researcher's ability to manipulate variables, we differentiate between experimental and ex post facto designs. In an **experiment,** the researcher attempts to control and/or manipulate the variables in the study. It is enough that we can cause variables to be changed or held constant in keeping with our research objectives. Experimental design is appropriate when one wishes to discover whether certain variables produce effects in other variables. Experimentation provides the most powerful support possible for a hypothesis of causation.

With an **ex post facto design,** investigators have no control over the variables in the sense of being able to manipulate them. They can only report what has happened or what is happening. It is important that the researchers using this design not influence the variables; to do so introduces bias. The researcher is limited to holding factors constant by judicious selection of subjects according to strict sampling procedures and by statistical manipulation of findings. MindWriter is planning this type of design.

The Purpose of the Study   The essential difference between descriptive and causal studies lies in their objectives. If the research is concerned with finding out *who, what, where, when,* or *how much,* then the study is **descriptive.** If it is concerned with learning *why*—that is, how one variable produces changes in another—it is causal. Research on crime is descriptive when it measures the types of crime committed, how often, when, where, and by whom. In a **causal study,** we try to explain relationships among variables—for instance, why the crime rate is higher in city A than in city B. At the outset, the MindWriter project is descriptive, although subsequent studies might be causal.

The Time Dimension   **Cross-sectional studies** are carried out once and represent a snapshot of one point in time. **Longitudinal studies** are repeated over an extended period. The advantage of a longitudinal study is that it can track changes over time. Jason and Myra's proposal describes a longitudinal study, with satisfaction measurements taken continuously over several months and reported monthly.

In longitudinal studies of the *panel* variety, the researcher may study the same people over time. In marketing, panels are set up to report consumption data on a variety of products. These data, collected from national samples, provide a major data bank on relative market share, consumer response to new products, and new promotional methods. Other longitudinal studies, such as *cohort groups,* use different subjects for each sequenced measurement. The service industry might have looked at the needs of aging baby boomers by sampling 40- to 45-year-olds in 1990 and 50- to 55-year-olds in 2000. Although each sample would be different, the population of 1945 to 1950 cohort survivors would remain the same.

Some types of information once collected cannot be collected a second time from the same person without the risks of bias. The study of public awareness of an advertising campaign over a six-month period would require different samples for each measurement.

While longitudinal research is important, the constraints of budget and time impose the need for cross-sectional analysis. Some benefits of a longitudinal study can be assured by adroit questioning about past attitudes, history, and future expectations. Responses to these kinds of questions should be interpreted with care, however.

The Topical Scope   The statistical study differs from the case study in several ways. **Statistical studies** are designed for breadth rather than depth. They attempt to capture a population's characteristics by making inferences from a sample's characteristics. Hypotheses are tested quantitatively. Generalizations about findings are presented based on the representativeness of the sample and the validity of the design. MindWriter plans a statistical study.

Case studies place more emphasis on a full contextual analysis of fewer events or conditions and their interrelations. Although hypotheses are often used, the reliance on qualitative data makes support or rejection more difficult. An emphasis on detail provides valuable insight for problem solving, evaluation, and strategy. This detail is secured from multiple sources of information. It allows evidence to be verified and avoids missing data. Remember the proposed observation study for MindWriter? If such a tracking of one or more laptops was done, then this could serve as a case study of the CompleteCare program.

Although case studies have been maligned as "scientifically worthless" because they do not meet minimal design requirements for comparison,[4] they have a significant scientific role. It is known that "important scientific propositions have the form of universals, and a universal can be falsified by a single counter-instance."[5] Thus, a single, well-designed case study can provide a major challenge to a theory and provide a source of new hypotheses and constructs simultaneously. Discovering new hypotheses to correct postservice complaints would be the major advantage of tracking a given number of damaged laptops through the case study design.

The Research Environment   Designs also differ as to whether they occur under actual environmental conditions or under other conditions. These are called **field conditions** and **laboratory conditions,** respectively.

To simulate is to replicate the essence of a system or process. **Simulations** are being used more in research, especially in operations research. The major characteristics of various conditions and relationships in actual situations are often represented in mathematical models. Role playing and other behavioral activities may also be viewed as simulations. A simulation for MindWriter might involve an arbitrarily damaged laptop being tracked through the call center and the CompleteCare program, monitoring results at each workstation. Another popularly used simulation is the retail service studies undertaken by "mystery shoppers."

Subjects' Perceptions   The usefulness of a design may be reduced when people in the study perceive that research is being conducted. **Subjects' perceptions** influence the outcomes of the research in subtle ways or more dramatically as we learned from the pivotal Hawthorne studies of the late 1920s. Although there is no widespread evidence of attempts to please researchers through successful hypothesis guessing or evidence of the prevalence of sabotage, when subjects believe that something out of the ordinary is happening, they may behave less naturally. There are three levels of perception:

1. Subjects perceive no deviations from everyday routines.
2. Subjects perceive deviations, but as unrelated to the researcher.
3. Subjects perceive deviations as researcher induced.[6]

In all research environments and control situations, researchers need to be vigilant to effects that may alter their conclusions. These serve as a reminder to classify one's study by type, to examine validation strength and weaknesses, and be prepared to qualify results accordingly.

Exploratory, descriptive, and causal research designs are discussed in the sections that follow. Other aspects of design are covered in later chapters after sufficient groundwork has been laid for those topics.

EXPLORATORY STUDIES

Exploration is particularly useful when researchers lack a clear idea of the problems they will meet during the study. Through **exploration** researchers develop concepts more clearly, establish priorities, develop operational definitions, and improve the final research design. Exploration may also save time and money. If the problem is not as important as first thought, research projects can be canceled.

Exploration serves other purposes. The area of investigation may be so new or so vague that a researcher needs to do an exploration just to learn something about the dilemma facing the manager. Important variables may not be known or thoroughly defined. Hypotheses for the research may be needed. Also, the researcher may explore to be sure it is practical to do a study in the area. A federal government agency proposed that research be done on how executives in a given industry made decisions about raw material purchases. Questions were planned asking how (and at what price spreads) one raw material was substituted for another in certain manufactured products. An exploration to discover if industry executives would divulge adequate information about their decision making on this topic was essential for the study's success.

Despite its obvious value, researchers and managers alike give exploration less attention than it deserves. There are strong pressures for quick answers. And exploration is sometimes linked to old biases about qualitative research: subjectiveness, nonrepresentativeness, and nonsystematic design. A wiser view is that exploration saves time and money and should not be slighted.

Qualitative Techniques

The objectives of exploration may be accomplished with different techniques. Both qualitative and quantitative techniques are applicable, although exploration relies more heavily on **qualitative techniques.** One author creates a verbal picture to differentiate the two:

> Quality is the essential character or nature of something; quantity is the amount. Quality is the what; quantity the how much. Qualitative refers to the meaning, the definition or analogy or model or metaphor characterizing something, while quantitative assumes the meaning and refers to a measure of it. . . . The difference lies in Steinbeck's [1941] description of the Mexican Sierra, a fish from the Sea of Cortez. One can count the spines on the dorsal fin of a pickled Sierra, 17 plus 15 plus 9. "But," says Steinbeck, "if the Sierra strikes hard on the line so that our hands are burned, if the fish sounds and nearly escapes and finally comes in over the rail, his colors pulsing and his tail beating the air, a whole new relational externality has come into being." Qualitative research would define the being of fishing, the ambiance of a city, the mood of a citizen, or the unifying tradition of a group.[7]

When we consider the scope of qualitative research, several approaches are adaptable for exploratory investigations of management questions:

1. In-depth interviewing (usually conversational rather than structured)
2. Participant observation (to perceive firsthand what participants in the setting experience)
3. Films, photographs, and videotape (to capture the life of the group under study)
4. Projective techniques and psychological testing (such as a Thematic Apperception Test, projective measures, games, or role-playing)
5. Case studies (for an in-depth contextual analysis of a few events or conditions)
6. Street ethnography (to discover how a cultural subgroup describes and structures its world at the street level)
7. Elite interviewing (for information from influential or well-informed people in an organization or community)
8. Document analysis (to evaluate historical or contemporary confidential or public records, reports, government documents, and opinions)
9. Proxemics and kinesics (to study the use of space and body motion communication, respectively)[8]

When these approaches are combined, four exploratory techniques emerge with wide applicability for the management researcher: (1) secondary data analysis, (2) experience surveys, (3) focus groups, and (4) two-stage designs.

Secondary Data Analysis

The first step in an exploratory study is a search of the secondary literature. Studies made by others for their own purposes represent **secondary data.** It is inefficient to discover anew through the collection of **primary data** or original research what has already been done.

Within secondary data exploration, a researcher should start first with an organization's own data archives. Reports of prior research studies often reveal an extensive amount of historical data or decision-making patterns. By reviewing prior studies, you can identify methodologies that proved successful and unsuccessful. Solutions that didn't receive attention in the past due to different environmental circumstances are revealed as potential subjects for further study. The researcher needs to avoid duplication in instances when prior collected data can provide sufficient information for resolving the current decision-making dilemma. While MindWriter's CompleteCare program is newly introduced, it is likely that one or more studies of the previous servicing practices and policies revealed customer attitudes on which MindWriter based the design of the current program.

The second source of secondary data is published documents prepared by authors outside the sponsor organization. There are tens of thousands of periodicals and hundreds of thousands of books on all aspects of business. Data from secondary sources help us decide what needs to be done and can be a rich source of hypotheses.

Special catalogs, subject guides, and electronic indices are available in most libraries that will help in this search. In many cases you can conduct a secondary search from your home or office using a computer, an online service, or an Internet gateway. Regarding MindWriter, thousands of articles have been written on customer service, and an Internet search using keywords *customer service* reveals tens of thousands of hits. We provide a detailed description of secondary data resources in Chapter 10 and Appendix A.

A search of secondary sources provides an excellent background and will supply many good leads if one is creative. If we confine the investigation to obvious subjects in bibliographic sources, we will often miss much of the best information. Suppose we are interested in estimating the outlook for the copper industry over the next 10 years. We could search through the literature under the headings "copper production" and "copper consumption." However, a search restricted to these two topics would miss more than it finds. When a creative search of the copper industry is undertaken, useful information turns up under the following reference headings: mines and minerals; nonferrous metals; forecasting; planning; econometrics; consuming industries such as automotive and communications; countries where copper is produced, such as Chile; and companies prominent in the industry, such as Anaconda and Kennecott.

Experience Survey

While published data are a valuable resource, seldom is more than a fraction of the existing knowledge in a field put into writing. A significant portion of what is known on a topic, while in writing, may be proprietary to a given organization and thus unavailable to an outside searcher. Also, internal data archives are rarely well organized, making secondary sources, even when known, difficult to locate. Thus, we will profit by seeking information from persons experienced in the area of study, tapping into their collective memories and experiences.

When we interview persons in an **experience survey,** we should seek their ideas about important issues or aspects of the subject and discover what is important across the subject's range. The investigative format we use should be flexible enough so that we can explore various avenues that emerge during the interview. What is being done? What has been tried in the past without success? How have things changed? What are the change-producing elements of the situation? Who is involved in decisions, and what roles do they play? What problem areas and barriers can be seen? What are the costs of the processes under study? Whom can we count on to assist and/or participate in the research? What are the priority areas?

The product of such questioning may be a new hypothesis, the discarding of an old one, or information about the practicality of doing the study. Probing may show whether certain facilities are available, what factors need to be controlled and how, and who will cooperate in the study.

Discovery is more easily carried out if the researcher can analyze cases that provide special insight. Typical of exploration, we are less interested in getting a representative cross-section than getting information from sources that might be insightful. Assume we are called to study an automobile assembly plant. It has a history of declining productivity, increasing costs, and growing numbers of quality defects. People who might provide insightful information include

1. Newcomers to the scene—employees or personnel who may have recently been transferred to this plant from similar plants.
2. Marginal or peripheral individuals—persons whose jobs place them on the margin between contending groups. First-line supervisors and lead workers are often neither management nor workers but something in between.
3. Individuals in transition—recently promoted employees who have been transferred to new departments.
4. Deviants and isolates—those in a given group who hold a different position from the majority—workers who are happy with the present situation, highly productive departments and workers, loners of one sort or another.
5. "Pure" cases or cases that show extreme examples of the conditions under study—the most unproductive departments, the most antagonistic workers, and so forth.
6. Those who fit well and those who do not—the workers who are well established in their organizations versus those who are not, those executives who fully reflect management views and those who do not.
7. Those who represent different positions in the system—unskilled workers, assemblers, superintendents, and so forth.[9]

Jason and Myra planned three interviews during the early phase of their research for MindWriter: with the manager of the service facility, the call center, and the contract courier service. Their emphasis should be not only on what has been done in the past but also on discovering the parameters of feasible change. They might want to expand their interviews to include long-term employees of the various departments, as their views are likely to be different from those of their managers. Because postpurchase service problems might be directly related to product design, expanding their experience survey to individuals associated with engineering and production should also be considered.

Focus Groups

With origins in sociology, focus groups became widely used in market research during the 1980s and are used for more diverse research applications today.[10] The most common application of focus group research continues to be in the consumer arena. However, many corporations are using focus group results for diverse exploratory applications.

The topical objective of a focus group is often a new product or product concept. The output of the session is a list of ideas and behavioral observations with recommendations of the moderator. These are often used for later quantitative testing. As a group interview tool, focus groups have applied-research potential for other functional areas of business, particularly where the generation and evaluation of ideas or assessment of needs is indispensable. In exploratory research, the qualitative data that focus groups produce may be used for enriching all levels of research questions and hypotheses and comparing the effectiveness of design options.

A **focus group** is a panel of people led by a trained moderator who meet for 90 minutes to 2 hours. The facilitator or moderator uses group dynamics principles to focus or guide the group in an exchange of ideas, feelings, and experiences on a *specific topic*. Typically the focus group panel is made up of 6 to 10 respondents. Too small or too large a group results in less effective participation. The facilitator introduces the topic and encourages the group to discuss it among themselves.

Following a topical guide, the moderator will steer the discussion to ensure that all the relevant information desired by the client is considered by the group. The facilitator also keeps gregarious indviduals from dominating the conversation, ensuring that each person enters the discussion. In ideal situations, the group's discussion will proceed uninterrupted; however, if the discussion begins to lag, the facilitator moves it along by introducing another facet of the topic that the group has not yet considered. In some groups a questionnaire is administered to the participants before the group begins to gather additonal data. Typically, one or more representatives of the client will sit behind a one-way mirror in the focus group room to observe the verbal and nonverbal interactions and responses of participants.

MindWriter could use focus groups involving employees (of the call center and service departments) to determine changes and provide an analysis of change ideas. They may want focus groups with customers (both dissatisfied and satisfied) to uncover what occurred in their different experiences. In other applications, when a large title insurance company was developing a computerized help system, they ran focus groups with their branch office administrators to discover their preferences for distributing files on their **intranet** (a company's proprietary network—behind a security "firewall" that limits access to authorized users). A small college used focus groups to develop a plan to attract more freshmen applications, and a blood center used a focus group to improve blood donations.[11]

Homogeneity Within the Focus Group

It is often preferable, depending on the topic, to run separate groups for different subsets of the population. For example, a study on nutritional advice may begin with separate consumer and physician focus groups to determine the best ways to provide the advice. This type of homogeneous grouping tends to promote more intense discussion and freer interaction.[12] For consumer groups, consideration should also be given to such factors as ethnicity, employment status, and education. In a recent exploratory study of discount shoppers, the attitudes about the economy and personal finances expressed by East Coast respondents and West Coast respondents were widely divergent. The client sponsor was able to use this information to build a market strategy tailored to the geographic area.[13]

Since most focus groups are homogeneous, locating respondents for focus groups is usually done through informal networks of colleagues, community agencies, and the target group. Sometimes researchers advertise to attract a wider range of opinions.[14]

Telephone Focus Groups

Traditional focus groups meet face to face and are run in large metropolitan areas using specialized facilities that enable respondents to interact in a comfortable setting while being observed by a sponsoring client. However, often there is a need to reach people that traditional focus groups cannot attract. With modern telephone conferencing facilities, telephone focus groups are particularly effective in these situations:

1. When it is difficult to recruit people: members of elite and hard-to-find respondents such as experts, professionals, physician specialists, high-level executives, and store owners

2. When target group members are rare, "low incidence," or widely dispersed geographically: directors of a medical clinic, celebrities, early adopters, and rural practitioners

3. When issues are so sensitive that anonymity is needed but respondents must be from a wide geographical area: people suffering from a contagious disease, people using nonmainstream products, high-income individuals, competitors

4. When you want to conduct only a couple of groups but want nationwide representation

Telephone groups are usually less expensive than face-to-face focus groups—up to 40 percent. In contrast to face-to-face groups, heterogeneous groups can be productive. People in traditionally superior-subordinate roles can be mixed as long as they are not from the same city. A telephone focus group can be used anywhere a face-to-face group is used except when participants need to handle a product, when an object cannot be sent through the mail in advance, for long sessions, and with groups of young children.

Online Focus Groups   An emerging technique for exploratory research is to approximate group dynamics using e-mail, Web sites, Usenet newsgroups, or an Internet chat room. Posting questions to a newsgroup with an interest in the research problem can generate considerable discussion. However, online discussions are not confidential unless they take place on an intranet. Although online forum discussions are unlikely to reflect the average participants, they can be a good way of getting in touch with populations that have special interests (e.g., BMW Club members, Little League coaches, or "power computer users").

Videoconferencing Focus Groups   The third type of non-face-to-face focus group is conducted via videoconferencing. Many anticipate growth for this medium. Like telephone focus groups, videoconferencing enables significant savings. By reducing the travel time for the facilitator and the client, it means more focus groups can be accomplished in a shorter time. However, videoconferencing retains the barrier between the moderator and participants, although less so than telephone groups. Since large corporations tend to have their own internal videoconferencing facilities, most videoconferencing focus groups will likely occur within this setting.

Recording, Analysis, and Reporting   In face-to-face settings, some moderators use large sheets of paper to record trends on the wall of the focus group room; others use a personal notepad. A videotape and audiotape are produced to enable a full analysis of the interview. The recorded conversations and moderator notes are summarized across several focus group sessions using *content analysis* (see Chapter 15). This provides the recipient of the research with a qualitative picture of the respondents' concerns, ideas, attitudes, and feelings.

Advantages and Disadvantages   The primary advantage of the focus group interview as an exploratory research tool is its ability to quickly and inexpensively grasp the core issues of a topic. Focus groups are brief, relatively inexpensive, and extremely flexible. They provide the manager, researcher, or client with a chance to observe reactions to their research questions in an open-ended group setting. Participants respond in their own words, rather than being force-fit into a formalized method. Because they can freely react to each other's responses, the unexpected often occurs.

Focus groups best enable the exploration of surprise information and new ideas. Agendas can be modified as the research team moves on to the next focus group. Even within an existing focus group, an adept facilitator can build on the ideas and insights of previous groups, getting to a greater depth of understanding. However, because they are qualitative devices, with limited sampling accuracy, results from focus groups should not be considered a replacement for quantitative analyses.

Two-Stage Design   A useful way to design a research study is as a **two-stage design.** With this approach, exploration becomes a separate first stage with limited objectives: (1) clearly defining the research question and (2) developing the research design. Thus, exploration can be a preliminary study of limited scope and budget.

In arguing for a two-stage approach, we recognize that much about the problem is not known but should be known before effort and resources are committed. In these circumstances, one is operating in unknown areas, where it is difficult to predict the problems and costs of the study. Proposals that acknowledge the practicality of this approach are particularly useful when the research budget is inflexible. A limited exploration for a specific, modest cost carries little risk for both parties and often uncovers information that reduces the total research cost. Sometimes the evidence uncovered in the exploration suggests that a major study is unnecessary.

The end of an exploratory study comes when the researchers are convinced they have established the major dimensions of the research task. They may have defined a set of subsidiary investigative questions that can be used as guides to a detailed research design. Or they may have developed several hypotheses about possible causes of a management dilemma. They may also have learned that certain other hypotheses are such remote possibilities they can be safely ignored in any subsequent study. Finally, researchers end exploration because they believe additional research is not needed or is not feasible.

In contrast to exploratory studies, formal studies are typically structured with clearly stated hypotheses or investigative questions. Formal studies serve a variety of research objectives: (1) descriptions of phenomena or characteristics associated with a subject population, (2) estimates of the proportions of a population that have these characteristics, (3) discovery of associations among different variables, and (4) discovery and measurement of cause-and-effect relationships among variables. The first three objectives are normally associated with descriptive studies, while the fourth calls for studies of causal relationships.

DESCRIPTIVE STUDIES

The objective of a descriptive study is to learn the *who, what, when, where,* and *how* of a topic. The study may be simple or complex; it may be done in many settings. Whatever the form, a descriptive study can be just as demanding of research skills as the causal study, and we should insist on the same high standards for design and execution.

The simplest **descriptive study** concerns a univariate question or hypothesis in which we ask about, or state something about, the size, form, distribution, or existence of a variable. In the account analysis at Center City Bank (see Chapter 3), we might be interested in developing a profile of savers. We may want first to locate them in relation to the main office. The question might be, "What percentage of the savers live within a two-mile radius of the office?" Using the hypothesis format, we might predict, "60 percent or more of the savers live within a two-mile radius of the office."

We may also be interested in securing information about other variables:

1. Relative size of accounts
2. Number of accounts for minors
3. Number of accounts opened within the last six months
4. Amount of activity (number of deposits and withdrawals per year) in accounts

Data on each of these variables, by themselves, may have value for management decisions. Bivariate relationships between these or other variables may be of even greater interest. Cross-tabulations between the distance from the branch and account activity may suggest that differential rates of activity are related to account owner location. A cross-tabulation of account size and gender of account owner may also show interrelation. Such correlative relationships do not necessarily imply a causal relationship.

Descriptive studies are often much more complex than this example. One study of savers began as described and then went into much greater depth. Part of the study included an observation of account records that revealed a concentration of nearby savers. Their accounts were typically larger and more active than those whose owners lived at a distance. A sample survey of savers provided information on stages in the family life cycle, attitudes toward savings, family income levels, and other matters. Correlation of this information with known savings data showed that women owned larger accounts. Further investigation suggested that women with larger accounts were often widowed or working single women who were older than the average account holder. Information about their attitudes and savings practices led to new business strategies at the bank.

Some evidence collected suggested causal relationships. The correlation between nearness to the office and the probability of having an account at the office suggested the question, "Why would people who live far from the office have an account there?" In this type of question a hypothesis makes its greatest contribution by pointing out directions that the research might follow. It might be hypothesized that

1. Distant savers (operationally defined as those with addresses more than two miles from the office) have accounts at the office because they once lived near the office; they were "near" when the account decision was made.
2. Distant savers actually live near the office, but the address on the account is outside the two-mile radius; they are "near," but the records do not show this.
3. Distant savers work near the office; they are "near" by virtue of their work location.
4. Distant savers are not normally near the office but responded to a promotion that encouraged savers to bank via computer; this is another form of "nearness" in which this concept is transformed into one of "convenience."

When these hypotheses were tested, it was learned that a substantial portion of the distant savers could be accounted for by hypotheses 1 and 3. Conclusion: Location was closely related to saving at a given association. The determination of cause is not so simple, however, and these findings still fall within the definition of a descriptive study.

MindWriter could benefit from a descriptive study that profiles satisfied service customers versus dissatisfied ones. Service customer characteristics could then be matched with specific types of service problems, which could lead to identifying changes in product design or customer training or service policies.

CAUSAL STUDIES

The correlation between location and probability of account holding at the savings and loan association looks like strong evidence to many, but the researcher with scientific training will argue that correlation is not causation. Who is right? The essence of the disagreement seems to lie in the concept of cause.

The Concept of Cause

One writer asserts, "There appears to be an inherent gap between the language of theory and research which can never be bridged in a completely satisfactory way. One thinks in terms of theoretical language that contains notions such as causes, forces, systems, and properties. But one's tests are made in terms of covariations, operations, and pointer readings."[15] The essential element of **causation** is that A "produces" B or A "forces" B to occur. But that is an artifact of language, not what happens. Empirically, we can never demonstrate an A-B causality with certainty. This is because we do not "demonstrate" such causal linkages deductively or use the form or validation of premises that deduction requires for conclusiveness. Unlike deductive syllogisms, empirical conclusions are inferences—inductive conclusions. As such, they are probabilistic statements based on what we observe and measure. But we cannot observe and measure all the processes that may account for the A-B relationship.

In Chapter 2 we discussed the example of a light failing to go on as the switch was pushed. Having ruled out other causes for the light's failure, we were left with one inference that was probably *but not certainly* the cause.

To meet the ideal standard of causation would require that one variable always caused another and no other variable had the same causal effect. The *method of agreement,* proposed by John Stuart Mill in the nineteenth century, states "When two or more cases of a given phenomenon have one and only one condition in common, then that condition may be regarded as the cause (or effect) of the phenomenon."[16] Thus, if we can find *Z* and only *Z* in every case where we find *C*, and no others (*A*, *B*, *D*, or *E*) are found with *Z*, then we can conclude that *C* and *Z* are causally related. Figure 6–1 illustrates this method.

An example of the method of agreement might be the problem of occasional high absenteeism on Mondays in a factory. A study of two groups with high absenteeism (No. 1 and No. 2 in Figure 6–1) shows no common job, department, demographic, or personal characteristics (*A*, *B*, *D*, and *E*). However, membership in a camping club (*C*) is common across both groups. The conclusion is that club membership is associated with high absenteeism (*Z*).

The method of agreement helps rule out some variables as irrelevant. In Figure 6–1, *A*, *B*, *D*, and *E* are unlikely to be causes of *Z*. However, there is an implicit assumption that there are no variables to consider other than *A*, *B*, *C*, *D*, and *E*. One can never accept this supposition with certainty because the number of potential variables is infinite. In addition, while *C* may be the cause, it may instead function only in the presence of some other variable not included.

The *negative canon of agreement* states that where the absence of *C* is associated with the absence of *Z*, there is evidence of a causal relationship between *C* and *Z*. Together with the method of agreement, this forms the basis for the *method of difference:* "if there are two or more cases, and in one of them observation *Z* can be made, while in the other it cannot; and if variable *C* occurs when observation *Z* is made, and does not occur when observation *Z* is not made; then it can be asserted that there is a causal relationship between *C* and *Z*."[17] For example, if Jason and Myra were to discover a particular servicing problem repeatedly occurred only when

FIGURE   6–1   Mill's Method of Agreement

FIGURE   6–2   Mill's Method of Difference

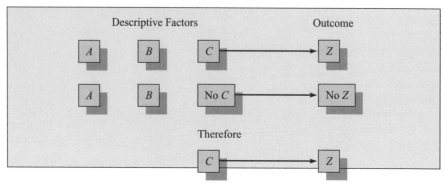

a single employee was involved in the servicing of customers' laptops and never when that employee was absent, an assumption of causation might be made. This method is illustrated in Figure 6–2. Although these methods neither ensure discovery of all relevant variables nor provide certain proof of causation, they help advance our understanding of causality by eliminating inadequate causal arguments.[18]

A more refined cause-and-effect model proposes that individual variables are not the cause of specific effects but that processes are the cause of processes.[19] Evidence for this position is illustrated in Figure 6–3. Here various cause-and-effect relationships between sales performance and feedback clarify the differences between simple and more complex notions of causality.[20]

In model A, we contend that feedback causes an increase in sales performance. An equally plausible explanation is shown in model B: Improvement in sales performance causes the salesperson to behave in a proactive way, seeking more feedback to apply to the next experience. Model C suggests the reinforcement history of the salesperson is the cause of both initiation of self-administered feedback and working harder to improve performance. In model D, we suggest that complex processes contribute to changes in feedback and performance. They are in the salesperson's environment and unique to the person. Other examples could show how positive versus negative reinforcement could create upward or downward sequences that would affect both feedback and performance. Yet all of them make predictions about presumed causal relationships among the variables. Contemporary authors describe the way researchers substitute "prediction" for "causation."

> When scientists speak of "causation," they are often referring to a kind of prediction. Predictions can be considered to reflect cause only when *all* the relevant information is considered. Of course, we can never know *all* the relevant information, so our predictions are consequentially presumptive. Hence the disillusionment in science with the concept of cause. Scientists do use the word "cause" from time to time, but do not be misled into thinking that they mean "cause" in the absolute sense.[21]

Causal inferences are going to be made. Although they are neither permanent nor universal, they allow us to build knowledge of presumed causes over time. Such

FIGURE   6–3   Possible Causal Models of Improved Sales Performance and Feedback

A. Feedback
   causes improved
   sales performance

Feedback ⟶ Improved
sales performance

B. Improved
   sales performance
   causes feedback

Improved ⟶ Feedback
sales performance

C. Motives (reinforcement
   history) cause improved
   sales performance and
   feedback

Motives ⟶ Feedback

⟶ Improved
sales performance

D. Complex processes
   contribute to improved
   sales and feedback

Environmental
Performance aids
Performance descriptions
Feedback results
Tools (equipment to do the job)
Consequences

Internal to Salesperson
Skills and knowledge
Capacity (intelligence,
   physical limitations,
   strengths)
Motives

⟶ Improved
sales
performance

⟶ Feedback

empirical conclusions provide us with successive approximations to the truth. Recognizing this caveat, let's look further at the types of causal relationships of interest to business researchers.

**Causal
Relationships**

Our concern in causal analysis is with how one variable affects, or is "responsible for," changes in another variable. The stricter interpretation of causation, found in experimentation, is that some external factor "produces" a change in the dependent variable. In business research, we often find that the cause-effect relationship is less explicit. We are more interested in understanding, explaining, predicting, and controlling relationships between variables than we are in discerning causes.

If we consider the possible relationships that can occur between two variables, we can conclude there are three possibilities. The relationships may be symmetrical, reciprocal, or asymmetrical.[22] A **symmetrical relationship** is one in which two variables fluctuate together but we assume the changes in neither variable are due to changes in the other. Symmetrical conditions are most often found when two variables are alternate indicators of another cause or independent variable. We might conclude that a correlation between low work attendance and active participation in a company camping club is the result of (dependent on) another factor such as a lifestyle preference.

A **reciprocal relationship** exists when two variables mutually influence or reinforce each other. This could occur if the reading of an advertisement leads to the use of a brand of product. The usage, in turn, sensitizes the person to notice and read more of the advertising of that particular brand.

Most research analysts look for **asymmetrical relationships.** With these we postulate that changes in one variable (the independent variable, or *IV*) is responsible for changes in another variable (the dependent variable, or *DV*). The identification of the *IV* and *DV* is often obvious, but sometimes the choice is not clear. In these latter cases we evaluate them on the basis of (1) the degree to which they may be altered and (2) the time order between them. Since age, social class, climate, world events, and present manufacturing technology are relatively unalterable we normally choose them as independent variables. In addition, when we can detect a time order, we usually find that the *IV* precedes the *DV*.

The types of asymmetrical relationships are

1. *Stimulus-response relationship.* This represents an event or force that results in a response from some object. A price rise results in fewer unit sales; a change in work rules leads to a higher level of worker output; or a change in government economic policy restricts corporate financial decisions. Experiments usually involve stimulus-response relationships.

2. *Property-disposition relationship.* A property is an enduring characteristic of a subject that does not depend on circumstances for its activation. Age, gender, family status, religious affiliation, ethnic group, and physical condition are personal properties. A disposition is a tendency to respond in a certain way under certain circumstances. Dispositions include attitudes, opinions, habits, values, and drives. Examples of property-disposition relationships are the effect of age on attitudes about saving, gender and its effect on attitudes toward social issues, or social class on opinions about taxation. Properties and dispositions are major concepts used in business and social science research.

3. *Disposition-behavior relationship.* Behavior responses include consumption practices, work performance, interpersonal acts, and other kinds of performance. Examples of relationships between dispositions and behavior include opinions about a brand and its purchase, job satisfaction and work output, and moral values and tax cheating. Much of ex post facto causal research involves relationships between properties, dispositions, and behaviors.

4. *Property-behavior relationship.* Examples include such relationships as the stage of the family life cycle and purchases of furniture, social class and family savings patterns, and age and sports participation. When thinking about possible causal relationships or proposing causal hypotheses, one must state the positional relationship, cause, and effect.

Testing Causal Hypotheses

While no one can ever be certain that variable *A* causes variable *B* to occur, one can gather some evidence that increases the belief that *A* leads to *B*. We seek three types of evidence:

1. Is there a predicted covariation between *A* and *B*? Do we find that *A* and *B* occur together in the way hypothesized? When *A* does not occur, is there also an absence of *B*? Or when there is less of *A*, does one also find more or less of *B*? When such conditions of covariation exist, it is an indication of a possible causal connection.

2. Is the time order of events moving in the hypothesized direction? Does *A* occur before *B*? If we find that *B* occurs before *A*, we can have little confidence that *A* causes *B*.

3. Is it possible to eliminate other possible causes of *B*? Can one determine that *C*, *D*, and *E* do not covary with *B* in a way that suggests possible causal connections?

Causation and Experimental Design   In addition to these three conditions, successful inference making from experimental designs must meet two other requirements. The first is referred to as **control.** All factors with the exception of the independent variable must be held constant and not confounded with another variable that is not part of the study. Second, each person in the study must have an equal chance for exposure to each level of the independent variable. This is **random assignment** of subjects to groups.

Here is a demonstration of how these factors are used to detect causation. Assume you wish to conduct a survey of a university's alumni to enlist their support for a new program. There are two different appeals, one largely emotional and the other much more logical in its approach. Before mailing out appeal letters to 50,000 alumni, you decide to conduct an experiment to see whether the emotional or the rational appeal will draw the greater response. You choose a sample of 300 names from the alumni list and divide them into three groups of 100 each. Two of these groups are designated as the experimental groups. One gets the emotional appeal and the other gets the logical appeal. The third group is the **control group** and it receives no appeal.

Covariation in this case is expressed by the percentage of alumni who respond in relation to the appeal used. Suppose 50 percent of those who receive the emotional appeal respond, while only 35 percent of those receiving the logical appeal respond. Control group members, unaware of the experiment, respond at a 5 percent rate. We would conclude that using the emotional appeal enhances response probability.

The sequence of events was not a problem. There could be no chance that the alumni support led to sending the letter requesting support. However, have other variables confounded the results? Could some factor other than the appeal have produced the same results? One can anticipate that certain factors are particularly likely to confound the results. One can control some of these to ensure they do not have this confounding effect. If the question studied is of concern only to alumni who attended the university as undergraduates, those who only attended graduate school are not involved. Thus, you would want to be sure the answers from the latter group did not distort the results. Control would be achieved by excluding graduate students.

A second approach to control uses **matching.** With alumni, there might be reason to believe that different ratios of support will come from various age groups. To control by matching, we need to be sure the age distribution of alumni is the same in all groups. In a similar way, control could be achieved by matching alumni from engineering, liberal arts, business, and other schools.

Even after using such controls, however, one cannot match or exclude other possible confounding variables. These are dealt with through random assignment.

Randomization is the basic method by which equivalence between experimental and control groups is determined. Experimental and control groups must be established so that they are equal. Matching and controlling are useful, but they do not account for all unknowns. It is best to assign subjects either to experimental or to control groups at random (this is not to say haphazardly—randomness must be secured in a carefully controlled fashion according to strict rules of assignment). If the assignments are made randomly, each group should receive its fair share of different factors. The only deviation from this fair share would be that which results from random variation (luck of the draw). The possible impact of these unknown extraneous variables on the dependent variables should also vary at random. The researcher, using tests of statistical significance, can estimate the probable effect of these chance variations on the *DV* and can then compare this estimated effect of extraneous variation to the actual differences found in the *DV* in the experimental and control groups.

We emphasize that random assignment of subjects to experimental and control groups is the *basic technique* by which the two groups can be made equivalent. Matching and other control forms are supplemental ways of improving the quality of measurement. In a sense, matching and controls reduce the extraneous "noise" in the measurement system and in this way improve the sensitivity of measurement of the hypothesized relationship.

Causation and Ex Post Facto Design   Most research studies cannot be carried out experimentally by manipulating variables. Yet we still are interested in the question of causation. Instead of manipulating and/or controlling exposure to an experimental variable, we study subjects who have been exposed to the independent factor and those who have not.

Consider the situation in which several workers in a plant have developed a pattern of absenteeism on Mondays. In searching for hypotheses to explain this phenomenon, we discover that some of these workers are members of a camping club formed a few months ago. Could it be that membership in the club caused increased absenteeism? It is not practical to set up an experiment. This would require us to assign persons to join the club and then determine whether this affected their work attendance.

The better approach would be to get the list of the club's membership and review the absence record of workers, concentrating on their record of work attendance on the Mondays after a camping event. We would also take a sample of

TABLE 6–1 Data on Employee Absenteeism

	Camping Club Member	
Absences	*Yes*	*No*
High	40	70
Low	10	280

employees who are not members of the club and calculate their Monday absence rates. The results might look something like those found in Table 6–1. The data suggest that membership in the camping club might be a cause of higher Monday absenteeism. Certainly the covariation evidence is consistent with this conclusion. But what other evidence will give us an even greater confidence in our conclusion?

We would like some evidence of the time order of events. It is logical to expect that if club membership causes higher absenteeism, there will be a temporal relationship. If high absenteeism were found only on the Monday immediately following a camping trip, it would be good evidence in support of our hypothesis. If absences from work occur before the camping trip, the time order does not support our hypothesis as well.

Of course, many other factors could be causing the high absenteeism among the club members. Here again, use control techniques to improve the ability to draw firm conclusions. First, in drawing a sample of nonmembers of the club, choose a random sample from the files of all employees. In this way, you can be more confident of a fair representation of average worker absence experiences.

We cannot use assignment of subjects in ex post facto research as we did in experimentation. However, we can gather information about potentially confounding factors and use these data to make cross-classification comparisons; determining whether there is a relationship between club membership, absenteeism, and other factors. Assume we also gather age data on the employees under study and introduce this as a cross-classification variable; the results might look like those in Table 6–2. These data suggest age is also a factor. Younger people are more likely to be among the high absentees. Part of the high absenteeism rate among club members seems to be associated with the fact that most club members are under 30 years of age. Within age groups, it is also apparent that club members have a higher incidence of excessive absenteeism than nonclub members of the same age. More will be said about the analysis of crosstabulation and the interpretation of relationships in later chapters.

TABLE 6–2 Data on Employee Absenteeism

	Club Member		Nonclub Member	
Age	*High Absentee*	*Low Absentee*	*High Absentee*	*Low Absentee*
Under 30 years	36	6	30	48
30 to 45	4	4	35	117
45 and over	0	0	5	115

CLOSE-UP

This "Close-Up" is an exercise in analyzing research designs. Its objectives are to help you (1) apply the design classifications and distinctions you have just learned to actual studies and (2) "reinvent" a selected study using the design information presented. We abstracted three studies to give you a flavor for the types of research reports that are appropriate for this exercise. You may choose from any of these or perhaps from a reading list for another course.

DIRECTIONS

1. Select a study from one of the following abstracts (or one suggested by your instructor) and secure a copy from your library.
2. Using the eight design descriptors, identify the characteristics of the selected study.
3. Suggest alternative designs that the researchers could have used (use four or more descriptors).
   a. How would the design look with your changes?
   b. In what ways would the alternative design be stronger? Weaker?
   c. Predict the effects on the results using your alternative design.

ABBREVIATED ABSTRACTS*

Study 1   This study argues the need to identify in advance those entrepreneurs who will create high-growth firms. The psychodynamics of successful entrepreneurs remain elusive despite considerable research. However, using task motivation theory, in contrast to hierarchic motivation, identification and prediction may be aided. The study's subjects were applicants for development grants under the

NSF Small Business Innovation Research Program. Data were obtained from 118 entrepreneurs who had founded firms and a comparison group of 41 manager/scientists who had applied but were not founders. Task motivation exhibited a substantial relationship to growth and differentiated entrepreneurs from nonentrepreneurs. Benefits to venture capitalists, investors, and improvement of the speed by which technological innovation could be brought to the marketplace through early identification of talent were cited as practical benefits. John B. Miner and Norman R. Smith, "Role of Entrepreneurial Task Motivation in the Growth of Technologically Innovative Firms." *Journal of Applied Psychology* 74, no. 4 (1989), pp. 554–60.

Study 2   Human resource managers have a difficult task balancing the employee's rights to fair treatment and due process against the employer's rights to manage the size and composition of the workforce. This study examines the effects of employment-at-will versus due-process personnel policies on organizational efforts to attract new employees. Using 101 undergraduate business students who had read fictitious company brochures, the findings indicated that future job applicants view companies that express employment-at-will policies as significantly less attractive than those who adhere to due-process policies; but that may not discourage them from gathering more information and pursuing further employment opportunities with the companies who have less-favored policies. The hypothesis that employers may be able to offset potential negative effects of employment-at-will by substantial compensation and benefits was partially supported. Catherine Schwoerer and Benson Rosen, "Effects of Employment-at-Will Policies and Compensation Policies on Corporate Image and Job Pursuit Intentions," *Journal of Applied Psychology* 74, no. 4 (1989), pp. 653–56.

Study 3 The self-fulfilling prophecy in interpersonal relationships is often referred to as the *Pygmalion effect*. Studied in a retail setting over a three-month period using newly hired salespeople and their first-level sales managers, this investigation examined the relationships between supervisor's expectations for a subordinate and the resulting performance. Little evidence of the Pygmalion effect was found in the overall sample although it was more operative in men than in women. The study's lack of significant findings in contrast to military and educational settings suggest that the process may be more complex than previously thought. Charlotte D. Sutton and Richard W. Woodman, "Pygmalion Goes to Work: The Effects of Supervisor Expectations in a Retail Setting," *Journal of Applied Psychology 74,* no. 6 (1989), pp. 943–50.

*These abstracts differ slightly from those appearing with the articles. Certain terminology was deleted for the purpose of the exercise. The authors' language is from the article.

The Post Hoc Fallacy   While researchers must necessarily use ex post facto research designs to address causal questions, a word of warning is in order. Club membership among persons with high absentee records is weak evidence for claiming a causal relationship. Similarly, the covariation found between variables must be interpreted carefully when the relationship is based on ex post facto analysis. The term *post hoc fallacy* has been used to describe these frequently unwarranted conclusions.

The ex post facto design is widely used in business research and often is the only approach feasible. In particular, one seeks causal explanations between variables that are impossible to manipulate. Not only can the variables not be manipulated, but the subjects usually cannot be assigned to treatment and control groups in advance. We often find that there are multiple causes rather than one. Be careful using the ex post facto design with causal reasoning. Thorough testing, validating of multiple hypotheses, and controlling for confounding variables are essential.

Summary

If the direction of a research project is not clear, it is often wise to follow a two-step research procedure. The first stage is exploratory, aimed at formulating hypotheses and developing the specific research design. The general research process contains three major stages: (1) exploration of the situation, (2) collection of data, and (3) analysis and interpretation of results.

A research design is the strategy for a study and the plan by which the strategy is to be carried out. It specifies the methods and procedures for the collection, measurement, and analysis of data. Unfortunately, there is no simple classification of research designs that cover the variations found in practice. Some major descriptors of designs are

- Exploratory versus formalized
- Observational versus interrogation/communication
- Experimental versus ex post facto

- Descriptive versus causal
- Cross-sectional versus longitudinal
- Case versus statistical
- Field versus laboratory versus simulation
- Subjects perceive no deviations, some deviations, or researcher-induced deviations

Exploratory research is appropriate for the total study in topic areas where the developed data are limited. In most other studies, exploration is the first stage of a project and is used to orient the researcher and the study. The objective of exploration is the development of hypotheses, not testing.

Formalized studies, including descriptive and causal, are those with substantial structure, specific hypotheses to be tested, or research questions to be answered. Descriptive studies are those used to describe phenomena associated with a subject population or to estimate proportions of the population that have certain characteristics.

Causal studies seek to discover the effect that a variable(s) has on another (or others) or why certain outcomes are obtained. The concept of causality is grounded in the logic of hypothesis testing, which, in turn, produces inductive conclusions. Such conclusions are probabilistic and thus can never be demonstrated with certainty. Current ideas about causality as complex processes improve our understanding over Mill's canons though we can never know all the relevant information necessary to prove causal linkages beyond doubt.

The relationships that occur between two variables may be symmetrical, reciprocal, or asymmetrical. Of greatest interest to the research analyst, the asymmetrical, is one of the following types:

- Stimulus-response
- Property-disposition
- Disposition-behavior
- Property-behavior

We test causal hypotheses by seeking to do three things. We (1) measure the covariation among variables, (2) determine the time order relationships among variables, and (3) ensure that other factors do not confound the explanatory relationships.

The problems of achieving these aims differ somewhat in experimental and ex post facto studies. Where possible, we try to achieve the ideal of the experimental design with random assignment of subjects, matching of subject characteristics, and manipulation and control of variables. Using these methods and techniques, we measure relationships as accurately and objectively as possible.

Key Terms

asymmetrical relationship	control group
case study	cross-sectional study
causal study (causation)	descriptive study
control	ex post facto design

experience survey	primary data
experiment	qualitative techniques
exploratory study (exploration)	random assignment
field conditions	randomization
focus group	reciprocal relationship
formal study	research design
interrogation/communication mode	secondary data
intranet	simulations
laboratory conditions	statistical study
longitudinal study	symmetrical relationship
matching	subjects' perception
observational study	two-stage design

Discussion Questions

1. Distinguish between the following:
   a. Exploratory and formal studies
   b. Experimental and ex post facto research designs
   c. Descriptive and causal studies

2. Establishing causality is difficult, whether conclusions have been derived inductively or deductively.
   a. Explain and elaborate on the implications of this statement.
   b. Why is ascribing causality more difficult when conclusions have been reached through induction?
   c. Correlation does not imply causation. Illustrate this point with examples from business.

3. You have been asked to determine how large corporations prepare for contract negotiations with labor unions. Since you know relatively little about this subject, how will you find out? Be as specific as possible.

4. You are the administrative assistant of a division chief in a large manufacturing organization. You and the division chief have just come from the general manager's office, where you were informed that the assemblers' performance is unsatisfactory. You had sensed tension among the workers but had not considered it unusual. The division chief calls you into the office after the meeting and instructs you to investigate. Suggest at least three different types of research that might be appropriate in this situation.

5. Using yourself as the subject, give an example of each of the following asymmetrical relationships:
   a. Stimulus-response
   b. Property-disposition
   c. Disposition-behavior
   d. Property-behavior

6. Why not use more control variables rather than depend on randomization as the means of controlling extraneous variables?

7. Propose one or more hypotheses for each of the following variable pairs, specifying which is the *IV* and which the *DV*. Then elaborate the basic hypothesis to include at least one moderating variable or intervening variable.

   a. The Index of Consumer Confidence and the business cycle

   b. Level of worker output and closeness of supervision of the worker

   c. Degree of personal friendship between customer and salesperson and the frequency of sales calls on the customer

8. Researchers seek causal relationships by either experimental or ex post facto research designs.

   a. In what ways are these two approaches similar?

   b. In what ways are they different?

9. Using the eight design descriptors, profile the MindWriter CompleteCare satisfaction study as described in this and preceding chapters.

Reference Notes

1. Reprinted with permission of Macmillan Publishing from *Social Research Strategy and Tactics,* 2nd ed., by Bernard S. Phillips, p. 93. Copyright © 1971 by Bernard S. Phillips.

2. Fred N. Kerlinger, *Foundations of Behavioral Research,* 3rd ed. (New York: Holt, Rinehart & Winston, 1986), p. 279.

3. The complexity of research design tends to confuse students as well as writers. The latter respond by forcing order on the vast array of design types through the use of classification schemes or taxonomies. Generally, this is helpful, but because the world defies neat categories, this scheme, like others, may either include or exclude too much.

4. Kerlinger, *Foundations of Behavioral Research,* p. 295.

5. Abraham Kaplan, *The Conduct of Inquiry* (San Francisco: Chandler, 1964), p. 37.

6. W. Charles Redding, "Research Setting: Field Studies," in *Methods of Research in Communication,* ed. Philip Emmert and William D. Brooks (Boston: Houghton Mifflin, 1970), pp. 140–42.

7. John Van Maanen, James M. Dabbs, Jr., and Robert R. Faulkner, *Varieties of Qualitative Research* (Beverly Hills, CA: Sage Publications, 1982), p. 32.

8. Catherine Marshall and Gretchen B. Rossman, *Designing Qualitative Research* (Newbury Park, CA: Sage Publications, 1989), pp. 78–108.

9. This classification is suggested in Claire Selltiz, Lawrence S. Wrightsman, and Stuart W. Cook, *Research Methods in Social Relations,* 3rd ed. (New York: Holt, Rinehart & Winston, 1976), pp. 99–101.

10. A comprehensive and detailed presentation may be found in Richard A. Krueger, *Focus Groups: A Practical Guide for Applied Research,* 2nd ed. (Thousand Oaks, CA: Sage Publications, 1994); and David L. Morgan, *Successful Focus Groups: Advancing the State of the Art* (Thousand Oaks, CA: Sage Publications, 1993). Also see Thomas L. Greenbaum, "Focus Group Spurt Predicted for the '90s," *Marketing News* 24, no. 1 (January 8, 1990), pp. 21–22.

11. "How Nonprofits Are Using Focus Groups," *Nonprofit World* 14, no. 5 (September/October 1996), p. 37.
12. P. Hawe, D. Degeling, and J. Hall, *Evaluating Health Promotion: A Health Worker's Guide* (Artarmon, N.S.W.: MacLennan & Petty, 1990).
13. "Shoppers Speak Out in Focus Groups," *Discount Store News* 36, no. 5 (March 3, 1997), pp. 23–26.
14. Hawe, Degeling, and Hall, *Evaluating Health Promotion*, p. 176.
15. Hubert M. Blalock, Jr., *Causal Inferences in Nonexperimental Research* (Chapel Hill: University of North Carolina Press, 1964), p. 5.
16. As stated in William J. Goode and Paul K. Hatt, *Methods in Social Research* (New York: McGraw-Hill, 1952), p. 75.
17. From *Methods in Social Research* by William J. Goode and Paul K. Hatt. Copyright © 1952, McGraw-Hill Book Company. Used with permission of McGraw-Hill Book Company.
18. Morris R. Cohen and Ernest Nagel, *An Introduction to Logic and Scientific Method* (New York: Harcourt, Brace, 1934), chap. 13; and Blalock, *Causal Inferences,* p. 14.
19. R. Carnap, *An Introduction to the Philosophy of Science* (New York: Basic Books, 1966).
20. Content adapted from Thomas F. Gilbert, *Human Competence* (New York: McGraw-Hill, 1978). Tabular concept based on Emanuel J. Mason and William J. Bramble, *Understanding and Conducting Research,* 2nd ed. (New York: McGraw-Hill, 1989), p. 13.
21. Mason and Bramble, *Understanding and Conducting Research,* p. 14.
22. Morris Rosenberg, *The Logic of Survey Analysis* (New York: Basic Books, 1968), p. 3.

Suggested Readings

1. Babbie, Earl R. *The Practice of Social Research,* 7th ed. Belmont, CA: Wadsworth, 1994. Contains a clear and thorough synopsis of design.
2. Krathwohl, David R. *Social and Behavioral Science Research: A New Framework for Conceptualizing, Implementing, and Evaluating Research Studies.* San Francisco: Jossey-Bass, 1985. Chapter 9 on causality is insightful, well reasoned, and highly recommended.
3. Mason, Emanuel J., and William J. Bramble. *Understanding and Conducting Research,* 2nd ed. New York: McGraw-Hill, 1989. Chapter 1 has an excellent section on causation; chapter 2 provides an alternative classification of the types of research.
4. Selltiz, Claire, Lawrence S. Wrightsman, and Stuart M. Cook. *Research Methods in Social Relations,* 3rd ed. New York: Holt, Rinehart & Winston, 1976. Chapters 4 and 5 discuss various types of research designs.
5. Templeton, Jane Farley. *The Focus Group: A Strategic Guide to Organizing, Conducting and Analyzing the Focus Group Interview,* 2nd ed. New York: Probus Publishing, 1994. A careful and thorough review of focus group applications.

7 MEASUREMENT

CHAPTER NAVIGATION

BRINGING RESEARCH TO LIFE

"I was a tourist here when the previous executive director, who had served for fifteen years, ran off to Vancouver with a violinist. He said he could not endure another year of our claustrophobic winters." The executive director gestured broadly at the still snow-capped Canadian Rockies that enveloped the White Ice Compound and discouraged casual visitation for most of the year. "Being a recent mugging victim—they took my wallet and broke my wrist—I was happy to stay for a while. And it has been three very happy years, though not easy on my ego since I let corporate North America intrude on our idyllic existence. Not that I blame them for my shortcomings."

"You mean the MindWriter people?" prompted Jason. "The ones who flew me up here? My clients?"

The executive director propelled Jason straight across a manicured lawn toward the refreshment tent, where her faculty and paying guests were basking in postconcert euphoria, following a stirring performance of Beethoven by the White Ice Summer Festival Orchestra.

"Please, don't misunderstand," said the executive director. "They have been fine tenants . . . good corporate citizens . . . generous contributors to our little community. When I rented them a part of our compound for use in corporate education, they were quite generously insistent that I avail myself of some of their training for midlevel managers. And I have to admit, now, that their managerial style makes me feel like an inadequate cellist with a stiff wrist, not an executive director evolving toward competence."

"Well, if we are going to help you," ventured Jason, "you had better tell us quickly what you do here. We have a 4 P.M. flight out."

"Surely. And I do appreciate this advice, especially as you have an insider's view of the Mind-Writer. We in White Ice have a simple, never-varying rhythm of activity. By the middle of September, the paying guests, the visiting artists, the musicians, and the tourists have left White Ice, and I bring in artisans for two weeks of intensive repairs

and renovations. Then I prepare financial and artistic reports for the three foundations that have endowed us and also draw up an agenda for capital improvements and special events, which become the basis for frantic proposal writing during the weeks preceding Christmas. From January to April, I am on the phone to travel agents from Mexico City to Juneau to arrange a tight reservation and scheduling process, so that we maximize the use of the facilities during our season. I have developed the ability to keep track of the cash flow, which is not easy, with Canadian and U.S. dollars mingled.

"During the winter my artistic directors, Frances Braun and Igor Starvinsky—they have been Mr. and Mrs. Braun-Starvinsky for thirty years, which will astonish you when you meet them—prepare the program and hire the musicians, coordinating closely with me on the budget. This is quite complicated, as most of the performing artists spend only two weeks with us, so that fully six hundred artists are part of this orchestra over the course of a summer.

"Then in the early spring I hear from the colleges in British Columbia, who send me their music scholarship students for summer employment as dishwashers, waiters, cleaners, and the like."

"Sounds as if you are right on top of the finances," said Jason, "and I suppose in your seminars with the MindWriter people they told you their theory of what to measure in any enterprise . . . and that cash flow is one of three things that must be watched most carefully."

"Oh, yes indeed," the executive director laughed. "Gauging cash flow is not the problem. I descend from a line of genteel poverty. Measuring customer satisfaction—one of the other critical three factors for the MindWriter folks—now that was a problem for me—at first. The care and frequency with which they measure customer satisfaction in the MindWriter seminars dumbfounded me. Halfway through a seminar, morning, afternoon, or evening, everyone breaks for coffee and is required to fill out a critique of the speaker. The results are tabulated by the time the last coffee cup has been picked up, *(continued)* and the seminar leader has been given feedback. Is he or she presenting material too slowly? Too quickly? Are there too many jokes or not enough? Are concrete examples being used often enough? Do the participants want hard copy of the slides? Really it is remarkable. They measure attitudinal data six times a day and even query you about the meals, including taste, appearance, cleanliness and speed, friendliness, and accuracy of service.

"We have a North American association of artistic and executive directors, and since experiencing the MindWriter seminars, I have every year hosted the fall subcommittee meeting on audience development. I take it right out of my budget, and show everyone a fine time—skiing, skating, and a frank exchange of ideas on measuring the customer."

"Smart," said Jason.

"My remaining problem is employee commitment, specifically commitment of the orchestral performers to the White Ice Festival. None of the other directors in my association has nearly the rapid turnover of performers we have here, so they are not much help in measuring commitment."

"Then the Braun-Starvinskys will have to be your eyes and ears. You must ask them to listen carefully to the performers. Employee satisfaction is the third leg of the three-legged stool on which performance is based. I'm quoting the MindWriter standard line, by the way," said Jason.

The executive director laughed ironically. "Jason," she said, "look over my shoulder. Directly behind me is a couple in their mid-sixties. Please describe as exactly as you can the behavior you observe. But lean forward and whisper, since they have the eyes of a hawk and the hearing of a lark."

"You mean the fellow in the sweatshirt and the woman with her hair in a bun?" whispered Jason. "I've been watching them all afternoon. They are remarkable, horrid, really. You say they are married? Why, he is sleeping. And the woman is nevertheless talking to him nonstop and every thirty seconds shaking him awake. Except he falls right back to sleep. And she does not stop talking, but simply chats a while longer and wakes him again."

"Yes, Jason, there you have them—my artistic directors. He stays up all night composing, and all

day, when he is not conducting, he snoozes. And she never stops expressing her opinions, be they lifelong prejudices or vagrant musings, and therefore she never listens well enough to later give a coherent report of anything she has heard or been told. If I have to rely on them for feedback, everything would be filtered and distorted beyond recognition. I might as well query the statue of Chief White Ice."

"Personally, I find untrained observers highly unreliable and inaccurate in measuring and reporting behavior," said Jason. "Have you tried a suggestion box?"

"No, but I do send a letter to each visiting performer soliciting bouquets and brickbats. Do you want to know what some of the performers have written?"

"Shoot," said Jason. "but, quickly, please. Don't want to fly through these mountains at night."

"They write, 'Starvinsky never listens to our ideas.' They write, 'A day under Braun feels like a week on a Los Angeles freeway.' They write, 'We are all highly trained college teachers of music, but we are treated like children.'

"And clearly our performers aren't our only concern. The restaurant employees, the hospitality staff, the stage carpenters, the. . . ."

"Hold on," said Jason, scribbling furiously on a napkin. "I can see you have a problem. I'm making a note to send you Patchen's Work Innovation Index and his Job Motivation Index. In fact, I'll send you all his indices, because he identifies and measures five different dimensions of worker attitudes. You'll find it interesting and maybe it is something you can use. Meanwhile, will you send me your customer satisfaction instrument for concert goers?"

"Of course, Jason. And be sure I shall act quickly on your suggestions. The *Vancouver Sun* has commented on our inability to sustain a steady tempo and tonation. When a businessperson fouls up, the mistake may not be evident for days or weeks. But when our orchestra strikes a sour note, six hundred audience members—guests, we call them, but they are potentially repeat customers—receive the message at the speed of sound."

THE NATURE OF MEASUREMENT

In everyday usage, measurement occurs when an established yardstick verifies the height, weight, or another feature of a physical object. How well you like a song, a painting, or the personality of a friend is also a measurement. In a dictionary sense, to measure is to discover the extent, dimensions, quantity, or capacity of something, especially by comparison with a standard. We measure casually in daily life, but in research the requirements are rigorous.

Measurement in research consists of assigning numbers to empirical events in compliance with a set of rules. This definition implies that measurement is a three-part process: (1) selecting observable empirical events, (2) using numbers or symbols to represent aspects of the events, and (3) applying a **mapping rule** to connect the observation to the symbol.[1] Figure 7–1 illustrates the components.

Assume you are studying people who attend an auto show where all of the year's new models are on display. You are interested in learning the male-to-female ratio among attendees. You observe those who enter the show area. If a person is female, you record an F; if male, an M. Any other symbols such as 0 and 1 or # and % could be used if you know what group the symbol identifies. Researchers might also want to measure the desirability of the styling of the new Espace van. They interview a sample of visitors and (with a different mapping rule) assign their opinions to the following scale:

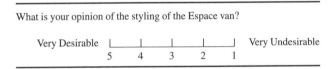

What is your opinion of the styling of the Espace van?

Very Desirable |___|___|___|___|___| Very Undesirable

            5   4   3   2   1

FIGURE 7–1   Characteristics of Measurement

All measurement theorists would call the opinion rating scale above a form of measurement, but some would challenge the male-female classification. Their argument is that measurement must involve quantification—that is, "the assignment of numbers to objects to represent amounts or degrees of a property possessed by all of the objects."[2] Our discussion endorses the more general view that numbers reflect qualitative and quantitative concepts.

Researchers deduce from a hypothesis that certain conditions should exist in the real world; then they measure for these conditions. If found, they lend support to the hypothesis; if not, researchers conclude the hypothesis is faulty. An important question at this point is, "Just what does one measure?"

What Is Measured?

Concepts used in research may be classified as objects or as properties. **Objects** include the things of ordinary experience, such as tables, people, books, and automobiles. Objects also include things that are not as concrete, such as genes, attitudes, neutrons, and peer-group pressures. **Properties,** on the other hand, are the characteristics of the objects. A person's physical properties may be stated in terms of weight, height, posture. Psychological properties include attitudes and intelligence. Social properties include leadership ability, class affiliation, or status. These and many other properties of an individual can be measured in a research study.

In a literal sense, researchers do not measure objects or properties. They measure indicants of the properties. Thus, they measure indicants of the properties of objects. It is easy to observe that A is taller than B and that C participates more than D in a group process. Or suppose you are analyzing members of a sales force of several hundred people to learn what personal properties contribute to sales success. The properties are age, years of experience, and number of calls made per week. The indicants in these cases are so accepted that one considers the properties to be observed directly.

In contrast, it is not easy to measure properties like motivation to succeed, ability to stand stress, problem-solving ability, and persuasiveness. Since they cannot be measured directly, one must infer their presence or absence by observing some indicant or pointer measurement. When you begin to make these inferences, there is often disagreement about how to operationalize the indicants.

Not only is it a challenge to measure such constructs, but a study's quality depends on what measures are selected or constructed and how they fit the circumstances. The nature of measurement scales, sources of error, and characteristics of sound measurement are considered next.

DATA TYPES

In measuring, one devises some mapping rule and then transfers the observation of property indicants using this rule. Several types of data are possible; the appropriate choice depends on what you assume about the mapping rules. Each data type has its own set of underlying assumptions about how the numerals correspond to real-world observations.

Data classifications employ the real numbers system. The most accepted basis for scaling has three characteristics:

1. Numbers are ordered. One number is greater than, less than, or equal to another number.
2. Differences between numbers are ordered. The difference between any pair of numbers is greater than, less than, or equal to the difference between any other pair of numbers.
3. The number series has a unique origin indicated by the number zero.

Combinations of these characteristics of order, distance, and origin provide the following widely used classification of measurement scales:

Type of Data	Characteristics of Data	Basic Empirical Operation
Nominal	No order, distance, or origin	Determination of equality
Ordinal	Order but no distance or unique origin	Determination of greater or lesser values
Interval	Both order and distance but no unique origin	Determination of equality of intervals or differences
Ratio	Order, distance, and unique origin	Determination of equality of ratios

Nominal Data

In business and social science research, nominal data are probably more widely collected than any other. When you collect **nominal data,** you partition a set into categories that are mutually exclusive and collectively exhaustive. In the camping club illustration used in the last chapter (see Table 6–1), persons were classified into four unique categories through cross-classification of club membership and degree of absenteeism. Each employee could be placed in one and only one of the four cells.

The counting of members in each group is the only possible arithmetic operation when a nominal scale is employed. If we use numbers to identify categories, they are recognized as labels only and have no quantitative value. Nominal classifications may consist of any number of separate groups if the groups are mutually exclusive and collectively exhaustive. Thus, one might classify the residents of a city according to their expressed religious preferences. Classification set A given in the accompanying table is not a sound nominal scale because it is not collectively exhaustive. Set B meets the minimum requirements, although this classification may be more useful for some research purposes than others.

Religious Preferences

A	B
Baptist	Catholic
Catholic	Jewish
Jewish	Protestant
Lutheran	Other
Methodist	None
Presbyterian	
Protestant	

Nominal scales are the least powerful of the four data types. They suggest no order or distance relationship and have no arithmetic origin. The scale wastes any information about varying degrees of the property being measured.

Since the only quantification is the number count of cases in each category (the frequency distribution), the researcher is restricted to the use of the mode as the measure of central tendency.[3] You can conclude which class has the most members, but that is all. There is no generally used measure of dispersion for nominal scales. Several tests for statistical significance may be utilized; the most common is the chi-square test. For measures of association, phi, lambda, or other measures may be appropriate. Significance tests and measures of association are presented in Chapters 16, 17, and Appendix E.

While nominal data are weak, they are still useful. If no other scale can be used, one can almost always classify one set of properties into a set of equivalent classes. Nominal measures are especially valuable in exploratory work where the objective is to uncover relationships rather than secure precise measurements. This data type is also widely used in survey and other ex post facto research when data are classified by major subgroups of the population. Classifications such as respondents' marital status, gender, political persuasion, and exposure to a certain experience abound. Cross-partitions of these and other variables provide insight into important data patterns.

Jason visited White Ice because of MindWriter's extensive research into customer satisfaction related to their manager training. His visit revealed White Ice's need for some nominal data on employee satisfaction. Orchestra performers could be divided into groups based on their appreciation of the Braun-Starvinskys (liked, not liked), on their attitude toward facilities (suitable, not suitable), or on their perception of how performers were treated (as adults, as children).

Ordinal Data

Ordinal data includes the characteristics of the nominal scale plus an indicator of order. Ordinal data is possible if the transitivity postulate is fulfilled. This postulate states: If a is greater than b and b is greater than c, then a is greater than c.[4] The use of an ordinal scale implies a statement of "greater than" or "less than" (an equality statement is also acceptable) without stating how much greater or less. Like a rubber yardstick, it can stretch varying amounts at different places along its length. Thus, the real difference between ranks 1 and 2 may be more or less than the difference between ranks 2 and 3.

An ordinal concept can be generalized beyond the simple illustration of $a > b > c$. Any number of cases can be ranked. While ordinal measurement speaks of "greater than" and "less than" measurements, other descriptors may be used—"superior to," "happier than," or "above." A third extension of the ordinal concept occurs when more than one property is of interest. We may ask a taster to rank varieties of carbonated soft drinks by flavor, color, carbonation, and a combination of these characteristics. We can secure the combined ranking either by asking the respondent to make such a ranking or by doing our own combining of the individual rankings. To develop an overall index, the researcher typically adds and averages ranks for each of the three dimensions. This procedure is technically incorrect and, especially for a given respondent, may yield misleading results. When the number of respondents is large, however, these errors average out. A more sophisticated way to combine a number of dimensions into a total index is to use a multidimensional scale (see Chapter 18).

The researcher faces another difficulty when combining the rankings of several respondents. Here again, it is not uncommon to use weighted sums of rank values for a combined index. If there are many observations, this approach will probably give adequate results, though it is not theoretically correct. A better way is to convert ordinal data into interval data, the values of which can then be added and averaged. One well-known example is *Thurstone's Law of Comparative Judgment.*[5] In its simplest form, Thurstone's procedure says the distance between scale positions of two objects, *A* and *B*, depends on the percentage of judgments in which *A* is preferred to *B*.

Examples of ordinal data include opinion and preference scales. The widely used paired-comparison technique uses ordinal data. Because the numbers of this scale have only a rank meaning, the appropriate measure of central tendency is the median. A percentile or quartile measure reveals the dispersion. Correlation is restricted to various rank-order methods. Measures of statistical significance are technically confined to that body of methods known as nonparametric methods.[6]

Researchers in the behavioral sciences differ about whether more powerful parametric significance tests are appropriate with ordinal measures. One position is that this use of parametric tests is incorrect on both theoretical and practical grounds:

> If the measurement is weaker than that of an interval scale, by using parametric methods tests the researcher would "add information" and thereby create distortions.[7]

At the other extreme, some behavioral scientists argue that parametric tests are usually acceptable for ordinal data:

> The differences between parametric and rank-order tests were not great insofar as significance level and power were concerned.[8]

A view between these extremes recognizes that there are risks in using parametric procedures on ordinal data, but these risks are usually not great:

> The best procedure would seem to be to treat ordinal measurements as though they were interval measurements but to be constantly alert to the possibility of *gross* inequality of intervals.[9]

Because nonparametric tests are abundant, simple to calculate, have good power efficiencies, and do not force the researcher to accept the assumptions of parametric testing, we advise their use with nominal and ordinal data. It is understandable, however, that because parametric tests (such as the *t*-test or analysis of variance) are so versatile, accepted, and understood, they will continue to be used with ordinal data when those data approach interval data characteristics.

Jason believed White Ice could potentially benefit from using Patchen's Work Innovation Index and his Job Motivation Index (see "Close-Up"). Both of these are constructed using ordinal data. Because of the constructs measured (work innovation, job motivation), we know after applying the test that one employee is more motivated than another, that one employee generates more ideas than another. By applying numerical scores to the variation in motivation, we can assume the collection of interval data.

Interval Data

Interval data has the power of nominal and ordinal data plus one additional strength: It incorporates the concept of equality of interval (the distance between 1 and 2 equals the distance between 2 and 3). Calendar time is such a scale. For example, the elapsed time between 3 and 6 A.M. equals the time between 4 and 7 A.M. One cannot say, however, 6 A.M. is twice as late as 3 A.M. because "zero time" is an arbitrary origin. Centigrade and Fahrenheit temperature scales are other examples of classical interval scales. Both have an arbitrarily determined zero point.

Many attitude scales are presumed to be interval. Thurstone's differential scale was an early effort to develop such a scale.[10] Users also treat intelligence scores, semantic differential scales, and many other multipoint graphical scales as interval.

When a scale is interval, you use the arithmetic mean as the measure of central tendency. You can compute the average time of first arrival of trucks at a warehouse or the average attitude value for union workers versus nonunion workers on an election. The standard deviation is the measure of dispersion for arrival times or worker opinions. Product moment correlation, *t*-tests, and *F*-tests and other parametric tests are the statistical procedures of choice.[11]

Ratio Data

Ratio data incorporates all of the powers of the previous data types plus the provision for absolute zero or origin. Ratio data represents the actual amounts of a variable. Measures of physical dimensions such as weight, height, distance, and area are examples. In the behavioral sciences, few situations satisfy the requirements of the ratio scale—the area of psychophysics offering some exceptions. In business research, we find ratio scales in many areas. There are money values, population counts, distances, return rates, productivity rates, and amounts of time in a time-period sense.

With the White Ice project, Jason could measure the relationship of job satisfaction with a performer's age, the number of years he or she had played professionally, the number of times he or she had participated in the White Ice summer festival. Each of these examples represent ratio data. For practical purposes, however, the analyst would make the same choice of statistical technique as with interval data.

All statistical techniques mentioned up to this point are usable with ratio scales. Other manipulations carried out with real numbers may be done with ratio-scale values. Thus, multiplication and division can be used with this scale but not with the others mentioned. Geometric and harmonic means are measures of central tendency, and coefficients of variation may also be calculated.

Researchers often encounter the problem of evaluating variables that have been measured at different data levels. The possession of a CPA by an accountant is a nominal, dichotomous variable, and salary is a ratio variable. Certain statistical techniques require the measurement levels to be the same. Since the nominal variable does not have the characteristics of order, distance, or point of origin, we cannot create them artificially after the fact. The ratio-based salary variable, on the other hand, can be reduced. Rescaling salary downward into high-low, high-medium-low, or another set of categories simplifies the comparison of nominal data. This example is generalizable to other measurement situations—that is, conversion or rescaling of a variable is unidirectional from the more powerful and robust measurement level to the lesser one, not the reverse.[12] The loss of measurement power accompanying such decisions is sometimes costly in that only nonparametric statistics can then be used in data analysis. Thus, the design of the measurement questions should anticipate such problems and avoid them when possible.

SOURCES OF MEASUREMENT DIFFERENCES

The ideal study should be designed and controlled for precise and unambiguous measurement of the variables. Since attainment of this ideal is unlikely, we must recognize the sources of potential error and try to eliminate, neutralize, or otherwise deal with them. Much potential error is systematic (results from a bias) while the remainder is random (occurs erratically). One authority has pointed out several sources from which measured differences can come.[13]

Assume you are conducting an ex post facto study of the residents of a major city. The study concerns the Prince Corporation, a large manufacturer with headquarters and several major plants located in the city. The objective of the study is to discover the public's opinions about the company and the origin of any generally held adverse opinions.

Ideally, any variation of scores among the respondents would reflect true differences in their opinions about the company. Attitudes toward the firm as an employer, as an ecologically sensitive organization, or as a progressive corporate citizen would be accurately expressed. However, four major error sources may contaminate the results. These sources are the respondent, the situation, the measurer, and the instrument.

Error Sources   **The Respondent as an Error Source**   Opinion differences will come from relatively stable characteristics of the respondent that affect the scores. Typical of these are employee status, ethnic group membership, social class, and nearness to plants. Many of these dimensions will be anticipated in the design, but others of a less obvious nature will not be. The latter variety might be a traumatic experience a given respondent had with the Prince Corporation or its personnel. The respondent may be reluctant to express strong negative feelings or may have little knowledge about Prince but be reluctant to admit ignorance. This reluctance can lead to an interview of "guesses."

Respondents may also suffer from temporary factors like fatigue, boredom, anxiety, or other distractions; these limit the ability to respond accurately and fully. Hunger, impatience, or general variations in mood may also have an impact.

Situational Factors   These potential problem areas are legion. Any condition that places a strain on the interview can have serious effects on the interviewer-respondent rapport. If another person is present, that person can distort responses by joining in, by distracting, or merely by being present. If the respondents believe anonymity is not ensured, they may be reluctant to express certain feelings. Curbside or intercept interviews are unlikely to elicit elaborate responses while in-home interviews more often do.

The Measurer as an Error Source   The interviewer can distort responses by rewording, paraphrasing, or reordering questions. Stereotypes in appearance and action introduce bias. Inflections of voice and conscious or unconscious prompting with smiles, nods, and so forth may encourage or discourage certain replies. Careless mechanical processing—checking of the wrong response or failure to record full replies—will obviously distort findings. In the data analysis stage, incorrect coding, careless tabulation, and faulty statistical calculation may introduce further errors.

Instrument as an Error Source   A defective instrument can cause distortion in two major ways. First, it can be too confusing and ambiguous. The use of complex words and syntax beyond respondent comprehension is typical. Leading questions, ambiguous meanings, mechanical defects (inadequate space for replies, response choice omissions, and poor printing), and multiple questions suggest the range of problems.

A more elusive type of instrument deficiency is poor sampling of the universe of content items. Seldom does the instrument explore all the potentially important issues. The Prince Corporation study might treat company image in areas of employment and ecology but omit the company management's civic leadership, its support of local education programs, or its position on minority issues. Even if the general issues are studied, the questions may not cover enough aspects of each area of concern. While we might study the Prince Corporation's image as an employer in terms of salary and wage scales, promotion opportunities, and work stability, perhaps such topics as working conditions, company management relations with organized labor, and retirement and other benefit programs should also be included.

THE CHARACTERISTICS OF SOUND MEASUREMENT

What are the characteristics of a good measurement tool? An intuitive answer to this question is that the tool should be an accurate counter or indicator of what we are interested in measuring. In addition, it should be easy and efficient to use. There are three major criteria for evaluating a measurement tool: validity, reliability, and practicality.

Validity refers to the extent to which a test measures what we actually wish to measure.

Reliability has to do with the accuracy and precision of a measurement procedure.

Practicality is concerned with a wide range of factors of economy, convenience, and interpretability.[14]

In the following sections, we discuss the nature of these qualities and how researchers can achieve them in their measurement procedures.

Validity

Many forms of validity are mentioned in the research literature, and the number grows as we expand the concern for more scientific measurement. This text features two major forms: external and internal validity.[15] The external validity of research findings refers to their ability to be generalized across persons, settings, and times; more will be said about this in Chapters 9 and 14.[16] In this chapter, we discuss only internal validity. Internal validity is further limited in this discussion to the ability of a research instrument to measure what it is purported to measure. Does the instrument really measure what its designer claims it does?

Validity in this context is the extent to which differences found with a measuring tool reflect true differences among respondents being tested. The difficulty in meeting this test is that usually one does not know what the true differences are; if one did, one would not do the measuring. Without direct knowledge of the dimension being studied, you must face the question, "How can one discover validity without direct confirming knowledge?" A quick answer is to seek other relevant evidence that confirms the answers found with the measurement device, but this leads to a second question, "What constitutes relevant evidence?" There is no quick answer this time. What is relevant depends on the nature of the research problem and the researcher's judgment. One way to approach this question is to organize the answer according to measure-relevant types. One widely accepted classification consists of three major forms: content, criterion-related, and construct (see Figure 7–2).[17]

Content Validity   The **content validity** of a measuring instrument is the extent to which it provides adequate coverage of the topic under study. If the instrument contains a representative sample of the universe of subject matter of interest, then content validity is good. To evaluate the content validity of an instrument, one must first agree on what elements constitute adequate coverage of the problem. In the Prince Corporation study, one must decide what knowledge, attitudes, and opinions are

FIGURE   7–2   Summary of Validity Estimates

Type	*What Is Measured*	*Methods*
Content	Degree to which the content of the items adequately represents the universe of all relevant items under study	Judgmental or panel evaluation with Content Validity Ratio
Criterion-related	Degree to which the predictor is adequate in capturing the relevant aspects of the criterion	Correlation
Concurrent	Description of the present; criterion data is available at same time as predictor scores	
Predictive	Prediction of the future; criterion is measured after the passage of time	
Construct	Answers the question, "What accounts for the variance in the measure?" Attempts to identify the underlying construct(s) being measured and determine how well the test represents them	Judgmental Correlation of proposed test with established one Convergent-discriminant techniques Factor analysis Multitrait-multimethod analysis

relevant to the measurement of corporate public image and then decide which forms of these opinions are relevant positions on these topics. In the White Ice study, Jason must first determine what factors are influencing employee satisfaction, before determining if Patchen's indices can be of value. If the questionnaire adequately covers the topics that have been defined as the relevant dimensions, we conclude the instrument has good content validity.

Determination of content validity is judgmental and can be approached in several ways. First, the designer may determine it through a careful definition of the topic of concern, the items to be scaled, and the scales to be used. This logical process is often intuitive and unique to each research designer. The management-research question hierarchy discussed in Chapter 3 helps to reduce research questions into specific investigative and measurement questions that have content validity. A second way to determine content validity is to use a panel of persons to judge how well the instrument meets the standards.

An operational example of how an instrument is content-validated comes from the employment setting. A panel independently assesses the test items for a performance test. They judge each item to be essential, useful but not essential, or not necessary in assessing performance of a relevant behavior. The "essential" responses on each item from each panelist are evaluated by a Content Validity Ratio, and those meeting a statistical significance value are retained. In both informal judgments and in this systematic process, "content validity is primarily concerned with inferences about test *construction* rather than inferences about test *scores*."[18]

It is important *not* to define *content* too narrowly. If you secure only superficial expressions of opinion in the Prince Corporation public opinion survey, it would probably not have adequate content coverage. The research should delve into the processes by which these opinions came about. How did the respondents come to feel as they did, and what is the intensity of feeling? The same would be true of MindWriter's evaluation of service quality and satisfaction. It is not enough to know a customer was dissatisfied. What processes, employees, parts, and time sequences within the CompleteCare program led to that dissatisfaction?

Criterion-Related Validity   **Criterion-related validity** reflects the success of measures used for prediction or estimation. You may want to predict an outcome or estimate the existence of a current behavior or condition. These are *predictive* and *concurrent validity,* respectively. They differ only in a time perspective. An opinion questionnaire that correctly forecasts the outcome of a union election has predictive validity. An observational method that correctly categorizes families by current income class has concurrent validity. While these examples appear to have simple and unambiguous validity criteria, there are difficulties in estimating validity. Consider the problem of estimating family income. There clearly is a knowable true income for every family. However, we may find it difficult to secure this figure. Thus, while the criterion is conceptually clear, it may be unavailable.

In other cases, there may be several criteria, none of which is completely satisfactory. Consider again the problem of judging success in a sales force. A researcher may want to develop a preemployment test that will predict sales success. There may be several possible criteria, none of which tells the full story. Total sales per salesperson may not adequately reflect territory market potential, competitive conditions, or the different profitability rates of various products. One might rely on the sales manager's overall evaluation, but how unbiased and accurate are those impressions? The researcher must ensure that the validity criterion used is itself "valid." One source suggests that any criterion measure must be judged in terms of four qualities: relevance, freedom from bias, reliability, and availability.[19]

A criterion is *relevant* if it is defined and scored in the terms we judge to be the proper measures of salesperson success. If you believe sales success is adequately measured by dollar sales volume achieved per year, then it is the relevant criterion. If you believe success should include a high level of penetration of large accounts, then sales volume alone is not fully relevant. In making this decision, you must rely on your judgment in deciding what partial criteria are appropriate indicants of salesperson success.

Freedom from bias is attained when the criterion gives each salesperson an equal opportunity to score well. The sales criterion would be biased if it did not show adjustments for differences in territory potential and competitive conditions.

A *reliable* criterion is stable or reproducible. An erratic criterion (highly variable sales performances from month to month) can hardly be considered a reliable standard by which to judge performances on a sales employment test. Yet an unreliable criterion is often relevant for the study's purpose because it is the only one available. In such a case, it is possible to use a *correction for attenuation* formula that lets you see what the correlation between the test and the criterion would be if they were made perfectly reliable.[20]

Finally, the information specified by the criterion must be *available*. If it is not available, how much will it cost and how difficult will it be to secure? The amount of money and effort that should be spent on development of a criterion depends on the importance of the problem for which the test is used.

Once there are test and criterion scores, they must be compared in some way. The usual approach is to correlate them. For example, you might correlate test scores of 40 new salespeople with first-year sales achievements adjusted to reflect differences in territorial selling conditions.

Construct Validity   One may also wish to measure or infer the presence of abstract characteristics for which no empirical validation seems possible. Attitude scales and aptitude and personality tests generally concern concepts that fall in this category. Although this situation is much more difficult, some assurance is still needed that the measurement has an acceptable degree of validity.

In attempting to evaluate **construct validity,** we consider both the theory and the measuring instrument being used. If we were interested in measuring the effect of ceremony on organizational culture, the way in which ceremony was operationally defined would have to correspond to an empirically grounded theory. Once assured that the construct was meaningful in a theoretical sense, we would next investigate the adequacy of the instrument. If a known measure of ceremony in organizational culture was available, we might correlate the results obtained using this measure with those derived from our new instrument. Such an approach would provide us with preliminary indications of *convergent* validity. If Jason were to develop a work innovation index for artistic personnel at White Ice and, when compared, the results revealed the same indications as Patchen's Index, Jason's instrument would have convergent validity. Similarly, if Jason and Myra developed an instrument to measure satisfaction with the CompleteCare program and the derived measure could be confirmed with a standarized customer satisfaction measure, convergent validity would exist.

Look again at the example to measure the impact of ceremony on organizational culture. Another method of validating the ceremony construct would be to separate it from other constructs in the theory or related theories. To the extent that ceremony could be separated from stories or symbols, we would have completed the first steps toward *discriminant* validity. Established statistical tools such as factor analysis and multitrait-multimethod analysis help determine the construct adequacy of a measuring device.[21]

In the Prince Corporation study, you may be interested in securing a judgment of "how good a citizen" the corporation is. Variations in respondent ratings may be drastically affected if the respondents have substantial differences in opinion about what constitutes proper corporate citizenship. One respondent may believe that any company is an economic organization designed to make profits for its stockholders. She sees relatively little role for corporations in the wide-ranging social issues of the day. Another respondent, at the other end of the continuum, views the corporation as a leader in solving social problems, even at the cost of profits.

Both of these respondents might understand Prince's role in the community but judge it quite differently in light of their views about what the role should be. If these different views were held, you would theorize that other information about these respondents would be logically compatible with their judgments. You might expect the first respondent to oppose high corporate taxes, to be critical of increased involvement of government in family affairs, and to believe that a corporation's major responsibility is to its stockholders. The second respondent would be more likely to favor high corporate income taxes, to opt for more governmental involvement in daily life, and to believe that a corporation's major responsibility is a social one.

Respondents may not be consistent on all questions because the measurements may be crude and the "theory" may be deficient. When hypothesized tests do not confirm the measurement scale, you are faced with a two-edged question: Is your measurement instrument invalid, or is your theory invalid? Answers require more information or the exercise of judgment.

The three forms of validity have been discussed separately, but they are interrelated, both theoretically and operationally. Predictive validity is important for a test designed to predict employee success. In developing such a test, you would probably first postulate the factors (constructs) that provide the basis for useful prediction. For example, you would advance a theory about the variable in employee success—an area for construct validity. Finally, in developing the specific items for inclusion in the success prediction test, you would be concerned with how well the specific items sample the full range of each construct (a matter of content validity).

In the corporate image study for the Prince Corporation, both content and construct validity considerations have been discussed, but what about criterion-related validity? The criteria are less obvious than in the employee success prediction, but judgments will be made of the quality of evidence about the company's image. The criteria used may be subjective (Does the evidence agree with what we believe?) and objective (Does the evidence agree with other research findings?). (See Figure 7–2.)

Reliability

Reliability means many things to many people, but in most contexts the notion of consistency emerges. A measure is reliable to the degree that it supplies consistent results. **Reliability** is a contributor to validity and is a necessary but not sufficient condition for validity. The relationship between reliability and validity can be simply illustrated with the use of a bathroom scale. If the scale measures your weight correctly (using a concurrent criterion such as a scale known to be accurate), then it is both reliable and valid. If it consistently overweighs you by six pounds, then the scale is reliable but not valid. If the scale measures erratically from time to time, then it is not reliable and therefore cannot be valid.

Reliability is concerned with estimates of the degree to which a measurement is free of random or unstable error. It is not as valuable as validity determination, but it is much easier to assess. Reliable instruments can be used with confidence that transient and situational factors are not interfering. Reliable instruments are robust; they work well at different times under different conditions. This distinction of time and condition is the basis for frequently used perspectives on reliability—**stability, equivalence,** and **internal consistency** (see Figure 7–3).

Stability   A measure is said to be stable if you can secure consistent results with repeated measurements of the same person with the same instrument. An observational

FIGURE   7–3   Summary of Reliability Estimates

Type	*Coefficient*	*What Is Measured*	*Methods*
Test-retest	Stability	Reliability of a test or instrument inferred from examinee scores. Same test is administered twice to same subjects over an interval of less than six months.	Correlation
Parallel forms	Equivalence	Degree to which alternative forms of the same measure produce same or similar results. Administered simultaneously or with a delay. Interrater estimates of the similarity of judges' observations or scores.	Correlation
Split-half KR20 Cronbach's alpha	Internal consistency	Degree to which instrument items are homogeneous and reflect the same underlying construct(s).	Specialized correlational formulas

procedure is stable if it gives the same reading on a particular person when repeated one or more times. It is often possible to repeat observations on a subject and to compare them for consistency. When there is much time between measurements, there is a chance for situational factors to change, thereby affecting the observations. The change would appear incorrectly as a drop in reliability of the measurement process.

Stability measurement in survey situations is more difficult and less easily executed than in observational studies. While you can observe a certain action repeatedly, you usually can resurvey only once. This leads to a test-retest arrangement—with comparisons between the two tests to learn how reliable they are. Difficulties occur beyond the time delay mentioned with the observation study. If the retest is given too quickly, the respondent will remember the answers already given and repeat them. This results in biased reliability indicators. The test-retest process may introduce bias if the respondent becomes savvy to the testing purpose. Or the first test sensitizes the respondent to the topic, and the respondent may then go on to learn more or form new and different opinions before the retest. Finally, opinions change from situational influences between the tests. In these cases, there is a downward bias in the stability scores.

A suggested remedy is to extend the interval between test and retest (from two weeks to a month). While this may help, the researcher must be alert to the chance an outside factor will contaminate the measurement and distort the stability score. Consequently, stability measurement through the test-retest approach has limited applications. More interest has centered on equivalence.

Equivalence   A second perspective on reliability considers how much error may be introduced by different investigators (in observation) or different samples of items being studied (in questioning or scales). Thus, while stability is concerned with personal and situational fluctuations from one time to another, equivalence is concerned with variations at one point in time among observers and samples of items. A good way to test for the equivalence of measurements by different observers is to compare their scoring of the same event. An example of this is the scoring of Olympic figure skaters by a panel of judges.

In studies where a consensus among experts or observers is required, the similarity of the judges' perceptions is sometimes questioned. How does a panel of supervisors render a judgment on merit raises, a new product's packaging, or future business trends? *Interrater* reliability may be used in these cases to correlate the observations or scores of the judges and render an index of how consistent their ratings are. In Olympic figure skating, a judge's relative positioning of skaters (by establishing a rank order for each judge and comparing each judge's ordering for all skaters) is a means of measuring equivalence.

The major interest with equivalence is typically not how respondents differ from item to item but how well a given set of items will categorize individuals. There may be many differences in response between two samples of items, but if a person is classified the same way by each test, then the tests have good equivalence.

One tests for item sample equivalence by using alternative or *parallel forms* of the same test administered to the same persons simultaneously. The results of the two tests are then correlated. Under this condition, the length of the testing process is likely to affect the subjects' responses through fatigue, and the inferred reliability of the parallel form will be reduced accordingly. Some measurement theorists recommend an interval between administrations to compensate for this problem. This approach, called *delayed* equivalent forms, is a composite of test-retest and the equivalence method. As in test-retest, one would administer form X followed by form Y to half the examinees and form Y followed by form X to the other half to prevent "order-of-presentation" effects.[22]

The test items to be included in any instrument are limited in number. This limitation implies that a sample of items from a content domain has been chosen and another sample producing a similar number will need to be drawn. It is frequently difficult to create this second set. Yet if the pool is initially large enough, the items may be randomly selected for each instrument. Even with more sophisticated procedures used by publishers of standardized tests, it is rare to find fully equivalent and interchangeable forms.[23]

Internal Consistency   A third approach to reliability uses only one administration of an instrument or test to assess consistency or homogeneity among the items. The *split-half* technique can be used when the measuring tool has many similar questions or statements to which the subject can respond. The instrument is administered and the results are separated by item into even and odd numbers or into randomly selected halves. If the results of the correlation are high, the instrument is said to have high reliability in an internal consistency sense; however, the longer the length of the test, the higher is the reliability. The Spearman-Brown correction formula is used to adjust for the effect of test length and to estimate reliability of the whole test.

A problem with this approach is that the way the test is split may influence the internal consistency coefficient. To remedy this, other indices are used to secure reliability estimates without splitting the test's items. The Kuder-Richardson Formula 20 and Cronbach's Coefficient Alpha are two frequently used examples. Cronbach's alpha has the most utility for multi-item scales at the interval level of measurement. The KR20 is the method from which alpha was generalized and is used to estimate reliability for dichotomous items. (See Figure 7–3.)

Improving Reliability   One can improve reliability if external sources of variation are minimized and the conditions under which the measurement occurs are standardized. You can achieve enhanced equivalence through improved investigator consistency by using only well-trained, supervised, and motivated persons to conduct the research. Much can be done to improve equivalence by broadening the sample of items used. You can do this by adding similar questions to the questionnaire or adding more observers or occasions to an observational study.

With measurement instruments such as achievement, attitude, or employment tests, we can often increase equivalence by improving the internal consistency of the test. This approach requires the assumption that a high total score reflects high performance and a low total score, low performance. One selects the extreme scorers—say, the top 20 percent and bottom 20 percent—for individual analysis. By this process, you can distinguish those items that differentiate high and low scorers. Items that have little discriminatory power can then be dropped from the test.

Practicality   The scientific requirements of a project call for the measurement process to be reliable and valid, while the operational requirements call for it to be practical. *Practicality* has been defined as *economy, convenience,* and *interpretability.*[24] While this definition refers to the development of educational and psychological tests, it is meaningful for business measurements as well.

Economy   Some trade-off is usually needed between the ideal research project and the budget. Instrument length is one area where economic pressures are quickly felt. More items give more reliability, but in the interest of limiting the interview or observation time (therefore costs), we hold the item number down. The choice of data collection method is also often dictated by economic factors. The use of long-distance telephone surveys has been strongly influenced by the rising costs of personal interviewing. In standardized tests, the cost of test materials alone can be such a significant expense that it encourages multiple reuse. Add to this the need for fast and economical scoring, and we see why computer scoring and scanning are attractive.

Convenience   A measuring device passes the *convenience* test if it is easy to administer. A questionnaire with a set of detailed but clear instructions, with examples, is easier to complete correctly than one that lacks these features. In a well-prepared study, it is not uncommon for the interviewer instructions to be several times longer than the interview questions. Naturally, the more complex the concepts, the greater is the need for clear and complete instructions. We can also make the instrument easier to administer by giving close attention to its design and layout. Crowding of material, poor reproductions of illustrations, and the carryover of items from one page to the next make completion of the instrument more difficult.

Interpretability   This aspect of practicality is relevant when persons other than the test designers must interpret the results. It is usually but not exclusively an issue with standardized tests. In such cases, several key pieces of information make interpretation possible:

- A statement of the functions the test was designed to measure and the procedures by which it was developed
- Detailed instructions for administration
- Scoring keys and scoring instructions
- Norms for appropriate reference groups
- Evidence about reliability
- Evidence on the intercorrelations of subscores
- Evidence on the relationship of the test to other measures
- Guides for test use

CLOSE-UP

Earlier, Jason Henry agreed to send the executive director at White Ice some useful tools for measuring job satisfaction and motivation. In reviewing his files, he found Martin Patchen's *Some Questionnaire Measures of Employee Motivation and Morale*, Monograph No. 41 (Ann Arbor: Institute for Social Research, University of Michigan, 1965). The table of contents showed that the monograph included indices on Interest in Work Innovation, Job Motivation, Acceptance of Job Changes, Willingness to Disagree with Supervisors, and Identification with the Work Organization.

Patchen's study had been conducted at five geographically separate units of the Tennessee Valley Authority, three divisions of an electronics company, and five departments of an appliance manufacturing company. The procedure for developing the measures was first to hold a number of informal interviews with supervisory and nonsupervisory employees. From the knowledge acquired, the researchers constructed the questions. These were then pretested and revised twice on separate groups of TVA employees. Out of this process came the six-item questionnaire on interest in work innovation shown in Figure 7–4. This instrument and the others were completed by employees of the three companies. Reliability of the Index of Interest in Work Innovation was measured by a test-retest of individual questions. The retest was done one month after the first test. Correlating the test-retest scores question by question gave the following results (see Chapter 17 for more information on computing a correlation coefficient):

Question	r
Q1	.72
Q2	.72
Q3	.64
Q4	.67
Q5	.54
Q6	.85

The researchers measured criterion-based validity by comparing worker scores on the six questions to ratings of the same workers by their supervisors. Supervisors were asked to "think of specific instances where employees in their units had suggested new or better ways of doing the job. They then ranked employees they personally knew on 'looking out for new ideas.'"[25] The median correlation between index scores and the supervisor ratings was about .35. At TVA, where there was an active suggestion system in operation, they also found that the index scores of those making suggestions were significantly higher than those not making suggestions.

Construct validity was evaluated by comparing scores on the Interest in Work Innovation Index to other job-related variables. Group mean scores on the index were computed for 90 work groups at TVA. These means were then correlated with group scores on other variables that were hypothesized to relate to interest in innovation. The results are shown in Table 7–1.

The researchers concluded, "The Index of Interest in Work Innovation, while a rough one, shows adequate reliability and sufficient evidence of validity to warrant its use in making rough distinctions among groups of people (or among units)."[26] In addition, they tested a short version of the index (items 1, 5, and 6) and found its validity to be almost equal to that of the longer form.

Having reviewed Patchen's research study with its derived indices, Jason forwarded what he

(continued)

FIGURE   7–4   Interest in Work Innovation Index*

1. In your kind of work, if a person tries to change his usual way of doing things, how does it generally turn out?
    - (1) _____ Usually turns out worse; the tried and true methods work best in my work.
    - (3) _____ Usually doesn't make much difference.
    - (5) _____ Usually turns out better; our methods need improvement.
2. Some people prefer doing a job in pretty much the same way because this way they can count on always doing a good job. Others like to go out of their way in order to think up new ways of doing things. How is it with you on your job?
    - (1) _____ I always prefer doing things pretty much in the same way.
    - (2) _____ I mostly prefer doing things pretty much in the same way.
    - (4) _____ I mostly prefer doing things in new and different ways.
    - (5) _____ I always prefer doing things in new and different ways.
3. How often do you try out, on your own, a better or faster way of doing something on the job?
    - (5) _____ Once a week or more often.
    - (4) _____ Two or three times a month.
    - (3) _____ About once a month.
    - (2) _____ Every few months.
    - (1) _____ Rarely or never.
4. How often do you get chances to try out your own ideas on the job, either before or after checking with your supervisor?
    - (5) _____ Several times a week or more.
    - (4) _____ About once a week.
    - (3) _____ Several times a month.
    - (2) _____ About once a month.
    - (1) _____ Less than once a month.
5. In my kind of job, it's usually better to let your supervisor worry about new or better ways of doing things.
    - (1) _____ Strongly agree.
    - (2) _____ Mostly agree.
    - (4) _____ Mostly disagree.
    - (5) _____ Strongly disagree.
6. How many times in the past year have you suggested to your supervisor a different or better way of doing something on the job?
    - (1) _____ Never had occasion to do this during the past year.
    - (2) _____ Once or twice.
    - (3) _____ About three times.
    - (4) _____ About five times.
    - (5) _____ Six to ten times.
    - (6) _____ More than ten times had occasion to do this during the past year.

*Numbers in parentheses preceding each response category indicate the score assigned to each response.
SOURCE: Martin Patchen, *Some Questionnaire Measures of Employee Motivation and Morale*, Monograph No. 41 (Ann Arbor, MI: Institute for Social Research, The University of Michigan, 1965), pp. 15–16.

found to the symphony director. She would decide if it was adaptable or if she should develop her own instrument. Managers and researchers frequently assume they need a device tailored to their unique situation. This decision can be costly and time-consuming. Reliability testing may be

TABLE 7–1   **Relation of Scores on Interest in Work Innovation Index* to Scores on Other Job-Related Variables† for 90 Work Groups at TVA (Pearson product-moment correlation coefficient, r)**

Variable Name

1. Job difficulty	.44‡
2. Identification with own occupation	.39‡
3. Control over work methods	.29‡
4. Perceived opportunity for achievement	.28‡
5. Feedback on performance	.19
6. Control over goals in work	.13
7. Need for achievement§	.06
8. Pressure from peers to do a good job	−.05
9. General job motivation	.36‡
10. Willingness to disagree with supervisors	.36‡
11. Acceptance of changes in work situation	.12
12. Identification with TVA	.00
13. Overall satisfaction (with pay, promotion, supervisors, and peers)	.21‖

*The shorter three-item Index B was used for these correlations.

†Variables listed are all indices; each index is composed of several specific questions.

‡$p < .01$, 2-tailed t-test.

§This is the Achievement Risk Preference Scale developed by P. O'Conner and J. W. Atkinson (1960).

‖$p < .05$, 2-tailed t-test.

SOURCE: Martin Patchen, *Some Questionnaire Measures of Employee Motivation and Morale*, Monograph No. 41 (Ann Arbor, MI: Institute for Social Research, The University of Michigan, 1965), p. 24.

ignored and validity assessments may be confined to impressions about content. Typically, there is no comparable evidence from other studies by which to calibrate the findings.

If Jason's recommendation proves to be inadequate, a further search of existing measures will reveal many established ones that might fit the director's needs. Most are copyrighted but available from commercial sources.

Summary

While people measure things casually in daily life, research measurement is more precise and controlled. In measurement, one settles for measuring properties of the objects rather than the objects themselves. An event is measured in terms of its duration. What happened during it, who was involved, where it occurred, and so forth, are all properties of the event. To be more precise, what are measured are indicants of the properties. Thus, for duration, one measures the number of hours and minutes recorded. For what happened, one uses some system to classify types of activities that occurred. Measurement typically uses some sort of scale to classify or quantify the data collected.

There are four scale types. In increasing order of power, they are nominal, ordinal, interval, and ratio. Nominal scales classify without indicating order, distance, or unique origin. Ordinal data show magnitude relationships of more than and less than but have no distance or unique origin. Interval scales have both order and distance but no unique origin. Ratio scales possess all features.

Instruments may yield incorrect readings of an indicant for many reasons. These may be classified according to error sources: (1) the respondent or subject, (2) situational factors, (3) the measurer, and (4) the instrument.

Sound measurement must meet the tests of validity, reliability, and practicality. Validity is the most critical and reveals the degree to which an instrument measures what it is supposed to measure. Three forms of validity are used to evaluate measurement scales. Content validity exists to the degree that a measure provides an adequate reflection of the topic under study. Its determination is primarily judgmental and intuitive. Criterion-related validity relates to our ability to predict some outcome or estimate the existence of some current condition. Construct validity is the most complex and abstract. A measure has construct validity to the degree that it conforms to predicted correlations of other theoretical propositions.

A measure is reliable if it provides consistent results. Reliability is a partial contributor to validity, but a measurement tool may be reliable without being valid. Three forms of reliability are stability, equivalence, and internal consistency. A measure meets the fourth criterion, practicality, if it is economical, convenient, and interpretable.

Key Terms

interval data	reliability
mapping rule	equivalence
measurement	internal consistency
nominal data	stability
objects	validity
ordinal data	construct
practicality	content
properties	criterion-related
ratio data	

Discussion Questions

1. What can we measure about the four objects listed below? Be as specific as possible.
   a. Laundry detergent
   b. Employees
   c. Factory output
   d. Job satisfaction

2. What are the essential differences among nominal, ordinal, interval, and ratio scales? How do these differences affect the statistical analysis techniques we can use?

3. You have data from a corporation on the annual salary of each of its 200 employees.

    a. Illustrate how the data can be presented as ratio, interval, ordinal, and nominal data.

    b. Describe the successive loss of information as the presentation changes from ratio to nominal.

4. Below are listed some objects of varying degrees of abstraction. Suggest properties of each of these objects that can be measured by each of the four basic types of scales.

    a. Store customers

    b. Voter attitudes

    c. Hardness of steel alloys

    d. Preference for a particular common stock

    e. Profitability of various divisions in a company

5. What are the four major sources of measurement error? Illustrate by example how each of these might affect measurement results in a face-to-face interview situation.

6. Do you agree or disagree with the following statements? Explain.

    a. Validity is more critical to measurement than is reliability.

    b. Content validity is the most difficult type of validity to determine.

    c. A valid measurement is reliable, but a reliable measurement may not be valid.

    d. Stability and equivalence are essentially the same thing.

7. You have been asked to design an instrument by which students can evaluate the quality and value of their various courses. How might you try to ensure that your instrument has

    a. Stability

    b. Equivalence

    c. Internal consistency

    d. Content validity

    e. Predictive validity

    f. Construct validity

8. A book titled *The 100 Best Companies to Work for in America* has just been published. In their study of companies, the authors chose five dimensions and rated each company on them, giving one to five stars to a firm on each dimension. What five dimensions would you use if you had designed their rating system?

9. You have been asked to develop an index of student morale at your school.

    a. What constructs or concepts might you employ?

    b. Choose several of the major concepts and specify their dimensions.

  c. Select observable indicators that you might use to measure these dimensions.

  d. How would you compile these various dimensions into a single index?

  e. How would you judge the reliability and/or validity of these measurements?

Reference Notes

1. Fred N. Kerlinger, *Foundations of Behavioral Research,* 3rd ed. (New York: Holt, Rinehart & Winston, 1986), p. 396; and S. Stevens, "Measurement, Statistics, and the Schemapiric View," *Science* (August 1968), p. 3844.

2. W. S. Torgerson, *Theory and Method of Scaling* (New York: Wiley, 1958), p. 19.

3. We assume the reader has had an introductory statistics course in which measures of central tendency such as arithmetic mean, median, and mode have been treated. Similarly, we assume familiarity with measures of dispersion such as the standard deviation, range, and interquartile range. For a brief review of these concepts, refer to Chapter 15 or see an introductory statistics text.

4. While this might intuitively seem to be the case, consider that one might prefer *a* over *b*, *b* over *c*, yet *c* over *a*. These results cannot be scaled ordinally because there is apparently more than one dimension involved.

5. L. L. Thurstone, *The Measurement of Values* (Chicago: University of Chicago Press, 1959).

6. Parametric tests are appropriate when the measurement is interval or ratio and when we can accept certain assumptions about the underlying distributions of the data with which we are working. Nonparametric tests usually involve much weaker assumptions about measurement scales (nominal and ordinal), and the assumptions about the underlying distribution of the population are fewer and less restrictive. More on these tests is found in Chapters 15, 16, 17, and Appendix E.

7. Sidney Siegel, *Nonparametric Statistics for the Behavioral Sciences* (New York: McGraw-Hill, 1956), p. 32.

8. Norman A. Anderson, "Scales and Statistics: Parametric and Nonparametric," *Psychological Bulletin* 58, no. 4, pp. 315–16.

9. Kerlinger, *Foundations,* p. 403.

10. See Chapter 8 for a discussion of the differential scale.

11. See Chapters 16 and 17 for a discussion of these procedures.

12. The exception involves the creation of a dummy variable for use in a regression or discriminant equation. A nonmetric variable is transformed into a metric variable through the assignment of a 0 or 1 and used in a predictive equation.

13. Claire Selltiz, Lawrence S. Wrightsman, and Stuart W. Cook, *Research Methods in Social Relations,* 3rd ed. (New York: Holt, Rinehart & Winston, 1976), pp. 164–69.

14. Robert L. Thorndike and Elizabeth Hagen, *Measurement and Evaluation in Psychology and Education,* 3rd ed. (New York: Wiley, 1969), p. 5.

15. Examples of other conceptualizations of validity are factorial validity, job-analytic validity, synthetic validity, rational validity, and statistical conclusion validity.

16. Thomas D. Cook and Donald T. Campbell, "The Design and Conduct of Quasi Experiments and True Experiments in Field Settings," in *Handbook of Industrial and Organizational Psychology,* ed. Marvin D. Dunnette (Chicago: Rand McNally, 1976), p. 223.

17. *Standards for Educational and Psychological Tests and Manuals* (Washington, D.C.: American Psychological Association, 1974), p. 26.
18. Wayne F. Cascio, *Applied Psychology in Personnel Management* (Reston, VA: Reston Publishing, 1982), p. 149.
19. Thorndike and Hagen, *Measurement,* p. 168.
20. See, for example, Cascio, *Applied Psychology,* pp. 146–47; and Edward G. Carmines and Richard A. Zeller, *Reliability and Validity Assessment* (Beverly Hills, CA: Sage Publications, 1979), pp. 48–50.
21. Emanuel J. Mason and William J. Bramble, *Understanding and Conducting Research* (New York: McGraw-Hill, 1989), pp. 260–63.
22. Cascio, *Applied Psychology,* pp. 135–36.
23. Mason and Bramble, *Understanding and Conducting Research,* p. 268.
24. Thorndike and Hagen, *Measurement,* p. 199.
25. Martin Patchen, *Some Questionnaire Measures of Employee Motivation and Morale,* Monograph No. 41 (Ann Arbor: Institute for Social Research, University of Michigan, 1965), p. 17.
26. Ibid., p. 25.

Suggested Readings

1. Cascio, Wayne F. *Applied Psychology in Personnel Management,* 4th ed. Englewood Cliffs, NJ: Prentice Hall, 1990.
2. Cook, Thomas D., and Donald T. Campbell. "The Design and Conduct of Quasi Experiments and True Experiments in Field Settings." In *Handbook of Industrial and Organizational Psychology,* ed. Marvin D. Dunnette. Chicago: Rand McNally, 1976, chap. 7.
3. Guilford, J. P. *Psychometric Methods,* 2nd ed. New York: McGraw-Hill, 1954.
4. Kerlinger, Fred N. *Foundations of Behavioral Research,* 3rd ed. New York: Holt, Rinehart & Winston, 1986, chaps. 25, 26, and 27.
5. Newmark, C. S. *Major Psychological Assessment Instruments.* Boston: Allyn and Bacon, 1989.
6. Nunnally, J. C. *Psychometric Theory,* 2nd ed. New York: McGraw-Hill, 1978.
7. Thorndike, Robert L., and Elizabeth Hagen. *Measurement and Evaluation in Psychology and Education,* 3rd ed. New York: Wiley, 1969.

8   SCALING DESIGN

CHAPTER NAVIGATION

BRINGING RESEARCH TO LIFE

They boarded the sleek corporate jet in Palm Beach and were taken aft to meet with the general manager of MindWriter, who was seated at a conference table that austerely held one sheaf of papers and a white telephone.

"I'm Jean-Claude Malraison," the general manager said. "Myra, please sit here . . . and you must be Jason Henry. On the flight up from Caracas I read your proposal for the CompleteCare project, and I am going to take my staff's word that it is OK, except maybe I don't like the schedule. Here is your contract, which I intend to sign if you answer one question to my satisfaction about the schedule.

"The rules are, I took marketing research in college and didn't like it, so you talk fast, straight, and plainly unless we both decide we need to get technical. If the phone rings, ignore it and keep talking. When you answer my one question I put you off the plane in the first Florida city that has a commercial flight back to . . . to. . . ."

"This is Palm Beach, Jean-Claude," said the steward.

"We'll let you off somewhere you can get home from. Fair enough?"

"Yes," said Jason and Myra.

"What I don't like is that you are going to hold everything up so you can develop a scale for the questionnaire. Scaling is what I didn't like in marketing research. It is complicated and it takes too much time. Why can't you use some of the scales our marketing people have been using? Why do you have to reinvent the wheel?" The manager jabbed a finger toward Myra.

"Our research staff agrees with us that it would be inappropriate to adopt surveys developed for use in our consumer products line," said Myra smoothly.

"OK. Computers are not the same as toaster ovens and VCRs. Gotcha. Jason, what is going to be different about the scales you intend to develop?"

"When we held focus groups with your customers, they continually referred to the need for your product service to 'meet expectations' or 'ex-

ceed expectations.' The hundredth time we heard this we realized . . . ."

"It's our company credo, 'Underpromise and exceed expectations.'"

"Well, virtually none of the scales developed for customer satisfaction deal with expectations. We want a scale that ranges in five steps from 'Met few expectations' to 'Exceeded expectations,' but we don't know what to name the in-between intervals so that the psychological spacing is equal between increments. We think 'Met many expectations' and 'Met most expectations' and 'Fully met expectations' will be OK, but we want to be sure."

"You are not being fussy here, are you, Jason?"

"No. Because of the way you are running your service operation, we want great precision and reliability."

"Justify that, please, Myra."

"Well, Jean-Claude, besides setting up your own repair force, you have contracted with an outside organization to provide repairs in certain areas, with the intention after six months of comparing the performance of the inside and outside repair organizations and giving the future work to whomever performs better. We feel that such an important decision, which involves the job security of your employees, must have full credibility."

"I can accept that. Good." The manager scribbled a signature on the contract. "You'll receive this contract in three days, after it has wended its way past the paper pushers. Meantime, you settle for a handshake. Nice job, so far, Myra. You seem to have gotten a quick start with MindWriter. Congratulations, Jason."

"We can put them down in Orlando," said the steward.

"No," said Jean-Claude. "We are only five minutes out. Turn the plane around and put these folks out where they got on. They can start working this afternoon. . . . Gosh, is that the beach out there? It looks great. I've got to get some sun one of these days."

"You do look pale," said Myra, sympathetically.

"Fais gaffe, tu m'fais mal!" he muttered under his breath.

183

THE NATURE OF SCALING

Business research concepts (constructs) are frequently complex and abstract while the available measurement tools can be crude or imprecise. We want a valid measurement, but we get something between the true score and the test score. When the object is a concrete concept and the measurement tool is standardized, the variation between the true and test scores will be small. This is like the accuracy you would expect in measuring the length of a table with a yardstick. If the concept is abstract (attitudes toward various institutions) and the measurement tool is not standardized (questions about attitudes), then you will not be confident that the test results reflect true scores. This is comparable to measuring a table using your forearm rather than a tape measure.

This chapter covers procedures that will help you understand and construct measurement scales. We concentrate on the problems of measuring attitudes and opinions. Similar principles hold for measuring in the physical realm.

Scaling Defined

Scaling is a "procedure for the assignment of numbers (or other symbols) to a property of objects in order to impart some of the characteristics of numbers to the properties in question."[1] Thus, one assigns a number scale to the various levels of heat and cold and calls it a thermometer.

What Is Scaled? Procedurally, we assign numbers to *indicants* of the properties of objects. If you want to measure the temperature of the air, you know that a property of temperature is that its variation leads to an expansion or contraction of materials such as mercury. You devise a glass tube arrangement with mercury. It provides an indicant of the temperature by the rise and fall of the mercury column in the tube as temperature changes.

In another context, you might devise a scale to measure the durability (property) of paint. You secure a machine with an attached scrub brush that applies a predetermined amount of pressure as it scrubs. You then count the number of brush strokes that it takes to wear through a 10-mil thickness of paint. The scrub count is the indicant of the paint's durability. Or you may judge a person's supervisory capacity (property) by asking a peer group to rate that person on various questions (indicants) that you create.

Scale Classification

Scaling may be reviewed in several ways, but we cover those approaches that are of greatest value for management research.[2] Selection of a scale requires decisions in six key areas.

Study Objective A scale may be designed to (1) measure the characteristics of the respondents who complete it or (2) use respondents as judges of the objects or stimuli presented to them. You might present people with a scale on government regulatory programs to capture their approval or disapproval of each program. If the respondents themselves are of primary interest, you might combine each person's answers to form an indicator of that person's conservatism or political orientation. The emphasis here is on measuring attitudinal differences among people. With the second study objective, you use the same data but are interested in how people view different government programs. In this instance, the emphasis is on the differences among regulatory programs.

Response Scales   Scales are either *rating* or *ranking.* **Rating scales** have multiple response categories and are also known as *category scales.* They are used when respondents score an object or attitude without making a direct comparison to another object or attitude. For example, they may be asked to rate the styling of a new automobile on a five-point scale. **Ranking scales** make comparisons among two or more attitudes or objects. Respondents may be asked to choose which one of a pair of cars has more attractive styling. They could also be asked to order the importance of comfort, ergonomics, performance, and price for the target vehicle.

Degree of Preference   Scaling approaches may involve *preference* measurement or *nonpreference* evaluation. In the former, respondents are asked to choose the object each favors or the solution each would prefer. In the latter, they are asked to judge which object has more of some characteristic or which solution takes the most resources, without reflecting any personal preference toward objects or solutions.

Scale Properties   Scaling approaches may also be viewed in terms of the data properties possessed by each scale. Chapter 7 said data are classified as nominal, ordinal, interval, or ratio. The assumptions underlying each data type determine how the scale created for that type of data could be used statistically.

Number of Dimensions   Scales are either *unidimensional* or *multidimensional.* With a **unidimensional scale,** one seeks to measure only one attribute of the respondent or object. One measure of employee potential is promotability. It is a single dimension. Several items may be used to measure this dimension, and by combining them into a single measure, a manager may place employees along a linear continuum of promotability. **Multidimensional scaling** recognizes that an object might be better described in an attribute space of *n* dimensions rather than on a unidimensional continuum. The employee promotability variable might be better expressed by three distinct dimensions—managerial performance, technical performance, and teamwork.

Scale Construction   We can classify scales by the methods used to build them. There are five scale design techniques.[3] The *arbitrary* approach develops the scale on an ad hoc basis. Such scales may measure the concepts for which they have been designed, but we have little evidence of this. Nevertheless, arbitrary construction is a universal practice.

A second construction approach is the *consensus* scale. A panel of judges evaluates the items to be included in the instrument based on topical relevance and lack of ambiguity. A third technique is through *item analysis.* Individual items are developed for a test that is given to a group of respondents. After administering the tests, total scores are calculated. Individual items are then analyzed to determine which ones discriminate between persons or objects with high total scores and low total scores.

Cumulative scales are chosen for their conformity to a ranking of items with ascending and descending discriminating power. In such a scale, the endorsement of an item that represents an extreme position results in the endorsement of all items of less extreme positions. Finally, *factor* scales are constructed from intercorrelations of items. Common factors account for the relationships. The relationships are measured statistically through factor analysis or cluster analysis.

The type of response scale and the scale's construction are key ingredients affecting selection for the business researcher. These topics form the basis for the remainder of the chapter.

RESPONSE METHODS

In Chapter 7, we said that questioning is a widely used stimulus for measuring concepts. A manager may be asked his or her views concerning an employee. The response is, " a good machinist," "a troublemaker," "a union activist," "reliable," or "a fast worker with a poor record of attendance." These answers represent different frames of reference for evaluating the worker and are often of limited value to the researcher.

Two approaches improve the usefulness of such replies. First, various properties may be separated and the respondent asked to judge each specific facet. Here, several questions are substituted for a single one. Second, we can replace the free-response reply with structuring devices. To quantify dimensions that are essentially qualitative, *rating scales* or *ranking scales* are used.

Rating Scales

One uses rating scales to judge properties of objects without reference to other similar objects. These ratings may be in such forms as "like-dislike," "approve-indifferent-disapprove," or other classifications using even more categories. There is little conclusive support for choosing a three-point scale over scales with five or more points. Some researchers think that more points on a rating scale provide an opportunity for greater sensitivity of measurement and extraction of variance. The most widely used scales range from three to seven points, but it does not seem to make much difference which number is used—with two exceptions.[4] First, a larger number of scale points is needed to produce accuracy with single-item versus multiple-item scales. Second, in cross-cultural measurement, the culture may condition respondents to a standard metric—a ten-point scale in Italy, for example.

Examples of rating scales are shown Figure 8–1. This figure amplifies the overview described in this section.[5] Later in the chapter, construction techniques for some commonly used rating scales are presented.

The **simple category scale** has two response choices. In Figure 8–1, they are *yes* and *no* but could just as easily be *important* and *unimportant, agree* and *disagree,* or another set of *discrete* categories had the question been different. This scale is particularly useful for demographic questions or where a *dichotomous* response is adequate.

FIGURE   8–1   Rating Scales

Simple Category Scale (dichotomous)	"I plan to purchase a MindWriter laptop in the next 12 months." ☐ yes ☐ no
Multiple Choice Single Response Scale	"What newspaper do you read most often for financial news?" ☐ East City Gazette ☐ West City Tribune ☐ Regional Newspaper ☐ National Newspaper ☐ Other (specify: _____)
Multiple Choice Multiple Response Scale	"Check *any* of the sources you consulted when designing your new home:" ☐ Online planning services ☐ Magazines ☐ Independent contractor/builder ☐ Developer's models/plans ☐ Designer ☐ Architect ☐ Other (specify: _____)

Likert Scale
Summated Rating

"The Internet is superior to traditional libraries for comprehensive searches."

STRONGLY AGREE	AGREE	NEITHER AGREE NOR DISAGREE	DISAGREE	STRONGLY DISAGREE
(5)	(4)	(3)	(2)	(1)

Semantic Differential
Scale

Lands' End Catalog

FAST ___ : ___ : ___ : ___ : ___ : ___ : ___ : SLOW
HIGH QUALITY ___ : ___ : ___ : ___ : ___ : ___ : ___ : LOW QUALITY

Numerical Scale

EXTREMELY FAVORABLE	5	4	3	2	1	EXTREMELY UNFAVORABLE

Employee's cooperation in teams ___
Employee's knowledge of task ___
Employee's planning effectiveness ___

FIGURE 8–1   (*concluded*)

Multiple Rating List Scale	"Please indicate how important or unimportant each service characteristic is:"

	IMPORTANT						UNIMPORTANT
Fast reliable repair	7	6	5	4	3	2	1
Service at my location	7	6	5	4	3	2	1
Maintenance by manufacturer	7	6	5	4	3	2	1
Knowledgeable technicians	7	6	5	4	3	2	1
Notification of upgrades	7	6	5	4	3	2	1
Service contract after warranty	7	6	5	4	3	2	1

Fixed Sum Scale

"Taking all the supplier characteristics we've just discussed and now considering *cost*, what is their relative importance to you (dividing 100 units between):"

Being one of the lowest cost suppliers	
All other aspects of supplier performance	
sum	100

Stapel Scale

(Company Name)

+5	+5	+5
+4	+4	+4
+3	+3	+3
+2	+2	+2
+1	+1	+1
Technology Leader	Exciting Products	World-Class Reputation
−1	−1	−1
−2	−2	−2
−3	−3	−3
−4	−4	−4
−5	−5	−5

Graphic Rating Scale

"How likely are you to recommend CompleteCare to others?" (place an X at the position along the line that best reflects your judgment)

VERY LIKELY |————————————————————————| VERY UNLIKELY

(alternative with graphic)

When there are multiple options for the rater and only one answer is sought, the **multiple choice, single response scale** is appropriate. Our example has five options. The primary alternatives should encompass 90 percent of the range with the "other" category completing the respondent's list. When there is no possibility for "other" or exhaustiveness of categories is not critical, this response may be omitted. Both this example and the *simple category scale* produce nominal data.

A variation, the **multiple choice, multiple response scale** allows the rater to select one or several alternatives. In this example we are asking seven questions, and it is possible that all seven sources for home design were consulted. The cumulative feature of this scale can be beneficial when a complete picture of the respondent's choices is desired, but it may also present a problem for reporting when readers expect the responses to sum to 100 percent. This scale generates nominal data.

The **Likert scale** is the most frequently used variation of the *summated rating scale*. Summated scales consist of statements that express either a favorable or unfavorable attitude toward the object of interest. The respondent is asked to agree or disagree with each statement. Each response is given a numerical score to reflect its degree of attitude favorableness, and the scores may be totaled to measure the respondent's attitude.

In this example, the respondent chooses one of five levels of agreement. The numbers indicate the value to be assigned to each possible answer with 1 the least favorable impression of Internet superiority and 5 the most favorable. These values are normally not printed on the instrument but are shown in Figure 8–1 to indicate the scoring system. Between 20 and 25 properly constructed questions about an attitude object would be required for a reliable Likert scale.

Likert scales help us compare one person's score with a distribution of scores from a well-defined group. They are also useful when we expect to conduct an experiment or undertake a program of change or improvement. We can measure attitudes before and after the experiment, or judge whether our efforts have had the desired effects. This scale produces interval data.

The **semantic differential** measures the psychological meanings of an attitude object. It is used by managers for brand image and other marketing studies of institutional images, political issues and personalities, and organizational studies. It is based on the proposition that an object can have several dimensions of connotative meaning. The meanings are located in multidimensional property space, called *semantic space.* The method consists of a set of bipolar rating scales, usually with seven points, by which one or more respondents rate one or more concepts on each scale item. In the example in Figure 8–1, two sets of bipolar pairs are shown, one from the traditional source and one adapted to the research purpose. Based on the construction requirements discussed later, we might choose 10 scales to score the "Lands' End Catalog."

The semantic differential has several advantages. It produces interval data. It is an efficient and easy way to secure attitudes from a large sample. These attitudes may be measured in both direction and intensity. The total set of responses provides a comprehensive picture of the meaning of an object and a measure of the subject doing the rating. It is a standardized technique that is easily repeated but escapes many problems of response distortion found with more direct methods.

Numerical scales have equal intervals that separate their numeric scale points. The verbal anchors serve as the labels for the extreme points. Numerical scales are often five-point scales, as shown in the example, but may be seven or ten. The respondent writes a number from the scale next to each item. If numerous questions about employee performance were included in the example, the scale would provide both an absolute measure of importance and a relative measure (ranking) of the various items rated. The scale's linearity, simplicity, and production of interval data make it popular for managers and researchers.

The **multiple rating list** is similar to the numerical scale but differs in two ways: (1) It accepts a circled response from the rater. (2) The layout allows visualization of the results. The advantage is that a mental map of the respondent's evaluations is evident to both the rater and the researcher. This scale produces interval data.

A scale that helps the researcher discover proportions is the **fixed sum scale.** In the example, two categories are presented that must sum to 100. Up to 10 categories may be used, but both respondent precision and patience suffer when too many stimuli are proportioned and summed. The advantage of the scale is its compatibility with percent (100%) and the fact that *continuous data* (versus *discrete* categories) can be compared for the alternatives. The scale is used to record attitudes, behavior, and behavioral intent.

The **stapel scale** is used as an alternative to the semantic differential, especially when it is difficult to find bipolar adjectives that match the investigative question. In the example in Figure 8–1 there are three attributes of corporate image. The scale is composed of the word (or phrase) identifying the image dimension and a set of 10 response categories for each of the three attributes. Fewer response categories are sometimes used. Respondents select a plus number for the characteristic that describes the named company. The more accurate the description, the larger is the positive number. Similarly, the less accurate the description, the larger is the negative number chosen. Ratings range from +5 to –5, very accurate to very inaccurate. Like the semantic differential, stapel scales produce interval data.

The **graphic rating scale** was created to enable researchers to discern fine differences. Theoretically, an infinite number of ratings is possible if the respondent is sophisticated enough to differentiate and record them. The respondent checks his or her response at any point along a continuum. Usually, the score is a measure of length (millimeters) from either end point. The results are usually treated as interval data. The difficulty is in coding and analysis that requires more time than scales with predetermined categories. Other graphic rating scales use pictures, icons, or other visuals to communicate with the rater.

Problems to Avoid with Rating Scales   The value of rating scales for measurement purposes depends on the assumption that a person can and will make good judgments. Before accepting respondents' ratings, we should consider their tendencies to make errors. Three of the most common are the errors of leniency, central tendency, and halo effect.[6]

The error of **leniency** occurs when a respondent is either an "easy rater" or a "hard rater." The latter is an error of **negative leniency.** Raters are inclined to score people higher whom they know well and with whom they are ego involved. There is also the opposite—where acquaintances are rated lower because one is aware of the leniency and attempts to counteract it. A way to deal with positive leniency is to design the rating scale to anticipate it. An example might be an asymmetrical scale that has only one unfavorable descriptive term and four favorable terms (poor—fair—good—very good—excellent). The scale designer expects that the mean ratings will be near "good" and that there will be a symmetrical distribution about that point.

Raters are reluctant to give extreme judgments, and this fact accounts for the error of **central tendency.** This is most often seen when the rater does not know the person being rated. Efforts to counteract this error are (1) adjusting the strength of descriptive adjectives, (2) spacing the intermediate descriptive phrases farther apart, (3) providing smaller differences in meaning between steps near the ends of the scale than between the steps near the center, and (4) using more points in the scale.

The **halo effect** is the systematic bias that the rater introduces by carrying over a generalized impression of the subject from one rating to another. You expect the student who does well on the first question of an examination to do well on the second. You conclude a report is good because you like its form, or you believe someone is intelligent because you agree with him or her. Halo is a pervasive error. It is especially difficult to avoid when the property being studied is not clearly defined, not easily observed, not frequently discussed, involves reactions with others, or is a trait of high moral importance.[7] One way to counteract the halo effect is to rate one trait at a time for all subjects or to have one trait per page.

Rating scales are widely used in management research and generally deserve their popularity. The results obtained with careful use compare favorably with other methods.

Ranking Scales

In ranking scales, the subject directly compares two or more objects and makes choices among them. Frequently, the respondent is asked to select one as the "best" or the "most preferred." When there are only two choices, this approach is satisfactory, but it often results in "ties" when more than two choices are found. For example, respondents are asked to select the most preferred among three or more models of a product. Assume that 40 percent choose model A, 30 percent choose model B, and 30 percent choose model C. "Which is the preferred model?" The analyst would be taking a risk to suggest that A is most preferred. Perhaps that interpretation is correct, but 60 percent of the respondents chose some model other than A. Perhaps all B and C voters would place A last, preferring either B or C to it. This ambiguity can be avoided by using some of the techniques described in this section.

Using the **paired-comparison scale,** the respondent can express attitudes unambiguously by choosing between two objects. Typical of paired comparisons would be the sports car preference example in Figure 8–2. The number of judgments required in a paired comparison is $[(n)(n-1)/2]$, where n is the number of stimuli or objects to be judged. There are four cars, resulting in six comparisons $[(4)(3)/2 = 6]$.

In another example we might compare two bargaining proposals available to union negotiators (see Table 8–1). Generally, there are more than two stimuli to

FIGURE   8–2   Ranking Scales

Paired-Comparison Scale

"For each pair of 2-seat sports cars listed, place a check beside the one you most prefer if you had to choose between the two."

____ BMW Z3   ____ Chevrolet Corvette
____ Porsche Boxster   ____ Porsche Boxster

____ Chevrolet Corvette   ____ Porsche Boxster
____ BMW Z3   ____ Dodge Viper

____ Chevrolet Corvette   ____ Dodge Viper
____ Dodge Viper   ____ BMW Z3

Forced Ranking Scale

"Rank the radar detection features in your order of preference. Place the number 1 next to the most preferred, 2 by the second choice, and so forth"

____ User programming
____ Cordless capability
____ Small size
____ Long range warning
____ Minimal false alarms

Comparative Scale

"Compared with your previous mutual fund's performance, the new one is:"

SUPERIOR		ABOUT THE SAME		INFERIOR
____	____	____	____	____
1	2	3	4	5

judge, resulting in a potentially tedious task for respondents. If 15 suggestions for bargaining proposals are available, 105 paired comparisons would be made.

Reducing the number of comparisons per respondent without reducing the number of objects can lighten this burden. You can present each respondent with only a sample of the stimuli. In this way, each pair of objects must be compared an equal number of times. Another procedure is to choose a few objects that are believed to cover the range of attractiveness at equal intervals. All other stimuli are then compared to these few standard objects. If 36 automobiles are to be judged, 4 may be selected as standards and the others divided into four groups of eight each. Within each group, the eight are compared to each other. Then the 32 are individually compared to each of the 4 standard automobiles. This reduces the number of comparisons from 630 to 240.

Paired comparisons run the risk that respondents will tire to the point that they give ill-considered answers or refuse to continue. Opinions differ about the upper

TABLE 8–1 Response Patterns of 200 Union Members' Paired Comparison on Five Suggestions for Bargaining Proposal Priorities

Paired-comparison data may be treated in several ways. If there is substantial consistency, we will find that if A is preferred to B, and B to C, then A will be consistently preferred to C. This condition of transitivity need not always be true but should occur most of the time. When it does, take the total number of preferences among the comparisons as the score for that stimulus. Assume a union bargaining committee is considering five major demand proposals. The committee would like to know how the union membership ranks these proposals. One option would be to ask a sample of the members to pair-compare the personnel suggestions. With a rough comparison of the total preferences for each option, it is apparent that B is the most popular.

	Suggestion				
	A	*B*	*C*	*D*	*E*
A	—	164*	138	50	70
B	36	—	54	14	30
C	62	146	—	32	50
D	150	186	168	—	118
E	130	170	150	82	—
Total	378	666	510	178	268
Rank order	3	1	2	5	4
M_p	0.478	0.766	0.610	0.278	0.368
Z_j	−0.060	0.730	0.280	−0.590	−0.340
R_j	0.530	1.320	0.870	0.000	0.250

*Interpret this cell, 164 members preferred suggestion *A* (column) to suggestion *A* (row)

limit, but 5 or 6 stimuli are not unreasonable when the respondent has other questions to answer. If the data collection consists only of comparisons, as many as 10 stimuli are reasonable.

While a paired comparison provides ordinal data, there are methods for converting it to interval data. The Law of Comparative Judgment involves converting the frequencies of preferences (such as in Table 8–1) into a table of proportions that are then transformed into a Z matrix by referring to the table of areas under the normal curve.[8] Guilford's *composite-standard* method is another alternative.[9]

The **forced ranking scale** shown in Figure 8–2 lists attributes that are ranked relative to each other. This method is faster than paired comparisons and is usually easier and more motivating to the respondent. With 5 items, it takes 10 paired comparisons to complete the task, and the simple forced ranking of 5 is easier. Also, ranking has no transitivity problem where *A* is preferred to *B*, and *B* to *C*, but *C* is preferred to *A*.

A drawback to forced ranking is the number of stimuli that can be handled by this method. Five objects can be ranked easily, but respondents may grow careless in ranking 10 or more items. In addition, rank-ordering produces ordinal data since the distance between preferences is unknown.

Often the manager or researcher is interested in benchmarking. This calls for a standard by which other programs, processes, brands, points of sale, or people can be compared. The **comparative scale** is ideal for such comparisons if the respondents are familiar with the standard. In the Figure 8–2 example, the standard is the respondent's previous mutual fund. The new fund is being assessed relative to it. The provision to compare yet other funds to the standard is not shown in the example but available to the researcher.

Some researchers treat the data produced by comparative scales as interval data since the scoring reflects an interval between the standard and what is being compared. We would treat the rank or position of the item as ordinal data unless the linearity of the variables in question could be supported.

None of the ranking methods covered is particularly useful when there are many items. The method of **successive intervals** is sometimes used to sort the items (usually one per card) into piles or groups representing a succession of values. From the sort, an interval scale can be developed.[10] This procedure is not used frequently and then only in unique studies.

SCALE CONSTRUCTION

Earlier, we classified scales by techniques used to construct them. Of the five techniques, three are used frequently; the *arbitrary* approach, *item analysis,* and *factor*-derived scales. They are emphasized in this section along with a preview of *multivariate* scales (described in more detail in Chapter 18). *Consensus* and *cumulative* methods receive less attention because they are time-consuming to construct or have fewer management applications. They are briefly mentioned because of their influence on current methods.

Arbitrary Scales   We design **arbitrary scales** by collecting several items that we believe are unambiguous and appropriate to a given topic. Some are chosen for inclusion in the instrument. To illustrate, consider a company image study. We choose a sample of items that we believe are the components of company image:

How do you regard (*name*) **Company's reputation**					
1. As a place to work?	Bad____	____	____	____	____Good
2. As a sponsor of civic projects?	Bad____	____	____	____	____Good
3. For ecological concern?	Bad____	____	____	____	____Good
4. As an employer of minorities?	Bad____	____	____	____	____Good

We might score each of these from 1 to 5, depending on the degree of favorableness reported. The results may be studied in several ways. Totals may be made by individual items, by company, by companies as places to work, for ecological concern, and so on. Totals for each company or for individuals may be calculated to determine how they compare to others. Based on a total for these four items, each company would receive from 4 to 20 points from each respondent. These data may also be analyzed from a respondent-centered point of view. Thus, we might use the attitude scores of each individual to study differences among individuals.

Arbitrary scales are easy to develop and inexpensive and can be designed to be highly specific. They provide useful information and are adequate if developed skillfully.

There are also weaknesses. The design approach is subjective. The researcher's insight and ability offer the only assurance that the items chosen are a representative sample of the universe of content (the totality of what constitutes "company image"). We have no evidence that respondents will view all items with the same frame of reference.

While arbitrary scales are often used, there has been a great effort to develop scale construction techniques that overcome some of their deficiencies. An early attempt was consensus scaling.

Consensus Scaling

Consensus scaling requires that items are selected by a panel of judges who evaluate them on (1) relevance to the topic area, (2) potential for ambiguity, and (3) the level of attitude they represent. A widely known form of this approach is the Thurstone **equal-appearing interval scale.** Also known as the *Thurstone scale*, this approach resulted in an interval rating scale for attitude measurement. Often 50 or more judges evaluate a large number of statements expressing different degrees of favorableness toward an object. There is one statement per card. The judges sort each card into 1 of 11 piles representing their evaluation of the degree of favorableness that the statement expresses. The judge's agreement or disagreement with the statement is not involved. Three of the 11 piles are identified to the judges by labels of "favorable" and "unfavorable" at the extremes and "neutral" at the midpoint. The eight intermediate piles are unlabeled to create the impression of equal-appearing intervals between the three labeled positions.

This method of scale construction is rarely used in applied management research these days. Its cost, time, and staff requirements make it impractical. The importance of this historic method, however, is its influence on Likert and the semantic differential scales.

Item Analysis

Item analysis is a procedure for evaluating an item based on how well it discriminates between those persons whose total score is high and whose total score is low. The most popular scale using this approach is the summated or Likert scale.

Item analysis involves calculating the mean scores for each scale item among the low scorers and high scorers. The item means between the high-score group and the low-score group are then tested for significance by calculating *t* values. Finally, the 20 to 25 items that have the greatest *t* values (significant differences between means) are selected for inclusion in the final scale.[11]

Likert-type scales are relatively easy to construct compared to the equal-appearing interval scale.[12] The first step is to collect a large number of statements that meet two criteria: (1) Each statement is believed to be relevant to the attitude being studied. (2) Each is believed to reflect a favorable or unfavorable position on that attitude. People similar to those who are going to be studied are asked to read each statement and to state the level of their agreement with it, using a five-point scale. A scale value of 1 might indicate a strongly unfavorable attitude; 5, a strongly favorable attitude (see Figure 8–1).

Each person's responses are then added to secure a total score. The next step is to array these total scores and select some portion representing the highest and lowest *total scores,* say, the top 25 percent and the bottom 25 percent. These two extreme groups represent people with the most favorable and least favorable attitudes toward the topic being studied. The extremes are the two criterion groups by which we evaluate individual statements. Through a comparative analysis of response patterns to each statement by members of these two groups, we learn which statements consistently correlate with low favorability and which correlate with high favorability attitudes.

This procedure is illustrated in Table 8–2. In evaluating response patterns of the high and low groups to the statement, "I consider my job exciting," we secure the re-

TABLE 8–2   Evaluating a Scale Statement by Item Analysis

Response Categories	Low Total Score Group				High Total Score Group			
	X	f	fX	fX^2	X	f	fX	fX^2
Strongly agree	5	3	15	75	5	22	110	550
Agree	4	4	16	64	4	30	120	480
Undecided	① 3	29	87	261	3	15	45	135
Disagree	2	22	44	88	2	4	8	16
Strongly disagree	1	15	15	15	1	2	2	2
Total		73	177	503 ← ② →	73	285	1,183
		n_L	ΣX_L	ΣX_L^2		n_H	ΣX_H	ΣX_H^2

$$\bar{X}_L = \frac{177}{73} = 2.42 \longleftarrow ③ \longrightarrow \bar{X}_H = \frac{285}{73} = 3.90$$

$$\Sigma(X_L - \bar{X}_L)^2 = 503 - \frac{(177)^2}{73} \longleftarrow ④ \longrightarrow \Sigma(X_H - \bar{X}_H)^2 = 1,183 - \frac{(285)^2}{73}$$

$$= 73.84 \qquad\qquad = 70.33$$

$$t = \frac{\bar{X}_H - \bar{X}_L}{\sqrt{\dfrac{\Sigma(X_H - \bar{X}_H)^2 + \Sigma(X_L - \bar{X}_L)^2}{n(n-1)}}} \longleftarrow ⑤$$

$$= \frac{3.90 - 2.42}{\sqrt{\dfrac{70.33 + 73.84}{73(73-1)}}}$$

$$= 8.92 \longleftarrow ⑥$$

LEGEND

1. For the statement, "I consider my job exciting," we select the data from the bottom 25% of the distribution (low total score group) and the top 25% (high total score group). There are 73 people in each group. The remaining 50% in the middle of the distribution is not considered for this analysis. For each of the response categories, the scale's value (X) is multiplied by the frequency or number of respondents (f) who chose that value. These values produce the product (fX). This number is then multiplied by X (fX^2). For example, there are 3 respondents in the low score group who scored a 5 (strongly agreed with the statement): (fX) = 5 × 3 = 15; (fX^2) = 15 × 5 = 75.

2. The frequencies, products, and squares are summed.

3. A mean score for each group is computed.

4. Deviation scores are computed, squared, and summed as required by the formula.

5. The data are tested in a modified t-test that compares the high and low scoring groups for the item. Notice the mean scores in the numerator of the formula.

6. The calculated value is compared with a criterion, 1.75. If the calculated value (in this case, 8.92) is equal to or exceeds the criterion, the statement is said to be a good discriminator of the measured attitude. (If it is less than the criterion, we would consider it a poor discriminator of the target attitude and delete it from the measuring instrument.) We then select the next item and repeat the process.

sults shown. After finding the *t* values for each statement, we rank-order them and select those statements with the highest *t* values. As an approximate indicator of a statement's discrimination power, Edwards suggests using only those statements whose *t* value is 1.75 or greater, provided there are 25 or more subjects in each group.[13] To safeguard against response-set bias, we should word approximately one-half of the statements to be favorable and the other half unfavorable.

The Likert scale has many advantages that account for its popularity. It is easy and quick to construct. Each item that is included has met an empirical test for discriminating ability. Since respondents answer each item, it is probably more reliable and it provides a greater volume of data than many other scales.

Cumulative Scales

Total scores on cumulative scales have the same meaning. Given a person's total score, it is possible to estimate which items were answered positively and negatively. A pioneering scale of this type was the **scalogram.** Scalogram analysis is a procedure for determining whether a set of items forms a unidimensional scale.[14] A scale is unidimensional if the responses fall into a pattern in which endorsement of the item reflecting the extreme position results also in endorsing all items that are less extreme.

Assume we are surveying opinions regarding a new style of running shoe. We have developed a preference scale of four items:

1. The *Airsole* is good looking.
2. I will insist on *Airsole* next time because it is great looking.
3. The appearance of *Airsole* is acceptable to me.
4. I prefer the *Airsole* style to other styles.

Respondents indicate whether they agree or disagree. If these items form a unidimensional scale, the response patterns will approach the ideal configuration shown in Table 8–3.

A score of 4 indicates all statements are agreed to and represents the most favorable attitude. Persons with a score of 3 should disagree with item 2 but agree with all others and so on. According to scalogram theory, this pattern confirms that the universe of content (attitude toward the appearance of this running shoe) is scalable.

TABLE 8–3   Ideal Scalogram Response Pattern

		Item		
2	*4*	*1*	*3*	*Respondent Score*
X	X	X	X	4
—	X	X	X	3
—	—	X	X	2
—	—	—	X	1
—	—	—	—	0

X = Agree.
— = Disagree.

The scalogram and similar procedures for discovering underlying structure are useful for assessing behaviors that are highly structured, such as social distance, organizational hierarchies, and evolutionary product stages.[15] Although used less often today, the scalogram retains potential for mangerial applications.

Factor Scales

Factor scales include a variety of techniques that have been developed for two problems: (1) how to deal with the universe of content that is multidimensional and (2) how to uncover underlying (latent) dimensions that have not been identified.

These techniques are designed to intercorrelate items so their degree of interdependence may be detected. There are many approaches that the advanced student will want to explore, such as latent structure analysis (of which the scalogram is a special case), factor analysis, cluster analysis, and metric and nonmetric multidimensional scaling. We limit the discussion in this section to the semantic differential (SD), which is based on factor analysis.[16]

Osgood and his associates developed the *semantic differential method* to measure the psychological meanings of an object to an individual.[17] They produced a long list of adjective pairs useful for attitude research. Searching *Roget's Thesaurus* for such adjectives, they located 289 pairs. These were reduced to 76 pairs that were formed into rating scales. They chose 20 concepts that evoked the psychological meanings they wished to probe. The concepts from this historical study illustrate the wide applicability of the technique to persons, abstract concepts (such as leadership), events, institutions, and physical objects.[18]

By factor analyzing the data, they concluded that semantic space is multidimensional rather than unidimensional. Three factors contributed most to meaningful judgments by respondents: (1) *evaluation*, (2) *potency*, and (3) *activity*. The evaluation dimension usually accounted for one-half to three-fourths of the extractable variance. (The evaluation dimension is the only dimension possessed by Likert scales.) Potency and activity are about equal and together accounted for a little over one-fourth of the extractable variance. Occasionally, the potency and activity dimensions combined to form "dynamism." Results of the *Thesaurus* study are shown in Table 8–4.

The SD scale should be adapted to each research problem. The first step in scale construction is to select the concepts. The concepts are nouns, noun phrases, or nonverbal stimuli such as visual sketches. Concepts are chosen by judgment and reflect the nature of the investigative question. In the MindWriter study, one concept might be "call center accessibility." Or in a study to evaluate multiple candidates for an executive position in an industry association, the concept would be a candidate, "Darnell Williams."

Next, select the original bipolar word pairs or pairs you adapt to your needs. If the traditional Osgood items are used, several criteria guide your selection. The first is the factor(s) composition. To use evaluation, potency, and activity, you need at least three bipolar pairs for each factor. Scores on these individual items should be averaged, by factor, to improve their test reliability. Second, the scale must be rele-

TABLE 8–4   Results of the *Thesaurus* Study

Evaluation	*Potency*	*Activity*
Good–bad	Hard–soft	Active–passive
Positive–negative	Strong–weak	Fast–slow
Optimistic–pessimistic	Heavy–light	Hot–cold
Complete–incomplete	Masculine–feminine	Excitable–calm
Timely–untimely	Severe–lenient	
	Tenacious–yielding	

Subcategories of Evaluation

Meek Goodness	*Dynamic Goodness*	*Dependable Goodness*	*Hedonistic Goodness*
Clean–dirty	Successful–unsuccessful	True–false	Pleasurable–painful
Kind–cruel	High–low	Reputable–disreputable	Beautiful–ugly
Sociable–unsociable	Meaningful–meaningless	Believing–skeptical	Sociable–unsociable
Light–dark	Important–unimportant	Wise–foolish	Meaningful–meaningless
Altruistic–egotistical	Progressive–regressive	Healthy–sick	
Grateful–ungrateful		Clean–dirty	
Beautiful–ugly			
Harmonious–dissonant			

SOURCE: Adapted from Charles E. Osgood, G. J. Suci, and P. H. Tannenbaum, *The Measurement of Meaning* (Urbana, IL: University of Illinois Press, 1957), Table 5, pp. 52–61.

vant to the concepts being judged. Choose adjectives that allow connotative perceptions to be expressed. Irrelevant concept-scale pairings yield neutral midpoint values that convey little information. Third, scales should be stable across subjects and concepts. A pair such as "large-small" may be interpreted by some to be denotative when judging a physical object such as "automobile" but may be used connotatively in judging abstract concepts such as "quality management." Fourth, scales should be linear between polar opposites and pass through the origin. A pair that fails this test is "rugged-delicate," which is nonlinear on the evaluation dimension. When used separately, both adjectives have favorable meanings.[19]

In Figure 8–3 we see the scale being used by a panel of corporate leaders to rate candidates for an industry leadership position. The selection of concepts in this case is simple; there are three candidates, plus a fourth—the ideal candidate.

The nature of the problem determines the selection of dimensions and bipolar pairs. Since the person who wins this position must influence business leaders, we decide to use all three factors. The candidate must deal with many people, often in a social setting; must have high integrity; and must take a leadership role in encouraging more progressive policies in the industry. The position will also involve a high degree of personal activity. Based on these requirements, we choose 10 scales to score the candidates from 7 to 1. The negative signs in the original scoring procedure (−3, −2, −1, 0, +1, +2, +3) were found to produce coding errors. Figure 8–3 illustrates the scale used for the research. The letters along the left side, which show

FIGURE 8–3   SD Scale for Analyzing Candidates for an Industry Leadership Position

(E) Sociable	(7): ____ : ____ : ____ : ____ : ____ :					(1) Unsociable
(P) Weak	(1): ____ : ____ : ____ : ____ : ____ :					(7) Strong
(A) Active	(7): ____ : ____ : ____ : ____ : ____ :					(1) Passive
(E) Progressive	(7): ____ : ____ : ____ : ____ : ____ :					(1) Regressive
(P) Yielding	(1): ____ : ____ : ____ : ____ : ____ :					(7) Tenacious
(A) Slow	(1): ____ : ____ : ____ : ____ : ____ :					(7) Fast
(E) True	(7): ____ : ____ : ____ : ____ : ____ :					(1) False
(P) Heavy	(7): ____ : ____ : ____ : ____ : ____ :					(1) Light
(A) Hot	(7): ____ : ____ : ____ : ____ : ____ :					(1) Cold
(E) Unsuccessful	(1): ____ : ____ : ____ : ____ : ____ :					(7) Successful

the relevant factor, would be omitted from the actual scale, as would the numerical values shown. Note also that the evaluation, potency, and activity scales are mixed, and about half are reversed to minimize the halo effect. To analyze the results, the set of evaluation (E) values is averaged, as are those for the potency (P) and activity (A) dimensions.

The data are plotted in Figure 8–4. Here the adjective pairs are reordered so evaluation, potency, and activity descriptors are grouped together with the ideal

FIGURE 8–4   Graphic Representation of SD Analysis

factor reflected by the left side of the scale. Profiles of the three candidates may be compared to each other and to the ideal.

Adapting SD Scales to the Management Question   One study explored a retail store image using 35 pairs of words or phrases classified into eight groups. These word pairs were especially created for the study. Excerpts from this scale are presented in Figure 8–5. Other categories of scale items were "general characteristics of the company," "physical characteristics of the store," "prices charged by the store," "store personnel," "advertising by the store," and "your friends and the store." Since the scale pairs are closely associated with the characteristics of the store and its use, one could develop image profiles of various stores.

Advanced Scaling Techniques

New approaches have removed many deficiencies of traditional scales. Some have evolved to handle specific management research applications. Most techniques mentioned in this section rely on complex computer algorithms and require an understanding of multivariate statistics. *Students interested in further information on these topics should refer to the statistical examples in Chapter 18 and the references.*

Multidimensional scaling (MDS) describes a collection of techniques that deal with property space in a more general manner than the semantic differential. With MDS, one can scale objects, people, or both in ways that provide a visual impression of the relationships among variables. The data-handling characteristics of MDS provide several options: ordinal input (with interval output), and fully metric (interval) and nonmetric modes. The various techniques use proximities as input data. A

FIGURE   8–5   **Adapting SD Scales for Retail Store Image Study**

Convenience of Reaching the Store from Your Location

nearby	___:	___:	___:	___:	___:	___:	___:	distant
short time required to reach store	___:	___:	___:	___:	___:	___:	___:	long time required to reach store
difficult drive	___:	___:	___:	___:	___:	___:	___:	easy drive
difficult to find parking place	___:	___:	___:	___:	___:	___:	___:	easy to find parking place
convenient to other stores I shop	___:	___:	___:	___:	___:	___:	___:	inconvenient to other stores I shop

Products Offered

wide selection of different kinds of products	___:	___:	___:	___:	___:	___:	___:	limited selection of different kinds of products
fully stocked	___:	___:	___:	___:	___:	___:	___:	understocked
undependable products	___:	___:	___:	___:	___:	___:	___:	dependable products
high quality	___:	___:	___:	___:	___:	___:	___:	low quality
numerous brands	___:	___:	___:	___:	___:	___:	___:	few brands
unknown brands	___:	___:	___:	___:	___:	___:	___:	well-known brands

SOURCE: Robert F. Kelly and Ronald Stephenson, "The Semantic Differential: An Information Source for Designing Retail Patronage Appeals," *Journal of Marketing* 31 (October 1967), p. 45.

proximity is an index of perceived similarity or dissimilarity between objects. The objects might be 20 nations (or 10 primary exports) that respondents are asked to judge in pairs of possible combinations as to their similarity. By means of a computer program, the ranked or rated relationships are then represented as points on a map in multidimensional space.[20]

We may think of three types of attribute space, each representing a multidimensional map. First, in *objective* space a product can be positioned in terms of, say, its price, taste, and brand image. Second, a person's perceptions may be also positioned in *subjective* space using similar dimensions. These maps do not always coincide, but they do provide information about perceptual disparities. Since the subjective maps vary over time, they also provide important trend data. Third, we can describe our preferences for the object's ideal attributes. All objects close to the ideal are more preferred than those farther away. These various configurations are said to reflect the "hidden structure" of the data and make complicated problems much easier to understand. In Figure 8–6 two dimensions are plotted, price and taste. The high-sodium beers are closest to the ideal beer on the price dimension while the imported beers are farthest away.

Another approach, representing a collection of techniques, is **conjoint analysis.** Conjoint analysis is used to measure complex decision making that requires multiattribute judgments. Its primary focus has been the explanation of consumer behavior with numerous applications in product development and marketing.[21]

When discovering and learning about products, consumers define a set of attributes or characteristics they use to compare competing brands or models in a

FIGURE   8–6   Multidimensional Map of Beer Preferences

product class. Using these attributes, they evaluate the product range and eliminate some brands. Then a final set of alternatives (including a nonpurchase or delayed purchase decision) is developed. These evaluations can change if there is new information about additional competitors, or corrections to attribute knowledge, or further thoughts about the attribute. Algebraic theory can be used to model these cognitive processes and develop statistical approximations that reveal the rules the consumer follows in decision making.[22]

For example, a consumer might be considering the purchase of a personal computer. One has a fast processing speed and a high price. The other has a low price and a slower processor. The consumer's choice will be evidence of the utility of the processing-speed attribute. Simultaneously, other attributes are being evaluated such as memory, portability, graphics support, and user friendliness.

Conjoint analysis can produce a scaled value for each attribute as well as a utility value for attributes that have levels (e.g., memory may have a range of 16 or 32 megabytes). Both ranking and rating inputs may be used to evaluate product attributes. Conjoint analysis is not restricted to marketing applications, nor should it be considered a single generalized technique (See Chapter 18).

Finally, advanced students who are interested in the above techniques may also wish to investigate *magnitude estimation scaling.*[23] Magnitude scales provide access to ratio measurement and open new alternatives to management problems previously addressed through ordinal scales alone. *Rasch models* also offer alternative approaches to a range of traditional measures from dichotomous responses to Likert-type response formats.[24]

CLOSE-UP

Myra and Jason had been working on scaling for the CompleteCare project for a week when the call came to Myra to report her progress to Mind-Writer's general manager, Jean-Claude. They had narrowed the choice to three scales: a Likert scale, a conventional rating scale with two verbal anchors, and their hybrid expectation scale. All were five-point scales that were presumed to measure at the interval level.

They needed a statement that could accompany the scale for preliminary evaluation. Returning to their list of investigative questions, they found a question that seemed to capture the essence of the repair process: "Are customers' problems resolved?" Translated into an assertion for the scale, the statement became, "Resolution of problems that prompted service/repair." They continued to labor over the wording of the verbal anchors after their meeting with Jean-Claude. It was important that the distance between the numbers would resemble the psychological distance implied by the words.

(continued)

Appropriate versions of the investigative question were constructed and then the scales were added:

Likert Scale

The problem that prompted service/repair was resolved.

Strongly Disagree	Disagree	Neither Agree nor Disagree	Agree	Strongly Agree
1	2	3	4	5

Conventional Likert Rating Scale (MindWriter's favorite)

To what extent are you satisfied that the problem that prompted service/repair was resolved?

Very Dissatisfied				Very Satisfied
1	2	3	4	5

Hybrid Expectation Scale

Resolution of the problem that prompted service/repair

Met few expectations	Met some expectations	Met most expectations	Met all expectations	Exceeded expectations
1	2	3	4	5

After consulting with MindWriter's research staff, Myra and Jason discussed the advantages of their scale. Myra suggested it was unlikely that CompleteCare would meet none of the customers' expectations. And, with errors of positive leniency, *none* should be replaced by the term *few* so the low end of the scale would be more relevant. Jason had read a *Marketing News* article that said Likert scales and scales similar to MindWriter's frequently produced a heavy concentration of 4s and 5s—a common problem in customer satisfaction research.

They also considered a seven-point scale to remedy this but in the end thought the term *exceeded* on the expectation scale could compensate for scores that clustered on the positive end, making the end point less susceptible to leniency.

They were ready for a pilot test. They decided to compare their hybrid expectation scale with MindWriter's conventional Likert rating scale. The Likert scale required that they create more potential items than they had room for on the postcard. Using the CompleteCare database, names, addresses, and phone numbers were selected. Thirty customers were selected at random from those who had recent service. They chose the delayed equivalent forms method for reliability testing (see Chapter 7). Myra administered the expectation scale followed by the satisfaction scale to half of the respondents and the satisfaction scale followed by the expectation scale to the other half. Each half sample experienced a time delay. No "order-of-presentation" effects were found. Subsequently, they correlated the satisfaction scores with the expectation scores and plotted the results.

Satisfaction and expectation were positively correlated for "problem resolution" ($r = .90$); reliability based on equivalence was supported. An assessment of test-retest reliability ($r = .93$) showed that the expectation scale had a higher degree of stability over the one-week interval than the satisfaction scale ($r = .75$). Their scale also produced linear results (as evidenced by the plot).

The decision was made. Myra and Jason would use the new hybrid expectation scale for the CompleteCare project.

Summary

Scaling describes the procedures by which we assign numbers to opinions, attitudes, and other concepts. Selection of a scale to best meet our needs involves six decisions:

1. *Study objective:* Do we measure the characteristics of the respondent or the stimulus object?
2. *Response form:* Do we measure with a rating scale or a ranking scale?
3. *Degree of preference:* Do we measure our preferences or make nonpreference judgments?
4. *Scale properties:* Do we measure with nominal, ordinal, interval, or ratio data?
5. *Number of dimensions:* Do we measure using a unidimensional or multidimensional scale?
6. *Scale construction technique:* Do we develop scales by arbitrary decision, consensus, item analysis, cumulative scaling, or factor analysis?

In this chapter, two classifications—the response form and scale construction techniques—were emphasized.

When using rating scales, one judges an object in absolute terms against certain specified criteria. Several scales were proposed: simple category, multiple choice–single response, multiple choice–multiple response, Likert scales, semantic differential, numerical scales, multiple rating lists, fixed sum scales, stapel scales, and graphic rating scales. When you use ranking methods, you make relative comparisons against other similar objects. Three well-known methods are the paired-comparison, forced ranking, and the comparative scale.

Scales are classified by the techniques used to construct them. Of the five techniques, three are used frequently: the *arbitrary* approach, *item analysis*, and *factor-derived* scales. *Consensus* and *cumulative* methods receive less attention because they are time-consuming to construct or have fewer business applications. Arbitrary scales are designed by the researcher's own subjective selection of items. These scales are simple to construct and have content validity only.

In the consensus method, a panel is used to judge the relevance, ambiguity, and attitude level of scale items. Those items that are judged best are then included in the final instrument. The Thurstone method of equal-appearing intervals is a historic consensus method that gave impetus for many current scales.

With the item analysis approach, one develops many items believed to express either a favorable or an unfavorable attitude toward some general object. These items are then pretested to decide which ones discriminate between persons with high total scores and those with low total scores on the test. Those items that meet this discrimination test are included in the final instrument. The most successful Likert scales are developed using this approach.

With cumulative scales, it is possible to estimate how a respondent has answered individual items by knowing the total score. The items are related to each other on a particular attitude dimension, so that if one agrees with a more extreme item, one will also agree with items representing less extreme views. The scalogram is the classic example.

Factor scales are developed through factor analysis or similar correlation techniques. They are particularly useful in uncovering latent attitude dimensions, and they approach scaling through the concept of multidimensional attribute space. The semantic differential scale is an example.

Other developments in scaling include multidimensional scaling and conjoint analysis. Each represents a family of related techniques with a variety of applications for handling complex judgments. Magnitude estimation and Rasch models provide an avenue for reconceptualizing traditional scaling techniques for greater efficiency and freedom from error.

Key Terms

arbitrary scales	forced ranking scale
central tendency (error)	graphic rating scale
comparative scale	halo effect
conjoint analysis	item analysis
consensus scaling	leniency (error)
equal-appearing interval scale	Likert scale
factor scales	multidimensional scaling
fixed sum scale	multiple choice, multiple response scale

multiple choice, single response scale
multiple rating list
negative leniency
numerical scale
paired-comparison scale
ranking scales
rating scales

scaling
scalogram
semantic differential
simple category scale
stapel scale
successive intervals
unidimensional scales

Case

BBQ Products Crosses over the Lines of Varied Tastes
(This is a case found in the optional casebook available with the text.)

Discussion Questions

1. Discuss the relative merits of and problems with

   a. Rating and ranking scales

   b. Likert and differential scales

   c. Unidimensional and multidimensional scales.

2. Suppose a researcher gives you a scale to complete on the U.S. economic system. What would the scale look like and how would it be developed if it were a

   a. Fixed sum scale

   b. Likert-type summated scale

   c. Semantic differential scale

   d. Stapel scale

   e. Forced ranking scale

3. An investigative question in your employee satisfaction study seeks to assess employee "job involvement." Create a measurement question that uses the following scales:

   a. A graphic rating scale

   b. A multiple rating list

   c. Which do you recommend and why?

4. You receive the results of a paired-comparison preference test of four soft drinks from a sample of 200 persons. The results are as follows:

	Koak	*Zip*	*Pabze*	*Mr. Peepers*
Koak	—	50*	115	35
Zip	150	—	160	70
Pabze	85	40	—	45
Mr. Peepers	165	130	155	—

*Read as 50 persons preferred Zip to Koak.

    a. How do these brands rank in overall preference in this sample?

    b. Develop an interval scale for these four brands.

5. One of the problems in developing rating scales is the choice of response terms to use. Below are samples of some widely used scaling codes. Do you see any problems with them?

    a. Yes _____ Depends _____ No _____

    b. Excellent _____ Good _____ Fair _____ Poor _____

    c. Excellent _____ Good _____ Average _____
        Fair _____ Poor _____

    d. Strongly Approve _____ Approve _____ Uncertain _____
        Disapprove _____ Stongly Disapprove_____

6. You are working on a consumer perception study of four brands of bicycles. You need

    a. An overall assessment of all the brands.

    b. A comparison of the brands for each of the following dimensions:

        —Styling

        —Durability

        —Gear quality

        —Brand image

    Develop measurement questions and scales to accomplish this. Explain which data levels (nominal, ordinal, interval, ratio) are appropriate and which quantitative techniques you will use.

7. Below is a Likert-type scale that might be used to evaluate your opinion of the educational program you are in. There are five response categories: Strongly Agree through Neither Agree nor Disagree to Strongly Disagree. If 5 represents the most positive attitude, how would the different items be valued?

    a. This program is not very challenging.

        SA—A—N—D—SD

    b. The general level of teaching is good.

        SA—A—N—D—SD

    c. I really think I am learning a lot from this program.

        SA—A—N—D—SD

    d. Students' suggestions are given little attention here.

        SA—A—N—D—SD

    e. This program does a good job of preparing one for a career.

        SA—A—N—D—SD

    f. This program is below my expectations.

        SA—A—N—D—SD

    Record your answers to the above items. In what two different ways could such responses be used? What would be the purpose of each?

Reference Notes

1. Bernard S. Phillips, *Social Research Strategy and Tactics,* 2nd ed. (New York: Macmillan, 1971), p. 205.

2. For a discussion of various scale classifications, see W. S. Torgerson, *Theory and Methods of Scaling* (New York: Wiley, 1958), chap. 3.

3. E. A. Suchman and R. G. Francis, "Scaling Techniques in Social Research," in *An Introduction to Social Research,* ed. J. T. Doby (Harrisburg, PA: Stackpole, 1954), pp. 126–29.

4. A study of the historic research literature found that more than three-fourths of the attitude scales used were of the five-point type. An examination of more recent literature suggests that the five-point scale is still common but there is a growing use of longer scales. For the historic study, see Daniel D. Day, "Methods in Attitude Research," *American Sociological Review* 5 (1940), pp. 395–410. Single versus multiple-item scaling requirements are discussed in Jum C. Nunnally, *Psychometric Theory* (New York: McGraw-Hill, 1967), chap. 14.

5. This section is adapted from Pamela L. Alreck and Robert B. Settle, *The Survey Research Handbook* (Burr Ridge, IL: Irwin, 1995), chap. 5.

6. J. P. Guilford, *Psychometric Methods* (New York: McGraw-Hill, 1954), pp. 278–79.

7. P. M. Synonds, "Notes on Rating," *Journal of Applied Psychology* 9 (1925), pp. 188–95.

8. See L. L. Thurstone, "A Law of Comparative Judgment," *Psychological Review* 34 (1927), pp. 273–86.

9. Guilford, *Psychometric Methods.*

10. See Milton A. Saffir, "A Comparative Study of Scales Constructed by Three Psychophysical Methods," *Psychometrica* 11, no. 3 (September 1937), pp. 179–98.

11. Allen L. Edwards, *Techniques of Attitude Scale Construction* (New York: Appleton-Century-Crofts, 1957), pp. 152–54.

12. One study reported that the construction of a Likert scale took only half the time required to construct a Thurstone scale. See L. L. Thurstone and K. K. Kenney, "A Comparison of the Thurstone and Likert Techniques of Attitude Scale Construction," *Journal of Applied Psychology* 30 (1946), pp. 72–83.

13. Edwards, *Techniques,* p. 153.

14. Louis Guttman, "A Basis for Scaling Qualitative Data," *American Sociological Review* 9 (1944), pp. 139–50.

15. John P. Robinson, "Toward a More Appropriate Use of Guttman Scaling," *Public Opinion Quarterly* 37 (Summer 1973), pp. 260–67.

16. For more on the process of factor analysis, see Chapter 18.

17. Charles E. Osgood, G. J. Suci, and P. H. Tannenbaum, *The Measurement of Meaning* (Urbana, IL: University of Illinois Press, 1957).

18. Ibid., p. 49. See also James G. Snider and Charles E. Osgood, eds., *Semantic Differential Technique* (Chicago: Aldine, 1969).

19. Ibid., p. 79.

20. See, for example, Joseph B. Kruskal and Myron Wish, *Multidimensional Scaling* (Beverly Hills, CA: Sage Publications, 1978); Paul Green and V. R. Rao, *Applied Multidimensional Scaling: A Comparison of Approaches and Algorithms* (New York: Holt, Rinehart & Winston, 1972); and Paul E. Green and F. J. Carmone, *Multidimensional Scaling in Marketing Analysis* (Boston: Allyn & Bacon, 1970).

21. See P. Cattin and D. R. Wittink, "Commercial Use of Conjoint Analysis: A Survey," *Journal of Marketing* 46 (1982), pp. 44–53; and Cattin and Wittink, "Commercial Use of Conjoint Analysis: An Update" (paper presented at the ORSA/TIMS Marketing Science Meetings, Richardson, TX, March 12–15, 1986).

22. Jordan J. Louviere, *Analyzing Decision Making: Metric Conjoint Analysis* (Beverly Hills, CA: Sage Publications, 1988), pp. 9–11.

23. See, for example, Milton Lodge, *Magnitude Scaling: Quantitative Measurement of Opinions* (Beverly Hills, CA: Sage Publications, 1981); and Donald R. Cooper and Donald A. Clare, "A Magnitude Estimation Scale for Human Values," *Psychological Reports* 49 (1981).

24. David Andrich, *Rasch Models for Measurement* (Beverly Hills, CA: Sage Publications, 1988).

Suggested Readings

1. Edwards, Allen L. *Techniques of Attitude Scale Construction.* New York: Appleton-Century-Crofts, 1957. Thorough discussion of basic unidimensional scaling techniques.

2. Kerlinger, Fred N. *Foundations of Behavioral Research,* 3rd ed. New York: Holt, Rinehart & Winston, 1986. Chapters 29, 31, and 32 cover various scaling and other data collection techniques, some of which are not discussed in this text.

3. Miller, Delbert C. *Handbook of Research Design and Social Measurement,* 5th ed. Thousand Oaks, CA: Sage Publications, 1991. Presents a large number of existing sociometric scales and indices as well as information on their characteristics, validity, and sources.

4. Osgood, Charles E., George J. Suci, and Percy H. Tannenbaum. *The Measurement of Meaning.* Urbana, IL: University of Illinois Press, 1957. The basic reference on SD scaling.

5. Summers, Gene F., ed. *Attitude Measurement.* Chicago: Rand McNally, 1970. An excellent collection of papers on various aspects of scaling.

CHAPTER

9   SAMPLING DESIGN

CHAPTER NAVIGATION

BRINGING
RESEARCH TO LIFE

"Jason, in business research, you need to accept the world as it is, not as you'd like it to be. The ideal subject is thoughtful, articulate, rational, and above all, cooperative. Real people, you quickly discover, are fractious, stubborn, ignorant, and even perverse. Nevertheless they are who you have to work with."

"Take a fellow I knew, my niece's son's college roommate. He was too haughty to be a really good researcher."

From 100 feet away, Eric Burbidge saw that the number 99 bus was filthy. It would smell on the inside, he was sure. Forty riders were docilely lined up to board—one was a letter carrier, and a collection of other blue-collar men and women comprised the rest. Some were idly thumbing through newspapers—Good! Very good!—some were chatting, and two were ruminating slowly on hero sandwiches, which he supposed they had picked up at the tavern across the street from the bus station.

Burbidge swept past the queued passengers, taking care not to make premature eye contact, and brusquely rapped his clipboard against the bus's folding door. With a whoosh the driver snapped the door open, and Burbidge heaved himself up onto the bus. No one tried to follow him up, which he would not have allowed anyway, as he needed time to interrogate the driver, to see if the man would be of any help.

"Good evening, driver. I am Mr. Burbidge, and I am from headquarters."

"That figures. We don't see many suits on route 99."

"Then you know why I have had to come out here." He'd been with the bus company for three months, and this was the first time he had been required to board and ride a bus. What is that smell? Machine oil . . . sandwich meats . . . what else do the route's demographics suggest would be tracked every day through this bus? Sweat, of course! "I am conducting a scientific survey to determine the newspaper readership, if any, of riders on this route."

"Yessir," murmured the driver, without enthusiasm.

"If you have been reading your employees' newsletter, you must know that the corporation is soon to announce a restructuring of the route system and schedule, pursuant to which we shall have to purchase advertising space in the leading media to reveal our new route structure, maps, and schedules."

"Won't that be a mess," muttered the driver, in the same flat tone. "And, yessir, I read your newsletter. For fifteen years I have read it."

"According to our records, you have been a driver on this very route for five years, and so you may have noticed that this route runs north-to-south equidistantly between the twin cities. . . ."

"The route runs north-south, with one city on the east and the other on the west, yessir. I caught on to that long ago, sir. It's right there on the route map, sir. Clean splits the line between East City and West City and never gets closer to one than the other. If you want to get to one city or the other, you transfer to another bus. My bus just goes straight north. Right up there on the route map, sir."

"As corporate research director," said Burbidge, gracefully emphasizing his point by pointing a forefinger roofward, "I take nothing for granted, but instead provide scientific methodology, in this instance to test my hypothesis that readership of newspapers on this route would be equally divided between the *East City Gazette* and the *West City Tribune*. To that very end I have prepared this survey of your riders, which with your complete cooperation I have selected to pass out along this route, on this day, at this time."

"Newspapers, you say," said the driver, showing a flicker of involvement. "I could tell you quite a lot about those newspapers. . . ."

"Not required! This is a scientific survey of riders on route 99, and anecdotal information is not appropriate. What I require of you is to let the passengers up onto the bus so I may give them these *(continued)* pencils and surveys, and then to refrain from swerving or unnecessarily agitating the bus while they are filling out my surveys. Do you think you can manage that?"

"I'd better turn on the inside lights, don't you think?"

"Well, of course, turn on the lights. That goes without saying."

The passengers boarded slowly, exchanging pleasantries with the driver. They were quite a little clan, Burbidge could see.

The bus rolled steadily northward, and Burbidge was pleased to see that riders hunched over his one-page survey, though he was struck by how long it took them to answer the simplest of questions. As each completed the survey, he or she shyly shuffled forward and proffered it to Burbidge without comment.

Just when he sensed everything was going as well as might be expected, two men stood up, one in the front by the driver, one in the rear, and spread their legs and straddled the aisles. A ball of newsprint was tossed into the aisle, and the passengers began whooping and batting the paper forward and back. "What is this, driver?" demanded Burbidge.

"Hockey. They are playing hockey. The idea is to knock the ball between this guy's legs or that guy's in the back."

"Aren't you going to stop them?"

"No harm done. These are a friendly bunch. Big sports fans. In fact," said the driver, whose voice had gained enthusiasm when evading discussion of company business, "the East City club is playing pro hockey tonight, so when I clean out the bus, most of the newspapers will be the *East City Gazette*." He rattled on, contributing to Burbidge's annoyance, explaining that the riders liked to study the night's pro game in advance, the better to discuss it among themselves, so newsstand sales were brisk in the terminal, but only for the newspaper that did the better job of covering the *sport du jour*. "Of course, tomorrow night there is pro basketball in West City, and most of the riders will pick up the *West City Tribune* at the newsstands."

"That's impossible to accept," shouted Burbidge. "Such behavior would bias my scientific survey, which asks for the paper they most recently purchased!"

"Well, you had better accept it. B'cause I've been cleaning out this bus for five years. It's the *Gazette* before hockey, and the *Trib* before basketball. This is a hockey crowd tonight, which means extra *Gazettes*."

Burbidge was mortified and hoped he wasn't revealing his distress to the driver. Surely the driver would not understand the consequences of this predicament in biasing the survey. But the driver added, "'Course, in the mornings these folks bring the papers that the newsboys toss on their lawns, so you don't see such a situation."

"That is very difficult to accept, driver. It means that by choosing between sampling this route—morning or evening—I get a systematically different set of results, and by choosing a hockey night or a basketball night, I further incline toward different results." Burbidge was thinking out loud, almost in a trance.

"Naturally," agreed the driver, with irritating enthusiasm.

"Be still, driver. I have to think." Burbidge was shaken.

The driver had now warmed to his exposition of trash-can sociological research. "Of course, by reading my newsletter, as I do, I know that by the time you announce the new routes and schedules, we will be finished with hockey and basketball and into the baseball season." Was there irony in the driver's chuckle?

"If you are furnishing me information that is at all reliable, driver, then the generalizability of my survey would be contingent on whether I ride in the morning or evening, on the professional sports schedule on a particular night, and on the season of the year."

"That's part of it, yessir."

"Part of it? Part of it? You mean, there's more? There is something else I haven't thought of?"

"Well, yessir, because, you see, most of these folks on the 5:15 bus are East City folks, and most of

(continued)

the people on the 5:45 bus are West City folks, so your outcomes would naturally depend on whether you took a survey on the 5:15 or 5:45 bus."

Burbidge was shaken and no longer able to muster a vigorous "impossible to accept" or even a "difficult to accept."

"How can this be? Tell me."

"Well, you see, the 5:15 bus on this route—the one you are on now—gets to Boght Corners at 5:55, and the East City folks transfer onto the eastbound bus that is waiting there for them. Most of the West City folks hang out in the bar across the street from the terminal, get on the 5:45 bus, and rendezvous at 6:25 with the westbound bus at Boght Corners."

"I see. I see." He was reconsidering the wisdom of this survey. "AND IS THERE ANYTHING ELSE you would care to share with me?"

"Only that the 5:45 boarders don't read the newspaper much at all, as they have been watching sports on the TV in the bar, are lightly soused, some of them, and can't read the small print because I don't turn on the inside lights."

"I might as well have stayed home," Burbidge cried in despair.

The driver stopped the bus and swiveled to face Burbidge. "Wouldn't that have been a pity, sir, as I would have been deprived of this excellent lesson in scientific research."

Burbidge studied the driver carefully, struggling to believe this last remark was not the unkindest cut of all. No, he concluded, the bumpkin is too disingenuous to be capable of irony.

THE NATURE OF SAMPLING

Most people intuitively understand the idea of sampling. One taste from a drink tells us whether it is sweet or sour. If we select a few employment records out of a complete set, we usually assume our selection reflects the characteristics of the full set. If some of our staff favors a flexible work schedule, we infer that others will also. These examples vary in their representativeness, but each is a sample.

The basic idea of **sampling** is that by selecting some of the elements in a population, we may draw conclusions about the entire population. A **population element** is the subject on which the measurement is being taken. It is the unit of study. For example, each office worker questioned about a flexible work schedule is a population element, and each business account analyzed is an element of an account population. A **population** is the total collection of elements about which we wish to make some inferences. All office workers in the firm compose a population of interest; all 4,000 files define a population of interest. A **census** is a count of all the elements in a population. If 4,000 files define the population, a census would obtain information from every one of them.

In studying customer satisfaction with the service operation for MindWriter, the popoulation of interest to Jason and Myra is all individuals who have had a laptop repaired while the CompleteCare program has been in effect. The population element is any one individual interacting with the service program.

Why Sample?   The economic advantages of taking a sample rather than a census are massive. Consider the cost of taking a census. Why should we spend thousands of dollars interviewing all 4,000 employees in our company if we can find out what we need to know by asking only a few hundred?

Deming argues that the quality of a study is often better with sampling than with a census. He suggests, "Sampling possesses the possibility of better interviewing (testing), more thorough investigation of missing, wrong, or suspicious information, better supervision, and better processing than is possible with complete coverage."[1] Research findings substantiate this opinion. More than 90 percent of the total survey error in one study was from nonsampling sources, and only 10 percent or less was from random sampling error.[2] The U.S. Bureau of the Census shows its confidence in sampling by taking sample surveys to check the accuracy of its census.

Sampling also provides much quicker results than does a census. The speed of execution reduces the time between the recognition of a need for information and the availability of that information. For every disgruntled customer that the MindWriter CompleteCare program generates, several prospective customers will move away from MindWriter to a competitor's laptop. So fixing the problems within the CompleteCare program will not only keep current customers coming back but encourage prospective customers from defecting to competitive brands due to negative word-of-mouth.

Some situations require sampling. When we test the breaking strength of materials, we must destroy them; a census would mean complete destruction of all materials. Sampling is also the only process possible if the population is infinite.

The advantages of sampling over census studies are less compelling when the population is small and the variability is high. Two conditions are appropriate for a census study: A census is (1) *feasible* when the population is small and (2) *necessary* when the elements are quite different from each other.[3] Consider North American manufacturers of stereo components. Fewer than 50 companies design, develop, and manufacture amplifier and loudspeaker products at the high end of the price range. The size of this population suggests a census is feasible. The diversity of their product offerings makes it difficult to accurately sample from this group. Some companies specialize in speakers, some amplifier technology, and others compact disk transports. Choosing a census in this situation is appropriate.

When the population is small and variable, any sample we draw may not be representative of the population from which it is drawn. The resulting values we calculate from the sample are incorrect as estimates of the population values. When the sample is drawn properly, however, some sample elements underestimate the parameters and others overestimate them. Variations in these values counteract each other; this counteraction results in a sample value that is generally close to the population value. For these offsetting effects to occur, however, there must be enough members in the sample, and they must be drawn in a way to favor neither overestimation nor underestimation.

What Is a Good Sample?

The ultimate test of a sample design is how well it represents the characteristics of the population it purports to represent. In measurement terms, the sample must be *valid.* Validity of a sample depends on two considerations.

Accuracy   First is the matter of *accuracy—the degree to which bias is absent from the sample.* An accurate (unbiased) sample is one in which the underestimators and the overestimators are balanced among the members of the sample. There is no **systematic variance** with an accurate sample. Systematic variance has been defined as "the variation in measures due to some known or unknown influences that 'cause' the scores to lean in one direction more than another."[4] Homes, for example, on the corner of the block are often larger and more valuable than those within the block. Thus, a sample that selects corner homes only will cause us to overestimate home values in the area. Burbidge learned that in selecting Route 99 for his newspaper readership sample, the time of day, day of the week, and season of the year of the survey dramatically reduced the accuracy and validity of his sample.

The classic example of a sample with systematic variance was the *Literary Digest* presidential election poll in 1936, in which more than 2 million persons participated. The poll said Alfred Landon would defeat Franklin Roosevelt for the presidency of the United States. Even the large size of this sample did not counteract its systematic bias. Later evidence showed that the poll drew its sample from the middle and upper classes, while Roosevelt's appeal was heavily among the much larger working class.

Precision   A second criterion of a good sample design is *precision of estimate.* No sample will fully represent its population in all respects. The numerical descriptors that describe samples may be expected to differ from those that describe populations because of random fluctuations inherent in the sampling process. This is called **sampling error** and reflects the influences of chance in drawing the sample members. Sampling error is what is left after all known sources of *systematic variance* have been accounted for. In theory, sampling error consists of random fluctuations only, although some unknown systematic variance may be included when too many or too few sample elements possess a particular characteristic. Let's say in drawing the MindWriter sample we inserted survey response cards in a sample of returned laptops and the list was alphabetized. As it works out, however, more than 80 percent of those surveyed had their laptops serviced by Max Jensen. And we know from our exploratory study that Max had more complaint letters about his work than any other technician. We have failed to truly randomize the sample and thus have increased our sampling error.

Precision is measured by the *standard error of estimate,* a type of standard deviation measurement; the smaller the standard error of estimate, the higher is the precision of the sample. The ideal sample design produces a small standard error of estimate. However, not all types of sample design provide estimates of precision, and samples of the same size can produce different amounts of error variance.

Types of Sample Design

A variety of sampling techniques is available. The one selected depends on the requirements of the project, its objectives, and funds available. In the discussion that follows, we will use three examples: (1) the Burbidge City Bus study introduced in the vignette at the beginning of this chapter, (2) the continuing MindWriter service satisfaction study, and (3) a study conducted by students taking an entrepreneurship class who are interested in starting a dining club near the campus of Metro University.

In the Metro U example their idea is to make a dining club's facilities available on a membership basis. To launch this venture, they will need to make a substantial investment. Research will allow them to reduce many risks. Thus the research question is: "Would the dining club be a viable enterprise?" An important general investigative question for their study might be, "Who would patronize the club and on what basis?" More detailed investigative questions that flow from the larger question are:

1. How many would join the club under various membership and fee arrangements?
2. How much would the average member spend per month?
3. What days would be most popular?
4. What menu and service formats would be most desirable?
5. What lunch times would be most popular?
6. Given the proposed price levels, how often per month would each member have lunch or dinner?
7. What percent of the people in the population say they would join the club, based on the projected rates and services?

We use the last three investigative questions for examples and focus on the last two for assessing the project's risks.

In decisions of sample design, the representation basis and the element selection techniques, as shown in Table 9–1, classify the different approaches.

Representation   The members of a sample are selected either on a probability basis or by another means. **Probability sampling** is based on the concept of *random selection—a controlled procedure that assures that each population element is given a known nonzero chance of selection.*

In contrast, **nonprobability sampling** is nonrandom and subjective. Each member does not have a known nonzero chance of being included. Allowing interviewers to choose sample members 'at random' (meaning 'as they wish' or 'wherever they find them') is not random sampling. Only probability samples provide estimates of

TABLE   9–1   Types of Sampling Designs

Element Selection	Representation Basis	
	Probability	*Nonprobability*
Unrestricted	Simple random	Convenience
Restricted	Complex random	Purposive
	Systematic	Judgment
	Cluster	Quota
	Stratified	Snowball
	Double	

precision. While we are not told how Burbidge selected the riders of Bus 99 as his sample, it's clear that he did not use probability sampling techniques.

Element Selection   Whether the elements are selected individually and directly from the population—viewed as a single pool—or whether additional controls are placed on element selection may also classify samples. When each sample element is drawn individually from the population at large, it is an *unrestricted sample. Restricted sampling* covers all other forms of sampling.

PROBABILITY SAMPLING

The unrestricted, simple random sample is the simplest form of probability sampling. Since all probability samples must provide a known nonzero chance of selection for each population element, the **simple random sample** is considered a special case in which each population element has a *known and equal chance* of selection. In this section, we use the simple random sample to build a foundation for understanding sampling procedures and choosing probability samples.

Steps in Sampling Design

There are several decisions to be made in securing a sample. Each requires unique information. While the questions presented here are sequential, an answer to one question often forces a revision to an earlier one. We will consider the following:

1. What is the relevant population?
2. What are the parameters of interest?
3. What is the sampling frame?
4. What is the type of sample?
5. What size sample is needed?
6. How much will it cost?

What Is the Relevant Population?   The definition of the population can be apparent from the management problem or the research question(s) but often is not. Is the population for the dining club at Metro University defined as full-time day students on the main campus of Metro U? Or should the population include all persons employed at Metro U? Or should townspeople who live in the neighborhood be included? Without knowing the target market chosen, it is not obvious which of these is the appropriate population.

There may also be confusion about whether the population consists of individuals, households, or families, or a combination of these. If a study concerns income, then the definition of the population element as individual or household can make quite a difference. Good operational definitions are critical at this point.

Assume the club is to be solely for the students and employees on the main campus. They might define the population as "all currently enrolled students and employees on the main campus of Metro U." However, this does not include family members. They may want to revise the definition to make it "current students and employees of Metro U, main campus, and their families."

In the nonprobability sample, Burbidge seems to have defined his relevant population as any rider of the City Bus system. He presumes he has an equal need to determine newspaper readership of both regular and infrequent City Bus riders, so that he might reach them with information about the new route structure, maps, and schedules. He can, however, easily reach regular riders by distributing information about the new routes via display racks on the bus for a period of time before the new routes are implemented. Infrequent riders, then, are the real interest of his newspaper readership study and should have been his population of interest.

What Are the Parameters of Interest?   **Population parameters** are summary descriptors (e.g., incidence, mean, variance) of variables of interest *in the population*. **Sample statistics** are descriptors of the relevant variables *computed from sample data*. Sample statistics are estimators of population parameters. They are the basis of our inferences about the population because they are the best estimates of the population.

When the variables of interest in the study are measured on interval or ratio scales, we use the sample mean to estimate the population mean and the sample standard deviation to estimate the population standard deviation. For Metro U investigative questions 5 and 6, the method of determining the sample—including the sample size calculation—is based on interval data estimators. In MindWriter, the rating of service (excellent, good, fair, etc.) by CompleteCare would be an example of an interval data estimator. Asking the City Bus riders about their number of days of ridership during the past 7 days would result in ratio data. Asking Metro U affiliates to reveal their frequency of eating on or near campus (less than 5 times per week, greater than 5 but less than 10 times per week, or greater than 10 times per week) would provide an interval data estimator.

Often a study may focus on nominally scaled data. In this event, a population proportion parameter would be of interest. The **population proportion** "is equal to the number of elements in the population belonging to the category of interest, divided by the total number of elements in the population."[5] Proportion measures are necessary for nominal data and are widely used for other measures as well. City Bus wanted to determine whether East City or West City had the most riders on Bus 99. MindWriter might want to know if men or women experienced the most problems with laptop model 9000. The most frequent concentration measure is the percentage; the variance equivalent is the *pq* ratio. In the Metro study, examples of nominal data are the proportion of a population that expresses interest in joining the club or the proportion of married students who report they now eat in restaurants at least five times a month. Investigative question 7 would be addressed with a proportion estimator. These procedures are discussed later in this chapter.

There may also be important subgroups in the population about whom we would like to make estimates. For example, we might want to draw conclusions about the extent of dining club use that could be expected from married students versus single students, residential students versus commuter students, and so forth. Such questions have a strong impact on the nature of the sampling frame we accept, the design of the sample, and its size. Burbidge should be more interested in reaching infrequent rather than regular City Bus riders with the newspaper advertising he plans. And in the MindWriter study, Jason may be interested in comparing responses of those who experienced poor service and those who experienced excellent service through the CompleteCare program.

What Is the Sampling Frame?   The **sampling frame** is closely related to the population. It is *the list of elements from which the sample is actually drawn.* Ideally, it is a complete and correct list of population members only. Jason should find limited problems obtaining a sampling frame of CompleteCare service users as MindWriter has maintained a database of all calls coming into the call center and all serial numbers of laptops serviced. As a practical matter, however, the sampling frame often differs from the theoretical population.

For the dining club study, the Metro U directory would be the logical choice as a sampling frame. Directories are usually accurate when published in the fall, but suppose the study is being done in the spring. The list will contain errors and omissions because some people will have left since the directory was published while others will have come to campus. You might use the directory anyway, ignoring the fact that it is not a fully accurate list. Just how much inaccuracy one can tolerate in choosing a sampling frame is a matter of judgment. Obviously, if the directory was a year old, the error might be unacceptable. One way to make the frame for the Metro study more representative would be to secure a supplemental list of the new students and employees from the Metro U Registrar's and Human Resources's databases.

A greater distortion would be introduced if a branch campus population were included in the Metro U directory. This would be an example of a too inclusive frame—that is, a frame that includes elements other than the ones in which we are interested. (Students and employees who have left since the directory was published are another example.)

Often you have to accept a sampling frame that includes people or cases beyond those in whom you are interested. You may have to use a telephone directory to draw a sample of business telephone numbers. Fortunately, this is easily resolved. You draw a sample from the larger population and screen out those who are not members of the group you wish to study.

The Metro U dining club survey is an example of a frame problem that is readily solved. Often one finds this task much more of a challenge. Suppose you need to sample the members of an ethnic group, say, Asians in Little Rock. There is probably no directory of this population. While you may use the general city directory, sampling from this too inclusive frame would be costly and inefficient. Asians probably represent only a small fraction of Little Rock's population, and the screening task would be monumental. Since ethnic groups frequently cluster in certain neighborhoods, you might identify these areas of concentration and then use a reverse area telephone or city directory to draw a sample. (City directories and reverse telephone directories are organized by street address.)

Burbidge had a definite problem as no sample frame of City Bus riders existed. While some regular riders used monthly passes, infrequent riders usually paid cash for their fares. It might have been possible for Burbidge to have anticipated this and developed over time a listing of customers. Bus drivers could have collected relevant contact information over a month, but the cost of contacting customers via phone or mail would have been much more expensive than the self-administered intercept approach Burbidge chose for data collection.

What Is the Type of Sample?

With personnel records available at a university and a population that is geographically concentrated, a probability sampling method is possible in the dining club study. University directories are generally available, and the costs of using a simple random sample would not be great here. Then, too, since the students are thinking of a major investment in the club, they would like to be confident they have a representative sample. The same analysis holds true for MindWriter: A sample frame is readily available, making a probability sample possible and likely.

Choosing a simple random sampling technique has several consequences. With this sample design, the students can make probability-based confidence estimates of various parameters. In using this method, they must also give careful attention to the execution of the sampling process. The selection must follow an appropriate procedure in which there is no chance for interviewers or others to modify the selections made. Strong efforts must be made to include all the elements in the original sampling frame, as no one other than those selected can be included in the study. The students must exclude substitutions except as clearly specified and controlled according to predetermined decision rules.

Despite all this care, the actual sample achieved will not match perfectly the sample that is originally drawn. Some people will refuse to participate, and others will be difficult to find. The latter represent the well-known "not-at-home" problem and require that enough callbacks be made to ensure they are adequately represented in the sample.

Due to the absence of a sampling frame of bus riders, Burbidge could have used a sampling frame of the bus routes. This would allow him to draw a sample using a cluster technique. Instead, it is obvious that Burbidge chose nonprobability sampling, arbitrarily choosing Bus 99 as a judgment sample and attempting to survey everyone riding the bus during the arbitrary times in which he chose to ride.

What Size Sample Is Needed?

Much folklore surrounds this question. One false belief is that a sample must be large or it is not representative. This is much less true than most people believe. Recall the *Literary Digest* example. A sample of more than 2 million voters failed to predict correctly a presidential election. In recent years, there has been controversy in congressional hearings about the representativeness of a national sample of TV viewers. Samples of 1,000 or more have been branded as inadequate by many critics but seldom, if ever, by a statistician. Sample size is only one aspect of representativeness. A sample of more than 2 million can be misleading while a sample of 1,000, drawn in the proper manner, can be more than adequate.

Often it is claimed that a sample should bear some proportional relationship to the size of the population from which it is drawn. One hears such views as, "A sample should be at least 10 percent or more of its population if it is to be credible." This is not true. The absolute size of a sample is much more important than its size compared with the population. *How large a sample should be is a function of the variation in the population parameters under study and the estimating precision needed by the researcher.* A sample of 400 may be appropriate sometimes, while more than 2,000 are required in other circumstances; in another case, perhaps a sample of only 40 is called for.

The basic formula for calculating sample size in probability sampling assumes an infinite population. Thus, a sample of 100 drawn from a population of 5,000 has roughly the same estimating precision as 100 drawn from a population of 200 million. The only problem with the sample from the larger population is the difficulty of drawing the sample. The most important factor in determining the size of a sample needed for estimating a population parameter is the size of the population variance. The greater the dispersion or variance in the population, the larger the sample must be to provide estimation precision. If we were asking opinions on a particular topic and everyone in the population held the same view, then a sample of one gives the complete picture of population opinion. If two opinions are possible, it takes a minimum of two in the sample to register them, and it takes a larger sample to estimate the relative frequency of the two views in the population. If a dozen views are possible, an even larger sample is needed to register them and estimate their frequency.

Just how large a sample the Metro U students need for their dining club study depends on how much precision they wish to secure. Since a sample can never reflect its population for certain, the researchers must decide how much precision they need. Precision is measured by (1) the interval range in which they would expect to find the parameter estimate and (2) the degree of confidence they wish to have in the estimate. More on these items later.

The size of the probability sample needed can be affected by the size of the population, but only when the sample size is large compared with the population. This so-called finite adjustment factor enters the calculation when the calculated sample is 5 percent or more of the population. The net effect of the adjustment is to reduce the size of the sample needed to achieve a given level of precision.[6] Other considerations often weigh heavily on the sample size decision. The conditions under which the sample is being conducted may suggest that only certain designs are feasible. One type of sample may be an inappropriate design because we have no lists of population elements and must therefore sample geographic units. This is what happened to Burbidge in his choice of Bus 99. Since various designs have differing statistical and economic efficiencies, the choice of design coupled with the other requirements mentioned above will also affect the size of the sample.

The researcher may also be interested in making estimates concerning various subgroups of the population; then the sample must be large enough for each of these subgroups to meet the desired level of precision. One achieves this in simple random sampling by making the total sample large enough to ensure that each critical subgroup meets the minimum size criterion. In more complex sampling procedures, the smaller subgroups are sampled more heavily, and then the parameter estimates drawn from these subgroups are weighted. Depending on the variety of causes of MindWriter complaints about repair service, Jason and Myra's sample size might be controlled by the number of models of laptops that MindWriter services.

How Much Will It Cost?   Cost considerations influence decisions about the size and type of sample and also the data collection methods. Almost all studies have some budgetary constraint, and this can mean a nonprobability sample must be used. Probability sample surveys incur callback costs, listing costs, and a variety of other costs that are not necessary when more haphazard methods are used.

Costs often dictate sample size. If there is a $2,000 budget for interviewing and it costs an estimated $25 to complete a personal interview using a simple random sample, the sample cannot exceed 80 respondents. By changing the design to a geographic cluster sample, we might be able to reduce this to $20 per interview, allowing a sample size of 100. A shift to a self-administered questionnaire might reduce costs to $12 per respondent, giving a sample of 167.[7]

Cost factors may also dictate abandoning personal interviewing in favor of either telephone or mail surveys. Thus, telephone interviews might cost $10 each, allowing a sample of 200. When the data collection method is changed, the amount and type of data that can be obtained also change.

For City Bus the cost of sampling riders' newspaper preferences to discover where to run the route-reconfiguration announcement must be significantly less than the cost of running ads in both East City and West City dailies. Thus the nonprobability judgment sampling procedure that Burbidge used was logical from a budget standpoint. The investment required to open the dining club at Metro U also justifies the more careful probability approach taken by the students. For MindWriter, an investment in CompleteCare has already been made; Myra would want to be highly confident that her recommendations to her supervising product manager to change CompleteCare procedures and policies would be on target and thoroughly supported by the data collected. These considerations justify a probability sampling approach.

Sampling Concepts

In this section, we discuss a few concepts that help in understanding probability sampling. Our treatment is largely intuitive, using Figures 9–1 and 9–2 and the student project at Metro U.

Figure 9–1 shows a population ($N = 20,000$) consisting of the values of 1, 2, 3, 4, and 5 for the preferred lunch times. The values represent 11:00 A.M., 11:30 A.M., 12:00 Noon, 12:30 P.M., and 1:00 P.M. The values have equal distances representing 30 minutes. The frequency of response (f) in the *population distribution,* shown beside the population, is what would be found if a census of the elements was taken. This information is unknowable, and we are pretending to be omniscient for the sake of the example. Normally, population data are unavailable or too costly to obtain.

Now assume we sample 10 data points from this population without knowledge of the population's characteristics. We use a sampling procedure from a statistical software program, a random number generator, or a table of random numbers. Our first sample ($n_1 = 10$) provides us with the frequencies shown in Figure 9–1. We also calculate a mean score, $\bar{X}_1 = 3.0$, for this sample. This mean would place the average preferred lunch hour at noon. The mean is a *point estimate* and our best predictor of the unknown population mean, μ (the arithmetic average of the population). Assume

FIGURE   9–1   Random Samples of Preferred Lunch Times

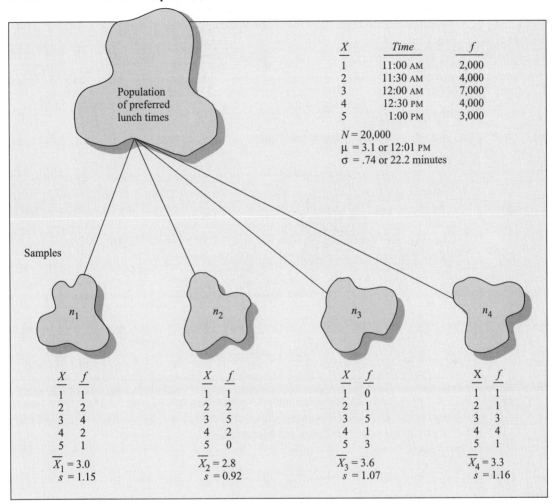

X	*Time*	f
1	11:00 AM	2,000
2	11:30 AM	4,000
3	12:00 AM	7,000
4	12:30 PM	4,000
5	1:00 PM	3,000

$N = 20,000$
$\mu = 3.1$ or 12:01 PM
$\sigma = .74$ or 22.2 minutes

Population of preferred lunch times

Samples

n_1

X	f
1	1
2	2
3	4
4	2
5	1

$\overline{X}_1 = 3.0$
$s = 1.15$

n_2

X	f
1	1
2	2
3	5
4	2
5	0

$\overline{X}_2 = 2.8$
$s = 0.92$

n_3

X	f
1	0
2	1
3	5
4	1
5	3

$\overline{X}_3 = 3.6$
$s = 1.07$

n_4

X	f
1	1
2	1
3	3
4	4
5	1

$\overline{X}_4 = 3.3$
$s = 1.16$

further that we return the first sample to the population and draw a second, third, and fourth sample by the same procedure. The frequencies, means, and standard deviations are shown in the figure. The means scores ($\overline{X}_1 = 3.0$, $\overline{X}_2 = 2.8$, $\overline{X}_3 = 3.6$, $\overline{X}_4 = 3.3$) form their own distribution, a *distribution of sample means*—to be used later. As the figure suggests, all the samples share some similarities with the population, but none are perfect duplications because no sample perfectly replicates its population.

We cannot judge which estimate is the true mean. We can say that each of the means is a point estimate of μ although none is likely to be exactly equal to μ. Again, the true population mean would be known with certainty only after completing a census. However, we can estimate the interval in which the true μ will fall by using any of the sample $\overline{X}$s. This is accomplished by using a formula that computes the **standard error of the mean.** The standard error of the mean measures the standard deviation of the distribution of sample means.

$$\sigma_{\overline{X}} = \frac{\sigma}{\sqrt{n}}$$

where

$\sigma_{\overline{X}}$ = Standard error of the mean or the standard deviation of all possible $\overline{X}$ values
σ = Population standard deviation
n = Sample size

The standard error of the mean varies directly with the standard deviation of the population from which it is drawn. If the population standard deviation were smaller—say, .37 instead of .74—the standard error would be only half as large. It also varies inversely with the square root of the sample size. If the square root of the sample size is doubled, the standard error is cut by one-half, provided the standard deviation remains constant. These relationships are shown:

	Reducing the Standard Deviation	*Doubling the Square Root of Sample Size*
$\sigma_{\overline{X}} = \frac{s}{\sqrt{n}}$	$\sigma_{\overline{X}} = \frac{.74}{\sqrt{10}} = .234$ $\sigma_{\overline{X}} = \frac{.37}{\sqrt{10}} = .117$	$\sigma_{\overline{X}} = \frac{.8}{\sqrt{25}} = .16$ $\sigma_{\overline{X}} = \frac{.8}{\sqrt{100}} = .08$

Let's now examine what happens when we apply sample data (n_1) from Figure 9–1 to the formula. The sample standard deviation will be used as an unbiased estimator of the population standard deviation.

$$\sigma_{\overline{X}} = \frac{s}{\sqrt{n}}$$

where

s = Standard deviation of the sample, n_1
$n_1 = 10$
$\overline{X}_1 = 3.0$
$s_1 = 1.15$
Substituting into the equation:

$$\sigma_{\overline{X}} = \frac{s}{\sqrt{n}} = \frac{1.15}{\sqrt{10}} = .36$$

How does this improve our prediction of μ from $\overline{X}$? The standard error creates the *interval range* that brackets the point estimate. In this example, μ is predicted to be 3.0 (the mean of n_1) $\pm$ .36. This range may be visualized on a continuum:

We would expect to find the true μ between 2.64 and 3.36—between 11:49 A.M. and 12:11 P.M. (If 2 = 11:30 and .64 (30 minutes) = 19.2 minutes, then 2.64 = 11:30 + 19.2 or 11:49.) Since we assume omniscience for this illustration, we know the population average value is 3.1. Further, because standard errors have characteristics like other standard scores, we have 68 percent confidence in this estimate—that is, one standard error encompasses ±1 Z or 68 percent of the area under the normal curve. Recall that the area under the curve also represents the confidence estimates that we make about our results. The combination of the interval range and the degree of confidence creates the **confidence interval.** To improve confidence to 95 percent, multiply the standard error of .36 by ±1.96 *(Z),* since 1.96 Z covers 95 percent of the area under the curve (see Table 9–2). Now, with 95 percent confidence, the interval in which we would find the true mean increases to ±.70 (from 2.3 to 3.7 or from 11:39 A.M. to 12:21 P.M.).

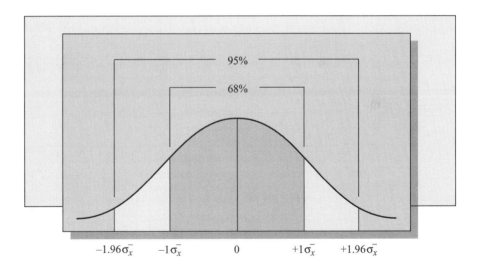

Parenthetically, if we compute the standard deviation of the *distribution of sample means* [3.0, 2.8, 3.6, 3.3], we will discover it to be .35. Compare this to the standard error from the formula (.36). The result is consistent with the second definition of the standard error: the *standard deviation of the distribution of sample means* (n_1, n_2, n_3, and n_4). It is, of course, impractical to draw repeated samples each time we want to generate an interval estimate for μ. Thus, the standard error formula is used. Now let's return to the dining club example and apply some of these concepts to the students' problem.

FIGURE   9–2   A Comparison of the Concepts of Population Distribution, Sample Distribution, and Distribution of Sample Means

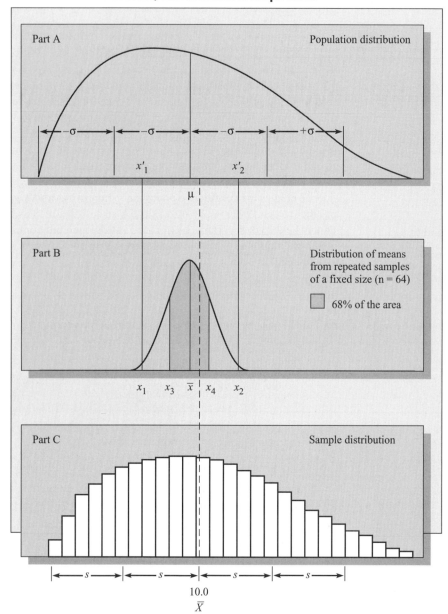

NOTE: The distributions in these figure are not to scale, but this fact is not critical to our understanding of the dispersion realtionships depicted.

If the students were to interview *all* the students and employees in the defined population, asking them, "How many times per month would you eat at the club?" they would get a distribution something like that shown in Part A of Figure 9–2. The responses would range from zero to as many as 30 lunches per month with a μ (mu) and σ (sigma).

However, they cannot take a census, so mu and sigma remain unknown. By sampling, the students find the mean to be 10.0 and the standard deviation to be 4.1. See Part C of Figure 9–2. Three observations about this sample distribution are consistent with our earlier illustration. First, it is shown as a histogram; it represents a frequency distribution of empirical data, while the smooth curve of Part A is a theoretical distribution. Second, the sample distribution (Part C) is similar in appearance but is not a perfect duplication of the population distribution (Part A). Third, the mean of the sample differs from the mean of the population.

Although the students will not draw repeated samples as we did earlier, if they did, they could plot the mean of each sample to secure the solid line distribution found in Part B. According to the **central limit theorem,** for sufficiently large samples ($n = 30$), the sample means will be distributed around the population mean approximately in a normal distribution. Even if the population is not normally distributed, the distribution of sample means will be normal if there is a large enough set of samples.

Estimating the Interval for the Students' Sample   Any sample mean will fall within the range of the distribution extremes shown in Part B of Figure 9–2. We also know that about 68 percent of the sample means in this distribution will fall between x_3 and x_4. Moving left to x_1 and right to x_2, about 95 percent will fall within this interval.

If we project points x_1 and x_2 up to the population distribution (Part A of Figure 9–2) at points x_1' and x_2', we see the interval where any given mean of a random sample of 64 is likely to fall 95 percent of the time. Since we do not know the population mean from which to measure the standard error, we infer that there is also a 95 percent chance that the population mean is within two standard errors of the sample mean (10.0). This inference enables us to find the sample mean, mark off an interval around it, and state a confidence likelihood that the population mean is within this bracket.

Because the students are considering an investment in this project, they would want some assurance that the population mean is close to the figure reported in any sample they take. To find out how close the population mean is to the sample mean, they must calculate the standard error of the mean and estimate an interval range within which the population mean is likely to be.

Given a sample size of 64, they still need a value for the standard error. Almost never will one have the value for the standard deviation of the population (σ), so we must use a proxy figure. The best proxy for σ is the standard deviation of the sample (*s*). Here the standard deviation ($s = 4.1$) was obtained from a pilot sample:

$$\sigma_{\bar{X}} = \frac{s}{\sqrt{n}} = \frac{4.1}{\sqrt{64}} = .51$$

If one standard error of the mean is equal to 0.51 visits, then 1.96 standard errors (95 percent) are equal to 1.0 visit. The students can estimate with 95 percent confidence that the population mean of expected visits is within 10.0 ± 1.0 visit, or from 9.0 to 11.0 meal visits per month.

Changing Confidence Intervals   This estimate may not be satisfactory in two ways. First, it may not represent the degree of confidence the students want in the interval estimate, considering their risk. They might want a higher degree of confidence than the 95 percent level used here. By referring to a table of areas under the normal curve, they can find various other combinations of probability. Table 9–2 summarizes some of those more commonly used. Thus, if the students want a greater confidence in the probability of including the population mean in the interval range, they can move to a higher standard error, say, $\bar{X} \pm 3\, \sigma_{\bar{X}}$. Now the population mean lies somewhere between $10.0 \pm 3 (0.51)$ or from 8.47 to 11.53. With 99.73 percent confidence, we can say this interval will include the population mean.

We might wish to have an estimate that will hold for a much smaller range, for example, 10.0 ± 0.2. To secure this smaller interval range, we must either (1) accept a smaller degree of confidence in the results or (2) take a sample large enough to provide this smaller interval with adequate confidence levels.

If one standard error is equal to 0.51 visits, then 0.2 visits would be equal to 0.39 standard errors (0.2/0.51). Referring to a table of areas under the normal curve, we find that there is a 30.3 percent chance that the true population mean lies within $\pm$ 0.39 standard errors of 10.0.[8] With a sample of 64, the sample mean would be subject to so much error variance that only 30 percent of the time could the students expect to find the population mean between 9.8 and 10.2. This is such a small degree of confidence that the students would normally move to the second alternative; they would increase the sample size until they could secure the desired interval estimate and degree of confidence.

Calculating the Sample Size for the Frequency of Patronage Question   We are ready to secure a sample size for the first key question in the entrepreneurship project. By way of review, decisions are needed on the following points:

1. The precision desired and how to quantify it:
   —Size of the interval estimate
   —The confidence we want with the estimate
2. The expected dispersion in the population for the question used to measure

TABLE   9–2   Estimates Associated with Areas under the Curve

Standard Error (Z)	Percent of Area*	Approximate Degree of Confidence	Interval Range of Dining Visits per Month
1.00	68.27	68%	μ is between 9.48 and 10.52
1.65	90.10	90%	μ is between 9.14 and 10.86
1.96	95.00	95%	μ is between 8.98 and 11.02
3.00	99.73	>99%	μ is between 8.44 and 11.56

*Includes both tails in a normal distribution.

precision

3. Whether a finite population adjustment should be used

The students have selected the investigative question, "frequency of patronage," because they believe it to be critical to the project's risks. Two subjective questions need to be answered to quantify the precision issue. One is how much confidence to place in the population interval estimate; the other is how large the estimating interval should be. The 95 percent confidence level is often used, but more or less confidence may be needed in light of project needs. *The students wanted 95 percent confidence.* This is equal to 1.96 Z.

Similarly, the size of the interval estimate for predicting the population parameter from the sample data should be decided. When a smaller interval is selected, we are saying that precision is vital. On a five-point measurement scale, one-tenth of a point is a very high degree of precision in comparison to a one-point interval. Both the degree of confidence and the desired interval are important determinants of sample size because they determine the standard error of the sample mean. *The students selected ±.5 meals per month per person as the interval estimate most consistent with the project's risks.*

The next factor that affects the size of the sample for a given level of precision is the population dispersion. The smaller the dispersion, the smaller is the sample needed to give a representative picture of population members. Suppose we were interested in the age of dining club members. If the population consists of ages ranging from 18 to 25, a smaller sample will give us a better estimate of the population's average age; with a population ranging from 18 to 65 years of age, a larger sample is needed for the same degree of confidence in the estimates. Since the population dispersion is unknowable, the standard deviation of the sample is used as a proxy figure. Typically, this figure is based on previous research on the topic, a pilot test, or a rule of thumb (one-sixth of the range). If the range is from 0 to 30 meals, the rule-of-thumb method would produce a standard deviation of five meals. *The students wanted more precision than the rule-of-thumb method provided, so they took a pilot sample of 25 and found the standard deviation to be 4.1 meals.*

A final factor affecting the size of a random sample is the size of the population. When the size of the sample exceeds 5 percent of the population, the finite limits of the population constrain the sample size needed. A correction factor is available in that event. *The students computed the sample as an infinite population because it did not need to be adjusted for a known 20,000-person population.*

The sample size is computed as

$$\sigma_{\bar{X}} = \frac{s}{\sqrt{n}}$$

$$\sqrt{n} = \frac{s}{\sigma}$$

$$n = \frac{s^2}{\sigma}$$

$$n = \frac{(4.1)^2}{(.255)^2}$$

$$n = 258.5 \text{ or } 259$$

where

$\sigma_X = 0.255$ from (0.5/1.96).

If we are willing to accept a larger interval range (± 1 meal), then $n = 65$.

Calculating the Sample Size for the Proportions Question   Up to this point, sample size has been discussed in terms of interval and ratio variables—measured as arithmetic means, standard deviations, and standard errors of the mean. Just as often, however, we deal with proportions data. An example is a CNN poll that projects the percentage of people who expect to vote for or against a proposition or a candidate. This is usually reported with a margin of error of ±5 percent.

The second key question concerning the dining club study was: "What percentage of the people in the population say they would join the dining club, based on the projected rates and services?" A sample answers this question using the same general procedure as before. But instead of the arithmetic mean, with proportions, it is p (the proportion of the population that has a given attribute).[9] And instead of the standard deviation, dispersion is measured in terms of $p \times q$ (in which q is the proportion of the population not having the attribute, and $q = (1 - p)$). The measure of dispersion of the sample statistic also changes from the standard error of the mean to the standard error of the proportion σ_p.

We calculate a sample size based on this data by making the same two subjective decisions—deciding on an acceptable interval estimate and the degree of confidence. Assume that 30 percent of the students say they will join the club. We decide to estimate the true proportion in the population within 10 percentage points of this figure ($p = 0.30 \pm 0.10$). Assume further that we want to be 95 percent confident that the population parameter is within ± 0.10 of the sample proportion. The calculation of the sample size proceeds as before:

±0.10   = Desired interval range within which the population proportion is expected (subjective decision)

1.96 σ_p = 95 percent confidence level for estimating the interval within which to expect the population proportion (subjective decision)

σ_p = 0.051= Standard error of the proportion (0.10/1.96)

pq = Measure of sample dispersion (used here as an estimate of the population dispersion)

$$\sigma_p = \sqrt{\frac{pq}{n}}$$

$$n = \frac{pq}{\sigma_p^{\,2}}$$

$$n = \frac{.03 \times .07}{(.051)^2}$$

$$n = 81$$

The sample size of 81 persons is based on an infinite population assumption. If the sample size is less than 5 percent of the population, there is little to be gained by using a finite population adjustment. The students interpreted the data found with a sample of 81 chosen randomly from the population as: "We can be 95 percent confident that 30 percent of the respondents would say they would join the club with a margin of error of ±10 percent."

Previously, the students used pilot testing to generate the variance estimate for the calculation. Suppose this is not an option. Proportions data have a feature concerning the variance that is not found with interval or ratio data. The *pq* ratio can never exceed 0.25. For example, if *p* = 0.5, then *q* = 0.5, and their product is 0.25. If either *p* or *q* is greater than 0.5, then their product is smaller than 0.25 ($0.4 \times 0.6 = 0.24$ and so on). When we have no information regarding the probable *p* value, we can assume that *p* = 0.5 and solve for the sample size.

$$n = \frac{pq}{\sigma_p^{\,2}}$$

$$n = \frac{0.25}{(.051)^2}$$

$$n = 96$$

If we use this maximum variance estimate in the dining club example, we find the sample needs to be 96. Because both investigative questions were of interest, the students would take the larger of the two sample sizes calculated, *n* = 259.

How to Choose a Random Sample   Selecting a random sample is accomplished with the aid of computer software, a table of random numbers, or a calculator with a random number generator. Drawing slips out of a hat or Ping-Pong balls from a drum serves as an alternative if every element in the sampling frame has an equal chance of selection. Mixing the slips (or balls) and returning them between every selection ensures that every element is just as likely to be selected as any other.

A table of random numbers (such as Appendix F, Table F–10) is a practical solution if no software program is available. Random number tables contain digits that have no systematic organization. Whether you look at rows, columns, or diagonals, you will find neither sequence nor order. Table F–10, in Appendix F, is arranged into 10 columns of five-digit strings, but this is solely for readability.

Assume the students in the entrepreneurship class want a special sample from the population of business school professors (of which there are 95). How will they begin? First the sampling frame is numbered consecutively. Then a random start in the table is found. (Dropping a pencil point-first onto the paper with closed eyes is sufficient.) Let's say the pencil dot lands on the eighth column from the left and 10 numbers down from the top of Table F–10, marking the five digits 05067. Further, the students agree to read the first two digits in this column downward until 10 faculty members are selected: 05, 27, 69, 94, 18, 61, 36, 85, 71, and 83. The digit 94 appeared twice and the second instance was omitted; 00 was omitted because the sampling frame started with 01. Other approaches to selecting digits are endless: horizontally right to left, bottom to top, diagonally across columns, and so forth. Computer selection of the sample would have been more efficient for the larger student project.

CLOSE-UP

"Do you know if the post office accepts checks?" asked Audrey, the business manager at the Chevron station.

"Couldn't say," Jason replied.

"Because I am going to spend a *fortune* on stamps and I don't want to carry a lot of cash down there." She waved a thick folio of three-up mailing labels. "I've got to survey our customers. Our banker insists. You know that new loan officer? The MBA? The one named Jasmine, who calls herself 'Jazz'?" We asked her for $50,000 so we can open at 5 A.M. and stay open until midnight— we have to put up a fence and some shrubbery, so as not to disturb the apartments in back, and install two new bays—and she told us to survey our customers to find out if many of them are retirees who go to bed early and wake up late and wouldn't use our service. And find out when the others leave for work in the morning and come home at night."

"So you have to do a survey."

"Yes. Three or four questions, maybe—nothing complicated. Like the two I mentioned and 'How long have you been our customer?'"

"How many years have you been our customer," Jason murmered reflexively.

"Oh, yeah, right. More precise, isn't it?" Audrey said. "But the point is, do you know what it costs to write to 1,000 customers?"

He crunched the numbers in his head. Postage to send out the survey. Postage prepaid to have it mailed back. Paper and printing. One envelope outbound and one inbound. Stuffing the outbound and opening and coding the inbound. "Minimum of $1.50 a survey," he said, "if your kids do the stuffing and opening and encoding. Maybe more. You generate labels from your computer, so you don't pay for labels, which saves a mint, maybe 25 cents a name."

"Right. A $1.50 times 1,000. Plus the kids' time, if I can pry them away from Little League, MTV, and personal calls."

"You don't need to survey 1,000 customers you know."

"Whaaat?"

"Pick 100 at random from your computer list. You'll get a 10 percent margin of error and save $1,350, plus the kids' time."

"That's hard to believe."

"But it's true," he said. "Look, why don't you take some of the money you save, and instead of just sampling 100 from your existing customer base, also do a separate survey of every 20th person from the Chamber of Commerce directory. You'll have one survey of customers and another of potential customers, and you'll still end up saving over $1,000."

She thought for a moment. "The banker will never believe this," she objected.

"The next time I make a deposit, I'll explain it to her."

"You do that," she said, "and we'll wax your car every three months for the next two years."

Jason was excited by the idea of having his car washed and waxed at no charge. He knew he was trading consulting services cheaply for automotive services, but it felt free, so the next day when he went to the bank he approached the new bank officer—the new market development V.P., actually—with carefully disguised excitement. This was going to be more fun than working for money.

Gosh, she was a tall woman. Jasmine Rogers. Thirty-five, he guessed, 6 feet 2 inches or even 6 feet 3. Hard to tell when she was sitting. She sat grandly behind a mahogany desk in a cubicle with three glass walls. But the back wall was covered—by sports memorabilia. A basketball shirt said, "Morgan State—African Tour, 1985," and there was another shirt that said, "Harvard B-School Intramurals." There were crossed field hockey sticks, too, and a boomerang, and a picture of her holding the boomerang with small folks he supposed were Australian nationals casting admiring glances at this tall American woman.

She came out to greet him and propelled him—almost lifted him—to a seat in her cubicle.

"So, what's up, Jason? Are we taking good care of you? Do you need another dozen computers? What?"

"I wanted to talk to you about the survey you asked Audrey to make. She and Juan own the Chevron station. . . ."

"Oh, sure. Audrey and Johnny. Good people . . . Say, if you are thinking of getting a BMW, I can give you a good rate on a loan."

"Well, I'm not in that bracket, Jazz. . . . Look, you told Audrey to take a survey of her customers, and that's what I wanted to discuss."

"I didn't intend her to have to hire a high-powered business consultant."

"Well, actually, this is more or less a favor, you see. . . ."

She chuckled. He thought she had a nice disposition for a banker. "A favor? By any means did she offer to wax your car about a million times for this favor? I had to turn down that particular offer, being her loan officer. Conflict of interest, you know. But if you want to help her, hey, I say that's great."

"Well, this is no big deal, Jazz. More or less a back-of-the-envelope computation, you see. Except I did it in my head, as there was no envelope handy."

"In your head? Impressive. I was on the math team in high school. . . ."

"Here's the thing. Audrey was about to do a census of her customers. . . ."

"A census? Surely not a survey of *all* her customers. I wanted just a sample. She must have misunderstood."

"Well, that's the thing. . . . I mean, I believe that a sample of maybe 100 customers will do the trick."

"I took marketing research in B-school, Jason, and while I certainly don't want to break Audrey's back, a sample of 100 seems kind of . . . well, thin."

"Maybe I can convince you."

"Maybe." She steepled her fingers thoughtfully and smiled wickedly. "Are you a betting man, Jason?" She placed a tall glass tumbler holding several dozen drinking straws between them. "I am willing to bet you cannot convince me."

"Then let me try. Take the first question you wanted. 'Are you currently retired from work?' This is what we call a proportions question. That is, a certain proportion of people will say they are retired."

"Yes," said the banker. "Suppose 20 percent of the existing customer base says they are retired. I would take that as a very bad omen for a station that opens early and closes late. Why would a retired person want to drop his car off at 6 A.M.?"

"Exactly . . . well, say 20 percent of the people sampled say they are retired. That's a proportion of .20, right? This means that, of the full 1,000-odd customers who comprise the 'population,' the actual proportion falls in a confidence interval centering around .20."

"Let me jump ahead here, Jason, because lunch approaches rapidly. I am willing to settle for a 95 percent chance of correctly locating the population proportion within an interval. . . ."

"So you will settle for a 95 percent confidence interval. You remember your statistics, I can see. Well, we need to compute the standard error of the proportion in order to compute the width of the confidence interval. To compute the standard error, we will use the formula. . . ."

Jazz leaned forward and grasped Jason's left hand with her right hand, to prevent him from writing formulas in the air, and held up the index finger of her left hand for attention. "One second, Jason. I am willing to bet you this," she extracted

(continued)

one drinking straw from the glass, "this valuable drinking straw, that I can tell you the formula to use. We take .2 and multiply by .8, and divide by 100 (which is your proposed number of subjects), and take the square root, which is, um . . . ," she rolled her eyes to the ceiling, "which is .04. And we multiply by 2. So the 95 percent confidence interval extends between .20 plus and minus 0.08, from .12 to .28." She laughed merrily and moved the straw closer to her side of the desk. "Come on, Jason, play this game to win. I won't take it out on Audrey."

"That's very good, Jazz, and I'm going to let you keep that straw. But you omitted to consider a significant factor. Would you care to improve your estimate?"

"Hah," she said, "I should have used 99 instead of 100. 'N − 1.' Hah!" and she reached for another straw from the tumbler, but Jason snatched the straw from her hands and set it on his side of the desk. Now each of them had a straw.

"That's too small a correction to matter. You lose."

"OK," she said with mock annoyance, "I should have multiplied by 1.96 instead of 2. That's it, isn't it?" And she reached for another straw, but Jason clapped his hand over the tumbler.

"Sorry," he said, "that's true, but again too small a correction to bother with. You should have allowed for the fact that she is sampling 100 out of a population of 1,000. That shrinks the standard error of the mean by the square root of 900/999, which comes to. . . ."

"Too small a correction to bother with," shouted Jazz with glee. "Take your hands away from my straws! OK, I'll give that to you, Jason, a sample of 100 will give me all the precision I want for that question. But what about the next question, 'What time do you leave your home in the morning to go to work?' "

"Well, we use a slightly different version of the formula this time. This time we divide the estimated standard deviation of the error by the square root of 100 to get the standard error of the mean."

She reached into the tumbler and withdrew another straw. "Wait just a second, Jason. I will bet you this straw that you don't know the standard error of the sample until after you have taken the sample."

"Well, then you are wrong. Because I happen to know that the morning rush hour extends from about 6:30 to 9:30, a period of 180 minutes, and applying the rule of thumb that the standard deviation is roughly one-sixth of the range, I arrived at a rough value of 30 minutes for the standard deviation, which gives a standard error of the mean of 3 minutes, which is all the precision you could possibly want." He reached for the straw, but this time she pulled it away.

"Wait a second, Mr. Statistician. Where did you get that rule of thumb?"

"I don't know," he admitted, "I picked it up during my graduate student days."

"Hah," she exulted. "Keep your straw-pickin' fingers away from my straws!"

"However," he said, "on returning to my office I did have a twinge of doubt about giving this advice to Audrey, so I called the planning department of the local bus company, which keeps enormously detailed statistical records as part of the requirement for their federal transportation subsidy, and they confirmed that the ridership of their number 45 bus through our town, and indeed the ridership of practically every other bus on the system, has a standard deviation of . . . 29 minutes." He extracted the straw. Now he had two, to her one.

"OK, Jason, you win. You have convinced me. If she can retrieve 100 surveys, I'll be satisfied. But I'll bet she will have to send out 200 surveys to get 100 replies."

"Not if her daughter makes follow-up phone calls," said Jason.

"OK, you win, this time. You have two straws to my one, which means I owe you a soda from the sandwich vendor who will pull his cart up outside in about one minute. Let me get my purse."

COMPLEX PROBABILITY SAMPLING

Simple random sampling is often impractical. It requires a population list that is often not available. The design may also be wasteful because it fails to use all the information about a population. In addition, the carrying out of a simple random design may be expensive in time and money. These problems have led to the development of alternative designs that are superior to the simple random design in statistical and/or economic efficiency.

A more efficient sample in a statistical sense is one that provides a given precision (standard error of the mean) with a smaller sample size. A sample that is economically more efficient is one that provides a desired precision at a lower dollar cost. We achieve this with designs that enable us to lower the costs of data collecting, usually through reduced travel expense and interviewer time.

In the discussion that follows, four alternative probability sampling approaches are considered: systematic, stratified, cluster, and double sampling.

Systematic Sampling

A versatile form of probability sampling is **systematic sampling.** In this approach, every kth element in the population is sampled, beginning with a random start of an element in the range of 1 to k. The major advantage of systematic sampling is its simplicity and flexibility. It is easier to instruct field workers to choose the dwelling unit listed on every kth line of a listing sheet than it is to use a random numbers table. With systematic sampling, there is no need to number the entries in a large personnel file before drawing a sample. Merely choose the total number of entries in the file, the sampling ratio, and the random start; then begin drawing a sample by choosing every kth entry. Invoices or customer accounts can be sampled by using the last digit or a combination of digits of an invoice or customer account number. Time sampling is also easily accomplished. This would be an appropriate technique for Mind-Writer's CompleteCare program evaluation.

While systematic sampling has some theoretical problems, from a practical point of view it is usually treated as a simple random sample. It is statistically more efficient than a simple random sample when similar population elements are grouped on the list. This might occur if the listed elements are ordered chronologically, by size, by class, and so on. Under these conditions, the sample approaches a proportional stratified sample. The effect of this ordering is more pronounced on the results of cluster samples than for element samples and may call for a proportional stratified sampling formula.[10]

A concern with systematic sampling is the possible *periodicity* in the population that parallels the sampling ratio. In sampling days of the week, a 1 in 7 sampling ratio would give biased results. A less obvious case might involve a survey in an area of apartment houses where the typical pattern is eight apartments per building. Many systematic sampling fractions, such as 1 in 8, could easily oversample some types of apartments and undersample others. The only protection against this is constant vigilance by the researcher.

Another difficulty may arise when there is a *monotonic trend* in the population elements. That is, the population list varies from the smallest to the largest element or vice versa. Even a chronological list may have this effect if a measure has trended in one direction over time. Whether a systematic sample drawn under these conditions provides a biased estimate of the population mean depends on the initial random draw. Assume that a list of 2,000 commercial banks is created, arrayed from the largest to the smallest, from which a sample of 50 must be drawn for analysis. A sampling ratio of 1 to 20 (begun with a random start at 16) and drawing every 20th bank would exclude the 15 largest banks and would give a downward size bias to the findings. There are ways to deal with this. One might randomize the population before sampling, change the random start several times in the sampling process, or replicate a selection of different samples.

Stratified Sampling

Most populations can be segregated into several mutually exclusive subpopulations, or strata. The process by which the sample is constrained to include elements from each of the segments is called **stratified random sampling.** University students can be divided by their class level, school, gender, and so forth. After a population is divided into the appropriate strata, a simple random sample can be taken within each stratum. The sampling results can then be weighted and combined into appropriate population estimates.

There are three reasons why a researcher chooses a stratified random sample. They are (1) to increase a sample's statistical efficiency, (2) to provide adequate data for analyzing the various subpopulations, and (3) to enable different research methods and procedures to be used in different strata.[11]

Stratification is usually more efficient statistically than simple random sampling and at worst is equal to it. With the ideal stratification, each stratum is homogeneous internally and heterogeneous with other strata. This might occur in a sample that includes members of several distinct ethnic groups. In this instance, stratification makes a pronounced improvement in statistical efficiency.

It is also useful when the researcher wants to study the characteristics of certain population subgroups. Thus, if one wishes to draw some conclusions about activities in the different classes of a student body, stratified sampling would be used. Stratification is also called for when different methods of data collection are applied in different parts of the population. This might occur when we survey company employees at the home office with one method but must use a different approach with employees scattered over the country.

If data are available on which to base a stratification decision, how shall we go about it?[12] The ideal stratification would be based on the primary variable under study. If the major concern is to learn how often per month patrons would use the dining club, then one would like to stratify on this expected number of use occasions. The only difficulty with this idea is that if we knew this information, we would not need to do the study. We must, therefore, pick a variable for stratifying that we believe will correlate with the frequency of club use per month.

Researchers often have several important variables about which they want to draw conclusions. A reasonable approach is to seek some basis for stratification that correlates well with the major variables. It might be a single variable (class level), or it might be a compound variable (class by gender). In any event, we will have done a good stratifying job if the stratification base maximizes the difference among strata means and minimizes the within-stratum variances for the variables of major concern.

The more strata used, the closer you come to maximizing interstrata differences and minimizing intrastratum variances. You must base the decision partially on the number of subpopulation groups about which you wish to draw separate conclusions. Costs of stratification also enter the decision. There is little to be gained in estimating population values when the number of strata exceeds six.[13]

The size of the strata samples is calculated with two pieces of information: (1) how large the total sample should be and (2) how the total sample should be allocated among strata. In deciding how to allocate a total sample among various strata, there are proportionate and disproportionate options.

Proportionate versus Disproportionate Sampling   In **proportionate stratified sampling,** each stratum is properly represented so the sample drawn from it is proportionate to the stratum's share of the total population. This approach is more popular than any other stratified sampling procedure. Proportionate sampling will generally have higher statistical efficiency than will a simple random sample. The method is also much easier to carry out than other stratifying methods. A third advantage is that such a sampling procedure provides a self-weighting sample; the population mean can be estimated simply by calculating the mean of all sample cases. On the other hand, proportionate stratified samples will often gain little in statistical efficiency if the strata means and variances are similar for the major variables under study.

Any stratification that departs from the proportionate relationship is **disproportionate.** There are several disproportionate allocation schemes. One type is a judgmentally determined disproportion based on the idea that each stratum is large enough to secure adequate confidence levels and interval range estimates for individual strata.

Decisions regarding disproportionate sampling, however, are usually made by considering how a sample will be allocated among strata. One author states,

In a given stratum, take a larger sample if

1. The stratum is larger.
2. The stratum is more variable internally.
3. Sampling is cheaper in the stratum.[14]

If one uses these suggestions as a guide, it is possible to develop an optimal stratification scheme. When there is no difference in within-stratum variances and when the costs of sampling among strata are equal, the optimal design is a proportionate sample.

While disproportionate sampling is theoretically superior, there is some question about whether it has wide applicability in a practical sense. If the differences in sampling costs or variances among strata are large, then disproportionate sampling is desirable. It has been suggested that "differences of several-fold are required to make disproportionate sampling worthwhile."[15]

Cluster Sampling

In a simple random sample, each population element is selected individually. The population can also be divided into groups of elements with some groups randomly selected for study. This is **cluster sampling.** An immediate question might be: How does this differ from stratified sampling? They may be compared as follows:

Stratified Sampling	Cluster Sampling
1. We divide the population into a few subgroups, each with many elements in it. The subgroups are selected according to some criterion that is related to the variables under study.	1. We divide the population into many subgroups, each with a few elements in it. The subgroups are selected according to some criterion of ease or availability in data collection.
2. We try to secure homogeneity within subgroups and heterogeneity between subgroups.	2. We try to secure heterogeneity within subgroups and homogeneity between subgroups, but we usually get the reverse.
3. We randomly choose elements from within each subgroup.	3. We randomly choose a number of the subgroups, which we then typically study in toto.

When done properly, cluster sampling also provides an unbiased estimate of population parameters. Two conditions foster the use of cluster sampling: (1) the need for more economic efficiency than can be provided by simple random sampling and (2) the frequent unavailability of a practical sampling frame for individual elements.

Statistical efficiency for cluster samples is usually lower than for simple random samples chiefly because clusters are usually homogeneous. Families in the same block (a typical cluster) are often similar in social class, income level, ethnic origin, and so forth.

While statistical efficiency in most cluster sampling may be low, economic efficiency is often great enough to overcome this weakness. The criterion, then, is the net relative efficiency resulting from the trade-off between economic and statistical factors. It may take 690 interviews with a cluster design to give the same precision as 424 simple random interviews. But if it costs only $2 per interview in the cluster situations and $4 in the simple random case, the cluster sample is more attractive ($1,380 versus $1,696).

Area Sampling   Much research involves populations that can be identified with some geographic area. When this occurs, it is possible to use **area sampling,** the most important form of cluster sampling. This method meets both the problems of high sampling cost and the unavailability of a practical sampling frame for individual elements. Area sampling methods have been applied to national populations, county populations, and even smaller areas where there are well-defined political or natural boundaries.

Suppose you want to survey the adult residents of a city. You would seldom be able to secure a listing of such individuals. It would be simple, however, to get a detailed city map that shows the blocks of the city. If you take a sample of these blocks, you are also taking a sample of the adult residents of the city.

Design   In designing cluster samples, including area samples, we must answer several questions:

1. How homogeneous are the clusters?
2. Shall we seek equal or unequal clusters?
3. How large a cluster shall we take?
4. Shall we use a single-stage or multistage cluster?
5. How large a sample is needed?

1. Clusters are homogeneous. This contributes to low statistical efficiency. Sometimes one can improve this efficiency by constructing clusters to increase intra-cluster variance. In the dining club study, the students might have constructed clusters that included members from all classes. In area sampling, they could combine adjoining blocks that contain different income groups or social classes. Area cluster sections do not have to be contiguous, but the cost savings is lost if they are not near each other.

2. A cluster sample may be composed of clusters of equal or unequal size. The theory of clustering is that the means of sample clusters are unbiased estimates of the population mean. This is more often true when clusters are equal. It is often possible to construct artificial clusters that are approximately equal, but natural clusters, such as households in city blocks, often vary substantially. While one can deal with clusters of unequal size, it may be desirable to reduce or counteract the effects of unequal size. There are several approaches to this.

One way to overcome the variation in cluster size is to combine small clusters and split large clusters until all approximate an average size. A second approach is to stratify clusters by size and choose clusters from each stratum. A third approach is size-stratified subsampling in which clusters are stratified by size and then sub-sampled, using varying sampling fractions to secure an overall sampling ratio. We may seek an overall sampling fraction of 1/60 and desire that subsamples be about five elements each. One group of clusters might average about 10 elements per cluster. In the "10 elements per cluster" stratum, we might choose 1 in 30 of the clusters and then subsample each chosen cluster at a 1/2 rate to secure the overall 1/60 sampling fraction. Among clusters of 120 elements, we might select clusters at a 1/3 rate and then subsample at a 1/20 rate to secure the 1/60 sampling fraction.[16]

3. The third question concerns the size of the cluster. There is no *a priori* answer to this question. Even with single-stage clusters, say, of 5, 20, or 50, it is not clear which size is superior. Some have found that in studies using single-stage clusters, the optimal cluster size is no larger than the typical city block.[17] To compare the efficiency of the above three cluster sizes requires that we discover the different costs for each size and estimate the different variances of the cluster means.

4. The fourth question concerns whether to use a *single-stage* or a *multistage* cluster design. For most area sampling, especially large-scale studies, the tendency is to use multistage methods.

> There are four reasons that justify subsampling, in preference to the direct creation of smaller clusters and their selection in one-stage cluster sampling: (1) *Natural clusters* may exist as convenient sampling units, yet larger than the desired economic size. . . . (2) We *can avoid the cost of creating smaller clusters* in the entire population and confine it to the selected sampling units. . . . (3) *The effect of clustering* . . . is often less in larger clusters. For example, a compact cluster of four dwellings from a city block may bring into the sample similar dwellings, perhaps from one building; but four dwellings selected separately can be spread around the dissimilar sides of the block. (4) The sampling *of compact clusters may present practical difficulties.* For example, independent interviewing of all members of a household may seem impractical.[18]

5. How large a sample is needed—that is, how many subjects must be interviewed or observed? The answer to this question depends heavily on the specific cluster design, and these details can be complicated. Unequal clusters and multistage samples are the chief complications, and their statistical treatment is beyond the scope of this book.[19] Here we will treat only single-stage samples with equal-size clusters (called simple cluster sampling). It is analogous to simple random sampling. The simple random sample is really a special case of simple cluster sampling. We can think of a population as consisting of 20,000 clusters of one student each, or 2,000 clusters of 10 students each, and so on. The only difference between a simple random and a simple cluster sample is the size of cluster. Since this is so, we should expect that the calculation of a probability sample size would be the same for both types.

Double Sampling

It may be more convenient or economical to collect some information by sample and then use this information as the basis for selecting a subsample for further study. This procedure is called **double sampling,** *sequential sampling,* or *multiphase sampling.* It is usually found with stratified and/or cluster designs. The calculation procedures are described in more advanced texts.

Double sampling can be illustrated by the dining club example. You might use a telephone survey or another inexpensive survey method to discover who would be interested in joining such a club and the degree of their interest. You might then stratify the interested respondents by degree of interest and subsample among them for intensive interviewing on expected consumption patterns, reactions to various services, and so on. Whether it is more desirable to gather such information by one-stage or two-stage sampling depends largely on the relative costs of the two methods.

Because of the wide range of sampling designs available, it is often difficult to select an approach that meets the needs of the research question and helps to contain the costs of the project. To help with these choices, Table 9–3 may be used to compare the various advantages and disadvantages of probability sampling. Nonprobability sampling techniques are covered in the next section. They are used frequently and offer the researcher the benefit of low cost. However, they are not based on a theoretical framework and do not operate from statistical theory; consequently, they

TABLE   9–3   Comparison of Probability Sampling Designs

Type	*Description*	*Advantages*	*Disadvantages*
Simple random	Each population element has an equal chance of being selected into the sample. Sample drawn using random number table/generator.	Easy to implement with automatic dialing (random digit dialing) and with computerized voice response systems.	Requires a listing of population elements. Takes more time to implement. Uses larger sample sizes. Produces larger errors. Expensive.
Systematic	Selects an element of the population at a beginning with a random start and following the sampling fraction selects every *k*th element.	Simple to design. Easier to use than the simple random. Easy to determine sampling distribution of mean or proportion. Less expensive than simple random.	Periodicity within the population may skew the sample and results. If the population list has a monotonic trend, a biased estimate will result based on the start point.
Stratified	Divide population into subpopulations or strata and use simple random on each strata. Results may be weighted and combined.	Researcher controls sample size in strata. Increased statistical efficiency. Provides data to represent and analyze subgroups. Enables use of different methods in strata.	Increased error will result if subgroups are selected at different rates. Expensive. Especially expensive if strata on the population have to be created.
Cluster	Population is divided into internally heterogeneous subgroups. Some are randomly selected for further study.	Provides an unbiased estimate of population parameters if properly done. Economically more efficient than simple random. Lowest cost per sample, especially with geographic clusters. Easy to do without a population list.	Often lower statistical efficiency (more error) due to subgroups being homogeneous rather than heterogeneous.
Double (sequential) (multiphase)	Process includes collecting data from a sample using a previously defined technique; based on the information found, selecting a subsample for further study.	May reduce costs if first stage results in enough data to stratify or cluster the population.	If indiscriminately used, it will increase costs.

produce selection bias and nonrepresentative samples. Despite these weaknesses, their widespread use demands their mention here.

NONPROBABILITY SAMPLING

Any discussion of the relative merits of probability versus nonprobability sampling clearly shows the technical superiority of the former. In probability sampling, researchers use a random selection of elements to reduce or eliminate sampling bias. Under such conditions, we can have substantial confidence that the sample is representative of the population from which it is drawn. In addition, with probability sample designs, we can estimate an interval range within which the population parameter is expected to fall. Thus, we not only can reduce the chance for sampling error but also can estimate the range of probable sampling error present.

With a subjective approach like **nonprobability sampling,** the probability of selecting population elements is unknown. There are a variety of ways to choose persons or cases to include in the sample. Often we allow the choice of subjects to be made by field workers on the scene. When this occurs, there is greater opportunity for bias to enter the sample selection procedure and to distort the findings of the study. Also, we cannot estimate any range within which to expect the population parameter. Given the technical advantages of probability sampling over nonprobability sampling, why would anyone choose the latter? There are some practical reasons for using these less precise methods.

Practical Considerations

We may use nonprobability sampling procedures because they satisfactorily meet the sampling objectives. While a random sample will give us a true cross section of the population, this may not be the objective of the research. If there is no desire or need to generalize to a population parameter, then there is much less concern about whether the sample fully reflects the population. Often researchers have more limited objectives. They may be looking only for the range of conditions or for examples of dramatic variations. This is especially true in exploratory research where one may wish to contact only certain persons or cases that are clearly atypical. Burbidge would have likely wanted a probability sample if the decision resting on the data was the actual design of the new City Bus routes and schedules. However, the decision of where and when to place advertising announcing the change is a relatively low-cost one in comparison.

Additional reasons for choosing nonprobability over probability sampling are cost and time. Probability sampling clearly calls for more planning and repeated callbacks to ensure that each selected sample member is contacted. These activities are expensive. Carefully controlled nonprobability sampling often seems to give acceptable results, so the investigator may not even consider probability sampling. Burbidge's results from Bus 99 would generate questionable data, but he seemed to realize the fallacy of many of his assumptions once he spoke with Bus 99's driver, something he should have done during exploration prior to designing the sampling plan.

While probability sampling may be superior in theory, there are breakdowns in its application. Even carefully stated random sampling procedures may be subject to careless application by the people involved. Thus, the ideal probability sampling may be only partially achieved because of the human element.

It is also possible that nonprobability sampling may be the only feasible alternative. The total population may not be available for study in certain cases. At the scene of a major event, it may be infeasible to even attempt to construct a probability sample. A study of past correspondence between two companies must use an arbitrary sample because the full correspondence is normally not available.

In another sense, those who are included in a sample may select themselves. In mail surveys, those who respond may not represent a true cross section of those who receive the questionnaire. The receivers of the questionnaire decide for themselves whether they will participate. There is some of this self-selection in almost all surveys because every respondent chooses whether to be interviewed.

Methods

Convenience   Nonprobability samples that are unrestricted are called **convenience samples.** They are the least reliable design but normally the cheapest and easiest to conduct. Researchers or field workers have the freedom to choose whomever they find, thus the name *convenience.* Examples include informal pools of friends and neighbors or people responding to a newspaper's invitation for readers to state their positions on some public issue.

While a convenience sample has no controls to ensure precision, it may still be a useful procedure. Often you will take such a sample to test ideas or even to gain ideas about a subject of interest. In the early stages of exploratory research, when you are seeking guidance, you might use this approach. The results may present evidence that is so overwhelming that a more sophisticated sampling procedure is unnecessary. In an interview with students concerning some issue of campus concern, you might talk to 25 students selected sequentially. You might discover that the responses are so overwhelmingly one-sided that there is no incentive to interview further.

Purposive Sampling   A nonprobability sample that conforms to certain criteria is called purposive sampling. There are two major types—judgment sampling and quota sampling.

Judgment sampling occurs when a researcher selects sample members to conform to some criterion. In a study of labor problems, you may want to talk only with those who have experienced on-the-job discrimination. Another example of judgment sampling occurs when election results are predicted from only a few selected precincts that have been chosen because of their predictive record in past elections. Burbidge chose Bus 99 because the current route led him to believe that he could get a representation of both East City and West City riders.

When used in the early stages of an exploratory study, a judgment sample is appropriate. When one wishes to select a biased group for screening purposes, this sampling method is also a good choice. Companies often try out new product ideas on their employees. The rationale is that one would expect the firm's employees to be more favorably disposed toward a new product idea than the public. If the product does not pass this group, it does not have prospects for success in the general market.

Quota sampling is the second type of purposive sampling. We use it to improve representativeness. The logic behind quota sampling is that certain relevant characteristics describe the dimensions of the population. If a sample has the same distribution on these characteristics, then it is likely representative of the population regarding other variables on which we have no control. Suppose the student body of

Metro U is 55 percent female and 45 percent male. The sampling quota would call for sampling students at a 55 to 45 percent ratio. This would eliminate distortions due to a nonrepresentative gender ratio. Burbidge could have improved his nonprobability sampling by considering time of day and day of week variations and chosen to distribute surveys to Bus 99 riders at various times, creating a quota sample.

In most quota samples, researchers specify more than one control dimension. Each should meet two tests: (1) It should have a distribution in the population that we can estimate. (2) It should be pertinent to the topic studied. We may believe that responses to a question should vary, depending on the gender of the respondent. If so, we should seek proportional responses from both men and women. We may also feel that undergraduates differ from graduate students, so this would be a dimension. Other dimensions such as the student's academic discipline, ethnic group, religious affiliation, and social group affiliation may be chosen. Only a few of these controls can be used. To illustrate, suppose we consider the following:

Gender—two categories—male, female

Class level—two categories—graduate and undergraduate

College—six categories—Arts and Science, Agriculture, Architecture, Business, Engineering, other

Religion—four categories—Protestant, Catholic, Jewish, other

Fraternal affiliation—two categories—member, nonmember

Family social-economic class—three categories—upper, middle, lower

In an extreme case, we might ask an interviewer to find a male undergraduate business student who is Catholic, a fraternity member, and from an upper-class home. All combinations of these five factors would call for 288 such cells to consider. This type of control is known as *precision control*. It gives greater assurance that a sample will be representative of the population. However, it is costly and too difficult to carry out with more than three variables.

When we wish to use more than three control dimensions, we should depend on *frequency control*. With this form of control, the overall percentage of those with each characteristic in the sample should match the percentage holding the same characteristic in the population. No attempt is made to find a combination of specific characteristics in a single person. In frequency control, we would probably find that the accompanying sample array is an adequate reflection of the population:

	Population	*Sample*
Male	65%	67%
Married	15	14
Undergraduate	70	72
Campus resident	30	28
Independent	75	73
Protestant	39	42

Quota sampling has several weaknesses. First, the idea that quotas on some variables assume a representativeness on others is argument by analogy. It gives no assurance that the sample is representative on the variables being studied. Often, the data used to provide controls may also be dated or inaccurate. There is also a practical limit on the number of simultaneous controls that can be applied to ensure precision. Finally, the choice of subjects is left to field workers to make on a judgmental basis. They may choose only friendly looking people, people who are convenient to them, and so forth.

Despite the problems with quota sampling, it is widely used by opinion pollsters and marketing and other researchers. Probability sampling is usually much more costly and time-consuming. Advocates of quota sampling argue that while there is some danger of systematic bias, the risks are usually not that great. Where predictive validity has been checked (e.g., in election polls), quota sampling has been generally satisfactory.

Snowball   This design has found a niche in recent years in applications where respondents are difficult to identify and are best located through referral networks. In the initial stage of **snowball sampling,** individuals are discovered and may or may not be selected through probability methods. This group is then used to locate others who possess similar characteristics and who, in turn, identify others. Similar to a reverse search for bibliographic sources, the "snowball" gathers subjects as it rolls along. Various techniques are available for selecting a nonprobability snowball with provisions for error identification and statistical testing. Let's consider a brief example.

The high end of the U.S. audio market is composed of several small firms that produce ultra-expensive components used in recording and playback of live performances. A risky new technology for improving digital signal processing is being contemplated by one firm. Through their contacts with a select group of recording engineers and electronics designers, the first-stage sample may be identified for interviewing. Subsequent interviewees are likely to reveal critical information for product development and marketing.

Variations on snowball sampling have been used to study drug cultures, teenage gang activities, power elites, community relations, insider trading, and other applications where respondents are difficult to identify and contact.

Summary

Sampling is based on two premises. One is that there is enough similarity among the elements in a population that a few of these elements will adequately represent the characteristics of the total population. The second premise is that while some elements in a sample underestimate a population value, others overestimate this value. The result of these tendencies is that a sample statistic such as the arithmetic mean is generally a good estimate of a population mean.

A good sample has both accuracy and precision. An accurate sample is one in which there is little or no bias or systematic variance. A sample with adequate precision is one that has a sampling error that is within acceptable limits for the study's purpose.

A variety of sampling techniques is available. They may be classified by their representation basis and element selection techniques as shown in the accompanying table.

| | **Representation Basis** | |
Element Selection	Probability	Nonprobability
Unrestricted	Simple random	Convenience
Restricted	Complex random	Purposive
	Systematic	Judgment
	Cluster	Quota
	Stratified	Snowball
	Double	

Probability sampling is based on random selection—a controlled procedure that ensures that each population element is given a known nonzero chance of selection. In contrast, nonprobability selection is "not random." When each sample element is drawn individually from the population at large, it is unrestricted sampling. Restricted sampling covers those forms of sampling in which the selection process follows more complex rules.

The simplest type of probability approach is simple random sampling. In this design, each member of the population has an equal chance of being included in a sample. In developing a probability sample, six procedural questions need to be answered:

1. What is the relevant population?
2. What are the parameters of interest?
3. What is the sampling frame?
4. What is the type of sample?
5. What size sample is needed?
6. How much will it cost?

Two kinds of estimates of a population parameter are made in probability sampling. First we make a point estimate that is the single best estimate of the population value. Then we make an interval estimate that covers the range of values within which we expect the population value to occur, with a given degree of confidence. All sample-based estimates of population parameters should be stated in terms of a confidence interval.

The specifications of the researcher and the nature of the population determine the size of a probability sample. These requirements are largely expressed in the following questions:

- What is the degree of confidence we want in our parameter estimate?
- How large an interval range will we accept?
- What is the degree of variance in the population?
- Is the population small enough that the sample should be adjusted for finite population?

Cost considerations are also often incorporated into the sample size decision.

Complex sampling is used when conditions make simple random samples impractical or uneconomical. The four major types of complex random sampling discussed in this chapter are systematic, stratified, cluster, and double sampling.

Systematic sampling involves the selection of every *k*th element in the population by beginning with a random start between elements from 1 to *k*. Its simplicity in certain cases is its greatest value.

Stratified sampling is based on dividing a population into subpopulations and then randomly sampling from each of these strata. This method usually results in a smaller total sample size than would a simple random design. Stratified samples may be proportionate or disproportionate.

In cluster sampling, we divide the population into convenient groups and then randomly choose the groups to study. It is typically less efficient from a statistical viewpoint than the simple random because of the high degree of homogeneity within the clusters. Its great advantage is the cost savings if the population is dispersed geographically or in time. The most widely used form of clustering is area sampling in which geographic areas are the selection elements.

At times it may be more convenient or economical to collect some information by sample and then use it as a basis for selecting a subsample for further study. This procedure is called double sampling.

Nonprobability sampling also has some compelling practical advantages that account for its widespread use. Often probability sampling is not feasible because the population is not available. Then, too, frequent breakdowns in the application of probability sampling discount its technical advantages. You find also that a true cross section is often not the aim of the researcher. Here the goal may be the discovery of the range or extent of conditions. Finally, nonprobability sampling is usually less expensive to conduct than is probability sampling.

Convenience samples are the simplest and least reliable forms of nonprobability sampling. Their primary virtue is low cost. One purposive sample is the judgmental sample in which one is interested in studying only selected types of subjects. The other purposive sample is the quota sample. Subjects are selected to conform to certain predesignated control measures that secure a representative cross section of the population. Snowball sampling uses a referral approach to reach particularly hard-to-find respondents.

Key Terms

area sampling	quota sampling
census	sample statistics
central limit theorem	sampling
cluster sampling	sampling error
confidence interval	sampling frame
convenience samples	simple random sample
double sampling	snowball sampling
judgment samples	standard error of the mean
nonprobability sampling	stratified random sampling
population	disproportionate
population element	proportionate
population parameters	systematic sampling
population proportion	systematic variance
probability sampling	

Case

Can This Survey Be Saved?
(This is a case found in the optional casebook available with the text.)

Discussion Questions

1. Distinguish between
    a. Statistic and parameter
    b. Sample frame and population
    c. Restricted and unrestricted sampling
    d. Standard deviation and standard error
    e. Simple random and complex random sampling
    f. Convenience and purposive sampling
    g. Sample precision and sample accuracy
    h. Systematic and error variance
    i. Variable and attribute parameters
    j. Point estimate and interval estimate
    k. Proportionate and disproportionate samples

2. Under what kind of conditions would you recommend
    a. A probability sample? A nonprobability sample?
    b. A simple random sample? A cluster sample? A stratified sample?
    c. Using the finite population adjustment factor?
    d. A disproportionate stratified probability sample?

3. You plan to conduct a survey using unrestricted sampling. What subjective decisions must you make?

4. You draw a random sample of 300 employee records from the personnel file and find that the average years of service per employee is 6.3, with a standard deviation of 3.0 years.
    a. What percentage of the workers would you expect to have more than 9.3 years of service?
    b. What percentage would you expect to have more than 5.0 years of service?

5. You want to interview a representative sample of undergraduate students but conclude there is no way to use probability sampling methods. You decide on a nonprobability method. The registrar gives you counts of freshmen, sophomores, juniors, and seniors, plus how many male and female students are in each class. How would you conduct a reasonably reliable nonprobability sample?

6. A manufacturer of precision gaskets makes gaskets in two grades: military and consumer automobile. In military applications the precise gasket thickness is far more critical than in consumer automobile applications. The production run for military applications is very small, whereas the production

run for consumer applications is very large. Explain how these facts affect decisions in sample design, confidence intervals, and sample size.

7. You wish to take an unrestricted random sample of undergraduate students at Cranial University to ascertain their levels of spending per month for food purchased off campus and eaten on the premises where purchased. You ask a test sample of nine students about their food expenditures and find that on the average they report spending $20, with two-thirds of them reporting spending from $10 to $30. What size sample do you think you should take? (Assume your universe is infinite.)

8. You wish to adjust your sample calculations to reflect the fact that there are only 2,500 students in your population. How does this additional information affect your estimated sample size in question 7?

9. Suppose you are going to take a sample survey and you want to estimate within a probable plus or minus 5 percent the proportion of people who have made a job change within the past year. What size of sample would you take if it were to be an unrestricted sample?

Reference Notes

1. W. E. Deming, *Sample Design in Business Research* (New York: Wiley, 1960), p. 26.
2. Henry Assael and John Keon, "Nonsampling Versus Sampling Errors in Survey Research," *Journal of Marketing Research* (Spring 1982), pp. 114–23.
3. A. Parasuraman, *Marketing Research,* 2nd ed. (Reading, MA: Addison-Wesley, 1991), p. 477.
4. Fred N. Kerlinger, *Foundations of Behavioral Research,* 3rd ed. (New York: Holt, Rinehart & Winston, 1986), p. 72.
5. Amir D. Aczel, *Complete Business Statistics* (Burr Ridge, IL: Irwin, 1996), p. 180.
6. The correction for a finite population is shown in the example below:
   If a finite population of 20,000 is considered, the sample size is 256 for an interval of ± .5 meals and 95 percent confidence.

   $$\sigma_{\bar{X}} = \frac{s}{\sqrt{n-1}} \times \sqrt{\frac{N-n}{N-1}} = 0.255 = \frac{4.1}{\sqrt{n-1}} \times \sqrt{\frac{20,000-n}{20,000-1}}$$

   or

   $$n = \frac{s^2 N + \sigma_{\bar{X}}^2 (N-1)}{s^2 + \sigma_{\bar{X}}^2 (N-1)}$$

   $$n = 256$$

   where
   N = size of the population
   n = size of the sample
7. All estimates of costs are hypothetical.
8. See Appendix F, Table F–1, at the back of the book.
9. A proportion is the mean of a dichotomous variable when members of a class receive the value of 1, and nonmembers receive a value of 0.
10. Leslie Kish, *Survey Sampling* (New York: Wiley, 1965), p. 188.
11. Ibid., pp. 76–77.

12. Typically, stratification is carried out before the actual sampling, but when this is not possible, it is still possible to stratify after the fact. Ibid., p. 90.
13. W. G. Cochran, *Sampling Techniques,* 2nd ed. (New York: Wiley, 1963), p. 134.
14. Ibid., p. 96.
15. Kish, *Survey Sampling,* p. 94.
16. For detailed treatment of these and other cluster sampling methods and problems, see Kish, *Survey Sampling,* pp. 148–247.
17. J. H. Lorie and H. V. Roberts, *Basic Methods of Marketing Research* (New York: McGraw-Hill, 1951), p. 120.
18. Kish, *Survey Sampling,* p. 156.
19. For specifics on these problems and how to solve them, the reader is referred to the many good sampling texts. Two that have already been mentioned are Kish, *Survey Sampling,* chaps. 5, 6, and 7; and Cochran, *Sampling Techniques,* chaps. 9, 10, and 11.

Suggested Readings

1. Deming, W. Edwards. *Sample Design in Business Research.* New York: Wiley, 1990. A classic by the late author, an authority on sampling.
2. Kalton, Graham. *Introduction to Survey Sampling.* Beverly Hills, CA: Sage Publications, 1983. An overview with particular attention to survey applications.
3. Kish, Leslie. *Survey Sampling.* New York: Wiley, 1995. A widely read reference on survey sampling recently updated.
4. Namias, Jean. *Handbook of Selected Sample Surveys in the Federal Government.* New York: St. John's University Press, 1969. A unique collection of illustrative uses of sampling for surveys carried out by various federal agencies. Of interest both for the sampling designs presented and for the information on the methodology used to develop various government statistical data.
5. Yates, F. *Sampling Methods for Censuses and Surveys,* 4th ed. New York: Oxford University Press, 1987. A readable text with emphasis on sampling practices.

THE SOURCES AND
COLLECTION OF DATA

BRINGING
RESEARCH TO LIFE

"Tell me what you know about big banks, Jason," Myra asked.

"Well, for my master's thesis I wrote an econometric model of the Federal Reserve System. . . ."

"Yes, yes. Swell," she said, impatiently. She dropped into a chair and locked her eyes onto his, a gesture that convinced him she was reading his thoughts before his mouth could say them. "Academic economic research, yes. Very impressive, I'm sure. But what do you know practically?" This acerbic remark she sweetened with a wry smile. "And you did some very clever stuff classifying the depositors of a small S&L by using ZIP code demographics. Yes, you did first-rate work there, too. As a numbers cruncher, you are a prodigy. No doubt about it. . . . But do you read the newspapers? What do you know about the political climate for big banks?" He murmured an evasion while he scanned his memory banks, his biocomputer as he called his brain.

Again, she prodded: "The political climate for banks. What do you know, Jason?"

"Well, Myra, it's never good for banks when liberals are running Congress and the White House. Is it?"

"The big banks can feel the eyes of Uncle Sam on them, morning, noon, and night. Which brings us to this." She produced his appointment planner from the top of his desk. "I stopped by today to drop off the draft of my final report for the economic council, the one you said you'd review and give me some feedback. Thought I'd pen myself into your planner for Wednesday and I could not help noticing you have an appointment this very noon with a Mr. Armand Croyand of Denver. Do you know who he is, this Mr. Croyand, who is coming from Denver?"

"No, not really. He identified himself as the principal of Croyand Associates and wanted a few minutes of my time over lunch, as he was swinging through town. I was free, and I said OK."

"Let me help you here. Saying yes to a meeting was a smart move. Leaving for the meeting without discovering in advance who Croyand is . . . well that would be dumb, wouldn't it?

"Since your telephone never sleeps, nor does your computer, nor does the online database of the *Rocky Mountain News,* a few minutes ago I dialed into that online database. Want to know what a few dollars of computer time discovered? It turns out that Mr. Croyand and his associates are the long-time research organization working for InterMountBanc, headquartered out there in Colorado, and he has a reputation for doing fine, deep, imaginative real estate research.

"Further rummaging in the *News's* database reveals that several of the directors recently resigned rather than face scrutiny of their private dealings, and that the new CEO of InterMount and the new directors are all Mr. Clean types who have publicly pledged to stand by the ethically highest standards.

"Now, the plot thickens, doesn't it? I dipped next into the online database of the *Miami Herald,* AND WHAT DO I FIND? I find that InterMount is heavily invested in that new Westridge development in the west county, the one that Ed Byldor is throwing up, the one that is now stopped dead in its tracks while the county commission, in all its wisdom, awaits recommendations from the county planners."

"You are telling me, then, that Mr. Armand Croyand is in town on business and I must treat this as a serious business lunch."

"I am telling you to go to lunch loaded for bear, because this could lead to a very big contract. How are you going to handle Mr. Croyand?"

"Well, first, I will go into the *Herald's* online database and see if the planning commission has taken a public position on Westridge." Myra nodded. "I have to swing by the Chamber of Commerce in an hour to drop off a final report of the aviation study, the one I did on a *pro bono* basis, and that will give me a chance to remind the various staff people there that they owe me a favor and to discover what they have picked up off the record about
(continued)

Westridge, the planning council, and the county commission. If they are sensitive to public opinion, that works in my favor, since I have a political polling background. If they are worried about real estate values, that is harder, but I suppose I can call the library and find out the address of some trade association that can give me a jump start.

"And since the county government center is within walking distance, I'll check the minutes of the county commission for any reports they have received from the planning council."

"Good. What else will you do while you are in the governmental center?"

"Something else?"

"Think."

He thought. "I'll check the bulletin board in the lobby and see when the planning council is due to hold its next public meeting, and I'll see if Westridge is on the agenda of the county commission for this coming Tuesday."

"OK, so far. And suppose you run into one of the commissioners. What will you do?"

"How would I know one if I met one?"

"Their pictures are in the lobby outside their commission chambers. Memorize them. But what if you run into one of the commissioners?"

"I'll say, 'Hello, Commissioner,' and keep going. I'm not a lobbyist: I'm a researcher, and besides I don't have a retainer yet from InterMountBanc."

"When you meet Croyand, concentrate on what he is telling you, and let him discover almost by accident that you are on top of the real estate situation in west county. Make him believe his prowess as a researcher directed him to you, and that he found exactly the right person to help him here in Florida. Let your secondary research scream quietly of your competence."

PRIMARY VERSUS SECONDARY DATA

What Are Secondary Data?

This chapter is about the problems and techniques of finding and using data already collected by others. More specifically, the chapter describes the nature of these data sources and how to use them.[1]

We classify information sources into primary and secondary types. **Primary data** are collected by you and agents known to you, especially to answer your research question—for instance, when you observe certain production operations and measure their cost, or when MindWriter surveys its CompleteCare customers to see what changes would improve customer satisfaction, or when the students at Metro U (introduced in Chapter 9) conduct a survey to see who would patronize a membership dining club. Studies made by others for their own purposes represent **secondary data** to you.

Primary and secondary sources each have strengths and weaknesses. Using primary sources, researchers can collect precisely the information they want. They usually can specify the operational definitions used and can eliminate, or at least monitor and record, the extraneous influences on the data as they are gathered. However, secondary sources are indispensable in other ways. There is nothing wrong with using primary data under many circumstances, or secondary data under different circumstances, or, rarely and prudently, substituting one for the other when either might be suitable. But the basis for substitution has to be well understood and good judgment applied.

Uses of Secondary Data

Secondary data are used for three research purposes. First, they fill a need for a specific reference or citation on some point—perhaps in a research proposal, to demonstrate why the proposed research fills a void in the knowledge base. Research typically calls for early exploration to learn if the past can contribute to the present study. Data from secondary sources help you decide what further research needs to be done and can be a rich source of hypotheses. Examples of secondary data include the estimated U.S. production of sulfuric acid last year, the population of Atlanta in 1990, and the current rate of return on government bonds.

For example, Jason didn't know that his lunch partner would be a fellow researcher for InterMountBanc. Without Myra's intervention he might have been blind-sided by questions on the Westridge land development debacle currently going on in the county commission.

You may also seek reference benchmarks against which to test other findings. From a sample survey, you could estimate the percentage of the population that has certain age and income characteristics. These estimates could then be checked against census data. Do *your data* seem consistent with *census data*?

Second, secondary data are an integral part of a larger research study or of a research report to justify having bypassed the costs and benefits of doing primary research. In essence, the researcher tries to keep from reinventing the wheel. Clearly, MindWriter could mine its existing databases (see "Data Mining" in Chapter 15) to discover patterns of service problems, models of laptops that experience more problems than others, distributors that sold laptops needing service, and environmental conditions during peak periods of calls to the call center. Each of these pieces of information collected initially to track divisional performance or supplier/distributor relationships would enable a clearer statement of the research question(s) or significantly reduce the list of investigative questions that would need to be translated into measurement questions.

Third, secondary data may be used as the sole basis for a research study, since in many research situations one cannot conduct primary research because of physical, legal, or cost influences. Historians' methods are the classic example but are hardly the only one. Retrospective research often requires the use of published data. The federal government frequently solves this problem for many organizations with the massive amount of data it publishes each year.

Advantages and Disadvantages of Secondary Data

Secondary sources can usually be found more quickly and cheaply than primary data, especially when national and international statistics are needed. Collecting primary data can be so costly and time-consuming as to be impractical. Can you imagine conducting primary research on the U.S. output of sulfuric acid? No, you cannot hope to gather primary information comparable to census reports and industry statistics, at any cost. Not only are these collections voluminous and detailed, but law provides for their collection. Most research on past events also has to rely on secondary data sources. Similarly, data about distant places often can be collected more cheaply through secondary sources.

However, not all secondary data is readily available or inexpensive. Data mining of company databases that are not designed for unstructured searches can be expensive due to the large amount of time such activities consume. After spending immense amounts of time, you may find that the data retrieved isn't useful for your study. Much of the research collected and reported by organizations is proprietary. Through a magazine article you learn that a study done by XYZ Company appears to hold much promise to help with your research project. Yet the next moment you find the XYZ report is not available to outsiders at any price. The United States has experienced a dramatic increase in information companies that track environmental trends or collect a wide variety of industry, product category, or country-specific data. While these companies will readily sell their data, the price tag is often beyond what many organizations can afford.

The most important limitation of secondary sources is that the information may not meet your specific needs. Others have collected source material for their own purposes. Operational definitions will differ and may not be available for evaluation, units of measure are different, and different times may be involved or environmental stimuli may not be compatible. It is difficult to assess the accuracy of the information because one knows little about the research design or the conditions under which the research occurred, unless the agent who collected the data is impeccably credentialed and has documented the procedures. Often, last year's data are not relevant today or are not relevant in the next county. When Hurricane Andrew devastated the heavily Hispanic residential areas south of Miami in Dade County, Florida, in September 1992 and displaced quite a few residents north to the area around Fort Lauderdale in Broward County, the 1990 census data for Hispanics in Broward County declined in usefulness.

Classifying Secondary Data

By Source   One way to classify data sources is as *internal* or *external* to your organization. Internal sources of organizational data are so varied that it is difficult to provide generalizations about their use. For some studies, internal sources may be the only source of information. For others they may be the starting points. Accounting and management information systems (MIS) create and store much of the internal data. Research and development, planning, and marketing functions also contribute. Examples are departmental reports, production summaries, financial and accounting reports, and marketing and sales studies.

The collection methods used are unique to the specific situation, and collection success depends on knowing just where and how to look. Sometimes the information may exist in central files (i.e., at headquarters), in data warehouses, in data marts, or in departmental chronological files. In other organizations, a central library keeps all relevant information. Systematic searches should be made through exploratory interviews with everyone who handles the information. Often company librarians, PR/communications, MIS, or departmental secretaries can help in pinpointing critical data sources. Internal data sources may be the only source of information for many studies.

One of the most productive ways to identify internal sources is to identify gatekeepers of those sources. Executive secretarial assistants are often knowledgeable about company documents because they oversee their preparation. Also, department heads will likely know of documents created within their divisions. Myra was urging Jason to memorize the names and faces of the county commissioners from their pictures in the government building lobby in order to make an internal document search easier in the future. The commissioners would likely have the latest and most accurate information on the Westridge land development issue, if not before Jason meets with the InterMountBanc researcher, then clearly later after he captures the InterMountBanc research contract.

The use of internal data has been steadily increasing and has accelerated sharply. **Intranets** (internal networks linking outward to the Internet but forbidding access from outside in) have begun to successfully eliminate the Tower of Babel effect that occurs when diverse computer systems are stitched together. Also, word/document processing, spreadsheet, and database programs are now linked directly to distributed organizational databases.

External sources are created outside the organization and are more varied than internal sources. They are seldom directly linked in corporate MIS, unless someone has recognized their value to the enterprise and licensed their inclusion in the MIS network. Although every enterprise has its peculiar way of structuring its MIS, there are also publicly understood methods for finding external secondary data. This discussion is restricted to published sources, where "published" is broadly construed to mean published in ink and paper or electronically, but certainly not hiding behind a corporate firewall.

By Category   A second way to classify sources of data is by five categories: databases, periodicals, books, government documents, and special collections. The first category consists of computerized databases on CD/DVD-ROMs or the Internet. They are composed of interrelated data files. The files are sets of records grouped together for storage on some medium. Online databases are often specialized and focus on information about a particular field. Often they are produced for resale or for access via a membership organization, so they may be public, but they are not free. Myra discovered InterMountBanc connections to the Westridge project in Florida through this category of sources.

CD/DVD-ROMs, the medium for many databases, are based on the compact disk and its successor, the digital videodisk. ROM is read-only memory. CD-ROM and DVD-ROM are inexpensive, accurate, high-information-density methods of dispensing text, data, audio, video, and other media for use by computers.

For reasons explained later, it is difficult to measure and count information technologies because they appear and disappear so quickly. We have included discussion questions to encourage you to search the Internet for facts and figures and see how quickly they change, how sources contradict one another, and how varied are the methods of arriving at the numbers.

Access to remote data files is now possible through a worldwide network called the **Internet.** Users can access **online public access catalogs (OPACs)** and other computerized files (some of which are in full-text form, i.e., not just abstracted but included whole) from remote locations.

FIGURE   10–1   University Online Public Access Catalog

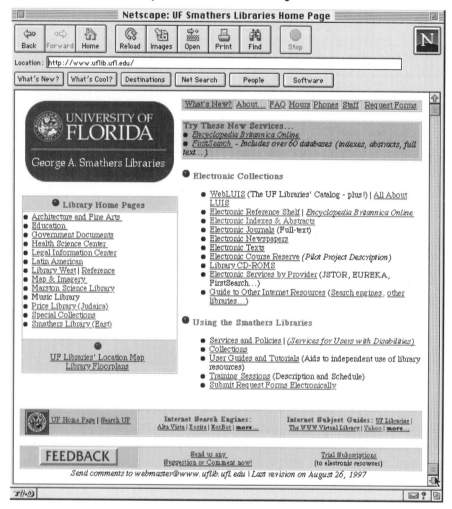

In Figure 10–1, we show the opening screen of a university's online public access catalog. The other four categories are listed below:

- Periodicals, as hard copy (paper and ink) or online, or, in some cases, as both hard copy and online.
- Books, which mostly are available as hard copy but are starting to appear online.
- Government documents, which are very soon going to be made available concurrently in hard copy and online, and eventually may not be available in hard copy. (Even maps may cease to appear as hard copy and be replaced by downloadable images.).

- Diverse materials in so-called **special collections.** In this category are many reference books, each a compendium of a range of information. A second group includes university publications, of which there are master's theses, doctoral dissertations, and research records. A third group includes company publications such as financial reports, company policy statements, speeches by prominent executives, sales literature, and product specifications. There are miscellaneous information sources consisting of the productions of various trade, professional, and other associations. These organizations often publish statistical compilations, research reports, and proceedings of meetings. Finally, there are personal documents. These are used in historical and other social science research, but less frequently in business studies.

By Medium   Another way to classify secondary data is as *hard copy, local-area online,* or *Internet.*[2]

What is the meaning of *online*? Consider the following five hypothetical instances:

1. If we own an ink-on-paper encyclopedia that fills a bookcase, it is in *hard copy,* a classification no one would dispute.
2. If the same encyclopedia resides as a disk in a CD/DVD-ROM player in our desktop personal computer, we probably would not call it online, though some might argue with us.
3. If the encyclopedia is in a CD/DVD-ROM player in a computer in the office down the hall or somewhere across campus, and we have access through a network, we can use a computerized search. Is the encyclopedia online? We would say it is **local-area online.**
4. If the CD/DVD-ROM is in a computer in the library and we have access through a client-server network (the library runs the server and we use the client), is it online? We would again say it is *local-area online.*
5. If we dial into the encyclopedia via the Internet (and probably pay a fee to a value-added subscription service), the encyclopedia is surely online. We would say it is *Internet-based.*

Cases 1 and 5 are easy, but cases 2, 3 and 4 are in the twilight zone. Here is our usage; Case 1 is a hard-copy text. Case 2 is a computerized database (because it is searchable) on CD/DVD-ROM in a personal computer. It is not online because it is not part of a network. Cases 3 and 4 describe CD/DVD-ROMs on local networks, and we will call them local-area online. Case (5) is an Internet encyclopedia.

By Database Format   Still another way to classify secondary data is by whether it is organized in a *database* or a *nondatabase format.* A **database** is a collection of records in a standard format. The record may consist of numerical or text data, or a combination of the two, and it may be as short as a single line, or it may be the full text of an article. In a bibliographic index, for instance, each record may consist of a list of authors, the title of an article, the journal the article appeared in, the volume, issue, and page numbers, the date the article appeared, an abstract or summary, and perhaps a list of standard key words or categories that a bibliographer decided the article belongs in.

Databases are thematically organized (all the records refer to magazine articles, or government grant programs, for instance), and the owner of the database (the individual or organization that compiles it, edits it, keeps it current, and perhaps copyrights it) provides the one and only searchable index. Databases are frequently extensive, comprehensive, and authoritative. Consequently, they may be proprietary, in which case a library may license them for use by its cardholders via local-area online, or an information vendor may sell access on a per minute basis via the Internet. Some databases are available free, such as the holding indexes of libraries and most of the federal databases.

Nondatabase information comprises most of the huge supply of the world's information, such as all the books, magazines, journals, and special collections contained in hard-copy libraries. Its authors and publishers do not index much of this material.

Because the Internet is practically wide open to the addition of material, there is no single index of its content. Instead various academic and commercial enterprises have undertaken the immense job of indexing it and providing the indices free to the public. Internet indices give exceedingly different results, as we will see later, so there is no one and only index of Internet documents, and the careful researcher uses several indices in parallel.

THE LIBRARY AND THE INTERNET

The Library: Not Just a Home for Paper

An important resource for collecting secondary data is the library, though it is no longer the obligatory first stop to make, nor is it necessarily the best source. Librarians, however, remain preeminent as sources of advice on finding secondary data. The library is where you must go to examine material in hard copy that the library happens to own, and to request the librarians to order through the department of **interlibrary loan (ILL)** documents from cooperating libraries. But think of a library not as a big house for paper but rather as a source of expert assistance, especially in the use of information technologies.

For instance, if you do not have an Internet account at home, in the office, through your academic program, the library may be able to arrange for a free account that gives you access to research data (though not to fun and games on the Net). Or you may be allowed to use a library terminal to access the Internet. Certain databases are available in the library on a **local area network(LAN).** Most of them will be free to library cardholders. Some coaching will be available from information specialists who probably hold master's degrees in library science. The library may act as a low-cost vendor of commercial CD/DVD-ROM and Internet databases or may allow cardholder searching at discounted rates made possible by mass purchasing of services from database vendors. Librarians and staff may offer telephone consultation about the best strategies for using the Internet from home or at the office. Do not expect help with strictly computer-related problems, such as how to install a modem.

The Internet: Not Just a Library Without Walls

Since you are probably familiar with your library, let's stop and discuss the Internet and then go to a discussion of library versus the Internet and which is more appropriate for secondary data research.

Superficially, you would not need to know what the Internet is. You would simply sit down and use it and encounter no difficulties. After all, how much do you care to know about how your telephone makes connections all over the world, or about the engineering details of your TV. You are pretty much in the dark. But as a practical matter, if you do not understand technical details about the Internet, you will wonder why your Internet connection runs slowly at some times and quickly at others; why certain sites and documents capriciously disappear from the Internet for short periods (or permanently); why the most useful sites are often the hardest ones to locate with search engines; and how to cope with the many distractions that might lure you away from your research to have fun.

The Internet is a much less mature technology than telephone and television, so the Internet is being reinvented every year and consequently displays various "bugs." While you may choose to think of the Internet as a computer screen hovering 18 inches in front of your nose, through which you stare out into the world's supply of information and fun, you will discover it pays to develop Net skills and insight.

The **Internet** is a giant network of computer systems (large and small), which in turn may consist of other systems—perhaps several computers networked together, perhaps a single computer standing alone on someone's desk. Connections and protocols among the computer systems allow a local computer (your computer) to connect to remote computers (other people's computers) anywhere in the world on the Internet.

Using your local computer, you may display documents; explore linkages of a document on your screen to other documents on other computers; retrieve information (download); upload information (the reverse of download, of course); view static images, animated images, and video; listen to audio, possibly audio-video; enter remote computers and run programs on them; allow remote computers to download programs that you can run on your computer; send carefully targeted messages or broadcast messages to all the world or to a considerable subset of the world's users; and carry out commercial transactions, such as spending electronic dollars or using your credit card. The applications of the Internet grow surprisingly and ceaselessly as the Internet engages the imagination of clever and commercially motivated people.

A remote computer you reach while browsing the Internet may be a dedicated "box" permanently connected to the Internet by a leased connection and provided with substantial bandwidth for handling many transactions an hour. Or it may be a hobbyist's desktop personal computer, connected to the Internet by telephone line and available to others when the personal computer and telephone line are not needed for the owner's other purposes. The occasional Internet user (and sometimes the expert user) will find it very difficult to be sure where the remote computer is located that he or she is connected to; whether it will be accessible at the same Internet address (called a **URL,** which stands for "uniform resource locater") in a month, week, day, or hour; whether its contents will remain stable from visit to visit; and whether it will appear to run fast or slow in the coming minutes, days, and months.

The Speed of the Internet   The Internet changes ceaselessly. Many new users join the Internet, and slow it by creating overloads and logjams. But attracted by the possibility of serving additional users, carriers and service providers add to Internet capacity, which tends to increase the speed. During certain hours the Internet is particularly jammed with traffic and runs slowly, and certain sites may be so overburdened that they become inaccessible and indeed invisible as the Internet erroneously reports that they do not exist.

New servers (computers dedicated to dispensing data) are added. Persons who were connected by slow modem and phone line are networked in to permanent high-speed connections. Persons add their content to the Internet, adding to the competition for browsers' attention. Everything is changing, and some changes increase speed, while others decrease it.

There is very little governance or attempt at governance of the Internet. Consequently the level of technical quality is uncertain (sites come and go and come back again, and sometimes they become overloaded). There is further no quality control of content, so it is your own responsibility to find or develop criteria for accuracy and reliability.

The Costs of Using the Internet   At home, you must add a modem to your personal computer ($100–$150) and pay an **Internet service provider (ISP)** about $20 a month for unlimited local dial-in connections (which means theoretically you can remain online always). You may wish to ask the phone company to install a second phone line (which you can share with a fax machine when you are not connected to the Internet). The ISP will provide software for the basic Internet interface. Setting up the software and modem to connect properly will be a one-time nightmare. There is no fee for long-distance calling if you use a local ISP, although signals may be skipping out to and in from computers all over the world. (You may examine your phone bill nervously after the first month if you have been downloading large files from around the world, but your only phone connection is a local call to the ISP.) After that, everything is routed around the world by your ISP and downstream technologies. Many of the documents you view and documents and data you download will be free, although there are also extra-cost vendors and services on the Internet. If you do not give your credit card number, you are not likely to encounter any surprise bills for Internet service.) The Electric Library, for an additional $10 a month, gives access to an encyclopedia (*Colliers*), a library of reference books, hundreds of magazines, hundreds of radio-TV transcripts, and a huge collection of local and nationally known newspapers, all very neatly indexed for rapid search and retrieval.[3]

At a business office, you may find your desktop computer is connected to a LAN which in turn is connected to the Internet by a high-speed line, experiencing faster input and output than a modem allows on a phone line. And the organization may foot the bill for the ISP and pay an MIS technician to set up and maintain your connection. Of course, you must suspect your company monitors or measures your use

CLOSE-UP

THE INTERNET EXPERIENCE, PART ONE

The Internet experience is difficult to capture in a single metaphor. People have described it as "an information wonderland," the "world's biggest library, continually under construction," and "a starship control panel for eggheads." Here is what one user said:

"When I use my Internet account, I usually start with an object firmly in mind. I start searching by using one of the search engines—I happen to like AltaVista—or one of the metasearch engines. I am immediately confronted with a list of one dozen to several hundred possible documents to visit, and I have to guess where to go first. I make my choice, and very likely, I am not satisfied with my first choice, and so I back up and try other suggestions.

"However, as I progress through my trips, I am constantly distracted. Many advertisements and offers pop up as I visit search engines that carry commercial advertisements. Also, my near misses produce many intriguing side possibilities, topics I would like to investigate. Here is an online magazine I mark to revisit when I feel not so pressed for time. There is an advertisement for a trial use of software that sounds as if it will solve my word-processing problems.

"No doubt the greatest distraction is my wish to expand my search to include ideas that occur to me as I browse. Also I begin to think of synonyms and alternative concepts for my search words, and I am tempted to go back to the search engine and try again.

"If I have not found what I hoped for within 15 or 20 minutes, I may become discouraged. One never knows when giving up is the better strategy."

of the Internet; but you have the luxury of staying permanently attached. In a university, such a LAN would serve faculty offices and student laboratories and provide free access to the libraries' online databases. Students and faculty attempting to dial in by using an Internet connection would be required to identify themselves by providing a password and library card to gain access to licensed databases. Casual visitors from the Internet might be allowed to inspect the catalog of databases, but without a library card they would be shut out of the databases that the library has licensed for cardholder use.

SEARCHING FOR SECONDARY DATA

A Strategy for Secondary Data

In its online public access catalog, one library suggests a six-step process for secondary data collection and analysis:

1. Select and analyze a topic. Think about your interests, time allowed, and what information is likely to be available. You may browse periodicals for ideas. What are specific issues within the topic? What kinds of library materials will be helpful? What time period will you need to cover?

2. Explore the topic and form a focus or state a hypothesis. Use encyclopedias, located in the references area of the library.

3. Get an overview and retrospective information. Use books. (Use the library catalog or a bibliography to get citations.)

4. Get more current or specific information. Use periodical articles. (Use periodical indexes to get citations.)

5. Get more in-depth information. Use research reports, conference proceedings, documents, and maps. (Use specialized indices to get citations.)

6. Evaluate and close the library research. Evaluate the information you have found to determine if it is relevant and appropriate for your needs, by asking questions such as: Is it right on target for my topic? Have I covered all aspects of the topic? Is the information at the appropriate level for me to understand? What are the qualifications of the authors? Is there a bias?

Strategy, Step by Step

Following this six-step model, we present a strategy for a search that is well balanced among hard copy, local-area online, and the Internet. Assume you have a topic and can go straight to step 2.

Explore the Topic and Form a Focus or State a Hypothesis   Using hard copy—consult an encyclopedia. The *Britannica* is the most comprehensive general encyclopedia, but the *Americana* is almost as comprehensive and is easier to use. For management research, beware of an encyclopedia more than three years past its last revision. Using an encyclopedia by local online: See if an online encyclopedia is available online, in a terminal in the library, on the campus network, or in student laboratories. Using the Internet: Online encyclopedias are generally up-to-date, and some libraries make them accessible by Internet to cardholders.[4]

At home, take a subscription to Electric Library and use its *Colliers* CD-ROM. Various Internet providers such as America Online and Prodigy provide online encyclopedias at no additional charge beyond that of the monthly connection.

Get an Overview and Retrospective Information   Using hard-copy books: Visit the library and use a terminal to locate materials on hand for inspection and borrowing. You may also use the terminal to link, through the Internet, to other libraries' OPACs, and you may ask the interlibrary loan department to order books for you, to borrow for two weeks to a month.[5]

Using the library terminal requires you to learn a search syntax. If you hold cards in several libraries that use different indexing methods, you may have to learn several syntaxes. Terminal search language/**syntax** is explained in Appendix A. If you use the Internet to visit OPACs at remote libraries, you may have to learn additional search languages/syntaxes. Generally, doing so is worth the effort. (Soon there may be a standard syntax or a master program that translates from natural language to the various search languages/syntaxes.)

There may be bibliographies of books and articles from periodicals (magazines and journals). The first step is for you to learn whether anyone has already prepared a bibliography on your subject. Bibliographies frequently accompany articles and books, and it would be wasteful to duplicate such effort. Therefore, ask a reference librarian if a recent bibliography is available. Be wary of anything older than six months. You can also search a library's catalog for bibliographies, using general business terms such as *finance, accounting, marketing, human resources, operations,* and *management.* Many of these bibliographies have subsections that cover more specific topics. If no bibliographies are available, you may develop your own by finding references to books, periodical articles (including newspapers, magazines, and journals), documents, and other miscellaneous sources through a computerized search.

One way to discover and download bibliographies is to go on the Internet and search for certain materials. Using the Internet: Visit your library's online search index (or visit the Library of Congress online to develop the widest possible overview of what books are available on a subject, and then visit interlibrary loan to borrow materials from a remote library). For the very latest books as they reach the bookstores, visit one of the mega-bookstores on the Internet's World Wide Web, such as amazon.com or Barnes and Noble. Figure 10–2 shows the opening screen of amazon.com's online bookstore. Notice in the upper left there is a search utility for jumping straight to desired authors, titles, and keywords.

Get More Current or Specific Information   The next important resource is **periodicals.** These include newspapers, magazines, and scholarly, professional, and trade journals. Recently, transcripts of radio and TV have become available for archival searching on the Internet. Using hard-copy periodical articles: Visit a large library and the room where the latest issues are set out for public browsing. This will give you a notion of the scope and depth of coverage of various topics.

Or, if you want to draw from the widest collection, from the library terminals, visit the listing of electronic abstracts and indices. (The list may be named differently in your library, so if in doubt, explain to a librarian that you need to search for articles by using a few subject areas and search words and phrases.) We explain in Appendix A how to use library terminals.[6]

So-called abstracting indices compile a searchable index of titles and abstracts (summaries) of articles. When you enter a search word or phrase, they return one or more citations containing the authors, article title, journal, date, and possibly an abstract. You may then decide to visit the shelved periodicals or ask the interlibrary loan department to obtain a copy. Some of the periodicals will be available through local-area online or the Internet. In some cases, the abstracting indices actually provide full text of the article (they are then full-text indices, not abstract indices).

Here is a list of indices beginning with the letter *A,* from a university list that indexes periodicals:

> ABI/INFORM (1985–   )
> Advanced Polymers Abstracts
> AGRICOLA (1970–   )
> AGRICOLA

AIDS & Cancer Research Abstracts

AIDSLINE (Florida Health Information Network – FHIN)

Anthropological Literature Index (In EUREKA)

Applied Science & Technology Index (1988–   )

Ant Bibliography (FORMIS) (1993 Version)

Art Index (1988–   )

ASFA: Aquatic Sciences & Fisheries Abstracts

ATLA Religion Database (American Theological Library Association)

Avery Index to Architectural Periodicals

FIGURE   10–2   Online Bookstore Reference

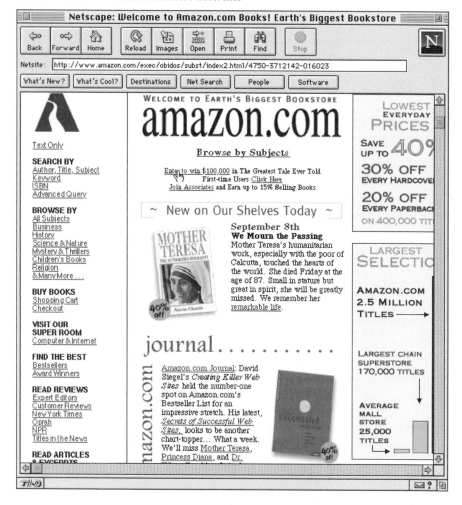

Figure 10–3 shows a screen shot of the "Electronic Indices and Abstracts" document of the University of Florida OPAC.

Although most periodicals still are published in hard copy, the periodical indices have migrated from hard copy to local-area online. Because a library may license these indices for use by its own cardholders, persons who visit the library by Internet OPAC will be shown a list of the indices but will not be permitted to use them.

Using local online periodicals: Your search starts at a library terminal with a local-area online search of the periodical abstracts.[7] You then proceed to attempt to access full-text databases on the local-area online system. Most typically, the full-text articles available online are nationally read newspapers (*New York Times, Washington Post, Wall Street Journal,* etc.) and local newspapers. Certain journals and magazines are also available through local-area online. From a library terminal, check for "Electronic Journal Full Text Resources," or ask a librarian for assistance.

FIGURE   10–3   Electronic Indices and Abstracts

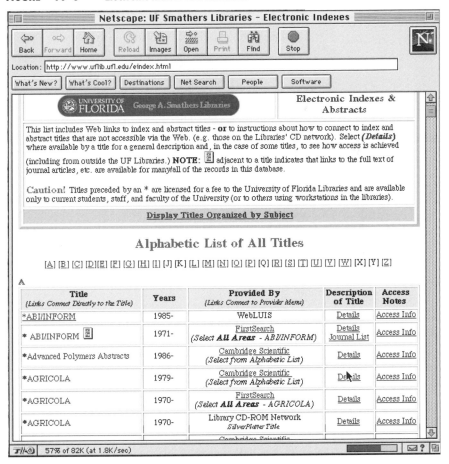

A problem with local-area online full-text is that holdings seldom extend backward past the early 1990s. There also may be a delay between paper-and-ink publication and production and mailing of the CD/DVD-ROM to the library. This is most acute in the case of newspapers, and local-area online access is mostly for historical review, since people who need up-to-date news will want to use Internet access. As the costs of ROM production fall and paper-and-ink costs rise, CD/DVD-ROM will displace hard copy altogether. Using the Internet lets you access periodicals from your home or office.

Get More In-Depth Information   We may classify newspapers as current and archival/historical. The Electric Library, a monthly service, contains newspapers from all over the United States (though not always the largest paper in each city), plus a collection of neighborhood and ethnic-oriented newspapers. Electric Library also includes a huge collection of magazines, transcripts from public radio and TV, and network public affairs programming. Electric Library is indexed and searchable. Except for a few items (e.g., transcripts of *Nightly Business Reports*, which appear within days), the Electric Library is slow to put material up and must be considered archival, starting in the mid-1990s.

Many newspapers are now available on the Internet a few days after they appear. These include *New York Times* and *Wall Street Journal.* Also on the Internet are the Reuters News Service and UP News Service. Generally, the fastest way to locate the news services is by accessing Lycos, Yahoo, or one of the other super-search engines. To check the availability of your local newspaper on the Internet, visit one of the World Wide Web sites listed in Appendix A.

Although the online newspapers may be up-to-date and timely, they are often lacking in historical/archival access. It is then necessary to access their archives by paying a fee. Managers can take an account with Dialog Information Services or an account with a particular newspaper or group of newspapers. This may be done on a purchase order or possibly (and more expensively) on a credit card.

Journals of scholarly, trade, and professional associations are starting to appear on the Internet. By and large, in the last few years existing hard-copy journals have remained in hard copy, new hard-copy journals have appeared, and new journals have appeared on the Internet with or without a hard-copy counterpart. The Electric Library has put several hard-copy journals on the Internet, furnishing their text but omitting their illustrations.

Magazines are not distinguished from journals by any hard and fast rule, except that journals are more likely to be published by a membership organization or be read by people in a discretely defined occupation, while magazines are of more general interest, are more likely to contain advertising, and perhaps pay more attention to layout and graphics. Certain magazines appear in both hard-copy and Internet versions; others are essentially creations of the Internet. If you are looking for an Internet version of a favorite magazine, see Appendix A for assistance.

Of enormous importance to the business researcher are **government documents.** The federal government is the sole agent with the authority and resources to collect certain data, most notably the national census that is carried out every ten years. Because of the requirements and expectations that the federal government will operate in the sunshine and be accountable and responsive to the people, Washington has made a massive effort to make its documents and programs available on the Internet concurrently with its hard-copy versions, and in many cases publishes information that is not available in hard copy.

The information available from the federal government includes directories of federal offices, with addresses, telephone numbers and fax numbers, e-mail addresses, and organization charts; databases of laws, proposed laws, regulations and proposed regulations, grants programs, and diverse database and nondatabase information limited only by the imagination of the citizens requesting information. A Web site called FedWorld is organized by the federal government as a gateway into the federal departments.

State government is not nearly so accessible, perhaps because no state has nearly so large a user base as the federal government. Several **World Wide Web documents** attempt to organize state and local government sites (county and city, for instance) that are quite difficult to find. Some state sites attempt to provide links down to the local sites.

It would be wrong to think that the local-area online and Internet services are "merely" replacing hard-copy services. Many of the search engines have virtual reference rooms that go far beyond their hard-copy versions in traditional libraries and include services that are impossible to render in hard copy. See our pointers in Appendix A.

In the traditional vein, there are conventional online dictionaries, such as *Bartlett's Familiar Quotations*. Online encyclopedias may contain multimedia links to sound clips and film clips. And online map rooms permit you to download maps, pan in and out from maps, and order road maps with superimposed driving directions from point to point. Visit the various search engines and study their reference rooms.

Evaluate and Close the Library Research   The final step is to evaluate the information for relevance and appropriateness for your needs.

Using Search Engines

Whether you are searching for hard-copy or online documents, you begin by using a searchable index. In the library, this will be the terminal that replaced the card catalog. On the Internet it will be one of several search engines that visit documents, read them, and index them so they can be searched. You will need a strategy for searching and one (almost certainly) or more search languages/syntaxes. Let's talk first about syntax. Since there are many different search engines on the Internet and in use in library terminals, we will start with the syntactical issues of online searching.

Searching Online Sources   A major problem of Internet use is to find useful and authoritative documents by sifting among millions of distracters—commercial advertisements, irrelevant documents that happen to contain the words you are searching for, items of dubious accuracy and authenticity, and well-intended pertinent material that is not quite good enough to be useful but would consume your time if you explored it in detail. You sharpen your searching by using the right tools and knowing which tool to use for a given task, by learning the rules (syntax), by allowing time to do the job right, and sticking to your objectives despite distractions on the World Wide Web.

Internet search engines are supercomputers that endeavor to visit every published document on every site that is not hiding behind a security firewall or inside an already-indexed database, read every bit of text and hypertext, and add documents to the engine's database.

The **search engine** consists of two elements. The first part is the Internet **robot/crawler**—"robot" or " 'bot" or "crawler" or "spider"—which crawls around the Internet reading documents and exploring the linked documents (documents pointed to by hypertext links), then reading documents it has visited and referring them for indexing.

The second part of the search engine is the *indexer,* which prepares searchable indices. Some of the most prominent search engines (crawler-indexers) are Lycos, AltaVista, and Excite. When you visit the search engine and enter a key word or phrase in its search form, the search engine returns a list of documents and addresses and provides *hypertext links* you can click on for immediate visits to the suggested document.

Searchableness is a good criterion for Internet effectiveness:

1. Text and hypertext documents are readable by Internet search engines because they consist of words and numbers. Text comprises the words and numbers that you will see on the screen if you read a document on the Internet. **Hypertext** consists of invisibly embedded words and numbers that instruct your browser how to display the text on your screen—that is, what to display in large fonts, in italics, in color, and so forth, and where on the screen to place graphics. More importantly, hypertext consists of instructions to the Internet on how documents link to other documents.

For instance, in Figure 10–1, much of the text constitutes links to other parts of the University of Florida OPAC; in Figure 10–2 the text items link to other parts of the amazon.com online bookstore; and in Figure 10–3, the text items link to various online indices. The linkage is achieved by invisible hypertext feeding instructions to a marvelously complicated and effective computer program. You cannot read the hypertext commands, but they make the Internet's World Wide Web work.

2. Text files are inaccessible to the Web robot/crawlers because they are within archival databases where the robot/crawlers cannot venture. These archival databases are indexed and searchable, however. What the search engines *are* able to index is not the actual contents of every database item but rather text descriptions of the database contents as provided by the database's owner. Naturally, a good deal of care has to be devoted by the owner to writing accurate and complete descriptions.

As a user, first you must use a search engine to find an archival database likely to contain what you need, and then you have to search within that database using its native indexer, to confirm your choice and retrieve your documents. This is an efficient way to search, because it does not clutter the search engine index with hundreds or thousands of documents on related topics. But it forces the user to deal with the syntax of one or more search engines (that point to the archival database), plus the native syntax of each archival database index.

3. Pictures and sound—static images, animated simple images, video, video-

with-audio, audio and binary files such as executable programs or data files in binary format — are not readable by the robot/crawlers (which are looking for text and hypertext), so their owners must provide text descriptions for the search engines. Graphics such as photographs and maps have always been important in business research, and now they are more accessible than ever. Other media may increase in value to researchers, once we discover how to use them.

Appendix A contains important tutorial material on search engines. For now, let us say that once a document has been visited by one of the robot/crawler search engines and its content read and indexed, the search engine makes it possible to request pages that contain a particular word ("Show me sites that contain *business.*"), several words in adjacency ("Show me sites that contain *business methods.*") or in propinquity ("*Show me sites that contain business* [any word] *methods.*"), a phrase (Show me sites that contain "*the latest edition of Business Research Methods,*" and other, so-called Boolean combinations ("Show me a site that contains *cheese* but not *chocolate.*" "Show me a site that contains *Swiss* and either *cheese* or *chocolate* or both but does not contain *Geneva.*").

You visit a search engine, and, using its native syntax, request a search for documents. Following a short wait, a menu of possibilities is offered, sites that meet the syntactical requirement, which you may visit by clicking on them. You then visit the sites and inspect them for suitability. Finding a suitable site, you may **bookmark** it (make a record of its address), print it, or download it to disk, and then you may investigate its outward links and perhaps find a site even more authentic, extensive, or attractive. Not finding a page useful, you may back up to the menu of choices found by the search engine and try others. Eventually, however successful or unsuccessful you are with a particular search engine, you should probably repeat the procedure using another search engine, because the engines do give different results.

Robot/crawler search engines are indiscriminate and index virtually every document they visit; hence they tend to be hypersensitive and hyperactive. When AltaVista was asked to search for the word *saw,* it offered 300,000 sites, some of which contained *saw* as the past tense of "to see" and some as "a tool used to cut hard material." So search engines serve well for finding the needle in the haystack. (AltaVista offered fewer than 70 sites on the phrase "chain saw safety," including one called "Info on Saw Chain for Non-professional Users ," which addressed our specific concerns about "chainsaw kickback.")

The polar opposite of robot/crawler engines is human-mediated search sites or **virtual libraries.** One of the best of the virtual libraries is the Argus Clearinghouse, whose opening screen is shown in Figure 10–4. Like all virtual libraries, Argus is hierarchically organized. In its opening screens, it offers visits to virtual folders on these topics:

Arts & Humanities

Business & Employment

Communication

Computers & Information Technology

Education

Engineering
Environment
Government & Law
Health & Medicine
Places & Peoples
Recreation

FIGURE   10–4   Virtual Library Page

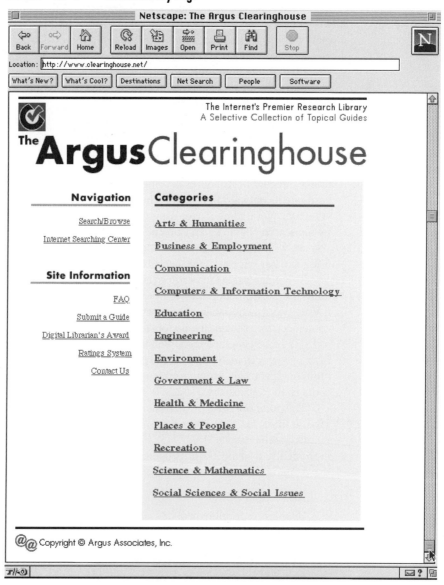

Science & Mathematics

Social Sciences & Social Issues

If we select the *Business & Employment* folder, we are offered several sub-folders;

banking and investment business

economics

employment

finance and credit

human resources

industry

marketing

Descending into the virtual business folder, we find these sub-subfolders.

agribusiness	imports
bar code	innovation policy
business cycle	international business
business directories	international development
business (general)	international trade
chambers of commerce	Internet commerce
commerce	meeting and event planning
companies	operations management
continuous improvement	organization
contract	quality improvement
corporate governance	quality standards
EDI (Electronic Data Interchange)	retailing
electronic commerce	shopping
entrepreneurship	small business
exports	TQM (Total Quality Management)
franchises	vendors
fundraising	Web space providers
home-based business	

If you choose *business cycle,* you are offered the screen shown in Figure 10–5, Argus's ultimate choice. It is a link out to the Internet, to a server at the University of Montreal.

Keeping Track of Your Research

When you use local-area online and the Internet, it is often cheap and fast to retain an almost complete record of your research. At home or in the office, you have the opportunity to turn on your printer and generate a printout of practically everything you read, plus the option to save the session to a floppy diskette or larger storage medium for later study on your personal computer.

FIGURE   10–5   Final Search Result

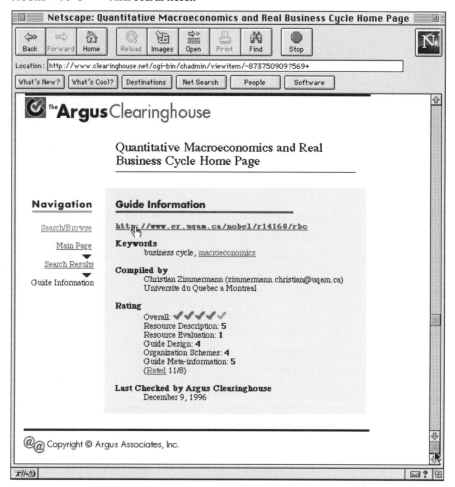

Gathering and recording information from sources are often viewed as simple chores within the competence of anyone. These tasks are frequently done poorly but may be improved in three ways. First, be selective in what you record. Some information will be useful and some will not; some will add to your collection and some will be repetitious. These decisions are guided by the research purpose. Set up an outline of the topic as quickly as possible, even knowing that it will probably change as you gather more information. The idea that "I'll gather all of the material and then decide how to organize it" is inefficient. Much interesting information that turns up is diversionary and unproductive.

Second, decide how to record what you will extract from the published material. Should you report it verbatim, paraphrase it, or outline it? More often than not, outlining is the most efficient method. You will wish to record specific important decisions or statements verbatim. In a few other instances, a paraphrase statement of the author's position is suitable.

Third, develop an orderly recording system. With it, you can have the extracted information available when needed, have a ready reference source for checking, and have maximum flexibility in organizing the information.

A recording system must be easy to use. Many researchers use a software program to record both bibliographic references and the notes taken from them. When the results can be imported into word processors, such a system is very efficient. Other researchers use cards. Recording information on cards allows for flexible handling and organizing. Some even advocate putting a single fact or idea on each individual card; this obviously promotes maximum flexibility, but it also fragments the information. The single-idea-per-card concept is probably most desirable in cases where the researcher does not have a clear idea of subject organization. It is, however, inefficient to transfer information using this approach.

CLOSE-UP

THE INTERNET EXPERIENCE, PART TWO

Some graduates came together to discover how they might "do well by going good" for their community.

Maps Online

Jeffrey G. was a real estate investor. He continually received offers to invest in sites at various locations and decided to take a flyer at investing in some low-income neighborhoods. In order to screen the possibilities, he used mapping software he discovered on the Internet. Given a street address, he is able to locate a ZIP code, and using a ZIP code he is able to consult the federal Census Bureau's Tiger map server to draw thematic census maps that reveal average household income, family size, and other indicators in individual census tracts.

Jeff wanted a bibliography for his work. He used the AltaVista search engine with the search

terms ["real estate investment" AND (bibliographies and bibliography)], and found a bibliography on "real estate investment" at the pages of the Evanston, Illinois, Public Library and a "Futures and Options Bibliography" by a professor of finance at Florida International University.

Jeff knew that so-called Usenet groups on the Internet discuss certain topics. He understood that to avoid explaining basics to "newbies" (new Internet users) the groups designate one or more members to post a document called **FAQ (Frequently Asked Questions).** He searched AltaVista using ["real estate" AND FAQ] but found nothing. However, he did find an Investment FAQ at Ohio State University.

Dead Ends Happen

Kathy K. majored in speech therapy and then took a health finance master's degree, with a specialty in nonprofit organizations. Now she is interested in opening her own clinic, which she intends to operate as a tax-exempt 501k(3) corporation, bringing in a physical therapist and an occupational therapist to provide skills and certifications

(continued)

she lacks. She hears a rumor that several large health insurance companies have established charitable foundations to support speech, hearing, and motor defect therapies for children.

Kathy wishes to apply for some of that foundation money. She appeals to the local library to do an online search of the Knight-Ridder GRANTS database of funding opportunities for nonprofits, and she compiles a list of foundations and corporate donations offices that are interested in funding projects for the disabled or for children. She resolves to query them, once IRS has given her a letter of determination of nonprofit status.

But Kathy is also very interested in discovering if there are *new* programs within the foundations or new foundations being formed, hoping to get in at the beginning of funding and becoming a permanent client. She uses various search engines with these terms:

["health insurance" AND (charity or charities)]
["insurance companies" AND (charity or charities)]
["insurance companies" AND (contributions)]

Although the search engines produce many apparent hits, none of them proves to be what she expects. Several of the sites she visits contain only public relations releases, and it occurrs to her that if new charities are being funded by insurance companies, the companies will wish to do some boasting through public relations. She then tries such search terms as

["health insurance" AND ("press releases")]
["insurance companies" AND ("news releases")]
["press releases" AND (children)]
["press releases" AND (charity or charities)]

All of them produces copious results, the last one leading her to a searchable database, *Philanthropic Digest,* placed on the Web by the Foundations Center, where she does in fact find some

interesting leads, but none of them a *new* foundation offering funding for children and the disabled.

Eventually she searches under ["health insurance" AND "trade associations"] and is led to the document of an insurance industry trade association in Washington, which she calls. The press officer there says he never heard of the new foundations Kathy is asking about— ones sponsored by insurance companies for disabled children.

Kathy's search time on the Internet was 8 hours; time spent in the library, 2 hours; time on the phone, 20 minutes. Output was several interesting leads, none of them related to the original object of the search—new foundations sponsored by insurance companies for disabled children.

"Maybe no such foundations have been founded," says Kathy. "Maybe they are one of those urban legends that blow about."

Moving the Homeless Out of the Business District

The group was concerned about the swelling ranks of homeless persons lingering around the retail districts. They organized a task force to determine what might be done. Wally Q. was asked to draw up a list of possibilities for a meeting in ten days. Wally decided to use the Excite Web engine, using a single key word, "homeless."

He was presented with a number of possibilities and, on a hunch, chose the Web page of the National Coalition for the Homeless. This document proved to be well suited to his task, since it contained a number of what appeared to be authoritative essays on the extent and causes of homelessness, as well as prospects for relieving it and possible sources of grant money. A phone call to his county's local coalition for the homeless verified his belief that the National Coalition was a reliable source.

His search time was about 30 minutes. Wally believes he was lucky to hit an extremely well-organized topical page so quickly. Kathy admits she is green with envy.

Reinventing the Business

Martina G. was interested in "reinventing" the family business, which she had taken over on her dad's retirement. It was her intention to restore the business's profitability and then implement her late father's wish to hire 25 percent minority employees. She used the key words "reinventing" and "re-invention" in various search engines and found hundreds of links, many of them dealing with reinventing government. After chopping through a thicket of links, many of which detailed rather narrowly focused reinvention efforts in particular companies, she visited amazon.com, a huge online bookstore, searching under "reinventing." She was able to locate several book descriptions and was able to place book orders on line for delivery by UPS.

After she had read a number of books, Martina G. decided to go into maintenance mode and read only new books. Consequently, she registered an interest in "reinventing" with the amazon book club, in order to be notified of new entries by electronic mail. Also, she used the Business Wire to search for news releases on "reinventing."

Summary

We classify information sources into primary and secondary types. Primary data are collected by you and agents known to you, especially to answer your research question. Studies made by others for their own purposes represent secondary data to you. Secondary data are used for three research purposes. They fill a need for a specific reference or citation on some point; they keep the researcher from "reinventing the wheel" ; and they may be used as the sole basis for a research study.

Secondary sources can usually be found more quickly and cheaply than primary data, especially when national and international statistics are needed. However, not all secondary data are readily available or inexpensive. The most important limitation of secondary sources is that the information may not meet your specific needs.

One way to classify data sources is as internal or external to your organization. Accounting and management information systems create and store much of the internal data. External sources are created outside the organization and are seldom directly linked in corporate MIS, unless someone has recognized their value to the enterprise.

A second way to classify sources of data is according to whether they are databases, periodicals, books, government documents, or special collections. Another is by medium—hard copy, local-area online, or Internet. Still another way to classify secondary data is as organized in a database or a nondatabase format.

An important resource for collecting secondary data is the library, though it no longer is the obligatory first stop or the best source. Certain databases are available in the library on a local-area network. Some assistance will be available from information specialists there. The library may act as a low-cost vendor of commercial CD/DVD-ROM and Internet access.

The Internet is not a mature technology and is being reinvented every year. The applications of the Internet grow surprisingly as the Internet engages the imaginations of clever and commercially motivated persons. Using a local computer, you may display documents; explore linkages of a document; retrieve information; upload information; view static images, animated images, and video; listen to audio, possibly audio-video; enter remote computers and run programs on them; allow remote computers to download programs that you can run on your computer; send carefully targeted messages or broadcast messages to all or a subset of the world's users; and carry out commercial transactions.

A six-step process for secondary data collection and analysis consists of (1) selecting and analyzing a topic, (2) exploring the topic and forming a focus or stating a hypothesis, (3) getting an overview and retrospective information, (4) getting more current or specific information, (5) getting more in-depth information, and (6) evaluating and closing the research.

Whether you are searching for hard-copy or online documents, start with a searchable index. In the library, this will be the terminal. On the Internet, it will be one of several search engines that visit documents and read and index them so they can be searched. You need a strategy for searching and facilitating with one or more search languages/syntaxes.

When you are using local-area online and the Internet, it is often cheap and fast to retain an almost complete record of your research. Record to your printer, save the session to a floppy diskette, or use a note system compatible with subsequent word processing.

Key Terms

bookmark	online public access catalog (OPAC)
CD/DVD-ROM	periodicals
database	primary data
Frequently Asked Questions (FAQ)	robot/crawler
government documents	search engine
hypertext	secondary data
interlibrary loan (ILL)	special collections
Internet	syntax
Internet service provider (ISP)	URL
intranets	virtual libraries
local-area online	World Wide Web document
local area network (LAN)	

Case

McDonald's Tests Catfish Sandwich
(This is a case found in the optional casebook available with the text.)

Discussion Questions

1. On the World Wide Web, visit the amazon.com bookstore, and use the search engine to locate books on the Nexis database service.
2. On the World Wide Web, locate one or more tutorials about the Nexis database service.

3. How big is the Internet? There are various measures, such as the number of distinct URLs (addressees) and the number of documents indexed by the various search engines. Go to one of the World Wide Web robot search engines and enter the following natural language query: "How big is the Internet?"

   a. What measures of size are cited?

   b. How were the figures arrived at (what methodology was used)?

   c. To what extent do the various sources contradict one another, and why?

   d. Do you trust figures older than three months, six months, or a year to be accurate?

   e. Have you found any trend data on the growth of the Internet?

4. Using the World Wide Web addresses provided in Appendix A, visit the Knight-Ridder Information site and count the number of databases available by Internet. How many are business-related? How many are also available in CD/DVD-ROM?

5. Locate the federal Census Bureau's Tiger map service, and experiment with drawing several thematic census maps. Specifically, locate your home town and overlay its map with a color scheme that reveals high- and low-income census tracts.

6. Some researchers find that their sole sources are secondary data. Why might this be? Name some management research questions for which secondary data sources are probably the only ones feasible.

7. Assume you are asked to investigate the use of mathematical programming in accounting applications. You decide to depend on secondary data sources. What search tools might you use? Which do you think would be the most fruitful? Sketch a flow diagram of your search sequence.

8. What problems of secondary data quality must researchers face? How can they deal with them?

9. Below are a number of requests that a staff assistant might receive. What specific tools or services would you expect to use to find the requisite information? (Appendix A may be helpful.)

   a. The president wants a list of six of the best references that have appeared on executive compensation during the last year.

   b. Has the FTC published any recent statements (within the last year) concerning its position on quality stabilization?

   c. I need a list of the major companies located in Greensboro, North Carolina.

   d. Please get me a list of the directors of General Motors, Microsoft, and Morgan Stanley & Co.

   e. Is there a trade magazine that specializes in the flooring industry?

   f. I would like to track down a study of small-scale service franchising that was recently published by a bureau of business research at one of the southern universities. Can you help me?

Reference Notes

1. This chapter is based on a manuscript contributed by Jay S. Mendell. While some tools are mentioned here, Appendix A contains a more detailed listing of important indices, guides, and other reference tools for secondary sources. Because the nature of secondary research is changing rapidly as data sources link to the Internet and new users eagerly use them, Appendix A will be maintained in an up-to-date form. The publisher's World Wide Web address is *http://www.mhhe.com/irwin/*. This site will link you to an independently maintained page containing new and improved tools. Should you have difficulty locating the book, go to the McGraw-Hill's onsite search tool at *http://www.mhhe.com/info/ search.mhtml*.

2. *Online* is a neologism that is used as a noun, adjective, or adverb. A document "on a network" was once said to be "on line" (an adverbial usage), but current usage is to say it is "online" (an adjectival usage). A document that is on line (online) was once called an "on-line" resource but now is known as an "online resource."

3. For the URL (Internet address) of every site mentioned in this chapter, see Appendix A.

4. Local-area online material is generally licensed for the use of cardholders, so most likely you will have to use it in the main or branch library, and you may have to show your card to an attendant or enter it in a terminal before you use the material. Some businesses license reference materials for use by employees working from hard-wired terminals (i.e., terminals that have unique network addresses, as opposed to Internet dial-in systems). If you are a university employee, your office may be hard-wired into the local-area system, permitting you to work from the office. Students may have access from student laboratories.

5. Interlibrary loan is an extraordinarily valuable service. It might cost as much as $25 a request if carried out through a private information retrieval consultant, but it is most often provided free or cheaply by a public or university library. You can fill out a written request or enter your request electronically.

6. Indices in the last few years have migrated from hard copy on the shelf to local online terminal availability. This change has perhaps been motivated by several factors. It is cheaper to publish a CD/DVD-ROM than a hard-copy book and cheaper to mail it from the publisher to the library. The cost of the computer hardware, software, and networks required to serve the CD/DVD-ROM indices is falling rapidly as technology improves and the user base increases, so all the momentum is away from hard copy. A local online index is able to serve users in a business or academic campus if the users are wired into a system. The local online material may be extended to Internet-using cardholders and password holders. Some computer intelligence is being brought to bear in the front-end searching tools, so less expertise is needed than before. Finally, computerized searching and retrieval has obvious advantages in poring through vast amounts of information.

   Despite the overwhelming advantages of online index searching, there is a downside for the researcher who prefers to hold onto old ways of searching. There is relatively little carryover from thumbing through hard-copy materials to using local-area online or the Internet to comb through available information. You must simply decide to invest in skill building.

7. In a university, a local-area online search may be available from various terminals around the campus, such as student laboratories and faculty offices.

Suggested Readings

1. Because the world of secondary data is changing so quickly, visit one of the online bookstores, such as Barnes and Noble or amazon.com, and search their offerings, using the key terms in this chapter. Or obtain the latest material from the World Wide Web, by using a search engine to locate documents using the search words "tutorials AND databases."
2. Daniells, Lorna M. *Business Information Sources,* 3rd ed. Berkeley: University of California Press, 1993.
3. Katz, W. A. *Introduction to Reference Work.* Vols. 1 and 2. New York: McGraw-Hill, 1996.

CHAPTER

11

SURVEY METHODS: COMMUNICATING WITH RESPONDENTS

 CHAPTER NAVIGATION

BRINGING
RESEARCH TO LIFE

"Jason, you gotta see this," Myra called as she arrived for her meeting on the economic council research. She was waving a letter above her head and smiling widely.

"You remember me telling you about my Aunt Edna, the not-so-retired attorney in Albany? Well, she sent this for my amusement, I guess. It's just so typical of how people, particularly physicians and even bright businesspeople, design questionnaires."

"Like me for MindWriter?" he murmured impatiently, looking up from the partially finished questionnaire on his computer screen.

"Come on, Jason, give it a rest. And read this," she prodded.

Edna Koogan, P.A.
Attorney at Law
P.O. Box 8219-2767
Albany, New York 12212-2767

Dr. Edith Coblenz, M.D.
3456 Barshoot Building
Albany, New York 12212

Dear Edith,

I want you to have my side of this morning's incident at the Albany Outpatient Laser Clinic Inc. I am sure you have by now heard from the business manager and the admissions director and possibly the anesthesiologist. You are a stockholder in the Center, I know, and as your former lawyer and current patient, I thought I owed you a warning and explanation.

You told me to report to the Center at 7 A.M. for a workup in preparation for eye surgery tomorrow. I caught a cab and was there at 6:55 promptly and was then obliged to stand outside in lightly drifting snow until the doors opened. (Yes, I set my watch by the radio the night before, so there is no possibility of an error. They were late opening the admissions department, and that's that.)

I identified myself as your patient, and at once the receptionist called someone from the back room and said, "Ms. Koogan's personal physician is Dr. Coblenz," which is, of course, not true, as you are my eye doctor, and my personal physician is Dr. Burke in Troy. But I was too cold to argue and there were people lined up behind me.

The fellow who had scooted in from the back insisted on taking my glasses and medications with him "for a workup," as he said. As soon as he had disappeared with my glasses the first admissions clerk disappeared and a second one appeared and handed me a "questionnaire" to fill out. You are going to think I am exaggerating, but it appeared to be a photocopy of a photocopy of a photocopy and was very faintly printed in small gray type on a light gray sheet. When I pointed out that I was about to be admitted for treatment of glaucoma, a leading cause of blindness, she told me, "Do the best you can." When I objected emphatically, she seemed taken aback. I suppose most of her 80-year-old patients are more compliant, but I guess I am an intractable old woman.

Was I wrong to object to the questionnaire being too faint and the type too small? Am I the first glaucoma patient who has ever been treated at the Laser Center? If I am, they must have opened yesterday, because what do you need the laser for if not eye surgery? If I am not, one would think they would understand you can't ask someone blind in one eye to fill out such a questionnaire. She finally, grudgingly, asked me to sit by her side, so she could help me.

There were several questions about my name, address, age, and occupation (which I had her list as "retired"). Then she wanted to know the name of the admitting physician and then the phone number (but not the name) of the physician who was most familiar with my health. I said the admitting physician was an eye doctor and the physician most familiar with my health was a GP, and asked, which did she want the phone number for, the eye doctor or

(continued)

the GP? She became very angry then and admonished me to try and "get over that bad attitude." Then she told me to go over and sit somewhere and fill out the form as best I could.

A very nice patient (hemorrhoids, no vision problems) heard our conversation and offered to help me. She began reading the questionnaire and came to the item, "Past Medical History: Yes or No." She didn't think this made any sense, and neither did I, because everyone has a past medical history, and no one would answer no; but after a while we decided that it meant I should answer yes or no to all of the questions underneath, such as did I have diabetes? Did I have heart disease? But I was beginning to have doubts about this questionnaire—or, more specifically, about whoever had written it and what sort of organization would pass out such a form.

But when we came to "Have you ever had or been treated for a recent cold or the flu?" we could not decide if it meant, have I ever had flu? Or have I had flu recently (I had flu six months ago, but is that "recent"?) so we asked the receptionist, and she became almost speechless and said she would get me some help.

After a while the "help" appeared—a nurse who wanted to measure my blood pressure and induce me to take a blue pill, which she said would be good for my "nerves." I refused and pointed out rather curtly that this was not a gulag but an admissions department, a place of business, for crying out loud, where they ought to be able to handle a little criticism from someone trained to elicit accurate information.

I went back to the questionnaire, and by then several nice people had pitched in to help me. But this made it even harder to decide on the answers, because we understood so many of the questions differently and couldn't agree. When we came to "Are all your teeth intact?" One man thought it meant "Do you have false teeth?" And another thought it meant "Do you have any broken dentures?" But a woman who assured me her son is a dentist said it meant

"Do you have any loose teeth?" We decided to settle that by eeny-meany-miney-moe.

Then there was the question, "Do you have limited motion of your neck?" and by then everyone was enjoying the incongruity of these questions. Of course I have limited motion of the neck. Doesn't everyone? We decided to save that question for later clarification.

After all of the yes-no questions there came various other stumpers, such as "Please list your current medications." The problem is, of course, that I have purple eye drops and yellow eye drops, but the young man had taken them away from me "for a workup," so I had no way of accurately answering the questions. I was pretty sure one of them was glucagon, so I guessed and put that down, but then I had second thoughts and scratched it out. (When I got home, I checked and it was betagan, not glucagon.)

There were four of us working on the questionnaire by then, and we were laughing and crowing and having a high time and discharging our anxieties, which got the admissions clerk very flustered and annoyed. So she called the anesthetist, a stuck-up young fellow who said he had written the questionnaire himself and had never had any problems at all with it. That is when I told him, if he had not had any problems with this questionnaire, this proved it was better to be lucky than smart.

He said he was going to overlook my "attitude" because he knew I was old and anxious about the coming operation, and I told him I was going to take my business somewhere else because of the bilaterality problem. What is that? he asked, what is the "bilaterality problem"? I said, I have two eyes, and if anyone as dumb as he went after me with a knife, he would probably take the wrong eye.

I caught a cab and sent my neighbor back for my glasses. As your lawyer, I urge you not to involve yourself with such fools.

Lovingly,

Edna

CHARACTERISTICS OF THE COMMUNICATION APPROACH

Research designs can be classified by the *approach* used to gather primary data. There are really only two alternatives. We can *observe* conditions, behavior, events, people, or processes. Or we can *communicate* with people about various topics. We begin this chapter by discussing the characteristics and applications of the communication approach. We then examine the strengths and weaknesses of three communication data collection modes—personal interviewing, telephone interviewing, and self-administered surveys (see Figure 11–1).

The **communication approach** is questioning or surveying people and recording their responses for analysis. (It differs significantly from the observational approach, described in Chapter 13.) The great strength of questioning—or conducting a **survey**—as a primary data collecting technique is its versatility. It does not require that there be a visual or other objective perception of the information sought by the researcher. Abstract information of all types can be gathered by questioning others. We seldom learn much about opinions and attitudes except by questioning. This is also true of intentions and expectations. Information about past events is often available only through questioning of people who remember the events.

Questioning is more efficient and economical than observation. A few well-chosen questions can yield information that would take much more time and effort to gather by observation. A survey that uses the telephone, mail, or the Internet as the medium of communication can expand geographic coverage at a fraction of the cost and time required by observation.

The questioning technique has its shortcomings, however. The major weakness is that the quality and quantity of information secured depends heavily on the ability and willingness of respondents to cooperate. Often, people refuse an interview or fail to reply to a mail survey. There may be many reasons for this unwillingness to cooperate. Certain people at certain times fail to see any value in participation; they may fear the interview experience for some personal reason; or they may view the topic as too sensitive and thus the interview as potentially embarrassing or intrusive.

Even if respondents do participate, they may not have the knowledge sought or even have an opinion on the topic of concern. Under these circumstances, their proper response should be "don't know" or "have no opinion." Too often, respondents feel obliged to express some opinion even if they do not have one. In those cases, it is difficult for researchers to know how true or reliable the answers are.

Respondents may also interpret a question or concept differently from what was intended by the researcher. This occurs when the respondent is answering a question different from the one being asked. Also, a respondent may intentionally mislead the researcher by giving false information. It is difficult for a researcher to identify these occasions. Thus, survey responses should be accepted for what they are—statements by others that reflect varying degrees of truth. Despite these weaknesses, communicating with research subjects is a principal method of management research.

Applications

The most appropriate applications are those where respondents are uniquely qualified to provide the desired information. We expect such facts as age, income, and immediate family situation to be appropriate topics on which to get good data.

FIGURE   11–1   Selecting a Communication Data Collection Method

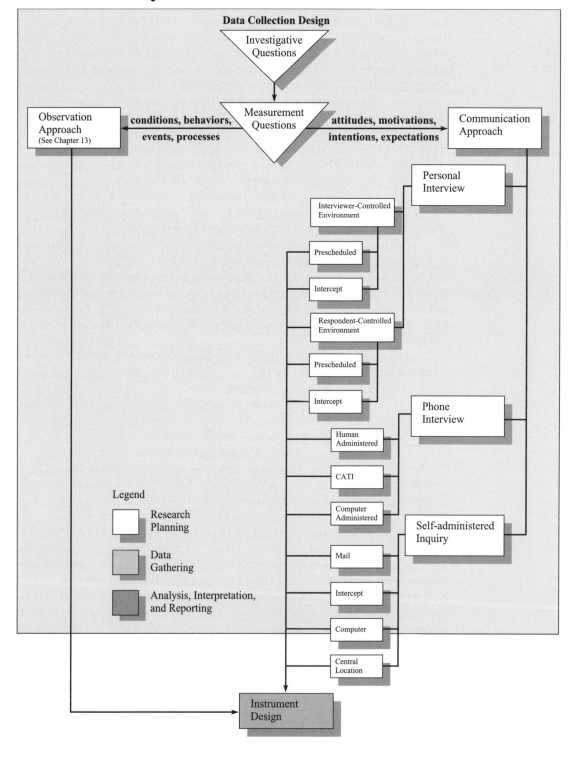

However, if we ask respondents to report on events that they have not personally experienced, we need to assess the replies carefully. If our purpose is to learn what the respondent understands to be the case, it is legitimate to accept the answers given. But if our intent is to learn what the event or situation was, we must recognize that the respondent is reporting second-hand data and the accuracy of the information declines. We should not depend on these second-hand sources if a more direct source can be found. A family member should be asked about another family member's experience only when there is no other way to get the information directly.

In the MindWriter study, only the individual who experiences difficulty with his or her laptop and goes through the CompleteCare program is privy to personal feelings and frustrations about the service process. While having shared some of what they experienced with others, no one but actual laptop owners are likely to give Jason or Myra as clear a picture of what works and what doesn't with CompleteCare. Aunt Edna, on the other hand, had a totally different experience when she went in for laser surgery to correct her vision problem. Answers to many of the questions on the patient survey might have been known by a caregiver, especially since Edna was over 80. And the clinic's admissions department could have been confident that such information was as accurate as if given by Edna herself.

Questions can be used to inquire about subjects that are exclusively internal to the respondent. We include here such items as attitudes, opinions, expectations, and intentions. Such information can be made available to the researcher if the right questions are asked of respondents. It becomes, finally, a matter of whether to ask direct or indirect questions to collect the most meaningful data. More is said about this topic in Chapter 12, "Instruments for Respondent Communication."

Besides these considerations, various means are used to secure information from subjects. Questioning can be carried out by personal interview, telephone, mail, computer, or a combination of these. While there are commonalties among these approaches, several considerations are unique to each. Before we explore them, let's revisit the research process model (Figure 3–1 in Chapter 3 and the inside front cover) to remind us of where we are in the process. In Chapter 3 we said that selecting a design and collecting information were complicated by the availability of a large variety of methods. In this chapter we are focusing on how our choices concerning the communication approach impact the research process. Figure 11–2 shows the selection of communication (versus observation) having the following effects:

- The creation and selection of the measurement questions
- Sampling issues (previously explored in Chapter 9), which drive contact and callback procedures
- Instrument design (to be discussed in Chapter 12), which incorporates attempts to reduce error and create respondent-screening procedures
- Data collection processes, which create the need for follow-up procedures (when self-administered instruments are used) and possible interviewer training (when personal or telephone interviewing methods are used)

FIGURE 11–2   **Data Collection Approach: Impact on the Research Process**

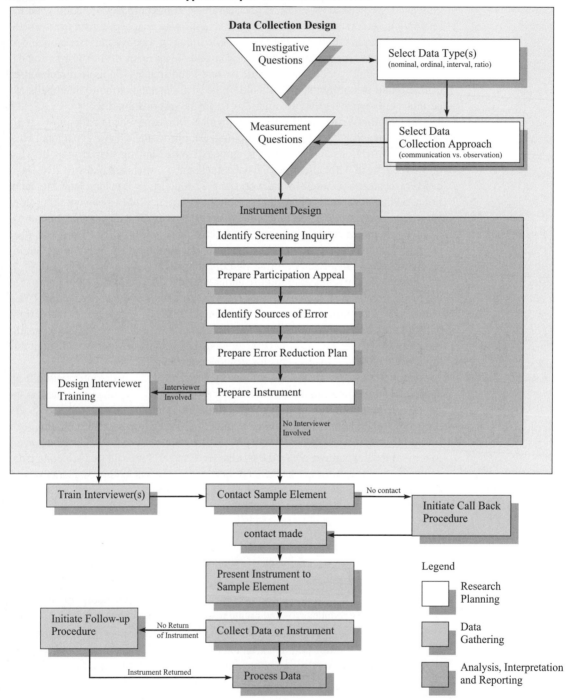

PERSONAL INTERVIEWING

A **personal interview** (i.e., face to face) is a two-way conversation initiated by an interviewer to obtain information from a respondent. The differences in roles of interviewer and respondent are pronounced. They are typically strangers, and the interviewer generally controls the topics and patterns of discussion. The consequences of the event are usually insignificant for the respondent. The respondent is asked to provide information and has little hope of receiving any immediate or direct benefit from this cooperation. Yet if the interview is carried off successfully, it is an excellent data collection technique. With her eyesight and the problems of question clarity that Edna experienced at the Albany Outpatient Laser Clinic, a personal interview rather than the intercept/self-administered questionnaire might have been a preferable communication method.

Evaluation of the Personal Interview

There are real advantages and clear limitations to personal interviewing. The greatest value lies in the depth of information and detail that can be secured. It far exceeds the information secured from telephone and self-administered studies via intercepts (e.g., in malls or, as with Edna, in a doctor's office), mail surveys, or computer (both intranet and Internet). The interviewer can also do more things to improve the quality of the information received than with another method.

The absence of assistance to interpret questions in the Albany clinic study was a clear weakness that would have been improved by the presence of an interviewer. Interviewers can note conditions of the interview, probe with additional questions, and gather supplemental information through observation. Edna was obviously in good spirits and very relaxed after she and her fellow patients had critiqued the questionnaire. This attitude would have been observed and noted by an interviewer. Of course, we're hopeful that the interviewer would correctly interpret laughter as a sign of humor and not as a negative attitude, as did the admissions clerk.

Interviewers also have more control than with other kinds of interrogation. They can prescreen to ensure the correct respondent is replying, and they can set up and control interviewing conditions. They can use special scoring devices and visual materials. Interviewers also can adjust to the language of the interview because they can observe the problems and effects the interview is having on the respondent.

With such advantages, why would anyone want to use any other survey method? Probably the greatest reason is that the method is costly, in both money and time. A personal interview may cost anywhere from a few dollars to several hundred dollars for an interview with a hard-to-reach person. Costs are particularly high if the study covers a wide geographic area or has stringent sampling requirements. An exception to this is the **intercept interview** that targets respondents in centralized locations such as shoppers in retail malls. Intercept interviews reduce costs associated with the need for several interviewers, training, and travel. Product and service demonstrations can also be coordinated, further reducing costs. Their cost-effectiveness, however, is offset when representative sampling is crucial to the study's outcome. The intercept interview would have been a possibility in the Albany clinic study, although more admissions clerks would likely have been needed if volunteers were not available to do this task.

Costs have risen rapidly in recent years for most communication methods because changes in the social climate have made personal interviewing more difficult. Many people have become reluctant to talk with strangers or permit visits in their homes. Interviewers are reluctant to visit unfamiliar neighborhoods alone, especially for evening interviewing. Finally, results of personal interviews can be affected adversely by interviewers who alter the questions asked or in other ways bias the results. As Edna and her friends discussed the Albany clinic survey, they each applied their own operational definitions to the concepts and constructs being asked. This confusion would have created a bias that might have been eliminated by a well-trained interviewer. More about interviewer bias is discussed later in the chapter. If we are to overcome these deficiencies, we must appreciate the conditions necessary for interview success.

Requirements for Success   Three broad conditions must be met to have a successful personal interview. They are (1) availability of the needed information from the respondent, (2) an understanding by the respondent of his or her role, and (3) adequate motivation by the respondent to cooperate. The interviewer can do little about the respondent's information level. Screening questions can qualify respondents when there is doubt about their ability to answer. This is the study designer's responsibility.

Interviewers can influence respondents in many ways. An interviewer can explain what kind of answer is sought, how complete it should be, and in what terms it should be expressed. Interviewers even do some coaching in the interview, although this can be a biasing factor.

Respondent motivation is a responsibility of the interviewer. Studies of reactions to many surveys show that respondents can be motivated to participate in personal interviews and, in fact, can even enjoy the experience. In one study, more than 90 percent of respondents said the interview experience was interesting, and three-fourths reported they were willing to be interviewed again.[1] In intercept/self-administered studies, the interviewer's primary role is to encourage participation as the respondent completes the survey on his or her own. Taking away Edna's glasses, along with the natural anxiety associated with eye surgery, would not have encouraged Edna's participation as a respondent. However, the "required" nature of the information (we assume surgery would not commence without prior completion of the questionnaire) guaranteed Edna's participation, no matter how grudgingly given.

A variety of forces affect respondent motivation in an interview. Many of these involve the interviewer. A graphic way to represent these various forces is presented in Figure 11–3.

Interviewing Technique[2]

At first, it may seem easy to question another person about various topics, but research interviewing is not so simple. What we do or say as interviewers can make or break a study. Respondents often react more to their feelings about the interviewer than to the content of the questions. It is also important for the interviewer to ask the questions properly, record the responses accurately, and probe meaningfully. To

FIGURE   11–3   Opposing Motivation Levels Affecting a Respondent in an Interview

SOURCE: Robert L. Kahn and Charles F. Cannell, "Interviewing," in David L. Sills, ed., *International Encyclopedia of the Social Sciences,* vol. 8, p. 153. Copyright © 1968 by Crowell Collier and Macmillan, Inc.

achieve these aims, the interviewer must be trained to carry out those procedures that foster a good interviewing relationship.

Increasing Respondent's Receptiveness   The first goal in an interview is to establish a friendly relationship with the respondent. Three factors will help with respondent receptiveness. The respondents must (1) believe the experience will be pleasant and satisfying, (2) think answering the survey is an important and worthwhile use of their time, and (3) have any mental reservations satisfied. Whether the experience will be pleasant and satisfying depends heavily on the interviewer. Typically, respondents will cooperate with an interviewer whose behavior reveals confidence and engages people on a personal level. Effective interviewers are differentiated not by demographic characteristics but by these interpersonal skills. By confidence, we mean that most respondents are immediately convinced they will want to participate in the study and cooperate fully with the interviewer. An engaging personal style is one where the interviewer instantly establishes credibility by adapting to the individual needs of the respondent.

For the respondent to think that answering the survey is important and worthwhile, some explanation of the study's purpose is necessary although the amount will vary. It is the interviewer's responsibility to discover what explanation is needed and to supply it. Usually, the interviewer should state the purpose of the study, tell how the information will be used, and suggest what is expected of the respondent. Respondents should feel that their cooperation would be meaningful to themselves and to the survey results. When this is achieved, more respondents will express their views willingly.

Respondents often have reservations about being interviewed that must be overcome. They may suspect the interviewer is a disguised salesperson, bill collector, or the like. In addition, they may also feel inadequate or fear the questioning will embarrass them. Techniques for successful interviewing of respondents in environments they control—particularly their homes—follow.

The Introduction   The respondent's first reaction to the request for an interview is at best a guarded one. Interviewer appearance and action are critical in forming a good first impression. Interviewers should immediately identify themselves by name and organization, and provide any special identification. Introductory letters or other information confirms the study's legitimacy. In this brief but critical period, the interviewer must display friendly intentions and stimulate the respondent's interest.

The interviewer's introductory explanations should be no more detailed than necessary. Too much information can introduce a bias. However, some respondents will demand more detail. For them, the interviewer might explain the objective of the study, its background, how the respondent was selected, the confidential nature of the interview (if it is), and the benefits of the research findings. Be prepared to deal with questions such as: "How did you happen to pick me?" "Who gave you my name?" "I don't know enough about this." "Why don't you go next door?" "Why are you doing this study?"[3]

The home interview typically involves two stages. The first occurs at the door when the introductory remarks are made, but this is not a satisfactory location for many interviews. In trying to secure entrance, the interviewer will find it more effective to suggest the desired action rather than to ask permission. "May I come in?" can be easily countered with a respondent's no. "I would like to come in and talk with you about X" is likely to be more successful.

If the Respondent Is Busy or Away   If it is obvious that the respondent is busy, it may be a good idea to give a general introduction and try to stimulate enough interest to arrange an interview at another time. If the designated respondent is not at home, the interviewer should briefly explain the proposed visit to the person who is contacted. It is desirable to establish good relations with intermediaries since their attitudes can help in contacting the proper respondent. Interviewers contacting respondents door to door often leave calling or business cards with their affiliation and a number where they can be reached to reschedule the interview.

Establishing a Good Relationship   The successful interview is based on rapport—meaning a relationship of confidence and understanding between interviewer and respondent. Interview situations are often new to respondents, and they need help in defining their roles. The interviewer can help by conveying that the interview is confidential (if it is) and important and that the respondent can discuss the topics with freedom from censure, coercion, or pressure. Under these conditions, the respondent can obtain much satisfaction in "opening up" without pressure being exerted.

Gathering the Data   To this point, the communication aspects of the interviewing process have been stressed. Having completed the introduction and established initial rapport, the interviewer turns to the technical task of gathering information. The interview centers on a prearranged questioning sequence. The technical task is well defined in studies with a structured questioning procedure (in contrast to an exploratory interview situation). The interviewer should follow the exact wording of the questions, ask them in the order presented, and ask every question that is specified. When questions are misunderstood or misinterpreted, they should be repeated.

A difficult task in interviewing is to make certain the answers adequately satisfy the question's objectives. To do this, the interviewer must learn the objectives of each question from a study of the survey instructions or by asking the research project director. It is important to have this information well in mind because many first responses are inadequate even in the best-planned studies.

The technique of stimulating respondents to answer more fully and relevantly is termed **probing.** Since it presents a great potential for bias, a probe should be neutral and appear as a natural part of the conversation. Appropriate probes (those that when used will elicit the desired information while injecting a limited amount of bias) should be specified by the designer of the data collection instrument. There are several different probing styles:

- *A brief assertion of understanding and interest.* With comments such as "I see" or "yes" or "uh-huh," the interviewer can tell the respondent that the interviewer is listening and is interested in more.

- *An expectant pause.* The simplest way to suggest to the respondent to say more is a pause along with an expectant look or a nod of the head. This approach must be used with caution. Some respondents have nothing more to say, and frequent pausing could create some embarrassing silences and make them uncomfortable, reducing their willingness to participate further.

- *Repeating the question.* This is particularly useful when the respondent appears not to understand the question or has strayed from the subject.

- *Repeating the respondent's reply.* The interviewer can do this while writing it down. Such repetition often serves as a good probe. Hearing thoughts restated often promotes revisions or further comments.

- *A neutral question or comment.* Such comments make a direct bid for more information. Examples are: "How do you mean?" "Can you tell me more about your thinking on that?" "Why do you think that is so?" "Anything else?"[4]

- *Question clarification.* When the answer is unclear or is inconsistent with something already said, the interviewer suggests the respondent failed to understand fully. Typical of such probes is, "I'm not *quite* sure I know what you mean by that—could you tell me a little more?" or "I'm sorry, but I'm not sure I understand. Did you say previously that . . . ?" It is important that the interviewer take the blame for failure to understand so as not to appear to be cross-examining the respondent.

A specific type of response that requires persistent probing is the "I don't know" answer. This is a satisfactory response if the respondent really does not know. But too often "I don't know" means the respondent does not understand, wants time to think, or is trying to evade the question. The interviewer can best probe this type of reply by using the expectant pause or by making some reassuring remark such as, "We are interested in your ideas about this."[5]

Recording the Interview   While the methods used in recording will vary, the interviewer usually writes down the answers of the respondent. Some guidelines can make this task more efficient. First, record responses as they occur. If you wait until later, you lose much of what is said. If there is a time constraint, the interviewer should use some shorthand system that will preserve the essence of the respondent's replies without converting them into the interviewer's paraphrases. Abbreviating words, leaving out articles and prepositions, and using only key words are good ways to do this.

Another technique is for the interviewer to repeat the response while writing it down. This helps to hold the respondent's interest during the writing and checks the interviewer's understanding of what the respondent said. Normally the interviewer should start the writing when the respondent begins to reply. The interviewer should also record all probes and other comments on the questionnaire in parentheses to set them off from responses.

Study designers sometimes create a special interview instrument for recording respondent answers. This may be integrated with the interview questions or a separate document. In such instances the likely answers are anticipated, allowing the interviewer to check respondent answers or to record ranks or ratings. However, all interview instruments must permit the entry of unexpected responses.

Selection and Training   The job requirements for interviewers include some college experience, good communication skills, flexible schedules, willingness to tolerate intermittent work hours, and mobility. This results in an interviewer profile that is largely composed of college-educated white females who have few child care responsibilities.[6] Little research evidence suggests that other profiles would increase performance or reduce error except in studies where the question directly involves ethnicity or religion or where volunteer interviewers are used. The former would imply that matching for race or religion should be considered, and the latter cautions against the use of volunteers because of attrition, recording error, and training-related problems.

Field interviewers receive varying degrees of training, ranging from brief written instructions to extensive sessions. Commercial research firms often provide lower levels of training, while governmental, educational, and similar research organizations provide more extensive training. Evidence supports the value of training. In one widely cited study, intensive training produced significant improvements in interviewer performance. The training effect was so great that performance of individual interviewers before training was a poor predictor of posttraining performance.[7]

Written instructions should be provided in all studies. Instructions should cover at least the general objectives of the study and mention something about the problems encountered in tests of the interview procedure and how they were solved. In addition, most questions should be discussed separately, giving the interviewer some insight into the purpose of the question, examples of adequate and inadequate responses, and other suggestions such as how to probe for more information. Definitions of concepts or constructs should be included so interviewers can explain and interpret in a standardized manner.

Several sources suggest an interview training program should do the following:

- Provide new interviewers with the principles of measurement; give them an intellectual grasp of the data collection function and a basis for evaluating interviewing behavior.
- Provide practice in introductions and introductory materials.
- Teach the techniques of interviewing.
- Teach wording and "skip" instructions to help with a smooth and consistent flow of questions.
- Teach how to probe.
- Provide experience in recording answers of different types and on different scales.
- Provide the opportunity for practice and evaluation by conducting interviews under controlled conditions.
- Offer careful evaluation of interviews, especially at the beginning of actual data collection. Such evaluation should include review of interview protocols.[8]

Interview Problems

In personal interviewing, the researcher must deal with bias and cost. While each is discussed separately, they are interrelated. Biased results grow out of three types of error: sampling error (discussed in Chapter 9), nonresponse error, and response error.

Nonresponse Error   In personal interviews, **nonresponse error** occurs when you cannot locate the person whom you are supposed to study or when you are unsuccessful in encouraging the person to participate. This is an especially difficult problem when you are using a probability sample of subjects. If there are predesignated persons to be interviewed; the task is to find them, and if you are forced to interview substitutes, an unknown but possibly substantial bias is introduced. One study of nonresponse found that only 31 percent of all first calls (and 20 percent of all first calls in major metropolitan areas) were completed.

The most reliable solution to nonresponse problems is to make **callbacks.** If enough attempts are made, it is usually possible to contact most target respondents, although unlimited callbacks are expensive.[9] An original contact plus three callbacks should usually secure about 85 percent of the target respondents. Yet in one study, 36 percent of central city residents still were not contacted after three callbacks.[10]

This problem relates to a second kind of nonresponse error—*accessibility.* In central cities where getting access to the respondent can be a problem, apartment security and locations that produce safety problems for nighttime follow-up may complicate household access.[11] In suburban areas, gated developments prohibit free access to interviewees.

One way to improve the productivity of callbacks is to vary them by time of day and day of the week. Sometimes neighbors can suggest the best time to call. An approach that has been used successfully is to treat all remaining nonrespondents as a new subpopulation after a few callbacks. A random sample is then drawn from this group, and every effort is made to complete this sample with a 100 percent response. These findings can then be weighted into the total population estimate.[12] In a survey in which central city residents are underrepresented, we can weight the results of interviews that are completed to give them full representation in the results. The weakness of this approach is that weighted returns often differ from those that would be secured if callbacks were made. Weighting for nonresponse after only one contact attempt will probably not overcome nonresponse bias, but respondent characteristics converge on their population values after two to three callbacks.[13]

A third way to deal with this nonresponse problem is *to substitute someone else for the missing respondent,* but this is dangerous. "At home" respondents are likely to differ from "not at home" persons in systematic ways. One study suggested that "not at home" persons are younger, better educated, more urban, and have a higher income than the average.[14]

If one must substitute, it is better for the interviewer to ask others in the household about the designated respondent. This approach has worked well "when questions are objective, when informants have a high degree of observability with respect to respondents, when the population is homogeneous, and when the setting of the interview provides no clear-cut motivation to distort responses in one direction or another."[15]

Response Error   When the data reported differ from the actual data, **response error** occurs. There are many ways these errors can happen. Errors can be made in the processing and tabulating of data. Errors occur when the respondent fails to report fully and accurately. One study found that liquid asset holdings were typically underestimated by as much as 25 to 50 percent. Other data, such as income and purchases of consumer durables, are more accurately reported. Respondents have difficulty in reporting fully and accurately on topics that are sensitive or involve ego matters. Consistent control or elimination of this bias is a problem that has yet to be solved. The best advice is to use trained interviewers who are knowledgeable about such problems.

Interviewer error is also a major source of response bias. From the introduction to the conclusion of the interview, there are many points where the interviewer's control of the process can affect the quality of the data. There are three different kinds of error concerning the interview techniques just discussed:

1. The sample loses credibility and is likely to be biased if interviewers do not do a good job of enlisting respondent cooperation. Certainly there is a question about the quality of the data collected from Edna during the Albany

clinic study. Toward the end of the communication, there is some doubt about the seriousness with which questions were answered. Stressing the importance of the information to the surgery that follows and having a receptionist serve as question interpreter/prober could reduce this type of error.

2. The precision of survey estimates will be reduced and there will be more error around estimates to the extent that interviewers are inconsistent in ways that influence the data. In the Albany clinic study, providing differing concept or construct definitions to different clinic patients would have created bias.

3. Answers may be systematically inaccurate or biased when interviewers fail to appropriately train and motivate respondents or fail to establish a suitable interpersonal setting.[16] Since the Albany clinic study asked for factual rather than attitudinal data, interviewer-injected bias would have been limited. If the clinic had required the admissions clerk (who insulted Edna by referring to her negative attitude) to also conduct a postsurgery study of patient satisfaction, the results of the latter study may have been influenced by interviewer bias.

Perhaps the most insidious form of interviewer error is cheating. Surveying is difficult work, often done by part-time employees, usually with only limited training and under little direct supervision. At times, falsification of an answer to an overlooked question is perceived as an easy solution to counterbalance the incomplete data. This seemingly easy, seemingly harmless first step can be followed by more pervasive forgery. It is not known how much of this occurs, but it should be of constant concern to research directors as they develop their data collection design.

It is also obvious that an interviewer can distort the results of any survey by inappropriate suggestions, word emphasis, tone of voice, and question rephrasing. These activities, whether premeditated or merely due to carelessness, are widespread. This problem was investigated with a simple structured questionnaire and planted respondents to report on the interviewers. The conclusion was "the high frequency of deviations from instructed behavior is alarming."[17]

Interviewers can influence respondents in many other ways also. Older interviewers are often seen as authority figures by young respondents, who modify their responses accordingly. Some research indicates that perceived social distance between interviewer and respondent has a distorting effect, although the studies do not fully agree on just what this relationship is.[18] In the light of the numerous studies on the various aspects of interview bias, the safest course for researchers is to recognize that there is a constant potential for response error.

Costs   While professional interviewers' wage scales are typically not high, interviewing is costly, and these costs continue to rise. Much of the cost results from the substantial interviewer time taken up with administrative and travel tasks. Respondents are often geographically scattered, and this adds to the cost. Repeated contacts (recommended at six to nine per household) are expensive. In recent years, some professional research organizations have attempted to gain control of these spiraling costs. Interviewers have typically been paid an hourly rate, but this method rewards inefficient interviewers and often results in field costs exceeding budgets.[19] The U.S. Bureau of the Census and the National Opinion Research Center have experimented with production standards and a formula pay system that provide an incentive for efficient interviewers. This approach has cut field costs about 10 percent and has improved the accuracy of the forecasts of fieldwork costs.

A second approach to the reduction of field costs has been to use the telephone to schedule personal interviews. Telephone calls to set up appointments for interviews are reported to reduce personal calls by 25 percent without reducing cooperation rates.[20] Telephone screening is also valuable when a study is concerned with a rare population. In one such case, where blind persons were sought, it was found that telephone screening of households was one-third the cost of screening on a face-to-face basis.[21]

A third means of reducing high field costs is to use self-administered questionnaires. In one study, a personal interview was conducted in the household with a self-administered questionnaire left for one or more other members of the household to complete. In this study, the cost per completed case was reduced by half when compared to conducting individual personal interviews. A comparison between a personal interview and a self-administered questionnaire seeking the same data showed that there was generally sufficient similarity of answers to enable them to be combined.[22]

TELEPHONE INTERVIEWING

The telephone can be helpful in arranging personal interviews and screening large populations for unusual types of respondents. Studies have also shown that making prior notification calls can improve the response rates of mail surveys. However, the **telephone interview** makes its greatest contribution in survey work as a unique mode of communication to collect information from respondents.

Evaluation of the Telephone Interview

Of the advantages that telephone interviewing offers, probably none ranks higher than its moderate cost. One study reports that sampling and data collection costs for telephone surveys can run from 45 to 64 percent lower than comparable personal interviews.[23] Much of the savings comes from cuts in travel costs and administrative savings from training and supervision. When calls are made from a single location, the researcher may use fewer yet more skilled interviewers. Telephones are especially economical when callbacks to maintain probability sampling are involved and respondents are widely scattered. Long-distance service options make it possible to interview nationally at a reasonable cost.

With the widespread use of computers, telephone interviewing can be combined with immediate entry of the responses into a data file by means of terminals, personal computers, or voice data entry. This brings added savings in time and money. **Computer-assisted telephone interviewing (CATI)** is used in research organiza-

tions throughout the world. A CATI facility consists of acoustically isolated interviewing carrels organized around supervisory stations. The telephone interviewer in
each carrel has a personal computer or terminal that is networked to the phone system and to the central data-processing unit. A software program that prompts the interviewers with introductory statements, qualifying questions, and precoded
questionnaire items drives questioning. These materials appear on the interviewers'
monitors. CATI works with a telephone number management system to select numbers, dial the sample, and enter responses. One facility, the Survey Research Center
at the University of Michigan, consists of 60 carrels with 100 interviewers working
in shifts from 8 A.M. to midnight (EST) to call nationwide. When fully staffed, they
produce more than 10,000 interview hours per month.[24]

Another means of securing immediate response data is the **computer-adminis-
tered telephone survey.** Unlike CATI, there is no interviewer. A computer calls the
phone number, conducts the interview, places data into a file for later tabulation, and
terminates the contact. The questions are voice-synthesized, and the respondent's answer and computer timing trigger continuation or disconnect. This mode is often
compared to the self-administered questionnaire (discussed later in the chapter) and
offers the advantage of respondent privacy. One study showed that the *noncontact
rate* for the electronic survey mode is similar to other telephone interviews when a
random phone list is used. It also found that rejection of this mode of data collection
affects the *refusal rate* (and thus nonresponse bias) because people hang up more
easily on a computer than on a human.[25] The **noncontact rate** is a ratio of potential
contacts (no answer, busy, answering machine, and disconnects but not refusals) to
all potential contacts. The **refusal rate** refers to the ratio of respondents who decline
the interview to all eligible contacts.

When compared to either personal interviews or mail surveys, the use of telephones brings a faster completion of a study, sometimes taking only a day or so for
the fieldwork. When compared to personal interviewing, it is also likely that interviewer bias, especially bias caused by the physical appearance, body language, and
actions of the interviewer, is reduced by using telephones.

Recent estimates of the percentage of U.S. households with at least one telephone are above 95 percent. In 13 states, 99 percent of all households are reported to
have phone service.[26] Access to respondents through low-cost, efficient means has
made telephone interviewing a very attractive alternative for marketing, public opinion, and academic researchers.

Finally, behavioral norms work to the advantage of telephone interviewing: If
someone is present, a ringing phone is usually answered, and it is the caller who decides the purpose, length, and termination of the call.[27] New technology, notably
caller identification systems where the receiver can decide whether a call is answered based on caller identity, is expected to increase the noncontract rate associated with telephone surveys.

There are also disadvantages to using the telephone for research. Obviously,
the respondent must be available by phone. Usage rates are not as high in households composed of single adults, less educated, poorer minorities, and individuals

employed as nonprofessional, nonmanagerial workers.[28] These variations can be a source of bias.

Because about 20 percent of American households move each year, there are always many obsolete numbers and new households for which numbers have not yet been published. In addition, it is estimated that about 22 percent of all household phone numbers are unlisted.[29] Another source says the highest incidence of nonlisting is in the West, in large metropolitan areas, among nonwhites, and for persons between 18 and 34 years of age.[30] Several methods have been developed to overcome the deficiencies of directories; among them are techniques for choosing phone numbers by using random-digit dialing or combinations of directories and random dialing.[31] **Random dialing procedures** normally require choosing phone exchanges or exchange blocks and then generating random numbers within these blocks for calling.[32]

A limit on interview length is another disadvantage of the telephone, but the degree of this limitation depends on the respondent's interest in the topic. Ten minutes has generally been thought of as ideal, but interviews of 20 minutes or more are not uncommon. Interviews ran for 1 1/2 hours in one long-distance survey.[33]

In telephone interviewing, it is not possible to use maps, illustrations, other visual aids, complex scales, or measurement techniques. The medium also limits the complexity of the questioning and the use of sorting techniques. One ingenious solution to not using scales, however, has been to employ a nine-point scaling approach and to ask the respondent to visualize this by using the telephone dial or keypad.[34]

Some studies suggest that the response rate in telephone studies is lower than for comparable face-to-face interviews. One reason is that respondents find it easier to terminate a phone interview. Telemarketing practices may also contribute. Public reaction to investigative reports of wrongdoing and unethical behavior within telemarketing activities places an added burden on the researcher trying to convince a respondent that the phone interview is not a pretext for soliciting contributions or selling products.

Telephone surveys can result in less thorough responses, and those interviewed by phone find the experience to be less rewarding to them than a personal interview. Respondents report less rapport with telephone interviewers than with personal interviewers. Given the growing costs and difficulties of personal interviews, it is likely that an even higher share of surveys will be by telephone in the future. Thus, it behooves management researchers using telephone surveys to attempt to improve the enjoyment of the interview. One authority suggests:

> We need to experiment with techniques to improve the enjoyment of the interview by the respondent, maximize the overall completion rate, and minimize response error on specific measures. This work might fruitfully begin with efforts at translating into verbal messages the visual cues that fill the interaction in a face-to-face interview: the smiles, frowns, raising of eyebrows, eye contact, etc. All of these cues have informational content and are important parts of the personal interview setting. We can perhaps purposefully choose those cues that are most important to data quality and respondent trust and discard the many that are extraneous to the survey interaction.[35]

Telephone Interview Trends

Future trends in telephone interviewing bear watching. Answering machines and multiline households will affect sampling. So will the variations among the 60 telephone companies' services and the degree of cooperation that will be extended to researchers. There is also concern for the ways in which random-digit dialing can be made to deal with nonworking and ineligible numbers.[36]

Answering machines could pose potentially complex response-rate problems since they are estimated to have substantial penetration in American households. A benchmark study discovered that most answering-machine households are accessible: The subsequent contact rate was greater in answering-machine households than in no-machine households and about equal with busy-signal households. Other findings suggested that (1) individuals with answering machines were more likely to participate, (2) machine use was more prevalent on weekends than on weekday evenings, and (3) machines were more commonplace in urban than in rural areas.

Newly developed voice-mail options by local phone service providers have less market penetration but are gaining increasing acceptance. Questions about the sociodemographics of users and nonusers and the relationship of answering-machine/voice-mail technology to the rapid changes in the wireless market remain to be answered.[37] The impact of caller identification technology and the assignment of facsimile machines or computer modems to dedicated phone lines is also expected to have an impact on the noncontact rate of phone interviews.

SELF-ADMINISTERED SURVEYS

The **self-administered questionnaire** has become ubiquitous in modern living. Service evaluations of hotels, restaurants, car dealerships, and transportation providers furnish ready examples. Often a short questionnaire is left to be completed by the respondent in a convenient location or is packaged with a product. User registrations, product information requests in magazines, warranty cards, the MindWriter repair study, and the Albany clinic study are self-administered. In this section, we focus on the **mail survey,** a self-administered questionnaire delivered by the Postal Service, facsimile, or a courier service.

Other delivery modalities include *computer-delivered* and *intercept* studies. Computer-delivered self-administered questionnaires use organizational intranets, the Internet, or online services to reach their respondents. Respondents may be targeted or self-selecting. Intercept studies may use a traditional questionnaire or a computerized instrument in a predetermined environment without interviewer assistance. All modes have special problems and unique advantages (see Table 11–1).

Mail Surveys

Mail surveys typically cost less than personal interviews. Telephone and mail costs are in the same general range, although in specific cases either may be lower. The more geographically dispersed the sample, the more likely it is that mail will be the

TABLE 11-1   Comparison of Communication Approaches

	Personal Interviews	Telephone Interviews	Self-Administered Surveys
Description	People selected to be part of the sample are interviewed in person by a trained interviewer.	People selected to be part of the sample are interviewed on the telephone by a trained interviewer.	Questionnaires are (a) mailed, faxed, or sent by courier to be self-administered—with return mechanism generally included; (b) computer delivered via intranet, Internet, and online services—computer stores/forwards completed instruments automatically; (c) people intercepted/studied via paper or computerized instrument in central location—without interviewer assistance.
Advantages	Good cooperation from respondents. Interviewer can answer questions about survey, probe for answers, use follow-up questions, and gather information by observation. Special visual aids and scoring devices can be used. Illiterate and functionally illiterate respondents can be reached. Interviewer can prescreen respondent to ensure he/she fits the population profile. CAPI—computer-assisted personal interviewing: Responses can be entered into a portable microcomputer to reduce error and cost.	Lower costs than personal interview. Expanded geographic coverage without dramatic increase in costs. Uses fewer, more highly skilled interviewers. Reduced interviewer bias. Fastest completion time. Better access to hard-to-reach respondents through repeated callbacks. Can use computerized random-digit dialing. CATI—computer-assisted telephone interviewing: Responses can be entered directly into a computer file to reduce error and cost.	Incentives may be used to increase response rate. Often lowest-cost option. Expanded geographic coverage without increase in costs (mail). Requires minimal staff (mail). Perceived as more anonymous (mail). Allows respondents time to think about questions (mail). Allows contact with otherwise inaccessible respondents (e.g., CEOs). Rapid data collection (computer delivered/intercept). More complex instruments can be used (computer delivered). Respondent who cannot be reached by phone(voice) may be accessible (intercept or computer delivered). Fast access to the computer-literate (computer delivered). Listing of viable locations rather than prospective respondents (computer delivered and intercept).
Disadvantages	High costs. Need for highly trained interviewers. Longer period needed in the field collecting data. May be wide geographic dispersion. Follow-up is labor intensive. Not all respondents are available or accessible. Some respondents are unwilling to talk to strangers in their homes. Some neighborhoods are difficult to visit. Questions may be altered or re-spondent coached by interviewers.	Response rate is lower than for personal interview. Higher costs if interviewing geographically dispersed sample. Interview length must be limited. Many phone numbers are unlisted or not working, making directory listings unreliable. Some target groups are not available by phone. Responses may be less complete. Illustrations cannot be used.	Low response rate in some modes. No interviewer intervention available for probing or explanation (mail). Cannot be long or complex (mail). Accurate mailing lists needed (mail). Often respondents returning survey represent extremes of the population—skewed responses (mail). Anxiety among some respondents (computer delivered). Directions/software instruction for progression through the instrument (computer delivered). Computer security (computer delivered). Need for low-distraction environment for survey completion (intercept).

low-cost method. A mail study can cost less because it is often a one-person job. Another value in using mail is that we can contact respondents who might otherwise be inaccessible. People such as major corporate executives are difficult to reach in any other way. When the researcher has no specific person to contact—say, in a study of corporations—the mail survey often will be routed to the appropriate respondent.

In a mail survey, the respondent can take more time to collect facts, talk with others, or consider replies at length than is possible with the telephone, personal interview, or intercept studies. Mail surveys are typically perceived as more impersonal, providing more anonymity than the other communication modes, including other methods for distributing self-administered questionnaires.

The major weakness of the mail survey is nonresponse error. Many studies have shown that better-educated respondents and those more interested in the topic answer mail surveys. A high percentage of those who reply to a given survey have usually replied to others, while a large share of those who do not respond are habitual nonrespondents.[38] Mail surveys with a return of about 30 percent are often considered satisfactory, but there are instances of more than 70 percent response.[39] In either case, there are many nonresponders, and we usually know nothing about how those who answer differ from those who do not answer.

The second major limitation of mail surveys concerns the type and amount of information that can be secured. We normally do not expect to obtain large amounts of information and cannot probe deeply into questions. Respondents will generally refuse to cooperate with a long and/or complex mail questionnaire unless they perceive a personal benefit. Returned mail questionnaires with many questions left unanswered testify to this problem, but there are also many exceptions. One general rule of thumb is that the respondent should be able to answer the questionnaire in no more than 10 minutes. On the other hand, a study of the general population found more than a 70 percent response to a questionnaire calling for 158 answers.[40]

Improving Returns

The research literature is filled with ways to improve mail survey returns. Seemingly every possible variable has been studied. Over 200 methodological articles have been published on efforts to improve mail response rates. Two review articles concluded that few variables consistently showed positive response rates.[41] Several practical suggestions emerge from the conclusions.[42]

Follow-ups. Follow-ups, or reminders, are very successful in increasing response rates. Since each successive follow-up produces more returns, the very persistent (and well-financed) researcher can potentially achieve an extremely high total response rate. However, the value of additional information thus obtained must be weighed against the costs required for successive contacts.

Preliminary Notification. There is evidence that advance notification, particularly by telephone, is effective in increasing response rates; it also serves to accelerate the rate of return. However, follow-ups are a better investment than preliminary notification.

Concurrent Techniques

1. *Questionnaire Length.* Although common sense suggests that short questionnaires should obtain higher response rates than longer questionnaires, research evidence does not support this view.

2. *Survey Sponsorship.* There is little experimental evidence concerning the influence of survey sponsorship on response rates; however, the sparse evidence that does exist suggests that official or "respected" sponsorship increases response rates.

3. *Return Envelopes.* The inclusion of a stamped, return envelope encourages response because it simplifies questionnaire return.

4. *Postage.* Many tests regarding postage are reported in the literature, but few studies have tested the same variables. The existing evidence shows that expedited delivery is very effective in increasing response rates. Findings do not show a significant advantage for first class over third class, for commemorative stamps over ordinary postage, for stamped mail over metered mail, or for multiple small denomination stamps over single larger denomination stamps.

5. *Personalization.* Personalization of the mailing has no clear-cut advantage in terms of improved response rates. Neither personal inside addresses nor individually signed cover letters significantly increased response rates; personally typed cover letters proved to be somewhat effective in most but not all cases cited. The one study that tested the use of a titled signature versus one without a title did show a significant advantage in favor of the title.

6. *Cover Letters.* The influence of the cover letter on response rates has received almost no experimental attention, although the cover letter is considered an integral part of the mail survey package. It is the most logical vehicle for persuading individuals to respond, yet the few studies that are reported offer no insights as to its formulation.

7. *Anonymity.* Experimental evidence shows that the promise of anonymity to respondents, either explicit or implied, has no significant effect on response rates.

8. *Size, Reproduction, and Color.* The few studies that examined the effects of questionnaire size, method of reproduction, and color found no significant difference in response rates.

9. *Money Incentives.* A monetary incentive sent with the questionnaire is very effective in increasing response rates. Larger sums bring in added response, but at a cost that may exceed the value of the added information.

10. *Deadline Dates.* The few studies that tested the impact of deadline dates found that they did not increase the response rate; however, they did serve to accelerate the rate of questionnaire return.

These suggestions and conclusions are equivocal because "the manipulation of one or two techniques independently of all others may do little to stimulate response."[43] Efforts should be directed toward the more important question of maximizing the overall probability of response. The Total Design Method (TDM), consisting of two parts, is proposed to meet this need.[44] First, one must identify the aspects of the survey process that affect the response rate, either qualitatively or quantitatively. Each aspect must be shaped to obtain the best response. Second, organize the survey effort so the design intentions are carried out in detail. The results achieved in 48 surveys using TDM showed response rates of 50 to 94 percent, with a median response rate of 74 percent.[45]

Maximizing the Mail Survey

To maximize the overall probability of response, attention must be given to each point of the survey process where the response may break down.[46] For example:

- The wrong address and wrong postage can result in nondelivery or nonreturn.
- The letter may look like junk mail and be discarded without being opened.
- Lack of proper instructions for completion leads to nonresponse.
- The wrong person opens the letter and fails to call it to the attention of the right person.
- A respondent finds no convincing explanation for completing the survey and discards it.
- A respondent temporarily sets the questionnaire aside and fails to complete it.
- The return address is lost so the questionnaire cannot be returned.

Efforts to overcome these problems will vary according to the circumstances, but some general suggestions can be made for mail surveys, and, by extension, for self-administered questionnaires using different delivery modes. A questionnaire, cover letter, and return mechanism are sent. Incentives, such as dollar bills, coins, or gift coupons are often attached to the letter in commercial studies. Follow-ups are usually needed to get the maximum response. Opinions differ about the number and timing of follow-ups. TDM uses the follow-ups described below; other timing should be adapted for different delivery modes:

1. *One week later*—A preprinted postcard is sent to all recipients thanking them for returns and reminding others to complete and mail the questionnaire.
2. *Three weeks after the original mailing*—A new questionnaire and a letter telling nonrespondents that the questionnaire has not been received and repeating the basic appeal of the original letter are sent.
3. *Seven weeks after the original mailing*—A third cover letter and questionnaire are sent by certified mail to the remaining nonrespondents.

An appeal for cooperation is essential and may be altruistic or more expedient. The former is often found when the questionnaire is short, easy to complete, and does not require much effort from a respondent. Anonymity may or may not be mentioned. A brief letter emphasizes the "Would you do me a favor?" approach. Often a token is sent to symbolize the researcher's appreciation. Sometimes this is not powerful enough. Then an appeal must stress how important the problem is to a group with which the respondent identifies.

The cover letter should also convey that the respondent's help is needed to solve a problem. Researchers are portrayed as reasonable people making a reasonable appeal for help. They are intermediaries between the person asked for help and an important issue. The total effect must be personalized to convey to respondents that they are important to the study. The standard is to make the appeal comparable in appearance and content to what one would expect in a business or professional letter.

Finally, a mixed model can be used to improve response. One study compared the use of "drop-off" delivery of a self-administered questionnaire to a mail survey.[47] Under the drop-off system, a lightly trained survey taker personally delivered the questionnaires to target households and returned in a couple of days for the completed instrument. Response rates for the drop-off system were typically above 70 percent—much higher than for comparable mail surveys. In addition, the cost per completed questionnaire was from 18 to 40 percent lower than for mail surveys.

Beyond a higher response rate and lower cost per response, the drop-off delivery gives greater control over sample design, permits thorough identification of the respondents' geographic location, and allows the researcher to eliminate those who fall outside a predefined sample frame (persons of the wrong age, income, or other characteristics). Additional information can also be gathered by observation on the visits. However, the cost advantage is probably restricted to studies where respondents can be reached with little travel.

Drop-off delivery has much in common with intercept studies that employ self-administered completion of a questionnaire. The researcher can encourage the selected respondent to complete the questionnaire, stressing the importance of his or her participation and the ease of completion, and then indicate the procedure for returning it. These activities are likely to increase response rates and reduce nonresponse error.

Self-Administered Survey Trends

Computer surveying is surfacing at trade shows, where participants complete surveys while making a visit to a company's booth. Continuous tabulation of results provides a stimulus for attendees to visit a particular exhibit as well as giving the exhibitor detailed information for evaluating the productivity of the show. This same technology easily transfers to other situations where large groups of people congregate.

Companies are now using intranet capabilities to evaluate employee policies and behavior. Ease of access to electronic mail systems makes it possible for both large and smaller organizations to use computer questioning with both internal and external respondent groups. Many techniques of traditional mail surveys can be easily adapted to computer-delivered questionnaires (e.g., follow-ups to nonrespondents are more easily executed and less expensive).

It is not unusual to find registration procedures and full-scale surveying being done on World Wide Web sites. University sites are asking prospective students about their interests, and university departments are evaluating current students' use of online materials. A short voyage on the Internet reveals organizations using their sites to evaluate customer service processes, build sales-lead lists, evaluate planned promotions and product changes, determine supplier and customer needs, discover interest in job openings, evaluate employee attitudes, and more. Advanced and easier-to-use software for designing modules for Web sites will encourage more organizations to engage in these activities.

SELECTING AN OPTIMAL METHOD

The choice of a communication method is not as complicated as it might first appear. By comparing your research objectives with the strengths and weaknesses of each method, you will be able to choose one that is suited to your needs. Table 11–1 presents a summary of the advantages and disadvantages of personal interviews, telephone interviews, and self-administered questionnaires that should be useful for making such a comparison.

When your investigative questions call for information from hard-to-reach or inaccessible respondents, the telephone interview or mail survey should be considered. However, if data must be collected very quickly, the mail survey would likely be ruled out because of lack of control over the returns. Alternatively, you may decide your objective requires extensive questioning and probing; then the personal interview should be considered.

If none of the choices turns out to be a particularly good fit, it is possible to combine the best characteristics of two or more alternatives into a *mixed mode*. Although this decision will incur the costs of the combined modes, the flexibility of tailoring a method to your unique needs is often an acceptable trade-off.

In the MindWriter study, Jason plans to insert a postcard questionnaire (a self-administered study delivered via courier) in each laptop returned by the Complete-Care repair service. Not all customers will return their questionnaires, creating nonresponse bias. The postcard format doesn't permit much space for encouraging customer response. Alerting customers to the importance of returning the response card by phone (to announce impending courier delivery of a repaired laptop) might improve the research design. Respondents would not be in the best frame of mind if they received a damaged laptop; dissatisfaction could lead to a decreased response rate and an increase in call center contacts. Combining the study with standard procedures for verifying delivery by the courier might also be needed.

Jason and Myra's proposal contains a follow-up procedure—telephoning nonrespondents to obtain their answers when response cards are not returned. This will likely decrease nonresponse error. Where most of the study respondents are answering measurement questions without assistance, telephone interviewing creates the possibility of interviewer bias at an unknown level for at least part of the data.

In the Albany clinic study, the researcher could have taken several actions to improve the quality of the data. Distributing the questionnaire to the patient's eye doctor or to the patient (by mail) prior to arrival would have increased the accuracy of identifying medications, diagnoses, hospitalizations, and so forth. The patient's eye doctor was in the best position to encourage compliance with the collection process but was not consulted. Having the patient bring the completed questionnaire to the admissions procedure, where the admissions clerk could review the completed instrument for accuracy and completeness, would have given the researcher the opportunity to clarify any confusion with the questions, concepts, and constructs. Finally, pretesting the instrument with a sample of patients would have revealed difficulties with the process and operational definitions. Edna's concerns could have been eliminated before they surfaced.

Ultimately, all researchers are confronted by the practical realities of cost and deadlines. Table 11–1 suggests that, on the average, personal interviews are the costliest and take the most field time unless a large field team is used. Telephone interviews are moderate in cost and offer the quickest option. Self-administered questionnaires are the least expensive and traditionally require a longer data collection period. The use of the computer to select respondents and reduce coding and processing time will continue to improve the cost-to-performance profiles of these methods in the future.

Two graphics help you make a decision about the best communication approach for your research. Table 11–1 reminds you of the strengths and weaknesses, and Figure 11–1 (at the beginning of the chapter) describes the environments, modalities, and resources required for data collection. Most of the time, an optimal method will be apparent. However, managers' needs for information often exceed their internal resources. Such factors as specialized expertise, a large field team, unique facilities, or a rapid turnaround prompt managers to seek assistance from research vendors of survey-related services.

Outsourcing Survey Services

Commercial suppliers of research services vary from full-service operations to specialty consultants. When confidentiality is likely to affect competitive advantage, the manager or staff will sometimes prefer to bid only a phase of the project. Alternatively, the organization's staff members may possess such unique knowledge of a product or service that they must fulfill a part of the study themselves. Regardless, the exploratory work, design, sampling, data collection, or processing and analysis may be contracted separately or as a whole.[48] Most organizations use a request for proposal (RFP) to describe their requirements and seek competitive bids (see Appendix C).

Research firms also offer special advantages that their clients do not typically maintain in-house. Centralized-location interviewing, focus group facilities, or computer-assisted telephone facilities may be particularly desirable for certain research needs. A professionally trained staff with considerable experience in similar management problems is another benefit. Data-processing and statistical analysis capabilities are especially important for some projects. Other vendors have specially designed software for interviewing and data tabulation.[49]

Panel suppliers provide another type of research service with emphasis on longitudinal survey work.[50] By using the same respondents over time, **panels** can track trends in attitudes toward issues or products, product adoption or consumption behavior, and a myriad of other research interests. Suppliers of panel data can secure information from personal and telephone interviewing techniques as well as from the mail and mixed modes. Diaries are a common means of chronicling events of research interest by the panel members. These are mailed back to the research organization. Point-of-sale terminals and scanners aid electronic data collection for panel-type respondent groups. And mechanical devices placed in the homes of panel members evaluate media usage.

Summary

The major advantages of personal interviewing are the ability to explore topics in great depth, to achieve a high degree of interviewer control, and to provide maximum interviewer flexibility for meeting unique situations. However, this method is costly and time-consuming, and the flexibility can result in excessive interviewer bias.

A successful interview requires that we seek information the respondent can provide and that the respondent understands his or her role and is motivated to play this role. Motivation, in particular, is a task for the interviewer. Good rapport with the respondent should be quickly established, and then the technical process of collecting data should begin. The latter often calls for skillful probing to supplement the answers volunteered by the respondent.

Two factors cause bias in interviewing. One is nonresponse. It is a concern with all types of surveys. Some studies show that first calls often secure less than 20 percent of the designated respondents. Various methods are useful for increasing this representation, the most effective being making callbacks until adequate numbers of completed interviews are secured. The second factor is response error, which occurs when the respondent fails to give a complete answer. The interviewer can contribute to the correction of this problem.

Telephone interviewing has become much more popular in recent years because of the diffusion of telephone service in American households and the low cost of this method compared with personal interviewing. Long-distance telephone interviewing has grown. There are also disadvantages to telephone interviewing. Many phone numbers are unlisted, and directory listings become obsolete quickly. There is also a limit on the length and depth of interviews using the telephone.

The self-administered questionnaire can be delivered by the Postal Service, facsimile, a courier service, a computer, or intercept. Computer-delivered self-administered questionnaires use organizational intranets, the Internet, or online services to reach their respondents. Respondents may be targeted or self-selecting. Intercept studies may use a traditional questionnaire or a computerized instrument in environments where interviewer assistance is minimal.

The optimal survey method is the one that is instrumental for answering your research question and dealing with the constraints imposed by time, budget, and human resources. The opportunity to combine several survey methodologies makes the use of the mixed mode desirable in many projects.

Outsourcing survey services offers special advantages to managers. A professionally trained research staff, centralized-location interviewing, focus group facilities, and computer-assisted facilities are among them. Specialty firms offer software and computer-based assistance for telephone and personal interviewing as well as mail and mixed modes. Panel suppliers produce data for longitudinal studies of all varieties.

Key Terms

callbacks	panels
communication approach	personal interview
computer-administered telephone survey	probing
computer-assisted telephone interviewing	random dialing procedures
intercept interview	refusal rate
interviewer error	response error
mail survey	self-administered questionnaire
noncontact rate	survey
nonresponse error	telephone interview

Case

Sturgel Division
(This is a case found in the optional casebook available with the text.)

Discussion Questions

1. Distinguish among response error, interviewer error, and nonresponse error.

2. Assume you are planning to interview shoppers in a shopping mall about their views on increased food prices and what the federal government should do about them. In what different ways might you try to motivate shoppers to cooperate in your survey?

3. In recent years, in-home personal interviews have grown more costly and more difficult to complete. Suppose, however, you have a project in which you need to talk with people in the home. What might you do to hold down the costs and increase the response rate?

4. How do environmental factors affect response rates in personal interviews? How can we overcome these environmental problems?

5. In the following situations, would you use a personal interview, telephone survey, or self-administered questionnaire? Give your reasons.

   a. A survey of the residents of a new subdivision on why they happened to select that area in which to live. You also wish to secure some information about what they like and do not like about life in the subdivision.

   b. A poll of students at Metro University on their preferences among three candidates who are running for presidency of the student government.

   c. A survey of 58 wholesale grocery companies, scattered over the eastern United States, on their personnel management policies for warehouse personnel.

   d. A survey of financial officers of the Fortune 500 corporations to learn their prediction for the economic outlook in their industries for next year.

   e. A survey of pharmacists in the state of Illinois to secure their opinions concerning a proposed state law to permit the advertising of prescription drugs.

6. You decide to take a telephone survey of 40 families in the 721-exchange area. You want an excellent representation of all subscribers in the exchange area. Explain how you will carry out this study.

7. You plan to conduct a mail survey of the traffic managers of 1,000 major manufacturing companies across the country. The study concerns their company policies regarding the payment of moving expenses for employees who are transferred. What might you do to improve the response rate of such a survey?

8. A major corporation agrees to sponsor an internal study on sexual harassment in the workplace. This is in response to concerns expressed by their female employees. How would you handle the following issues:

   a. Sample selection

   b. The communication approach (self-administered, telephone, personal interview, mixed)

   c. The purpose: fact finding, awareness, relationship building, and change

   d. Minimization of response and nonresponse error

Reference Notes

1. Robert L. Kahn and Charles F. Cannell, *The Dynamics of Interviewing* (New York: Wiley, 1957), pp. 45–51.

2. One of the top research organizations in the world is the Survey Research Center of the University of Michigan. The material in this section draws heavily on the *Interviewer's Manual*, rev. ed. (Ann Arbor, Survey Research Center, University of Michigan, 1976); and Floyd J. Fowler, Jr., *Survey Research Methods* (Beverly Hills, CA: Sage Publications, 1988), chap. 7.

3. Survey Research Center, *Interviewer's Manual,* p. 8.

4. Ibid., pp. 15–16.

5. Ibid., p. 17.

6. Fowler, *Survey Research Methods,* p. 112.

7. S. A. Richardson, B. S. Dohrenwend, and D. Klein, *Interviewing: Its Forms and Functions* (New York: Basic Books, 1965), pp. 328–58.

8. Reprinted by special permission from Charles F. Cannell and Robert L. Kahn, "Interviewing," in *The Handbook of Social Psychology,* 2nd ed., vol. 2, eds. G. Lindzey and E. Aronson (Reading, MA: Addison-Wesley, 1968). See also, Fowler, *Survey Research Methods,* p. 115; and P. J. Guenzel, T. R. Berkmans, and Charles F. Cannell, *General Interviewing Techniques* (Ann Arbor: Institute for Social Research, University of Michigan, 1983).

9. In one study, 5.5 percent of white respondents and 11 percent of nonwhite respondents were still not contacted after six calls. See W. C. Dunkelberg and G. S. Day, "Nonresponse Bias and Callbacks in Sample Surveys," *Journal of Marketing Research* (May 1974), table 3.

10. Ibid.
11. Fowler, *Survey Research Methods,* p. 50.
12. C. H. Fuller, "Weighting to Adjust for Survey Nonresponse," *Public Opinion Quarterly* (Summer 1974), pp. 239–46.
13. Dunkleberg and Day, "Nonresponse Bias," table 3.
14. Ibid., pp. 160–68.
15. Eleanore Singer, "Agreement Between Inaccessible Respondents and Informants," *Public Opinion Quarterly* (Winter 1972–73), pp. 603–11.
16. Fowler, *Survey Research Methods,* p. 111.
17. B. W. Schyberger, "A Study of Interviewer Behavior," *Journal of Marketing Research* (February 1967), p. 35.
18. B. S. Dohrenwend, J. A. Williams, Jr., and C. H. Weiss, "Interviewer Biasing Effects: Toward a Reconciliation of Findings," *Public Opinion Quarterly* (Spring 1969), pp. 121–29.
19. Seymour Sudman, *Reducing the Costs of Surveys* (Chicago: Aldine, 1967), p. 67.
20. Ibid., p. 59.
21. Ibid., p. 63.
22. Ibid., p. 53.
23. Robert M. Groves and Robert L. Kahn, *Surveys by Telephone* (New York: Academic Press, 1979), p. 223.
24. Institute for Social Research, *ISR Newsletter* (Ann Arbor: University of Michigan, 1991–92), p. 3.
25. Michael J. Havice, "Measuring Nonresponse and Refusals to an Electronic Telephone Survey," *Journalism Quarterly,* (Fall 1990), pp. 521–30.
26. Paul J. Lavrakas, *Telephone Survey Methods: Sampling, Selection, and Supervision* (Beverly Hills, CA: Sage Publications, 1987), pp. 14–15.
27. See, for example, J. H. Frey, Jr., *Survey Research by Telephone* (Beverly Hills, CA: Sage Publications, 1983).
28. See, for example, Groves and Kahn, *Surveys by Telephone.*
29. R. W. Graves, "An Empirical Comparison of Two Telephone Sample Designs," *Journal of Marketing Research* (November 1978), p. 622.
30. G. J. Glasser and G. D. Metzger, "National Estimates of Nonlisted Telephone Households and Their Characteristics," *Journal of Marketing Research* (August 1975), p. 360.
31. G. J. Glasser and G. D. Metzger, "Random Digit Dialing as a Method of Telephone Sampling," *Journal of Marketing Research* (February 1972), pp. 59–64; and Seymour Sudman, "The Uses of Telephone Directories for Survey Sampling," *Journal of Marketing Research* (May 1973), pp. 204–7.
32. A block is defined as an exchange group composed of the first four or more digits of a seven-digit number such as 721–0, 721–1, and so forth.
33. Sudman, *Reducing the Costs of Surveys,* p. 65.
34. J. J. Wheatley, "Self-Administered Written Questionnaires or Telephone Interviews," *Journal of Marketing Research* (February 1973), pp. 94–95.
35. Groves and Kahn, *Survey by Telephone,* p. 223.
36. Lavrakas, *Telephone Survey Methods,* p. 16.
37. Peter S. Tuckel and Barry M. Feinberg, "The Answering Machine Poses Many Questions for Telephone Survey Researchers," *Public Opinion Quarterly* (Summer 1991), pp. 200–217.
38. D. Wallace, "A Case for and Against Mail Questionnaires," *Public Opinion Quarterly* (Spring 1954), pp. 40–52.

39. Don A. Dillman, "Increasing Mail Questionnaire Response in Large Samples of the General Public," *Public Opinion Quarterly* (Summer 1972), pp. 254–57.

40. Don A. Dillman, *Mail and Telephone Surveys* (New York: Wiley, 1978), p. 6.

41. Leslie Kanuk and Conrad Berenson, "Mail Surveys and Response Rates: A Literature Review," *Journal of Marketing Research* (November 1975), pp. 440–53; and Arnold S. Linsky, "Stimulating Responses to Mailed Questionnaires: A Review," *Public Opinion Quarterly* 39 (1975), pp. 82–101.

42. Kanuk and Berenson, "Mail Surveys," p. 450. Reprinted from the *Journal of Marketing Research,* published by the American Marketing Association.

43. Dillman, *Mail and Telephone Surveys,* p. 8.

44. Ibid., p. 12.

45. Ibid., pp. 22–24.

46. Ibid., pp. 160–61.

47. C. H. Lovelock, Ronald Still, David Cullwick, and Ira M. Kaufman, "An Evaluation of the Effectiveness of Drop-Off Questionnaire Delivery," *Journal of Marketing Research* (November 1976), pp. 358–64.

48. For an excellent discussion of the sources and types of research services, see the section on primary data collection and panel vendors in Duane Davis, *Business Research for Decision Making,* 4th ed. (Belmont, CA: Wadsworth, 1996), pp. 278–83.

49. There are a number of sources for research services, some of which are annotated. For current listings, consult the latest edition of the *Marketing Services Guide & The American Marketing Association Membership Directory* (Chicago: American Marketing Association); *Consultants and Consulting Organizations Directory* (Detroit: Gale Research Corporation); or the research section of *Marketing News.* Also see "Software for Marketing and Marketing Research," *Marketing News,* February 14, 1986, pp. 9–22.

50. A list of panel vendors is provided by Davis, *Business Research for Decision Making,* p. 283. For an evaluation of the panel process, see Seymour Sudman and Robert Ferber, *Consumer Panels* (Chicago: American Marketing Association, 1979).

Suggested Readings

1. Barabba, Vincent P. "The Market Research Encyclopedia." *Harvard Business Review* 90, no. 1 (1990), pp. 105–17. A set of reference tables for managers and researchers. Of particular interest is the second table, which compares mail, telephone, personal, and mixed-mode interviews on several dimensions including response rates, costs, and probability versus nonprobability sampling decisions.

2. Dexter, Louis A. *Elite and Specialized Interviewing.* Evanston, IL: Northwestern University Press, 1970. Discusses the techniques and problems of interviewing "people in important or exposed positions."

3. Dillman, Don A. *Mail and Telephone Surveys.* New York: Wiley, 1978. A practical book on mail and telephone survey projects. The entire book is recommended. It includes an extensive bibliography.

4. Fowler, Floyd J., Jr. *Survey Research Methods,* 2nd ed. Thousand Oaks, CA: Sage Publications, 1993. An excellent overview of all aspects of the survey process.

5. Groves, R. M., et al. *Telephone Survey Methodology.* New York: Wiley, 1989. An important reference on telephone collection techniques.

6. Lavrakas, Paul J. *Telephone Survey Methods: Sampling, Selection, and Supervision,* 2nd ed. Thousand Oaks, CA: Sage Publications, 1993. This specialized work takes an applied perspective of interest to students and managers. Chapters 3, 5, and 6 on supervision are particularly useful.

INSTRUMENTS FOR RESPONDENT COMMUNICATION

CHAPTER NAVIGATION

BRINGING
RESEARCH TO LIFE

"While visiting my hometown, I was invited to a dinner meeting . . . at the country club no less . . . to plan our high school reunion."

Myra frowned, "Jason, you hated high school. Naturally you declined."

"As a matter of fact, no. My wife and mother were away for a few days at a surgical convention, and I thought I would see how the country club crowd lived."

"So, you overcame your deeply ingrained *reverse* snobbery?" asked Myra.

"Let's say that I was curious to see how they had turned out, the bunch I'd detested in high school. At our planning dinner, I was not disappointed by the turnout of snobs and social climbers: The ones I loved least turned up for our meeting, especially Stanton."

"Stanton?"

"Most especially Stanton. I'd been the unsociable one of the class, the one with no leadership skills, no musical skills, no sports skills, no car. I'd been the outcast. Stanton was the class scoundrel, whose dad happened to own the bank. As repulsive as he was, he had the right car, the right clothes, the right address. Ten years ago, I kidded myself and pretended I did not resent the bunch of them and Stanton the most, and Stanton pretended he did not resent my brains."

"Then it turned out to be a miserable meeting, this dinner at the country club?"

"It started poorly. I arrived during cocktail hour, feeling altogether out of place among the crowd. My clothes weren't fashionable enough. I was not sure what to ask for when the waiter asked for our drink orders. Wine? A cocktail? What? I was afflicted by doubt. The old resentments returned. Then Stanton shambled over to me. He had become fleshy and dissipated, but he was dressed beautifully, as they all were. And the moment he condescended to notice me, my attitude softened. When he clapped his meaty paw heartily on my shoulder,

I felt an electrical thrill of . . . acceptance. Nina, the beautiful Nina, whose father had been mayor for as long as anyone remembered and publisher of the newspaper, smiled at me, the whole bunch of them turned ever so slightly toward me, and suddenly . . . suddenly I belonged."

"Remarkable, Jason," said Myra. "You are so gullible!"

"Stanton—he wanted me to call him Stan!—was executive vice president at the bank, Nina was an associate publisher, and the others owned auto dealerships, radio stations, majority shares in airlines, sports franchises, and were doing remarkably well. And what about me, what about Jason? Stanton said he had been *following my career closely*, and discussing me with the others, and that by all accounts I was doing *brilliantly* in economics research for *major corporations* and *federal agencies*, and they had received reports that I was consulting with CEOs *person-to-person* on matters of *top policy*."

"Stanton was buttering you up."

"Yes, extravagantly flattering me. And I believed every hyperbole as if they were describing my actual life. By and by, Stanton asked about my opinion polling. And Nina chimed in, actually stood close and looked at me as if I were a human being. Stanton would now and then offer to buy me a cocktail, but I'm not a heavy drinker, and I was intoxicated by the attention. Stanton wanted to know if I collected information about people's incomes, their banking, their 'love lives'. . . ."

"Really? Stanton asked about. . . ."

"Nina, too, asked about *that* topic, though also about whether I polled people's reading habits and TV watching.

"As to the reunion, the fundamentals were easy enough to plan . . . chicken *or* roast beef . . . hold it here at the Club . . . a Saturday night in June would be fine . . . a band that a few of the current students had thrown together. But we came inevitably to the question of publicity . . . what, who, and how? And that was when Stanton said, 'We all know that
(continued)

Jason here is a hot-shot pollster with a gold-plated reputation, and I am sure we can count on him to do something special.'

"With those words, 'count on him to do something special,' Stanton sunk the hook in this fish's mouth. Before I knew it, I had volunteered to, or Stanton and Nina had maneuvered me into, taking a mail poll of our entire class, which would become the basis of a citywide barrage of newspaper publicity. (Have I mentioned that I had a terrific crush on Nina, and that ten years later she was still standing on a pedestal for me?)"

"I figured that out long ago, Jason. And shame on you. We won't tell Dorrie."

"We would ask in my mail poll about graduates' lives and livelihoods to place a story on the business page and ask about their families and avocations for the lifestyle section, and we would no doubt find some angle by which to grub for space in the national media. I was to draft a dozen questions and forward them to Stanton for duplication and mailing. The surveys would be mailed back to Stanton and coded by his secretary. Then a data diskette would be mailed to me for analysis."

"Well," said Myra, "It was simple and straightforward, and you have done this several times for church groups and nonprofits, though I recollect that in each instance you grumbled about entrusting such sensitive work to 'laymen.' I can't see where this is headed, but it appears you acted impulsively, egged on by flattery. Stanton sounds like a master of manipulation. Are you going to reveal what he did to you that turned this into a disaster?"

"Yes," said Jason, "but he was not just manipulative. He was despicable, too."

"How so?"

"On the Monday following our dinner, the program committee wrote a letter to all our graduates, in which they laid out their plans in a general sort of way and also trumpeted that one of their own alumni was an important consultant to the nation's 50 top companies who would be conducting a scientific and authoritative mail survey, toward having ready for the reunion a picture of where the class had traveled and how high it had risen since gradu-

ation. Again they flattered me, and they urged every member of the class to respond fully and openly. The hoopla must have been extensive, because my mother called to tell me that she had encountered some of my classmates in the supermarket and even the classmates' parents, and all had expressed considerable excitement. I've got to admit that I began to believe my own press clippings. I was the scientific wunderkind of our graduating class. I would penetrate the veil of secrecy and reveal us for who we were. As to the questions, when I wrote them they turned out to be fairly innocuous, items from the University of Michigan's general social survey from the previous year, not original with me, but used by permission. I sent them to Stanton.

"Four weeks passed. I chafed with eagerness to receive the data diskettes, but did not even receive my own questionnaire to fill out and return. This was strange, I thought; I had heard nothing. Stanton and Nina failed to return my calls.

"Then my mother phoned and asked me if I had been a 'naughty boy.' *What?* I asked. Mom said she'd seen Lucia in the supermarket, and Lucia said she thought I was a pig. Now Lucia's brother was my best pal, and I'd taken Lucia to the senior dance and had been a perfect gentleman. She teaches kindergarten now, and she called me a pig. And later another fellow—a semi-thug who had played football—told mother I had better not come back to town, because there was a bunch who planned to 'set me straight' if they saw me. And one day the principal saw Mom coming down the street and ran into the men's room of a service station—to avoid her, mother is pretty certain."

"Really? Have you discovered what was going on?"

"Of course. Half of the town are mother's patients. They will tell her anything when she is drilling their teeth. After asking a few of the right people and cajoling them (buzz, buzz!), she extracted a copy of the survey, as Stanton had sent it out.

"Look here." He reached into his desk and passed Myra a sheet that had been angrily torn, then taped together. "It appears that without asking me, Stanton and Nina added a few questions to satisfy their own prurient curiosities."

Myra licked her lips. The type was smaller than she would have recommended in a mail survey, so she carried the sheet to her desk where the light was better and she found her eyeglasses. She ran her finger down the sheet, at first reading each item approvingly. She recognized familiar academic questions from the University of Michigan.

Suddenly her finger paused over one question, then advanced slowly over several others. Her mouth dropped open in astonishment, and she slowly blushed, turning progressively more florid, from brow to shoulders. She dropped the survey sheet and covered her mouth, but was unable to stifle first a gasp, then a giggle, then a guffaw.

"Why they most certainly were naughty, Jason, weren't they? Why look at these questions they added. I would never ask anyone such questions, no, not ever—I would not admit that people in a small town had even heard of these things. No!" She removed her eyeglasses and studied his unhappy face. ". . . And you say this went out over your name?"

"Yes. So you can understand why I will not set foot in that town . . . for years. I am going to have to write a letter of apology and hope that Nina allows it to run in her father's newspaper. I'll make up a cock-and-bull story about a mistake at the printer's. . . . "

"Nobody will ever believe that story."

"I've made a mess of things, Myra. To save the cost of printing and mailing the survey and coding the data, I allowed Stanton to take control and insert his creepy questions. My reputation is ruined in the town where I grew up, people will be looking strangely at Mom, and we have lost the opportunity to learn about the fortunes of my classmates. The worst part is, of course, that I let my emotions cloud my good scientific judgment. No, and I can't tell the truth, because if I blame it all on her and Stanton, Nina will not let my apology letter run in her father's paper."

DEVELOPING THE INSTRUMENT DESIGN STRATEGY: PHASE 1

New researchers often want to draft questions immediately. They are reluctant to go through the preliminaries that make for successful surveys. Figure 12–1 is a suggested flowchart for instrument design. The procedures to follow in developing an instrument vary from study to study, but the flowchart suggests three phases. Each phase is discussed in this chapter, starting with a review and "Close-Up" and ending with procedures for pretesting the completed instrument.

Management-Research Question Hierarchy Revisited

How to refine a management dilemma and take it through the research process was discussed in Chapter 3 and depicted in Figure 3–1. We revisit the hierarchy here because it is the foundation of successful instrument development. The process of moving from the general management dilemma to specific measurement questions goes through four question levels:

1. *The management question*—the dilemma, stated in question form, that the manager needs resolved.
2. *Research question(s)*—the fact-based translation of the question the researcher must answer to contribute to the solution of the management question.

3. *Investigative questions*—specific questions the researcher must answer to provide sufficient detail and coverage of the research question. Within this level, there may be several questions as the researcher moves from the general to the specific.

4. *Measurement questions*—questions respondents must answer if the researcher is to gather the needed information and resolve the management question.

Addressing the *management-research question hierarchy* is the first step in planning for the collection of data. Investigative questions are the core of the researcher's information needs. In many studies, an exploratory investigation helps the researcher understand all dimensions of the subject. In the Prince Corporation image study (see

FIGURE   12–1   Flowchart for Instrument Design

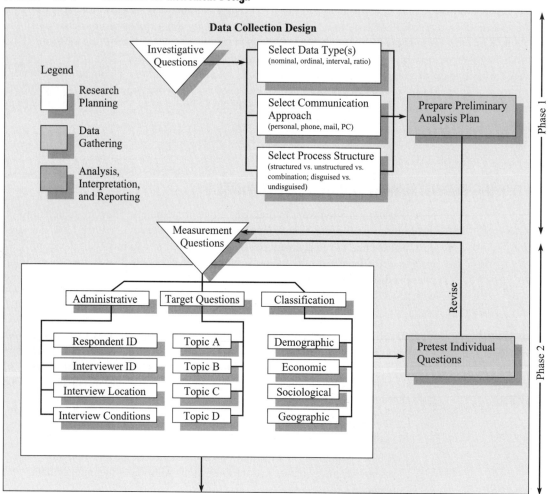

Chapter 7), many exploratory interviews were needed to ensure all investigative topics were covered. In the Albany Outpatient Laser Clinic study (see Chapter 11), the eye surgeon would know from experience the types of medical complications that could result in poor recovery. Thus, the list of information needs (investigative questions) would be specific and easily developed without extensive exploration studies. The co-chairs of Jason's high school reunion planning committee obviously had a hidden agenda. Jason had one list of investigative questions, and they had a distinctly different list. In the MindWriter project, exploration was limited to several interviews and an in-depth study of company service records because the concepts were not complicated and the researchers had experience in the industry.

The MindWriter "Close-Up" reveals the thinking leading to the final questionnaire and shows you the direction of this chapter. Normally, once the researcher understands the connection between the investigative questions and the potential measurement questions, a strategy for the survey is the next logical step. This precedes

FIGURE   12–1   (continued)

CLOSE-UP

Replacing an imprecise management question with specific measurement questions is an exercise in analytical reasoning. We described that process incrementally in the MindWriter "Close-Up" sections of Chapters 3, 4, and 8. In Chapter 3, Myra and Jason's fact finding at MindWriter resulted in their ability to state the management dilemma as management, research, and investigative questions. Adding context to the questions allowed them to construct the proposal described in Chapter 4. In Chapter 8, they returned to the list of investigative questions and selected one question to use in testing their scaling approach. Here is a brief review of the steps Jason and Myra have taken and the measurement questions that resulted.

Synopsis of the Problem   MindWriter Corporation's new service and repair program, CompleteCare, for laptop computers was designed to provide a rapid response to customers' service problems. Management has received several complaints. Management needs information on the program's effectiveness and its impact on customer satisfaction. There is also a shortage of trained technical operators in the company's telephone center. The package courier is uneven in executing its pickup and delivery contract. Parts availability problems exist for some machine types. Occasionally, customers receive units that are either not fixed or damaged in some way.

Management Question   What should be done to improve the CompleteCare program for MindWriter laptop repairs and servicing to enhance customer satisfaction?

Research Questions

1. Should the technical representatives be given more intensive training, or not?
2. Should ABC Courier Service be replaced by an overnight air-transport service, or not?
3. Should the repair diagnostic and repair sequencing operations be modified, or not?
4. Should the return packaging be modified to include premolded rigid foam inserts, conforming-expandable foam protection, or neither?
5. Should metropolitan repair centers be established to complement or replace in-factory repair facilities, or not?

Investigative Questions

a. Are customers' expectations being met in terms of the time it takes to repair the systems? What is the customers' overall satisfaction with CompleteCare service program and with the MindWriter product?

b. How well is the call center helping customers? Is it helping them with instructions? What percentage of customers' technical problems is it solving without callbacks or subsequent repairs? How long do customers wait on the phone?

c. How good is the transportation company? Do they pick up and deliver the system responsively? How long do customers wait for them? Was the laptop damage due to package handling?

d. How good is the repair group? What problems are most common? What repair processes are involved in fixing these problems? For what percentage of laptops is the repair complete within the promised time limit? Are customers' problems fully resolved? Are there new problems with newer models? How quickly are problems diagnosed?

e. How are repaired laptops packaged for returned shipping? What is the cost of alternative rigid foam inserts and expandable-foam packaging? Would new equipment be required if packaging were changed? Would certain shipping-related complaints be avoided with new packaging materials?

The extensive scope of the research questions and resulting measurement questions forced MindWriter to reassess the scope of the desired initial research study, to determine where to concentrate the enhancement efforts. Management chose a descriptive rather than a prescriptive scope.

Measurement Questions   The measurement questions used for the self-administered package insert instrument are shown in Figure 12–2.[1] Of the investigative questions in *b*, the first two are addressed as "responsiveness" and "competence" with telephone assistance in the questionnaire. The second two investigative questions may be answered by accessing the company's service database. The questionnaire's three-part question on courier service parallels investigative question *c*. Specific service deficiencies will be recorded in the "Comments/Suggestions" section. Investigative questions under *d* and *e* are covered with questionnaire items 3, 4, and 5. Since deficiencies in item 5 may be attributed to both the repair facility and the courier, the reasons will be cross-checked during analysis. Questionnaire item 6 uses the same language as the last investigative question in *a*. Questionnaire item 7 is an extension of item 6 but attempts to secure an impression of behavioral intent to use CompleteCare again. Finally, the last item will make known the extent to which change is needed in CompleteCare by revealing repurchase intention as linked to product and service experience.

FIGURE   12–2   Measurement Questions for the MindWriter Study

MindWriter personal computers offer you ease of use and maintenance. When you need service, we want you to rely on *CompeteCare,* wherever you may be. That's why we're asking you to take a moment to tell us how well we've served you.	
	Met **few** expectations Met **some** expectations Met **most** expectations Met **all** expectations **Exceeded** expectations 1 2 3 4 5

1. Telephone assistance with your problem:
   - a. Responsiveness   1   2   3   4   5
   - b. Technical competence   1   2   3   4   5
2. The courier service's effectiveness:
   - a. Arrangements   1   2   3   4   5
   - b. Pickup speed   1   2   3   4   5
   - c. Delivery speed   1   2   3   4   5
3. Speed of the overall repair process.   1   2   3   4   5
4. Resolution of the problem that prompted service/repair.   1   2   3   4   5
5. Condition of your MindWriter on arrival.   1   2   3   4   5
6. Overall impression of CompleteCare's effectiveness.   1   2   3   4   5
7. Likelihood of using CompleteCare on another occasion.
   - (**1 = very unlikely   3 = neither likely nor unlikely   5 = very likely**)   1   2   3   4   5
8. Likelihood of repurchasing a MindWriter based on:
   - (**1 = very unlikely   3 = neither likely nor unlikely   5 = very likely**)
   - a. Service/repair experience   1   2   3   4   5
   - b. Product performance   1   2   3   4   5

Comments/Suggestions: _____

_____

_____

How may we contact you to follow up on any problems you have experienced?

		(_____)	
Last Name	First Name		Phone
	City	State	Zip
			Service Code

getting down to the particulars of instrument design. Prominent among the strategic concerns are

1. What type of data is needed to answer the management question?
2. What communication approach will be used?
3. Should the questions be structured, unstructured, or some combination?
4. Should the questioning be undisguised or disguised and, if so, to what degree?

Type of Data

Data type determines the analytical procedures that are possible during data analysis. Chapter 7 discussed nominal, ordinal, interval, and ratio data and how the characteristics of each type influence the analysis (statistical choices and hypothesis testing). Chapters 15 through 18 show you how to code and extract the data from the instrument, select appropriate descriptive measures or tests, and analyze the results.

Communication Approach

Surveying may be conducted by personal interview, telephone, mail, computer, or some combination of these, as we said in Chapter 11. Decisions on which method to use as well as where to interact with the respondent (at home, at a neutral site, at the sponsor's place of business, etc.) will affect the design of the instrument. In personal interviewing and computer questioning, it is possible to use graphics and other questioning tools more easily than by mail or phone. The differing delivery mechanisms result in different introductions, instructions, instrument layout, and conclusions.

In the MindWriter example, these decisions were easy. The dispersion of respondents, the necessity of a service experience, and budget limitations all dictated a mail survey where the respondent received the instrument either at home or at work. The danger in using a telephone survey as a follow-up to questionnaires that weren't returned is that memory decay might alter respondents' answers due to the passage of time between return of the laptop and MindWriter contact with the respondent by telephone.

Some of the same issues dictated a mail survey in Jason's reunion study; we could add to the previous list the sensitivity of the prurient questions added by Stanton and Nina and the desire of most respondents to maintain anonymity in the face of such questions. In the Prince Corporation study, there was a desire to use telephone interviews because of cost savings. However, the study objectives called for data that could not easily be collected by telephone. Edna would probably have preferred a personal interview to the self-administered study provided by the Albany clinic.

Question Structure

The degree of question and response structure must also be decided. *Response strategy decisions (the type of question used) depend more on the content and objectives of specific questions. Question wording is affected largely by the communication mode chosen and attempts to control bias.* Questionnaires and interview schedules (**interview schedule** is an alternative term for the questionnaire used in an interview) can range from those that have a great deal of structure to those that are essentially unstructured. Both questionnaires and interview schedules contain three types of measurement questions. **Administrative questions** identify the respondent, interviewer, interview location, and conditions. **Classification questions** are usually sociological-demographic variables that allow respondents' answers to be grouped. **Target questions** address the investigative questions of a specific study. Target questions may be **structured** (they present the respondents with a fixed set of choices, often called *closed questions*) or **unstructured** (they do not offer a limited set of responses but do provide a frame of reference for respondents' answers, sometimes referred to as *open-ended questions*).

In the MindWriter self-administered mail questionnaire, it was necessary to use structured questions to get the most information possible from the limited space. In the exploratory stages of the Prince Corporation study, both questions and responses were unstructured, but in the final project both were largely structured. At the Albany clinic, Edna faced a series of open-ended questions, because anticipating medications and health history for a wide variety of individuals would be a gargantuan task for a researcher and would take up far too much space. Jason's reunion study was limited to twelve questions from the University of Michigan's lifestyle index, all of which are structured questions to facilitate analysis of data from large numbers of respondents on a repeat basis.

The type of interview also affects question structure. In extremely unstructured interviews, the interviewer's task is to encourage the respondent to talk in-depth about a set of topics. The **in-depth interview** encourages respondents to share as much information as possible in an unconstrained environment. The interviewer uses a minimum of prompts and guiding questions.

With more focused in-depth interviews, the researcher provides additional guidance by using a set of questions to promote discussion and elaboration by the respondent. In these interviews, the researcher guides the topical direction and coverage. Whether the interview is focused or more in-depth, the aim is to provide a relaxed environment in which the respondent will be open to fully discuss topics. This kind of questioning is often used in exploratory research or where the investigator is dealing with complex topics that do not lend themselves to structured interviewing. If we were doing case research among various participants in a major event, a substantial portion of the questioning would be unique to each respondent and would benefit from an unstructured approach.

Interviews of **focus groups** are widely used in exploratory research. As we noted (see Chapter 6), the interviewer-moderator generally has a list of specific points he or she would like to see discussed, and these are used to prompt the group members. When the discussion stays within these bounds, the interviewer lets group members continue their interaction.

Disguising Objectives and Sponsors

Another consideration in communication instrument design is whether the purpose of the study should be disguised. Some degree of disguise is often present in survey questions, especially to shield the study's sponsor. A **disguised question** is designed to conceal the question's true purpose. We disguise the sponsor and the objective of a study if the researcher believes that respondents will respond differently than they would if both or either is known.

The accepted wisdom is that often we must disguise the study's objective or sponsor or abandon the research. The decision about when to use disguised questioning may be made easier by identifying four situations where disguising the study objective is or is not an issue:

1. When asking for information from respondents who know it at a conscious level and are willing to provide it. Example: "Have you attended the showing of a foreign language film in the last six months?" Either disguised or undisguised questions may be used, but the situation rarely requires disguised techniques. In the MindWriter study, the questions revealed in Figure 12–2 ask for information which the respondent should know and be willing to provide.

2. When asking for information from respondents who know it at a conscious level but are unwilling to provide it. Example: "Are you in favor of recycling household waste materials?" When we ask for an opinion on some topic on which respondents may hold a socially unacceptable view, we often use projective techniques (a disguised questioning method). In the high school reunion study, the objective for collecting information on classmates' love lives was not disclosed—in part that is why most people did not return the study. As the researcher, Jason surely wishes that his identity was not disclosed.

3. When asking for information that is knowable at a conscious level but respondents may not consciously have given the issue much thought. Example: "What is it about air travel during stormy weather that attracts you?" Asking about individual attitudes when they know they hold the attitude but have not explored why they hold the attitude may encourage the use of disguised questions.

4. When asking for information that respondents do not know at a conscious level although they have the information at some deeper level. Example: interview probes—"Would you say, then, that the attitude you just expressed indicates you oppose or favor requiring adult drivers to declare their position on being an organ donor at the time of license renewal?" Seeking insight into the basic motivations underlying attitudes or consumption practices may or may not require disguised techniques.

The first situation seldom needs disguised questions, but in the second, respondents may not give their true feelings or may give stereotyped answers. The researcher can encourage more accurate answers by phrasing the questions in a hypothetical way or by asking how "people around here feel about this topic." The assumption is that responses to these questions will indirectly reveal the respondent's opinions.

In the MindWriter study, the questions were direct, and the specific information sought was undisguised. Customers knew they were evaluating their experience with the service and repair program at MindWriter; thus the purpose of the study and its sponsorship were also undisguised. While the sponsorship of the study that Burbidge conducted for City Bus was revealed, the objective of the study (where and when advertising should be run to announce changes in bus route and schedules) was not revealed. In the Prince Corporation study, the questions concerned only a few companies, giving the sponsor only a limited disguise. Many questions sought direct answers, but sometimes indirect questioning was used to seek answers on sensitive topics or to reduce stereotypical answers. While the sponsor of the Albany clinic study was obvious, multiple interpretations from several questions suggest that the study's objective was not apparent.

Indirect questioning and analysis may often be needed to achieve the research objective in the third situation. A classic example is a study of government bond buying during World War II.[2] A survey sought reasons why some people bought more war bonds than others with equal ability to buy. Frequent buyers had been personally solicited to buy bonds while most infrequent buyers had not received personal solicitation. No direct *why* question to respondents could have provided the answer to this question because respondents did not know they were receiving differing solicitation approaches.

The last situation represents an in-depth study that may or may not be disguised. **Projective techniques** (such as sentence completion tests, cartoon or balloon tests, and word association tests) thoroughly disguise the study objective, but they are often difficult to interpret.

Preliminary Analysis Plan

Researchers are concerned with adequate coverage of the topic and with securing the information in its most usable form. A good way to test how well the study plan meets these needs is to develop "dummy" tables that display the data one expects to secure. This serves as a check on whether the planned measurement questions meet the data needs of the research question. It also helps the researcher determine the type of data needed for each question—a preliminary step to developing measurement questions for investigative questions (review Figure 11–2 in Chapter 11).

CONSTRUCTING AND REFINING THE MEASUREMENT QUESTIONS: PHASE 2

Communication instruments normally include three types of questions. The most important of these are the *target* questions: facts, attitudes, preferences, and expectations about the central topic(s) of the study. A second type, *classification,* concerns the respondent characteristics (socio-demographic factors and some behavior information) needed for classification or grouping used in analysis. Gender, age, family life cycle stage, household income, social class, and attitudes toward topics allied to the study's subject are included. Other classification data depend on the particular study and its research objectives. A third type of information is *administrative.* This includes respondent identification; interviewer identification; and date, place, and conditions of the interview.

Drafting the questions begins once you develop a complete list of investigative questions and decide on the collection processes to be used. In developing a survey instrument, keep in mind four major question-related decision areas. The first three (question content, question wording, and response strategy) are described in Phase 2 of instrument design and the last (question sequence) in Phase 3. These are discussed sequentially, although in practice the process is not orderly. For this discussion, we assume the questions are structured.

Question Content

You begin actual instrument design by drafting specific measurement questions to produce the type of data you need for your data analysis (as spelled out in your preliminary analysis plan). You must consider the subject content, the degree of disguise, and the wording of each question. Be careful in defining constructs and concepts. A wide variety of question types (response strategies) can be created for the same subject content. Four questions, covering numerous issues, guide the instrument designer in selecting appropriate question content:

- Should this question be asked?
- Is the question of proper scope and coverage?
- Can the respondent adequately answer this question, as asked?
- Will the respondent willingly answer this question, as asked?

Should This Question Be Asked?   *Issue 1: Purposeful versus Interesting*   Questions that merely produce "interesting information" cannot be justified on either economic or research grounds. Challenge each question's function. Does it contribute significant information toward answering the research question? Will its omission limit or prevent the thorough analysis of other data? Can we infer the answer from another question? A good question designer knows the value of learning more from fewer questions.

Is the Question of Proper Scope and Coverage?   *Issue 2: Incomplete or Unfocused*   We can test this content issue by asking, "Will this question reveal all we need to know?" We sometimes ask respondents to reveal their motivations for particular behaviors or attitudes by asking them "Why?" This simple question is inadequate to probe the range of most causal relationships. When studying product use behavior, for example, direct two or three questions on product use to the heavy-use consumer and only one question to the light user.

Questions are also inadequate if they do not provide the information you need to interpret responses fully. If you ask about the Prince Corporation's image as an employer, have you recognized that different groups of employees may have different reactions? Do you need to ask the same question about other companies so you can evaluate relative attitudes?

In the Albany clinic study, Edna was asked, "Have you ever had or been treated for a recent cold or flu?" If Edna answers yes, what exactly has she told the researcher that would be of use to her eye surgeon? Wouldn't it be likely that the surgeon is interested in medication taken to treat colds or flu within, say, the prior ten days? This question also points to two other problems of scope and coverage, the multiple question and the imprecise question.

Issue 3: Multiple Questions   Does the question request so much content that it should be broken into two or more questions? While reducing the overall number of questions in a study is highly desirable, don't try to ask **double-barreled questions:** two or more questions in one that the respondent might need to answer differently to preserve the accuracy of the data. The question posed to Edna fires more than two barrels. It asks four questions in all. Here's another common example posed to menswear retailers: "Are this year's shoe sales *and* gross profits higher than last year's?" Couldn't sales be higher with stagnant profits, or profits higher with level or lower sales? This second example is more typical of the problem of multiple questions. A less obvious **multiple question** is the question we ask to identify a family's TV station preference. A better question would ask the station preference of each family member separately or, alternatively, screen for the member who most often controls channel selection on Monday evenings during prime time. Also, it's highly probable that no one station would serve as an individual's preferred station when we cover a wide range of time (8–11 P.M.). This reveals another problem, the imprecise question.

Issue 4: Precision   To test a question for precision ask, "Does the question ask precisely what we want and need to know?" We sometimes ask for a respondent's income when we really want to know the family's total annual income before taxes. We ask what a respondent purchased "last week" when we really want to know what he or she purchased in a "typical 7-day period during the past 90 days." Edna was asked her cold and flu history during the time frame "ever." It is hard to imagine an 80-year-old woman who has never experienced a cold or flu and equally hard to assume Edna hasn't been treated for one or both at some time in her life.

A second precision issue deals with common vocabulary between researcher and respondent. To test your question for this problem, ask, "Do I need to offer operational definitions of concepts and constructs used in the question?"

Can the Respondent Answer Adequately?   ***Issue 5: Time for Thought***   Although the question may address the topic, is it asked in such a way that the respondent will be able to frame an answer, or is it reasonable to assume that the respondent can determine the answer? This is also a question that drives sample design, but once the ideal sample unit is determined, researchers often assume that respondents who fit the sample profile have all the answers, preferably on the tip of their tongues. To frame a response to some questions takes time and thought; such questions are best left to self-administered questionnaires.

Issue 6: Participation at the Expense of Accuracy   Respondents typically want to cooperate in interviews; thus they assume giving any answer is more helpful than denying knowledge of a topic. Their desire to impress the interviewer may encourage them to give answers based on no information. A classic illustration of this problem occurred with the following question:[3] "Which of the following statements most closely coincides with your opinion of the Metallic Metals Act?" The response pattern shows that 70 percent of those interviewed had a fairly clear opinion of the Metallic Metals

Act; however, *there is no such act.* The respondents apparently assumed that if a question is asked, they should provide an answer. Given reasonable-sounding choices, they selected one even though they knew nothing about the topic.

To counteract this tendency to respond at any cost, **filter questions** are used to qualify the respondent's knowledge. If the MindWriter service questionnaire was distributed via mail to all recent purchasers of MindWriter products, we might ask, "Have you required service for your machine since its purchase?" Only those for whom service was provided could provide the detail and scope of the responses indicated in the investigative question list. If such a question were asked in a phone interview, we would call the question a **screen,** because it is being used to determine whether the person on the other end of the phone line is a qualified sample unit.

Assuming that respondents have prior knowledge or understanding may be risky. The risk is getting many answers that have little basis in fact. The Metallic Metals Act illustration may be challenged as unusual, but in another case, a Gallup report revealed that 45 percent of the persons surveyed did not know what a "lobbyist in Washington" was, and 88 percent could not give a correct description of "jurisdictional strike."[4] This points to the need for operational definitions as part of question wording,

Issue 7: Presumed Knowledge

The question designer should consider the respondents' information level when determining the content and appropriateness of a question. In some studies, the degree of respondent expertise can be substantial, and simplified explanations are inappropriate and discourage participation. In asking the public about gross margins in menswear stores, we would want to be sure the "general public" respondent understands the nature of "gross margin." If our sample unit was a merchant, explanations might not be needed. A high level of knowledge among our sample units, however, may not eliminate the need for operational definitions. Among merchants, gross margin per unit in dollars is commonly accepted as the difference between cost and selling price; but when offered as a percentage rather than a dollar figure, it can be calculated as a percentage of unit selling price or as a percentage of unit cost. A respondent answering from the "cost" frame of reference would calculate gross margin at 100 percent; another respondent, using the same dollars and the "selling price" frame of reference, would calculate gross margin at 50 percent. If a construct is involved and differing interpretations of a concept are feasible, operational definitions may still be needed.

Issue 8: Recall and Memory Decay

The adequacy problem also occurs when you ask questions that overtax respondents' recall ability. People cannot recall much that has happened in their past, unless it was dramatic. Your mother may remember everything about your arrival if you were her first child: the weather, time of day, even what she ate prior to your birth. If you have several siblings, her memory of subsequent births may be less complete. If the events surveyed are of incidental interest to respondents, they will probably be unable to recall them correctly even a short time later. An unaided recall question, "What radio programs did you listen to last night?" might identify as few as 10 percent of those individuals who actually listened to a program.[5]

Issue 9: Balance (General or Specific)   Answering adequacy also depends on the proper balance between generality and specificity. We often ask questions in terms too general and detached from respondents' experiences. Asking for average annual consumption of a product may make an unrealistic demand for generalization on people who do not think in these terms. Why not ask how often the product was used last week or last month? Too often respondents are asked to recall individual use experiences over an extended time and to average them for us. This is asking respondents to do the researcher's work and encourages substantial response errors. It may also contribute to a higher refusal rate and higher discontinuation rate.

There is a danger in being too narrow in the time frame applied to behavior questions. We may ask about movie attendance for the last 7 days, although this is too short a time span on which to base attendance estimates. It may be better to ask about attendance, say, for the last 30 days. There are no firm rules about this generality-specificity problem. Developing the right level of generality depends on the situation and the art and experience of the question designer.

Issue 10: Objectivity   The ability of respondents to answer adequately is also often distorted by questions whose content is biased by what is included or omitted. The question may explicitly mention only the positive or negative aspects of the topic or make unwarranted assumptions about the respondent's position. Consider an experiment in which the following two forms of a question were asked:

A.   What is your favorite brand of ice cream? _____
B.   Some people have a favorite brand of ice cream while others do not have a favorite brand.
In which group are you? (please check)

                _____I have a favorite brand of ice cream.

                _____I do not have a favorite brand of ice cream.

What is your favorite (if you have a favorite)? _____

Fifty-seven randomly chosen graduate business students answered version A, and 56 answered version B. Their responses are shown in the accompanying table.

Response	*Version A*	*Version B*
Named a favorite brand	77%*	39%*
Named a favorite flavor rather than a brand	19	18
Had no favorite brand	4	43
Total	100%	100%
	n = 57	56

*Significant difference at the 0.001 level.

The probable cause of the difference in brand preference is that A is a **leading question.** It assumes and suggests that everyone has a favorite brand of ice cream and will report it. Version B indicates the respondent need not have a favorite.

A deficiency in both versions is that about one respondent in five misinterpreted the meaning of *brand.* This misinterpretation cannot be attributed to low education, low intelligence, or lack of exposure to the topic. The subjects were students who had taken at least one course in marketing in which branding was prominently treated. Word confusion difficulties are discussed in greater detail later in this chapter.

Will the Respondents Answer Willingly?   *Issue 11: Sensitive Information*   Even if respondents have the information, they may be unwilling to give it. Some topics are considered too sensitive to discuss with strangers. These vary from person to person, but one study suggests the most sensitive topics concern money matters and family life.[6] More than one-fourth of those interviewed mentioned these as the topics about which they would be "least willing to answer questions." Respondents of lower socioeconomic status also included political matters in this "least willing" list.

Respondents may also be unwilling to give correct answers for ego reasons. Many exaggerate their incomes, the number of cars they own, their social status, and the amount of high-prestige literature they read. They also minimize their ages and the amount of low-prestige literature they read. Many respondents are reluctant to try to give an adequate response. Often this will occur when they see the topic as irrelevant to their own interests or to their perception of the survey's purpose. They participate halfheartedly, often answer with "don't know," give negative replies, refuse to be interviewed, or give stereotypical responses. The lack of response to Jason's high school reunion survey was attributed to the inclusion of questions about classmate's lascivious activities. This information was far too sensitive to risk being mentioned in a potentially embarrassing article in the hometown paper.

Question Wording

It is frustrating when people misunderstand a question that has been painstakingly written. This is partially a problem of the lack of a shared vocabulary. The difficulty of understanding long and complex sentences or involved phraseology aggravates the problem further. Our dilemma arises from the requirements of question design (the need to be explicit, to present alternatives, and to explain meanings). All contribute to longer and more involved sentences.[7]

The difficulties caused by question wording exceed most other sources of distortion in surveys. They have led one social scientist to conclude:

> To many who worked in the Research Branch it soon became evident that error or bias attributable to sampling and to methods of questionnaire administration were relatively small as compared with other types of variations—especially variation attributable to different ways of wording questions.[8]

While it is impossible to say which wording of a question is best, we can point out several areas that cause respondent confusion and measurement error. The diligent question designer will put a given question through many revisions before it satisfies these criteria.[9]

- Is the question stated in terms of a shared vocabulary?
- Does the question contain vocabulary with a single meaning?
- Does the question contain unsupported or misleading assumptions?

- Does the question contain biased wording?
- Is the question correctly personalized?
- Are adequate alternatives presented within the question?

The Albany clinic study illustrated several of these problems. The multiple question about Edna's "referring physician" and "physician most knowledgeable about her health" was further distorted by a request for a phone number. Edna didn't know which doctor's phone number was being requested. By offering space for only one number, the data collection instrument implied that both parts of the question might refer to the same doctor. The questions about past medical history did not offer clear directions. Questions (about having the flu) did not include time frames or had unrealistic time frames (the term "ever"). The question about "intact teeth" generated several plausible interpretations. Another question about neck movement assumed every respondent had the same operational definition for "limited motion of your neck." A talented researcher did not design the clinic's study.

The MindWriter study (see Figure 12–2) simplified the process by using the same response strategy for each factor the respondent was asked to evaluate. The study basically asks, "How did our CompleteCare service program work for you when you consider each of the following factors?" It accomplishes this as it sets up the questioning with "take a moment to tell us how well we've served you." Because the sample includes CompleteCare users only, the underlying assumption that respondents have used the service is acceptable. The language is appropriate for the respondent's likely level of education. And the open-ended question used for "comments" adds flexibility to capture any unusual circumstances not covered by the structured factor list.

Issue 12: Shared Vocabulary   Because surveying is an exchange of ideas between interviewer and respondent, each must understand what the other says, and this is possible only if the vocabulary used is common to both parties.[10] Two problems arise. First, the words must be simple enough to allow adequate communication with persons of limited education. This is dealt with by reducing the level of word difficulty to simple English words and phrases (more is said about this in the section on word clarity).

Technical language is the second issue. Even highly educated respondents cannot answer questions stated in unfamiliar technical terms. Technical language also poses difficulties for interviewers. In one study of how corporation executives handled various financial problems, interviewers had to be conversant with technical financial terms. This necessity presented the researcher with two alternatives—hiring people knowledgeable in finance and teaching them interviewing skills or teaching financial concepts to experienced interviewers.[11]

A great obstacle to effective question wording is the choice of words. Questions to be asked of the public should be restricted to the 2,000 most common words in the English language.[12] Even the use of simple words is not enough. Many words have vague references or meanings that must be gleaned from their context. In a repair study, technicians were asked, "How many radio sets did you repair last month?" This question may seem unambiguous, but respondents interpreted it in two ways. Some viewed it as a question of them alone; others interpreted "you" more inclusively, as referring to the total output of the shop. There is also the possibility of misinterpreting-interpreting "last month," depending on the timing of the questioning. Using "during the last 30 days" would be much more precise and unambiguous. Typical of the many problem words are *any, could, would, should, fair, near, often, average,* and *regular.* One author recommends that after stating a question as precisely as possible, we should test each word against this checklist:

- Does the word chosen mean what we intend?
- Does the word have multiple meanings? If so, does the context make the intended meaning clear?
- Does the word chosen have more than one pronunciation? Is there any word with similar pronunciation that the chosen word might be confused?
- Is a simpler word or phrase suggested or possible?[13]

In the Prince Corporation study, what percentage of the population would understand the terms *conglomerate* or *multinational company?* We cause other problems when we use abstract concepts that have many overtones or emotional qualifications.[14] Without concrete referents, meanings are too vague for the researcher's needs. Examples of such words are *business, government,* and *society.* Suppose that in the Prince Corporation study we asked the question, "How involved is business in the affairs of our society?" What is meant by "involved"? What parts of "society"? Is there such a thing as "business" per se?

Issue 13: Unsupported Assumptions   Unwarranted assumptions contribute to many problems of question wording. A metropolitan newspaper in the Midwest attempting to discover what readers would like in the redesigned lifestyle section did a study. One notable question asked readers: "Who selects your clothes? You or the man in your life?" In this age of educated, working, independent women, the question managed to offend a significant portion of the female readership. In addition, the news daily discovered that many of its female readers were younger than researchers originally assumed and the only man in their lives was their father, not the spousal or romantic relationship alluded to by the questions that followed. Once men reached this question, they assumed that the paper was interested in serving only the needs of female readers. The unwarranted assumptions built into the questionnaire caused a significantly smaller response rate than should have been expected and caused several of the answers to be uninterpretable.

Issue 14: Frame of Reference   Inherent in word meaning problems is also the matter of a frame of reference. Each of us understands concepts, words, and expressions in the light of our own experience. The U.S. Bureau of the Census wanted to know how many people were in the labor market. To learn whether a person was employed, it asked, "Did you do any work for pay or profit last week?" The researchers erroneously assumed there would be a common frame of reference between the interviewer and respondents on the meaning of *work.* Unfortunately, many persons viewed themselves primarily or foremost as homemakers or students. They failed to report that they also worked at a job during the week. This difference in frame of reference resulted in a consistent underestimation of the number of people working in the United States.

In a subsequent version of the study this question was replaced by two questions, the first of which sought a statement on the respondent's major activity during the week. If the respondent gave a nonwork classification, a second question was asked to determine if he or she had done any work for pay besides this major activity. This revision increased the estimate of total employment by more than 1 million people, half of them working 35 hours or more per week.[15]

The frame of reference can be controlled in two ways. First, the interviewer may seek to learn the frame of reference used by the respondent. When asking respondents to evaluate their reasons for judging a labor contract offer, the interviewer must learn the frames of reference they use. Is the contract offer being evaluated in terms of the specific offer, the failure of management to respond to other demands, the personalities involved, or the personal economic pressures that have resulted from a long strike?

Second, it is useful to specify the frame of reference for the respondent. In asking for an opinion about the new labor contract offer, the interviewer might specify that the question should be answered based on the respondent's opinion of the size of the offer, the sincerity of management, or another frame of reference of interest.

Issue 15: Biased Wording   Bias is the distortion of responses in one direction. It can result from many of the problems already discussed, but word choice is often the major source. Obviously such words or phrases as *politically correct* or *fundamentalist* must be used with great care. Strong adjectives can be particularly distorting. One alleged opinion survey concerned with the subject of preparation for death included the following question: "Do you think that decent, low-cost funerals are sensible?" Who could be against anything that is decent or sensible? There is a question about whether this was a legitimate survey or a burial service sales campaign, but it shows how suggestive an adjective can be.

Congressional representatives have been known to use surveys as a means of communicating with their constituencies. "Would you have me vote for a balanced budget if it means higher costs for supplemental Social Security benefits which you have already earned?" Questions are often worded, however, to imply the issue stance that the representative favors.

We can also strongly bias the respondent by using prestigious names in a question. In a historic survey on whether the War and Navy Departments should be combined into a single Defense Department, one survey said, "General Eisenhower says the Army and Navy should be combined," while the other version omitted his name. Given the first version (name included), 49 percent of the respondents approved of having one department; given the second version, only 29 percent favored one department.[16]

We also can bias response through the use of superlatives, slang expressions, and fad words. These are best excluded unless they are critical to the objective of the question. Ethnic references should also be stated with care.

Issue 16: Personalization   How personalized should a question be? Should we ask, "What would *you* do about . . .?" Or should we ask, "What would *people with whom you work* do about . . .?" The effect of personalization is shown in a classic example reported by Cantril.[17] A split test was made of a question concerning attitudes about the expansion of U.S. armed forces in 1940:

> Should the United States do any of the following at this time?
> A. Increase our armed forces further, even if it means more taxes.
> B. Increase our armed forces further, even if you have to pay a special tax.

Eighty-eight percent of those answering question A thought the armed forces should be increased, while only 79 percent of those answering question B favored increasing the armed forces.

These and other examples show that personalizing questions changes responses, but it is not clear whether this change is for better or for worse. We often cannot tell which answer is superior. Perhaps the best that can be said is that when either form is acceptable, we should choose that which appears to present the issues more realistically. If there are doubts, then split survey versions should be used.

Issue 17: Adequate Alternatives   Have we adequately expressed the alternatives with respect to the point of the question? It is usually wise to express each alternative explicitly to avoid bias. This is illustrated well with a pair of questions that were asked of matched samples of respondents.[18] Theses forms were used:

> A. Do you think most manufacturing companies that lay off workers during slack periods could arrange things to avoid layoffs and give steady work right through the year?
> B. Do you think most manufacturing companies that lay off workers in slack periods could avoid layoffs and provide steady work right through the year, or do you think layoffs are unavoidable?

	A	B
Company could avoid layoffs	63%	35%
Could not avoid layoffs	22	41
No opinion	15	24

Response Strategy   A third major decision area in question design is the degree and form of structure imposed on the respondent. The various response strategies offer options that include **unstructured response** (**open-ended response** = free choice of words) and **structured response** (**closed response** = specified alternatives provided). Free responses, in turn, range from those in which the respondents express themselves extensively to those in which respondents' latitude is restricted by space, layout, or instructions to choose one word or phrase, as in a "fill-in" question. Closed responses typically are categorized as dichotomous, multiple-choice, checklist, rating, or ranking response strategies.

Situational Determinants of Response Strategy Choice   Several situational factors affect the decision of whether to use open-ended or closed questions.[19] The decision is also affected by the degree to which these factors are known to the interviewer. The factors are (1) objectives of the study, (2) respondent's level of information about the topic, (3) degree to which respondent has thought through the topic, (4) ease with which respondent communicates, and (5) respondent's motivation level to share information.

If the objective of the question is only to classify the respondent on some stated point of view, then the closed question will serve well. Assume you are interested only in whether a respondent approves or disapproves of a certain corporate policy. A closed question will provide this answer. This response strategy ignores the full scope of the respondent's opinion and its antecedents. If the objective is to explore a wider territory, then an open-ended question (free-response strategy) is preferable.

Open-ended questions are appropriate when the objective is to discover opinions and degrees of knowledge. They are also appropriate when the interviewer seeks sources of information, dates of events, and suggestions, or when probes are used to secure more information. When the topic of a question is outside the respondent's experience, the open-ended question may offer the better way to learn his or her level of information. Open-ended questions also help to uncover certainty of feelings and expressions of intensity, although well-designed closed questions can do the same.

Finally, it may be better to use open-ended questions when the interviewer does not have a clear idea of the respondent's frame of reference or level of information. Such conditions are likely to occur in exploratory research or in pilot testing. Closed questions are better when there is a clear frame of reference, the respondent's level of information is predictable, and the researcher believes the respondent understands the topic.

Issue 18: Thoroughness of Prior Thought   If a respondent has developed a clear opinion on the topic, a closed question does well. If an answer has not been thought out, an open-ended question may give the respondent a chance to ponder a reply, then elaborate on and revise it.

Issue 19: Communication Skill   Open-ended questions require a stronger grasp of vocabulary and a greater ability to frame responses than do closed questions.

Issue 20: Respondent Motivation   Experience has shown that closed questions typically require less motivation and answering them is less threatening to respondents. But the response alternatives sometimes suggest which answer is appropriate; for this reason, closed questions may be biased.

While the open-ended question offers many advantages, closed questions are generally preferable in large surveys. They reduce the variability of response, make fewer demands on interviewer skills, are less costly to administer, and are much easier to code and analyze. After adequate exploration and testing, we can often develop closed questions that will perform as effectively as open-ended questions in many situations. Experimental studies suggest that closed questions are equal or superior to open-ended questions in many more applications than is commonly believed.[20]

**Response
Strategies
Illustrated**

The characteristics of respondents, the nature of the topic(s) being studied, the type of data needed, and your analysis plan dictate the response strategy. Examples of the strategies described below are found in Table 12–1.

Free-Response Questions   **Free-response questions,** also known as *open-ended questions,* ask the respondent a question, and the interviewer pauses for the answer (which is unaided), or the respondent records his or her ideas in his or her own words in the space provided on a questionnaire.

Dichotomous Response Questions   A topic may present clearly *dichotomous* choices: Something is a fact or it is not; a respondent can either recall or not recall information; a respondent attended or didn't attend an event. **Dichotomous questions** suggest opposing responses, but this is not always the case. One response may be so unlikely that it would be better to adopt the middle-ground alternative as one of the two choices. For example, if we ask respondents whether they are underpaid or overpaid, we are not likely to get many selections of the latter choice. The better alternatives to present to the respondent might be "underpaid" and "fairly paid."

In many two-way questions, there are potential alternatives beyond the stated two alternatives. If the respondent cannot accept either alternative in a dichotomous question, he or she may convert the question to a multiple-choice or rating question by writing in his or her desired alternative. For example, the respondent may prefer an alternative such as "don't know" to a yes-no question, or "no opinion" when faced with a favor-oppose option. In other cases, when there are two opposing or complementary choices, the respondent may prefer a qualified choice ("yes, if X doesn't occur," or "sometimes yes and sometimes no," or "about the same"). Thus, two-way questions may become multiple-choice or rating questions and these additional responses should be reflected in your revised analysis plan. Dichotomous questions generate nominal data.

Multiple-Choice Questions   **Multiple-choice questions** are appropriate where there are more than two alternatives or where we seek gradations of preference, interest, or agreement; the latter situation also calls for rating questions. While such questions offer more than one alternative answer, they request the respondent to make a single choice. Multiple-choice questions can be efficient, but they also present unique design problems.

Assume we ask whether mine safety rules should be determined by the (1) mine companies, (2) miners, (3) federal government, or (4) state government. One type of problem occurs when one or more responses have not been anticipated. For example,

TABLE 12-1   Alternative Response Strategies

Free response	What factors influenced your enrollment in Metro U?

Dichotomous selection

Did you attend either of the "A Day at College" programs at Metro U?

❏ Yes   ❏ No

(paired comparison dichotomous selection)

In your decision to attend Metro U, which was more influential: the *semester calendar* or the *many friends attending from your home town*?

❏ Semester calendar
❏ Many friends attending from home town

Multiple choice

Which one of the following factors was *most influential* in your decision to attend Metro U?

❏ Good academic reputation
❏ Specific program of study desired
❏ Enjoyable campus life
❏ Many friends from home attend
❏ High quality of the faculty

Checklist

Which of the following factors encouraged you to apply to Metro U? (Check all that apply.)

❏ Tuition cost
❏ Specific program of study desired
❏ Parent's preferences
❏ Opinion of brother or sister
❏ Many friends from home attend
❏ High school counselor's recommendation
❏ High quality of the faculty
❏ Good academic reputation
❏ Enjoyable campus life
❏ Closeness to home

Rating

Each of the following factors has been shown to have some influence on a student's choice in applying to Metro U. Using your own experience, for each factor please tell us whether the factor was "strongly influential," "somewhat influential," or "not at all influential."

	Strongly Influential	Somewhat Influential	Not at All Influential
Good academic reputation	❏	❏	❏
Enjoyable campus life	❏	❏	❏
Many friends from home attend	❏	❏	❏
High quality of the faculty	❏	❏	❏
Semester calendar	❏	❏	❏

Ranking

Please rank-order your top three factors from the following list based on their influence in encouraging you to apply to Metro U. Use 1 to indicate the most encouraging factor, 2 the next most encouraging factor, etc.

_____ Closeness to home
_____ Enjoyable campus life
_____ Good academic reputation
_____ High quality of the faculty
_____ High school counselor's recommendation
_____ Many friends from home attend
_____ Opinion of brother or sister
_____ Parent's preferences
_____ Specific program of study desired
_____ Tuition cost

the union has not been mentioned in the alternatives on mine safety rules. Many respondents might combine this alternative with "miners," but others will view "unions" as a distinct alternative. Exploration prior to drafting the measurement question attempts to identify the most likely choices.

A second problem occurs when the list of choices is not exhaustive. Respondents may want to give an answer that is not offered as an alternative. This may occur when the desired response is one that combines two or more of the listed individual alternatives. Many people may believe the federal government and the miners acting jointly should set mine safety rules, but the question does not include this response. When the researcher tries to provide for all possible options, the list of alternatives can become exhausting. We guard against this by discovering the major choices through exploration and *pretesting* (discussed in detail below). We may also add the category "other (please specify)" as a safeguard to provide the respondent an acceptable alternative for all other options. In analysis of a self-administered questionnaire we may create a combination alternative.

Yet another problem occurs when the respondent divides the question of mine safety into several questions, each with different alternatives. Some respondents may believe rules dealing with air quality should be set by a federal agency, while those dealing with length of workday or number of workers per square foot should be set by mine company and union representatives. Still others want local management-worker committees to make rules. To address this problem, the instrument designer would need to divide the question. Pretesting should reveal if a multiple-choice question is really a multiple question.

Another challenge in alternative selection occurs when the choices are not mutually exclusive (the respondent thinks two or more responses overlap). In a multiple-choice question that asks students, "'Which one of the following factors was most influential in your decision to attend Metro U?" the following response alternatives might be listed:

1. Good academic reputation
2. Specific program of study desired
3. Enjoyable campus life
4. Many friends from home attend
5. High quality of the faculty

Some respondents might view items 1 and 5 as overlapping, and some may see items 3 and 4 in the same way.

It is also important to seek a fair balance in choices. One study showed that an off-balance presentation of alternatives biases the results in favor of the more heavily offered side.[21] If four gradations of alternatives are on one side of an issue and two are offered reflecting the other side, responses will tend to be biased toward the better-represented side.

It is necessary in multiple-choice questions to present reasonable alternatives—particularly when the choices are numbers or identifications. If we ask, "Which of the following numbers is closest to the number of students enrolled in American colleges and universities today?" the following choices might be presented:

1. 75,000
2. 750,000
3. 7,500,000
4. 25,000,000
5. 75,000,000

It should be obvious to most respondents that at least three of these choices are not reasonable, given general knowledge about the population of the United States.

The order in which choices are given can also be a problem. Numbers are normally presented in order of magnitude. This practice introduces a bias. The respondent assumes that if there is a list of five numbers, the correct answer will lie somewhere in the middle of the group. Researchers are assumed to add a couple of incorrect numbers on each side of the correct one. To counteract this tendency to choose the central position, put the correct number at an extreme position more often when you design a multiple-choice question.

Order bias with non-numeric alternatives often leads the respondent to choose the first alternative (primacy effect) or the last alternative (recency effect) over the middle ones. Using the split-ballot technique can counteract this bias. To implement this strategy in face-to-face interviews, list the alternatives on a card to be handed to the respondent when the question is asked. Cards with different choice orders can be alternated to ensure positional balance. Leave the choices unnumbered on the card so respondents reply by giving the choice itself rather than its identifying number. It is a good practice to use cards like this any time there are four or more choice alternatives. This saves the interviewer's reading time and ensures a more valid answer by keeping the full range of choices in front of the respondent.

In most multiple-choice questions, there is also a problem of ensuring that the choices represent a unidimensional scale—that is, the alternatives to a given question should represent different aspects of the same *conceptual dimension*. In the college selection example, the list included features associated with a college that might be attractive to a student. This list, while not exhaustive, illustrated aspects of the concept "college attractiveness factors within the control of the college." The list did not mention other factors that might affect a school attendance decision. Parents and peer advice, local alumni efforts, and high school adviser's suggestions may influence the decision, but these represent a different conceptual dimension of "college attractiveness factors"—those not within the control of the college.

Multiple-choice questions usually generate nominal data. When the choices are numbers, this response structure will produce at least interval and sometimes ratio data. When the choices represent ordered numerical ranges (for example, a question on family income) or a verbal rating scale (for example, a question on how you prefer your steak prepared: well done, medium well, medium rare, or rare), the multiple-choice question generates ordinal data.

Checklist Strategies   When you want a respondent to give multiple responses to a single question, you will ask the question in one of three ways. If relative order is not important, the **checklist** is the logical choice. Questions like "Which of the following factors encouraged you to apply to Metro U? (Check all that apply.)" force the respondent to exercise a dichotomous response (yes, encouraged; no, didn't encourage) to each factor presented. Of course you could have asked for the same information as a series of dichotomous selection questions, one for each individual factor, but that would have been time- and space-consuming. Checklists are more efficient. Checklists generate nominal data.

Rating Strategies   **Rating questions** ask the respondent to position each factor on a companion scale, either verbal, numeric, or graphic. "Each of the following factors has been shown to have some influence on a student's choice to apply to Metro U. Using your own experience, for each factor please tell us whether the factor was 'strongly influential,' 'somewhat influential,' or 'not at all influential'." Generally, rating-scale structures generate ordinal data; some carefully crafted scales generate interval data.

Ranking Strategies   When relative order of the alternatives is important, the **ranking question** is ideal. "Please rank-order your top three factors from the following list based on their influence in encouraging you to apply to Metro U. Use 1 to indicate the most encouraging factor, 2 the next most encouraging factor, etc." The checklist strategy would provide the three factors of influence, but we would have no way of knowing the importance the respondent places on each factor. Even in a personal interview, the order in which the factors are mentioned is not a guarantee of influence. Ranking as a response strategy solves this problem.

One concern surfaces with ranking activities. How many presented factors should be ranked? If you listed the 15 brands of potato chips sold in a given market, would you have the respondent rank all 15 in order of preference? In most instances it is helpful to remind yourself that while respondents may have been selected for a given study due to their experience or likelihood of having desired information, this does not mean that they have knowledge of all conceivable aspects of an issue, only with some. It is always better to have respondents rank only those elements with which they are familiar. If you want motivation to remain strong, avoid asking a respondent to rank a list longer than seven items. Ranking generates ordinal data.

All types of response strategies have their advantages and disadvantages. Several different strategies are often found in the same questionnaire, and the situational factors mentioned earlier are the major guides in this matter. There is a tendency, however, to use closed questions instead of the more flexible open-ended type. Table 12–2 summarizes some important considerations in choosing between the various response strategies.

Sources of Existing Questions

The tools of data collection should be adapted to the problem, not the reverse. Thus, the focus of this chapter has been on crafting an instrument to answer specific investigative questions. But inventing and refining questions demands considerable time and effort. For some topics, a careful review of the related literature and an examination of existing instrument sourcebooks can shorten this process.

TABLE   12–2   Characteristics of Response Strategies

Characteristic	Dichotomous	Multiple Choice	Checklist	Rating	Rank Ordering	Free Response
Type of data generated	Nominal	Nominal, ordinal, or ratio	Nominal	Ordinal or interval	Ordinal	Nominal or ratio
Usual number of answer alternatives provided	2	3 to 10	10 or fewer	3 to 7	10 or fewer	None
Used to provide . . .	Classification	Classification, order, or specific number	Classification	Order or distance	Order	Classification, order, or specific number or idea

TABLE   12–3   Sources of Questions

Author(s)	Title	Source
Philip E. Converse, Jean D. Dotson, Wendy J. Hoag, and William H. McGee III, eds.	*American Social Attiudes Data Sourcebook 1947–1978*	Cambridge, MA: Harvard University Press, 1980
George H. Gallup	*The Gallup Poll: 1935–1971*	New York: Random House, 1935–1971; Wilmington, DE: Scholarly Resources, Inc., 1972–1985
George H. Gallup, Jr., ed.	*The Gallup Poll: Public Opinion* [annual series]	Wilmington, DE: Scholarly Resources, Inc., 1986–1993
Elizabeth H. Hastings and Philip K. Hastings, eds.	*Index to International Public Opinion 1986–1987*	Westport, CT: Greenwood Press, 1988
Philip K. Hastings and Jessie C. Southwick, eds.	*Survey Data for Trend Analysis: An Index to Repeated Questions in the U.S. National Surveys Held by the Roper Public Opinion Research Center*	Storrs, CT: Roper Center for Public Public Opinion Research, Inc., 1974
Elizabeth Martin, Diana McDuffee, and Stanley Presser	*Sourcebook of Harris National Surveys: Repeated Questions 1963–1976*	Chapel Hill: Institute for Research in Social Science, University of North Carolina Press, 1981
National Opinion Research Center	*General Social Surveys 1972–1985: Cumulative Code Book*	Chicago: NORC, 1985
John P. Robinson, Robert Athanasiou, and Kendra B. Head	*Measures of Occupational Attitudes and Occupational Characteristics*	Ann Arbor: Institute for Social Research, University of Michigan, 1968
John P. Robinson and Philip R. Shaver	*Measures of Social-Psychological Attitudes,* rev. ed.	Ann Arbor: Institute for Social Research, University of Michigan, 1973

A review of literature will reveal instruments used in similar studies that may be obtained by writing the researchers or, if copyrighted, purchased through a clearinghouse. Many instruments are available through compilations and sourcebooks. While these tend to be oriented to social science applications, they are a rich source of ideas for tailoring questions to meet the manager's needs. Several compilations are recommended; we have suggested them in Table 12–3.[22]

Borrowing items from existing sources is not without risks. It is quite difficult to generalize the reliability and validity of selected items or portions of a questionnaire that have been taken out of the original context. Retesting is also warranted if it is necessary to report the reliability and validity of the instrument being constructed. Time and situation-specific fluctuations should be scrutinized. Remember that the original estimates are only as good as the sampling and testing procedures, and many researchers you borrow from may not have reported that information.

Language, phrasing, and idioms can also pose problems. Questions tend to age and may not appear (or sound) as relevant to the respondent as freshly worded ones would. Integrating existing and newly constructed questions is problematic. When adjacent questions are relied on to carry context in one questionnaire and then are not selected for the customized application, the newly selected question is left without necessary meaning.[23] Whether an instrument is constructed from scratch or adapted from the ideas of others, pretesting is recommended.

DRAFTING AND REFINING THE INSTRUMENT: PHASE 3

Once the questions are formulated, you need to do the following: (1) Develop the respondent-screening process (personal or phone interview) along with the introduction. (2) Arrange the measurement question sequence, which includes (a) identifying topic groups, (b) establishing a logical sequence for the question groups and questions within groups, and (c) developing transitions between these groups. (3) Prepare and insert instructions—for the interviewer or respondent—including termination, skip directions, and probes. (4) Create and insert a conclusion, along with a survey disposition statement. The final step in Phase 3 is pretesting.

Introduction and Respondent Screening

The introduction must supply the sample unit with the motivation to participate in the study. It must reveal enough about the forthcoming questions, usually by revealing some or all of the topics to be covered, for respondents to judge their interest level and their ability to provide the desired information. In any communication study, the introduction also reveals the amount of time participation is likely to take. In a personal or phone interview, the introduction usually contains a filter or screen question to determine if the potential respondent has the knowledge or experience necessary to participate in the study. The introduction also reveals the research organization or sponsor (unless the study is disguised) and possibly the objective of the study. At a minimum, a phone or personal interviewer will introduce himself or herself to help establish critical rapport with the potential respondent. Table 12–4 provides a sample introduction for the MindWriter telephone study of nonrespondents to the self-administered mail survey.

Measurement Question Sequencing

Often the content of one question (called a **branched question**) assumes other questions have been asked and answered. The psychological order of the questions is also important; question sequence can encourage or discourage commitment and promote or hinder the development of researcher-respondent rapport.

The design of survey questions is influenced by the need to relate each question to the others in the instrument. The basic principle to guide sequence decisions is: *The nature and needs of the respondent must determine the sequence of questions and the organization of the interview schedule.* Four guidelines may be suggested to implement this principle:

1. The question process must quickly awaken interest and motivate the respondent to participate in the interview. Put the more interesting topical target questions early.

2. The respondent should not be confronted by early requests for information that might be considered personal or ego threatening. Put questions that might influence the respondent to discontinue or terminate the questioning process near the end.

TABLE   12–4   Sample Components of Communication Instruments

Introduction	Good evening. May I please speak with (*name of respondent*)? Mr. (*respondent's last name*), I'm (*your name*) calling on behalf of MindWriter Corporation. You recently had your MindWriter laptop serviced at our CompleteCare Center. Could you take five minutes to tell us what you thought of the service provided by the center?
Transition	The next set of questions asks about your family and how you enjoy spending your nonworking or personal time.
Instructions for . . .	
a. Terminating (following filter or screen question)	I'm sorry, today we are only talking with individuals who eat cereal at least three days per week, but thank you for speaking with me. (*Pause for respondent reply.*) Good-bye.
b. Respondent discontinue	Would there be a time I could call back to complete the interview? (*Pause; record time.*) We'll call you back then at (*repeat day, time*). Thank you for talking with me this evening. *Or.* I appreciate your spending some time talking with me. Thank you.
c. Skip directions (between questions or groups of questions)	3. Did you purchase boxed cereal in the last 7 days? ❏ Yes ❏ No (skip to question 7)
d. Disposition instructions	A postage-paid envelope was included with your survey. Please refold your completed survey and mail it to us in the postage-paid envelope.
Conclusion	
a. Phone or personal interview	That's my last question. Your insights and the ideas of other valuable customers will help us to make the CompleteCare program the best it can be. Thank you for talking with us this evening. (*Pause for respondent reply*). Good evening.
b. Self-administered (usually precedes the disposition instructions)	Thank you for sharing your ideas about the CompleteCare program. Your insights will help us serve you better.

3. The questioning process should begin with simple items and move to the more complex, and move from general items to the more specific. Put taxing and challenging questions later in the questioning process.

4. Changes in the frame of reference should be small and should be clearly pointed out. Use transition statements between different topics of the target question set.

The first challenge is to awaken the respondent's interest in the study and motivate participation. We try to bring this about by choosing questions that are attention getting and not controversial. If the questions have human-interest value, so much the better. It is possible that the early questions will contribute hard data to the major study objective, but their major task is to overcome the motivational barrier.

The second guideline concerns requests for sensitive information too early in the process. Two forms of this error are common. There is usually a need to ask for personal classification information about respondents. They normally will provide these data, but the request should be made toward the end. If made immediately, it often causes respondents to feel threatened, dampening their interest and motivation to continue. It is also dangerous to ask any question at the start that is too personal. For example, respondents in one survey were asked whether they suffered from insomnia. When the question was asked immediately after the interviewer's introductory remarks, about 12 percent of those interviewed admitted to having insomnia. When a matched sample was asked the same question after two **buffer questions** (neutral questions designed chiefly to establish rapport with the respondent), 23 percent admitted suffering from insomnia.[24]

The third guideline concerns placing simpler questions first and moving progressively to more complex ones. Even simple questions that require much thought should be deferred until later. These recommendations can help reduce the number of "don't know" responses that are so prevalent early in interviews.

The procedure of moving from general to more specific questions is sometimes called the **funnel approach.** The objectives of this procedure are to learn the respondent's frame of reference and to extract the full range of desired information while limiting the distortion effect of earlier questions on later ones. This process may be illustrated with the following series of questions:

1. How do you think this country is getting along in its relations with other countries?
2. How do you think we are doing in our relations with Russia?
3. Do you think we ought to be dealing with Russia differently than we are now?
4. *(If yes)* What should we be doing differently?
5. Some people say we should get tougher with Russia and others think we are too tough as it is; how do you feel about it?[25]

The first question introduces the general subject and provides some insight into the respondent's frame of reference. The second question narrows the concern to a single country, while the third and fourth seek views on how the United States should deal with Russia. The fifth question illustrates a specific opinion area and would be asked only if this point of toughness had not been covered in earlier responses. Question 4 is an example of a *branched question;* the response to the previous question determines whether or not question 4 is asked of the respondent.

There is also a risk of interaction whenever two or more questions are related. Question-order influence is especially problematic with self-administered questionnaires, because the respondent is at liberty to refer back to questions previously answered. In an attempt to "correctly align" two responses, accurate opinions and attitudes may be sacrificed. The two questions shown in this table were asked in a national survey at the start of World War II:[26]

	Percent Answering Yes	
Question	*A Asked First*	*B Asked First*
A. Should the United States permit its citizens to join the French and British Armies?	45%	40%
B. Should the United States permit its citizens to join the German army?	31%	22%

Apparently, some respondents who first endorsed enlistment with the Allies felt obliged to extend this privilege to joining the German army. Where the decision was first made against joining the German army, a percentage of the respondents felt constrained from approving the option to join the Allies.

The last question-sequencing guideline suggests that questions be arranged so there is a minimum of shifting in subject matter and frame of reference. Respondents often interpret questions in the light of earlier questions and miss shifts of perspective or subject unless they are clearly stated. Respondents fail to listen carefully and frequently jump to conclusions about the import of a given question before it is completely stated. Their answers are strongly influenced by their frame of reference. Any change in subject by the interviewer may not register with them unless it is made strong and obvious. Most questionnaires that cover a range of topics are divided into sections with clearly defined transitions between sections to alert the respondent to the change in frame of reference. Table 12–4 provides a sample of a transition in the high school reunion study when measurement questions changed from work- or career-related questions to personal and family-related questions.

Instructions

Instructions to the interviewer or respondent attempt to ensure that all respondents are treated equally, thus avoiding building error into the results. Two principles form the foundation for good instructions: clarity and courtesy. Instruction language needs to be unfailingly simple and polite.

Instruction topics include (1) how to terminate an interview when the respondent does not correctly answer the screen or filter questions, (2) how to conclude an interview when the respondent decides to discontinue, (3) skip directions for moving between topic sections of an instrument when movement is dependent on the answer to specific questions or when branched questions are used, and (4) telling the respondent to a self-administered intrument about the disposition of the completed questionnaire. In a self-administered questionnaire, instructions must be contained within the survey instrument. Personal interviewer instructions sometimes are in a document separate from the questionnaire (a document thoroughly discussed during interviewer training) or are distinctly and clearly marked (highlighted, printed in colored ink, or boxed on the computer screen) on the data collection instrument itself. Sample instructions are presented in Table 12–4.

Conclusion

The role of the conclusion is to leave the respondent with the impression that his or her participation has been valuable. Subsequent researchers may need this individual to participate in new studies. If every interviewer or instrument expresses appreciation for participation, cooperation in subsequent studies is more likely. A sample conclusion is shown in Table 12–4.

Overcoming Instrument Problems

There is no substitute for a thorough understanding of question-wording, question-content, and sequencing issues. However, the researcher can do several things to help improve survey results: (1) build rapport with the respondent, (2) redesign the questioning process, (3) explore alternative response strategies, and (4) use methods other than questioning to secure the data. Also, by pretesting the instrument, the researcher can test and refine all the survey elements.

Building Rapport with the Respondent   Most information can be secured by direct undisguised questioning if rapport has been developed. Rapport is particularly useful in building respondent interest in the project, and the more interest respondents have, the more cooperation they will give. One can also overcome respondent unwillingness by providing some material compensation for cooperation. This approach has been especially successful in mail surveys.

The assurance of confidentiality can also increase respondents' motivation. One approach is to give discrete assurances, both by question wording and interviewer comments and actions, that all types of behavior, attitudes, and positions on controversial or sensitive subjects are acceptable and normal. Where you can say so truthfully, *guarantee* that respondents' answers will be used only in combined statistical totals. If respondents are convinced that their replies contribute to some important purpose, they are more likely to be candid, even about taboo topics.

Redesigning the Questioning Process   You can redesign the questioning process to improve the quality of answers by modifying the administrative process and the response strategy. We might show that confidentiality is indispensable to the administration of the survey by using a group administration of questionnaires, accompanied by a ballot-box collection procedure. Even in face-to-face interviews, the respondent may fill in the part of the questionnaire containing sensitive information and then seal the entire instrument in an envelope. While this does not guarantee confidentiality, it does suggest it.

We can also develop appropriate questioning sequences that will gradually lead a respondent from "safe" questions to those that are more sensitive. Indirect questioning (using projective techniques) is a widely used approach for securing opinions on sensitive topics. The respondents are asked how "other people" or "people around here" feel about a topic. It is assumed the respondents will reply in terms of their own attitudes and experiences, but this outcome is hardly certain. Indirect questioning may give a good measure of the majority opinion on a topic but fail to reflect the views either of the respondent or of minority segments.

With certain topics, it is possible to secure answers by using a proxy code. When we seek family income classes, we can hand the respondent a card with income brackets like these:

A. Under $25,000 per year

B. $25,000 to $49,999 per year

C. $50,000 to $74,999 per year

D. $75,000 and over per year

The respondent is then asked to report the appropriate bracket as either A, B, C, or D. For some reason, respondents are more willing to provide such an obvious proxy measure than to verbalize actual dollar values.

Exploring Alternative Response Strategies   At the original question drafting, try developing positive, negative, and neutral versions of each type of question. This practice dramatizes the problems of bias, helping you select question wording that minimizes the problems. Sometimes use an extreme version of a question rather than the expected one.

Minimize nonresponses to particular questions by recognizing the sensitivity of certain topics. In a self-administered instrument, for example, asking a multiple-choice question about income or age, where incomes and ages are offered in ranges, is usually more successful than using a free-response question (such as, What is your age, please? _____).

Using Methods Other Than Questioning   Sometimes questioning will not secure the information needed. A classic example concerns a survey to discover magazines read by respondents. An unusually high rate was reported for prestigious magazines, and an unusually low rate was reported for tabloid magazines. The study was revised so that the subjects, instead of being interviewed, were asked to contribute their old magazines to a charity drive. The collection gave a more realistic estimate of readership of both types of magazines.[27] Another study on the use of similar unobtrusive measures cites many other types of research situations where unique techniques have been used to secure more valid information than was possible from a survey.[28] (See Chapter 13, "Observational Studies.")

The Value of Pretesting

The final step toward improving survey results is pretesting (see Figure 12–1). There are abundant reasons for pretesting individual questions, questionnaires, and interview schedules. In this section we discuss several and raise questions to help you plan an effective test of your instrument. Most of what we know about pretesting is prescriptive. According to contemporary authors,

> There are no general principles of good pretesting, no systematization of practice, no consensus about expectations, and we rarely leave records for each other. How a pretest was conducted, what investigators learned from it, how they redesigned their question-naire on the basis of it—these matters are reported only sketchily in research reports, if at all.[29]

Nevertheless, conventional wisdom suggests that **pretesting** not only is an estab-lished practice for discovering errors but also is useful for training the research team. Ironically, professionals who have participated in scores of studies are more likely to pretest an instrument than is a beginning researcher hurrying to complete a project. Revising questions five or more times is not unusual. Yet inexperienced researchers often underestimate the need to follow the design-test-revise process.

Respondent Interest   An important purpose of pretesting is to discover the respondents' reactions to the questions. If respondents do not find the experience stimulating when an interviewer is physically present, how will they react on the phone or in the self-administered mode? Pretesting should help to discover where repetitiveness or redun-dancy is bothersome or what topics were not covered that the respondent expected. An alert interviewer will look for questions or even sections that the respondent perceives to be sensitive or threatening or topics about which the respondent knows nothing.

Meaning   Questions that we borrow or adapt from the work of others carry an authori-tativeness that may prompt us to avoid pretesting them, but they are often most in need of examination. Are they still timely? Is the language relevant? Do they need context from adjacent questions? Newly constructed questions should be similarly checked for meaningfulness to the respondent. Does the question evoke the same meaning as that intended by the researcher? How different is the researcher's frame of reference from that of the average respondent? Words and phrases that trigger a "what do you mean?" response from the respondent need to be singled out for further refinement.

Question Transformation   Respondents do not necessarily process every word in the question. They also may not share the same definitions for the terms they hear. When this happens, respondents modify the question to make it fit their own frame of refer-ence or simply change it so it makes sense to them. Probing is necessary to discover how respondents have transformed the question when this is suspected.[30]

Continuity and Flow   In self-administered questionnaires, questions should read ef-fortlessly and flow from one to another and from one section to another. In personal and telephone interviews, the sound of the question and its transition must be fluid as well. A long set of questions with nine-point scales that worked well in a mail instru-ment would not be effective on the telephone unless you ask respondents to visualize the scale as the touch keys on their phone. Moreover, the types of transitions that may appear redundant in a self-administered questionnaire may be exactly the ones that need to be heard in personal or telephone interviewing.

Question Sequence   Question arrangement can play a significant role in the success of the instrument. Many authorities recommend starting with stimulating questions and placing sensitive questions last. Since questions concerning income and family life are most likely to be refused, this is often good advice for building trust before getting into a refusal situation. However, interest-building questions need to be tested first to be sure they are stimulating. And when background questions are asked earlier in the interview, some demographic information will be salvaged if the interview stops unexpectedly. Pretesting with a large enough group permits some experimentation with alternating these sequences.

Skip Instructions   In interviews and questionnaires, **skip patterns** and their contingency sequences may not work as envisioned on paper. Skip patterns are designed to route or sequence the response to another question contingent on the answer to the previous question (branched questions). Pretesting in the field helps to identify problems with box-and-arrow schematics that the designers may not have thought of. By correcting them in the revision stage, we also avoid problems with flow and continuity.

Variability   With a small group of respondents, pretesting cannot provide definitive quantitative conclusions but will deliver an early warning about items that may not discriminate among respondents or places where meaningful subgrouping may occur in the final sample. With 25 to 100 respondents in the pretest group, statistical data on the proportion of respondents answering yes or no or marking "strongly agree" to "strongly disagree" can supplement the qualitative information noted by the interviewers. This information is useful for sample size calculations and getting preliminary indications of reliability problems with scaled questions.

Length and Timing   Most draft questionnaires or interview schedules suffer from lengthiness. By timing each question and section, the researcher is in a better position to make decisions about modifying or cutting material. In personal and telephone interviews, labor is a project expense. Thus, if the budget influences the final length of the questionnaire, an accurate estimate of elapsed time is essential. Videotaped or audiotaped pretests may also be used for this purpose. Their function in reducing errors in data recording is widely accepted.

Pretesting Options

There are various ways that pretesting can be used to refine an instrument. They range from informal reviews by colleagues to creating conditions similar to those of the final study.

Researcher Pretesting   Designers typically test informally in the initial stages and build more structure into the tests along the way. Fellow instrument designers can do the first-level pretest. Their many differences of opinion are likely to create numerous suggestions for improvement. Usually at least two or three drafts can be effectively developed by bringing research colleagues into the process.

Respondent Pretesting   Respondent pretests require that the questionnaire be field-tested by sample respondents or respondent surrogates (individuals with characteristics and backgrounds similar to the desired respondents).

Field pretests also involve distributing the test instrument exactly as the actual instrument will be distributed. Most studies use two or more pretests. National projects may use one trial to examine local reaction and another to check for regional differences. Although many researchers try to keep pretest conditions and times close to what they expect for the actual study, personal interview and telephone limitations make it desirable to test in the evenings or on weekends in order to interview people who are not available for contact at other times.

Test mailings are useful, but it is often faster to use a substitute procedure. In the MindWriter example, the managers who were interviewed in the exploratory study were later asked to review the pilot questionnaire. The interviewers left them alone and returned later. Upon their return, they went over the questions with each manager. They explained that they wanted the manager's reactions to question clarity and ease of answering. After several such interviews, the instrument was revised and the testing process repeated with customers. With minor revision, the questionnaire was reproduced and prepared for inserting into the computer packing material.

Collaborative Pretests   Different approaches taken by interviewers and the respondents' awareness of those approaches affect the pretest. If the researcher alerts respondents to their involvement in a preliminary test of the questionnaire, the respondents are essentially being enlisted as collaborators in the refinement process. Under these conditions, detailed probing of the parts of the question, including phrases and words, is appropriate. Because of the time required for probing and discussion, it is likely that only the most critical questions will be reviewed. The respondent group may therefore need to be conscripted from colleagues and friends to secure the additional time and motivation needed to cover an entire questionnaire. If friends or associates are used, experience suggests that they introduce more bias than strangers, argue more about wording, and generally make it more difficult to accomplish other goals of pretesting such as timing the length of questions or sections.[31]

Occasionally, a highly experienced researcher may improvise questions during a pretest. When this occurs, it is essential to record the interview or take detailed notes so the questionnaire may be reconstructed later. Ultimately, a team of interviewers would be required to follow the interview schedule's prearranged sequence of questions. Only experienced investigators should be free to depart from the interview schedule during a pretest and explore respondents' answers by adding probes.

Noncollaborative Pretests   When the researcher does not inform the respondent that the activity is a pretest, it is still possible to probe for reactions but without the cooperation and commitment of time provided by collaborators. The comprehensiveness of the effort also suffers because of flagging cooperation. The virtue of this approach is that the questionnaire can be tested under conditions approaching those of the final study. This realism is similarly useful for training interviewers.

Summary

The versatility of the communication approach is its greatest strength. It is an exceptionally practical way to gather opinions, knowledge, and behavioral intentions. Its dependence on the respondent's verbal behavior is its greatest weakness. Not only may intentionally false information be given, but verbal behavior can also be dramatically changed in many ways.

Several choices must be made in designing a communication study instrument. Surveying can be a face-to-face interview, or it can be much less personal, using indirect media and self-administered questionnaires. The questioning process can be unstructured as in in-depth interviewing, or the questions can be clearly structured. Responses may be unstructured and open-ended or structured with the respondent choosing from a list of possibilities. The degree to which the objectives and intent of the questions should be disguised must also be decided.

The instrument design process flows through three phases: (1) developing the instrument design strategy, (2) constructing and refining the measurement questions, and (3) drafting and refining the instrument. Question development will be easier if the designer follows the research question hierarchy, which begins with the management question, then moves toward greater specificity with the research question, the investigative questions, and finally the measurement questions.

Instruments obtain three general classes of information. Target questions address the investigative questions and are the most important. Classification questions concern respondent characteristics and allow respondents' answers to be grouped for analysis. Administrative questions identify the respondent, interviewer, and interview location and conditions.

Question construction has three critical decision areas. They are (1) question content, (2) question wording, and (3) response strategy. Question content should pass the following tests: Should the question be asked? Is it of proper scope? Can and will the respondent answer adequately?

Question-wording difficulties exceed most other sources of distortion in surveys. Retention of a question should be confirmed by answering: Is the question stated in terms of a shared vocabulary? Does the vocabulary have a single meaning? Does the question contain misleading assumptions? Is the wording biased? Is it correctly personalized? Are adequate alternatives presented?

The study's objective and respondent factors affect the decision of whether to use open-ended or closed questions. Respondent factors include level of information about the topic, degree to which the topic has been thought through, ease of communication, and motivation to share information. The decision is also affected by the interviewer's perception of respondent factors.

Both two-way and multiple-choice questions are valuable, but on balance, the latter are preferred if only because few questions have only two possible answers. Checklist, rating, and ranking strategies are also common.

Question sequence can drastically affect respondent willingness to cooperate and the quality of responses. Generally, the sequence should begin with efforts to awaken the respondent's interest in continuing the interview. Early questions should be simple rather than complex, easy rather than difficult, nonthreatening, and obviously germane to the announced objective of the study. Frame-of-reference changes should be minimal, and questions should be sequenced so early questions do not distort the replies to later ones.

Sources of questions for the construction of questionnaires include the literature on related research and sourcebooks of scales and questionnaires. Borrowing items has attendant risks such as time and situation-specific reliability and validity problems. Incompatibility of language and idiom also needs to be considered.

Pretesting the instrument is recommended to identify problems before the actual collection of data begins. Insights and ideas for refining instruments result from thoroughness in pretesting. Effective revision is the result of determining respondent interest, discovering if the questions have meaning for the respondent, checking for respondent modification of a question's intent, examining question continuity and flow, experimenting with question-sequencing patterns, evaluating skip instructions for the interviewers, collecting early warning data on item variability, and fixing the length and timing of the instrument.

Key Terms

administrative question	interview schedule
branched question	leading question
buffer question	multiple-choice question
checklist	multiple question
classification question	open-ended question/response
closed question/response	pretesting
dichotomous question	projective techniques
disguised question	ranking question
double-barreled question	rating question
filter question	screen question
focus group	skip pattern
free-response question	structured question/response
funnel approach	target question
in-depth interview	unstructured question/response

Cases

T-Shirt Designs
Violence on TV
(These are cases found in the optional case book available with the text.)

Discussion
Questions

1. Distinguish between:
   a. Direct and indirect questions
   b. Open-ended and closed questions
   c. Research, investigative, and measurement questions
   d. Alternative response strategies

2. Why is the survey technique so popular? When is it not appropriate?

3. What special problems do open-ended questions have? How can these be minimized? In what situations is the open-ended question most useful?

4. Why might a researcher wish to disguise the objective of a study?

5. One of the major reasons why survey research may not be effective is that the survey instruments are less useful than they should be. What would you say are the four major faults of the survey instrument designer?

6. Why is it desirable to pretest survey instruments? What information can you secure from such a pretest? How can you find the best wording for a question on a questionnaire?

7. One design problem in the development of survey instruments concerns the sequence of questions. What suggestions would you give to people designing their first questionnaire?

8. One of the major problems facing the designer of a survey instrument is the assumptions made. What are the major "problem assumptions"?

9. Below are six questions that might be found on questionnaires. Comment on each as to whether or not it is a good question. If it is not, tell why. (Assume that no lead-in or screening questions are required for these. Judge each question on its own merits.)
   a. Do you read *National Geographic* magazine regularly?
   b. What percentage of your time is spent asking for information from others in your organization?
   c. When did you first start chewing gum?
   d. How much discretionary buying power do you have each year?
   e. Why did you decide to attend Big State University?
   f. Do you think the president is doing a good job now?

10. A student class project developed a brief self-administered questionnaire by which students might quickly evaluate a professor. One student

submitted the following instrument. Evaluate the questions asked and the format of the instrument.

Professor Evaluation Form

1. Overall, how would you rate this professor?

    _____ good   _____ fair   _____ poor

2. Does this professor

    a. Have good class delivery? _____

    b. Know the subject? _____

    c. Have a positive attitude toward the subject? _____

    d. Grade fairly? _____

    e. Have a sense of humor? _____

    f. Use audiovisuals, case examples, or other classroom aids? _____

    g. Return exams promptly? _____

3. What is the professor's strongest point? _____

4. What is the professor's weakest point? _____

5. What kind of class does the professor teach? _____

6. Is this course required? _____

7. Would you take another course from this professor? _____

11. Below is a copy of the letter and mail questionnaire received by a professor who is a member of the American Society of Training Directors. Please evaluate the usefulness and tone of the letter and the questions and format of the instrument.

    Dear ASTD Member: In partial fulfillment of master's degree work, I have chosen to do a descriptive study of the industrial trainer in our area. Using the roster of the ASTD as a mailing list, your name came to me. I am enclosing a short questionnaire and a return envelope. I hope you will take a few minutes and fill out the questionnaire as soon as possible, as the sooner the information is returned to me, the better.

    Sincerely,

    Questionnaire

    Directions: Please answer as briefly as possible.

    1. With what company did you enter the field of training? _____

    2. How long have you been in the field of training? _____

    3. How long have you been in the training department of the company with which you are presently employed? _____

    4. How long has the training department in your company been in existence? _____

    5. Is the training department a subset of another department? If so, what department? _____

    6. For what functions (other than training) is your department responsible? _____

    7. How many people, including yourself, are in the training department of your company? (Local plant or establishment) _____

    8. What degrees do you hold and from what institutions? _____ Major _____ Minor _____

    9. Why were you chosen for training? What special qualifications do you have that prompted your entry into training? _____

       _____

       _____

   10. What experience would you consider necessary for an individual to enter into the field of training with your company? Include both educational requirements and actual experience. _____

       _____

Reference Notes

1. The MindWriter questionnaire used in this example is based on an actual questionnaire copyrighted by Cooper Research Group, Inc., 1993, for an unidentified client who shares the intellectual property rights. No part of the format, question wording, sequence, scale, or references to MindWriter © 1997 may be produced or transmitted in any form or by any means, electronic or mechanical, including photocopy, recording, or any information storage and retrieval system, without permission in writing from Cooper Research Group, Inc. Reprinted with permission.

2. Dorwin Cartwright, "Some Principles of Mass Persuasion," *Human Relations* 2 (1948), p. 266.

3. Sam Gill, "How Do You Stand on Sin?" *Tide,* March 14, 1947, p. 72.

4. Stanley L. Payne, *The Art of Asking Questions* (Princeton, NJ: Princeton University Press, 1951), p. 18.

5. Unaided recall gives respondents no clues as to possible answers. Aided recall gives them a list of radio programs that played last night and then asks them which ones they heard. See Harper W. Boyd, Jr., and Ralph Westfall, *Marketing Research,* 3rd ed. (Homewood, IL: Irwin, 1972), p. 293.

6. Gideon Sjoberg, "A Questionnaire on Questionnaires," *Public Opinion Quarterly* 18 (Winter 1954), p. 425.

7. More will be said on the problems of readability in Chapter 19; "Presenting Results: Written and Oral Reports."

8. S. A. Stouffer et al., *Measurement and Prediction: Studies in Social Psychology in World War II,* vol. 4 (Princeton, NJ: Princeton University Press, 1950), p. 709.

9. An excellent example of the question revision process is presented in Payne, *The Art of Asking Questions,* pp. 214–25. This example illustrates that a relatively simple question can go through as many as 41 different versions before being judged satisfactory.

10. Robert L. Kahn and Charles F. Cannell, *The Dynamics of Interviewing* (New York: Wiley, 1957), p. 108.

11. Ibid., p. 110.

12. Payne, *The Art of Asking Questions,* p. 140.

13. Ibid., p. 141.

14. Ibid., p. 149.

15. Gertrude Bancroft and Emmett H. Welch, "Recent Experiences with Problems of Labor Force Measurement," *Journal of the American Statistical Association* 41 (1946), pp. 303–12.

16. National Opinion Research Center, *Proceedings of the Central City Conference on Public Opinion Research* (Denver, CO: University of Denver, 1946), p. 73.

17. Hadley Cantril, ed., *Gauging Public Opinion* (Princeton, NJ: Princeton University Press, 1944), p. 48.

18. Payne, *The Art of Asking Questions,* pp. 7–8.

19. Kahn and Cannell, *Dynamics of Interviewing,* p. 132.

20. Barbara Snell Dohrenwend, "Some Effects of Open and Closed Questions on Respondents' Answers," *Human Organization* 24 (Summer 1965), pp. 175–84.

21. Cantril, *Gauging Public Opinion,* p. 31.

22. Jean M. Converse and Stanley Presser, *Survey Questions: Handcrafting the Standardized Questionnaire* (Beverly Hills, CA: Sage Publications, 1986), pp. 50–51.

23. Ibid., p. 51.

24. Frederick J. Thumin, "Watch for These Unseen Variables," *Journal of Marketing* 26 (July 1962), pp. 58–60.

25. F. Cannell and Robert L. Kahn, "The Collection of Data by Interviewing," in *Research Methods in the Behavioral Sciences,* eds. Leon Festinger and Daniel Katz (New York: Holt, Rinehart & Winston, 1953), p. 349.

26. Cantril, *Gauging Public Opinion,* p. 28.

27. Perceival White, *Market Analysis* (New York: McGraw-Hill, 1921).

28. Eugene J. Webb, Donald T. Campbell, Richard D. Schwartz, and Lee Sechrest, *Unobtrusive Measures: Nonreactive Research in the Social Sciences* (Chicago: Rand McNally, 1966).

29. Converse and Presser, *Survey Questions,* p. 52.

30. W. R. Belson, *The Design and Understanding of Survey Questions* (Aldershot, England: Gower, 1981), pp. 76–86.

31. The sections on methods and purposes of pretesting are largely adapted from Converse and Presser, *Survey Questions,* pp. 51–64; and Survey Research Center, *Interviewer's Manual,* rev. ed. (Ann Arbor: Institute for Social Research, University of Michigan, 1976), pp. 133–34. For an extended discussion of the phases of pretesting, see Converse and Presser, *Survey and Questions,* pp. 65–75.

Suggested Readings

1. Converse, Jean M., and Stanley Presser. *Survey Questions: Handcrafting the Standardized Questionnaire.* Beverly Hills, CA: Sage Publications, 1986. A worthy successor to Stanley Payne's classic. Advice on how to write survey questions based on professional experience and the experimental literature.

2. Dillman, Don A. *Mail and Telephone Surveys.* New York: Wiley, 1978. Chapters 3, 4, and 6 are on question construction. Extensive bibliography.

3. Kahn, Robert L., and Charles F. Cannell. *The Dynamics of Interviewing.* New York: Wiley, 1957. Chapters 5 and 6 cover questionnaire design.
4. Payne, Stanley L. *The Art of Asking Questions.* Princeton, NJ: Princeton University Press, 1951. An enjoyable book on the many problems found in developing useful survey questions. A classic resource.
5. Selltiz, Claire, Lawrence S. Wrightsman, and Stuart W. Cook. *Research Methods in Social Relations,* 3rd ed. New York: Holt, Rinehart & Winston, 1976. Appendix B is an especially well-organized set of guides for questionnaire development.
6. Sudman, Seymour, and Norman N. Bradburn. *Asking Questions: A Practical Guide to Questionnaire Design.* San Francisco: Jossey-Bass, 1982. This book covers the major issues in writing individual questions and constructing scales. The emphasis is on structured questions and interview schedules.

CHAPTER 13 OBSERVATIONAL STUDIES

CHAPTER NAVIGATION

BRINGING RESEARCH TO LIFE

Their conversation turned to most frightening experiences. Myra took the first turn.

"I was a foreign correspondent," said Myra. "Not a war correspondent, mind you—I hadn't signed on for anything risky—when a coterie of local thugs got their hands on some high-quality plastique and declared themselves freedom fighters. They found my reports unsympathetic and three times in one month, I lost my hotel—just came home and found my digs reduced to rubble—and this happened three times. The funny thing is, I would have stayed on for a fourth or fifth hotel, but I could not afford to replace my typewriters on the local black market."

"That is scary," said Dorrie Madison-Henry. "I have nothing to equal it. During my internship, I had to resuscitate three people in one night. Brought each of them back from clinical death. But that was exciting more than scary. For scariness, nothing matches Jason's experience with Otto Darnell."

"You mean *the* Otto Darnell, the infamous 'O Darn,' who dropped the winning pass in the Rose Bowl?"

"That Otto, yes," said Jason. "He dropped the pass with twenty seconds to go—and in the end zone—and all he could say was, 'O, darn,' hence his nickname. Otto was tall and broad and fast, and he had huge hands, and he was one of the smartest guys I have met. So on paper he looked like an All-American wide receiver. But he was always dropping things, and if he were here I would not offer him a cup of coffee over Dorrie's white carpet.

"Otto's uncle owned an electronics assembly plant in the northwest part of the state. He made miniature TV cameras for industrial and bank security and such. Right after the Rose Bowl, he asked us up, to maybe take Otto's mind off his football foul-up and also to brainstorm a production problem. Around 5 every afternoon, the quality of assembled cameras deteriorated. Uncle had six women assembling the cameras—good, loyal, hard workers—and he could not pinpoint the quality problem. If he sat and watched them, they were on their best behavior and followed standard operating procedures, and their quality stayed up. Likewise, if they knew he was spying on them with one of his cameras. But if they suspected that he'd stopped watching, bugs began to creep into quality, and always around 5 P.M.

"Otto and I questioned the women. They denied deviating from the standards, and, of course, they were not going to 'rat out' anybody in their group."

"Wouldn't expect them to."

"So we didn't bother asking them to inform on each other. But Otto was watching carefully and told me later that five of the women took covert glances at a sixth, Bertha, who looked fidgety. She was a huge, good-natured, serious woman, ferociously devoted to an honest day's work, to my uncle, and to the company; but she looked nervous, Otto said, blinking her eyes and twitching her lips, as if she were close to tears from keeping a dirty secret. And she would not look Otto in the eyes. I, myself, didn't notice this behavior. . . ."

"Because you were probably reading questions from a clipboard and not looking up," added Myra.

"I suppose. . . . Well, the window in the assembly room was what you call mirrored glass. Otto got the idea of unscrewing all the 60-watt bulbs inside the room and replacing them with 200-watters, so that after the sun went down, we could look in through the windows and observe the six women, without much likelihood that they would see us, so long as we didn't attract their attention to the window.

"The problem was, this was a fifth-story window, so we could not stand outside and point the camera in. We had to run up to the sixth story, to an empty room, and cable a TV to a video monitor-recorder, and crank open the sixth-floor window and lower the TV camera down to the fifth story on a pole. I was supposed to watch the monitor and tell Otto, 'pan left,' 'pan right,' until we had rolled enough tape to see where the problem was.

"No sooner had Otto opened the window than I heard, 'Oh, darn.' He had dropped the camera, and I could see it swinging below the window by its

(continued)

thread of an optical cable. So I leaned way out the window to snare it, knowing that if Otto were to set his hands on it, he would surely make matters worse. Not that they weren't bad enough—as time was flying.

"When I tell you what happened next, remember that Otto was very ego involved in this observation idea and could not stand the thought of letting down his side, not again, not so soon after the bowl game. I felt him grab me by the ankles and he lowered me out the window. In a stage whisper he said, `Grab it, and hold it, and pan it left and right, very slowly.'

"So there I was upside down and trying not to look down, at the five-and-a-half-story drop into a snowbank.

"Someday I'll show you the video recording. You can see the six women at work, and, in particular, you can see that every now and then Bertha would dip her hand into her left smock pocket and bring her hand up to her mouth and then down to pick up a chip and then press the chip into the circuit board. This was not standard operations.

"This was fairly scary, but was soon to get scarier by far. The camera happened to be pointed toward Bertha when I carelessly let it rap against the window. In the video, you can see Bertha glance up and reach for the switch to stop the assembly line and warily stroll over to the window and crank it open. All of this was against standard procedures, of course—stopping the line, leaving the workstation, opening the window, and I had a very bad feeling about what was going to happen next. And I was dizzy, and nauseous, and cold.

"She sees me, and with the camera pointing straight in her face, you see her reach back into her hair and withdraw a hat pin which is holding her bandanna in place, and thrust out and jam the hat pin toward me. The hatpin goes past the camera and her arm goes past, up to the elbow.

"She stuck the huge pin in Otto's big ham of a hand, and that was when he yelped, `Oh, darn,' and let go of my left ankle.

"Now the video goes black, as I let go of the camera and it breaks loose from its cable. There I am, swinging around, first looking in the window, looking at the moon, looking at the parking lot, looking down at the snowbank maybe forty feet below, all at the same time, it seemed.

"I must have grabbed Bertha, because I remember that Otto was pulling up and Bertha was pulling back, and Bertha won, thank goodness! and we fell backward, me on top of Bertha.

"After the scuffling and hollering and then everyone calming down when they recognized me, we had the good wits to check the contents of Bertha's pocket. It was full of greasy, salted peanuts. The poor gal was not able to wait until her 6 P.M. dinner break and was feeding herself secretly and quietly. Then with the greasy fingers she was picking up a chip and pressing the greasy pins into the circuit board.

"Uncle advanced the supper hour to 4:45 and the problem disappeared."

"Quite a triumph of observation," said Myra.

"It was craziness," said Jason. "I was a lunatic to trust Otto to lean out the window and not drop the camera. It took us two guys half an hour the next morning to dig the camera out of a snowbank, and I could not stop thinking, this might be me, buried head down in the snow. Overall, it was no great coup of observation. I mean, ask yourself, why hadn't the people in quality control noticed grease on the circuit boards?"

THE USES OF OBSERVATION

Much of what we know comes from observation. We notice co-workers' reactions to political intrigue, the sounds of the assembly area, the smell of perfume, the taste of office coffee, the smoothness of the vice president's marble desk, and a host of other stimuli. While such observation may be a basis for knowledge, the collection processes are often haphazard.

Observation qualifies as scientific inquiry when it is specifically designated to answer a research question, is systematically planned and executed, uses proper controls, and provides a reliable and valid account of what happened. The versatility of observation makes it an indispensable primary source method and a supplement for other methods. Many academics have a limited view of observation, relegating it to a minor technique of field data collection. This ignores its potential for forging business decisions and denies its historic stature as a creative means to obtain primary data.

In Chapter 11, we said that research designs are classified by the *approach* used to gather primary data: We can *observe,* or we can *communicate.* Figure 13–1 describes the conditions under which observation is an appropriate method for data collection. It also contrasts those conditions with ones we are familiar with from the communication modes—personal inteview, telephone inteview, and self-administered survey (see Figure 11–1).

Besides collecting data visually, observation involves listening, reading, smelling, and touching. Behavioral scientists define observation in terms of animal

FIGURE   13–1   Selecting the Data Collection Method

or human behavior, but this too is limiting. As used in this text, **observation** includes the full range of monitoring behavioral and nonbehavioral activities and conditions, which can be classified roughly as follows:

1. Nonbehavioral observation
   a. Record analysis
   b. Physical condition analysis
   c. Physical process analysis
2. Behavioral observation
   a. Nonverbal analysis
   b. Linguistic analysis
   c. Extralinguistic analysis
   d. Spatial analysis

Nonbehavioral Observation

A prevalent form of observation research is **record analysis.** This may involve historical or current records and public or private records. They may be written, printed, sound-recorded, photographed, or videotaped. Historical statistical data are often the only sources used for a study. Analysis of current financial records and economic data also provides a major data source for studies. Other examples of this type of observation are the *content analysis* (described in Chapter 15) of competitive advertising and the analysis of personnel records.

Physical condition analysis is typified by store audits of merchandise availability, studies of plant safety compliance, analysis of inventory conditions, and analysis of financial statements. **Process** or **activity analysis** includes time/motion studies of manufacturing processes, and analysis of traffic flows in a distribution system, paperwork flows in an office, and financial flows in the banking system.

Behavioral Observation

The observational study of persons can be classified into four major categories.[1] **Nonverbal behavior** is the most prevalent of these and includes body movement, motor expressions, and even exchanged glances. At the level of gross body movement, one might study how a salesperson travels a territory. At a fine level, one can study the body movements of a worker assembling a product or time-sample the activity of a department's workforce to discover the share of time each worker spends in various ways. More abstractly, one can study body movement as an indicator of interest or boredom, anger or pleasure in a certain environment. Motor expressions such as facial movements can be observed as a sign of emotional states. Eye blink rates are studied as indicators of interest in advertising messages. Exchanged glances are of interest in studies of interpersonal behavior.

Linguistic behavior is a second frequently used form of behavior observation. One simple type, familiar to most students, is the tally of "ahs" or other annoying sounds or words a professor makes or uses during a class. More serious applications are the study of a sales presentation's content or the study of what, how, and how much information is conveyed in a training situation. A third form of linguistic behavior involves interaction processes that occur between two people or in small groups. Bales has proposed one widely used system for classifying such linguistic interactions.[2]

Behavior may also be analyzed on an extralinguistic level. Sometimes **extralinguistic behavior** is as important a means of communication as linguistic behavior. One author has suggested there are four dimensions of extralinguistic activity.[3] They are (1) vocal, including pitch, loudness, and timbre; (2) temporal, including the rate of speaking, duration of utterance, and rhythm; (3) interaction, including the tendencies to interrupt, dominate, or inhibit; and (4) verbal stylistic, including vocabulary and pronunciation peculiarities, dialect, and characteristic expressions. These dimensions could add substantial insight to the linguistic content of the interactions between supervisors and subordinates or salespeople and customers.

A fourth type of behavior study involves **spatial relationships,** especially how a person relates physically to others. One form of this study, *proxemics,* concerns how people organize the territory about them and how they maintain discrete distances between themselves and others. A study of how salespeople physically approach customers and a study of the effects of crowding in a workplace are examples of this type of observation.

Often in a study, the researcher will be interested in two or more of these types of information and will require more than one observer. In these forms of behavior study, it is also important to consider the relationship between observers and subjects.

EVALUATION OF THE OBSERVATIONAL METHOD

Observation is the only method available to gather certain types of information. The study of records, mechanical processes, and lower animals falls into this category. Most small children and illiterate and functionally illiterate people cannot be surveyed effectively or subjected to experimentation.

Another value of observation is that we can collect the original data at the time they occur. We need not depend on reports by others. Every respondent filters information no matter how well intentioned he or she is. Forgetting occurs, and there are reasons why the respondent may not want to report fully and fairly. Observation overcomes many of these deficiencies of questioning.

A third strength is that we can secure information that most participants would ignore either because it is so common and expected or because it is not seen as relevant. For example, if you are observing buying activity in a store, there may be conditions important to the research study that the shopper does not notice or consider important, such as: What is the weather? What is the day of the week, the time of day? How heavy is customer traffic? What is the level of promotional activity in competing stores? We can expect to learn only a few of the answers to these questions from most respondents.

The fourth advantage of observation is that it alone can capture the whole event as it occurs in its natural environment. Whereas the environment of an experiment may seem contrived to subjects, and the number and types of questions limit the range of responses from respondents, observation is less restrictive than most primary collection methods. Also, the limitations on the length of data collection activities imposed by surveys or experiments are relaxed for observation. You may be interested in all the conditions surrounding a confrontation at a bargaining session between union and management representatives. These sessions may extend over time, and any effort to study the unfolding of the negotiation is facilitated by observation. Questioning could seldom provide the insight of observation for many aspects of the negotiation process.

Finally, subjects seem to accept an observational intrusion better than they respond to questioning. Observation is less demanding of them and normally has a less biasing effect on their behavior than does questioning. In addition, it is also possible to conduct disguised and unobtrusive observation studies much more easily than disguised questioning.

There are some research limitations of the observational method. The observer normally must be at the scene of the event when it takes place, yet it is often impossible to predict where and when the event will occur. One way to guard against missing an event is to observe for prolonged periods until it does occur, but this strategy brings up a second disadvantage. Observation is a slow and expensive process that requires either human observers or costly surveillance equipment.

A third limitation of observation is that its most reliable results are restricted to information that can be learned by overt action or surface indicators. To go below the surface, the observer must make inferences. Two observers will probably agree on the nature of various surface events, but the inferences they draw from such data are much more variable.

Fourth, the research environment is more likely suited to subjective assessment and recording of data than to controls and quantification of events. When control is exercised through active intervention by the researchers, their participation may threaten the validity of what is being assessed. Even when sample sizes are small, the observation records can be disproportionately large and difficult to analyze.

Fifth, observation is limited as a way to learn about of the past. It is similarly limited as a method by which to learn what is going on in the present at some distant place. It is also difficult to gather information on such topics as intentions, attitudes, opinions, or preferences.

Nevertheless any consideration of the merits of observation confirms its value when used with care and understanding.

THE OBSERVER-SUBJECT RELATIONSHIP

Interrogation presents a clear opportunity for interviewer bias. The problem is less pronounced with observation but is still real. The relationship between observer and subject may be viewed from three perspectives: (1) whether the observation is direct or indirect, (2) whether the observer's presence is known or unknown to the subject, and (3) what role the observer plays.

Directness of Observation

Direct observation occurs when the observer is physically present and personally monitors what takes place. This approach is very flexible because it allows the observer to react to and report subtle aspects of events and behavior as they occur. He or she is also free to shift places, change the focus of the observation, or concentrate on unexpected events if they occur. A weakness of this approach is that observers' perception circuits may become overloaded as events move quickly, and observers must later try to reconstruct what they were not able to record. Also, observer fatigue, boredom, and distracting events can reduce the accuracy and completeness of observation.

Indirect observation occurs when the recording is done by mechanical, photographic, or electronic means. For example, a special camera that takes one frame every second is mounted in a department of a large store to study customer and employee movement. Indirect is less flexible than direct observation, but also much less biasing and may be less erratic in accuracy. Another advantage of indirect observation is that the permanent record can be reanalyzed to include many different aspects of an event. Electronic recording devices, which have improved in quality and declined in cost, are being used more frequently in observation research.

Concealment

A second factor affecting the observer-subject relationship concerns whether the presence of the observer should be known to the subjects. When the observer is known, there is a risk of atypical activity by the subjects. The initial entry of an observer into a situation often upsets activity patterns of the subjects, but this influence usually dissipates quickly, especially when subjects are engaged in some absorbing activity or the presence of observers offers no potential threat to the subjects' self-interest. The potential bias from subject awareness of observers is always a matter of concern, however.

Observers use **concealment** to shield themselves from the object of their observation. Often, technical means are used such as one-way mirrors, hidden cameras, or microphones. These methods reduce the risk of observer bias but bring up a question of ethics. Hidden observation is a form of spying, and the propriety of this action must be reviewed carefully.

A modified approach involves partial concealment. The presence of the observer is not concealed, but the objectives and subject of interest are. A study of selling methods may be conducted by sending an observer with a salesperson who is making calls on customers. However, the observer's real purpose may be hidden from both the salesperson and the customer (e.g., she may pretend she is analyzing the display and layout characteristics of the stores they are visiting).

Participation

The third observer-subject issue is whether the observer should participate in the situation while observing. A more involved arrangement, **participant observation,** exists when the observer enters the social setting and acts as both an observer and a participant. Sometimes he or she is known as an observer to some or all of the participants; at other times the true role is concealed. While reducing the potential for bias, this again raises an ethical issue. Often subjects will not have given their consent and will not have knowledge of or access to the findings. After being deceived and having their privacy invaded, what further damage could come to the subjects if the results became public? This issue needs to be addressed when concealment and covert participation are used.

Participant observation makes a dual demand on the observer. Recording can interfere with participation, and participation can interfere with observation. The observer's role may influence the way others act. Because of these problems, participant observation is less used in business research than, say, in anthropology or sociology. It is typically restricted to cases where nonparticipant observation is not practical—for example, a study of the functioning of a traveling auditing team.

CONDUCTING AN OBSERVATIONAL STUDY

The Type of Study   Observation is found in almost all research studies, at least at the exploratory stage. Such data collection is known as **simple observation.** Its practice is not standardized, as one would expect, because of the discovery nature of exploratory research. The decision to use observation as the major data collection method may be made as early as the moment the researcher moves from research questions to investigative questions. The latter specify the outcomes of the study—the specific questions the researcher must answer with collected data. If the study is to be something other than exploratory, **systematic observation** employs standardized procedures, trained observers, schedules for recording, and other devices for the observer that mirror the scientific procedures of other primary data methods. Systematic studies vary in the emphasis placed on recording and encoding observational information:

> At one end of the continuum are methods that are unstructured and open-ended. The observer tries to provide as complete and nonselective a description as possible. On the other end of the continuum are more structured and predefined methods that itemize, count, and categorize behavior. Here the investigator decides beforehand which behavior will be recorded and how frequently observations will be made. The investigator using structured observation is much more discriminating in choosing which behavior will be recorded and precisely how they are to be coded.[4]

One author classifies observational studies by the degree of structure in the environmental setting and the amount of structure imposed on the environment by the researcher:[5]

Research	Environment
1. Completely unstructured	Natural setting
2. Unstructured	Laboratory
3. Structured	Natural setting
4. Completely structured	Laboratory

The researcher conducting a class 1, completely unstructured, study would be in a natural or field setting endeavoring to adapt to the culture. A typical example would be an ethnographic study in which the researcher, as a participant-observer, becomes a part of the culture and describes in great detail everything surrounding the event or activity of interest. Donald Roy, in the widely used case in organizational behavior, "Banana Time," took a punch press job in a factory to describe the rituals that a small work group relied on to make their highly repetitive, monotonous work bearable.[6] With other purposes in mind, business researchers may use this type of study for hypothesis generation.

Class 4 studies—completely structured research—are at the opposite end of the continuum from completely unstructured field investigations. The research purpose of class 4 studies is to test hypotheses; therefore, a definitive plan for observing specific, operationalized behavior is known in advance. This requires a measuring instrument, called an **observational checklist,** analogous to a questionnaire. Checklists should possess a high degree of precision in defining relevant behavior or acts and have mutually exclusive and exhaustive categories. The coding is frequently closed, thereby simplifying data analysis. The subject groups being observed must be comparable and the laboratory conditions identical. The classic example of a class 4 study was Bales's investigation into group interaction.[7] Many team-building, decision-making, and assessment center studies follow this structural pattern.

The two middle classes emphasize the best characteristics of either researcher-imposed controls or the setting. In class 2, the researcher uses the facilities of a laboratory—videotape recording, two-way mirrors, props, and stage sets—to introduce more control into the environment while simultaneously reducing the time needed for observation. In contrast, a class 3 study takes advantage of a structured observational instrument in a natural setting.

Content Specification

Specific conditions, events, or activities that we want to observe determine the observational reporting system (and correspond to measurement questions). To specify the observation content, we should include both the major variables of interest and any other variables that may affect them. From this cataloging, we then select those items we plan to observe. For each variable chosen, we must provide an operational definition if there is any question of concept ambiguity or special meanings. Even if the concept is a common one, we must make certain that all observers agree on the measurement terms by which to record results. For example, we may agree that variable W will be reported by count, while variable Y will be counted and the effectiveness of its use judged qualitatively.

Observation may be at either a *factual* or an *inferential* level. Table 13–1 shows how we could separate the factual and inferential components of a salesperson's presentation. This table is suggestive only. It does not include many other variables that might be of interest, including data on customer purchase history; company, industry, and general economic conditions; the order in which sales arguments are presented; and specific words used to describe certain product characteristics. The particular content of observation will also be affected by the nature of the observation setting.

Observer Training

There are a few general guidelines for selection. The observer must have sufficient concentration powers to function in a setting full of distractions. The ability to remember the details of an experience is also an asset. There is also a need to select people who will be unobtrusive in the situation. An obviously attractive observer will be a distraction in some settings but ideal in others. The same can be said for age or ethnic background.

TABLE   13–1   Content of Observation: Factual Versus Inferential

Factual	Inferential
Introduction/identification of salesperson and customer.	Credibility of salesperson. Qualified status of customer.
Time and day of week.	Convenience for the customer. Welcoming attitude of the customer.
Product presented.	Customer interest in product.
Selling points presented per product.	Customer acceptance of selling points per product
Number of customer objections raised per product.	Customer concerns about features and benefits.
Salesperson's rebuttal of objection.	Effectiveness of salesperson's rebuttal attempts.
Salesperson's attempt to restore controls.	Effectiveness of salesperson's control attempt. Consequences for customer who prefers interaction.
Length of interview.	Customer's/salesperson's degree of enthusiasm for the interview.
Environmental factors interfering with the interview.	Level of distraction for the customer.
Customer purchase decision.	General evaluation of sales presentation skill.

If observation is at the surface level and involves a simple checklist or coding system, then experience is less important. Inexperience may even be an advantage if there is a risk that experienced observers may have preset convictions about the topic. Regardless, most observers are subject to fatigue, halo effects, and **observer drift,** a decay in reliability or validity over time that affects the coding of categories.[8] Only intensive videotaped training relieves these problems.

The observers should be thoroughly versed in the requirements of the specific study. Each observer should be informed of the outcomes sought and the precise content elements to be studied. Observer trials with the instrument and sample videotapes should be used until a high degree of reliability is apparent in their observations. When there are interpretative differences between observers, they should be reconciled.

Data Collection

The data collection plan specifies the details of the task. In essence it answers the questions *who, what, when,* and *how.*

Who Are the Targets?   What qualifies a subject to be observed? Must each subject meet a given criterion—those who initiate a specific action? Who are the contacts to gain entry (in an ethnographic study), the intermediary to help with introductions, the contacts to reach if conditions change or trouble develops? Who has responsibility for the various aspects of the study? Who fulfills the ethical responsibilities to the subjects?

What?   The characteristics of the observation must be set as sampling elements and units of analysis. This is achieved when an event-time dimension and "act" terms are defined. In **event sampling,** the researcher records selected behavior that answers the investigative questions. In **time sampling,** the researcher must choose among a time-point sample, continuous real-time measurement, or a time-interval sample. For a time-point sample, recording occurs at fixed points for a specified length. With continuous measurement, behavior or the elapsed time of the behavior is recorded. Like continuous measurement, time-interval sampling records every behavior in real time but counts the behavior only once during the interval.[9]

Assume the observer is instructed to observe a quality control inspection for ten minutes out of each hour (a duration of two minutes each for five times). Over a prolonged period, if the samples are drawn randomly, time sampling can give a good estimate of the pattern of activities. In a time-interval sampling of workers in a department, the outcome may be a judgment of how well the department is being supervised. In a study of sales presentations using continuous real-time sampling, the research outcome may be an assessment of a given salesperson's effectiveness or the effectiveness of different types of persuasive messages.

Other important dimensions are defined by *acts.* What constitutes an act is established by the needs of the study. It is the basic unit of observation, such as (1) a single expressed thought, (2) a physical movement, (3) a facial expression, or (4) a motor skill. Although acts may be well defined, they often present difficulties for the observer. A single statement from a sales presentation may include several thoughts about product advantages, a rebuttal to an objection about a feature, or some remark about a competitor. The observer is hard-pressed to sort out each thought, decide whether it represents a separate unit of observation, and then record it quickly enough to follow continued statements.

When?   Is the time of the study important, or can any time be used? In a study of out-of-stock conditions in a supermarket, the exact times of observation may be important. Inventory is shipped to the store on certain days only, and buying peaks occur on other days. The likelihood of a given product being out of stock is a function of both time-related activities.

How?   Will the data be directly observed? If there is more than one observer, how will they divide the task? How will the results be recorded for later analysis? How will the observers deal with various situations that may occur—when expected actions do not take place or when someone challenges the observer in the setting?

Observers face unlimited variations in conditions. Fortunately, most problems do not occur simultaneously. When the plans are thorough and the observers well trained, observational research is quite successful.

UNOBTRUSIVE MEASURES

Up to this point, our discussion has focused on direct observation as a traditional approach to data collection. Like surveys and experiments, some observational studies—particularly participant observation—require the observer to be physically present in the research situation. This contributes to a **reactivity response,** a phenomenon where subjects alter their behavior in response to the researcher. (You are familiar with the

CLOSE-UP

The design of an observational study follows the same pattern as other research. Once the researcher has specified the investigative questions, it is often apparent that the best way to conduct the study is through observation. Guidance for conducting an observation and translating the investigative question(s) into an observational checklist is the subject of this section. We first review the procedural steps and then explain how to create a checklist.

Most studies that use the observational method follow a general sequence of steps that parallel the research process. Here we adapt to the terminology of the observational method:

- Define the content of the study.
- Develop a data collection plan that identifies subjects, sampling strategy, and acts (operationalized as a checklist or coding scheme).
- Secure and train observers.
- Collect the data.
- Analyze the data.

In "Bringing Research to Life," we recounted a humorous incident in a quality control situation that used observation. Assume our concerns are more serious. We have limited resources, so the study will be small. Management is concerned about a deterioration of quality in its assembled product, security cameras, toward the end of each day. The management question is, "Why are products failing quality assurance in the afternoon?" The research question might be stated, "What factors affect the quality of assembled cameras?" Although we presume that management is correct about the time, we will allow the data to confirm this. The investigative questions could then include: "What is the variability due to changes in parts vendors? Inventory? Does the manufacturing pro-

cedure change during the day? Is it shift dependent? To what extent is the failure rate contingent on time? What is the role of workplace conditions? Is it linked to assembler performance?"

Further assume that through interviewing, we isolate the *content of the study* to assembler behavior in the natural environment. The major variables of interest will be operationalized from the assembler's job description and the environmental conditions of the assembly area.

The *observational targets* will be the assemblers and their *acts* (physical behavior consistent with the job description). We have chosen to sample during the late afternoon, initially, and we will use *time sampling* on a *continuous* basis. This allows us to record all relevant behavior and complete an environmental checklist. The observation will be *direct*, and we will operate from *concealment* using the one-way mirror on the door to the assembly area.

A tour of the assembly area reveals a rectangular room with east- and west-facing windows. The workstations run the length of the rectangle, splitting the room in half and facing north. Comfortable chairs are present, and parts bins are to the right of each workstation, requiring the assembler to turn westward to select parts. The windows have shades, and there is both general and task lighting.

The variables to be measured (measurement questions) were derived from the investigative questions on workplace conditions and assembler performance. Notes taken on the tour improved our understanding of contextual variables. By examining the workplace first, we can assess and begin to rule out environmental variables (lighting, temperature, noise, and other variables controlled by the production facility) before moving on to behavioral characteristics. Both checklists will be revised after pretesting. The *observational checklist* for the assembly environment features a range of measures from graphic rating scales to category scales. It is shown in Figure 13–2.

FIGURE   13–2   Environmental Observation Checklist

ProSec Electronics: Assembly Observational Study

Time Stamp: _____   **Observer:** _____

Lights: General Area ☐ On ☐ Off ☐ Malfunction   **Comments:**

                         Workstations ☐ On ☐ Off ☐ Malfunction

Lighting (general)   Irregularly   Uniformly   Uniformly   Uniformly   Irregularly
                         Bright   Bright   Even   Dim   Dim
                         ☐   ☐   ☐   ☐   ☐

                              (Note locations for discrepancies)

Shades (Estimate and color in)   **Temperature**

               (West)   (East)   Cold   Standard   Hot

                                                   ├────────┼────────┼────────┤
                                                   65°   70°   75°   80°

Example   % Used _____ % Used _____
70%

Cleanliness Very ├───┼───┼───┼───┤ Very   Very ├───┼───┼───┼───┤ Very
(Circle)   Clean 1   2   3   4   5 Dirty   Clean 1   2   3   4   5 Dirty
                        General Area   **Workstation**
                                                   (Note individual deficiencies below)

Noise Level   Quiet   Loud
(decibels: mark scale per reading)   ├────────┼────────┤
                              50   75   100

Assemblers at Workstations during Observation   Virginia ☐ Yes ☐ No
                                                       Bertha   ☐ Yes ☐ No
                                                       Gladys   ☐ Yes ☐ No
                                                       Maria   ☐ Yes ☐ No
                                                       Helen   ☐ Yes ☐ No
                                                       Roberta ☐ Yes ☐ No

Nonassembly Personnel in Room: **Activities of Nonassemblers:**

Comments:

(continued)

The assemblers are subject to periodic and unscheduled supervisory visits and normal workplace rules for a drug-free environment. Nevertheless, the foremost ethical concern is restricting the observations to assembly activities. Using the company's cameras, we will run one on wide angle for context and the other zoomed-in to capture individual assembler behavior on a *time-interval* sampling. The observation will be videotaped so a consistent stimulus may be used to train observers, pretest and refine the checklists, and have a benchmark for later comparison. The behavioral checklist will be devised after studying the job descriptions and viewing the preliminary videotape.

historic research at Western Electric and the so-called Hawthorne effect and to the reactions interviewers produce in respondents that bias the findings of a study.)

Webb and his colleagues have given us an insight into some very innovative observational procedures that can be both nonreactive and inconspicuously applied. Called **unobtrusive measures,** this set of approaches encourages creative and imaginative forms of indirect observation, archival searches, and variations on simple and contrived observation.[10] Of particular interest are measures involving indirect observation based on **physical traces** that include *erosion* (measures of wear) and *accretion* (measures of deposit).

Natural erosion measures are illustrated by the frequency of replacement of vinyl floor tile in front of museum exhibits as an indicator of exhibit popularity. The study of wear and tear on book pages is a measure of library book use. Counting the remaining brochures in a car dealer's display rack after a favorable magazine review suggests consumer interest.

Physical traces also include natural accretion such as discovering the listenership of radio stations by observing car radio settings as autos are brought in for service. Another type of unobtrusive study involves estimating liquor and magazine consumption by collecting and analyzing family trash. An interesting application compared beer consumption reports acquired through interviews with the findings of sampled trash. If the interview data were valid, the consumption figures for the area were at 15 percent. However, the validity was questioned when the beer can count from trash supported a 77 percent consumption rate.[11]

William Rathje is a professor of archaeology at the University of Arizona and founder of the Garbage Project in Tucson. His study of trash, refuse, rubbish, and litter resulted in the subdiscipline that the *Oxford English Dictionary* has called *garbology.* By excavating landfills, he has gained insight into human behavior and cultural patterns—sometimes sorting the contents of up to 150 coded categories. His previous studies have shown that "people will describe their behavior to satisfy cultural expectations, like the mothers in Tucson who unanimously claimed they made their baby food from scratch, but whose garbage told a very different tale."[12]

Physical trace methods present a strong argument for use based on their ability to provide low-cost access to frequency, attendance, and incidence data without contamination from other methods or reactivity from subjects. They are excellent "triangulation" devices for cross-validation. Thus, they work well as supplements to other methods. Designing an unobtrusive study can test a researcher's creativity, and one must be especially careful about inferences made from the findings. Erosion results may have occurred because of wear factors not considered, and accretion material may be the result of selective deposit or survival.

Summary

Observation is one of the few options available for studying records, mechanical processes, lower animals, small children, and complex interactive processes. We can gather data as the event occurs and can come closer to capturing the whole event than with interrogation. On the other hand, we have to be present to catch the event or have some recording device on the scene to do the job.

Observation includes a variety of monitoring situations that cover nonbehavioral and behavioral activities.

The strengths of observation as a data collection method include (1) securing information about people or activities that cannot be derived from experiments or surveys, (2) avoiding respondent filtering and forgetting, (3) securing environmental context information, (4) optimizing the naturalness of the setting, and (5) reducing obtrusiveness.

Observation may be limited by (1) the difficulty of waiting for long periods to capture the relevant phenomena, (2) the expense of observer costs and equipment, (3) the reliability of inferences from surface indicators, (4) the problems of quantification and disproportionately large records, and (5) limitation to present activities and inferences about cognitive processes.

We can classify observation in terms of the observer-subject relationship. This relationship may be viewed from three perspectives: (1) Is the observation direct or indirect? (2) Is the observer's presence known or unknown? (3) Is the observer a participant or nonparticipant?

The design of an observational study follows the same general pattern as other research. Observational studies fall into four general types based on the degree of structure and the nature of the observational environment. The researcher must define the content of the study; develop a data collection plan that identifies subjects, sampling strategy, and "acts" (often operationalized as a checklist or coding scheme); secure and train observers; and launch the study.

Unobtrusive measures offer an unusual and creative approach to reducing reactivity in observational research by indirect observation and other methods. Measures of erosion and accretion serve as ways to confirm the findings from other methods or operate as singular data sources.

Key Terms

concealment	observation
event sampling	direct
extralinguistic behavior	indirect
linguistic behavior	simple
nonverbal behavior	systematic

observational checklist
observer drift
participant observation
physical condition analysis
physical trace
process (activity) analysis

reactivity response
record analysis
spatial relationships
time sampling
unobtrusive measures

**Discussion
Questions**

1. Compare the advantages and disadvantages of the survey to those of observation. Under which circumstances could you make a case for using observation?

2. What ethical risks are involved in observation? In the use of unobtrusive measures?

3. The observer-subject relationship is an important consideration in the design of observational studies. What kind of relationship would you recommend in each of the following cases?

    a. Observations of professional conduct in the classroom by the student author of a course evaluation guide

    b. Observation of retail shoppers by a researcher who is interested in determining customer purchase time by type of good purchased

    c. Observation of a focus group interview by a client

    d. Effectiveness of individual farm worker organizers in their efforts to organize employees of grape growers

4. Assume you are to set up an observational study in which you will observe five students engaging in a discussion of the question, "How should students organize a network that will be beneficial for postcollege employment connections?"

    a. What are the varieties of information that might be observed in such a setting?

    b. Select a limited number of content areas for study, and operationally define the observation acts that should be measured.

5. Develop a checklist to be used by observers in the previous study.

    a. Determine how many observers you need, and assign two or three to a specific observation task.

    b. Compare the results of the group members' checklists for stability of recorded perceptions.

6. Based on present or past work experience, suggest problems that could be resolved by using observation-based data.

7. You wish to analyze the pedestrian traffic that passes a given store in a major shopping center. You are interested in determining how many shoppers pass by this store, and you would like to classify these shoppers on various relevant dimensions. Any information you secure should be obtainable from observation alone.

    a. What other information might you find useful to observe?

    b. How would you decide what information to collect?

     c. Devise the operational definitions you would need.

     d. What would you say in your instructions to the observers you plan to use?

     e. How might you sample this shopper traffic?

  8. Distinguish between the following:

     a. The relative value of communication and of observation

     b. Nonverbal, linguistic, and extralinguistic analysis

     c. Factual and inferential observation

Reference Notes

1. K. E. Weick, "Systematic Observational Methods," in *The Handbook of Social Psychology,* vol. 2, eds. G. Lindzey and E. Aronson (Reading, MA: Addison-Wesley, 1968), p. 360.
2. R. Bales, *Interaction Process Analysis* (Reading, MA: Addison-Wesley, 1950).
3. Weick, "Systematic Observational Methods," p. 381.
4. Louise H. Kidder and Charles M. Judd, *Research Methods in Social Relations,* 5th ed. (New York: Holt, Rinehart & Winston, 1986), p. 292.
5. Kenneth D. Bailey, *Methods of Social Science,* 2nd ed. (New York: Free Press, 1982), pp. 252–54.
6. Donald F. Roy, " 'Banana Time,' Job Satisfaction, and Informal Interaction," *Human Organization* 18, no. 4 (Winter 1959–60), pp. 151–68.
7. Robert F. Bales, *Personality and Interpersonal Behavior* (New York: Holt, Rinehart & Winston, 1970).
8. Kidder and Judd, *Research Methods in Social Relations,* pp. 298–99.
9. Ibid., p. 291.
10. E. J. Webb, D. T. Campbell, R. D. Schwartz, L. Sechrest, and J. B. Grove, *Nonreactive Measures in the Social Sciences,* 2nd ed. (Boston: Houghton Mifflin, 1981).
11. W. L. Rathje and W. W. Hughes, "The Garbage Project as a Nonreactive Approach: Garbage in . . . Garbage Out?" In *Perspectives on Attitude Assessment: Surveys and Their Alternatives,* eds. H. W. Sinaiko and L. A. Broedling (Washington, D.C.: Smithsonian Institution, 1975).
12. William Grimes, "If It's Scientific, It's 'Garbology,'" *International Herald Tribune,* August 15–16, 1992, p. 17.

Suggested Readings

1. Bailey, Kenneth D. *Methods of Social Research,* 4th ed. New York: Free Press, 1994. Includes a thorough discussion of observational strategies.
2. Bales, Robert F. *Personality and Interpersonal Behavior.* New York: Holt, Rinehart & Winston, 1970. From a pioneer in interaction process analysis, a model for structured observation, checklists, and coding schemes.
3. Kidder, Louise H., and Charles M. Judd. *Research Methods in Social Relations,* 5th ed. New York: Holt, Rinehart & Winston, 1986. Chapter 12 gives a fine overview of observational types and sampling plans.
4. Webb, E. J., D. T. Campbell, R. D. Schwartz, L. Sechrest, and J. B. Grove. *Nonreactive Measures in the Social Sciences,* 2nd ed. Boston: Houghton Mifflin, 1981. The classic source of information on all aspects of unobtrusive measures. Excellent examples and ideas for planning projects.

CHAPTER

14 EXPERIMENTATION

CHAPTER NAVIGATION

BRINGING
RESEARCH TO LIFE

"Let me put my hand on your tummy."

"What?"

"Oh, did I wake you?"

"You know you did."

"I want to put my hand on your tummy."

"Of course, you woke me. What time is it? Midnight? . . . All right. Place your hand on my abdomen." All he felt was the arrhythmic pulsating of peristalsis.

"It's not time," she said. "May I go back to sleep?"

"Dorrie, hon', I've been thinking. . . ."

"What?"

"I've been thinking . . . we should not wait. We should give them names . . . now."

"How will we know the right names?"

"Suppose we call them Terry and Robin. They don't have to be boys or girls. The names will fit, don't you see? Either way, the names will fit."

They lay side by side in the darkness, in silence. Silence maybe meant he was thinking and would rouse her again. No use fighting to regain sleep. Hear him out. "Why the hurry, Jason?"

"I want you to talk to them. I want you to say, 'Robin, dearest, this is your mommy,' and 'Terry, your mommy and daddy love you terrifically much.'"

"Nice. May I go back to sleep?"

Again he was silent in the darkness. Then, "This has possibilities, you know. . . ."

"Possibilities." Please, no possibilities. No twilight zone ideas, grasped at in the gray area between conscious and unconscious, wakefulness and sleep, and proposed with utter seriousness.

"Say, you read poetry to Robin. You say, `Robin, this is for you, and it is by a very famous poet, William Blake. . . .'

" 'Tyger, tyger, burning bright. . . .'

"That's the idea. Say you read poetry to Robin and maybe sing to Terry. Well, maybe it is not so good an idea letting you sing to little Terry, because you do not sing nearly as well as you read poetry.

We would want the differential treatments to be delivered with more or less equal efficacy, wouldn't we? So, maybe you should read Shakespeare to Terry and Blake to Robin, and then, in puberty, we will see if one has a preference for Shakespeare over Blake."

She rolled over on an elbow. "I see. You are suggesting, that if the twins are monozygous . . . share the same genetic makeup . . . they will differentially emphasize contrasting environmental stimuli administered during the earliest development of their central nervous systems."

"Yes."

"You woke me for this?"

"Yes, whatever treatment . . . stimuli . . . remarks . . . you direct to them through internal dialogue, such as poetry by Blake and Shakespeare, will fall on almost identically genetically endowed organisms. . . . Of course, I would have to trust you to adhere to the experimental protocols we devise."

He did not hear her angry gasp.

When she regained her composure, she ventured, "Following your line of thought, perhaps Blake and Shakespeare would not be good alternative treatments, since they wrote in different styles and were not contemporaries . . . assuming we take all of this seriously . . . which I am certain I do not do."

"I am not sure I have heard you express equal enthusiasm for Blake and Shakespeare, so you will surely bias the administration of the treatment in favor of Blake, your favorite."

"Let me understand this, sweetheart." She was fully awake now and sitting up. "I might not stick to the protocols, and you do not trust me to avoid bias in administering the 'treatments' with equal enthusiasm."

"Well, at the conscious level, I have to trust you, because you are a doctor . . .

". . . and my wife and life's companion . . . and the parent of *our* children . . .

". . . and you understand the importance of nice clean experimentation. But, yes, biases might be present at the subconscious level and remain difficult to control."

(continued)

She sat up. "Wanting to call the babies by name is a sentimental impulse. My heart says it is sweet of you to want me to talk to them, but my brain says this is a cruel experiment. Nevertheless, let's talk about 'nice clean experimentation,' as you call it.

"Jason, *Tales from the Petri Dish* may have ethicists and the public spinning, but we are talking about our children here, not genetically created identical twin embryos, not even gene-spliced tomato experiments. First, you cannot differentially direct treatment to one or the other. Never—no, not in my wildest dreams—should I believe one of my unborn babies knows he is Robin or Terry. Second, when they reach an age when they attend nursery school, we will totally lose our ability to differentially apply stimuli. . . ."

"Would you consider home schooling?"

"I'm a public health doctor, Jason. Doctors don't work at home! That's why we have hospitals! And, third, I would have no way, after their birth, to know I am not reading Blake to the very one to whom I was reading Shakespeare in the womb, and vice versa."

"OK, OK. No need to get huffy."

"Jason," she struggled for self-control, "Jason, I am experiencing the joys and pains of a multiple pregnancy. There are certain hormonal changes . . . yes . . . which I have heard you indelicately call 'gland things,' but I am a professional person and am well aware of my responsibilities—to the public, to you, to my unborn children, and to myself—to maintain my emotional equilibrium. So lay off, Jason!"

"I'm sorry I woke you. OK?"

"Waking me is only part of the problem. It's what you woke me for—this lame idea that just popped into your head, this notion to manipulate your own offspring, which you forced on me without any critical thinking in advance."

"Well, I was curious, that's all. I was brainstorming."

"If you were doing research in the university or hospital, you would not float such a lame idea, because a human subjects committee would roast you for such an ethically questionable idea, starting with . . . I don't know . . . starting with whether unborn children are able to give informed consent, whether I am able to give consent on their behalf, and ending up, maybe, by asking what right you have to try to alter the artistic sensibilities of anyone's offspring. You don't get away with crazy ideas like this in business research, do you?"

There was a long silence. "Swell," he said. "Can we get back to sleep, then?"

"Let's hope so. But let me explain something. Experimentation is not about ideas that pop into your head because you cannot sleep." She pulled his face close, so that by the light shining in from a street lamp he could see how rigid her lips were. "Experimentation is about needing to know something so badly that you cannot live without an answer, because others cannot live without an answer.

"This year I am part of a program to administer treatments to 150 mortally ill subjects. They know that 75 of them are receiving an experimental treatment and 75 receiving colored saline solution. It's a double-blind experiment, so I have no idea who is receiving the placebo.

"Do you have an idea what it means to know you are withholding the promise of life from 75 human beings? Do you grasp what it means to look into their eyes and have them look back and maybe cry, so an unspoken message passes— 'Don't let me die.'

"This is not what I expected in medical school, Jason. I expected, then, to do my best to save every life. But my fellow doctors are counting on me for proof, Jason, so they may justify the treatment and request funding. I am not playing games with people, Jason. I am letting people die so others may live.

"What experimentation is about is not having a brainstorm, not scratching a mental itch. Experimentation is responsibility."

WHAT IS EXPERIMENTATION?

Why do events occur under some conditions and not under others? Research methods that answer such questions are called "causal" methods. (Recall the discussion of causality in Chapter 6.) Ex post facto research designs, where a researcher interviews respondents or observes what is or what has been, also have the potential for discovering causality. The distinction between these methods and experimentation is that the researcher is required to accept the world as it is found, whereas an experiment allows the researcher to alter systematically the variables of interest and observe what changes follow.

In this chapter we define experimentation and discuss its advantages and disadvantages. An outline for the conduct of an experiment is presented as a vehicle to introduce important concepts. The questions of internal and external validity are also examined: Does the experimental treatment determine the observed difference, or was some extraneous variable responsible? And, how can one generalize the results of the study across times, settings, and persons? The chapter concludes with a review of the most widely accepted designs and a "Close-Up" example.

Experiments are studies involving intervention by the researcher beyond that required for measurement. The usual intervention is to manipulate some variable in a setting and observe how it affects the subjects being studied (e.g., people or physical entities). The researcher manipulates the independent or explanatory variable and then observes whether the hypothesized dependent variable is affected by the intervention.

An example of such an intervention is the study of bystanders and thieves.[1] In this experiment, students were asked to come to an office where they had an opportunity to see a fellow student steal some money from a receptionist's desk. A confederate of the experimenter, of course, did the stealing. The major hypothesis concerned whether people observing a theft would be more likely to report it (1) if they observed the crime alone or (2) if they were in the company of someone else.

There is at least one **independent variable (IV)** and one **dependent variable (DV)** in a causal relationship. We hypothesize that in some way the IV "causes" the DV to occur. The independent or explanatory variable in our example was the state of either being alone when observing the theft or being in the company of another person. The dependent variable was whether the subjects reported observing the crime. The results suggested that bystanders were more likely to report the theft if they observed it alone rather than in another person's company.

On what grounds did the researchers conclude that people who were alone were more likely to report crimes observed than people in the company of others? Three types of evidence form the basis for this conclusion. First, there must be an agreement between independent and dependent variables. The presence or absence of one is associated with the presence or absence of the other. Thus, more reports of the theft (DV) came from lone observers (IV_1) than from paired observers (IV_2).

Second, beyond the correlation of independent and dependent variables, the time order of the occurrence of the variables must be considered. The dependent variable should not precede the independent variable. They may occur almost simultaneously, or the independent variable should occur before the dependent variable. This requirement is of little concern since it is unlikely that people could report a theft before observing it.

The third important support for the conclusion comes when researchers are confident that *other extraneous variables did not influence the dependent variable.* To ensure that these other variables are not the source of influence, researchers control their ability to confound the planned comparison. Under laboratory conditions, standardized conditions for control can be arranged. The crime observation experiment was carried out in a laboratory set up as an office. The entire event was staged without the observers' knowledge. The receptionist whose money was to be stolen was instructed to speak and act in a specific way. Only the receptionist, observers, and the "criminal" were in the office. The same process was repeated with each trial of the experiment.

While such controls are important, further precautions are needed so the results achieved reflect the influence of the independent variable alone on the dependent variable.

AN EVALUATION OF EXPERIMENTS

Advantages

When we elaborated on the concept of cause in Chapter 6, we said causality could not be proved with certainty but the probability of one variable being linked to another could be established convincingly. The experiment comes closer than any primary data collection method to accomplishing this goal. The foremost advantage is the researcher's ability to manipulate the independent variable. The probability that changes in the dependent variable are a function of that manipulation consequently increases. Also, a control group serves as a comparison to assess the existence and potency of the manipulation.

The second advantage of the experiment is that contamination from extraneous variables can be controlled more effectively than in other designs. This helps the researcher isolate experimental variables and evaluate their impact over time. Third, the convenience and cost of experimentation are superior to other methods. These benefits allow the experimenter opportunistic scheduling of data collection and the flexibility to adjust variables and conditions that evoke extremes not observed under routine circumstances. In addition, the experimenter can assemble combinations of variables for testing rather than having to search for their fortuitous appearance in the study environment.

Fourth, **replication**— repeating an experiment with different subject groups and conditions—leads to the discovery of an average effect of the independent variable across people, situations, and times. Fifth, researchers can use naturally occurring events and, to some extent, field experiments to reduce subjects' perceptions of the researcher as a source of intervention or deviation in their everyday lives.

Disadvantages

The artificiality of the laboratory is arguably the primary disadvantage of the experimental method. However, many subjects' perceptions of a contrived environment can be improved by investment in the facility. Second, generalization from nonprobability samples can pose problems despite random assignment. The extent to which a study can be generalized from college students to managers or executives is open to question. And when an experiment is unsuccessfully disguised, volunteer subjects are often those with the most interest in the topic.

Third, despite the low costs of experimentation, many applications of experimentation far outrun the budgets for other primary data collection methods. Fourth, experimentation is most effectively targeted at problems of the present or immediate future. Experimental studies of the past are not feasible, and studies about intentions or predictions are difficult. Finally, management research is often concerned with the study of people. There are limits to the types of manipulation and controls that are ethical.

CONDUCTING AN EXPERIMENT[2]

In a well-executed experiment, researchers must complete a series of activities to carry out their craft successfully. Although the experiment is the premier scientific methodology for establishing causation, the resourcefulness and creativeness of the researcher are needed to make the experiment live up to its potential. In this section, we discuss seven activities the researcher must accomplish to make the endeavor successful:

1. Select relevant variables.
2. Specify the level(s) of the treatment.
3. Control the experimental environment.
4. Choose the experimental design.
5. Select and assign the subjects.
6. Pilot-test, revise, and test.
7. Analyze the data.

Selecting Relevant Variables

Throughout the book we have discussed the idea that a research problem can be conceptualized as a hierarchy of questions starting with a management problem. The researcher's task is to translate an amorphous problem into the question or hypothesis that best states the objectives of the research. Depending on the complexity of the problem, investigative questions and additional hypotheses can be created to address specific facets of the study or data that need to be gathered. Further, we mentioned that a **hypothesis** is a relational statement because it describes a relationship between two or more variables. It must also be **operationalized,** a term we used earlier in discussing how concepts are transformed into variables to make them measurable and subject to testing.

Consider the following research question as we work through the seven points:

Does a sales presentation that describes product benefits in the introduction of the message lead to improved retention of product knowledge?

Since a hypothesis is a tentative statement—a speculation—about the outcome of the study, it might take this form:

> Sales presentations in which the benefits module is placed in the introduction of a 12-minute message produce better retention of product knowledge than those where the benefits module is placed in the conclusion.

The researchers' challenges at this step are to (1) select variables that are the best operational representations of the original concepts, (2) determine how many variables to test, and (3) select or design appropriate measures for them. The researchers would need to select variables that best operationalize the concepts *sales presentation, product benefits, retention,* and *product knowledge.* The product's classification and the nature of the intended audience should also be defined. In addition, the term *better* could be operationalized statistically by means of a significance test.

The number of variables in an experiment is constrained by the project budget, the time allocated, the availability of appropriate controls, and the number of subjects being tested. For statistical reasons, there must be more subjects than variables.[3]

The selection of measures for testing requires a thorough review of the available literature and instruments. In addition, measures must be adapted to the unique needs of the research situation without compromising their intended purpose or original meaning.

Specifying the Levels of Treatment

The **treatment levels** of the independent variable are the distinctions the researcher makes between different aspects of the treatment condition. For example, if salary is hypothesized to have an effect on employees exercising stock purchase options, it might be divided into high, middle, and low ranges to represent three levels of the independent variable.

The levels assigned to an independent variable should be based on simplicity and common sense. In the sales presentation example, the experimenter should not select 8 minutes and 10 minutes as the starting points to represent the two treatment levels if the average message about the product is 12 minutes long. Similarly, if the benefits module is placed in the first and second minutes of the presentation, observable differences may not occur because the levels are too close together. Thus, in the first trial, the researcher is likely to position the midpoint of the benefits module the same interval from the end of the introduction as from the end of the conclusion.

Under an entirely different hypothesis, several levels of the independent variable may be needed to test order-of-presentation effects. Here we use only two. Alternatively a **control group** could provide a base level for comparison. The control group is composed of subjects who are not exposed to the independent variable(s), in contrast to those who receive the **experimental treatment** [manipulation of the independent variable(s)].

Controlling the Experimental Environment

Chapter 2 discussed the nature of extraneous variables and the need for their control. In our sales presentation experiment, extraneous variables can appear as differences in age, gender, race, dress, communications competence, and many other characteristics of the presenter, the message, or the situation. These have potential for distorting the effect of the treatment on the dependent variable and must be controlled or eliminated. However, at this stage, we are principally concerned with **environmental control,** holding constant the physical environment of the experiment. The introduction of the experiment to the subjects and the instructions would likely be videotaped for consistency. The arrangement of the room, the time of administration, the experimenter's contact with the subjects, and so forth, must all be consistent across each administration of the experiment.

Other forms of control involve subjects and experimenters. When subjects do not know if they are receiving the experimental treatment, they are said to be **blind.** When the experimenters do not know if they are giving the treatment to the experimental group or to the control, the experiment is **double blind.** Both approaches control unwanted complications such as subjects' reactions to expected conditions or experimenter influence.

Choosing the Experimental Design

Unlike the general descriptors of research design that were discussed in Chapter 6, experimental designs are unique to the experimental method. They serve as positional and statistical plans to designate relationships between experimental treatments and the experimenter's observations or measurement points in the temporal scheme of the study. Many of these designs are diagrammed and described later in this chapter. In the conduct of the experiment, the researchers apply their knowledge to select one design that is best suited to the goals of the research. Judicious selection of the design improves the probability that the observed change in the dependent variable was caused by the manipulation of the independent variable and not by another factor. It simultaneously strengthens the generalizability of results beyond the experimental setting.

Selecting and Assigning Subjects

The subjects selected for the experiment should be representative of the population to which the researcher wishes to generalize. This may seem self-evident, but we have witnessed several decades of experimentation with college sophomores that contradict that assumption. In the sales presentation example, corporate buyers, purchasing managers, or others in a decision-making capacity would provide better generalizing power than undergraduate college students *if* the product in question was targeted for industrial use rather than to the consumer.

The procedure for random sampling of experimental subjects is similar in principle to the selection of respondents for a survey (we discussed random sampling in Chapter 9). The researcher first prepares a sampling frame and then assigns the subjects for the experiment to groups using a randomization technique. Systematic sampling may be used if the sampling frame is free from any form of periodicity that parallels the sampling ratio. Since the sampling frame is often small, experimental subjects are recruited; thus they are a self- selecting sample. However, if randomization is used, those assigned to the experimental group are likely to be similar to those assigned to the control group. **Random assignment** to the groups is required to make the groups as comparable as possible with respect to the dependent variable.

Randomization does not guarantee that if a pretest of the groups was conducted before the treatment condition, the groups would be pronounced identical; but it is an assurance that those differences remaining are randomly distributed. In our example, we would need three randomly assigned groups—one for each of the two treatments and one for the control group.

When it is not possible to randomly assign subjects to groups, **matching** may be used. Matching employs a nonprobability quota sampling approach. The object of matching is to have each experimental and control subject matched on every characteristic used in the research. This becomes more cumbersome as the number of variables and groups in the study increases. Since the characteristics of concern are only those that are correlated with the treatment condition or the dependent variable, they are easier to identify, control, and match.[4] In the sales presentation experiment, if a large part of the sample was composed of businesswomen who had recently completed communications training, we would not want the characteristics of gender, business experience, and communication training to be disproportionately assigned to one group.

Some authorities suggest a **quota matrix** as the most efficient means of visualizing the matching process.[5] In Figure 14–1, one-third of the subjects from each cell of the matrix would be assigned to each of the three groups. If matching does not alleviate the assignment problem, a combination of matching, randomization, and increasing the sample size would be used.

Pilot Testing, Revising, and Testing

The procedures for this stage are similar to those of other forms of primary data collection. Pilot testing is intended to reveal errors in the design and improper control of extraneous or environmental conditions. Pretesting the instruments permits refinement before the final test. This is the researcher's best opportunity to revise scripts, look for control problems with laboratory conditions, and scan the environment for factors that might confound the results. In field experiments, researchers are sometimes caught off guard by events that have a dramatic effect on subjects: the test marketing of a competitor's product announced before an experiment, or a reduction in force, reorganization, or merger before a crucial organizational intervention. The experiment should be timed so subjects are not sensitized to the independent variable by factors in the environment.

Analyzing the Data

If adequate planning and pretesting have occurred, the experimental data will take an order and structure uncommon to surveys and unstructured observational studies. It is not that data from experiments are easy to analyze; they are simply more conveniently arranged because of the levels of the treatment condition, pretests and posttests, and the group structure. The choice of statistical techniques is commensurately simplified.

Researchers have several measurement and instrument options with experiments. Among them are (1) observational techniques and coding schemes, (2) paper-and-pencil tests, (3) self-report instruments with open or closed questions, (4) scaling techniques (e.g., Likert scales, semantic differentials, Q-sort), and (5)

FIGURE   14–1   Quota Matrix Example

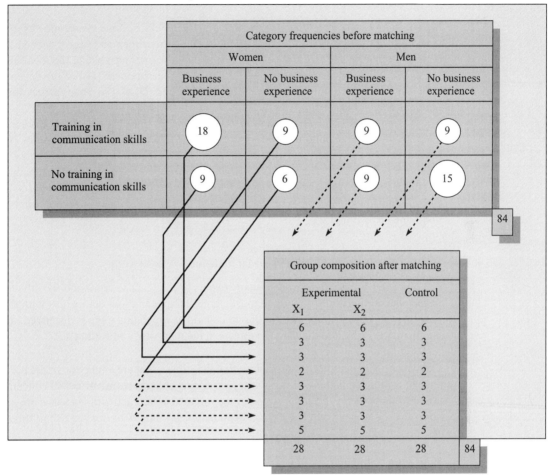

physiological measures (e.g., galvanic skin response, EKG, voice pitch analysis, eye dilation).

VALIDITY IN EXPERIMENTATION

Even when an experiment is the ideal research design, it is not without problems. There is always a question about whether the results are true. We have previously defined validity as whether a measure accomplishes its claims. While there are several different types of validity, here only the two major varieties are considered: **internal validity**—do the conclusions we draw about a demonstrated experimental relationship truly imply cause? **External validity**—does an observed causal relationship generalize across persons, settings, and times?[6] Each type of validity has specific threats we need to guard against.

Internal Validity   Among the many threats to internal validity, we consider seven.

History   During the time that an experiment is taking place, some events may occur that confuse the relationship being studied. In many experimental designs, we take a control measurement (O_1) of the dependent variable before introducing the manipulation (X). After the manipulation, we take an after-measurement (O_2) of the dependent variable. Then the difference between O_1 and O_2 is the change that the manipulation has caused.

A company's management may wish to find the best way to educate its workers about the financial condition of the company before this year's labor negotiations. To assess the value of such an effort, managers give employees a test on their knowledge of the company's finances (O_1). Then they present the educational campaign (X) to these employees, after which they again measure the knowledge level (O_2). This design, known as a preexperiment because it is not a very strong design, can be diagrammed as follows:

$$O_1 \qquad X \qquad O_2$$

Pretest   Manipulation   Posttest

Between O_1 and O_2, however, many events could occur to confound the effects of the education effort. A newspaper article might appear about companies with financial problems, a union meeting might be held at which this topic is discussed, or another occurrence could distort the effects of the company's education test.

Maturation   Changes may also occur within the subject that are a function of the passage of time and are not specific to any particular event. These are of special concern when the study covers a long time, but they may also be factors in tests that are as short as an hour or two. A subject can become hungry, bored, or tired in a short time, and this condition can affect response results.

Testing   The process of taking a test can affect the scores of a second test. The mere experience of taking the first test can have a learning effect that influences the results of the second test.

Instrumentation   This threat to internal validity results from changes between observations, in measuring instrument or in observer. Using different questions at each measurement is an obvious source of potential trouble, but using different observers or interviewers also threatens validity. There can even be an instrumentation problem if the same observer is used for all measurements. Observer experience, boredom, fatigue, and anticipation of results can all distort the results of separate observations.

Selection   An important threat to internal validity is the differential selection of subjects for experimental and control groups. Validity considerations require that the groups be equivalent in every respect. If subjects are randomly assigned to experimental and control groups, this selection problem can be largely overcome. Additionally, matching the members of the groups on key factors can enhance the equivalence of the groups.

Statistical Regression   This factor operates especially when groups have been selected by their extreme scores. Suppose we measure the output of all workers in a department for a few days before an experiment and then conduct the experiment with only those workers in the top 25 percent and bottom 25 percent of productivity scores. No matter what is done between O_1 and O_2, there is a strong tendency for the average of the high scores at O_1 to decline at O_2 and for the low scores at O_1 to increase. This tendency results from imperfect measurement that, in effect, records some persons abnormally high and abnormally low at O_1. In the second measurement, members of both groups score more closely to their long-run mean scores.

Experiment Mortality   This occurs when the composition of the study groups changes during the test. Attrition is especially likely in the experimental group, and with each dropout, the group changes. Because members of the control group are not affected by the testing situation, they are less likely to withdraw. In a compensation incentive study, some employees might not like the change in compensation method and withdraw from the test group; this action could distort the comparison with the control group that has continued working under the established system, perhaps without knowing a test is under way.

All the threats mentioned to this point are generally, but not always, dealt with adequately in experiments by random assignment. However, five added threats to internal validity are independent of whether one randomizes.[7] The first three have the effect of equalizing experimental and control groups.

1. *Diffusion or imitation of treatment.* If people in the experimental and control groups talk, then those in the control group may learn of the treatment, eliminating the difference between the groups.
2. *Compensatory equalization.* Where the experimental treatment is much more desirable, there may be an administrative reluctance to deprive the control group members. Compensatory actions for the control groups may confound the experiment.
3. *Compensatory rivalry.* This may occur when members of the control group know they are in the control group. This may generate competitive pressures, causing the control group members to try harder.
4. *Resentful demoralization of the disadvantaged.* When the treatment is desirable and the experiment is obtrusive, control group members may become resentful of their deprivation and lower their cooperation and output.
5. *Local history.* The regular history effect already mentioned impacts both experimental and control groups alike. However, when one assigns all experimental persons to one group session and all control people to another, there is a chance for some idiosyncratic event to confound results. This problem can be handled by administering treatments to individuals or small groups that are randomly assigned to experimental or control sessions.

External Validity

Internal validity factors cause confusion about whether the experimental treatment (*X*) or extraneous factors are the source of observation differences. In contrast, external validity is concerned with the interaction of the experimental treatment with other factors and the resulting impact on abilities to generalize to (and across) times, settings, or persons. Among the major threats to external validity are the following interactive possibilities.

The Reactivity of Testing on *X*   The reactive effect is one of sensitizing subjects by the pretest so they respond to the experimental stimulus in a different way. A before-measurement of the level of knowledge about the ecology programs of a company will often sensitize the subject to the various experimental communication efforts that might then be made about the company. This before-measurement effect can be particularly significant in attitude studies.

Interaction of Selection and *X*   The process by which test subjects are selected for an experiment may be a threat to external validity. The population from which one selects subjects may not be the same as the population to which one wishes to generalize results. Suppose you use a selected group of workers in one department for the test of the piecework incentive system. The question may remain about whether you can extrapolate the results to all production workers. Or consider a study in which you ask a cross-section of a population to participate in an experiment, but a substantial number refuse. If you do the experiment only with those who agree to participate, can the results be generalized to the total population?

Other Reactive Factors   The experimental settings themselves may have a biasing effect on a subject's response to *X*. An artificial setting can obviously give results that are not representative of larger populations. Suppose the workers who are given the incentive pay are moved to a different work area to separate them from the control group. These new conditions alone could create a strong reactive condition.

If subjects know they are participating in an experiment, there may be a tendency to role-play in a way that distorts the effects of *X*. Another reactive effect is the possible interaction between *X* and subject characteristics. An incentive pay proposal may be more effective with persons in one type of job, with a certain skill level, or with a certain personality trait.

Problems of internal validity can be solved by the careful design of experiments, but this is less true for problems of external validity. External validity is largely a matter of generalization, which, in a logical sense, is an inductive process of extrapolating beyond the data collected. In generalizing, we estimate the factors that can be ignored and that will interact with the experimental variable. Assume the closer two events are in time, space, and measurement, the more likely they are to follow the same laws. As a rule of thumb, first seek internal validity. Try to secure as much external validity as is compatible with the internal validity requirements by making experimental conditions as similar as possible to conditions under which the results will apply.

EXPERIMENTAL RESEARCH DESIGNS

The many experimental designs vary widely in their power to control contamination of the relationship between independent and dependent variables. The most widely accepted designs are based on this characteristic of control: (1) preexperiments, (2) true experiments, and (3) field experiments. (See Figure 14–2.)

FIGURE   14–2   Key to Design Symbols

X	An X represents the introduction of an experimental stimulus to a group. The effects of this independent variable(s) are of major interest.
O	An O identifies a measurement or observation activity.
R	An R indicates that the group members have been randomly assigned to a group.

The X's and O's in the diagram are read from left to right in temporal order.

$$O \; X \; O \; O$$
$$\overrightarrow{}$$
Time

X's and O's vertical to each other indicate that the stimulus and/or observation take place simultaneously.

$$X \; \underset{O}{\overset{O}{|}}$$

Time
q

Parallel rows that are not separated by dashed lines indicate that comparison groups have been equalized by the randomization process.

$$X \; O$$
$$O$$

Those separated with a dashed line have not been so equalized.

$$\underline{O \; X \; O}$$
$$-----$$
$$O$$

Preexperimental Designs

All three preexperimental designs are weak in their scientific measurement power—that is, they fail to control adequately the various threats to internal validity. This is especially true of the one-shot case study.

One-Shot Case Study   This may be diagrammed as follows:

$$X \qquad\qquad O$$

| Treatment or manipulation of independent variable | Observation or measurement of dependent variable | **(1)** |

An example is an employee education campaign about the company's financial condition without a prior measurement of employee knowledge. Results would reveal only how much the employees know after the education campaign, but there is no way to judge the effectiveness of the campaign. How well do you think this design would meet the various threats to internal validity? The lack of a pretest and control group makes this design inadequate for establishing causality.

One-Group Pretest-Posttest Design   This is the design used earlier in the educational example. It meets the various threats to internal validity better than the one-shot case study, but it is still a weak design. How well does it control for history? Maturation? Testing effect? The others?

$$O \qquad\qquad X \qquad\qquad O$$

Pretest   Manipulation   Posttest   **(2)**

Static Group Comparison   This design provides for two groups, one of which receives the experimental stimulus while the other serves as a control. In a field setting, imagine this scenario. A forest fire or other natural disaster is the experimental treatment, and psychological trauma (or property loss) suffered by the residents is the measured outcome. A pretest before the forest fire would be possible, but not on a large scale (as in the California fires). Moreover, timing of the pretest would be problematic. The control group, receiving the posttest, would consist of residents whose property was spared.

$$
\begin{array}{cc}
X & O_1 \\
\text{-------} & \text{-------} \\
& O_2
\end{array}
\qquad \textbf{(3)}
$$

The addition of a comparison group makes a substantial improvement over the other two designs. Its chief weakness is that there is no way to be certain that the two groups are equivalent.

True Experimental Designs

The major deficiency of the preexperimental designs is that they fail to provide comparison groups that are truly equivalent. The way to achieve equivalence is through matching and random assignment. With randomly assigned groups, we can employ tests of statistical significance of the observed differences.

It is common to show an X for the test stimulus and a blank for the existence of a control situation. This is an oversimplification of what really occurs. More precisely, there is an X_1 and an X_2, and sometimes more. The X_1 identifies one specific independent variable while X_2 is another independent variable that has been chosen, often arbitrarily, as the control case. Different levels of the same independent variable may also be used, with one level serving as the control.

Pretest-Posttest Control Group Design   This design consists of adding a control group to the design number 2 *one-group pretest-posttest* and assigning the subjects to either of the groups by a random procedure. The diagram is:

$$R \quad O_1 \quad X \quad O_2$$
$$R \quad O_3 \quad \quad O_4$$

(4)

The effect of the experimental variable is

$$E = (O_2 - O_1) - (O_4 - O_3)$$

In this design, the seven major internal validity problems are dealt with fairly well, although there are still some difficulties. Local history may occur in one group and not the other. Also, if communication exists between people in test and control groups, there can be rivalry and other internal validity problems.

Maturation, testing, and regression are handled well because one would expect them to be felt equally in experimental and control groups. Mortality, however, can be a problem if there are different dropout rates in the study groups. Selection is adequately dealt with by random assignment.

The record of this design is not as good on external validity. There is a chance for a reactive effect from testing. This might be a substantial influence in attitude change studies where pretests introduce unusual topics and content. Nor does this design ensure against reaction between selection and the experimental variable. Even random selection may be defeated by a high decline rate by subjects. This would result in using a disproportionate share of people who are essentially volunteers who may not be typical of the population. If this occurs, we will need to replicate the experiment several times with other groups under other conditions before we can be confident of external validity.

Posttest-Only Control Group Design   In this design, the pretest measurements are omitted. Pretests are well established in classical research design but are not really necessary when it is possible to randomize. The design is:

$$R \quad X \quad O_1$$
$$R \quad \quad O_2$$

(5)

The experimental effect is measured by the difference between O_1 and O_2. The simplicity of this design makes it more attractive than the pretest-posttest control group design. Internal validity threats from history, maturation, selection, and statistical regression are adequately controlled by random assignment. Since the subjects are measured only once, the threats of testing and instrumentation are reduced, but different mortality rates between experimental and control groups continue to be a potential problem. The design reduces the external validity problem of testing interaction effect, although other problems remain.

Extensions of True Experimental Designs

True experimental designs have been discussed in their classical forms, but researchers normally use an operational extension of the basic design. These extensions differ from the classical design forms in (1) the number of different experimental stimuli that are considered simultaneously by the experimenter and (2) the extent to which assignment procedures are used to increase precision.

Before we consider the types of extensions, some terms that are commonly used in the literature of applied experimentation are introduced. **Factor** is widely used to denote an independent variable. Factors are divided into *treatment levels,* which represent various subgroups. A factor may have two or more levels such as (1) male and female; (2) large, medium, and small; or (3) no training, brief training, and extended training. These levels should be operationally defined.

Factors may also be classified by whether the experimenter can manipulate the levels associated with the subject. **Active factors** are those the experimenter can manipulate by causing a subject to receive one level or another. Treatment is used to denote the different levels of active factors. With the second type, the **blocking factor,** the experimenter can only identify and classify the subject on an existing level. Gender, age group, customer status, and organizational rank are examples of blocking factors, because the subject comes to the experiment with a preexisting level of each.

Up to this point, the assumption is that experimental subjects are people, but this is often not so. A better term for subject is **test unit;** it can refer equally well to an individual, organization, geographic market, animal, machine type, mix of materials, and innumerable other entities.

Completely Randomized Design

The basic form of the true experiment is a completely randomized design. To illustrate its use, and that of more complex designs, consider a decision now facing the pricing manager at the Top Cannery. He would like to know what the ideal difference in price should be between the Top's private brand of canned vegetables and national brands such as Del Monte and Stokely's.

It is possible to set up an experiment on price differentials for canned green beans. Eighteen company stores and three price spreads (treatment levels) of 7 cents, 12 cents, and 17 cents between the company brand and national brands are used for the study. Six of the stores are assigned randomly to each of the treatment groups. The price differentials are maintained for a period, and then a tally is made of the sales volumes and gross profit of the canned green beans for each group of stores.

This design can be diagrammed as follows:

$$R \quad O_1 \quad X_1 \quad O_2$$
$$R \quad O_3 \quad X_3 \quad O_4 \qquad \textbf{(6)}$$
$$R \quad O_5 \quad X_5 \quad O_6$$

Here, O_1, O_3, and O_5 represent the total gross profits for canned green beans in the treatment stores for the month before the test. X_1, X_3, and X_5 represent 7-cent, 12-cent, and 17-cent treatments, while O_2, O_4, and O_6 are the gross profits for the month after the test started.

It is assumed that the randomization of stores to the three treatment groups was sufficient to make the three store groups equivalent. Where there is reason to believe this is not so, we must use a more complex design.

Randomized Block Design   When there is a single major extraneous variable, the randomized block design is used. Random assignment is still the basic way to produce equivalence among treatment groups, but something more is needed for two reasons. The more critical reason is that the sample being studied may be so small that it is risky to depend on random assignment alone to guarantee equivalence. Small samples, such as the 18 stores, are typical in field experiments because of high costs or because few test units are available. Another reason for blocking is to learn whether treatments bring different results among various groups of subjects.

Consider again the canned green beans pricing experiment. Assume there is reason to believe that lower-income families are more sensitive to price differentials than are higher-income families. This factor could seriously distort our results unless we stratify the stores by customer income. Each of the 18 stores is assigned to one of three income blocks and randomly assigned, within blocks, to the price difference treatments. The design is shown in the accompanying table.

In this design, one can measure both **main effects** and **interaction effects.** The main effect is the average direct influence that a particular treatment has independent of other factors. The interaction effect is the influence of one factor on the effect of another. The main effect of each price differential is secured by calculating the impact of each of the three treatments averaged over the different blocks. Interaction effects occur if you find that different customer income levels have a pronounced influence on customer reactions to the price differentials. (See Chapter 16, "Hypothesis Testing.")

		Blocking Factor—Customer Income			
Active Factor—Price Difference		*High*	*Medium*	*Low*	
7 cents	R	X_1	X_1	X_1	
12 cents	R	X_2	X_2	X_2	(7)
17 cents	R	X_3	X_3	X_3	

NOTE: The O's have been omitted. The horizontal rows no longer indicate a time sequence, but various levels of the blocking factor. However, before-and-after measurements are associated with each of the treatments.

Whether the randomized block design improves the precision of the experimental measurement depends on how successfully the design reduces the variance within blocks and maximizes the variance between blocks. If the response patterns are about the same in each block, there is little value to the more complex design. Blocking may be counterproductive.

Latin Square Design   The Latin square may be used when there are two major extraneous factors. To continue with the pricing example, assume we decide to block on the size of store and on customer income. It is convenient to consider these two blocking factors as forming the rows and columns of a table. Each factor is divided into three levels to provide nine groups of stores, each representing a unique combination of the two blocking variables. Treatments are then randomly assigned to these cells so a given treatment appears only once in each row and column. Because of this restriction, a Latin square must have the same number of rows, columns, and treatments. The design looks like the table below.

	Customer Income		
Store Size	*High*	*Medium*	*Low*
Large	X_3	X_1	X_2	
Medium	X_2	X_3	X_1	(8)
Small	X_1	X_2	X_3	

Treatments can be assigned by using a table of random numbers to set the order of treatment in the first row. For example, the pattern may be 3, 1, 2 as shown above. Following this, the other two cells of the first column are filled similarly, and the remaining treatments are assigned to meet the restriction that there can be no more than one treatment type in each row and column.

The experiment is carried out, sales results are gathered, and the average treatment effect is calculated. From this, we can determine the main effect of the various price spreads on the sales of company and national brands. With cost information, we can discover which price differential produces the greatest margin.

A limitation of the Latin square is that we must assume there is no interaction between treatments and blocking factors. Therefore, we cannot determine the interrelationships among store size, customer income, and price spreads. This limitation exists because there is not an exposure of all combinations of treatments, store sizes, and customer income groups. To do so would take a table of 27 cells, while this one has only 9. This can be accomplished by repeating the experiment twice to furnish the number needed to provide for every combination of store size, customer income, and treatment. If one is not especially interested in interaction, the Latin square is much more economical.

Factorial Design   One misconception that many have about experiments is that the researcher can manipulate only one variable at a time. This is not true; with factorial designs, you can deal with more than one treatment simultaneously. Consider again the pricing experiment. The president of the chain might also be interested in finding the effect of posting unit prices on the shelf to aid shopper decision making. The accompanying table can be used to design an experiment to include both the price differentials and the unit pricing.

	Price Spread		
Unit Price Information?	*7 Cents*	*12 Cents*	*17 Cents*
Yes	X_1Y_1	X_1Y_2	X_1Y_3
No	X_2Y_1	X_2Y_2	X_2Y_3

(9)

This is known as a 2×3 factorial design in which we use two factors: one with two levels and one with three levels of intensity. The version shown here is completely randomized, with the stores being randomly assigned to one of six treatment combinations. With such a design, it is possible to estimate the main effects of each of the two independent variables and the interactions between them. The results can give answers to the following questions:

1. What are the sales effects of the different price spreads between company and national brands?
2. What are the sales effects of using unit-price marking on the shelves?
3. What are the sales-effect interrelations between price spread and the presence of unit-price information?

Covariance Analysis   We have discussed direct control of extraneous variables through blocking. It is also possible to apply some degree of indirect statistical control on one or more variables through analysis of covariance. Even with randomization, one may find that the before-measurement shows an average knowledge level difference between experimental and control groups. With covariance analysis, one can adjust statistically for this before-difference. Another application might occur if the canned green beans pricing experiment was carried out with a completely randomized design, only to reveal a contamination effect from differences in average customer income levels. With covariance analysis, one can still do some statistical blocking on average customer income even after the experiment has been run.

Field Experiments: Quasi- or Semi-Experiments[8]

Under field conditions, we often cannot control enough of the extraneous variables or the experimental treatment to use a true experimental design. Because the stimulus condition occurs in a natural environment, a **field experiment** is required.

A modern version of the bystander and thief field experiment, mentioned at the beginning of the chapter, involves the use of electronic article surveillance to prevent shrinkage due to shoplifting. In a proprietary study, a shopper came to the optical counter of an upscale mall store and asked the salesperson to see special designer frames. The salesperson, a confederate of the experimenter, replied that she would get them from a case in the adjoining department and disappeared. The "thief" selected two pairs of sunglasses from an open display, deactivated the security tags at the counter, and walked out of the store.

Thirty-five percent of the subjects (store customers) reported the theft upon the return of the salesperson. Sixty-three percent reported it when the salesperson asked about the shopper. Unlike previous studies, the presence of a second customer did not reduce the willingness to report a theft.

This study was not possible with a control group, a pretest, or randomization of customers, but the information gained was essential and justified a compromise of true experimental designs. We use the preexperimental designs previously discussed or quasi-experiments to deal with such conditions. In a quasi-experiment, we often cannot know when or to whom to expose the experimental treatment. Usually, however, we can decide when and whom to measure. A quasi-experiment is inferior to a true experimental design but is usually superior to preexperimental designs. In this section, we consider a few common quasi-experiments.

Nonequivalent Control Group Design   This is a strong and widely used quasi-experimental design. It differs from the pretest-posttest control group design, because the test and control groups are not randomly assigned. The design is diagrammed as follows:

$$O_1 \qquad X \qquad O_2$$
$$\text{-----} \quad \text{-----} \quad \text{-----} \qquad \textbf{(10)}$$
$$O_3 \qquad\qquad O_4$$

There are two varieties. One is the *intact equivalent design,* in which the membership of the experimental and control groups is naturally assembled. For example, we may use different classes in a school, membership in similar clubs, or customers from similar stores. Ideally, the two groups are as alike as possible. This design is especially useful when any type of individual selection process would be reactive.

The second variation, the *self-selected experimental group design,* is weaker because volunteers are recruited to form the experimental group, while nonvolunteer subjects are used for control. Such a design is likely when subjects believe it would be in their interest to be a subject in an experiment—say, an experimental training program.

Comparison of pretest results $(O_1 - O_3)$ is one indicator of the degree of equivalence between test and control groups. If the pretest results are significantly different, there is a real question about the groups' comparability. On the other hand, if pretest observations are similar between groups, there is more reason to believe internal validity of the experiment is good.

Separate Sample Pretest-Posttest Design   This design is most applicable when we cannot know when and to whom to introduce the treatment but we can decide when and whom to measure. The basic design is:

$$R \qquad O_1 \qquad (X)$$
$$R \qquad\qquad X \qquad O_2 \qquad \textbf{(11)}$$

The bracketed treatment (X) is irrelevant to the purpose of the study but is shown to suggest that the experimenter cannot control the treatment.

This is not a strong design because several threats to internal validity are not handled adequately. History can confound the results but can be overcome by repeating the study at other times in other settings. In contrast, it is considered superior to true experiments in external validity. Its strength results from its being a field experiment in which the samples are usually drawn from the population to which we wish to generalize our findings.

We would find this design more appropriate if the population is large, or a before-measurement is reactive, or there is no way to restrict the application of the treatment. Assume a company is planning an intense campaign to change its employees' attitudes toward energy conservation. It might draw two random samples of employees, one of which is interviewed about energy use attitudes before the information campaign. After the campaign the other group is interviewed.

Group Time Series Design A time series introduces repeated observations before and after the treatment and allows subjects to act as their own controls. The single treatment group design has before-after measurements as the only controls. There is also a multiple design with two or more comparison groups as well as the repeated measurements in each treatment group.

The time series format is especially useful where regularly kept records are a natural part of the environment and are unlikely to be reactive. The time series approach is also a good way to study unplanned events in an ex post facto manner. If the federal government would suddenly begin price controls, we could still study the effects of this action later if we had regularly collected records for the period before and after the advent of price control.

The internal validity problem for this design is history. To reduce this risk, we keep a record of possible extraneous factors during the experiment and attempt to adjust the results to reflect their influence.

CLOSE-UP

A JOB ENRICHMENT QUASI-EXPERIMENT[9]

One theory of job attitudes holds that ``hygiene'' factors, which include working conditions, pay, security, status, interpersonal relationships, and company policy, can be a major source of dissatisfaction among workers but have little positive motivational power. This theory says that the positive motivator factors are intrinsic to the job; they include achievement, recognition for achieve-

ment, the work itself, responsibility, and growth or advancement.[10]

A study of the value of job enrichment as a builder of job satisfaction was carried out with laboratory technicians, or ``experimental officers'' (EOs), in a British chemical company. The project was a multiple group time series quasi-experiment. The project is diagrammed at the end of the "Close-Up."

Two sections of the department acted as experimental groups and two as control groups. It is not clear how these groups were chosen, but there was no mention of random assignment. One of the experimental groups and one of the control

(continued)

groups worked closely together, while the other two groups were separated geographically and were engaged in different research. Hygiene factors were held constant during the research, and the studies were kept confidential to avoid the tendency of participants to act in artificial ways.

A before-measurement was made using a job reaction survey instrument. This indicated the EOs typically had low morale, and many wrote of their frustrations. All EOs were asked to write monthly progress reports, and these were used to assess the quality of their work. The assessment was made against eight specifically defined criteria by a panel of three managers who were not members of the department. These assessors were never told which laboratory technicians were in the experimental group and which were in the control group.

The study extended over a year, with the treatments introduced in the experimental groups at the start of the 12-month study period. Changes

were made to give experimental group EOs important chances for achievement; these changes also made the work more challenging. Recognition of achievement was given, authority over certain aspects was increased, new managerial responsibilities were assigned to the senior EOs, added advancements were given to others, and the opportunity for self-initiated work was provided. After about six months, these same changes were instituted with one of the control groups, while the remaining group continued for the entire period as a control. Several months of EO progress reports were available as a prior base line for evaluation. The results of this project are shown in Figure 14–3.

FIGURE 14–3 Assessment of EOs' Monthly Reports

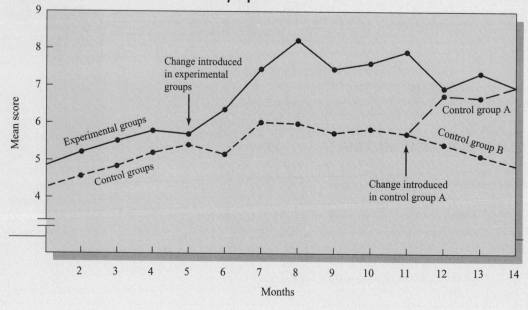

Summary

Experiments are studies involving intervention by the researcher beyond that required for measurement. The usual intervention is to manipulate a variable (the independent variable) and observe how it affects the subjects being studied (the dependent variable).

An evaluation of the experimental method reveals several advantages: (1) the ability to uncover causal relationships, (2) provisions for controlling extraneous and environmental variables, (3) convenience and low cost of creating test situations rather than searching for their appearance in business situations, (4) replicating findings to rule out idiosyncratic or isolated results, and (5) the ability to exploit naturally occurring events.

Some advantages of other methods are liabilities for the experiment: (1) the artificial setting of the laboratory, (2) generalizability from nonprobability samples, (3) disproportionate costs in select business situations, (4) a focus restricted to the present and immediate future, and (5) ethical issues related to manipulation and control of human subjects.

Consideration of the following activities is essential for the execution of a well-planned experiment:

1. Select relevant variables for testing.
2. Specify the levels of treatment.
3. Control the environmental and extraneous factors.
4. Choose an experimental design suited to the hypothesis.
5. Select and assign subjects to groups.
6. Pilot test, revise, and conduct the final test.
7. Analyze the data.

We judge various types of experimental research designs by how well they meet the tests of internal and external validity. An experiment has high internal validity if one has confidence that the experimental treatment has been the source of change in the dependent variable. More specifically, a design's internal validity is judged by how well it meets seven threats. These are history, maturation, testing, instrumentation, selection, statistical regression, and experiment mortality.

External validity is high when the results of an experiment are judged to apply to some larger population. Such an experiment is said to have high external validity regarding that population. Three potential threats to external validity are testing reactivity, selection interaction, and other reactive factors.

Experimental research designs include (1) preexperiments, (2) true experiments, and (3) quasi-experiments. The main distinction among these types is the degree of control that the researcher can exercise over validity problems.

Three preexperimental designs were presented. They represent the crudest form of experimentation and are undertaken only when nothing stronger is possible. Their weakness is the lack of an equivalent comparison group, and as a result, they fail to meet many internal validity criteria. They are the (1) one-shot control study, (2) one-group pretest-posttest design, and (3) static group comparison.

Two forms of the true experiment were also presented. Their central characteristic is that they provide a means by which we can assure equivalence between experimental and control groups through random assignment to the groups. These designs are (1) pretest-posttest control group and (2) posttest-only control group.

The classical two-group experiment can be extended to multigroup designs in which different levels of the test variable are used as controls rather than the classical nontest control. In addition, the true experimental design is extended into more sophisticated forms that use blocking. Two such forms, the randomized block and the Latin square, were discussed. Finally, the factorial design was discussed in which two or more independent variables can be accommodated.

Between the extremes of preexperiments, with little or no control, and true experiments, with random assignment, there is a gray area in which we find quasi-experiments. These are useful designs when some variables can be controlled, but equivalent experimental and control groups usually cannot be established by random assignment. There are many quasi-experimental designs, but only three were covered in this chapter: (1) nonequivalent control group design, (2) separate sample pretest-posttest design, and (3) group time series design.

Key Terms

active factors	hypothesis
blind	independent variable
blocking factors	interaction effects
control group	internal validity
dependent variable	main effects
double blind	matching
environmental control	operationalized
experimental treatment	quota matrix
experiments	random assignment
external validity	replication
factor	test unit
field experiment	treatment level

Case

Retailers Unhappy with Displays from Manufacturer
(This is a case found in the optional casebook available with the text.)

Discussion Questions

1. Distinguish between the following:
   a. Internal validity and external validity
   b. Preexperimental design and quasi-experimental design
   c. History and maturation
   d. Random sampling, randomization, and matching

    e. Active factors and blocking factors

    f. Environmental variables and extraneous variables

2. Compare the advantages of experiments with the advantages of survey and observational methods.

3. A lighting company seeks to study the percentage of defective glass shells being manufactured. Theoretically, the percentage of defectives is dependent on temperature, humidity, and the level of artisan expertise. Complete historical data is available on a daily basis for a year:

    a. Temperature (high, normal, low)

    b. Humidity (high, normal, low)

    c. Artisan expertise level (expert, average, mediocre)

    Some experts feel that defectives also depend on production supervisors. However, data on supervisors in charge is available for only 242 of the 365 days. How should this study be conducted?

4. Describe how you would operationalize variables for experimental testing in the following research question: What are the performance differences between 10 microcomputers connected in a local-area network (LAN) and one minicomputer with 10 terminals?

5. A pharmaceuticals manufacturer is testing a drug developed to treat cancer. During the final stages of development the drug's effectiveness is being tested on individuals for different (1) dosage conditions and (2) age groups. One of the problems is patient mortality during experimentation. Justify your design recommendations through a comparison of alternatives and in terms of external and internal validity.

    a. Recommend the appropriate design for the experiment.

    b. Explain the use of control groups, blinds, and double blinds if you recommend them.

6. What ethical problems do you see in conducting experiments with human subjects?

7. Why would a noted business researcher say, "It is essential that we always keep in mind the model of the controlled experiment, even if in practice we have to deviate from an ideal model"?

8. What essential characteristics distinguish a true experiment from other research designs?

9. You are asked to develop an experiment for a study on the effect that compensation has on the response rates secured from personal interview subjects. This study will involve 300 people who will be assigned to one of the following conditions: (1) no compensation, (2) $1 compensation, and (3) $3 compensation. A number of sensitive issues will be explored concerning various social problems, and the 300 people will be drawn from the adult population. Describe how your design would be set up if it were a completely randomized design, a randomized block design, a Latin square, a

factorial design (suggest another active variable to use). Which would you use? Why?

10. What type of experimental design would you recommend in each of the following cases? Suggest in some detail how you would design each study:

   a. A test of three methods of compensation of factory workers. The methods are hourly wage, incentive pay, and weekly salary. The dependent variable is direct labor cost per unit of output.

   b. The effects of various levels of advertising effort and price reduction on the sale of specific branded grocery products by a retail grocery chain.

   c. It is claimed that the use of fast-paced music played over a store's public address system will speed the shopping rate of customers without an adverse effect on the amount spent per customer.

Reference Notes

1. Bibb Latane and J. M. Darley, *The Unresponsive Bystander: Why Doesn't He Help?* (New York: Appleton-Century-Crofts, 1970), pp. 69–77. Research into the responses of bystanders who witness crimes was stimulated by an incident in New York City where Kitty Genovese was attacked and killed in the presence of 38 witnesses who refused to come to her aid or summon authorities.

2. This section is largely adapted from Julian L. Simon and Paul Burstein, *Basic Research Methods in Social Science,* 3rd ed. (New York: Random House, 1985), pp. 128–33.

3. For a thorough explanation of this topic, see Helena C. Kraemer and Sue Thiemann, *How Many Subjects? Statistical Power Analysis in Research* (Beverly Hills, CA: Sage Publications, 1987).

4. Kenneth D. Bailey, *Methods of Social Research,* 2nd ed. (New York: Free Press, 1982), pp. 230–33.

5. The concept of a quota matrix and the tabular form for Figure 14–1 were adapted from Earl R. Babbie, *The Practice of Social Research,* 5th ed. (Belmont, CA: Wadsworth, 1989), pp. 218–19.

6. Donald T. Campbell and Julian C. Stanley, *Experimental and Quasi-Experimental Designs for Research* (Chicago: Rand McNally, 1963), p. 5.

7. Thomas D. Cook and Donald T. Campbell, "The Design and Conduct of Quasi-Experiments and True Experiments in Field Settings," in *Handbook of Industrial and Organizational Psychology,* ed. Marvin D. Dunnette (Chicago: Rand McNally, 1976), p. 223.

8. For an in-depth discussion of many quasi-experiment designs and their internal validity, see ibid., pp. 246–98.

9. William J. Paul, Jr., Keith B. Robertson, and Frederick Herzberg, "Job Enrichment Pays Off," *Harvard Business Review* (March–April 1969), pp. 61–78.

10. Frederick J. Herzberg, "One More Time: How Do You Motivate Employees?" *Harvard Business Review* (January–February 1968), pp. 53–62.

Suggested Readings

1. Campbell, Donald T., and Julian C. Stanley. *Experimental and Quasi-Experimental Designs for Research.* Chicago: Rand McNally, 1963. A universally quoted discussion of experimental designs in the social sciences.

2. Cook, Thomas D., and Donald T. Campbell. "The Design and Conduct of Quasi-Experiments and True Experiments in Field Settings." In *Handbook of Industrial and Organizational Psychology,* 2nd ed., edited by Marvin D. Dunnette and Leaetta M. Hough. Palo Alto, CA: Consulting Psychologists Press, 1990. *Quasi-Experimentation: Design and Analysis Issues for Field Settings.* Chicago: Rand McNally, 1979. Major authoritative works on both true and quasi-experiments and their design. Already classic references.

3. Edwards, Allen. *Experimental Design in Psychological Research,* 4th ed. New York: Holt, Rinehart & Winston, 1972. A complete treatment of experimental design with helpful illustrative examples.

4. Green, Paul E., Donald S. Tull, and Gerald Albaum. *Research for Marketing Decisions,* 5th ed. Englewood Cliffs, NJ: Prentice-Hall, 1988. A definitive text with sections on the application of experimentation to marketing research.

5. Kirk, Roger E. *Experimental Design: Procedures for the Behavioral Sciences,* 3rd ed. Belmont, CA: Brooks/Cole, 1994. An advanced text on the statistical aspects of experimental design.

6. Krathwohl, David R. *Social and Behavioral Science Research: A New Framework for Conceptualizing, Implementing, and Evaluating Research Studies.* San Francisco: Jossey-Bass, 1985. Chapters 3, 4, and 5 present a convincing argument for reformulating internal and external validity into broader concepts. A conceptually refreshing approach.

ANALYSIS AND PRESENTATION OF DATA

BRINGING RESEARCH TO LIFE

Dorrie Henry arrived for lunch, joining Jason and Myra, who were wrapping up a MindWriter meeting. The conversation naturally turned to one of Jason's early research projects.

"As a public health doctor," said Dorrie, "I work with statistics. Call me a consumer—if not an expert, at least an educated consumer. I am able to scan Jason's work and offer advice. More importantly, I understand his perfectionism and why he carries it to such extremes. You know how 'difficult' he can be when he is under stress."

Myra responded by arching her eyebrows and laughing mirthlessly.

"I can see this turning into a bashing Jason story," Jason groaned.

"My insight into the stress of doing high-quality business research has allowed us to stay together when a lay person might have walked out. Has Jason told you about our near blowup over the bus line survey? No? Before we moved down here and he connected with you, Jason was retained by a bus line up north to assist in a sample survey of 2,000 passengers. The line had just dismissed its research director, a horrible chap name Burbidge, who could not relate to the blue-collar ridership. I believe he has subsequently bounced around in research positions with the royal airlines of the oil-producing Gulf states. Well, no matter.

"The point is Jason had a 20-question survey of 2,000 randomly selected riders, a total of 40,000 items to be coded, some of them multiple choice, some of them numerical entry, some free-response. He estimated this would take 15 seconds an item, on the average, a total of 10,000 minutes, which he rounded up to 12,000 minutes. Call it 200 person-hours, then. He decided to hire 25 temporary personnel for one 8-hour data entry shift."

"That sounds reasonable, " said Myra.

"Well, of course it was quite reasonable. When the trouble started between Jason and me was when he discovered that since it received a county subsidy, the bus line had to follow county purchasing procedures and put the data entry out for competitive bidding. I was a board member of a nonprofit organization that provided temporary employment for former mental patients."

"You are not a psychiatrist, are you?"

"No, but I was a member of the board of directors, out of my concern for the way society stigmatizes persons who can very well cope with the widest range of occupations. Well, to make a story short, I insisted on bidding for the data entry work, over Jason's strongest objections. He had never expressed any objections to my finding work for these persons, but when I wanted them involved in his own work, he become prickly, hostile, self-pitying, irritable, and hypercritical."

"I've seen that side of Jason," grinned Myra.

"Would you like me to leave so you can shred me without compunction?" replied Jason.

"I'm certain you have," said Dorrie ignoring Jason, "and certainly you know what motivated it—the most intense desire for accuracy and reliability."

"Which as his client, I not only appreciate but demand," supported Myra. "See, Jason, Dorrie's not really telling tales."

"Thanks to his association with you, Myra, he has learned to moderate the acting-out of his anxieties, for which I thank you. But on the inside he ceaselessly worries about threats to validity.

"Well, back to the bus company. I won the contract, and Jason had no choice. My men and women were to be his temporary employees for data entry. Our plan was to bring my crew in at 5 P.M. on a Friday evening to bus line HQ, putting each in a separate office, using 25 networked computers in employee offices. Jason procured a data entry program, which we ran off the system server. Each member of the crew, sitting in a separate office, was given 80 surveys to encode, 10 an hour, for 8 hours. The system server put on the screen of each computer a data entry screen, a program very cleverly contrived to prevent errors of data entry, so far as possible.

(continued)

"For instance, if a survey item—a question—called for choosing between `Ride the bus less than twice a week,' `Ride the bus at least twice but less than 8 times,' or `Ride the bus 8 or more times,' the data clerk would put a cursor over the correct answer and press ENTER. Making a mistake would be difficult, because the screen would closely resemble the printed page. If the item called for "Enter your age," and the clerk entered a one- or three-digit number, the computer would beep loudly, to indicate that ages less than 10 and greater than 99 were considered suspect.

"Jason continued to face the prospect of DEN—data entry night—with thinly disguised opposition. He grumbled that my crew would ruin the results of his carefully crafted research. I reminded him that these people were not visually impaired and had no intellectual deficits. They were just folks who were not yet ready to reenter the workplace or were ready but suffered unreasonable discrimination, of exactly the sort Jason was showing."

"You are going to tell the part where I redeem myself, aren't you?" asked Jason plaintively.

"Don't ruin my fun, Jason. Anyway, while it was prudent to warn the HQ staff to secure their offices, Jason went overboard and infected the office staff with his nervousness and negativity about my crew coming in to use their computers. At 4:45 P.M., when a special bus arrived with me and my crew and a supervisory social worker, my crew was confronted by a stream of departing office workers carrying out their potted plants. Can you imagine? Did they think my crew were herbivores? It was a flagrant insult, and I felt awful.

"Jason exhibited a fundamental preoccupation with human error. He decided to double-check the data entry by staying up all night long and pulling one-twentieth of the surveys at random for checking. A twenty-sixth crew member ran up and down the halls all night retrieving randomly sampled surveys, which Jason compared with the already entered data in the server. He warned me that if he found more than a certain error rate he intended to stop the operation and send everyone home. He was working himself into a lather, looking for trouble he was not going to find.

"He was furiously recoding forms and checking them against already entered data. As he was pulling the forms generated by 25 workers, he had to work at least as fast as any one of them to keep up, slightly faster in fact, and very frankly I had serious doubts that he would not make more errors than my crew and blame the errors on my own people. He skipped supper at 8 P.M., although I had made us sandwiches, and worked steadily and crankily and drank too much black coffee. He did not allow himself bathroom breaks or stretch breaks, and although I noticed that his irritation seemed to increase steadily after 9 P.M., I ascribed it to fatigue. But at 10 P.M., five hours into our eight-hour shift, he threw down his surveys, smiled broadly, murmured 'darn good,' strolled off to the bathroom, returned, ate two peanut butter and jelly sandwiches and made a few dumb jokes."

"It seems," continued Dorrie, " the discrepancy rate between his coding and my crew was less than 1 percent for the first five hours. He spent the next two hours humming 'Strangers in the Night,' over and over again and running preliminary frequency distributions and cross-tabulations.

"In the end, he expressed considerable satisfaction with my crew. The HQ office workers came back Monday morning, toting their philodendrons, and word of mouth said that they found their offices clean and orderly. Each of my crew had cleaned the keyboards and monitor screens with little sanitized towelettes they had brought along, and consequently the offices even smelled minty."

INTRODUCTION

Once the data begin to flow in, attention turns to data analysis. If the project has been done correctly, the analysis planning is already done. Back in the research design stage or at least by completion of the proposal or the pilot test, decisions should have been made about how to analyze the data. Unfortunately, many researchers wait until the analysis stage to decide what to do. This results in the late discovery that some data will not be collected, will be collected in the wrong form, or will exhibit unanticipated characteristics.

This chapter addresses three major topics. The first is *data preparation,* which includes editing, coding, and data entry. These activities ensure the accuracy of the data and its conversion from raw form to reduced and classified forms that are more appropriate for analysis. Second, *exploring, displaying, and examining data* involves breaking down, inspecting, and rearranging data to start the search for meaningful descriptions, patterns, and relationships. Third, *data mining* is used to extract patterns and predictive trends from databases. Data mining combines exploration and discovery with confirmatory analysis. It also bridges primary and secondary types of data.

Before concluding this introduction, we must comment briefly on several assumptions of this part of the book. This book was developed for and with graduate students. It may be used successfully with undergraduates if an elementary statistics course was a prerequisite. Without that grounding, some of the ideas presented here may require remedial study. Students should be able to prepare data, explore it, and complete a preliminary analysis after reading this chapter. We have tried to make it easy to use. Readers whose research objectives are reporting or basic description will find that this coverage is sufficient for their data analysis needs. Others, whose research goals are explanation or prediction, will want to continue on to hypothesis testing. For them, this chapter is an indispensable prelude to the remainder of the book.

EDITING

The customary first step in analysis is to edit the raw data. **Editing** detects errors and omissions, corrects them when possible, and certifies that minimum data quality standards are achieved. The editor's purpose is to guarantee that data are (1) accurate, (2) consistent with other information, (3) uniformly entered, (4) complete, and (5) arranged to simplify coding and tabulation.

In the following question asked of military officers, one respondent checked two categories, indicating that he was in the reserves and currently serving on active duty.

Please indicate your current military status:
- ☑ Active duty officer
- ❏ National Guard officer
- ☑ Reserve officer
- ❏ Separated officer
- ❏ Retired officer

The editor's responsibility is to decide which of the responses is consistent with the intent of the question or other information in the survey and is most accurate for this individual respondent.

Field Editing

During the stress of data collection, the researcher often uses ad hoc abbreviations and special symbols. Soon after the interview, experiment, or observation the investigator should review the reporting forms. It is difficult to complete what was abbreviated or written in shorthand or noted illegibly if the entry is not caught that day. When gaps are present from interviews, a callback should be made rather than guessing what the respondent "probably would have said." Self-interviewing has no place in quality research.

In large projects, field editing review is a responsibility of the field supervisor. It, too, should be done soon after the data have been gathered. A second important control function of the field supervisor is to validate the field results. This normally means he or she will reinterview some percentage of the respondents, at least on some questions. Many commercial research firms will recontact about 10 percent of the respondents.

Central Editing

At this point, the data should get a thorough editing. For a small study, the use of a single editor produces maximum consistency. In large studies, the tasks may be broken down so each editor can deal with one entire section. This approach will not identify inconsistencies between answers in different sections. However, this problem can be handled by identifying points of possible inconsistency and having one editor check specifically for them.

Sometimes it is obvious that an entry is incorrect, is entered in the wrong place, or states time in months when it was requested in weeks. When replies clearly are inappropriate or missing, the editor can sometimes detect the proper answer by reviewing the other information in the schedule. This practice, however, should be limited to those few cases where it is obvious what the correct answer is. It may be better to contact the respondent for correct information, if time and budget allow. Another alternative is for the editor to strike out the answer if it is clearly inappropriate. Here an editing entry of "no answer" or "unknown" is called for.

Another editing problem concerns faking. Armchair interviewing is difficult to spot, but the editor is in the best position to do so. One approach is to check responses to open-ended questions. These are most difficult to fake. Distinctive response patterns in other questions will often emerge if faking is occurring. To uncover this, the editor must analyze the instruments used by each interviewer.

Here are some useful rules to guide editors in their work:

- Be familiar with instructions given to interviewers and coders.
- Do not destroy, erase, or make illegible the original entry by the interviewer. Original entries should be crossed out with a single line to remain legible.
- Make all entries on an instrument in some distinctive color and in a standardized form.

- Initial all answers changed or supplied.
- Place initials and date of editing on each instrument completed.

CODING

Coding involves assigning numbers or other symbols to answers so the responses can be grouped into a limited number of classes or categories. The classifying of data into limited categories sacrifices some data detail but is necessary for efficient analysis. Instead of requesting the word *male* or *female* in response to a question that asks for the identification of one's gender, we could use the codes "M" or "F." Normally this variable would be coded 1 for male and 2 for female or 0 and 1. If we use *M* and *F*, or other letters, in combination with numbers and symbols, the code is *alphanumeric*. When numbers are used exclusively, the code is *numeric*.

Coding helps the researcher to reduce several thousand replies to a few categories containing the critical information needed for analysis. In coding, *categories* are the partitioning of a set; and *categorization* is the process of using rules to partition a body of data.

Coding Rules

Four rules guide the establishment of category sets. The categories should be

- Appropriate to the research problem and purpose
- Exhaustive
- Mutually exclusive
- Derived from one classification principle

Appropriateness Categories must provide the best partitioning of data for testing hypotheses and showing relationships. Year-by-year age differences may be important to the question being researched. If so, wider age classifications hamper the analysis. If specific income, attitude, or reason categories are critical to the testing relationship, then we must choose the best groupings. In particular, choose class boundaries that match those being used for comparisons. It is disheartening, late in a study, to discover that age, income, or other frequency classes do not precisely match those of the data with which we wish to make comparisons.

Exhaustiveness A large number of "other" responses suggests our classification set may be too limited. In such cases, we may not be tapping the full range of information in the data. Failure to present an adequate list of alternatives is especially damaging when multiple-choice questions are used. Any answer that is not specified in the set will surely be underrepresented in the tally.

While the exhaustiveness requirement in a single category set may be obvious, a second aspect is less apparent. Does the one set of categories fully capture all the information in the data? For example, responses to an open-ended question about family economic prospects for the next year may originally be classified only in terms of being optimistic or pessimistic. It may also be enlightening to classify responses in terms of other concepts such as the precise focus of these expectations (income or jobs) and variations in responses between family heads and others in the family.

Mutual Exclusivity   Another important rule is that category components should be mutually exclusive. This standard is met when a specific answer can be placed in one and only one cell in a category set. For example, in an occupation survey, the classifications may be (1) professional, (2) managerial, (3) sales, (4) clerical, (5) crafts, (6) operatives, and (7) unemployed. Some respondents will think of themselves as being in more than one of these groups. The person who views selling as a profession and spends time supervising others may fit in three of these categories. A function of operational definitions is to provide categories that are composed of mutually exclusive elements. Here, operational definitions of the occupations to be classified in "professional," "managerial," and "sales" should clarify the situation. The problem of how to handle an unemployed salesperson brings up a fourth rule of category design.

Single Dimension   The need for a category set to follow a single classificatory principle means every class in the category set is defined in terms of one concept. Returning to the occupation survey example, the person in the study might be both a salesperson and unemployed. The "salesperson" label expresses the concept *occupation type;* the response "unemployed" is another dimension concerned with *current employment status* without regard to the respondent's normal occupation. When a category set uses more than one dimension, it will normally not be mutually exclusive unless the cells in the set combine the dimensions (employed manager, unemployed manager, and so on).

Codebook Construction

A **codebook,** or *coding scheme,* contains each variable in the study and specifies the application of coding rules to the variable. It is used by the researcher or research staff as a guide to make data entry less prone to error and more efficient. It is also the definitive source for locating the positions of variables in the data file during analysis. In many statistical programs, the coding scheme is integral to the data file. Most codebooks—computerized or not—contain the question number, variable name, location of the variable's code on the input medium, descriptors for the response options, and whether the variable is alpha or numeric. An example of a paper-based codebook is shown in Figure 15–1. When pilot testing has been conducted, there should be sufficient information about the variables to prepare a codebook. A preliminary codebook used with pilot data may reveal coding problems that will need to be corrected before the data for the final study are collected and processed.

Coding Closed Questions

The responses to closed questions include scaled items and others for which answers can be anticipated. When codes are established early in the research process, it is possible to precode the questionnaire. **Precoding** is particularly helpful for data entry because it makes the intermediate step of completing a coding sheet unnecessary. The data are accessible directly from the questionnaire. A respondent, interviewer, field supervisor, or researcher (depending on the data collection method) is

FIGURE   15–1   Sample Codebook for Questionnaire Items

Project _____

Question Number	Variable Number	Column Location	Code Descriptors	Software Variable Name
_____	_____	1	Record number	RECNUM
_____	_____	2–4	Respondent number	RESPID
1	1	5–9	Zip code 99999 = Missing	ZIP
2	2	10–11	Birth year 99 = Missing	BIRTH
3	3	12	Gender 1 = Male 2 = Female 9 = Missing	GENDER
4	4	13	Marital status 1 = Married 2 = Widow(er) 3 = Divorced 4 = Separated 5 = Never married 9 = Missing	MARITAL
5	5	14	Own–Rent 1 = Own 2 = Rent 3 = Provided 9 = Missing	HOUSING
6	6	15	Purchase reason(s) 1 = Mentioned 0 = Not mentioned	PURCH
6	7	16	Bought home	REASON
		17	Birth of child	
		18	Death of relative or friend	
		19	Promoted	
		20	Changed job/career	
		21	Paid college expenses	
		22	Acquired assets	
		23	Retired	
		24	Changed marital status	
		25	Started business	
		26	Expanded business	
		27	Parent's influence	
		28	Contacted by agent	
		29	Other	

able to assign an appropriate numerical response on the instrument by checking, circling, or printing it in the proper coding location.

Figure 15–2 shows questions in the sample codebook. When precoding is used, editing may precede data processing. Note question 4 where the respondent may choose between five characteristics of marital status and enter the number of the item best representing present status in the unshaded portion of the questionnaire. This code is later transferred to an input medium for analysis.

Coding Open Questions

Closed questions are favored by researchers over open questions for their efficiency and specificity. They are easier to measure, record, code, and analyze. But there are situations where insufficient information or lack of a hypothesis prohibits preparing

FIGURE   15–2   Sample Questionnaire Items

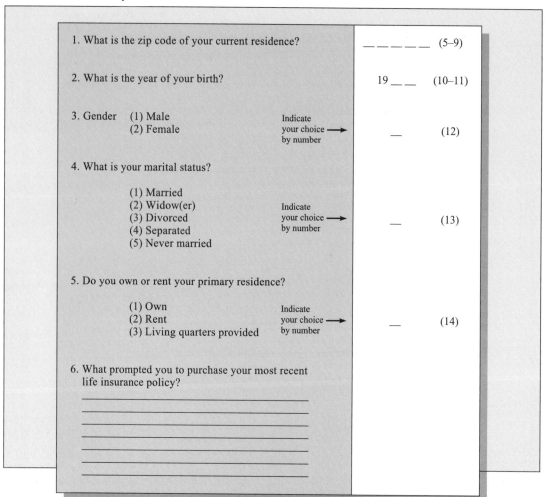

1. What is the zip code of your current residence?   _ _ _ _ _ (5–9)

2. What is the year of your birth?   19 _ _   (10–11)

3. Gender   (1) Male
              (2) Female   Indicate
                                      your choice ⟶   _   (12)
                                      by number

4. What is your marital status?

        (1) Married
        (2) Widow(er)
        (3) Divorced   Indicate
        (4) Separated   your choice ⟶   _   (13)
        (5) Never married   by number

5. Do you own or rent your primary residence?

        (1) Own
        (2) Rent   Indicate
        (3) Living quarters provided your choice ⟶   _   (14)
                                      by number

6. What prompted you to purchase your most recent
   life insurance policy?
   _____
   _____
   _____
   _____
   _____
   _____

response categories in advance. Other reasons for using open-ended responses include the need to measure sensitive or disapproved behavior, to discover salience, or to encourage natural modes of expression.[1]

In Figure 15–2, question 6 illustrates the use of an open question for which advance knowledge of response options was not available. The answer to "What prompted you to purchase your most recent life insurance policy?" was filled in by the respondent as a short-answer essay. After preliminary evaluation, response categories (shown in the codebook, Figure 15–1) were created for that item. Although most responses could be accounted for by the derived categories, an "other" category was established to meet the coding rule of exhaustiveness.

Using Content Analysis for Open Questions

Content analysis measures the semantic content or the *what* aspect of a message. Its breadth makes it a flexible and wide-ranging tool that may be used as a methodology or as a problem-specific technique. Trend-watching organizations like the BrainReserve, the Naisbitt Group, SRI International, and Inferential Focus use variations on content analysis for selected projects, often spotting changes from newspapers or magazine articles before they can be confirmed statistically. The Naisbitt Group's content analysis of 2 million local newspaper articles compiled over a 12-year period resulted in the publication of *Megatrends*. After a brief review of the characteristics of content analysis, we will consider one of its many problem-specific applications: handling open questions.

Content analysis has been described as "a research technique for the objective, systematic, and quantitative description of the manifest content of a communication."[2] Because this definition is sometimes confused with simply counting obvious message aspects such as words or attributes, more recent interpretations have broadened the definition to include latent as well as manifest content, the symbolic meaning of messages, and qualitative analysis. One author states:

> In any single written message, one can count letters, words, or sentences. One can categorize phrases, describe the logical structure of expressions, ascertain associations, connotations, denotations, elocutionary forces, and one can also offer psychiatric, sociological, or political interpretations. All of these may be simultaneously valid. In short, a message may convey a multitude of contents even to a single receiver.[3]

Content analysis follows a systematic process starting with the selection of a unitization scheme. The units may be syntactical, referential, propositional, or thematic. *Syntactical* units are illustrated by words, which are the smallest and most reliable units. *Referential* units may be objects, events, persons, and so forth, to which an expression refers. An advertiser may refer to a product as a "classic," a "power performer," or "ranked first in safety"—each denoting the same object. *Propositional* units use several frameworks. One might show the relationships among the actor, the mode of acting, and the object—for example, "subscribers [actor] to this periodical save [mode of acting] $15 [object of the action] over the single issue rate." *Thematic* units are higher-level abstractions inferred from their connection to a unique structure or pattern in the content. A response to a question about working conditions may reflect a temporal theme: the past ("how good things used to be here"), the present ("the need to talk with management now before production gets worse"), or the future ("employee expectations to be involved in planning and goal setting").

Other aspects of the methodology include selection of a sampling plan, development of recording and coding instructions, data reduction, inferences about the context, and statistical analysis. Content analysis guards against selective perception of the content, has provision for the rigorous application of reliability and validity criteria, and is amenable to computerization.

The data to be content-analyzed include materials of interest to management researchers: books, chapters, historical documents, speeches, interviews, advertisements, promotional brochures, group interactions, paragraphs, and words. Any recorded activity with its own syntax and semantics is subject to measurement and analysis. Thus, content analysis may be used to analyze written, audio, or video data from experiments, observations, surveys, and secondary data studies.

Let's look at an informal application of content analysis to a problematic, open question. In this truncated example, suppose employees in the assembly operation of a unionized manufacturing firm are asked, "How can management-employee relations be improved?" A sample of the responses yields the following:

1. Management should treat the worker with more respect.
2. Managers should stop trying to speed up the assembly line.
3. Working conditions in the shop are terrible. Managers should correct them.
4. The foreman should be fired. He is unfair in his treatment of workers.
5. Managers should form management-worker councils in the department to iron out problems and improve relations.
6. Management should stop trying to undermine union leadership.
7. Management should accept the union's latest proposals on new work rules.

The first step in analysis requires that the units developed reflect the objectives for which the data were collected. The research question is concerned with learning what the assemblers think is the locus of responsibility for improving company-employee relations. The categories selected are keywords and referential units. The first pass through the data produces a few general categories, shown in Figure 15–3. These categories are mutually exclusive and contain only one concept dimension. The use of "other" makes the category set exhaustive. If the sample suggested that

FIGURE   15–3   Open Question Coding Example (before revision)

Question: "How can management-employee relations be improved?"

Locus of Responsibility	Mentioned	Not Mentioned
A. Management	_____	_____
B. Union	_____	_____
C. Worker (other than union)	_____	_____
D. Joint management–union	_____	_____
E. Joint management–workers	_____	_____
F. Other	_____	_____

many respondents identified the need for action by the public, government, or regulatory bodies, then including all of them in "other" would ignore much of the richness of the data.

Since responses to this type of question often suggest specific actions, the second evaluation of the data uses propositional units. This identifies action objects and the actors previously discovered. If we used only the set of categories in Figure 15–3, the analysis would omit a considerable amount of information. The second analysis produces categories for action planning:

1. Human relations
2. Production processes
3. Working conditions
4. Other action areas
5. No action area identified

How can we categorize a response suggesting a combined management-production process? Figure 15–4 illustrates a combination of alternatives. By taking the categories of the first list with the action areas, it is possible to get an accurate frequency count of the joint classification possibilities for this question.

"Don't Know" Responses

The **"don't know" (DK) response** presents special problems for data preparation. When the DK response group is small, it is not troublesome. But there are times when it is of major concern, and it may even be the most frequent response received. Does this mean the question that elicited this response is useless? The answer is, "It

FIGURE 15–4   Open Question Coding (after revision)

Question: "How can management-employee relations be improved?"

Locus of Responsibility	*Frequency (n = 100)*
A. Management	
1. Human relations	15
2. Production processes	45
3. Working conditions	25
4. Other action areas	10
5. No action area identified	5
B. Union	
1. Human relations	10
2. Production processes	10
3. Working conditions	65
4. Other action areas	15
5. No action area identified	0
C. Worker (other than union)	
D.	
E.	
F. Other	

all depends." Most DK answers fall into two categories.[4] First, there is the legitimate DK response when the respondent does not know the answer. This response meets our research objectives; we expect DK responses and consider them to be useful answers.

In the second situation, a DK reply illustrates the researcher's failure to get the appropriate information. Consider the following illustrative questions:

1. Who developed the Managerial Grid concept?
2. Do you believe the new president's fiscal policy is sound?
3. Do you like your present job?
4. Which of the various brands of chewing gum do you believe has the best quality?
5. How often each year do you go to the movies?

It is reasonable to expect that some legitimate DK responses will be made to each of these questions. In the first question, the respondents are asked for a level of information that they often will not have. There seems to be little reason to withhold a correct answer if known. Thus, most DK answers to this question should be considered as legitimate. A DK response to the second question presents a different problem. It is not immediately clear whether the respondent is ignorant of the president's fiscal policy or knows the policy but has not made a judgment about it. The researchers should have asked two questions: In the first, they would have determined the respondent's level of awareness of fiscal policy. If the interviewee passed the awareness test, then a second question would have secured judgment on fiscal policy.

In the remaining three questions, DK responses are more likely to be a failure of the questioning process, although some will surely be legitimate. The respondent may be reluctant to give the information. A DK response to question 3 may be a way of saying, "I do not want to answer that question." Question 4 might also elicit a DK response in which the reply translates to, "This is too unimportant to talk about." In question 5, the respondents are being asked to do some calculation about a topic to which they attach little importance. Now the DK may mean, "I do not want to do that work for something of so little consequence."

Dealing with Undesired DK Responses   The best way to deal with undesired DK answers is to design better questions at the beginning. The interviewers, however, must deal with the problem in the field. Before interviewing, they should identify the questions for which a DK response is unsatisfactory. Several actions are then possible. First, good interviewer-respondent rapport will motivate respondents to provide more usable answers. When interviewers recognize an evasive DK response, they can repeat the question or probe for a more definite answer. The interviewer may also record verbatim any elaboration by the respondent and buck the problem on to the editor.

If the editor finds many undesired responses, little can be done unless the verbatim comments can be interpreted. Understanding the real meaning relies on clues from the respondent's other questions. One way to do this is to estimate the alloca-

TABLE   15–1   Handling "Don't Know" Responses

	Do You Like Your Present Job?		
Years of Service	*Yes*	*No*	*Don't Know*
Less than 1 year	10%	40%	38%
1–3 years	30	30	32
4 years or more	60	30	30
Total	100%	100%	100%
n =	650	150	200

tion of DK answers from other data in the questionnaire. The pattern of responses may parallel income, education, or experience levels. Suppose a question concerning whether employees like their present jobs elicits the answers in Table 15–1. The correlation between years of service and the "don't know" answers and the "no" answers suggests that most of the "don't knows" are disguised "no" answers.

There are several ways to handle "don't know" responses in the tabulations. If there are only a few, it does not make much difference how they are handled, but they will probably be kept as a separate category. If the DK response is legitimate, it should remain as a separate reply category. When we are not sure how to treat it, we should keep it as a separate reporting category and let the reader make the decision.

Another way to treat DK responses is to assume they occur almost randomly. Using this approach, we distribute them among the other answers in the same ratio that the other answers occur. This assumes that those who reply "don't know" are proportionally distributed among all of the groups studied. This can be achieved either by prorating the DK responses or by excluding all DK replies from the tabulation. The latter approach is better since it does not inflate the actual number of other responses.

DATA ENTRY

Researchers have profited from new and more efficient ways of speeding up the research process (see Figure 15–5). **Data entry** converts information gathered by secondary or primary methods to a medium for viewing and manipulation. Keyboard entry remains a mainstay for researchers who need to create a data file immediately and store it in a minimal space on a variety of media.

Optical scanning instruments—the ubiquitous choice of testing services—have improved efficiency. Examinees darken small circles, ellipses, or sets of parallel lines to choose a test answer. Optical scanners process the marked-sensed questionnaires and store the answers in a file. This technology has been adopted by questionnaire designers for the most routine data collection. It reduces the number of times data are handled, thereby reducing the number of errors that are introduced.

Voting procedures used in several states are another example of direct response entry. With a specially prepared punch card, citizens cast their votes by pressing a pen-shaped instrument against the card next to the preferred candidate. This opens a

FIGURE   15–5   Methods of Data Entry

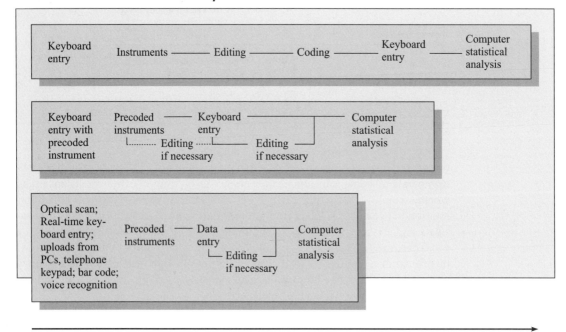

Time required for completion

small hole in a specific column and row of the card. The cards are collected and placed directly into a card reader. This method also removes the coding and entry steps. Another governmental application is the 1040EZ form used by the Internal Revenue Service. It is designed for computerized number and character recognition. Similar character recognition techniques are employed for many forms of data collection. Again, both approaches move the response from the question to data analysis with little handling.

The cost of technology has allowed most researchers access to desktop or portable computers or a terminal linked to a larger computer. This technology enables computer-assisted telephone or personal interviews to be completed with answers entered directly for processing, eliminating intermediate steps and errors.

The increase in computerized random-digit dialing encouraged other data collection innovations. **Voice recognition** and response systems, while still far from mature, are providing some interesting alternatives for the telephone interviewer. Such systems can be used with software that is programmed to call specific three-digit prefixes and randomly generated four-digit numbers, reaching a random sample within a set geographical area. Upon getting a voice response, the computer branches into a questionnaire routine. Currently, the systems are programmed to record the verbal answers, but voice recognition is improving quickly enough so that these systems will soon translate voice responses into data files. Telephone keypad response is another capability made possible by computers linked to telephone lines. Using the telephone keypad (touch tone), the respondent answers questions by pressing the appropriate number. The computer captures the data by "listening," decoding the tone's electrical signal, and storing the numeric or alphabetic answer in a data file.

Field interviewers can use portable computers or electronic notebooks instead of clipboards and pencils. With a built-in communications modem or cellular link, their files can be sent directly to another computer in the field or to a remote site. This lets supervisors inspect data immediately or simplifies processing at a central facility.

Bar code readers are used in several applications: at point-of-sale terminals, for inventory control, for product and brand tracking, and at busy rental car locations to speed the return of cars and generate invoices. This technology can be used to simplify the interviewer's role as a data recorder. Instead of writing (or typing) information about the respondents and their answers by hand, the interviewer can pass a bar code wand over the appropriate codes. The data are recorded in a small, lightweight unit for translation later.

Even with these time reductions between data collection and analysis, continuing innovations in multimedia technology are being developed by the personal computer business. The capability to integrate visual images, audio, and data may soon replace video equipment as the preferred method for recording an experiment, interview, or focus group. A copy of the response data could be extracted for data analysis, but the audio and visual images would remain intact for later evaluation.

Other techniques on the horizon will continue to improve research efficiency and effectiveness. Although technology will never replace researcher judgment, it can reduce data-handling errors, decrease time between data collection and analysis, and help provide more usable information.

Data Entry Formats

A full-screen editor, where an entire data file can be edited or browsed, is a viable means of data entry for statistical packages like SPSS, SAS, or SYSTAT. The same software makes accessing data from databases, spreadsheets, data warehouses, or data marts effortless.

For large projects, database programs serve as valuable data entry devices. A **database** is a collection of data organized for computerized retrieval. Programs allow users to define data fields and link files so storage, retrieval, and updating are simplified. The relationship between data fields, records, files, and databases is illustrated in Figure 15–6. A company's personnel records serve as an example of a database. Employee information may be kept in several files: salary and position, education, benefits, and home and family. The data are separated so authorized people can see only those parts pertinent to their needs. However, the files may be linked so that when, say, a woman changes her name, the change is entered once and all the files are updated.

Researchers consider database entry when they have large amounts of potentially linked data that will be retrieved and tabulated in different ways over time. Another application of a database program is as a "front-end" entry mechanism. A telephone interviewer may ask the question, "How many children live in your home?" The computer's software has been programmed to accept any answer between 0 and 20. If a

FIGURE   15–6   Data Fields, Records, Files, and Databases

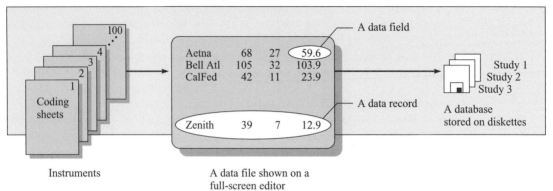

Instruments

A data file shown on a
full-screen editor

Data fields represent single elements of information (e.g., an answer to a question, a description, a number, a statement, etc.). Data fields can contain numeric, alphabetic, or symbolic information. A **record** is a set of data fields that are related. Records are the rows of a data file or spreadsheet program worksheet. **Data files** are sets of records that are grouped together for storage on diskettes, disks, tapes. CD-ROM, or optical disks. **Databases** are made up of one or more data fields that are interrelated.
SOURCE: Company data: Public domain.

"P" is accidentally struck, the program will not accept the answer and will return the interviewer to the question. With a precoded online instrument, much of the editing needed previously is done by the program. In addition, the program can be set for automatic conditional branching. In the example, an answer of 1 or greater causes the program to prompt the questioner to ask the ages of the children. A 0 causes the age question to be automatically skipped. Although this option is available whenever interactive computing is used, front-end processing is typically done within the database design. The database will then store the data into a set of linked files that allow the data to be easily sorted. Descriptive statistics and tables are readily generated from within the base.

Spreadsheets are a specialized type of database. For data that need organizing, tabulating, and simple statistics, spreadsheets provide an easy-to-learn mechanism. They also offer some database management, graphics, and presentation capabilities. Data entry on a **spreadshe**et uses numbered rows and letter columns with a matrix of thousands of cells into which an entry may be placed. Spreadsheets allow you to type numbers, formulas, and text into appropriate cells. Many statistics programs for personal computers and also charting and graphics applications have data editors similar to the spreadsheet format shown in Figure 15–7. This is a convenient and flexible means for entering and viewing the data.

A **data warehouse** organizes large volumes of data into categories to facilitate retrieval, interpretation, and sorting by end-users. The data warehouse provides an accessible archive to support dynamic organizational intelligence applications. The contents of departmental computers are duplicated in a central repository where standard architecture and consistent data definitions are applied. These data are available to departments or cross-functional teams for direct analysis, or through intermediate storage facilities, **data marts,** that compile locally required information.

FIGURE   15–7   Data Entry Using Spreadsheets and Editors

Spreadsheet Data Entry: Lotus 1-2-3 ®

| File Edit | Worksheet | Range | Graph | Data | Style | Tools | Window |

A:A2: [W4]   @IF(@CELL("type",B2..B17)="1",A1+1,@S(AH2..AH2))

CompleteCare

	A	A	B	C	D	E	F	G	H	I	J	K	L	M	N
	1	Card	Received	1a.	1b.	2a.	2b.	2c.	3.	4.	5.	6.	7.	8a.	8b.
2	1	2-20	5	5	4	5	5	5	5	5	5	5	3	5
3	2	2-20	4	4	4	2	5	4	4	4	4	3	5	5
4	3	2-20	4	4	4	4	4	3	5	4	5	5	4	5
5	4	2-20	4	4	3	1	4	5	3	3	4	4	5	5
6	5	2-20	5	4	5	5	5	4	4	5	5	5	4	3
7	6	2-20	3	3	1	3	1	2	4	1	2	5	4	3
8	7	2-20	4	4	5	4	4	5	5	5	5	4	3	5
9	8	2-20	5	5	5	4	5	5	5	1	5	5	5	3
10	9	2-20	5	5	2	5	5	5	5	5	5	4	5	5
11	10	2-20		4	4	4	4	1	3	5	3	5	3	5
12	11	2-21	4	4	1	4	4	4	4	4	5	5	4	5
13	12	2-21	4	5	5			5	4	4	4	5	4	5
14	13	2-21	4	5	3	5	5	5	4	4	5	3	5	5
15	14	2-21	3	4	4	4	4	4	4	4	4	5	5	4
16	15	2-21	5	4	4	4	4	3	4	4	4	4	5	5
17	16	2-21	1	4	5	4	4	4	4	2	3	5	3	4
18	17	2-21	5	4	4	5	5	5	5	4	5	4	4	5
19	18	2-21	5	5	4	5	5	5	5	5	5	4	4	5

Statistical Program Data Editor: Data Desk ®

Company	Assets	Sales	Market Value
Rockwell Int'l	9033	12534	5491
Sundstrand	1503	1595	1341
Alco Standard	1546	4207	1290
Comdisco	4293	1758	1091
General Signal	1324	1918	1029
Tecumseh Products	1034	1510	697
Timken	1566	1533	895
FMC	2819	3415	1253

The entire system must be constructed for integration and compatibility among the different data marts.

Data warehouse tools are of two types: (1) transformation and cleaning and (2) end-user access tools. Both primary and secondary data can be warehoused. With survey responses, for example, one transformation process involves *binning* the classification variables. A respondent's occupation could have a value from 1 to 20. If each occupational code was allowed to remain a discrete value, the information might be lost because of sparse data in that category. Binned responses provide more data points and increase the information within each essential category. Data quality is a problem during transformation and cleaning. To avoid useless information, the data should have few missing values. The key is to continually monitor data as it is added to the data warehouse, using the preliminary data analysis techniques described in the next section of this chapter. End user access tools for data warehousing are discussed later in the chapter in conjunction with data mining.

EXPLORING, DISPLAYING, AND EXAMINING DATA

The convenience of data entry via spreadsheet or with the data editor of a statistical program makes it tempting to move directly to statistical analysis. Why waste time finding out if the data confirm the hypothesis that motivated the study? Why not begin with statistical summaries and then hypothesis tests?

In Chapter 2, we said research conducted scientifically is a puzzle-solving activity. We also noted that an attitude of curiosity, suspicion, and imagination was essential to the discovery process. It is natural, then, that exploration of the data would be an integral part of our perspective. When the study's purpose is not the production of causal inferences, confirmatory data analysis is not required. When it is, we advocate discovering as much as possible about the data before selecting the appropriate means of confirmation.

An Exploratory Data Analysis Approach

Exploratory data analysis (EDA) is a data analysis perspective and set of techniques.[5] In **exploratory data analysis,** the data guide the choice of analysis—or a revision of the planned analysis—rather than the analysis presuming to overlay its structure on the data without the benefit of the analyst's scrutiny. This is comparable to our position that research should be problem oriented rather than tool driven. The flexibility to respond to the patterns revealed by successive iterations in the discovery process is an important attribute of this approach. By comparison, **confirmatory data analysis** occupies a position closer to classical statistical inference in its use of significance and confidence. But confirmatory analysis may also differ from traditional practices by using information from a closely related data set or by validating findings through the gathering and analyzing of new data.[6]

One authority compared exploratory data analysis to the role of police detectives and other investigators and confirmatory analysis to that of judges and the judicial system. The former are involved in the search for clues and evidence; the latter are preoccupied with evaluating the strength of what is found. Exploratory data analysis is the first step in the search for evidence, without which confirmatory analysis has nothing to evaluate.[7] Consistent with that analogy, EDA shares a commonality with exploratory designs, not formalized ones. Because it doesn't follow a rigid structure, it is free to take many paths in unraveling the mysteries in the data—to sift the unpredictable from the predictable.

A major contribution of the exploratory approach lies in the emphasis on visual representations and graphical techniques over summary statistics. Summary statistics, as you will see momentarily, may obscure, conceal, or even misrepresent the underlying structure of the data. When numerical summaries are used exclusively and accepted without visual inspection, the selection of confirmatory models may be precipitous, based on flawed assumptions, and may consequently produce erroneous conclusions.[8] For these reasons, preliminary analysis should begin with visual inspection, not numerical summaries. After that, it is not only possible but also desirable to cycle between exploratory and confirmatory approaches.

In the following sections, we will survey the fundamentals of EDA with respect to distributions, displays, and techniques. But first, in the "Close-Up," we review descriptive statistics and start building a case for doing something wiser than taking a quick look at number summaries and wading into inferential statistics.

CLOSE-UP
DESCRIPTIVE STATISTICS

DESCRIBING DISTRIBUTIONS

In the first part of the chapter, we discussed how responses can be coded and entered. When nominal measurements are involved (e.g., company classifications like high-tech consumer products, retailing), each category is represented by its own numerical code. With ordinal data, the item's rank, reflecting a position in the range from the lowest to the highest, is entered. The same is true with interval-ratio scores. When these data are tabulated, they may be arrayed from the lowest to the highest scores on their scales. Together with the frequency of occurrence, the observations form a **distribution** of values.

Many variables of interest have distributions that approximate a **standard normal distribution.** This distribution, shown in Part A of Figure 15–8, is the most significant theoretical distribution in statistics. It is a standard of comparison for describing distributions of sample data and is used with inferential statistics that assume normally distributed variables.

The characteristics of location, spread, and shape describe distribution. Their definitions, applications, and formulas fall under the heading of **descriptive statistics.** Although the definitions will be familiar to most readers, the review takes the following perspective on distributional characteristics:

1. A distribution's shape is just as consequential as its location and spread.
2. Visual representations are superior to numerical ones for discovering a distribution's shape.
3. The choice of summary statistics to describe a singe variable is contingent on the appropriateness of those statistics for the shape of the distribution.[9]

MEASURES OF LOCATION

The common **measures of location,** often called **central tendency** or *center*, include the mean, median, and mode.

Mean

The **mean** is the arithmetic average. It is the sum of the observed values in the distribution divided

(*continued*)

FIGURE   15–8   Characteristics of Distributions

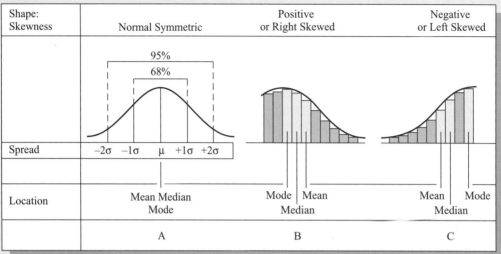

Shape: Skewness	Normal Symmetric	Positive or Right Skewed	Negative or Left Skewed
Spread	-2σ -1σ μ $+1\sigma$ $+2\sigma$		
Location	Mean Median Mode	Mode Mean Median	Mean Mode Median
	A	B	C

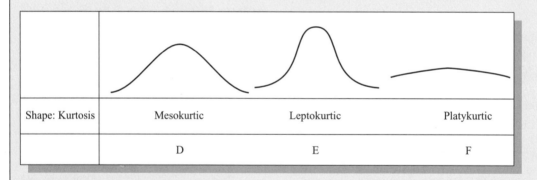

Shape: Kurtosis	Mesokurtic	Leptokurtic	Platykurtic
	D	E	F

by the number of observations. It is the location measure most frequently used for interval-ratio data but can be misleading when the distribution contains extreme scores, large or small. The symbol for the sample mean is $\overline{X}$. The Greek letter mu (μ) is used to represent the population.

$$\overline{X} = \sum_{i=1}^{n} \frac{X_i}{n}$$

Median

The **median** is the midpoint of the distribution. Half of the observations in the distribution fall above and the other half fall below the median.

When the distribution has an even number of observations, the median is the average of the two middle scores. The median is the most appropriate locator of center for ordinal data and has resistance to extreme scores, thereby making it a preferrred measure for interval-ratio data—particularly those with asymmetric distributions. The median is sometimes symbolized, *M* or *mdn*.

Mode

The **mode** is the most frequently occurring value. When there is more than one score that has the highest yet equal frequency, the distribution is bi-modal or multimodal. When every score has an equal number of observations, there is no mode. The mode is the location measure for normal data and a point of reference along with the median and mean for examining spread and shape.

MEASURES OF SPREAD

The common **measures of spread,** alternatively referred to as *dispersion* or **variability,** are the variance, standard deviation, range, interquartile range, and quartile deviation. They describe how scores cluster or scatter in a distribution.

Variance

The **variance** is the average of the squared deviation scores from the distribution's mean. It is a measure of score dispersion about the mean. If all the scores are identical, the variance is 0. The greater the dispersion of scores, the greater is the variance. Both the variance and the standard deviation are used with interval-ratio data. The symbol for the sample variance is s^2, and the population variance is the Greek letter sigma squared (σ^2).

$$s^2 = \sum_{i=1}^{n} \frac{(X_i - \bar{X})^2}{n-1}$$

Standard Deviation

The **standard deviation** is the positive square root of the variance. It is perhaps the most frequently used measure of spread because it improves interpretability by removing the variance's square and expressing deviations in their original units (e.g., net profits in dollars, not dollars squared). Like the mean, the standard deviation is affected by extreme scores. The symbol for the sample standard deviation is *s*, and a population standard deviation is σ. Alternatively, it is labeled *std. dev.*

$$s = \sqrt{s^2}$$

Range

The **range** is the difference between the largest and smallest score in the distribution. Unlike the standard deviation, it is computed from only the minimum and maximum scores; thus, it is a very rough measure of spread. With the range as a point of comparison, it is possible to get an idea of the homogeneity (small std. dev.) or heterogeneity (large std. dev.) of the distribution. For homogeneous distribution, the ratio of the range to the standard deviation should be between 2 and 6. A number above 6 would indicate a high degree of heterogeneity. The range provides useful but limited information for all data. It is mandatory for ordinal data.

Interquartile Range

The **interquartile range** (IQR) is the difference between the first and third quartiles of the distribution. It is also called the *midspread.* Ordinal or ranked data use this measure in conjunction with the median. It is also used with interval-ratio data when asymmetrical distributions are suspected or for exploratory analysis. Recall the following relationships. The minimum value of the distribution is the 0th percentile; the maximum, the 100th percentile. The first quartile (Q_1) is the 25th percentile; it is also known as the *lower hinge* when used with boxplots. The median, or Q_2, is the 50th percentile. The third quartile (Q_3) is the 75th pecentile; it is also known as the *upper hinge.* The IQR is the distance between the hinges.[10]

Quartile Deviation

The **quartile deviation,** or semi-interquartile range, is expressed as

(continued)

$$Q = \frac{Q_1 - Q_3}{2}$$

The quartile deviation is always used with the median for ordinal data. It is helpful for interval-ratio data of a skewed nature. In a normal distribution, the median plus one quartile deviation (Q) on either side encompasses 50 percent of the observations. Eight Qs cover approximately the range. Q's relationship with the standard deviation is constant (Q = .6745s) when scores are normally distributed.

MEASURES OF SHAPE

The **measures of shape,** *skewness* and *kurtosis,* describe departures from the symmetry of a distribution and its relative flatness (or peakedness), respectively. They are related to statistics known as *moments*, which use deviation scores $(X - \bar{X})$. The variance, for example, is a second power moment. The measures of shape use third and fourth power deviations for their computations and are often difficult to interpret when extreme scores are in the distribution. Generally, shape is best communicated through visual displays.

Skewness

Skewness is a measure of a distribution's deviation from symmetry. In a symmetrical distribution, the mean, median, and mode are in the same location. A distribution that has cases stretching toward one tail or the other is called *skewed*. As shown in Figure 15–8, when the tail stretches to the left, to smaller values, it is negatively skewed. Scores stretching toward the right, toward larger values, skew the distribution positively. Note the relationship between the mean, median, and made in asymmetrical distributions. The symbol for skewness is *sk*.

$$sk = \frac{m_3}{m_2\sqrt{m_2}} = \frac{\Sigma x^3 / N}{\left(\sqrt{\Sigma x^2 / N}\right)^3}$$

When a distribution approaches symmetry, *sk* is approximately 0. With a positive skew, *sk* will be a positive number; with negative skew, *sk* will be negative.

Kurtosis

As illustrated in Figure 15–8, **kurtosis** is a measure of a distribution's peakedness (or flatness). Distributions where scores cluster heavily or pile up in the center (along with more observations than normal in the extreme tails) are peaked or *leptokurtic*. Flat distributions with scores more evenly distributed and tails fatter than a normal distribution are called *playtykurtic*. Intermediate or *mesokurtic* distributions are neither too peaked nor too flat. The symbol for kurtosis is *ku*.

$$ku = \frac{m_4}{m_2^2} - 3 = \frac{\Sigma x^4 / N}{\left(\Sigma x^2 / N\right)^2} - 3$$

The value of *ku* for a normal or mesokurtic distribution is 0. A leptokurtic distribution will have a positive value, and the platykurtic will be negative. As with skewness, the larger the absolute value of the index, the more extreme is the characteristic.

Frequency Tables, Bar Charts, and Pie Charts[11]

Several useful techniques for displaying data are not new to EDA. They are essential to any preliminary examination of the data. For example, a **frequency table** is a simple device for arraying data. An example is presented in Table 15–2. It arrays data from the lowest value to the highest, with columns for percent, percent adjusted for missing values, and cumulative percent. Sector, the nominal variable that describes

TABLE 15–2   A Frequency Table of Market Sector

Value Label	Value	Frequency	Percent	Valid Percent	Cum. Percent
Chemicals and materials	1	10	10.0	10.0	10.0
Consumer products	2	8	8.0	8.0	18.0
Durables/capital equipment	3	7	7.0	7.0	25.0
Energy	4	13	13.0	13.0	38.0
Financial	5	24	24.0	24.0	62.0
Health	6	4	4.0	4.0	66.0
High-tech	7	11	11.0	11.0	77.0
Insurance	8	6	6.0	6.0	83.0
Retailing	9	7	7.0	7.0	90.0
Other	10	10	10.0	10.0	100.0
Total		100	100.0	100.0	

Valid cases   100   Missing cases   0

the business classifications or markets of the sampled corporations, provides the observations for this table. Although there are 100 observations, the small number of categories makes the variable easily tabled. The same data are presented in Figure 15–9 using a bar chart and a pie chart. The values and percentages are more readily understood in this graphic format, and visualization of the sector categories and their relative sizes is improved.

When the variable of interest is measured on an interval-ratio scale and is one with many potential values, these techniques are not particularly informative. Table 15–3 is a condensed frequency table of the highest total return to investors measured in percentages of the top 48 companies in this category taken from Fortune 500.[12] Only two values, 59.9 and 66 have a frequency greater than 1. Thus, the primary contribution of this table is an ordered list of values. If the table were converted to a bar chart, it would have 48 bars of equal length and two bars with two occurrences. And bar charts do not reserve spaces for values where no observations occur within the range. Constructing a pie chart for this variable would also be pointless.

Histograms

The histogram is a conventional solution for the display of interval-ratio data. **Histograms** are used when it is possible to group the variable's values into intervals. Histograms are constructed with bars (or asterisks that represent data values) where each value occupies an equal amount of area within the enclosed area. Data analysts find histograms useful for (1) displaying all intervals in a distribution, even those without observed values, and (2) examining the shape of the distribution for skewness, kurtosis, and the modal pattern. When looking at a histogram, one might ask: Is there a single hump (a mode)? Are subgroups identifiable when multiple modes are present? Are straggling data values detached from the central concentration?[13]

The values for the return to investors variable presented in Table 15–3 were measured on a ratio scale and are easily grouped. Other variables possessing an underlying order are similarly appropriate for histograms. A histogram would not be

FIGURE 15–9 **Nominal Variable Displays**

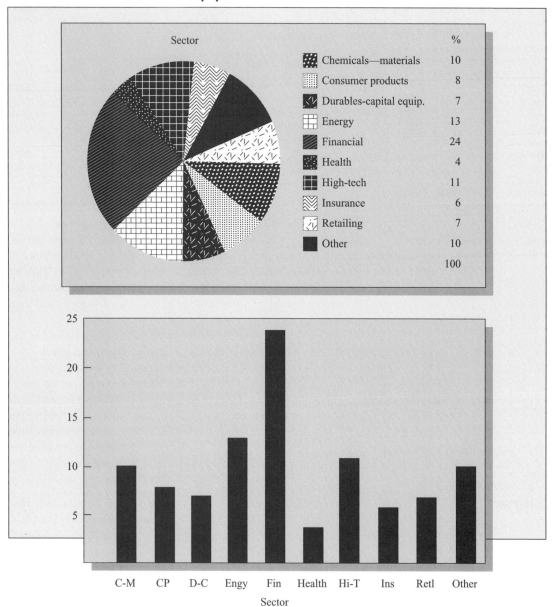

used for a nominal variable like sector (Figure 15–9) that has no order to its categories.

A histogram of the return to investors variable taken from the Fortune 500 ranked by performance listing is shown in Figure 15–10. The midpoint for each interval for the variable of interest, return to investors, is shown on the horizontal axis, the fre-

TABLE   15–3   Data Display of the Top 48 in the Fortune 500.

Row	Value	Frequency	Percent	Cum. Percent	Row	Value	Frequency	Percent	Cum. Percent
1	54.9	1	2	2	25	75.6	1	2	54
2	55.4	1	2	4	26	76.4	1	2	56
3	55.6	1	2	6	27	77.5	1	2	58
4	56.4	1	2	8	28	78.9	1	2	60
5	56.8	1	2	10	29	80.9	1	2	62
6	56.9	1	2	12	30	82.2	1	2	64
7	57.8	1	2	14	31	82.5	1	2	66
8	58.1	1	2	16	32	86.4	1	2	68
9	58.2	1	2	18	33	88.3	1	2	70
10	58.3	1	2	20	34	102.5	1	2	72
11	58.5	1	2	22	35	104.1	1	2	74
12	59.9	2	4	26	36	110.4	1	2	76
13	61.5	1	2	28	37	111.9	1	2	78
14	62.6	1	2	30	38	118.6	1	2	80
15	64.8	1	2	32	39	123.8	1	2	82
16	66.0	2	4	36	40	131.2	1	2	84
17	66.3	1	2	38	41	140.9	1	2	86
18	67.6	1	2	40	42	146.2	1	2	88
19	69.1	1	2	42	43	153.2	1	2	90
20	69.2	1	2	44	44	163.2	1	2	92
21	70.5	1	2	46	45	166.7	1	2	94
22	72.7	1	2	48	46	183.2	1	2	96
23	72.9	1	2	50	47	206.9	1	2	98
24	73.5	1	2	52	48	218.2	1	2	100

quency or number of observations in each interval on the vertical axis. We erect a vertical bar above the midpoint of each interval on the horizontal scale. The height of the bar corresponds with the frequency of observations in the interval above which it is erected. This histogram was constructed with intervals 20 increments wide, and the last interval contains only two observations, 206.9 and 218.2. These values are found in the frequency table (Table 15–3). Intervals with 0 counts show gaps in the data and alert the analyst to look for problems with spread. When the upper tail of the distribution is compared with the frequency table, we find three extreme values (183.2, 206.9, and 218.2). Along with the peaked midpoint and reduced number of observations in the upper tail, this histogram warns us of irregularities in the data.

Stem-and-Leaf Displays[14]

The **stem-and-leaf display** is an EDA technique that is closely related to the histogram. It shares some of its features but offers several unique advantages. It is easy to construct by hand for small samples or may be produced by computer programs.

In contrast to histograms, which lose information by grouping data values into intervals, the stem-and-leaf presents actual data values that can be inspected directly without the use of enclosed bars or asterisks as the representation medium. This feature reveals the distribution of values within the interval and preserves their rank order for finding the median, quartiles, and other summary statistics. It also eases linking a specific observation back to the data file and to the subject that produced it.

FIGURE   15–10   Histogram of the Return to Investors

Return to Investors (%)

Visualization is the second advantage of stem-and-leaf displays. The range of values is apparent at a glance, and both shape and spread impressions are immediate. Patterns in the data are easily observed such as gaps where no values exist, areas where values are clustered, or outlying values that differ from the main body of the data.

In order to develop a stem-and-leaf display for the data in Table 15–3, the first digits of each data item are arranged to the left of a vertical line. Next, we pass through the return to investor percentages in the order they were recorded and place the last digit for each item (the unit position, 1.0) to the right of the vertical line. Note that the digit to the right of the decimal point is ignored. The last digit for each item is placed on the horizontal row corresponding to its first digit(s). Now it is a simple matter to rank-order the digits in each row, creating the stem-and-leaf display shown in Figure 15–11.

Each line or row in this display is referred to as a *stem,* and each piece of information on the stem is called a *leaf.* The first line or row is

5 | 4 5 5 6 6 6 7 8 8 8 8 9 9

The meaning attached to this line or row is that there are 13 items in the data set whose first digit is five: 54, 55, 55, 56, 56, 56, 57, 58, 58, 58, 58, 59, and 59. The second line,

6 | 1 2 4 6 6 6 7 9 9

shows that there are nine return to investors percentage values whose first digit is six: 61, 62, 64, 66, 66, 66, 67, 69, 69. The stem is the digit(s) to the left of the vertical line

FIGURE   15–11   A Stem-and-Leaf Display

5	4 5 5 6 6 6 7 8 8 8 8 9 9
6	1 2 4 6 6 6 7 8 9
7	0 2 2 3 5 6 7 8
8	0 2 2 6 8
9	
10	2 4
11	0 1 8
12	3
13	1
14	0 6
15	3
16	3 6
17	
18	3
19	
20	6
21	8

(6 for this example), and the leaf is the digit(s) to the right of the vertical line (1, 2, 4, 6, 6, 6, 7, 9, 9).

When the stem-and-leaf display shown in Figure 15–11 is turned upright (rotated ninety degrees to the left), the shape is the same as that of the histogram shown in Figure 15–10.

Boxplots[15]

The **boxplot,** or *box-and-whisker plot,* is another technique used frequently in exploratory data analysis.[16] A boxplot reduces the detail of the stem-and-leaf display and provides a different visual image of the distribution's location, spread, shape, tail length, and outliers. Boxplots are extensions of the **five-number summary** of a distribution. This summary consists of the median, upper and lower quartiles, and the largest and smallest observations. The median and quartiles are used because they are particularly **resistant statistics.** *Resistance* is a characteristic that "provides insensitivity to localized misbehavior in data."[17] Resistant statistics are unaffected by outliers and change only slightly in response to the replacement of small portions of the data set.

Recall the previous discussion of the mean and standard deviation in the "Close-Up." Now assume we take the data set [5,6,6,7,7,7,8,8,9]. The mean of the set is 7, the standard deviation 1.23. If the 9 is replaced with 90, the mean becomes 16 and the standard deviation increases to 27.78. The mean is now two times larger than most of the numbers in the distribution, and the standard deviation is more than 22 times its original size. Changing only one of nine values has disturbed the location and spread summaries to the point where they no longer represent the other eight values. Both the mean and the standard deviation are considered **nonresistant statistics;** they are susceptible to the effects of extreme values in the tails of the distribution and do not represent typical values well under conditions of asymmetry. The standard deviation is particularly problematic because it is computed from the squared deviations from the mean.[18] In contrast, the median and quartiles are highly resistant to change. When we changed the 9 to 90, the median remained at 7 and the lower and upper quartiles stayed at 6 and 8, respectively. Because of the nature of quartiles, up to 25 percent of the data can be made extreme without perturbing the median, the rectangular composition of the plot, or the quartiles themselves. These characteristics of resistance are incorporated into the construction of boxplots.

Boxplots may be constructed easily by hand or by computer programs. The basic ingredients of the plot are the (1) rectangular plot that encompasses 50 percent of the data values, (2) a center line (or other notation) marking the median and going through the width of the box, (3) the edges of the box, called hinges, and (4) the whiskers that extend from the right and left hinges to the largest and smallest values. These values may be found within 1.5 times the interquartile range (IQR) from either edge of the box. These components and their relationships are shown in Figure 15–12.

We can create a boxplot of the return to investors variable from the information provided in Table 15–3. With the five-number summary, we have the basis for a skeletal plot.

Minimum	Lower Hinge	Median	Upper Hinge	Maximum
54.9	60.3	74.55	111.52	218.2

The plot shown in Figure 15–13 started with these data and the following calculations. Beginning with the box, the ends are drawn using the lower and upper quartile

FIGURE   15–12   Boxplot Components

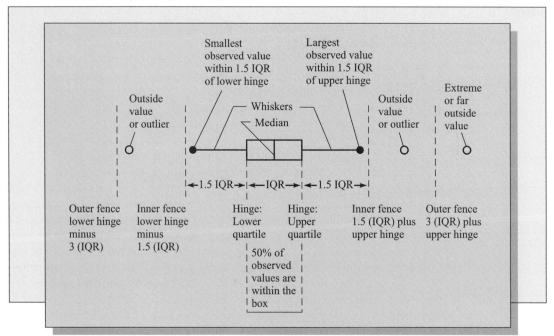

FIGURE   15–13   Boxplot of Return to Investors

(hinge) data. The median is drawn in at 74.55. Then the IQR is calculated (111.52 – 60.3 = 51.22). From this we can locate the lower and upper fences. The fences are –16.53 and +188.35. Next, the smallest and largest data values from the distribution within the fences are used to determine the whisker length. These values are 54.9 and 183.2. We are now able to see the outliers in relation to the "main body" of the data. **Outliers** are data points that exceed + 1.5 IQRs of a boxplot's hinges. Data values for the outliers are added, and identifiers may be provided for interesting values. The completed boxplot is shown in Figure 15–13.

		Fence	
IQR	*Distance to*	*(–)*	*(+)*
51.22	* (±1.5) = 76.83	60.3 – 76.83 = –16.53	111.52 + 76.83 = 188.35

In preliminary analysis, it is important to separate legitimate outliers from errors in measurement, editing, coding, and data entry. Outliers that reflect unusual cases are an important source of information for the study. They are displayed or given special statistical treatment, or other portions of the data set are sometimes shielded from their effects. Outliers that are mistakes should be corrected or removed.

Figure 15–14 summarizes several comparisons that are of help to the analyst. Boxplots are an excellent diagnostic tool, especially when graphed on the same scale. The upper two plots in the figure are both symmetric, but one is larger than the other. Larger box widths are sometimes used when the second variable, from the same measurement scale, comes from a larger sample size. The box widths should be proportional to the square root of the sample size, but not all plotting programs account for this.[19] Right- and left-skewed distributions and those with reduced spread are also presented clearly in the plot comparison. Finally, groups may be compared by means of multiple plots. One variation, in which a notch at the median marks off a confidence interval to test the equality of group medians, takes us a step closer to hypothesis testing.[20] Here the sides of the box return to full width at the upper and lower confidence intervals. When the intervals do not overlap, we can be confident, at a specified confidence level, that the medians of the two populations are different.

FIGURE   15–14   Diagnostics with Boxplots

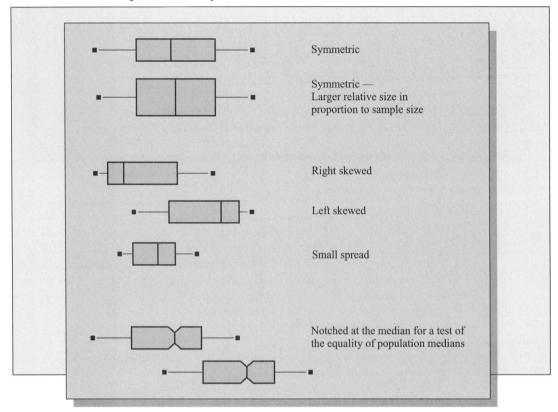

In Figure 15–15, multiple boxplots compare five sectors on the return to investors variable. The overall impression is one of potential problems for the analyst: unequal variances, skewness, and extreme outliers. Note the similarities of the profiles of finance and retailing in contrast the to high-tech and insurance sectors. If hypothesis tests are planned, further examination of this plot for each sector would require a stem-and-leaf display and a five-number summary. From this, we could make decisions on test selection and whether the data should be transformed or reexpressed before further analysis.

Transformation[21]   Some of the examples in this section have departed from normality. While this makes for good illustrations, such data pose special problems in preliminary analysis. Transformation is one solution to this problem. **Transformation** is the reexpression of data on a new scale using a single mathematical function for each data point. Although nominal and ordinal data may be transformed, the procedures are beyond the scope of this book. We will consider only interval-ratio scale transformations here.

The fact that data collected on one scale are found to depart from the assumptions of normality and constant variance does not preclude reexpressing them on another scale. What is discovered, of course, must be linked to the original data.

FIGURE   15–15   Boxplot Comparison of Sectors

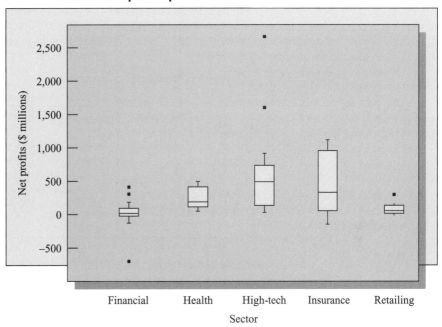

We transform data for several reasons: (1) to improve interpretation and compatibility with other data sets, (2) to enhance symmetry and stabilize spread, and (3) to improve linear relationships between and among variables. We improve interpretation when we find alternate ways to understand the data and discover patterns or relationships that may not have been revealed on the original scales. A **standard score,** or *Z score,* may be calculated to improve compatibility among variables that come from different scales and require comparison. *Z* scores convey distance in standard deviation units with a mean of 0 and a standard deviation of 1. This is accomplished by converting the raw score, X_i, to

$$Z = \frac{X_i - \overline{X}}{s}$$

Z scores improve interpretation through their reference to the normal curve and our understanding of the areas under it.

Conversion of centimeters to inches, stones to pounds, liters to gallons, or Celsius to Fahrenheit are examples of linear conversions that change the scale but do not change symmetry or spread. Many statisticians consider these data manipulations instead of transformations.

Nonlinear transformations are often needed to satisfy the other two reasons for reexpressing data. Normality and constancy of variance are important assumptions for many parametric statistical techniques. A transformation to reduce skewness and stabilize variance makes it possible to use various confirmatory techniques without violating their assumptions. Analysis of the relationship between variables also benefits from transformation. Improved predictions and better diagnostics of fit and residuals (as in regression analysis) are frequent payoffs.

Transformations are defined with power, p, as the reexpression of x with x^p.[22] Table 15–4 shows the most frequently used power transformations.

TABLE   15–4   Frequently Used Power Transformations

Power	Transformation
3	Cube
2	Square
1	No charge: existing data
1/2	Square root
0	Logarithm (usually Lg_{10})
–1/2	Reciprocal root
–1	Reciprocal
–2	Reciprocal square
–3	Reciprocal cube

We use *spread-and-level* plots to guide our choice of a power transformation. By plotting the log of the median against the log of the interquartile range, we can find the slope of the plot: where p, the power we are seeking, is equal to $1 -$ slope. Although 1/4 and 1/3 powers often result—and are sometimes preferred—many computer programs require rounding the transformation to the nearest half power.

The return to investors variable is used to illustrate this concept. The data distribution shows a right skew. The five-number summary (data in millions of dollars) reveals an extreme score as the maximum data point:

Minimum	Lower Hinge	Median	Upper Hinge	Maximum
54.9	60.3	74.55	111.52	218.2

The largest observation, 218.2, is only approximately 0.5 IQRs beyond the main body of data, and there is only one other value beyond the fence.

A quick calculation of the ratio of the largest observation to the smallest (218.2/54.9 = 3.97) serves as the final confirmation that transformation might not be worthwhile. It is desirable that this informal index is greater than 20; with ratios less than 2, transformation is not practical.[23] From this information, we might conclude that the return to investors variable is not a good candidate for transformation.

When researchers communicate their findings to management, the advantages of reexpression must be balanced against pragmatism: Some transformed scales have no familiar analogies. Logarithmic dollars can be explained, but how about reciprocal root dollars? Attitude and preference scales might be better understood transformed, but the question of interpretation remains.

Throughout this section we have exploited the visual techniques of exploratory data analysis to look beyond numerical summaries and gain insight into the behavior of the data. Few of the approaches have stressed the need for advanced mathematics, and all have an intuitive appeal for the analyst. When the more common ways of summarizing location, spread, and shape have conveyed an inadequate picture of the data, we have used more resistant statistics to protect us from the effects of extreme scores and occasional errors. We have also emphasized the value of transforming the original scale of the data during preliminary analysis rather than at the point of hypothesis testing.

CROSSTABULATION

The last section focused primarily on single-variable distributions where observations were collected on interval-ratio scales. Frequency tables were introduced for tabulating counts or percentages, and exploratory data analysis techniques were recommended for graphical display and examination of distributions. Many studies would be content to conclude data analysis at this point. Other studies, particularly those with variables composed of category data (frequency counts of nominally scaled variables), may need to inspect the relationships between and among those variables. This analysis is commonly done with crosstabulation.

Crosstabulation is a technique for comparing two classification variables, such as gender and selection by one's company for an overseas assignment. The technique uses tables having rows and columns that correspond to the levels or values of each variable's categories. Table 15–5 is an example of a computer-generated crosstabulation. This table has two rows for gender and two columns for assignment selection. The combination of the variables with their values produces four **cells.** Each cell contains a count of the cases of the joint classification and also the row, column, and

TABLE   15–5   Sample SPSS Crosstabulation of Gender by Overseas Assignment Opportunity

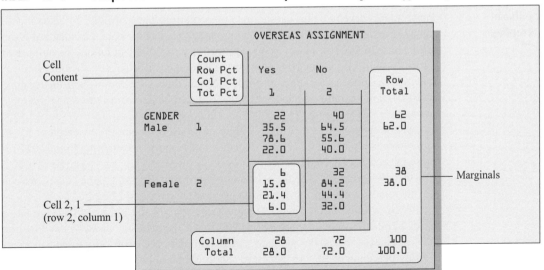

TABLE   15–6   Comparison of Percentages in Crosstabulation Studies of Gender by Overseas Assignment

		Study 1						Study 2		
		OVERSEAS ASSIGNMENT						OVERSEAS ASSIGNMENT		
	Count Row Pct Col Pct Tot Pct	Yes 1	No 2	Row Total			Count Row Pct Col Pct Tot Pct	Yes 1	No 2	Row Total
GENDER Male	1	22 35.5 78.6 22.0	40 64.5 55.6 40.0	62 62.0		GENDER Male	1	225 25.0 62.5 15.0	675 75.0 59.2 45.0	900 60.0
Female	2	6 15.8 21.4 6.0	32 84.2 44.4 32.0	38 38.0		Female	2	135 22.5 37.5 9.0	465 77.5 40.8 31.0	600 40.0
Column Total		28 28.0	72 72.0	100 100.0		Column Total		360 24.0	1140 76.0	1500 100.0

total percentages. The number of row cells and column cells is often used to designate the size of the table, as in this 2 × 2 table. The cells are individually identified by their row and column numbers, as illustrated. Row and column totals, called **marginals,** appear at the bottom and right "margins" of the table. They show the counts and percentages of the separate rows and columns.

When tables are constructed for statistical testing, we call them **contingency tables,** and the test determines if the classification variables are independent. Of course, tables may be larger than 2 × 2.

The Use of Percentages

Percentages serve two purposes in data presentation. They simplify by reducing all numbers to a range from 0 to 100. Second, they translate the data into standard form, with a base of 100, for relative comparisons. In a sampling situation, the number of cases that fall into a category is meaningless unless it is related to some base. A count of 28 overseas assignees has little meaning unless we know it is from a sample of 100. Using the latter as a base, we conclude that 28 percent of this study's sample has an overseas assignment.

While the above is useful, it is even more useful when the research problem calls for a comparison of several distributions of data. Assume the previously reported data was collected five years ago and the present study had a sample of 1,500, of which 360 were selected for overseas assignments. By using percentages, we can see the relative relationships and shifts in the data (see Table 15–6).

With two-dimension tables, the selection of a row or column will accentuate a particular distribution or comparison. This raises the question about which direction the percentages should be calculated. Most computer programs offer options for presenting percentages in both directions and interchanging the rows and columns of the table. But in situations when one variable is hypothesized to be the presumed cause, is thought to affect or predict a response, or is simply antecedent to the other variable, we label it the *independent* variable. Percentages should then be computed in the direction of this variable. Thus, if the independent variable is placed on the row, select row percentages; if it is on the column, select column percentages.[24] In which direction should the percentages run in the previous example? If only the column percentages are reported, we imply that assignment status has some effect on gender. This is implausible. When percentages are reported by rows, the implication is that gender influences selection for overseas assignments.

Care should be taken in interpreting percentages from tables. Consider again the data in Table 15–6. From the first to the second study, it is apparent that the percentage of females selected for overseas assignment rose from 6 to 9 percent of their respective samples. This is not to be confused with the percentage of women in the samples who happen to be assignees. Among all *women eligible* for selection in the first study, 15.8 percent were assigned and 84.2 percent were not. Among all *overseas selectees* in the first study, 21.4 percent were women. Similar comparisons can be made for the other categories.

Percentages are used by virtually everyone dealing with numbers—and often incorrectly. The following guidelines, if used during analysis, will prevent errors in reporting.[25]

1. *Averaging percentages.* Percentages cannot be averaged unless each is weighted by the size of the group from which it is derived. Thus, a simple average will not suffice; it is necessary to use a weighted average.

2. *Use of too large percentages.* This often defeats the purpose of percentages—to simplify. A large percentage is difficult to understand and is confusing. If a 1,000 percent increase is experienced, it is better to describe this as a tenfold increase.

3. *Using too small a base.* Percentages hide the base from which they have been computed. A figure of 60 percent when contrasted with 30 percent would appear to suggest a sizable difference. Yet if there are only three cases in the one category and six in the other, the differences would not be as significant as they have been made to appear with percentages.

4. *Percentage decreases can never exceed 100 percent.* This is obvious, but this type of mistake occurs frequently. The higher figure should always be used as the base. For example, if a price was reduced from $1 to $.25, the decrease would be 75 percent (75/100).

Other Table-Based Analysis

The recognition of a meaningful relationship between variables generally signals a need for further investigation. Even if one finds a statistically significant relationship, the questions of why and under what conditions remain. The introduction of a **control variable** to interpret the relationship is often necessary. Crosstabulation tables serve as the framework.

Statistical packages like Minitab, SAS, SPSS, and SYSTAT have among their programs many options for the construction of *n*-way tables with provision for mul-

TABLE   15–7   SPSS Crosstabulation with Control and Nested Variables

	Control variable				
	category 1			category 2	
	Nested variable			Nested variable	
	cat 1	cat 2	cat 3	cat 1	cat 2	cat 3
Stub...	Cells...				

	SEX OF EMPLOYEE			
	MALES		FEMALES	
	MINORITY CLASSIFICATION		MINORITY CLASSIFICATION	
	WHITE	NONWHITE	WHITE	NONWHITE
EMPLOYMENT CATEGORY				
CLERICAL	16%	7%	18%	7%
OFFICE TRAINEE	7%	3%	17%	2%
SECURITY OFFICER	3%	3%		
COLLEGE TRAINEE	7%	0%	1%	
EXEMPT EMPLOYEE	6%	0%	0%	
MBA TRAINEE	1%	0%	0%	
TECHNICAL	1%			

tiple control variables. Suppose you are interested in creating a crosstabulation of two variables with one control. Whatever the number of values in the primary variables, the control variable with five values determines the number of tables. For some applications, it is appropriate to have five separate tables; for others, it might be preferable to have adjoining tables or have the values of all the variables in one. Management reports are of the latter variety. Table 15–7 presents an example in which all three variables are handled under the same banner. Programs such as this one can handle far more complex tables and statistical information.[26]

An advanced variation on *n*-way tables is **automatic interaction detection (AID)**. AID is a sequential partitioning procedure that begins with a dependent variable and a set of predictors. It searches among up to 300 variables for the best single division according to each predictor variable, chooses one, and splits the sample using chi-square tests to create multiway splits. These subgroups then become separate samples for further analysis. The search procedure is repeated to find the variable that, when split into parts, makes the next largest contribution to the reduction of unexplained variation in each subsample, and so on.

Figure 15–16 shows the tree diagram that resulted from an AID study of Mind-Writer's CompleteCare repair service. The initial dependent variable is the overall

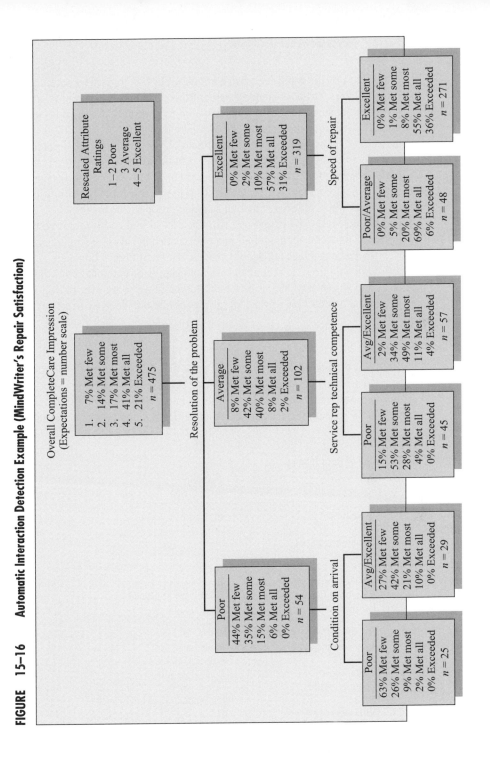

impression of the repair service. This variable was measured on an interval scale. The variables that contribute to perceptions of repair effectiveness were also measured on the same scale but were rescaled to nominal data for this example (1-2 = poor, 3= average, and 4-5= excellent). The top box shows that 62% of the respondents rated the repair service as excellent (41% + 21%). The best predictor of effectiveness is "resolution of the problem." On the left side of the tree, customers who rated "resolution of the problem" as poorly have fewer expectations being met or exceeded than the average (6% versus 62%). A poor rating on "condition on arrival" exacerbates this, reducing the total satisfied group to 2%.

On the right side of the tree, for those customers who rated "resolution of the problem" as excellent, the repair met or exceeded the average respondent (88% versus 62%). Excellent scores on "speed of repair" further improve this rating, taking the total satisfaction up to 91%. This analysis would alert decision makers at MindWriter to the best- and worst-case scenarios for the service, how to recover during a problematic month, and which "key drivers" of the process should receive corrective resources.

DATA MINING

The term **data mining** describes the concept of discovering knowledge from databases. The idea behind data mining is the process of identifying valid, novel, useful, and ultimately understandable patterns in data.[27] Similar to traditional mining, where we search beneath the surface for valuable ore, data mining searches large databases

TABLE   15–8   The Evolution of Data Mining

Evolutionary Step	Investigative Question	Enabling Technologies	Characteristics
Data collection (1960s)	"What was my average total revenue over the last five years?"	Computers, tapes, disks	Retrospective, static data delivery
Data access (1980s)	"What were unit sales in California last December?"	Relational databases (RDBMS), structured query language (SQL), ODBC	Retrospective, dynamic data delivery at record level
Data navigation (1990s)	"What were unit sales in California last December? Drill down to Sacramento."	Online analytic processing (OLAP), multidimensional databases, data warehouses	Retrospective, dynamic data delivery at multiple levels
Data mining (2000)	"What's likely to happen to Sacramento unit sales next month? Why?"	Advanced algorithms, multiprocessor computers, massive databases	Prospective, proactive information delivery

for indispensable information for managing an organization. Both require sifting a large amount of material to discover a profitable vein. Data mining is a useful tool, a new approach that combines discovery with analysis.

Traditional database queries are unidimensional and historical—for example, "How much beer was sold during December 1997 in the Sacramento area?" In contrast, data mining attempts to discover patterns and trends in the data and to infer rules from these patterns. For example, analysis of retail sales can identify products that are often purchased together—like beer and diapers—although they may appear to be unrelated. With the rules discovered from the data mining, a manager is able to support, review, and/or examine decisions.

Evolution of Data Mining

The complex algorithms used in data mining have existed for two decades. The U.S. government has employed customized data-mining software using neural networks, fuzzy logic, and pattern recognition to spot tax fraud, eavesdrop on foreign communications, and process satellite imagery.[28] Until recently, these tools have been available only to very large corporations or agencies due to their high costs. However, this is rapidly changing.

In the evolution from *business data* to *information,* each new step has built on previous ones. For example, large database storage is crucial to the success of data mining. The four steps listed in Table 15–8 were revolutionary because each allowed new management questions to be answered accurately and quickly. [29]

FIGURE   15–17   Data Mining in Business

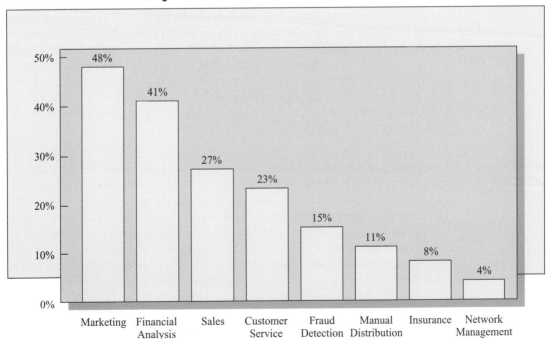

Management Research Uses

The process of extracting information from data has been done in some industries for years. Insurance companies often compete by finding small market segments where the premiums paid greatly outweigh the risks. They issue specially priced policies to a particular segment with profitable results. However, two problems limited the effectiveness: Getting the data was both difficult and expensive, and processing it into information took time—making it historical rather than predictive. Now, instead of recurring high data collection costs, secondary data are available, having been collected for other purposes.

Functional areas of management and select industries are currently driving data-mining projects: marketing, customer service, administrative/financial analysis, sales, manual distribution, insurance, fraud detection, and network management (see Figure 15–17).[30] Data-mining technology provides two unique capabilities to the researcher or manager.

Pattern Discovery   Data-mining tools can be programmed to sweep regularly through databases and identify previously hidden patterns. An example of pattern discovery is the detection of stolen credit cards based on analysis of credit card transaction records. MasterCard processes 12 million transactions daily and uses data mining to detect fraud.[31] Other uses include finding retail purchase patterns, identifying call center volume fluctuations (for staffing), and locating anomalous data that could represent data entry errors.

Predicting Trends and Behaviors   A typical example of a predictive problem is targeted marketing. Using data from past promotional mailings to identify the targets most likely to maximize return on investment, future mailings can be more effective. Bank of America and Mellon Bank both use data-mining software to pinpoint marketing programs that attract high-margin, low-risk customers. Bank of America focuses on credit lines and retail lending; Mellon Bank has used data mining to optimize its home equity line of credit marketing to existing customers.[32] Other predictive problems include forecasting bankruptcy and loan default and finding population segments with similar responses to a given stimulus. Data-mining tools can also be used to build risk models for a specific market, such as discovering the top ten most significant buying trends each week (see Table 15–9).

Data-Mining Techniques[33]

Statistics are essential to the data-mining process. Data-mining tools perform exploratory and confirmatory statistical analysis to discover and validate relationships. Data-mining tools even extend confirmatory statistical approaches by allowing the automated examination of large numbers of hypotheses. Suppose there are twelve variables in the MindWriter survey and we have a process whose outcome can be predicted when three variables are in a particular range. But we are unfamiliar with the repair process and don't know which variables are relevant. With this small problem there are $12 \times 11 \times 10 = 1,320$ combinations. If you spent a minute examining a plot of each pair of variables, you could easily spend twenty-two hours on the problem.

TABLE 15–9   Sample Data-Mining Applications

Banking and finance	The Canadian Imperial Bank of Commerce, based in Toronto, Canada, uses data-mining for statistical modeling of customer traffic to aid in staffing, time analysis of cash transactions to manage currency holding, and the market-basket analysis of products sold to plan marketing strategies.*
Retailing and sales	The Army and Air Force Exchange Service uses data mining to predict how much a particular customer will spend annually, given the customer's age, number of dependents, and income.[†]
Health care	Aetna provides data analysis capabilities to its business partners and affiliates. Hospitals and other health care providers use a multidimensional tool to measure and assess their performance.[≠]
Sports and recreation	In the small-boat industry, trade association data from member manufacturers assessed sales by state. The findings showed a growing trend in northern states like Pennsylvania and a slowing trend in southern states like North Carolina and Florida. Personal watercraft sales were flat in Florida. Bombardier increased its share of the Florida market with Sea-Doo personal watercraft with 43 percent of all units sold. Yamaha WaveRunners composed the next biggest chunk of Florida sales, followed by Polaris, Kawasaki, and Tigershark.
Insurance	Metrohealth Insurance Corp. of Roanoke, created a pictorial directory of health care providers on a CD-ROM to help its agents. Linking its data warehouse with MapInfo's geographic system, MetroHealth's directory enables geographically oriented queries. Agents accessing the CD see a color-coded map of their city indicating the population density of health care providers.[§]

• SAS Institute Inc., "Data Warehousing, "Web site: http://www.sas.com.

† Information Discovery Inc., Web site: http://www.idi.com.

≠ B. DePompe, "There's Gold in Databases," CMP Publications (January 8, 1996),Web site: http://techweb.cmp.com/iwk.

§ L. Connor, "Data Warehousing: Mining for Data," CMP Publications, (February 12, 1996), Web site: http://techweb.cmp.com/cw/021296/close596.htm.

Numerous techniques are used in data mining; often they are used together. The type of data available and the nature of information sought determine the technique used.

Data Visualization   By viewing aggregated data on multiple dimensions (e.g., product, brand, date of sale, and region), both the analyst and the end-user gain a deeper, intuitive understanding of the data in picture form. A multidimensional database typically contains three axes: (1) *dimensions,* like the fields in a table; (2) *measurements,* aggregate computations to be viewed; and (3) *hierarchies,* which impose structure on the dimensions. The set {month, quarter, year} is a time-based hierarchy.[34] Using this approach, the researcher views the data at various levels ("drill down / drill up"). Starting with a total of sales of breakfast cereal by region, she observes that one region is more profitable than others. Next, she drills down to sales by store and discovers that one store is outperforming all others. Looking deeper yet reveals that this store spends the most on training stocking personnel.

Data visualization uses two types of interactive queries. The first type is usually available to the end user via a query language. The second, for complex queries that go beyond traditional two-dimensional row and column data analysis, uses online analytical processing (OLAP) tools. Multidimensional analysis, another phrase for OLAP, provides fast, flexible data summarization, analyses, and reporting capabilities with the ability to view trends over time. So, complex queries such as, "How much coffee did we sell last month in Sacramento, compared to the same month last year?" can be answered quickly.

Clustering   **Clustering** enables the researcher to segment a population. This approach assigns each record to a group or segment. The assignment process is performed automatically by clustering algorithms that identify the similar characteristics in the data set and then partition them into groups often referred to as the "nearest neighbors" (see "Cluster Analysis" in Chapter 18).

Clustering is often used as the first step in data mining. For example, clustering may be used to segment a customer database for further analysis of customers' buying habits to decide which segments to target for a new sales campaign.

Neural Networks   **Neural networks,** or *artificial neural networks (ANN),* are collections of simple processing nodes that are connected. Each node operates only on its local data and on the inputs it receives via the connections. The result is a nonlinear predictive model that resembles biological neural networks and learns through training.

The neural model has to train its network on a training data set. One drawback is that no explanation of the results is available. Neural networks are best used where a predictive model is more useful than an explanatory model. For database marketing, a neural network can be constructed that predicts whether a specific person is likely to purchase a particular product. This enables the marketing organization to be very specific in its target marketing, reducing costs and dramatically improving sales "hits."

Tree Models   This technique segregates data by using a hierarchy of if-then statements based on the values of the variables and creates a tree-shaped structure that represents the segregation decisions. **Decision tree models** are faster and easier to understand than neural networks, but the data must be interval or categorical. Specific decision tree methods include classification and regression trees (CART) and chi-square automatic interaction detection (CHAID), a type of AID model previously discussed.

Classification   Classification uses a set of preclassified examples to develop a model that can classify the population of records at large. Fraud detection and risk assessments of credit applications are particularly well suited to this type of analysis. Classification frequently employs decision trees or neural network-based classification algorithms (see descriptions, below).

Classification begins with training the software with a set of preclassified sample transactions. For a fraud detection application, this would include complete records of both fraudulent and valid activities. The algorithm uses these cases as criteria to set the parameters for proper discrimination. Once developed, the model can correctly classify new records into the same predefined classes. For example, a model capable of classifying loan applicants may generate a rule stating "if applicant earns $\geq$ \$45,000, is between 35–45 years old, and lives in a specific zip code, then the applicant is a good credit risk." **Estimation** is a variation of classification. Instead of using a binary classifier (e.g., a loan applicant is a good risk or a bad risk) estimation generates a score of (e.g., creditworthiness), based on a prescored training set.

Other Mining Techniques   The process used to recognize and understand patterns in the data is **association.** The goal is to find, across large numbers of small transactions, trends that can be used to understand and exploit natural buying patterns.

The most common form of association is **market-basket analysis**. A classic example of market-basket analysis was the discovery that beer and diapers are often purchased during the evening in the same transaction. Presumably this is not because babies like beer before bed, but because the baby's father buys the diapers and chooses to purchase beer at the same time. Information from market-basket analysis can lead stores to change their layout, adjust their inventories, or introduce a targeted promotional campaign. In the financial sector, association can be used to analyze customers' accounts. The patterns identified may be to create a "bundle" of service offerings.

Results from association analyses are often expressed in terms of confidence, such as, "Seventy-five percent of all transactions in which soft drinks were purchased also included potato chips." The results of the association analysis often trigger additional analysis to help the manager to understand why the association exists.

A variant of traditional market-basket analysis, **sequence-based analysis** ties together a series of activities or purchases (for example, using an account number, a credit card, or a frequent-flyer number). The association algorithm takes into account not only the combination of items but also the order of the items. Rules derived from these relationships can be used to predict a specific purchase based on previous purchases. In health care, such methods can be used to predict the course of a disease and order preventive care.

Fuzzy logic, genetic algorithms, and fractal transforms are used in more complex mining operations. **Fuzzy logic,** an extension of conventional (Boolean) logic, handles the concept of partial truth—truth values between "completely true" and "completely false." **Genetic algorithms** are optimization techniques that use processes analogous to mutation, natural selection, and genetics for search and identification of meaningful relationships. Fractal geometry was originally applied to the compression of topographic images. It is a mathematical means of compressing data with no data. Models using **fractal-based transformation** can work on many gigabytes of data, offering the possibility of identifying tiny subsets of data that have common characteristics. For example, fractal based transformations would enable a researcher to discover the five customers out of five million who responded to a Neiman Marcus catalog offering.

Data-Mining Process

Data mining involves a five-step process.[35] To better visualize the connections between the techniques just described and the process steps listed in this section, readers may want to download a demonstration version of data-mining software from the Internet.

FIGURE   15–18   Data-Mining Process

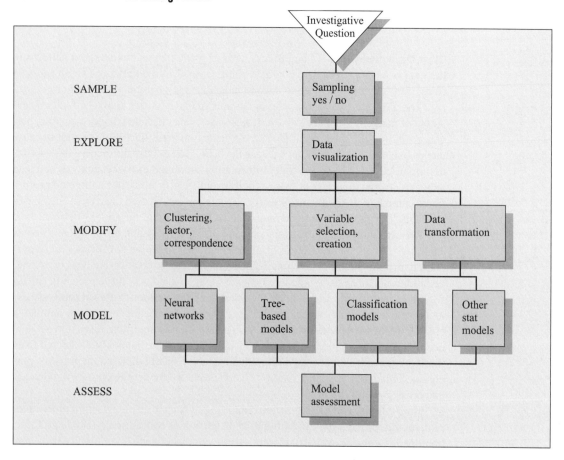

Sample   Figure 15–18 suggests that the researcher must decide whether to use the entire data set or a sample of the data.[36] If the data set in question is not large, if the processing power is high, or if it is important to understand patterns for every record in the database, sampling should not be done. However, if the data warehouse is very large (terabytes of data), the processing power is limited, or speed is more important than complete analysis, it is wise to draw a sample. In some instances, researchers may use a data mart for their sample—with local data that is appropriate for their geography. Alternatively, an appropriate sampling technique (see Chapter 9) could be selected. Since fast turnaround for decisions is often more important than absolute accuracy, sampling is appropriate.

If general patterns exist in the data as a whole, they will be found in the sample. If a niche is so tiny that it is not represented in a sample yet so important that it influences the big picture, it would have been found using exploratory data analysis. EDA techniques were described earlier.

Explore   After the data are sampled, the next step is to explore them visually or numerically for trends or groups. Both visual and statistical exploration (data visualization) can be used to identify trends. The researcher also looks for outliers to see if the data need to be cleaned, cases need to be dropped, or a larger sample needs to be drawn.

Modify   Based on the discoveries in the exploration phase, the data may require modification. Clustering, fractal-based transformation, and application of fuzzy logic are completed during this phase as appropriate. A data reduction program such as factor analysis, correspondence analysis, and clustering may be used (see Chapter 18). If important constructs were discovered, new factors would be introduced to categorize the data into these groups. In addition, variables based on combinations of existing variables may be added, recoded, transformed, or dropped.

At times, descriptive segmentation of the data is all that is required to answer the investigative question. However, if a complex predictive model is needed, the researcher will move to the next step of the process.

Model   Once the data are prepared, construction of a model begins. Modeling techniques in data mining include neural networks, decision tree models, sequence-based models, classification and estimation models, and genetic-based models.

Assess   The final step in data mining is to assess the model to estimate how well it performs. A common method of assessment involves applying a portion of data that was not used during the sampling stage. If the model is valid, it will work for this "holdout" sample. Another way to test it is to run the model against known data. For example, if you know which customers in a file have high loyalty and your model predicts loyalty, you can check to see whether the model selected these customers accurately.

Summary

The first step in data preparation is to edit the collected raw data to detect errors and omissions that would compromise quality standards. The editor is responsible for making the data accurate, consistent with other data, uniformly entered, and ready for coding. In survey work, it is common to use both field and central editing.

Coding is the process of assigning numbers and other symbols to answers so we can classify the responses into categories. Categories should be appropriate to the research problem, exhaustive of the data, mutually exclusive, and unidimensional. The reduction of information through coding requires the researcher to design category sets carefully, using as much of the data as possible. Codebooks are guides to reduce data entry error and serve as a compendium of variable locations and other information for the analysis stage.

Closed questions include scaled items and other items for which answers are anticipated. Precoding of closed items avoids tedious completion of coding sheets for each response. Coding open questions is more difficult since answers are not prepared in advance, but it does encourage disclosure of complete information. A systematic method to analyze open questions is called content analysis. It uses preselected sampling units to produce frequency counts and other insights on data patterns.

"Don't know" replies are evaluated in the light of the question's nature and the respondent. While many DKs are legitimate, some result from questions that are ambiguous or from an interviewing situation that is not motivating. It is better to report DKs as a separate category unless there are compelling reasons to treat them otherwise.

Data entry is accomplished by keyboard entry from precoded instruments, optical scanning, real-time keyboarding, telephone pad data entry, bar codes, voice recognition, and data transfers from electronic notebooks and laptop computers. Database programs, spreadsheets, and editors in statistical software programs offer flexibility for entering, manipulating, and transferring data for analysis, warehousing, and mining.

The objective of preliminary data analysis is to learn as much as possible about the data. Exploratory data analysis (EDA) simplifies this goal by providing a perspective and set of tools to search for clues and patterns. EDA augments rather than supplants traditional statistics. In addition to numerical summaries of location, spread, and shape, EDA uses visual displays to provide a complete and accurate impression of distributions and variable relationships.

Frequency tables array data from highest to lowest values with counts and percentages. They are most useful for inspecting the range of responses and their repeated occurrence. Bar charts and pie charts are appropriate for relative comparisons of nominal data. Histograms are optimally used with continuous variables where intervals group the responses.

Stem-and-leaf displays and boxplots are EDA techniques that provide visual representations of distributions. The former present actual data values using a histogram-type device that allows inspection of spread and shape. Boxplots use the five-number summary to convey a detailed picture of a distribution's main body, tails, and outliers. Both stem-and-leaf displays and boxplots rely on resistant statistics to overcome the limitations of descriptive measures that are subject to extreme scores. Transformation may be necessary to reexpress metric data to reduce or remove problems of asymmetry, inequality of variance, or other abnormalities.

Preliminary evaluation of relationships involving nominally scaled variables employs crosstabulation. The tables used for this purpose consist of cells and marginals. The cells contain combinations of count, row, column, and total percentages. The tabular structure is the framework for later statistical testing.

Computer software for cross-classification analysis makes table-based analysis with one or more control variables an efficient tool for decision making. An advanced variation on n-way tables is automatic interaction detection (AID).

Data mining describes the concept of discovering knowledge from databases. Data-mining technology provides two unique capabilities to the researcher or manager: pattern discovery and predicting trends and behaviors. Data-mining tools perform exploratory and confirmatory statistical analysis to discover and validate relationships. These tools even extend confirmatory statistical approaches by allowing the automated examination of large numbers of hypotheses. The type of data available and the nature of information sought determine which of the numerous data-mining techniques to select. Data mining involves a five-step process: sample, explore, modify, model, and assess.

Key Terms

association
automatic interaction detection (AID)
bar code
boxplot
cells
central tendency
clustering
codebook
coding
confirmatory data analysis
content analysis
contingency tables
control variable
crosstabulation
data entry
data fields
data files
data mart
data mining
data visualization
data warehouse
database
decision tree models
descriptive statistics
distribution
DK (don't know) response
editing
estimation
exploratory data analysis
five-number summary
fractal based transformation
frequency table

fuzzy logic
genetic algorithms
histogram
interquartile range
kurtosis
marginal
market-basket analysis
mean
measures of location
measures of shape
measures of spread
median
mode
neural networks
optical scanning
outliers
precoding
quartile deviation
range
record
resistant /nonresistant statistics
sequence-based analysis
skewness
spreadsheet
standard deviation
standard normal distribution
standard scores (Z scores)
stem-and-leaf display
transformation
variability
variance
voice recognition

Cases

Xerox Abuses
Healthy Lifestyles
AIDS Rates for Females
Agri Comp
(These are cases found in the optional casebook available with the text.)

Discussion Questions

1. Define or explain:
   a. Coding rules
   b. Spreadsheet data entry
   c. Alphanumeric variables
   d. Precoded instruments
   e. Nonresistant statistics
   f. Measures of shape
   g. The five-number summary
   h. Notched boxplots
   i. Spread-and-level plots

2. How should the researcher handle "don't know" responses?

3. A problem facing shoe store managers is that many shoes must eventually be sold at markdown prices. This prompts us to conduct a mail survey of shoe store managers in which we ask, "What methods have you found most successful for reducing the problem of high markdowns?" We are interested in extracting as much information as possible from these answers to better understand the full range of strategies that store managers use. Establish what you think are category sets to code 500 responses similar to the 14 below. Try to develop an integrated set of categories that reflects your theory of markdown management. After developing the set, use it to code the 14 responses.

   a. Have not found the answer. As long as we buy style shoes, we will have markdowns. We use PMs on slow merchandise, but it does not eliminate markdowns. (PM stands for "push-money"—special item bonuses for selling a particular style of shoe.)

   b. Using PMs before too old. Also reducing price during season. Holding meetings with salespeople indicating which shoes to push.

   c. By putting PMs on any slow-selling items and promoting same. More careful check of shoes purchased.

   d. Keep a close watch on your stock, and mark down when you have to—that is, rather than wait, take a small markdown on a shoe that is not moving at the time.

   e. Using the PM method.

   f. Less advance buying—more dependence on in-stock shoes.

   g. Sales—catch bad guys before it's too late and close out.

   h. Buy as much good merchandise as you can at special prices to help make up some markdowns.

   i. Reducing opening buys and depending on fill-in service. PMs for salespeople.

   j. Buy more frequently, better buying, PM on slow-moving merchandise.

    k. Careful buying at lowest prices. Cash on the buying line. Buying close-outs, FDs, overstock, "cancellations." (FD stands for "factory-discontinued style.")

    l. By buying less "chanceable" shoes. Buy only what you need, watch sizes, don't go overboard on new fads.

    m. Buying more staple merchandise. Buying more from fewer lines. Sticking with better nationally advertised merchandise.

    n. No successful method with the current style situation. Manufacturers are experimenting, the retailer takes the markdowns—cuts gross profit by about 3 percent—keep your stock at lowest level without losing sales.

4. How do the following detect errors in the data?

    a. Histogram

    b. Stem-and-leaf display

    c. Boxplot

    d. Crosstabulation

5. Use the data in Table 15–3 to construct a stem-and-leaf display.

    a. Where do you find the main body of the distribution?

    b. How many values reside outside the inner fence(s)?

6. Select the sales variable from Table 15–10.

    a. Create a five-number summary.

    b. Construct a boxplot.

    c. Interpret the distribution and results with summary measures and descriptive statistics.

    d. Transform the variable into Z scores.

    e. Identify and comment on outliers, if any.

7. Select the market value variable from Table 15–10, and construct a histogram with available software.

    a. What is the gain in information with 5,000-, 2,000-, or 1,000-unit intervals?

    b. Which would be the best interval to convey results to management?

    c. Why would this data need reexpression?

    d. What is the optimal power transformation for this data?

8. Define a small sample of class members, work associates, or friends and ask them to answer the following in a paragraph or two: "What are your career aspirations for the next five years?" Use one of the four basic units of content analysis to analyze their responses. Describe your findings as frequencies for the unit of analysis selected.

9. Suppose you were preparing two-way tables of percentages for the following pairs of variables. How would you run the percentages?

TABLE 15–10   Data Table for Discussion Questions 6–7

	Market Value	Sales	Sector		Market Value	Sales	Sector
1	24983.00	8966.00	2	26	9009.00	17533.00	4
2	31307.00	126932.00	3	27	7842.00	11113.00	2
3	57193.00	54574.00	7	28	5431.00	19671.00	8
4	57676.00	86656.00	4	29	5811.00	11389.00	5
5	60345.00	62710.00	7	30	16257.00	15242.00	2
6	22190.00	96146.00	3	31	16247.00	10211.00	7
7	36566.00	39011.00	2	32	18548.00	9593.00	7
8	44646.00	36112.00	7	33	13620.00	9691.00	7
9	25022.00	50220.00	4	34	10750.00	12844.00	3
10	26043.00	25099.00	1	35	12450.00	18398.00	2
11	13152.00	53794.00	2	36	16729.00	20276.00	7
12	11234.00	25047.00	5	37	16532.00	8730.00	7
13	26666.00	23966.00	4	38	5111.00	17635.00	10
14	20747.00	17424.00	7	39	9116.00	8588.00	4
15	25826.00	13996.00	7	40	26325.00	25922.00	2
16	15423.00	32416.00	4	41	8249.00	16103.00	2
17	15263.00	14150.00	8	42	8407.00	14083.00	3
18	18146.00	17600.00	1	43	18537.00	11990.00	10
19	18739.00	15351.00	4	44	23866.00	29443.00	4
20	7875.00	22605.00	2	45	6872.00	19532.00	7
21	8122.00	37970.00	5	46	4319.00	10018.00	5
22	18072.00	11557.00	5	47	9505.00	12937.00	7
23	6404.00	11449.00	7	48	3891.00	15654.00	8
24	16056.00	20054.00	8	49	8090.00	7492.00	4
25	16056.00	13211.00	7	50	11119.00	12345.00	7

a. Age and consumption of breakfast cereal

b. Family income and confidence about the family's future

c. Marital status and sports participation

d. Crime rate and unemployment rate

10. You study the attrition between students who enter college as freshmen and those who stay to graduate. You find the following relationships between attrition, aid, and distance of home from school.

	Aid		Home Near Aid		Home Far Aid	
	Yes	No	Yes	No	Yes	No
Drop out	25%	20%	5%	15%	30%	40%
Stay	75	80	95	85	70	60

What is your interpretation? Consider all variables and relationships.

11. A local health agency is experimenting with two appeal letters, A and B, with which to raise funds. It sends out 400 of the A appeal and 400 of the B appeal (divided equally among working-class and middle-class neighborhoods). The agency secures the following results:

	Appeal A		Appeal B	
	Middle Class	*Working Class*	*Middle Class*	*Working Class*
Contribution	20%	40%	15%	30%
No contribution	80	60	85	70
	100	100	100	100

    a. Which appeal is the best?

    b. Which class responded better?

    c. Is appeal or social class a more powerful independent variable?

12. Assume you have collected data on employees of a large organization in a major metropolitan area. You analyze the data by type of work classification, education level, and whether the workers were raised in a rural or urban setting. The results are shown below. How would you interpret them?

Annual Employee Turnover per 100 Employees

	Part A		Part B			
			High Education		Low Education	
	Salaried	*Wage*	*Salaried*	*Wage*	*Salaried*	*Wage*
Rural	8	16	6	14	18	18
Urban	12	16	10	12	19	20

Reference Notes

1. Jean M. Converse and Stanley Presser, *Survey Questions: Handcrafting the Standardized Questionnaire* (Beverly Hills, CA.: Sage Publications, 1986), pp. 34–35.

2. B. Berelson, *Content Analysis in Communication Research* (New York: Free Press, 1952), p. 18.

3. Klaus Krippendorff, *Content Analysis: An Introduction to Its Methodology* (Beverly Hills, CA: Sage Publications, 1980), p. 22.

4. Hans Zeisel, *Say It with Figures,* 6th ed. (New York: Harper & Row, 1985), pp. 48–49.

5. John W. Tukey, *Exploratory Data Analysis* (Reading, MA.: Addison-Wesley, 1977).

6. David C. Hoaglin, Frederick Mosteller, and John W. Tukey, eds., *Understanding Robust and Exploratory Data Analysis* (New York: John Wiley & Sons, 1983), p. 2.

7. Tukey, *Exploratory Data Analysis,* pp. 2–3.

8. Frederick Hartwig with Brian E. Dearing, *Exploratory Data Analysis* (Beverly Hills, CA: Sage Publications, 1979), pp. 9–12.

9. Ibid., p. 15.

10. Different definitions of quartiles are based on variations in their calculation. We use Q_1, 25th percentile, and *lower hinge* synonymously, and Q_3, 75th percentile, and *upper hinge*, similarly. There are technical differences, although they do not make much of a difference in this context.

11. The figures and tables in this section were created with statistical and graphic programs whose modules or subroutines are particularly suited to exploratory data analysis. The authors gratefully acknowledge the following vendors for evaluation and use of their products: SPSS Inc., 444 N. Michigan Ave., Chicago, IL 60611; and Data Desk 4.0, Data Description, P.0. Box 4555, Ithaca, NY 14852 .

12. "Fortune 500 Ranked by Performance," *The Fortune 500,* April 28, 1997, p. F-30.

13. Paul F. Velleman and David C. Hoaglin, *Applications, Basics, and Computing of Exploratory Data Analysis* (Boston: Duxbury Press, 1981), p. 13.

14. John Hanke, Eastern Washington University, contributed this section. For further references to stem-and-leaf displays, see John D. Emerson and David C. Hoaglin, "Stem-and-Leaf Displays," in *Understanding Robust and Exploratory Data Analysis,* pp. 7–31; and Velleman and Hoaglin, *Applications,* pp. 1–13.

15. This section is adapted from the following excellent discussions of boxplots: Velleman and Hoaglin, *Applications,* pp. 65–76; Hartwig, *Exploratory Data Analysis,* pp. 19–25; John D. Emerson and Judith Strenio, "Boxplots and Batch Comparison," in *Understanding Robust and Exploratory Data Analysis,* pp. 59–93; and Amir D. Aczel, *Complete Business Statistics* (Homewood, IL: Irwin, 1989), pp. 723–28.

16. Tukey, *Exploratory Data Analysis,* pp. 27–55.

17. Hoaglin et al., *Understanding Robust and Exploratory Data Anlaysis,* p. 2.

18. Several robust estimators that are suitable replacements for the mean and standard deviation we do not discuss here—for example, the trimmed mean, trimean, and the M-estimators (such as Huber's, Tukey's, Hampel's, and Andrew's estimators) and the median absolute deviation (MAD). See Hoaglin et al., *Understanding Robust and Exploratory Data Analysis,* chap. 10; and Marija J. Norusis/SPSS, Inc., *SPSS for Windows Base System User's Guide, Release 6.0* (Chicago: SPSS, Inc., 1993), chap. 9.

19. R. McGill, J. W. Tukey, and W. A. Larsen, "Variations of Box Plots," *The American Statistician* 32 (1978), pp. 12–16.

20. See J. Chambers, W. Cleveland, B. Kleiner, and P. Tukey, *Graphical Methods for Data Analysis* (Boston: Duxbury Press, 1983).

21. This section is based on the discussion of transformation in John D. Emerson and Michael A. Stoto, "Transforming Data," in *Understanding Robust and Exploratory Data Analysis,* pp. 97–127; and Velleman and Hoaglin, *Applications,* pp. 48–53.

22. Hoaglin et al., *Understanding Robust and Exploratory Data Analysis,* p. 77.

23. Ibid., p. 125.

24. Norusis, *Base System User's Guide,* p. 203.

25. Harper W. Boyd, Jr., and Ralph Westfall, *Marketing Research,* 3rd ed. (Homewood, IL: Irwin, 1972), p. 540.

26. SPSS-X Tables software with their systems file: Bank Data.

27. R. Srikant and R. Agrawal, "Mining Sequential Patterns: Generalizations and Performance Improvements," *Proceedings,* 5th International Conference on Extending Database Technology, Paris, France, March 1996.

28. B. DePompe,"There's Gold in Databases," CMP Publications (January 8, 1996), Web site: http://techweb.cmp.com/iwk.

29. Table adapted from DIG White Paper 95/01, "An Overview of Data Mining at Dun & Bradstreet," Data Intelligence Group, Pilot Software, Cambridge, MA, (September 1995).

30. "Data Mining: Plumbing the Depths of Corporate Databases," *Computerworld Customer Publication,* insert to *Computerworld,* April 21, 1997, p. 12.

31. DePompe, CMP Publications, Web site: http://techweb.cmp.com/iwk.

32. "Data Mining: Plumbing the Depths of Corporate Databases," pp. 6, 18.

33. The section on data-mining techniques was adapted from Bruce Moxon, "Defining Data Mining," DBMS Data Warehouse Supplement, *DBMS Online* (August 1996), http://www.dbmsmag.com; Mark Kantrowitz, Erik Horstkotte, and Cliff Joslyn ,"Fuzzy Logic FAQ," http://comp.ai.fuzzy newsgroup; DIG White Paper95/01and Michael Bell, "A Data Mining FAQ," Quintillion Corporation, Web page: http://www.qwhy.com/dmfaq.htm.

34. Information Discovery Inc. , Web site: http://www.idi.com.

35. SAS Institute Inc., "Data Mining," Web site: http://www.sas.com.

36. Figure 15–18 was adapted from SAS Institute Inc., "Data Mining," Web site: http://www.sas.com.

Suggested Readings

1. Fayyad, U. M., and G. Piatesky-Shapiro. *Advances in Knowledge Discovery and Data Mining.* Cambridge, MA: AAAI Press-MIT Press, 1996. An excellent text that provides an overview of knowledge discovery and data mining using statistical methods.

2 Hartwig, Frederick, with Brian E. Dearing. *Exploratory Data Analysis.* Beverly Hills, CA: Sage Publications, 1979. Chapter 4 on data transformation is particularly informative.

3. Hoaglin, David C., Frederick Mosteller, and John W. Tukey, eds. *Understanding Robust and Exploratory Data Analysis.* New York: Wiley, 1983. A complete and advanced treatment of the subject. Especially well-organized topical coverage.

4. Velleman, Paul F., and David C. Hoaglin. *Applications, Basics, and Computing of Exploratory Data Analysis.* Boston: Duxbury Press, 1981. The basics of EDA are presented in a straightforward style with helpful examples and excellent connections to computer applications.

5. Zeisel, Hans. *Say It with Figures,* 6th ed. New York: Harper & Row, 1985. The entire book is worth reading for its excellent discussion of numerical presentation.

CHAPTER 16

HYPOTHESIS TESTING

CHAPTER NAVIGATION

BRINGING
RESEARCH TO LIFE

"I want you to know, I do not believe in such things as ghosts," said Jason.

"Certainly not, Jason. You are too much the scientist."

"It is one thing, you understand, to believe in things that go bump in the night, and quite another to simply tell an amusing story on Halloween evening." He nodded at the window, through which could be seen diminutive apparitions scuttling beneath streetlights and toting trick-or-treat bags.

He leaned toward Myra, a smile flickering on his lips. She had never heard him tell a ghost story and decided to remain for one more glass of apple cider. She replied, "Well if there happens to be an interesting Halloween story, and if it happens to make good telling . . ."

". . . if it makes good telling on a moonless Halloween night . . ."

". . . well, then, what would be the harm? So, here it is, the Tale of the Carpet of Burley Hall. Back in my grad student days, in Burley Hall, in the business college, there was a fellow named Don Ticker who annoyed me very much. Don was a nice enough fellow, I suppose, but talking to Don was nothing but an exercise in futility, as he seemed to absorb no advice or learning. What especially annoyed me was that no matter how often I explained this to him, he never caught on to the idea of statistical post hoc analysis. . . ."

"Which would be what, in plain English?"

"I'll give you an example. Don would find himself a set of data with 100 interval variables, say, and put his statistics program to work at calculating the Pearson correlation coefficients among all the variables. In a set of 100 variables, there would be quite a few such correlations generated in almost no time at all. . . . If you have 100 variables, every one of them will have 99 other variables to correlate with . . . assuming they are all what we call interval or ratio-level variables . . . that makes 9,900 possibles. Except you have to divide by two, because the correlation of *X* with *Y* is the same as *Y* with *X*. Which leaves you with 4,950 actual computations for the statistics program to print out. The program will give you 4,950 Pearson correlation coefficients, therefore 4,950 statistical tests of significance."

"If you say so, Jason."

He saw her interest was flagging. "Do you follow me so far? Whether a relationship is statistically significant is a very big issue."

"No doubt it is . . . to a statistician. Your point is what, Jason? Something to do with a Halloween story, remember?"

"My point is, if you instruct your statistics program to flag all the results that appear to be significant at the level of $p = .05$, then even if the data originated in a table of random numbers the program would flag more or less 0.05 times 4,950 of the computations as being apparently significant. That's almost 250 of the calculations that will be flagged as significant, though they may signify nothing more than sampling error."

"I'm not sure I follow, but get on with the Halloween story, would you?"

"In a moment. I want you to understand this concept. Choosing .05 as the probability level of statistical significance means you have consciously decided to risk that .05 or 1/20 of the results flagged as significant may actually be spurious, due to sampling error, a law of nature. Now if the data set actually contains any real correlations, these would add additional significant results that were not spurious. But you would have no way of telling which of the flagged results were spurious and which were due to real effects. Yet Don would always get awfully excited, believing he had hit the mother lode of statistical discoveries, when it was really sampling error that produced the results, not his prowess in doing research. Ticker would take out his Day-Glo™ yellow marker and circle all the ostensibly significant results, and whip himself into a frenzy. But try and explain to Don that you cannot mass-produce statistics. Futility! It is a fundamental statistical idea, but he'd taken an undergraduate *(continued)* major in journalism, and wasn't fully committed to understanding statistics at the deepest levels."

"I suppose God created journalism majors for statisticians to laugh at. How often have I heard it said that journalists are from Mars and statisticians are from Uranus."

Jason failed to notice the gibe. "He would grab his printout and come running down the hallway with the printout streaming along behind, whooping and wanting to show his results around. He would always launch himself from the far end of the hall and hit warp speed as he passed the little cubbyhole the professors had given me for my work, and I don't mind telling you his raspy, whiny voice would unnerve me, because just as he was passing my open door is when he would let loose his first holler. I would be deep in thought, on the edge of my consciousness I would hear Don's sneakers pounding down the hall, and right outside my office he would loose the most horrifying of shrieks of joy, which cut down to my very bones. And, of course, I knew Ticker was up to his old tricks. If he had preplanned his analysis, based on logical hypotheses, he would have saved countless hours and reams of computer paper. But, no, Ticker would never have done that. No."

"What this has to do with Halloween, I fail to see."

"Well, I want you to understand that I was badly wrought-up by Ticker's obtuseness, the more so by his getting away with it. Some of the senior faculty who were weak in statistics had begun to ask for his assistance in testing hypotheses of the most dubious sort, and took to belittling those who did not appear to be mining copious results from faculty data. Why, one tenure-hungry assistant professor preparing for a journalists' conference on health finance reform brought in bushels of data, various dollar amounts from various lines of the IRS form 1040, to be correlated with cranial capacity, femur length, and other anatomical measurements. Only a charlatan like Ticker would dare to crank so many variables through a computer in the hope of discovering spurious correlations. So I was stuck sitting in a miserable airless cubbyhole, hunched over an obsolete

personal computer, programming obscure bits of code for offbeat statistical inquiries, while Don sat in an office with a view of the quadrangle and air-conditioning that worked all year round. His obtuseness was unfairly rewarded, and I was angry."

"I have seen you petulant, Jason, and it's not a pretty sight. You must have been ugly as a toad, stewing over . . . over post hoc analysis. I can see you working up a fury over . . . post hoc analysis."

"Well," he snapped, "I was. And I *am!*" He continued. "It was on the afternoon before Halloween, that I was deep in studying an intricate fragment of code that had been returning error messages all the day long, when I felt the thrill of discovery flickering at the fringes of my consciousness. I was about to break through to a solution when I was jolted by one of Don's dashes down the hall. Though I was only millimeters from my own real revelation, Don's phony science and whooping and hooting had once again derailed the train of my thoughts. That was when I resolved that Donald must pay for his transgressions. I thought of walling him up in his own office, to expire from lack of air or water; I thought of smothering him and of crushing him. In short, I reviewed all of my favorite writers of the bizarre, Edgar Allan Poe, H. P. Lovecraft, Stephen King, the other masters of the macabre, but found no suitable punishment."

"You are *so-o-o* bad. Even then you were *so-o-o* bad."

"The issue, Myra, was not just the interruptions, It was the principle of things, the darned fishing expeditions among the data that were making him comfortable and respected while I was crouching, practically, in a broom closet. That afternoon, late, the sky was dark, Myra, and there was a chill. Even on the path home to my meager, chilly, and ratty little furnished room, I could perceive small dark creatures squealing and scuttling among the bushes. And as I drove home, bright, beady red eyes peered out of the bushes that bordered the road. There was a moon, but it had hid itself behind leaden clouds, and when it appeared, it threw shadows of the most bizarre shapes that I would only reveal to a counselor. No matter how you try, on that one night of the year, you had to wonder if retributive justice were not available. For it was Halloween."

"The truth is," Myra said, "it was just a little bit of fun for a graduate student with not much of a life, it was just a bit of a tingle to believe that on this night powerful things were loose in the world, and that the Don Tickers of the world, with their post hoc analyses and spurious results, might encounter one of them. . . ."

"Quite right. On arriving home, I took a sniff of brandy and immediately tumbled onto the sofa, intending to catch a few winks, followed by a full night of number crunching for my term project. Yet I descended into one of those oppressively lucid dreams in which one knows one is dreaming but cannot gain control or float upward to consciousness. I was back in Burley Hall: I had floated back to reengage that problem that Donald Ticker had interrupted with his stupid post hoc analysis. But when I stood in the dark hallway and attempted to enter my cubbyhole, the door was pulled open from within, by a specter dressed all in a black shroud, his face covered by a black veil. He was tall, at least seven feet, and he held a shepherd's crook, which he wielded effortlessly despite its length and thickness. I was fearful. I knew I was about to be part of some awful act, one fully justified by Ticker's despicable actions, but awesome nevertheless.

"Abruptly, my dream shifted into slow motion. I heard footsteps in the hallway, spaced as deliberate steps, as if in slow motion, and down the hall came Donald Ticker. His printout trailed behind him, but it was in this dream outrageously long, twenty-five or thirty feet long, and it must have held thousands of spurious results, the yellow highlights glowing as pale fireflies in the darkness of the hall. The usual Ticker holler was deflated and prolonged to a long and awful moan, and down the hall he came in long slow bounds."

Myra was transfixed. She had no idea Jason was capable of such storytelling.

"The specter waited until the last moment, and though Ticker was moving in slow motion, the mysterious figure was himself quick and agile. It did not seem a fair match, but I was too angry with Ticker's phony science to care about fairness. I longed for the denouement.

"The specter thrust the shepherd's crook between Ticker's knees and hooked the near knee, and as he disappeared from sight, Ticker became fully airborne and passed out of my field of vision almost entirely horizontal, sailing slowly three feet off the floor.

"At this point, I snapped awake. It was 6 A.M. I was cold, but sweating. I was filled with trepidation, not reassured by rationality. Hot instant coffee, which had never failed to buoy me, was likewise futile. Nothing would do but to visit the Hall, as rapidly as possible.

"Even at 6:15 Burley Hall is a busy place, what with students who have stayed up all night in the computer lab and the assistant professors eager to arrive before the senior faculty. As I pulled open the front door and stepped across the threshold, I knew something was dreadfully wrong. I heard excited chattering coming from halfway up the hallway, which would place it outside my office.

"I could barely force myself to move forward. Suddenly I was again in slow motion. The premonition was awful but the guilt was worse. Surely post hoc data analysis was a practice to be discouraged but a venial sin at worst. I promised myself I would never wish ill to anyone over a philosophical dispute, and I forced myself forward. It seemed to take forever, the short walk to my office.

"A knot of students and junior faculty were gathered outside my cubbyhole. To one side leaned the crook as I remembered it, long and sturdy. But the focus of attention was something far more frightening and bizarre."

By now, Myra was leaning forward, transfixed. "It was Ticker, wasn't it? It was Ticker's mangled corpse."

"Ticker. Oh, no. Ticker in fact was missing, and to this day has not reappeared, although there are rumors he is in Sioux City, attempting to complete his degree through distance learning. No, but there in the carpet, outside my office, exactly where the

(continued)

dream took place . . . right there . . . as clearly as could be, we could see embossed in the carpet the face—the nose and eyebrows, the lips, even—and two handprints—all ten digits showing distinctly—of a human being!!! Don Ticker's face, in broadest outline, had been imprinted in the Carpet of Burley Hall!"

He paused to light his pipe. Myra's pupils had swollen to pie plates.

He chuckled. At first Myra was speechless. Then she ventured, "You are a lying little sadist, Jason. And a prevaricating sociopath. But a great storyteller."

"So?" he said. "Do you disbelieve me, Myra? I knew you would. Yet, I can prove it, every word of

it. Come, we will take flashlights and go out into the backyard to the woodshed. Don't fear, the wolves in this part of the country are not aggressive and the rats fear the light, even on Halloween, and I have made a pact with both the dead and the undead. Now you will see: I have that shepherd's crook: yes, I have kept it to this day. You can see it for yourself, and then you must believe."

"Forget it, Jason. You spin a good yarn. And I can believe you working up a fuss over someone taking credit for spurious results. But an old piece of wood means nothing, and I am not going to risk a raccoon bite to look at an old tree branch."

INTRODUCTION

In Chapter 15, we discussed the procedures for data preparation and preliminary analysis. The next step for many studies is hypothesis testing.

Just as your understanding of scientific reasoning was an important foundation in the last chapter, recollection of the specific differences between induction and deduction is fundamental to hypothesis testing. *Inductive reasoning* moves from specific facts to general, but tentative conclusions. We can never be absolutely sure that inductive conclusions are flawless. With the aid of probability estimates, we can qualify our results and state the degree of confidence we have in them. Statistical inference is an application of inductive reasoning. It allows us to reason from evidence found in the sample to conclusions we wish to make about the population.

Inferential statistics is the second of two major categories of statistical procedures, the other being descriptive statistics. We used descriptive statistics in Chapter 15 when exploration and description of distributions were emphasized. Under the heading **inferential statistics,** two topics are discussed in this book. The first, estimation of population values, was used with sampling in Chapter 9, but we will return to it here briefly. The second, testing statistical hypotheses, is the primary subject of this chapter.

In the next few sections, we will refresh your memory of hypothesis testing and look at selected statistical tests. Many are basic, but they illustrate the diverse types of data and situations a researcher may encounter. A section on nonparametric techniques in Appendix E provides further study for readers with a special interest in nominal and ordinal variables.

HYPOTHESIS TESTING

Testing Approaches   There are two approaches to hypothesis testing. The more established is the classical or sampling-theory approach; the second is known as the Bayesian approach. **Classical statistics** are found in all of the major statistics books and are widely used in research applications. This approach represents an objective view of probability in which the decision making rests totally on an analysis of available sampling data. A hypothesis is established; it is rejected or fails to be rejected, based on the sample data collected.

      Bayesian statistics are an extension of the classical approach. They also use sampling data for making decisions, but they go beyond them to consider all other available information. This additional information consists of subjective probability estimates stated in terms of degrees of belief. These subjective estimates are based on general experience rather than on specific collected data. They are expressed as a prior distribution that can be revised after sample information is gathered. The revised estimate, known as a *posterior distribution*, may be further revised by additional information, and so on. Various decision rules are established, cost and other estimates can be introduced, and the expected outcomes of combinations of these elements are used to judge decision alternatives.

      The Bayesian approach, based on the centuries-old Bayes theorem, has emerged as an alternative hypothesis-testing procedure since the mid-1950s. An example of Bayesian decision making is presented in Appendix B on the topic of valuing research information. The reader interested in learning more about Bayesian statistics is referred to the suggested readings at the end of this chapter.

Statistical Significance   Following the sampling-theory approach, we accept or reject a hypothesis on the basis of sampling information alone. Since any sample will almost surely vary somewhat from its population, we must judge whether these differences are statistically significant or insignificant. A difference has **statistical significance** if there is good reason to believe the difference does not represent random sampling fluctuations only. For example, the controller of a large retail chain may be concerned about a possible slowdown in payments by the company's customers. She measures the rate of payment in terms of the average age of receivables outstanding. Generally, the company has maintained an average of about 50 days with a standard deviation of 10 days. Suppose the controller has all of the customer accounts analyzed and finds the average is now 51 days. Is this difference statistically significant from 50? Of course it is because the difference is based on a census of the accounts and there is no sampling involved. It is a fact that the population average has moved from 50 to 51 days. While it is of statistical significance, whether it is of **practical significance** is another question. If the controller judges that this variation has no real importance, then it is of little practical significance.

      Since it would be too expensive to analyze all of a company's receivables frequently, we normally resort to sampling. Assume a sample of 25 accounts is randomly selected and the average number of days outstanding is calculated to be 54. Is this statistically significant? The answer is not obvious. It is significant if there is good reason to believe the average age of the total group of receivables has moved up from 50. Since the evidence consists of only a sample, consider the second possibility, that this is only a random sampling error and thus not significant. The task is to judge whether such a result from this sample is or is not statistically significant. To answer this question, one needs to consider further the logic of hypothesis testing.

The Logic of Hypothesis Testing

In classical tests of significance, two kinds of hypotheses are used. The **null hypothesis** is used for testing. It is a statement that no difference exists between the parameter and the statistic being compared to it. Analysts usually test to determine whether there has been no change in the population of interest or whether a real difference exists. Why not state the hypothesis in a positive form? Why not state that any difference between the sample statistic and the population parameter is due to some reason? Unfortunately, this type of hypothesis cannot be tested definitively. Evidence that is consistent with a hypothesis stated in a positive form can almost never be taken as conclusive grounds for accepting the hypothesis. A finding that is consistent with this type of hypothesis might be consistent with other hypotheses too, and thus does not demonstrate the truth of the given hypothesis.

For example, suppose a coin is suspected of being biased in favor of heads. The coin is flipped 100 times and the outcome is 52 heads. It would not be correct to jump to the conclusion that the coin is biased simply because more than the expected number of 50 heads resulted. The reason is that 52 heads is consistent with the hypothesis that the coin is fair. It would not be surprising to flip a fair coin 100 times and observe 52 heads. On the other hand, flipping 85 or 90 heads in 100 flips would seem to contradict the hypothesis of a fair coin. In this case there would be a strong case for a biased coin.

In the controller example, the null hypothesis states that the population parameter of 50 days has not changed. A second, or **alternative hypothesis,** holds that there has been a change in average days outstanding (i.e., the sample statistic of 54 indicates the population value probably is no longer 50). The alternative hypothesis is the logical opposite of the null hypothesis.

The accounts receivable example can be explored further to show how these concepts are used to test for significance. The null hypothesis (H_0) is: There has been no change from the 50 days average age of accounts outstanding. The alternative hypothesis (H_A) may take several forms, depending on the objective of the researchers. The H_A may be of the "not the same" form:. The average age of accounts has changed from 50 days. A second variety may be of the "greater than" or "less than" form: The average age of receivables has increased (decreased) from 50 days.

These types of alternative hypotheses correspond with two-tailed and one-tailed tests. A **two-tailed test,** or *nondirectional test,* considers two possibilities: The average could be more than 50 days, or it could be less than 50 days. To test this hypothesis, the regions of rejection are divided into two tails of the distribution. A **one-tailed test,** or *directional test,* places the entire probability of an unlikely outcome into the tail specified by the alternative hypothesis. In Figure 16–1, the first diagram represents a nondirectional hypothesis, and the second is a directional hypothesis of the "greater than" variety. Hypotheses for the example may be expressed in the following form:

Null	$H_0 : \mu \text{ (mu)}$	$=$	50 days
Alternative	$H_A : \mu$	$\neq$	50 days (not the same case)
or	$H_A : \mu$	$>$	50 days (greater than case)
or	$H_A : \mu$	$<$	50 days (less than case)

In testing these hypotheses, adopt this decision rule: Take no corrective action if the analysis shows that one cannot reject the null hypothesis. Note "not to reject"

FIGURE   16–1   One- and Two-Tailed Tests at the 5% Level of Significance

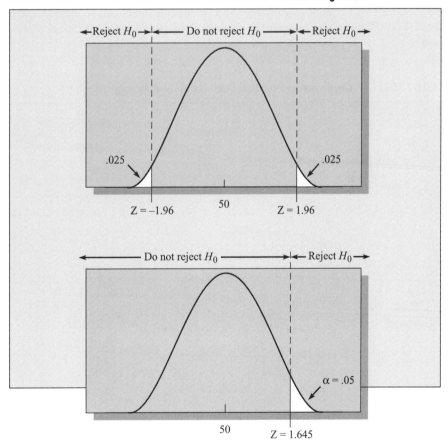

rather than "accept" the null hypothesis. It is argued that a null hypothesis can never be proved and therefore cannot be "accepted." Here, again, we see the influence of inductive reasoning. Unlike deduction, where the connections between premises and conclusions provide a legitimate claim of "conclusive proof," inductive conclusions do not possess that advantage. Statistical testing gives only a chance to (1) disprove (reject) or (2) fail to reject the hypothesis. Despite this terminology, it is common to hear "accept the null" rather than the clumsy "fail to reject the null." In this discussion, the less formal "accept" means "fail to reject" the null hypothesis.

If we reject a null hypothesis (finding a statistically significant difference), then we are accepting the alternative hypothesis. In either accepting or rejecting a null hypothesis, we can make incorrect decisions. A null hypothesis can be accepted when it should have been rejected or rejected when it should have been accepted.

These problems are illustrated with an analogy to the American legal system.[1] In our system of justice, the innocence of an indicted person is presumed until proof of guilt beyond a reasonable doubt can be established. In hypothesis testing, this is the null hypothesis; there should be no difference between the presumption

TABLE   16–1   Comparison of Statistical Decisions to Legal Analogy

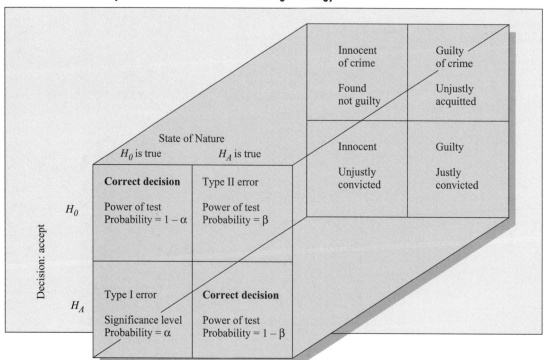

and the outcome unless contrary evidence is furnished. Once evidence establishes beyond reasonable doubt that innocence can no longer be maintained, a just conviction is required. This is equivalent to rejecting the null hypothesis and accepting the alternative hypothesis. Incorrect decisions or errors are the other two possible outcomes. We can unjustly convict an innocent person, or we can acquit a guilty person.

Table 16–1 compares the statistical situation to the legal one. One of two conditions exists in nature—either the null hypothesis is true or the alternative hypothesis is true. An indicted person is innocent or guilty. Two decisions can be made about these conditions: one may accept the null hypothesis or reject it (thereby accepting the alternative). Two of these situations result in correct decisions; the other two lead to decision errors.

When a **Type I error** (α) is committed, a true null hypothesis is rejected; the innocent person is unjustly convicted. The α value is called the *level of significance* and is the probability of rejecting the true null. With a **Type II error** (β), one fails to reject a false null hypothesis; the result is an unjust acquittal with the guilty person going free. In our system of justice, it is more important to reduce the probability of convicting the innocent than acquitting the guilty. Similarly, hypothesis testing places a greater emphasis on Type I errors than on Type II. We shall examine each of these errors in more detail.

Type I Error   Assume the controller's problem is deciding whether the average age of accounts receivable has changed. Assume the population mean is 50 days, the standard deviation of the population is 10 days, and the size of the sample is 25 accounts. With this information, one can calculate the standard error of the mean (σ_X) (the standard deviation of the distribution of sample means). This hypothetical distribution is pictured in Figure 16–2. The standard error of the mean is calculated to be 2 days.

$$\sigma_{\overline{X}} = \frac{\sigma}{\sqrt{n}} = \frac{10}{\sqrt{25}} = 2$$

If the decision is to reject H_0 with a 95 percent confidence interval ($\alpha = .05$), a Type I error of .025 in each tail is accepted (assumes a two-tailed test). In Part A of Figure 16–2, see the **regions of rejection** indicated by the shaded areas. The area between these two regions is known as the **region of acceptance.** The dividing points between rejection and acceptance areas are called **critical values.** Since the distribution of sample means is normal, the critical values can be computed in terms of the standardized random variable,[2] where

$$
\begin{aligned}
Z &= 1.96 \text{ (significance level} = .05) \\
\overline{X}_c &= \text{The critical value of the sample mean} \\
\mu &= \text{The population value stated in } H_0 = 50 \\
\sigma_{\overline{X}} &= \text{The standard error of a distribution of means of samples of 25}
\end{aligned}
$$

FIGURE   16–2   Probability of Making a Type I Error Given H_0 Is True

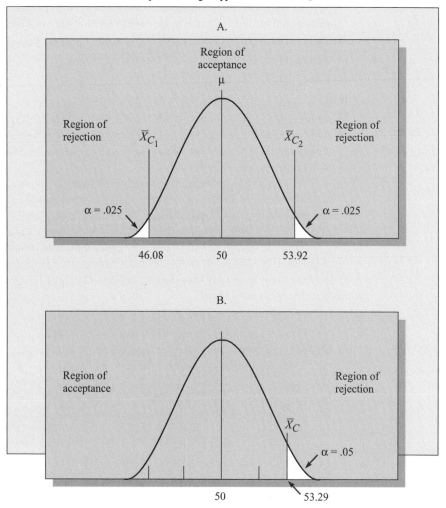

$$Z = \frac{\bar{X} - \mu}{\sigma_{\bar{X}}}$$

$$-1.96 = \frac{\bar{X}_{C_1} - 50}{2}$$

$$\bar{X}_{C_1} = 46.08$$

$$1.96 = \frac{\bar{X}_{C_2} - 50}{2}$$

$$\bar{X}_{C_2} = 53.92$$

The probability of a Type I error is

$$\alpha = .05, \text{ or } 5\%$$

The probability of a correct decision if the null hypothesis is true is 95 percent. By changing the probability of a Type I error, you move critical values either closer to or farther away from the assumed parameter of 50. This can be done if a smaller or larger α error is desired and critical values are moved to reflect this. You can also change the Type 1 error and the regions of acceptance by changing the size of the sample. For example, if you take a sample of 100, the critical values that provide a Type I error of .05 are 48.04 and 51.96.

The alternative hypothesis concerned a change in either direction from 50, but the controller may be interested only in increases in the age of receivables. For this, one uses a one-tailed (greater than) H_A and places the entire region of rejection in the upper tail of the distribution. One can accept a 5 percent α risk and compute a new critical value (X_c). (See Appendix Table F–1 to find the Z value of 1.645 for the area of .05 under the curve.) Substitute this in the Z equation and solve for X_c.

$$Z = 1.645 = \frac{\overline{X}_C - 50}{2}$$

$$\overline{X}_C = 53.29$$

This new critical value, the boundary between the regions of acceptance and rejection, is pictured in Part B of Figure 16–2.

Type II Error   The controller would commit a Type II error (β) by accepting the null hypothesis ($\mu = 50$) when in truth it had changed. This kind of error is difficult to detect. The probability of committing a β error depends on five factors: (1) the true value of the parameter, (2) the α level we have selected, (3) whether a one- or two-tailed test was used to evaluate the hypothesis, (4) the sample standard deviation, and (5) the size of the sample. We secure a different β error if the new β moves from 50 to 54 than if it moves only to 52. We must compute separate β error estimates for each of a number of assumed new population parameters and $\overline{X}_c$ values.

To illustrate, assume μ has actually moved to 54 from 50. Under these conditions, what is the probability of our making a Type II error if the critical value is set at 53.29? This may be expressed in the following fashion:

$P(A_2|S_1) = \alpha = .05$ (assume a one-tailed alternative hypothesis)
$P(A_1|S_2) = \beta = ?$

If the new μ is 54, then

$$\sigma_{\overline{X}} = \frac{\sigma}{\sqrt{n}} = \frac{10}{\sqrt{25}} = 2$$

$$Z = \frac{\overline{X} - \mu}{\sigma_{\overline{X}}} = \frac{53.29 - 54}{2} = -.355$$

Using Table F–1 in Appendix F, we interpolate between .35 and .36 Z scores to find the .355 Z score. The area between the mean and Z is .1387. β is the tail area, or the area below the Z, and is calculated as

$$\beta = .50 - .1387 = .36$$

This condition is shown in Figure 16–3. With an α of .05 and a sample of 25, there is a 36 percent probability of a Type II (β) error if the μ is 54. We also speak of the **power of the test**—that is $(1 - \beta)$. For this example, the power of the test equals 64 percent $(1 - .36)$—that is, we will correctly reject the false null hypothesis with a 64 percent probability. A power of 64 percent is less than the 80 percent minimum percentage usually needed.

There are several ways to reduce a Type II error. We can shift the critical value closer to the original μ of 50; but to do this, we must accept a bigger α. Whether to take this action depends on the evaluation of the relative α and β risks. It might be desirable to enlarge the acceptable α risk because a worsening of the receivables situation would probably call for increased efforts to stimulate collections. Committing a Type I error would mean only that we engaged in efforts to stimulate collections when the situation had not worsened. This act probably would not have many adverse effects even if the days of credit outstanding had not increased.

A second way to reduce Type II error is to increase sample size. For example, if the sample were increased to 100, the power of the test would be much stronger.

$$\sigma_{\bar{X}} = \frac{\sigma}{\sqrt{n}} = \frac{10}{\sqrt{100}} = 1$$

$$Z = \frac{\bar{X} - \mu}{\sigma_{\bar{X}}} = \frac{53.29 - 54}{1} = -.71$$

$$\beta = .50 - .2612 = .24$$

This would reduce the Type II error to 24 percent and increase the power of the test to 76 percent.

A third method seeks to improve both α and β errors simultaneously and is difficult to accomplish. We know that measuring instruments, observations, and recording produce error. By using a better measuring device, tightening the observation and recording processes, or devising a more efficient sample, we can reduce the variability of observations. This diminishes the standard error of estimate and in turn reduces the sampling distributions' spread. The net effect is that there is less tail area in the error regions.

Statistical Testing Procedures

Testing for statistical significance follows a relatively well-defined pattern, although authors differ in the number and sequence of steps. One six-stage sequence is as follows:

1. *State the null hypothesis.* While the researcher is usually interested in testing a hypothesis of change or differences, the null hypothesis is always used for statistical testing purposes.

2. *Choose the statistical test.* To test a hypothesis, one must choose an appropriate statistical test. There are many tests from which to choose, and there are at

FIGURE   16–3   Probability of Making a Type II Error

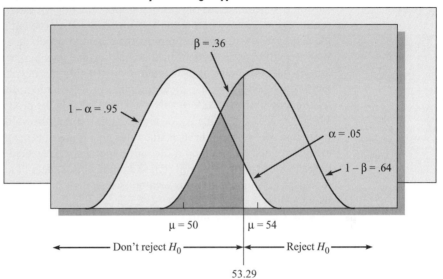

least four criteria that can be used in choosing a test. One is the power efficiency of the test. A more powerful test provides the same level of significance with a smaller sample than a less powerful test. In addition, in choosing a test, one can consider how the sample is drawn, the nature of the population, and the type of measurement scale used. For instance, some tests are useful only when the sequence of scores is known or when observations are paired. Other tests are appropriate only if the population has certain characteristics; still other tests are useful only if the measurement scale is interval or ratio. More attention is given to test selection later in the chapter.

3. *Select the desired level of significance.* The choice of the **level of significance** should be made before we collect the data. The most common level is .05, although .01 is also widely used. Other α levels such as .10, .025, or .001 are sometimes chosen. The exact level to choose is largely determined by how much α risk one is willing to accept and the effect that this choice has on β risk. The larger the α, the lower is the β.

4. *Compute the calculated difference value.* After the data are collected, use the formula for the appropriate significance test to obtain the calculated value.

5. *Obtain the critical test value.* After we compute the calculated t, χ^2, or other measure, we must look up the critical value in the appropriate table for that distribution. The critical value is the criterion that defines the region of rejection from the region of acceptance of the null hypothesis.

6. *Make the decision.* For most tests if the calculated value is larger than the critical value, we reject the null hypothesis and conclude that the alternative hypothesis is supported (although it is by no means proved). If the critical value is larger, we conclude we have failed to reject the null.[3]

Probability Values (p Values)

According to the "make the decision" step of the statistical test procedure, the conclusion is stated in terms of rejecting or not rejecting the null hypothesis based on a reject region selected before the test is conducted. A second method of presenting the results of a statistical test reports the extent to which the test statistic disagrees with the null hypothesis. This method has become popular because analysts want to know what percentage of the sampling distribution lies beyond the sample statistic on the curve, and most statistical computer programs report the results of statistical tests as probability values (p values). The p value is the probability of observing a sample value as extreme as, or more extreme than, the value actually observed, given that the null hypothesis is true. This area represents the probability of a Type I error that must be assumed if the null hypothesis is rejected. The p value is compared to the significance level (α), and on this basis the null hypothesis is either rejected or not rejected. If the p value is less than the significance level, the null hypothesis is rejected (if p value < α, reject null). If p is greater than or equal to the significance level, the null hypothesis is not rejected (if p value > α, don't reject null).

Statistical data analysis programs commonly compute the p value during the execution of a hypothesis test. The following example will help illustrate the correct way to interpret a p value.

In Part B of Figure 16–2 the critical value was shown for the situation where the controller was interested in determining whether the average age of accounts receivable had increased. The critical value of 53.29 was computed based on a standard deviation of 10, sample size of 25, and the contoller's willingness to accept a 5 percent α risk. Suppose that the sample mean equaled 55. Is there enough evidence to reject the null hypothesis? If the p value is less than .05, the null hypothesis will be rejected. The p value is computed as follows.

The standard deviation of the distribution of sample means is 2. The appropriate Z value is

$$Z = \frac{\overline{X} - \mu}{\sigma_{\overline{X}}}$$

$$Z = \frac{55 - 50}{2}$$

$$Z = 2.5$$

The p value is determined using the standard normal table. The area between the mean and a Z value of 2.5 is .4938. The p value is the area above the Z value (shown in Part B of Figure 16–2). The probability of observing a Z value at least as large as 2.5 is only .0062 (.5000 − .4932 = .0062) if the null hypothesis is true.

This small p value represents the risk of rejecting the null hypothesis. It is the probability of a Type I error if the null hypothesis is rejected. Since the p value (p = .0062) is smaller than α = .05, the null hypothesis is rejected. The controller can conclude that the average age of the accounts receivable has increased. The probability that this conclusion is wrong is .0062.

TESTS OF SIGNIFICANCE

This section provides an overview of statistical tests that are representative of the vast array available to the researcher. After a review of the general types and their assumptions, the procedures for selecting an appropriate test are discussed. The remainder of the section contains examples of parametric and nonparametric tests for one-sample, two-sample, and *k*-sample cases. Readers needing a comprehensive treatment of significance tests are referred to the suggested readings at the end of this chapter.

Types of Tests

There are two general classes of significance tests: parametric and nonparametric. **Parametric tests** are more powerful because their data are derived from interval and ratio measurements. **Nonparametric tests** are used to test hypotheses with nominal and ordinal data. Parametric techniques are the tests of choice if their assumptions are met. Assumptions for parametric tests include the following:

1. The observations must be independent—that is, the selection of any one case should not affect the chances for any other case to be included in the sample.
2. The observations should be drawn from normally distributed populations.
3. These populations should have equal variances.
4. The measurement scales should be at least interval so that arithmetic operations can be used with them.

The researcher is responsible for reviewing the assumptions pertinent to the chosen test. Performing diagnostic checks on the data allows the researcher to select the most appropriate technique. The normality of a distribution may be checked in several ways. We have previously discussed the measures of location, shape, and spread for preliminary analysis and considered graphic techniques for exploring data patterns and examining distributions. Another diagnostic tool is the **normal probability plot.** This plot compares the observed values with those expected from a normal distribution.[4] If the data display the characteristics of normality, the points will fall within a narrow band along a straight line. An example is shown in the upper left panel of Figure 16–4.

An alternative way to look at this is to plot the deviations from the straight line. These are shown in a "detrended" plot in the upper right panel of the figure. Here we would expect the points to cluster without pattern around a straight line passing horizontally through 0. In the bottom two panels of Figure 16–4, there is neither a straight line in the normal probability plot nor a random distribution of points about 0 in the detrended plot. Visually, the bottom two plots tell us the variable is not normally distributed. In addition, two separate tests of the hypothesis that the data come from normal distributions are rejected at a significance level of less than .01.[5]

If we wished to check another assumption—say, one of equal variance—a spread-and-level plot would be appropriate. Statistical software programs often provide diagnostic tools for checking assumptions. These may be nested within a spe-

FIGURE   16–4   Probability Plots and Tests of Normality

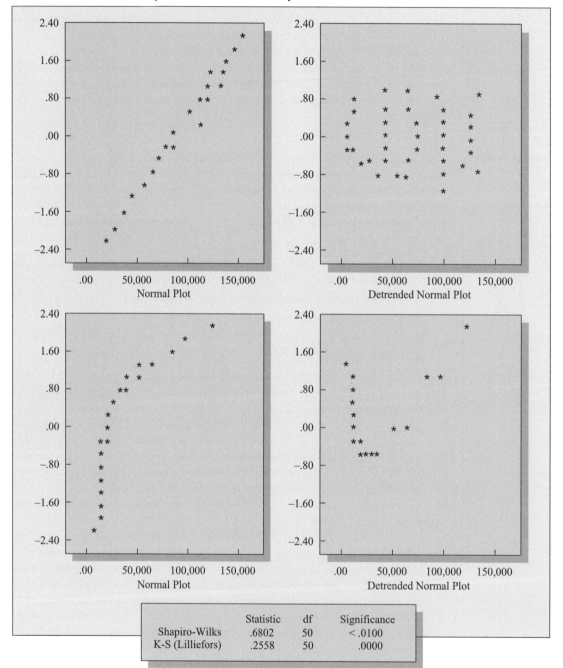

	Statistic	df	Significance
Shapiro-Wilks	.6802	50	< .0100
K-S (Lilliefors)	.2558	50	.0000

cific statistical procedure, such as analysis of variance or regression, or provided as a general set of tools for examining assumptions.

Parametric tests place different emphasis on the importance of assumptions. Some tests are quite robust and hold up well despite violations. For others, a departure from linearity or equality of variance may threaten the validity of the results.

Nonparametric tests have fewer and less stringent assumptions. They do not specify normally distributed populations or homogeneity of variance. Some tests require independence of cases; others are expressly designed for situations with related cases. Nonparametric tests are the only ones usable with nominal data; they are the only technically correct tests to use with ordinal data, although parametric tests are sometimes employed in this case. Nonparametric tests may also be used for interval and ratio data, although they waste some of the information available. Nonparametric tests are also easy to understand and to use. Parametric tests have greater efficiency when their use is appropriate, but even in such cases nonparametric tests often achieve an efficiency as high as 95 percent. This means the nonparametric test with a sample of 100 will provide the same statistical testing power as a parametric test with a sample of 95.

How to Select a Test

In attempting to choose a particular significance test, the researcher should consider at least three questions:

1. Does the test involve one sample, two samples, or *k* samples?
2. If two samples or *k* samples are involved, are the individual cases independent or related?
3. Is the measurement scale nominal, ordinal, interval, or ratio?

Additional questions may arise once answers to these are known: What is the sample size? If there are several samples, are they of equal size? Have the data been weighted? Have the data been transformed? Often such questions are unique to the selected technique. The answers can complicate the selection, but once a tentative choice is made, most standard statistics textbooks will provide further details.

Decision trees provide a more systematic means of selecting techniques. One widely used guide from the Institute for Social Research starts with questions about the number of variables, nature of the variables (continuous, discrete, dichotomous, independent, dependent, and so forth), and level of measurement. It goes through a tree structure asking detailed questions about the nature of the relationships being searched, compared, or tested. Over 130 solutions to data analysis problems are paired with commonly asked questions.[6]

An expert system offers another approach to choosing appropriate statistics. Capitalizing on the power and convenience of personal computers, expert system programs provide a comprehensive search of the statistical terrain just as a computer search of secondary sources does. Most programs ask about your research objectives, the nature of your data, and the intended audience for your final re-

FIGURE 16–5 **Recommended Statistical Techniques by Measurement Level and Testing Situation**

Measurement Level	One-Sample Case	Two-Samples Case		k-Samples Case	
		Related Samples	*Independent Samples*	*Related Samples*	*Independent Samples*
Nominal	Binomial χ^2 One-sample	McNemar	Fisher exact test χ^2 Two-samples test	Cochran Q	χ^2 for k samples
Ordinal	Kolmogorov-Smirnov one-sample test Runs test	Sign test Wilcoxon matched pairs	Median test Mann-Whitney U test Kolmogorov-Smirnov Wald-Wolfowitz	Friedman two-way ANOVA	Median estension Kruskal-Wallis one-way ANOVA
Interval and ratio	*t* test *Z* test	*t* test for paired samples	*t* test *Z* test	Repeated-measures ANOVA	One-way ANOVA N-way ANOVA

port. When you are not 100 percent confident of your answers, you can bracket them with an estimate of the degree of your certainty. One such program, Statistical Navigator, covers eight categories of statistics from exploratory data analysis through reliability testing and multivariate data analysis. In response to your answers, a report is printed containing recommendations, rationale for selections, references, and the statistical packages that offer the suggested procedure.[7]

In this chapter, we used the above three criteria to develop a classification of the major parametric and nonparametric tests and measures. This is shown in Figure 16–5.[8] For example, if your testing situation involves two samples, the samples are independent, and the data are interval, the figure suggests the *t* test of differences as the appropriate choice. The most frequently used of the tests listed in Figure 16–5 are covered next. For additional examples see Appendix E.

One-Sample Tests

One-sample tests are used when we have a single sample and wish to test the hypothesis that it comes from a specified population. In this case we encounter questions such as these:

1. Is there a difference between observed frequencies and the frequencies we would expect, based on some theory?
2. Is there a difference between observed and expected proportions?
3. Is it reasonable to conclude that a sample is drawn from a population with some specified distribution (normal, Poisson, and so forth)?
4. Is there a significant difference between some measures of central tendency $(\overline{X})$ and its population parameter (μ)?

A number of tests may be appropriate in this situation. The parametric test is discussed first.

Parametric Tests   The Z or t test is used to determine the statistical significance between a sample distribution mean and a parameter.

The **Z distribution** and **t distribution** differ. The t has more tail area than that found in the normal distribution. This is a compensation for the lack of information about the population standard deviation. Although the sample standard deviation is used as a proxy figure, the imprecision makes it necessary to go farther away from 0 to include the percentage of values in the t distribution necessarily found in the standard normal.

When sample sizes approach 120, the sample standard deviation becomes a very good estimate of σ; beyond 120, the t and Z distributions are virtually identical.

Some typical real-world applications of the one-sample test are

1. Finding the average monthly balance of credit card holders compared to the average monthly balance five years ago
2. Comparing the failure rate of computers in a 20-hour test of quality specifications
3. Discovering the proportion of people who would shop in a new district compared to the assumed population proportion
4. Comparing the average income taxes collected this year to last year's income tax revenues

Example   To illustrate the application of the t test to the one-sample case, consider again the controller's problem mentioned earlier. With a sample of 100 accounts, she finds that the mean age of outstanding receivables is 52.5 days, with a standard deviation of 14. Do these results indicate the population mean might still be 50 days?

In this problem, we have only the sample standard deviation (s). This must be used in place of the population standard deviation (σ). When we substitute s for σ, we use the t distribution, especially if the sample size is less than 30. We define t as

$$t = \frac{\overline{X} - \mu}{s / \sqrt{n}}$$

This significance test is conducted by following the six-step procedure recommended earlier.

1. *Null hypothesis.* H_0: = 50 days.
   H_A: > 50 days (one-tailed test).
2. *Statistical test.* Choose the t test because the data are ratio measurements. Assume the underlying population is normal and we have randomly selected the sample from the population of customer accounts.
3. *Significance level.* Let α = .05, with n = 100.
4. *Calculated value.*

$$t = \frac{52.5 - 50}{14 / \sqrt{100}} = \frac{2.5}{1.4} = 1.786; \ \text{d.f.} = n - 1 = 99$$

5. *Critical test value.* We obtain this by entering the table of critical values of *t* (see Appendix Table F–2 at back of book), with 99 d.f. and a level of significance value of .05. We secure a critical value of about 1.66 (interpolated between d.f. = 60 and d.f. = 120 in Table F–2).

6. *Decision.* In this case, the calculated value is greater than the critical value (1.786 > 1.66), so we reject the null hypothesis and conclude that the average accounts receivable outstanding has increased.

Nonparametric Tests   A variety of nonparametric tests may be used in a one-sample situation, depending on the measurement scale used and other conditions. If the measurement scale is nominal (classificatory only), it is possible to use either the binomial test or the chi-square (χ^2) one-sample test. The binomial test is appropriate when the population is viewed as only two classes, such as male and female, buyer and nonbuyer, and successful and unsuccessful, and all observations fall into one or the other of these categories. The binomial test is particularly useful when the size of sample is so small that the χ^2 test cannot be used.

Chi-Square Test   Probably the most widely used nonparametric test of significance is the **chi-square (χ^2) test**. It is particularly useful in tests involving nominal data but can be used for higher scales. Typical are cases where persons, events, or objects are grouped in two or more nominal categories such as "yes-no," "favor-undecided-against," or class "A, B, C, or D."

Using this technique, we test for significant differences between the *observed* distribution of data among categories and the *expected* distribution based on the null hypothesis. Chi-square is useful in cases of one-sample analysis, two independent samples, or *k* independent samples. It must be calculated with actual counts rather than percentages.

In the one-sample case, we establish a null hypothesis based on the expected frequency of objects in each category. Then the deviations of the actual frequencies in each category are compared with the hypothesized frequencies. The greater the difference between them, the less is the probability that these differences can be attributed to chance. The value of χ^2 is the measure that expresses the extent of this difference. The larger the divergence, the larger is the χ^2 value.

The formula by which the χ^2 test is calculated is

$$\chi^2 = \sum_{i=1}^{k} \frac{(O_i - E_i)^2}{E_i}$$

in which

O_i = Observed number of cases categorized in the *i*th category

E_i = Expected number of cases in the *i*th category under H_0

k = The number of categories

There is a different distribution for χ^2 for each number of degrees of freedom (d.f.), defined as $(k-1)$ or the number of categories in the classification minus 1.

$$\text{d.f.} = k - 1$$

With chi-square contingency tables of the two-sample or *k*-sample variety, we have both rows and columns in the cross-classification table. In that instance, d.f. is defined as rows minus 1 $(r-1)$ times columns minus 1 $(c-1)$.

$$\text{d.f.} = (r-1)(c-1)$$

In a 2×2 table there is 1 d.f., and in a 3×2 table there are 2 d.f. Depending on the number of degrees of freedom, we must be certain the numbers in each cell are large enough to make the χ^2 test appropriate. When d.f. = 1, each expected frequency should be at least 5 in size. If d.f. > 1, then the χ^2 test should not be used if more than 20 percent of the expected frequencies are smaller than 5, or when any expected frequency is less than 1. Expected frequencies can often be increased by combining adjacent categories. Four categories of freshmen, sophomores, juniors, and seniors might be classified into upper class and lower class. If there are only two categories and still there are too few in a given class, it is better to use the binomial test.

Assume a survey of student interest in the dining club that was discussed in Chapter 9 is taken. We have interviewed 200 students and learned of their intentions to join such a club. We would like to analyze the results by living arrangement (type and location of student housing and eating arrangements). The 200 responses are classified into the four categories shown in the accompanying table. Do these variations indicate there is a significant difference among these students, or are these sampling variations only? Proceed as follows:

1. *Null hypothesis H_0: $O_i = E_i$.* The proportion in the population who intend to join the club is independent of living arrangement. In H_A: $O_i \neq E_i$, the proportion in the population who intend to join the club is dependent on living arrangement.

2. *Statistical test.* Use the one-sample χ^2 to compare the observed distribution to a hypothesized distribution. The χ^2 test is used because the responses are classified into nominal categories, and there are sufficient observations.

3. *Significance level.* Let $\alpha = .05$.

4. *Calculated value.*

$$\chi^2 = \sum_{i=1}^{k} \frac{(O_i - E_i)^2}{E_i}$$

Calculate the expected distribution by determining what proportion of the 200 students interviewed were in each group. Then apply these proportions to the number who intend to join the club. Then calculate the following:

$$\chi^2 = \frac{(16-27)^2}{27} + \frac{(13-12)^2}{12} + \frac{(16-12)^2}{12} + \frac{(15-9)^2}{9}$$

$$= 4.48 + 0.08 + 1.33 + 4.0$$

$$= 9.89$$

$$\text{d.f.} = (4-1)(2-1) = 3$$

5. *Critical test value.* Enter the table of critical values of χ^2 (see Appendix Table F–3), with 3 d.f., and secure a value of 7.82 for $\alpha = .05$.

6. *Decision.* The calculated value is greater than the critical value, so the null hypothesis is rejected.

Living Arrangement	Intend to Join	Number Interviewed	Percent (No. Interviewed/200)	Expected Frequencies (Percent × 60)
Dorm/fraternity	16	90	45	27
Apartment/rooming house, nearby	13	40	20	12
Apartment/rooming house, distant	16	40	20	12
Live at home	15	30	15	9
Total	60	200	100	60

Two Independent Samples Tests

The need to use **two independent samples tests** is often encountered in business research. We might compare the purchasing predispositions of a sample of subscribers from two magazines to discover if they are from the same population. Similarly, a test of output methods from two production lines or the price movements of common stock from two samples could be compared. A study of worker productivity from two groups or different samples from a public opinion poll would also use this method.

Parametric Tests   The Z and t tests are frequently used parametric tests for independent samples, although the F test can be used.

The **Z test** is used with large sample sizes (exceeding 30 for both independent samples) or with smaller samples when the data are normally distributed and population variances are known. The formula for the Z test is

$$Z = \frac{(\bar{X}_1 - \bar{X}_2) - (\mu_1 - \mu_2)0}{\sqrt{\dfrac{S_1^2}{n_1} + \dfrac{S_2^2}{n_2}}}$$

With small sample sizes, normally distributed populations, and assuming equal population variances, the *t* **test** is appropriate:

$$t = \frac{(\bar{X}_1 - \bar{X}_2) - (\mu_1 - \mu_2)0}{\sqrt{S_p^2 \left(\frac{1}{n_1} + \frac{1}{n_2} \right)}}$$

where

$(\mu_1 - \mu_2)$ is the difference between the two population means

S_p^2 is associated with the pooled variance estimate:

$$S_p^2 = \frac{(n_1 - 1)S_1^2 + (n_2 - 1)S_2^2}{n_1 + n_2 - 2}$$

To illustrate this application, consider a problem that might face a manager who wishes to test the effectiveness of two methods for training new salespeople. The company selects 22 sales trainees who are randomly divided into two experimental groups. One receives type A and the other type B training. The salespeople are then assigned and managed without regard to the training they have received. At the year's end, the manager reviews the performances of salespeople in these groups and finds the following results:

	A Group	*B Group*
Average weekly sales	$\bar{X}_1 = \$1,500$	$\bar{X}_2 = \$1,300$
Standard deviation	$s_1 = 225$	$s_2 = 251$

Following the standard testing procedure, we will determine whether one training method is superior to the other.

1. *Null hypothesis.* H_0: There is no difference in sales results produced by the two training methods.

   H_A: Training method A produces sales results superior to those of method B.

2. *Statistical test.* The *t* test is chosen because the data are at least interval and the samples are independent.

3. *Significance level.* $\alpha = .05$ (one-tailed test).

4. *Calculated value.*

$$t = \frac{(1,500 - 1,300) - 0}{\sqrt{\frac{(10)(225)^2 + (10)(251)^2}{20} \left(\frac{1}{11} + \frac{1}{11} \right)}}$$

$$= \frac{200}{101.63} = 1.97, \text{ d.f.} = 20$$

There are $n - 1$ degrees of freedom in each sample, so total
d.f. $= (11 - 1) + (11 - 1) = 20$.

5. *Critical test value.* Enter Appendix Table F–2 with d.f. = 20, one-tailed test, $\alpha = .05$. The critical value is 1.725.

6. *Decision.* Since the calculated value is larger than the critical value (1.97 > 1.725), reject the null hypothesis and conclude that training method A is superior.

Nonparametric Tests   The chi-square (χ^2) test is appropriate for situations in which a test for differences between samples is required. It is especially valuable for nominal data but can be used with ordinal measurements. When parametric data have been reduced to categories, they are frequently treated with χ^2 although this results in a loss of information. Preparing to solve this problem is the same as presented earlier although the formula differs slightly:

$$\chi^2 = \sum_i \sum_j \frac{(O_{ij} - E_{ij})^2}{E_{ij}}$$

in which

O_{ij} = Observed number of cases categorized in the *ij*th cell
E_{ij} = Expected number of cases under H_0 to be categorized in the *ij*th cell

Suppose a manager implementing a smoke-free workplace policy is interested in whether smoking affects worker accidents. Since the company has complete reports of on-the-job accidents, she draws a sample of names of workers who were involved in accidents during the last year. A similar sample from among workers who had no reported accidents in the last year is drawn. She interviews members of both groups to determine if they are smokers or not. The results appear in the following table.

Smoker	Count Expected Values	On-the-Job Accident		Row Total
		Yes	No	
Heavy		12	4	16
		8.24	7.75	
Moderate		9	6	15
		7.73	7.27	
Nonsmoker		13	22	35
		18.03	16.97	
Column Total		34	32	66

The expected values have been calculated and are shown. The testing procedure is:

1. *Null hypothesis.* H_0: There is no difference in on-the-job accident occurrences between smokers and nonsmokers.

   H_A: There is a difference in on-the-job accident occurrences between smokers and nonsmokers.

2. *Statistical test.* χ^2 is appropriate but it may waste some of the data because the measurement appears to be ordinal.

3. *Significance level.* $\alpha = .05$, with d.f. $= (3 - 1)(2 - 1) = 2$.

4. *Calculated value.* The expected distribution is provided by the marginal totals of the table. If there is no relationship between accidents and smoking, there will be the same proportion of smokers in both accident and nonaccident classes. The numbers of expected observations in each cell are calculated by multiplying the two marginal totals common to a particular cell and dividing this product by n. For example,

$$\frac{34 \times 16}{66} = 8.24, \text{ the expected value in cell } (1,1)$$

$$\chi^2 = \frac{(12 - 8.24)^2}{8.24} + \frac{(4 - 7.75)^2}{7.75} + \frac{(9 - 7.73)^2}{7.73} + \frac{(6 - 7.72)^2}{7.72}$$

$$+ \frac{(13 - 18.03)^2}{18.03} + \frac{(22 - 16.97)^2}{16.97}$$

$$= 6.86$$

5. *Critical test value.* Enter Appendix Table F–3 and find the critical value 5.99 with $\alpha = .05$ and d.f. $= 2$.

6. *Decision.* Since the calculated value is greater than the critical value, the null hypothesis is rejected.

For chi-square to operate properly, data must come from random samples of multinomial distributions, and the expected frequencies should not be too small. We previously noted the traditional caution that expected frequencies below 5 should not compose more than 20 percent of the cells, and no cell should have an E_i of less than 1. Some research has argued that these restrictions are too severe.[9]

In another type of χ^2, the 2×2 table, a correction known as *Yates' correction for continuity* is often applied when sample sizes are greater than 40 or when the sample is between 20 and 40 and the values of E_i are 5 or more. The formula for this correction is

$$\chi^2 = \frac{n\left(|AD - BC| - \frac{n}{2}\right)^2}{(A + B)(C + D)(A + C)(B + D)}$$

where the letters represent the cells designated as

A	B
C	D

When the continuity correction is applied to the data shown in Figure 16–6, a χ^2 value of 5.25 is obtained. The observed level of significance for this value is .02192. If the level of significance had been set at .01, we would accept the null hypothesis. However, had we calculated χ^2 without correction, the value would have been 6.25, which has an observed level of significance of .01242. Some researchers may be tempted to reject the null at this level. (But note that the critical value of χ^2 at .01 with 1 d.f. is 6.64. See Appendix Table F–3.) The literature is in conflict regarding the merits of Yates' correction, but this example suggests one should take care when interpreting 2×2 tables.[10] To err on the conservative side would be in keeping with our prior discussion of Type I errors.

The Mantel-Haenszel test and the Likelihood Ratio also appear in Figure 16–6. The former is used with ordinal data, so it does not apply; the latter, based on maximum likelihood theory, produces results similar to Pearson's chi-square.

Two Related Samples Tests

The **two related samples tests** concern those situations in which persons, objects, or events are closely matched or the phenomena are measured twice. One might

FIGURE 16–6   Comparison of Corrected and Noncorrected Chi-Square Results Using SPSS Procedure Crosstab

```
INCOME  Income by CPA Possession of a CPA

                              CPA
                  Count
                        Yes       No
                                            Row
                         1        2        Total
        INCOME     ─────────────────────
                  High 1    30       30       60
                                             60.0

                  Low 2    10       30       40
                                             40.0

                  Column    40       60      100
                  Total    40.0     60.0    100.0
```

Chi Square	Value	D.F.	Significance
Pearson	6.25000	1	.01242
Continuity Correction	5.25174	1	.02192
Likelihood Ratio	6.43786	1	.01117
Mantel-Haenszel	6.18750	1	.01287

Minimum Expected Frequency: 16.000

compare the output of specific workers before and after vacations, the performance of the same stocks at two intervals, or the effects of an experimental stimulus when persons were randomly assigned to groups and given pretests and posttests. Both parametric and nonparametric tests are applicable under these conditions.

Parametric Tests   The t test for independent samples would normally be inappropriate for this situation because one of its assumptions is that observations are independent. This problem is solved by a formula where the difference is found between each matched pair of observations, thereby reducing the two samples to the equivalent of a one-sample case—that is, there are now several differences, each independent of the other, for which one can compute various statistics.

In the following formula, the average difference, $\overline{D}$, corresponds to the normal distribution when the σ difference is known and the sample size is sufficient. The statistic t with $(n - 1)$ degrees of freedom is defined as

$$t = \frac{\overline{D}}{S_D / \sqrt{n}}$$

where

$$\overline{D} = \frac{\Sigma D}{n}$$

$$S_D = \sqrt{\frac{\Sigma D^2 - \frac{(\Sigma D)^2}{n}}{n - 1}}$$

To illustrate this application, we use sales data (in millions of dollars) for 1988 and 1989 from 10 companies of the Forbes Super50 found in Table 16–2.

TABLE   16–2   Sales Data for Paired-Samples *t* Test (dollars in millions)

Company	Sales 1989	Sales 1988	Difference D	D^2
GM	126932	123505	3427	11744329
GE	54574	49662	4912	24127744
Exxon	86656	78944	7712	59474944
IBM	62710	59512	3192	10227204
Ford	96146	92300	3846	14791716
AT&T	36112	35173	939	881721
Mobil	50220	48111	2109	4447881
DuPont	35099	32427	2632	6927424
Sears	53794	49975	3819	14584761
Amoco	23966	20779	3187	10156969
Totals			$\Sigma D = 35781$	$\Sigma D^2 = 157364693$

FIGURE 16–7   **Sample SPSS Output for Paired-Samples *t* Test**

```
                    ---t-tests for paired samples---

                Number                   Standard      Standard
 Variable      of cases     Mean         Deviation      Error

89 Sales          10      62620.9000    31777.649    10048.975
88 Sales          10      62620.8000    31072.871     9836.104


(Difference  Standard   Standard               2-tail    t     Degrees of  2-tail
   Mean)     Deviation   Error     Corr.       Prob.   Value    Freedom     Prob.

 3582.1000   1803.159   570.209    .999        .000    6.28       9         .000
```

1. *Null hypothesis.* H_0: $\mu = 0$; there is no difference between the two years' sales records. H_A: $\neq 0$; there is a difference between sales for 1988 and 1989.

2. *Statistical test.* The matched- or paired-samples *t* test is chosen because there are repeated measures on each company, the data are not independent, and the measurement is ratio.

3. *Significance level.* Let $\alpha = .01$, with $n = 10$ and d.f. $= n - 1$.

4. *Calculated value.*

$$t = \frac{\overline{D}}{S_D / \sqrt{n}} = \frac{3,578.10}{570.93} = 6.28; \ \text{d.f.} = 9$$

5. *Critical test value.* Enter Appendix Table F–2, with d.f. = 9, two-tailed test, $\alpha = .01$. The critical value is 3.25.

6. *Decision.* Since the calculated value is greater than the critical value (6.28 > 3.25), reject the null hypothesis and conclude there is a statistically significant difference between 1989 and 1988 sales.

A computer solution to the problem is illustrated in Figure 16–7. Notice that an *observed significance level* is printed for the calculated *t* value. With SPSS, this is often rounded and would be interpreted as significant at the .0005 level. The correlation coefficient, to the left of the *t* value, is a measure of the relationship between the two pairs of scores. In situations where matching has occurred (such as husbands' and wives' scores), it reveals the degree to which the matching has been effective in reducing the variability of the mean difference.

Nonparametric Tests   The McNemar test may be used with either nominal or ordinal data and is especially useful with before-after measurement of the same subjects.

Test the significance of any observed change by setting up a fourfold table of frequencies to represent the first and second set of responses:

	After	
Before	*Do Not Favor*	*Favor*
Favor	A	B
Do not favor	C	D

Since $A + D$ represents the total number of people who changed (B and C are no-change responses), the expectation under a null hypothesis is that $1/2 (A + D)$ cases change in one direction and the same proportion in the other direction. The McNemar test uses the following transformation of the χ^2 test:

$$\chi^2 = \frac{(|A - D| - 1)^2}{A + D} \text{ with d.f.} = 1$$

The "minus 1" in the equation is a correction for continuity since the χ^2 is a continuous distribution and the observed frequencies represent a discrete distribution.

To illustrate this test's application, we use survey data from a large corporation whose management decided to tell employees of the "values of teamwork" in an internal education campaign. Managers took a random sample of their employees before the campaign, asking them to complete a questionnaire on their attitudes on this topic. On the basis of their responses, the workers were divided into equal groups reflecting their favorable or unfavorable views of teamwork. After the campaign, the same 200 employees were asked again to complete the questionnaire. They were again classified as to favorable or unfavorable attitudes. The testing process is:

1. *Null hypothesis.* H_0: $P(A) = P(D)$.
   H_A: $P(A) \neq P(D)$.
2. *Statistical test.* The McNemar test is chosen because nominal data are used, and the study involves before-after measurements of two related samples.
3. *Significance level.* Let $\alpha = .05$, with $n = 200$.
4. *Calculated value.*

$$\chi^2 = \frac{(|10 - 40| - 1)^2}{10 + 40} = \frac{29^2}{50} = 16.82; \text{ d.f.} = 1$$

	After	
Before	*Unfavorable*	*Favorable*
Favorable	10	90
Unfavorable	60	40

5. *Critical test value.* Enter Appendix Table F–3, and find the critical value to be 3.84 with $\alpha = .05$ and d.f. = 1.

6. *Decision.* The calculated value is greater than the critical value ($16.82 > 3.84$), indicating one should reject the null hypothesis. In fact, χ^2 is so large that it would have surpassed an α of .001.

k Independent Samples Tests

In management and economic research, we often use *k* **independent samples tests** when three or more samples are involved. Under this condition, we are interested in learning whether the samples might have come from the same or identical populations. When the data are measured on an interval-ratio scale and we can meet the necessary assumptions, analysis of variance and the *F* test are used. If preliminary analysis shows the assumptions cannot be met or if the data were measured on an ordinal or nominal scale, a nonparametric test should be selected.

As with the two-samples case, the samples are assumed to be independent. This is the condition of a completely randomized experiment when subjects are randomly assigned to various treatment groups. It is also common for an ex post facto study to require comparison of more than two independent sample means.

Parametric Tests　　The statistical method for testing the null hypothesis that the means of several populations are equal is **analysis of variance (ANOVA).** *One-way analysis of variance* is described in this section. It uses a single-factor, fixed-effects model to compare the effects of one factor (brands of coffee, varieties of residential housing, types of retail stores) on a continuous dependent variable. In a fixed-effects model, the levels of the factor are established in advance, and the results are not generalizable to other levels of treatment. For example, if coffee were Jamaican grown, Colombian grown, and Honduran grown, we could not extend our inferences to coffee grown in Guatemala or Mexico.

To use ANOVA, certain conditions must be met. The samples must be randomly selected from normal populations, and the populations should have equal variances. In addition, the distance from one value to its group's mean should be independent of the distances of other values to that mean (independence of error). ANOVA is reasonably robust, and minor variations from normality and equal variance are tolerable. Nevertheless, the analyst should check the assumptions with the diagnostic techniques previously described.

Analysis of variance, as the name implies, breaks down or partitions total variability into component parts. Unlike the *t* test, which uses sample standard deviations, ANOVA uses squared deviations of the variance so computation of distances of the individual data points from their own mean or from the grand mean can be summed (recall that standard deviations sum to zero).

In an ANOVA model, each group has its own mean and values that deviate from that mean. Similarly, all the data points from all of the groups produce an overall *grand mean*. The total deviation is the sum of the squared differences between each data point and the overall grand mean.

The total deviation of any particular data point may be partitioned into *between-groups variance* and *within-groups variance*. The between-groups variance represents the effect of the **treatment** or factor. The differences of between-group means imply that each group was treated differently, and the treatment will appear as deviations of the sample means from the grand mean. Even if this were not so, there would still be some natural variability among subjects and some variability attributable to sampling. The within-groups variance describes the deviations of the data points within each group from the sample mean. This results from variability among subjects and from random variation. It is often called *error*.

Intuitively, we might conclude that when the variability attributable to the treatment exceeds the variability arising from error and random fluctuations, the viability of the null hypothesis begins to diminish. And this is exactly the way the test statistic for analysis of variance works.

The test statistic for ANOVA is the **F ratio.** It compares the variance from the last two sources:

$$F = \frac{\text{Between-groups variance}}{\text{Within-groups variance}} = \frac{\text{Mean square}_{between}}{\text{Mean square}_{within}}$$

where

$$\text{Mean square}_{between} = \frac{\text{Sum of squares}_{between}}{\text{Degrees of freedom}_{between}}$$

$$\text{Mean square}_{within} = \frac{\text{Sum of squares}_{within}}{\text{Degrees of freedom}_{within}}$$

To compute the F ratio, the sum of the squared deviations for the numerator and denominator are divided by their respective degrees of freedom. By dividing, we are computing the variance as an average or mean, thus the term *mean square*. The degrees of freedom for the numerator, the mean square between groups, is one less than the number of groups ($k - 1$). The degrees of freedom for the denominator, the mean square within groups, is the total number of observations minus the number of groups ($n - k$).

If the null hypothesis is true, there should be no difference between the populations, and the ratio should be close to 1. If the population means are not equal, the numerator should manifest this difference, and the F ratio should be greater than 1. The F distribution determines the size of ratio necessary to reject the null hypothesis for a particular sample size and level of significance.

To illustrate one-way ANOVA, consider the travel industry magazine that received several reports from international travelers about the quality of in-flight service on various carriers from the United States to Europe. Before writing a feature story coinciding with a peak travel period, the magazine decided to retain a researcher to secure a more balanced perspective on the reactions of travelers. The researcher selected passengers who had current impressions of the meal service, comfort, and friendliness of a major carrier. Three airlines were chosen and 20 passengers were randomly selected for each airline. The data, found in Table 16–3,[11] are used for this and the next two examples. For the one-way analysis of

TABLE 16–3   Data Table: Analysis of Variance Examples

Subject	Flight Service Rating 1	Rating 2	Airline	Class	Subject	Flight Service Rating 1	Rating 2	Airline	Class
1	40	36	1	1	32	70	80	2	2
2	28	28	1	1	33	73	79	2	2
3	36	30	1	1	34	72	88	2	2
4	32	28	1	1	35	73	89	2	2
5	60	40	1	1	36	71	72	2	2
6	12	14	1	1	37	55	58	2	2
7	32	26	1	1	38	68	67	2	2
8	36	30	1	1	39	81	85	2	2
9	44	38	1	1	40	78	80	2	2
10	36	35	1	1	41	92	95	3	1
11	40	42	1	2	42	56	60	3	1
12	68	49	1	2	43	64	70	3	1
13	20	24	1	2	44	72	78	3	1
14	33	35	1	2	45	48	65	3	1
15	65	40	1	2	46	52	70	3	1
16	40	36	1	2	47	64	79	3	1
17	51	29	1	2	48	68	81	3	1
18	25	24	1	2	49	76	69	3	1
19	37	23	1	2	50	56	78	3	1
20	44	41	1	2	51	88	92	3	2
21	56	67	2	1	52	79	85	3	2
22	48	58	2	1	53	92	94	3	2
23	64	78	2	1	54	88	93	3	2
24	56	68	2	1	55	73	90	3	2
25	28	69	2	1	56	68	67	3	2
26	32	74	2	1	57	81	85	3	2
27	42	55	2	1	58	95	95	3	2
28	40	55	2	1	59	68	67	3	2
29	61	80	2	1	60	78	83	3	2
30	58	78	2	1					
31	52	65	2	2					

Airline 1 = Delta; 2 = Lufthansa; 3 = KLM
Class 1 = Economy; 2 = Business.
All data are hypothetical.

variance problem, we are concerned only with the columns labeled "Flight Service Rating 1" and "Airline." The factor, airline, is the grouping variable for three carriers.

Again, we follow the procedure:

1. *Null hypothesis.* H_0: $\mu_{A1} = \mu_{A2} = \mu_{A3}$.

   H_A: $\mu_{A1} \neq \mu_{A2} \neq \mu_{A3}$.

2. *Statistical test.* The F test is chosen because we have k independent samples, accept the assumptions of analysis of variance, and have interval data.

3. *Significance level.* Let $\alpha = .05$, and d.f. = [numerator $(k - 1) = (3 - 1) = 2$], [denominator $(n - k) = (60 - 3) = 57$] = 2, 57).

4. *Calculated value.*

$$F = \frac{MS_b}{MS_w} = \frac{5822.017}{205.695} = 28.304, \text{ d.f. } (2,57)$$

See summary in Table 16–4.

5. *Critical test value.* Enter Appendix Table F–9, with d.f. (2, 57), $\alpha = .05$. The critical value is 3.16.

6. *Decision.* Since the calculated value is greater than the critical value (28.3 > 3.16), we reject the null hypothesis and conclude there are statistically significant differences between two or more pairs of means. Note in Table 16–4 that the *p* value equals .0001. Since the *p* value (.0001) is less than the significance level (.05), we have a second method for rejecting the null hypothesis.

The ANOVA model summary in Table 16–4 is a standard way of summarizing the results of analysis of variance. It contains the sources of variation, degrees

TABLE 16–4   Summary Tables for One-Way ANOVA Example

Model Summary

Source		d.f.	Sum of Squares	Mean Square	F Value	p Value
Model	Airline	2	11644.033	5822.017	28.304	.0001
Residual	Error	57	11724.550	205.694		
Total		59	23368.583			

Factor: Airline
Dependent: Flight Service Rating 1

Means Table

	Count	Mean	Std. Dev.	Std. Error
Delta	20	38.950	14.006	3.132
Lufthansa	20	58.900	15.089	3.374
KLM	20	72.900	13.902	3.108

Scheffé's S Multiple Comparison Procedure

	Vs.	Diff.	Crit. Diff.	p Value	
Delta	Lufthansa	19.950	11.400	.0002	S
	KLM	33.950	11.400	.0001	S
Lufthansa	KLM	14.000	11.400	.0122	S

S = Significantly different at this level.
Significance level: .05
All data are hypothetical.

of freedom, sum of squares, mean squares, and calculated F value. The probability of rejecting the null hypothesis is computed up to 100 percent α—that is, the probability value column reports the exact significance for the F ratio being tested.

A Priori Contrasts   When we compute a t test, it is not difficult to discover the reasons why the null is rejected. But with one-way ANOVA, how do we determine which pairs are not equal? We could calculate a series of t tests, but they would not be independent of each other and the resulting Type I error would increase substantially. Obviously, this is not recommended. If we decided in advance that a comparison of specific populations was important, a special class of tests known as *a priori* **contrasts** could be used after the null was rejected with the F test (*a priori* because the decision was made before the test).[12]

A modification of the F test provides one approach for computing contrasts:

$$F = \frac{\mathrm{MS_{CON}}}{\mathrm{MS_W}}$$

The denominator, the within-groups mean square, is the same as the error term of the one-way's F ratio (recorded in the summary table, Table 16–4). We have previously referred to the denominator of the F ratio as the error variance estimator. The numerator of the contrast test is defined as

$$\mathrm{MS_{CON}} = \mathrm{SS_{CON}} = \frac{\left(\sum_j C_j \overline{X}_j\right)^2}{\sum_j \dfrac{C_j^2}{n}}$$

where

  C_j is the contrast coefficient for the group j

  n_j is the number of observations recorded for group j

A contrast is useful for experimental and quasi-experimental designs when the researcher is interested in answering specific questions about a subset of the factor. For example, in a comparison of coffee products, we have a factor with six levels. The levels, blends of coffee, are meaningfully ordered. Assume we are particularly interested in two Central American grown blends and one Colombian blend. Rather than looking at all possible combinations, we can channel the power of the test into fewer degrees of freedom by stating the comparisons of interest. This increases our likelihood of detecting differences if they really exist.

Multiple Comparison Tests   For the probabilities associated with the contrast test to be properly used in the report of our findings, it is important that the contrast strategy be devised ahead of the testing. In the airline study, we had no theoretical reason for an *a priori* contrast. However, examining the means table (Table 16–4) revealed that the airline means were quite disparate. Comparisons after the results are compared require post hoc tests or **multiple comparison procedures.** Multiple comparison tests use group means and incorporate the MS_{error} term of the F ratio. Together they produce confidence intervals for the population means and a criterion score. Differences between the mean values may be compared.

There are roughly a dozen such tests with different optimization goals: maximum number of comparisons, unequal cell size compensation, cell homogeneity, α or β error reduction, and so forth. The example in Table 16–4 is Scheffé's S. It is a conservative test that is robust to violations of assumptions.[13] The computer calculated the critical difference criterion as 11.4; all the differences between the pairs of means exceed this. The null hypothesis for the Scheffé was tested at the .05 level. Therefore, conclude that all combinations of flight service mean scores differ from each other.

While the table provides information for understanding the rejection of the one-way null hypothesis and the Scheffé null, in Figure 16–8 we use plots for the comparisons. The means plot shows relative differences among the three levels of the factor. The means by standard deviations plot reveals lower variability in the opinions recorded by the hypothetical Delta and KLM passengers. Nevertheless, these two groups are sharply divided on the quality of in-flight service, and that is apparent in the upper plot.

Exploring the Findings with Two-Way ANOVA   Is the airline on which the passengers traveled the only factor influencing perceptions of in-flight service? By extending the one-way ANOVA, we can learn more about the service ratings. There are many possible explanations. We have chosen to look at the fare class of the travelers in the interest of brevity.

Recall that in Table 16–3, data were entered for the variable fare class: economy and business-class travelers. Adding this factor to the model, we have a *two-way* analysis of variance. Now three questions may be considered with one model:

1. Are differences in flight service ratings attributable to airlines?
2. Are differences in flight service ratings attributable to fare class?
3. Do the airline and the fare class interact with respect to flight service ratings?

The third question reveals a distinct advantage of the two-way model. A separate one-way model on airlines averages out the effects of class. Similarly, a single factor test of class averages out the effects of the airline. But an interaction test of airline by class considers them *jointly*.

Table 16–5 reports a test of the hypotheses for these three questions. The significance level was established at the .01 level. We first inspect the interaction effect, airline by class, since the individual *main effects* cannot be considered separately if factors operate jointly. The interaction was not significant at the .01 level, and the null is accepted. Now the separate main effects, airline and class, can be verified. As with the one-way ANOVA, the null for the airline factor was rejected, and class was also found significant at .0001.

FIGURE   16–8   One-Way Analysis of Variance Plots

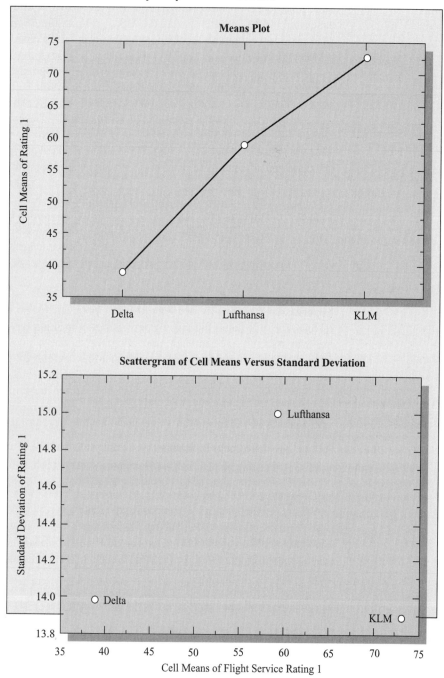

TABLE 16–5   Summary Table for Two-Way ANOVA Example

Model Summary

Source	d.f.	Sum of Squares	Mean Square	F Value	p Value
Airline	2	11644.033	5822.017	39.178	.0001
Class	1	3182.817	3182.817	21.418	.0001
Airline * Class	2	517.033	258.517	1.740	.1853
Residual	54	8024.700	148.606		

Main effects:
  Airline.
  Class.
Dependent: Flight Service Rating 1.

Means Table Effect: Airline * Class

	Count	Mean	Std. Dev.	Std. Error
Delta Economy	10	35.600	12.140	3.839
Delta Business	10	42.300	15.550	4.917
Lufthansa Economy	10	48.500	12.501	3.953
Lufthansa Business	10	69.300	9.166	2.898
KLM Economy	10	64.800	13.037	4.123
KLM Business	10	81.000	9.603	3.037

All data are hypothetical.

Means and standard deviations listed in the table are plotted in Figure 16–9. We note a band of similar deviations for economy-class travelers and a band of lower variability for business class—with the exception of one carrier. The plot of cell means confirms visually what we already know from the summary table: There is no interaction between airline and class ($p = .185$). If an interaction had occurred, the lines connecting the cell means would have crossed rather than displaying a parallel pattern.

Analysis of variance is an extremely versatile and powerful method that may be adapted to a wide range of testing applications. Discussions of further extensions in n-way and experimental designs may be found in the list of suggested readings.

Nonparametric Tests   When there are k independent samples for which nominal data have been collected, the chi-square test is appropriate. It can also be used to classify data at higher measurement levels, but metric information is lost when reduced. The k-sample χ^2 test is an extension of the two independent samples cases treated earlier. It is calculated and interpreted in the same way.

The Kruskal-Wallis test is appropriate for data that are collected on an ordinal scale or for interval data that do not meet F-test assumptions, that cannot be transformed, or that for another reason prove to be unsuitable for a parametric test. Kruskal-Wallis is a one-way analysis of variance by ranks. It assumes

FIGURE   16–9   Two-Way Analysis of Variance Plots

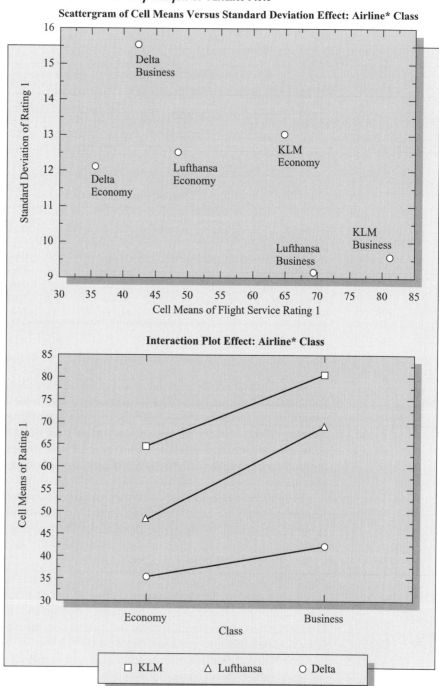

random selection and independence of samples, and an underlying continuous distribution.

Data are prepared by converting ratings or scores to ranks for each observation being evaluated. The ranks range from the highest to the lowest of all data points in the aggregated samples. The ranks are then tested to decide if they are samples from the same population. An application of this technique is provided in Appendix E.

k Related Samples Case

Parametric Tests   A *k* **related samples test** is required for situations where (1) the grouping factor has more than two levels, (2) observations or subjects are matched or the same subject is measured more than once, and (3) the data are at least interval. In experimental or ex post facto designs with *k* samples, it is often necessary to measure subjects several times. These repeated measurements are called **trials.** For example, multiple measurements are taken in studies of stock prices, products evaluated by quality assurance, inventory, sales, and measures of

TABLE 16–6   Summary Tables for Repeated-Measures ANOVA

Model Summary

Source	d.f.	Sum of Squares	Mean Square	F Value	p Value
Airline	2	35527.550	17763.775	67.199	.0001
Subject (Group)	57	15067.650	264.345		
Ratings	1	625.633	625.633	14.318	.0004
Ratings *Air. . . .	2	2061.717	1030.858	23.592	.0001
Ratings * Subj. . . .	57	2490.650	43.696		

Dependent: Flight Service Ratings 1 and 2.

Means Table Ratings * Airline

	Count	Mean	Std. Dev.	Std. Error
Rating 1, Delta	20	38.950	14.006	3.132
Rating 1, Lufthansa	20	58.900	15.089	3.374
Rating 1, KLM	20	72.900	13.902	3.108
Rating 2, Delta	20	32.400	8.268	1.849
Rating 2, Lufthansa	20	72.250	10.572	2.364
Rating 2, KLM	20	79.800	11.265	2.519

Means Table Effect: Ratings

	Count	Mean	Std. Dev.	Std. Error
Rating 1	60	56.917	19.902	2.569
Rating 1	60	61.483	23.208	2.996

All data are hypothetical.

FIGURE   16–10   Repeated Measures ANOVA Plot

All data are hypothetical.

human performance. Hypotheses for these situations may be tested with a univariate or multivariate general linear model. The latter is beyond the scope of this discussion.

The repeated-measures ANOVA is a special type of *n*-way analysis of variance. In this design, the repeated measures of each subject are related just as they are in the related *t* test when only two measures are present. In this sense, each subject serves as its own control requiring a within-subjects variance effect to be assessed differently than the between-groups variance in a factor like airline or fare class. The effects of the correlated measures are removed before calculation of the *F* ratio.

This model is an appropriate solution for the data presented in Table 16–3. You will remember that the one-way and two-way examples considered only the first rating of in-flight service. Assume a second rating was obtained after a week by reinterviewing the same respondents. We now have two trials for the dependent variable, and we are interested in the same general question as with the one-way ANOVA, with the addition of how the passage of time affects perceptions of in-flight service.

Following the testing procedure, we state:

1. *Null hypotheses*
   - (1) Airline: H_0: $\mu_{A1} = \mu_{A2} = \mu_{A3}$.
   - (2) Ratings: H_0: $\mu_{R1} = \mu_{R2}$.
   - (3) Ratings × Airline: H_0: $(\mu_{R2A1} - \mu_{R2A2} - \mu_{R2A3})$
     $= (\mu_{R1A1} - \mu_{R1A2} - \mu_{R1A3})$.

   For the alternative hypotheses, we will generalize to the statement that not all the groups have equal means for each of the three hypotheses.

2. *Statistical test.* The F test for repeated measures is chosen because we have related trials on the dependent variable for k samples, accept the assumptions of analysis of variance, and have interval data.

3. *Significance level.* Let $\alpha = .05$ and d.f. = [airline (2, 57), ratings (1, 57), ratings by airline (2, 57)].

4. *Calculated values.* See summary in Table 16–6.

5. *Critical test value.* Enter Appendix Table F–9, with d.f. (2, 57), $\alpha = .05$ and (1, 57), $\alpha = .05$. The critical values are 3.16 (2, 57) and 4.01 (1, 57).

6. *Decision.* The statistical results are grounds for rejecting all three null hypotheses and concluding there are statistically significant differences between means in all three instances. We conclude the perceptions of in-flight service were significantly affected by the different airlines, the interval between the two measures had a significant effect on the ratings, and the measures' time interval and the airlines interacted to a significant degree.

The ANOVA summary table in Table 16–6 records the results of the tests. A means table provides the means and standard deviations for all combinations of ratings by airline. A second table of means reports the differences between flight service ratings 1 and 2. In Figure 16–10, there is an interaction plot for these data. Note that the second in-flight service rating was improved in two of the three groups after one week, and for the third carrier, there was a decrease in favorable response. The intersecting lines in the interaction plot reflect this finding.

Nonparametric Tests   When the k related samples have been measured on a nominal scale, the Cochran Q test is a good choice.[14] This test extends the McNemar test, discussed earlier, for studies having more than two samples. It tests the hypothesis that the proportion of cases in a category is equal for several related categories.

When the data are at least ordinal, the Friedman two-way analysis of variance is appropriate. It tests matched samples, ranking each case and calculating the mean rank for each variable across all cases. It uses these ranks to compute a test statistic. The product is a two-way table where the rows represent subjects and the columns represent the treatment conditions.[15]

Summary

There are two approaches to hypothesis testing—classical or sampling theory statistics and the Bayesian approach. With classical statistics, we make inferences about a population based on evidence gathered from a sample. Although we cannot state unequivocally what is true about the entire population, representative samples allow us to make statements about what is probably true and how much error is likely to be encountered in arriving at a decision. The Bayesian approach also employs sampling statistics but has an additional element of prior information to improve the decision maker's judgment. With prudent use of prior probabilities, the Bayesian approach will also provide good results.

A difference between two or more sets of data is statistically significant if it actually occurs in a population. To have a statistically significant finding based on sampling evidence, we must be able to calculate the probability that some observed difference is large enough that there is little chance it could result from random sampling. Probability is the foundation for deciding on the acceptability of the null hypothesis, and sampling statistics facilitate acquiring the estimates.

Hypothesis testing can be viewed as a six-step procedure:

1. Establish a null hypothesis as well as the alternative hypothesis. It is a one-tailed test of significance if the alternative hypothesis states the direction of difference. If no direction of difference is given, it is a two-tailed test.

2. Choose the statistical test on the basis of the assumption about the population distribution and measurement level. The form of the data can also be a factor. In the light of these considerations, one typically chooses the test that has the greatest power efficiency or ability to reduce decision errors.

3. Select the desired level of confidence. While $\alpha = .05$ is the most frequently used, many others are also used. The α is the significance level that we desire and is typically set in advance of the study. Alpha or Type I error is the risk of rejecting a true null hypothesis and represents a decision error. The β or Type II error is the decision error that results from accepting a false null hypothesis. Usually, one determines a level of acceptable α error then seeks to reduce the β error by increasing the size sample, shifting from a two-tailed to a one-tailed significance test, or both.

4. Compute the actual test value of the data.

5. Obtain the critical test value, usually by referring to a table for the appropriate type of distribution.

6. Make the decision by comparing the actual test value with the critical test value.

Parametric and nonparametric tests are applicable under the various conditions described in the chapter. They were also summarized in Figure 16–5. Parametric tests operate with interval and ratio data and are preferred when their assumptions can be met. Diagnostic tools examine the data for violations of those assumptions. Nonparametric tests do not require stringent assumptions about population distributions and are useful with less powerful nominal and ordinal measures.

In selecting a significance test, one needs to know, at a minimum, the number of samples, their independence or relatedness, and the measurement level of the data.

Statistical tests emphasized in the chapter were the *Z* and *t* tests, analysis of variance, and chi-square. The *Z* and *t* tests may be used to test for the difference between two means. The *t* test is chosen when the sample size is small. Variations on the *t* test are used for both independent and related samples.

One-way analysis of variance compares the means of several groups. It has a single grouping variable, called a factor, and a continuous dependent variable. Analysis of variance (ANOVA) partitions the total variation among scores into between-groups (treatment) and within-groups (error) variance. The *F* ratio, the test statistic, determines if the differences are sufficiently large to reject the null hypothesis. ANOVA may be extended to two-way, *n*-way, repeated measures, and multivariate applications.

Chi-square is a nonparametric statistic that is used frequently for crosstabulation or contingency tables. Its applications include testing for differences between proportions in populations and testing for independence. Corrections for chi-square were discussed.

Key Terms

alternative hypothesis	one-tailed test
analysis of variance (ANOVA)	parametric tests
a priori contrasts	power of the test
Bayesian statistics	practical significance
chi-square (χ^2) test	regions of acceptance
classical statistics	regions of rejection
critical value	statistical significance
F ratio	*t* distribution
inferential statistics	treatment (factor)
k independent samples test	trials (repeated measures)
k related samples tests	*t* test
level of significance	two independent samples tests
multiple comparison (post hoc) tests	two related samples tests
nonparametric tests	two-tailed test
normal probability plot	Type I error (α)
null hypothesis	Type II error (β)
one-sample tests	*Z* distribution
	Z test

Cases

HiTech Engineering
Violence on TV
Rubbergate
Waste Paper
Performance Evaluations
(These are cases found in the optional casebook available with the text.)

Discussion Questions

1. Distinguish between the following:

   a. Parametric tests and nonparametric tests

   b. Type I error and Type II error

   c. Null hypothesis and alternative hypothesis

   d. Acceptance region and rejection region

   e. One-tailed tests and two-tailed tests

   f. Type II error and the power of the test

2. Suggest situations where the researcher should be concerned more with Type II error than with Type I.

   a. How can the probability of a Type I error be reduced? A Type II error?

   b. How does practical significance differ from statistical significance?

   c. Suppose you interview all members of the freshman and senior classes and find that 65 percent of the freshmen and 62 percent of the seniors favor a certain ecological proposal. Is this difference significant?

3. What hypothesis-testing procedure would you use in the following situations:

   a. A test classifies applicants as accepted or rejected. On the basis of data on 200 applicants, we test the hypothesis that success is not related to gender.

   b. A production batch of 26 gaskets must be evaluated on thickness specifications: A 3-mm thickness is specified by the quality control department.

   c. A company manufactures automobiles at two different facilities. We want to know if the gas mileage is the same for vehicles from both facilities. There are samples of 45 units from each facility.

   d. A company has three categories of managers: (1) with professional qualifications but without work experience, (2) with professional qualifications and with work experience, (3) without professional qualifications but with work experience. A study exists that measures each manager's motivation level (classified as high, normal, and low). A hypothesis of no relation between manager category and motivation is to be tested.

   e. A company has 24 salespersons. The test must evaluate whether their sales performance is unchanged or has improved after a training program.

   f. A company has to evaluate whether it should attribute increased sales to product quality, advertising, or an interaction of product quality and advertising.

4. You conduct a survey of a sample of 25 members of this year's graduating class and find that their average GPA is 3.2. The standard deviation of the sample is 0.4. Over the last 10 years, the average GPA has been 3.0. Is the

GPA of this year's class significantly different from the long-run average? At what alpha level would it be significant?

5. You are curious about whether the professors and students at your school are of different political persuasions. So you take a sample of 20 professors and 20 students drawn randomly from each population. You find that 10 professors say they are conservative and 6 students say they are conservative. Is this a statistically significant difference?

6. Summarize the steps of hypothesis testing. What is the virtue of this procedure?

7. In analysis of variance, what is the purpose of the mean square between and the mean square within? If the null hypothesis is accepted, what do these quantities look like?

8. Describe the assumptions for ANOVA, and explain how they may be diagnosed.

9. You contact a random sample of 36 graduates of Western University and learn that their starting salaries were $28,000 last year. You then contact a random sample of 40 graduates from Eastern University and find that their average starting salary was $28,800. In each case, the standard deviation of the sample was $1,000.

   a. Test the null hypothesis that there is no difference between average salaries received by the graduates of the two schools.

   b. What assumptions are necessary for this test?

10. A random sample of students is interviewed to determine if there is an association between class and attitudes toward corporations. With the following results, test the hypothesis that there is no difference among students on this attitude.

	Favorable	*Neutral*	*Unfavorable*
Freshmen	100	50	70
Sophomores	80	60	70
Juniors	50	50	80
Seniors	40	60	90

11. You do a survey of business school students and liberal arts school students to find out how many times a week they read a daily newspaper. In each case, you interview 100 students. You find the following:

$$X_b = 4.5 \text{ times per week}$$
$$s_b = 1.5$$
$$X_{la} = 5.6 \text{ times per week}$$
$$s_{la} = 2.0$$

Test the hypothesis that there is no significant difference between these two samples.

Computer Problems

1. One-Koat Paint Company has developed a new type of porch paint that it hopes will be the most durable on the market. The R&D group tests the new product against the two leading competing products by using a machine that scrubs until it wears through the coating. One-Koat runs five trials with each product and secures the following results (in thousands of scrubs):

Trial	One-Koat	Competitor A	Competitor B
1	37	34	24
2	30	19	25
3	34	22	23
4	28	31	20
5	29	27	20

Test the hypothesis that there are no differences between the means of these products ($\alpha = .05$).

2. Test the assumptions for ANOVA in the preceeding problem, using what graphical diagnostic checks may be available in your computer software.

3. Using the data in Table 16–3 for the variables Flight Service Rating 2 and Airline (2, 3), test the hypothesis of no difference between means.

4. A computer manufacturer is introducing a new product specifically targeted at the home market and wishes to compare the effectiveness of three sales strategies: computer stores, home electronics stores, and department stores. Numbers of sales by 15 salespeople are recorded below:

   Electronics store: 5, 4, 3, 3, 3

   Department store: 9, 7, 8, 6, 5

   Computer store: 7, 4, 8, 4, 3

   a. Test the hypothesis that there is no difference between the means of the retailers ($\alpha = .05$).

   b. Select a post hoc test, if necessary, to determine which groups differ in mean sales ($\alpha = .05$).

5. A financial analyst is interested in whether there was a significant change in profits for utilities from one period to another. A random sample of 11 companies from the Forbes 500 contributed the following data:

Company	Profits 1988	Profits 1989
Ohio Edison	218.9	361.0
Kentucky Utilities	79.4	82.3
PSI Holdings	99.1	125.2
Idaho Power	49.0	84.7
NY State E & G	171.5	157.8
Northeast Utilities	224.8	203.2
Southwestern Public Service	105.0	124.9
Pacific Corp.	446.8	465.6
Scana	120.7	122.6
Puget Sound Power & Light	128.2	117.7
Public Service Colorado	124.9	148.8

SOURCE: *Forbes,* April 30, 1990.

    a. Should a test of independent or related samples be used?

    b. Is there a difference in profits between the two years?

6. A consumer testing firm is interested in testing two competing antivirus products for personal computers. They want to know how many strains of virus will be removed. The data are:

	Removed by Q-Cure?	
Removed by Anti-V?	Yes	No
Yes	45	33
No	58	20

    Are Anti-V and Q-Cure equally effective ($\alpha = .05$)?

7. A researcher for an auto manufacturer is examining preferences for styling features on larger sedans. Buyers were classified as "first-time" and "repeat," resulting in the following table.

	Preference	
	European Styling	Japanese Styling
Repeat	40	20
First-time	8	32

    a. Test the hypothesis that buying characteristic is independent of styling preference ($\alpha = .05$).

    b. Should the statistic be adjusted?

Reference Notes

1. A more detailed example is found in Amir D. Aczel, *Complete Business Statistics,* 3rd ed. (Burr Ridge, IL: Irwin, 1996), pp. 243–45.

2. The standardized randomized variable, denoted by Z, is a deviation from expectancy and is expressed in terms of standard deviation units. The mean of the distribution of a

standardized random variable is 0, and the standard deviation is 1. With this distribution, the deviation from the mean by any value of X can be expressed in standard deviation units.

3. Procedures for hypothesis testing are reasonably similar across authors. This outline was influenced by Sidney Siegel, *Nonparametric Statistics for the Behavioral Sciences* (New York: McGraw-Hill, 1956), chap. 2.

4. Marija J. Norusis/SPSS, Inc., *SPSS for Windows Base System User's Guide, Release 6.0* (Chicago: SPSS, Inc., 1993), pp. 601–6.

5. For further information on these tests, see ibid., pp. 187–88.

6. F. M. Andrews, L. Klem, T. N. Davidson, P. M. O'Malley, and W. L. Rodgers, *A Guide for Selecting Statistical Techniques for Analyzing Social Science Data* (Ann Arbor: Institute for Social Research, University of Michigan, 1976).

7. Statistical Navigator™ is an IBM-PC/compatible product from The Idea Works, Inc., 100 West Briarwood, Columbia, MO 65203.

8. The figure is partially adapted from Siegel, *Nonparametric Statistics,* flyleaf.

9. See B. S. Everitt, *The Analysis of Contingency Tables* (London: Chapman and Hall, 1977).

10. The critiques are represented by W. J. Conover, "Some Reasons for Not Using the Yates Continuity Correction on 2×2 Contingency Tables," *Journal of the American Statistical Association* 69 (1974), pp. 374–76; and N. Mantel, "Comment and a Suggestion on the Yates Continuity Correction," *Journal of the American Statistical Association* 69 (1974), pp. 378–80.

11. This data table and the analysis of variance tables and plots in this section were prepared with SuperANOVA™.

12. See, for example, Roger E. Kirk, *Experimental Design: Procedures for the Behavioral Sciences* (Belmont, CA: Brooks/Cole, 1982), pp. 115–33. An exceptionally clear presentation for step-by-step hand computation is found in James L. Bruning and B. L. Kintz, *Computational Handbook of Statistics,* 2nd ed. (Glenview, IL: Scott, Foresman, 1977), pp. 143–68. Also, when you use a computer program, the reference manual typically provides helpful advice in addition to the set-up instructions.

13. Kirk, *Experimental Design,* pp. 90–115. Alternatively, see Bruning and Kintz, *Computational Handbook of Statistics,* pp. 113–32.

14. For a discussion and example of the Cochran test, see Sidney Siegel and N. J. Castellan, Jr., *Nonparametric Statistics for the Behavioral Sciences,* 2nd ed. (New York: McGraw-Hill, 1988).

15. For further details, see ibid.; and Aczel, *Complete Business Statistics,* pp. 659–63.

Suggested Readings

1. Aczel, Amir D. *Complete Business Statistics,* 3rd ed. Burr Ridge, IL: Irwin, 1996. This excellent text is characterized by highly lucid explanations and numerous examples.

2. Berenson, Mark L., David M. Levine, and David Rindskopf. *Applied Statistics: A First Course.* Englewood Cliffs, NJ: Prentice-Hall, 1988. For students or managers without recent statistical coursework, this text provides an excellent review.

3. DeFinetti, Bruno. *Probability, Induction, and Statistics.* New York: Wiley, 1972. A highly readable work on subjective probability and the Bayesian approach.

4. Kirk, Roger E. *Experimental Design: Procedures for the Behavioral Sciences,* 3rd ed. Belmont, CA: Brooks/Cole, 1994. An advanced text on the statistical aspects of experimental design.

5. Norusis, Marija J., SPSS, Inc. *SPSS for Windows Base System User's Guide, Release 6.0.* Chicago: SPSS, Inc., 1993. Application-oriented instruction in basic methods from one of the best-documented software packages.

6. Siegel, Sidney, and N. J. Castellan, Jr. *Nonparametric Statistics for the Behavioral Sciences,* 2nd ed. New York: McGraw-Hill, 1988. The classic book on nonparametric statistics.

7. Winer, B. J. *Statistical Principles in Experimental Design,* 2nd ed. New York: McGraw-Hill, 1971. Another classic source. Thorough coverage of analysis of variance and experimental design.

MEASURES OF ASSOCIATION

CHAPTER NAVIGATION

BRINGING
RESEARCH TO LIFE

Myra arrived for an analysis meeting with Jason and found a round, bald little man sitting at Jason's desk, studying the screen of a laptop computer, stroking his gray beard and smiling broadly.

"Myra," said Jason, "meet my Uncle Jack."

"Really? At last I meet the famous or should I say infamous Uncle? I feared you were imaginary."

"Reports of my being imaginary are greatly exaggerated, if I may paraphrase Mark Twain."

It seemed to her he should have been taller. The ex-biggest painting contractor on Long Island ought to be more ample, she felt. Maybe he had shrunk upon retiring to Florida. Uncle Jack was the kind of unassuming diminutive old fellow who often proved to have money, or power, or both, though no one would have guessed.

Uncle Jack began to rub his laptop computer and grin even more broadly. "I wanted Jason to see that I am taking *good care* of this Mindwriter." Myra saw nothing special about that particular laptop computer, as she and Jason owned two apiece, Mindwriter being the link that kept them together. It was a great "box," but what made this one so special?

"This little computer," said Uncle Jack, "has made me the political kingpin of the Boca Beach Condominium Association, Phases One *and* Two. Not to mention all the widows who want to meet with me. Which I had better not mention, as I have only been widowed for a short while and don't want this getting back to my boys on Long Island. I gave the painting business to my three boys and—hey, I'm seventy-five and deserve some fun—I moved to Boca Raton. For three months I played golf in the morning and sat by the pool and played cards in the after-

noon. For three months, seven days, I did this. Do I have to tell you? I was going crazy.

"Then my next-door neighbor Marty 'headed south,' and his wife gave me his Mindwriter."

Myra tried to imagine what was south of Florida and why Marty would go there without his wife. Uncle Jack saw the confusion and explained, "She 'planted him,' is what I mean. Do you follow me? He died, he met his 'necessary end,' if I may quote from *Julius Caesar.* And what was a widow going to do with this computer?

"So now I had a laptop, and what was I going to do with it? Jason came through Boca Raton, and copied me a program from his computer, but it was a statistical program, free from the Internet. That's all he had that he that could give me without breaking the copyright law, a statistical program from the Internet. And me the guy who had to take statistics three times at Brooklyn College in 1948, to get a lousy C+.

"Something developed pretty soon. We had a dirty guy, Sandy Plover, who had come down from being a big electrical contractor in Jersey and got himself into condo politics. Sandy had not become successful up North without developing a sense of who holds power, what their weaknesses are, and how the politicians agitate the electorate. Being a natural-born troublemaker, he waited for his chance to agitate. Well, the sheriff had launched a statistics-reporting program, and the statistical results had started to come in. Now, it happens there is a creek that divides our condominium into two halves of roughly equal population, Oceanside and Gladeside, the former being slightly tonier. And it further happens that the incidence of arrests resulting from police calls to Oceanside, where he lives, is higher than in Gladeside."

(continued)

Uncle Jack wrote the following:

H_1: Gladeside residents get special treatment when it comes to solving crimes and thus live in a safer environment due to their higher incomes and greater political power.

H_0: Gladeside and Oceanside receive the same attention from the police.

In Gladeside:	Police calls without arrest	46	
	Police calls resulting in arrests	4	50
In Oceanside:	Police calls without arrest	40	
	Police calls resulting in arrests	10	50

"I doubt that Sandy would have paid attention, except that in both sides of the condo association the total number of police calls happened to be fifty, which made it easy for him to see that in Oceanside the rate of arrests was twice that in Gladeside."

"Actually," said Myra, "I'm surprised there would be any police calls in such a tony condo community."

"We are old," said Uncle Jack, "but not dead.

"In any case, Sandy's finely honed political instincts told him he was going to go nowhere by trying to turn the condo against the sheriff. It would be much, much better, he saw, to try and turn voters of Oceanside against those in Gladeside. And so he decided to complain about the disparate impact of arrests, though being self-educated, he had never heard that expression, 'disparate.' All he knew is that here was an opportunity to make trouble and thereby make a name, because in Oceanside were mostly folks moved down from Brooklyn, and in Gladeside folks from the Bronx, and there was an undercurrent, if you know what I mean."

"But the ethics. . . ."

". . . meant nothing to Sandy. He told me, 'I think am gonna kick some butt and make a name for myself down here.'

"Right away, you can see his strategy. Sandy thought he would make more mileage by whipping our side of the association against the other. This had something to do with his wanting to run in a jurisdiction where elections were not done at large but on a single-district basis, and something to do

with his rabble-rousing instincts, which had always been impeccable."

Jason interrupted with a mini-lecture on the politics of statistics. "The trouble with the police calls as an issue is that sheriffs' offices nowadays are well staffed with statistically educated analysts who know very well how to rebut oddball claims."

"Personally, I miss the old days, when if you worked for the cops, you busted bad guys' heads and never mind statistics. But I understand nowadays you don't mess with crime statistics without one of the pencil-heads rebutting you. So I punched the numbers into this Mindwriter here to double-check the stats. I did the obvious first, just what I supposed a police analyst would have done. I ran a crosstabulation and a chi-square test of the hypothesis that the arrests in Oceanside were disproportionate to those in Gladeside."

"But," said Myra, "you only have to look at the numbers to see they are."

"Yes, but what you have there is the 'eyeball' fallacy, as my dear old professor called it almost fifty years ago. As I explained to Sandy, one hundred police encounters resulting in a few arrests is nothing, *nada*, not a large enough sample to trust a quick peek and a leap to a conclusion. You run it through the computer, and, sure enough, although the ratios seem to be out of whack, they are not statistically significant. You cannot support disparate impact. No way."

Jason said, "Granting that 10 arrests per 50 is bigger than 4 per 50, Uncle Jack saw that a statistician would say that it is not *significantly* bigger, would say that it is not disproportionate enough to convince a *scientist* that the police were acting differently in the two sides of town. A statistician would say, wait and see, let the story unfold, collect a bigger sample."

"How did Sandy accept your explanation, Jack?"

"Like the mad dog he was. To quote my favorite poet, 'There are chords in the hearts of the most reckless which cannot be touched without emotion.'"

"Emerson?" asked Myra.

"Poe," said Uncle Jack. "Underrated as a poet, overrated as a mystery writer. Well, as for Sandy, he was ready to shoot the messenger, very much bothered, at first, that I would not support his political strategy, and he grumbled that I did not understand such things, that you had to do bad to do good, which I am not sure I agree with, and that I was maybe too much overeducated to ever understand the need just to get on with investing issues. Me, overeducated, an English major!

"But I was not interested in right and wrong, I said, and he could be pretty sure the sheriff would come roaring back with a statistical analysis to throw cold water over Sandy."

"Did you bring him around?"

"That jerk, come around? Never. He ran to the papers, they splashed his numbers all over the third page of the local section on Monday, and Tuesday the sheriff came back with his experts and made Sandy look like a fool . . . except that it was a slow news day on Tuesday and the paper gave the story plenty of ink, on page one, if you can believe it. So Sandy was washed up, and I am now the resident genius. What I do is look at the opponents' polling results and deny their validity for the newspapers and TV. If the opposing party is ahead by a few poll points, I scoff at the thinness of the margin. If their lead is wide, I belittle the size of the sample and intimate that any statistician would see through them."

Jason provided the scholarly footnote. "Uncle Jack is colorful, amusing, and good-natured in debunking his opponents' polls, and the newspaper writers, who understand less statistics than anyone, have never challenged him to substantiate his claims. What he learned from me is that statistics is so complicated, and scares so many people, that you can claim or deny anything. And he is usually right to debunk the polls, since for a preelection political poll to be taken seriously there has to be a large enough sample to produce significant results. And there has to be a big enough spread between winners and losers to protect against a last-minute shift in voter sentiment. In the small, closely contested voting precincts of condominium politics, hardly any poll can meet two such stringent criteria."

"Right, Jason. I sit in the clubhouse and people come over and want to know what I think about the Middle East, campaign reform, everything. When you have a computer, to paraphrase Tevya, 'they think you really know.'"

INTRODUCTION

Research questions in business frequently revolve around the study of relationships between two or more variables. Various objectives may be served by such analysis. The strength, direction, shape, and other features of the relationship may be discovered. Or tactical and strategic questions may be answered by predicting the values of one variable from those of another. Let's look at some typical management questions:

1. In the mail-order business, excessive catalog costs quickly squeeze margins. Many mailings fail to reach receptive or active buyers. What is the relationship between various categories of mailings that delete inactive customers and the improvement in profit margins?

2. Medium-sized companies often have difficulty attracting the cream of the MBA crop, and when they are successful, they have trouble retaining them. What is the relationship between the ranking of candidates based on executive interviews and the ranking obtained from testing and assessment?

3. Retained cash flow, undistributed profits plus depreciation, is a critical source of funding for equipment investment. During a period of decline, capital spending suffers. What is the relationship between retained cash flow and equipment investment over the last year? Between cash flow and dividend growth?

4. Aggressive U.S. high-tech companies have invested heavily in the European chip market, and their sales have grown 20 percent over the three largest European firms. Can we predict next year's sales based on present investment?

All these questions may be evaluated by means of measures of association. And all call for different techniques based on the level at which the variables were measured or the intent of the question. Problems 1 through 3 require nominal, ordinal, and interval measures, respectively. Problem 4 is answered through simple bivariate regression.

With correlation, one calculates an index to measure the nature of the relationship between variables. With regression, an equation is developed to predict the values of a dependent variable. Both are affected by the assumptions of measurement level and the distributions that underlie the data.

Table 17–1 lists some common measures and their uses. The chapter follows the progression of the table, first covering bivariate linear correlation, then simple regression, and concluding with nonparametric measures of association. Exploration of data through visual inspection and diagnostic evaluation of assumptions continue to be emphasized.

BIVARIATE CORRELATION ANALYSIS

Bivariate correlation analysis differs from nonparametric measures of association and regression analysis in two important ways. First, parametric correlation requires two continuous variables measured on an interval or ratio scale. Second, the coefficient does not distinguish between independent and dependent variables. It treats the variables symmetrically since the coefficient r_{xy} has the same interpretation as r_{yx}.

Pearson's Product Moment Coefficient r

The **Pearson** (product moment) **correlation coefficient** varies over a range of +1 through 0 to –1. The designation r symbolizes the coefficient's estimate of linear association based on sampling data. The coefficient ρ represents the population correlation.

TABLE   17–1   Commonly Used Measures of Association

Measurement	Coefficient	Comments and Uses
Interval and Ratio	**Pearson product moment**	For continuous linearly related variables.
	Correlation ratio (eta)	For nonlinear data or relating a main effect to a continuous dependent variable.
	Biserial	One continuous and one dichotomous variable with an underlying normal distribution.
	Partial correlation	Three variables; relating two with the third's effect taken out.
	Multiple correlation	Three variables; relating one variable with two others.
	Bivariate linear regression	Predicting one variable from another's scores.
Ordinal	**Gamma**	Based on concordant-discordant pairs: (P – Q); proportional reduction in error (PRE) interpretation.
	Kendall's tau *b*	P – Q based; adjustment for tied ranks.
	Kendall's tau *c*	P – Q based; adjustment for table dimensions.
	Somers's *d*	P – Q based; asymmetrical extension of gamma.
	Spearman's rho	Product moment correlation for ranked data.
Nominal	**Phi**	Chi-square (CS) based for 2 × 2 tables.
	Cramer's *V*	CS based; adjustment when one table dimension > 2.
	Contingency coefficient	CS based; flexible data and distribution assumptions.
	Lambda	PRE-based interpretation.
	Goodman & Kruskal's tau	PRE-based with table marginals emphasis.
	Uncertainty coefficient	Useful for multidimensional tables.
	Kappa	Agreement measure.

Statistics covered are in **boldface**.

Correlation coefficients reveal the magnitude and direction of relationships. The *magnitude* is the degree to which variables move in unison or opposition. The size of a correlation of +.40 is the same as one of −.40. The sign says nothing about size. The degree of correlation is modest. The coefficient's sign signifies the *direction* of the relationship. Direction tells us whether large values on one variable are associated with large values on the other (and small values with small values). When the values correspond in this way, the two variables have a positive relationship: As one increases, the other also increases. Family income, for example, is positively related to household food expenditures. As income increases, food expenditures increase.

Other variables are inversely related. Large values on the first variable are associated with small values on the second (and vice versa). The prices of products and services are inversely related to their scarcity. In general, as products decrease in available quantity, their prices rise. The absence of a relationship is expressed by a coefficient of approximately zero.

Scatterplots for Exploring Relationships

Scatterplots are essential for understanding the relationships between variables. They provide a means for visual inspection of data that a list of values for two variables cannot. Both the direction and the shape of a relationship are conveyed in a plot. With a little practice, the magnitude of the relationship can be seen.

FIGURE 17–1   Scatterplots of Correlations between Two Variables

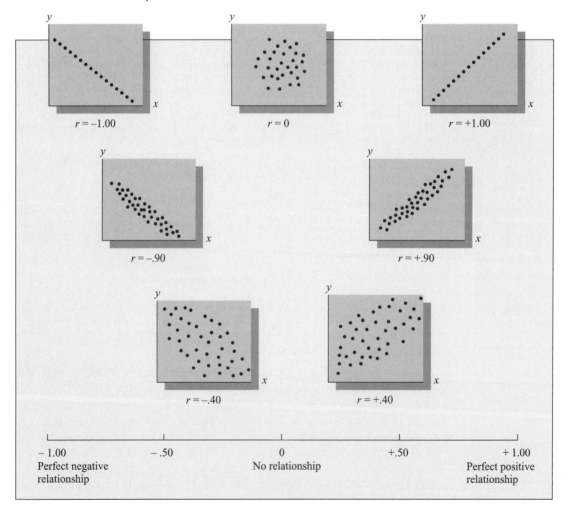

Figure 17–1 contains a series of scatterplots that depict some relationships across the range *r*. The three plots on the left side of the figure have their points sloping from the upper left to the lower right of each *X*–*Y* plot.[1] They represent different magnitudes of negative relationships. On the right side of the figure, three plots have opposite patterns and show positive relationships.

When stronger relationships are apparent (for example, the ±.90 correlations), the points cluster close to an imaginary straight line passing through the data. The weaker relationships (±.40) depict a more diffuse data cloud with points spread farther from the line.

The shape of linear relationships is characterized by a straight line, whereas nonlinear relationships have curvilinear, parabolic, and compound curves representing their shapes. Pearson's *r* measures relationships in variables that are linearly related. It cannot distinguish linear from nonlinear data. Summary statistics alone do not reveal the appropriateness of the data for the model, as the following example illustrates.

One author constructed four small data sets possessing identical summary statistics but displaying strikingly different patterns.[2] Table 17–2 contains these data. Figure 17–2 exhibits plots of the data. In Plot 1 of the figure, the variables are positively related. Their points follow a superimposed straight line through the data. This example is well suited to correlation analysis. In Plot 2, the data are curvilinear in relation to the line, and *r* is an inappropriate measure of their relationship. Plot 3 shows the presence of an influential point that changed a coefficient that would have otherwise been a perfect +1.0. The last plot displays constant values of *X* (similar to what you might find in an animal or quality-control experiment). One leverage point establishes the fitted line for this data.

We will return to these concepts and the process of drawing the line when we discuss regression. For now, comparing plots 2 through 4 with 1 suggests the importance of visually inspecting correlation data for underlying patterns. Careful analysts make

TABLE 17–2   **Four Data Sets with the Same Summary Statistics**

Ss	X_1	Y_1	X_2	Y_2	X_3	Y_3	X_4	Y_4
1	10	8.04	10	9.14	10	7.46	8	6.58
2	8	6.95	8	8.14	8	6.77	8	5.76
3	13	7.58	13	8.74	13	12.74	8	7.71
4	9	8.81	9	8.77	9	7.11	8	8.84
5	11	8.33	11	9.26	11	7.81	8	8.47
6	14	9.96	14	8.10	14	8.84	8	7.04
7	6	7.24	6	6.13	6	6.08	8	5.25
8	4	4.26	4	3.10	4	5.39	19	12.50
9	12	10.84	12	9.13	12	8.15	8	5.56
10	7	4.82	7	7.26	7	6.42	8	7.91
11	5	5.68	5	4.74	5	5.73	8	6.89
Pearson's *r*		.81642		.81624		.81629		.81652
r^2		.66654		.66624		.66632		.66671
Adjusted r^2		.62949		.62916		.62925		.62967
Standard error		1.23660		1.23721		1.23631		1.23570

FIGURE   17–2   Different Scatterplots for the Same Summary Statistics

scatterplots an integral part of the inspection and exploration of their data. Although small samples may be plotted by hand, statistical software packages save time and offer a variety of plotting procedures.

The Assumptions of r

Like other parametric techniques, correlation analysis makes certain assumptions about the data. Many of these assumptions are necessary to test hypotheses about the coefficient.

The first requirement for r is **linearity.** All of the examples in Figure 17–1 with the exception of $r = 0$ illustrate a relationship between variables that can be described by a straight line passing through the data cloud. When $r = 0$, no pattern is evident that could be described with a single line. Parenthetically, it is also possible to find coefficients of 0 where the variables are highly related but in a nonlinear form. As we have seen, plots make such findings evident.

The second assumption for correlation is a **bivariate normal distribution**— that is, the data are from a random sample of a population where the two variables are normally distributed in a joint manner.

Often these assumptions or the required measurement level cannot be met. Then the analyst should select a nonlinear or nonparametric measure of association, many of which are described later in this chapter.

Computation and Testing of *r*

The formula for calculating Pearson's *r* is

$$r = \frac{\Sigma(X - \bar{X})(Y - \bar{Y})}{(N-1)s_x s_y} \tag{1}$$

where

    N is the number of pairs of cases

    s_x, s_y are the standard deviations for *X* and *Y*

Alternatively,

$$r = \frac{\Sigma xy}{\sqrt{(\Sigma x^2)(\Sigma y^2)}} \tag{2}$$

since

$$s_x = \sqrt{\frac{\Sigma x^2}{N}} \qquad s_y = \sqrt{\frac{\Sigma y^2}{N}}$$

If the numerator of equation (2) is divided by N, we have the *covariance,* the amount of deviation that the *X* and *Y* distributions have in common. With a positive covariance, the variables move in unison; with a negative one, they move in opposition. When the covariance is 0, there is no relationship. The denominator for equation (2) represents the maximum potential variation that the two distributions share. Thus, correlation may be thought of as a ratio.

Table 17–3 contains a random subsample of 10 firms of the Forbes 500 sample. The variables chosen to illustrate computation of *r* are cash flow and net profits. Beneath each variable is its mean and standard deviation. In columns 4 and 5 we obtain the deviations of the *X* and *Y* values from their means, and in column 6 we find the product. Columns 7 and 8 are the squared deviation scores.

Substituting into the formula, we get

$$r = \frac{224777.23}{\sqrt{138419.71} * \sqrt{422139.76}} = .9298$$

In this subsample, net profits and cash flow are positively related and have a very high coefficient. As net profits increase, cash flow increases; the opposite is also true. Linearity of the variables may be examined with a scatterplot such as the one shown in Figure 17–3. The data points fall along a straight line.

TABLE   17–3   Computation of Pearson's Product Moment Correlation

| Corporation | Net Profit ($ mil.) X | Cash Flow ($ mil.) Y | Deviations from Means | | | | |
			$(X - \bar{X})\, x$	$(Y - \bar{Y})\, y$	xy	x^2	y^2
1	82.6	126.5	−93.84	−178.64	16763.58	8805.95	31912.25
2	89.0	191.2	−87.44	−113.94	9962.91	7645.75	12982.32
3	176.0	267.0	−0.44	−38.14	16.78	0.19	1454.66
4	82.3	137.1	−94.14	−168.04	15819.29	8862.34	28237.44
5	413.5	806.8	237.06	501.66	118923.52	56197.44	251602.56
6	18.1	35.2	158.34	−269.94	42742.30	25071.56	72867.60
7	337.3	425.5	160.86	120.36	19361.11	25875.94	14486.53
8	145.8	380.0	−30.64	74.86	−2293.71	938.81	5604.02
9	172.6	326.6	−3.84	21.36	−82.02	14.75	456.25
10	247.2	355.5	70.76	50.36	3563.47	5006.98	2536.13

$\bar{X} = 176.44$ $\bar{Y} = 305.14$ $\Sigma xy = 224777.23$

$s_x = 216.59$ $s_y = 124.01$ $\Sigma x^2 = 138419.71$

$\Sigma y^2 = 422139.76$

Common Variance as an Explanation   The amount of common variance in X (net profits) and Y (cash flow) may be summarized by r^2, the **coefficient of determination.** As Figure 17–4 shows, the overlap between the two variables is the proportion of their common or shared variance.

FIGURE   17–3   Plot of Net Profits with Cash Flow

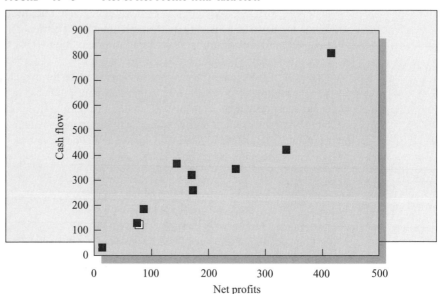

FIGURE   17–4   **Diagram of Common Variance**

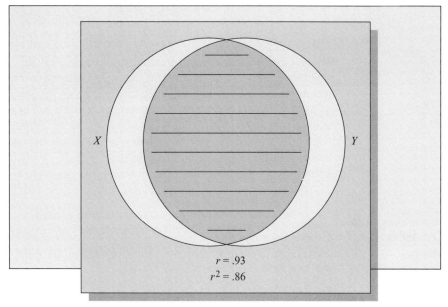

$r = .93$
$r^2 = .86$

The lined area represents the percentage of the total relationship accounted for by one variable or the other. So 86 percent of the variance in X is explained by Y, and vice versa.

Testing the Significance of *r*   Is the coefficient representing the relationship between net profits and cash flow real, or does it occur by chance? This question tries to discover whether our r is a chance deviation from a population p of zero. In other situations, the researcher may wish to know if significant differences exist between two or more rs. In either case, r's significance should be checked before r is used in other calculations or comparisons. For this test, we must have independent random samples from a bivariate normal distribution. Then the Z or t test may be used for the null hypothesis, $p = 0$.

The formula for small samples is

$$t = \frac{r}{\sqrt{\dfrac{1 - r^2}{n - 2}}}$$

where

$r = .93$
$n = 10$

Substituting into the equation, we calculate t:

$$t = \frac{.93}{\sqrt{\dfrac{1 - .86}{8}}} = 7.03$$

With $n - 2$ degrees of freedom, the statistical program calculates the value of t (7.03) at a probability less than .005 for the one-tailed alternative, H_A: $\rho > 0$. We reject the hypothesis that there is no linear relationship between net profits and cash flow in the population. The above statistic is appropriate when the null hypothesis states a correlation of 0. It should be used only for a one-tailed test.[3] However, it is often difficult to know in advance whether the variables are positively or negatively related, particularly when a computer removes our contact with the raw data. Software programs produce two-tailed tests for this eventuality. The observed significance level for a one-tailed test is half of the printed two-tailed version in most programs.

Correlation Matrix

A **correlation matrix** is a table used to display coefficients for more than two variables. Table 17–4 shows the intercorrelations among six variables for the full Forbes 500 data set.[4]

It is conventional for a symmetrical matrix to report findings in the triangle below the diagonal. The diagonal contains coefficients of 1.00 that signify the relationship of each variable with itself. Journal articles and management reports often show matrices with coefficients at different probability levels. A symbol beside the coefficient keys the description of differences to a legend. The practice of reporting tests of the null hypothesis, $r = 0$, was followed in Table 17–4.

Correlation matrices have utility beyond bivariate correlation studies. Interdependence among variables is a common characteristic of most multivariate techniques. Matrices form the basis for computation and understanding of the nature of relationships in multiple regression, discriminant analysis, factor analysis, and many others. Such applications call for variations on the standard matrix. Pooled within-groups covariance matrices average the separate covariances for several groups and

TABLE   17–4   Correlation Matrix for Forbes 500 Sample

	Assets ($ mil.)	Cash Flow ($ mil.)	Number Employed (thousands)	Market Value ($ mil.)	Net Profits ($ mil.)	Sales ($ mil.)
Assets	1.0000					
Cash flow	.3426	1.0000				
Employed	.3898	.8161	1.0000			
Market value	.3642	.9353	.8106	1.0000		
Net profits	.2747	.9537	.7467	.9101	1.0000	
Sales	.5921	.7990	.8831	.7485	.7261	1.0000

NOTES:

All coefficients are statistically significant, p < .01.

$n = 100$.

array the results as coefficients. Total or overall correlation matrices treat coefficients as if they came from a single sample.

Interpretation of Correlations

A correlation coefficient of any magnitude or sign, whatever its statistical significance, does not imply causation. Increased net profits may cause an increase in market value, or improved satisfaction may cause improved performance in certain situations, but correlation provides no evidence of cause and effect. Several alternate explanations may be provided for correlation results: (1) X causes Y, (2) Y causes X, (3) X and Y are activated by one or more other variables, or (4) X and Y influence each other reciprocally. Ex post facto studies seldom possess sufficiently powerful designs to *demonstrate* which of these conditions could be true. By controlling variables under an experimental design, we may obtain more rigorous evidence of causality.

Take care to avoid so-called **artifact correlations** where distinct groups combine to give the impression of one. The upper panel of Figure 17–5 shows data from two business sectors. If all the data points for the X and Y variables are aggregated and a correlation is computed for a single group, a positive correlation results. Separate calculations for each sector (note that points for Sector A form a circle, as do points for Sector B) reveal *no* relationship between the X and Y variables. A second example shown in the lower panel contains a plot of data on assets and sales. We have enclosed and highlighted the data for the financial sector. This is shown as a narrow band enclosed by an ellipse. These companies score high on assets and low in sales—all are banks. When the data for banks are removed and treated separately, the correlation is nearly perfect (.99). When banks are returned to the sample, and the correlation is recalculated, the overall relationship drops to the mid .80s. In short, data hidden or nested within an aggregated set may present a radically different picture.

Another issue affecting interpretation of coefficients concerns practical significance. Even when a coefficient is statistically significant, it must be practically meaningful. In many relationships, other factors combine to make the coefficient's meaning misleading. For example, in nature we expect rainfall and the height of reservoirs to be positively correlated. But in states where water management and flood control mechanisms are complex, an apparently simple relationship may not hold. Techniques like partial and multiple correlation or multiple regression are helpful in sorting out confounding effects.

With large samples, even exceedingly low coefficients can be statistically significant. This "significance" only reflects the likelihood of a linear relationship in the population. Should magnitudes less than .30 be reported when they are significant? It all depends. We might consider the correlations between variables such as cash flow, sales, market value, or net profits to be interesting revelations of a particular phenomenon whether they were high, moderate, or low. The nature of the study, the characteristics of the sample, or other reasons will be determining factors. But a coefficient is not remarkable simply because it is statistically significant.

By probing the evidence of direction, magnitude, statistical significance, and common variance together with the study's objectives and limitations, we reduce the chances of reporting trivial findings. Simultaneously, the communication of practical implications to the reader will be improved.

FIGURE   17–5   Artifact Correlations

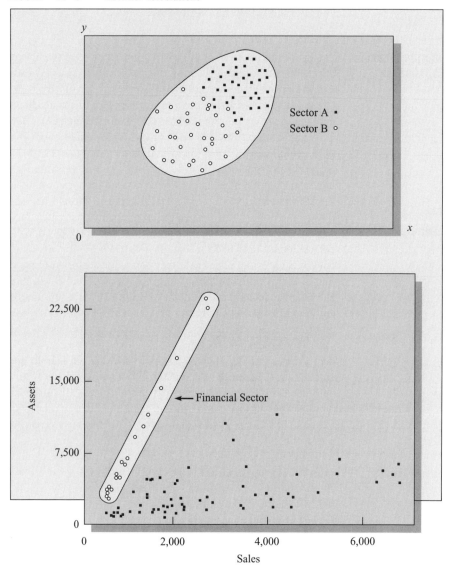

BIVARIATE LINEAR REGRESSION[5]

In the previous section, we focused on relationships between variables. The product moment correlation was found to represent an index of the magnitude of the relationship, the sign governed the direction, and r^2 explained the common variance. Relationships also serve as a basis for estimation and prediction.

FIGURE   17–6   Comparison of Bivariate Linear Correlation and Regression

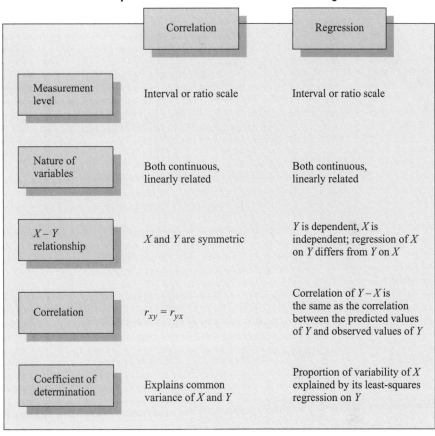

When we take the observed values of X to estimate or predict corresponding Y values, the process is called *simple prediction*.[6] When more than one X variable is used, the outcome is a function of multiple predictors. Simple and multiple predictions are made with a technique called **regression analysis.**

The similarities and differences of regression and correlation are summarized in Figure 17–6. Their relatedness would suggest that beneath many correlation problems is a regression analysis that could provide further insight about the relationship of Y with X.

The Basic Model   A straight line is fundamentally the best way to model the relationship between two continuous variables. The bivariate linear regression may be expressed as

$$Y = \beta_0 + \beta_1 X_i$$

where the value of the dependent variable Y is a linear function of the corresponding

FIGURE   17–7   Examples of Different Slopes

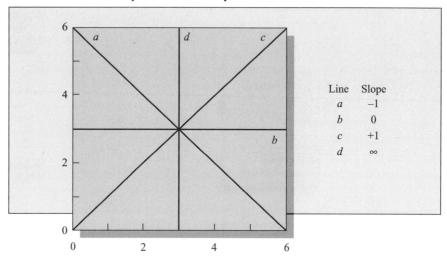

Line	Slope
a	−1
b	0
c	+1
d	∞

value of the independent variable X_i in the ith observation. The slope, β_1, and the Y intercept, β_0, are known as **regression coefficients.** The **slope,** β_1, is the change in Y for a one-unit change in X. It is sometimes called the "rise over run." This is defined by the formula

$$\beta_1 = \frac{\Delta Y}{\Delta X}$$

This is the ratio of change (Δ) in the rise of the line relative to the run or travel along the X axis. Figure 17–7 shows a few of the many possible slopes you may encounter.

The **intercept,** β_0, is the value for the linear function when it crosses the Y axis; it is the estimate of Y when $X = 0$. A formula for the intercept based on the mean scores of the X and Y variables is

$$\beta_0 = \bar{Y} - \beta_1 \bar{X}$$

Concept Application

The price of investment-grade red wine is influenced in several ways, not the least of which is tasting. Tasting from the barrel is a major determinant of market *en primeur* or futures contracts, which represent about 60 percent of the harvest. After the wine rests for 18 to 24 months in oak casks, further tasting occurs, and the remaining stock is released.

Weather is widely regarded as responsible for pronouncements about wine quality. A Princeton economist has elaborated on that notion. He suggested that just a few facts about local weather conditions may be better predictors of vintage French red wines than the most refined palates and noses.[7] The regression model developed predicts an auction price index for about 80 wines from winter and harvest rainfall amounts and average growing-season temperatures. Interestingly, the calculations suggested that the 1989 Bordeaux would be one of the best since 1893. The "guardians of tradition" reacted hysterically to these methods yet agreed with the conclusion.

While this application of regression analysis requires multiple predictors, our first example will use one predictor with highly simplified data. Let X represent the average growing-season temperature in degrees Celsius and Y the price of a 12-bottle case in French francs. The data appear below.

X	Y
Average Temperature Celsius	*Price per Case (FF)*
12	2000
16	3000
20	4000
24	5000
$\bar{X} = 18$	$\bar{Y} = 3500$

The plotted data in Figure 17–8 show a linear relationship between the pairs of points and a perfect positive correlation, $r_{yx} = 1.0$. The slope of the line is calculated:

$$\beta_1 = \frac{Y_i - Y_j}{X_i - X_j} = \frac{4000 - 3000}{20 - 16} = \frac{1000}{4} = 250$$

where the $X_i Y_i$ values are the data points (20, 4000) and $X_j Y_j$ are points (16, 3000). The intercept β_0 is –1000, the point at which $X = 0$ in this plot. This area is off the graph and appears in an insert on the figure.

$$\beta_0 = \bar{Y} - \beta_1 \bar{X} = 3500 - 250(18) = -1000$$

Substituting into the formula, we have the simple regression equation

$$Y = -1000 + 250X_i$$

We could now predict that a warm growing season with 25.5°C temperatures would bring a case price of 5375 French francs. $\hat{Y}$ (called Y-hat) is the predicted value of Y.

$$\hat{Y} = -1000 + 250(25.5) = 5375$$

Unfortunately, one rarely comes across a data set composed of four paired values, a perfect correlation, and an easily drawn line. A model based on such data is *deterministic* in that for any value of X, there is only one possible corresponding value of Y. It is more likely that we will collect data where the values of Y vary for each X value. Considering Figure 17–9, we should expect a distribution of price values for the temperature $X = 16$, another for $X = 20$, and another for *each* value of X.

FIGURE   17–8   Plot of Wine Price by Average Growing Temperature

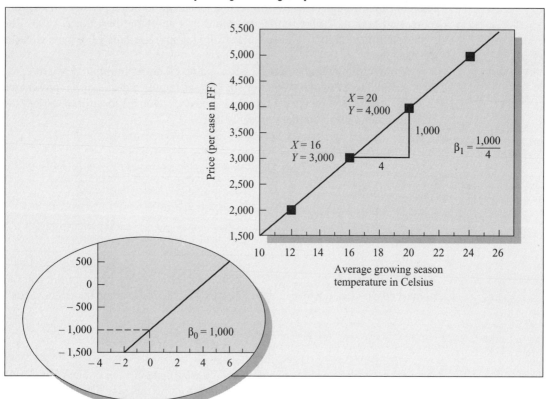

The means of these Y distributions will also vary in some systematic way with X. These variabilities lead us to construct a *probabilistic* model that also uses a linear function.[8] This function is written

$$Y_i = \beta_0 + \beta_1 X_i + \varepsilon_1$$

where ε symbolizes the deviation of the ith observation from the mean, $\beta_0 + \beta_1 X_i$.

As shown in Figure 17–9, the actual values of Y may be found above or below the regression line represented by the mean value of Y ($\beta_0 + \beta_1 X_i$) for a particular value of X. These deviations are the error in fitting the line and are often called the **error term.**

Method of Least Squares

Table 17–5 contains a new data set for the wine price example. Our prediction of Y from X must now account for the fact that the X and Y pairs do not fall neatly along the line. Actually, the relationship could be summarized by several lines. Figure

FIGURE   17–9   Distribution of Y for Observations of X

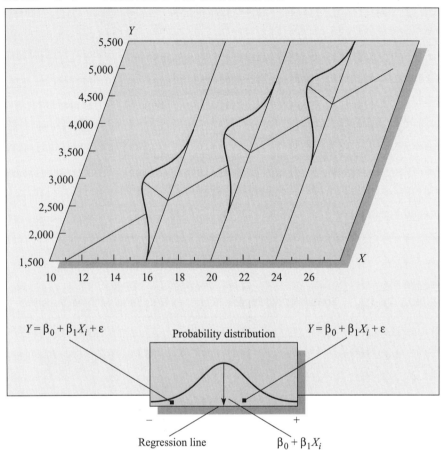

17–10 suggests a few alternatives based on visual inspection—all of which produce errors, or vertical distances from the observed values to the line. The **method of least squares** allows us to find a regression line, or line of best fit, which will keep these errors to a minimum. It uses the criterion of minimizing the total squared errors of estimate. When we predict values of Y for each X_i, the difference between the actual Y_i and the predicted $\hat{Y}$ is the error. This error is squared and then summed. The line of best fit is the one that minimizes the total squared errors of prediction.[9]

$$\sum_{i=1}^{n} e_i^2 \text{ minimized}$$

Regression coefficients β_0 and β_1 are used to find the least-squares solution. They are computed as follows:

TABLE   17–5   Data for Wine Price Study

	Y Price (FF)	X Temperature (C°)	XY	Y^2	X^2	y^2	x^2
1	1813.00	11.80	21393.40	3286969.00	139.24	3186225.00	61.00
2	2558.00	15.70	40160.60	6543364.00	246.49	1081600.00	15.29
3	2628.00	14.00	36792.00	6906384.00	196.00	940900.00	31.47
4	3217.00	22.90	73669.30	10349089.00	524.41	145161.00	10.82
5	3228.00	20.00	64560.00	10419984.00	400.00	136900.00	0.15
6	3629.00	20.10	72942.90	13169641.00	404.01	961.00	0.24
7	3886.00	17.90	69559.40	15100996.00	320.41	82944.00	2.92
8	4897.00	23.40	114589.80	23980609.00	547.56	1687401.00	14.36
9	4933.00	24.60	121351.80	24334489.00	605.16	1782225.00	24.90
10	5199.00	25.70	133614.30	27029601.00	660.49	2563201.00	37.09
Σ	35988.00	196.10	748633.50	141121126.00	4043.77	11607518.00	198.25
Mean	3598.80	19.61					
s	1135.66	4.69					
Sum of squares (SS)	11607511.59	198.25	42908.82				

FIGURE   17–10   Scatterplot and Possible Regression Lines Based on Visual Inspection

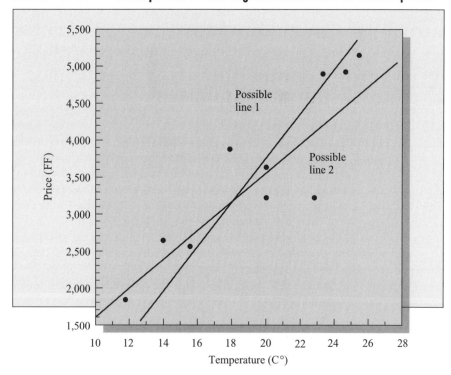

$$\beta_1 = \frac{\Sigma XY = \dfrac{(\Sigma X)(\Sigma Y)}{n}}{\Sigma X^2 - \dfrac{(\Sigma X)^2}{n}}$$

$$\hat{\beta}_0 = \overline{Y} - \hat{\beta}1\overline{X}$$

Substituting into both formulas with data from Table 17–5, we get

$$\beta_1 = \frac{748633.5 - \dfrac{(196.1)(35988)}{10}}{4043.77 - \dfrac{(196.1)^2}{10}} = 216.439$$

$$\hat{\beta}_0 = 3598.8 - (216.439)(19.61) = -645.569$$

The predictive equation is now $\hat{Y} = -645.57 + 216.44\,X_i$.

Drawing the Regression Line   Before drawing the regression line, we select two values of X to compute. Using values 13 and 24 for X_i, the points are

$$\hat{Y} = -645.57 + 216.44(13) = 2168.15$$

$$\hat{Y} = 645.57 + 216.44(24) = 4548.99$$

Comparing the line drawn in Figure 17–11 to the trial lines in Figure 17–10, one can readily see the success of the least-squares method in minimizing the error of prediction.

Residuals   We now turn our attention to the plot of standardized residuals in Figure 17–12. A **residual** is what remains after the line is fit or $(Y_i - \hat{Y}_i)$. When standardized, residuals are comparable to Z scores with a mean of 0 and a standard deviation of 1. In this plot, the standardized residuals should fall between 2 and –2, be randomly distributed about zero, and show no discernible pattern. All these conditions say the model is applied correctly.

   In our example, we have one residual at –2.2, a random distribution about zero, and few indications of a sequential pattern. It is important to apply other diagnostics to verify that the regression assumptions are met. Various software programs provide plots and other checks of normality, linearity, equality of variance, and independence of error.[10]

Predictions   If we wanted to predict the price of a case of investment-grade red wine for a growing season that averages 21°C, our prediction would be

$$\hat{Y} = -645.57 + 216.44(21) = 3899.67$$

FIGURE   17–11   Drawing the Least-Squares Line

$$Y = -645.57 + 216.44X$$

FIGURE   17–12   Plot of Standardized Residuals

Case	−3.0	0.0	3.0	Y Price	Predicted price	Residual
1		* .		1,813	1,908.4112	−95.4112
2		* .		2,558	2,752.5234	−194.5234
3		. *		2,628	2,384.5771	243.4229
4	*	.		3,217	4,310.8844	−1,093.8844
5		* .		3,228	3,683.2112	−455.2112
6		*		3,629	3,704.8551	−75.8551
7		. *		3,886	3,228.6893	657.3107
8		. *		4,897	4,419.1039	477.8961
9		. *		4,933	4,678.8307	254.1693
10		. *		5,199	4,916.9137	282.0863

−3.0   0.0   3.0

This is a *point prediction* of Y and should be corrected for greater precision. As with other confidence estimates, we establish the degree of confidence desired and substitute into the formula

$$\hat{Y} \pm t_{\alpha/2}s\sqrt{1 + \frac{1}{10} + \frac{(X - \overline{X})^2}{SS_x}}$$

where
    $t_{\alpha/2}$ is the two-tailed critical value for t at the desired level (95 percent in this example)
    s is the standard error of estimate (also the square root of the mean square error from the analysis of variance of the regression model) (see Table 17–6).
    SS_x is the sum of squares for X (Table 17–5).

$$3899.67 \pm (2.306)(538.559)\sqrt{1 + \frac{1}{10} + \frac{(21 - 19.61)^2}{198.25}}$$

$$3899.67 \pm 1308.29$$

We are 95 percent confident of our prediction that a case of investment-quality French red wine grown in a particular year at 21°C average temperatures will be initially priced at 3899.67 ± 1308.29, or from approximately 2591 to 5208 FF. The comparatively large band width results from the amount of error in the model (reflected by r^2), some peculiarities in the Y values, and the use of a single predictor.

It is more likely that we would want to predict the average price of *all* cases grown at 21°C. This prediction would use the same basic formula omitting the first digit (the 1) under the radical. A narrower *confidence* band is the result since the average of all Y values is being predicted from a given X. In our example, the confidence interval for 95 percent is 3899.67 ± 411.42, or from 3488 to 4311 FF.

The predictor we selected, 21°C, was close to the mean of X (19.61). Because the **prediction and confidence bands** are shaped like a bow tie, predictors farther from the mean have larger band widths. For example, X values of 15, 20, and 25 produce confidence bands of ±565, ±397, and ±617, respectively. This is illustrated in Figure 17–13. The farther one's selected predictor is from X, the wider is the prediction interval.

Testing the Goodness of Fit

With the regression line plotted and a few illustrative predictions, we should now gather some evidence of **goodness of fit**—how well the model fits the data,. The most important test in bivariate linear regression is whether the slope, β_1, is equal to zero.[11] We have already observed a slope of zero in Figure 17–6, line *b*. Zero slopes result from various conditions: (1) Y is completely unrelated to X, and no systematic pattern is evident; (2) there are constant values of Y for every value of X; or (3) the data are related but represented by a nonlinear function.

FIGURE 17–13 Prediction and Confidence Bands Based on Proximity to X

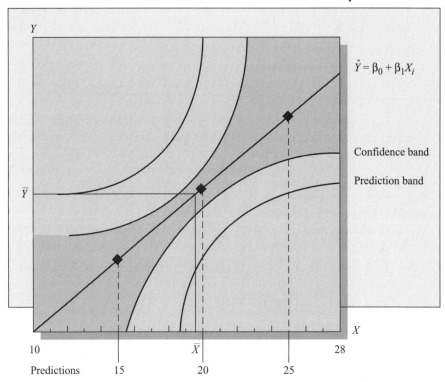

The *t* Test To test whether $\beta_1 = 0$, we use a two-tailed test (since the actual relationship is positive, negative, or zero). The test follows the t distribution for $n - 2$ degrees of freedom.

$$t = \frac{b_1}{s(b_1)} = \frac{216.439}{38.249} = 5.659$$

where

b_1 was previously defined as the slope β_1.

$s(b_1)$ is the standard error of β_1.[12]

We reject the null, $\beta_1 = 0$ because the calculated t is greater than any t value for 8 degrees of freedom and $\alpha = .01$.

The *F* Test Computer printouts generally contain an analysis of variance (ANOVA) table with an F test of the regression model. In bivariate regression, t and F tests produce the same results since t^2 is equal to F. In multiple regression, the F test has an overall role for the model, and each of the independent variables is evaluated with a separate t test. From the last chapter, recall that ANOVA partitions vari-

FIGURE   17–14   Components of Variation

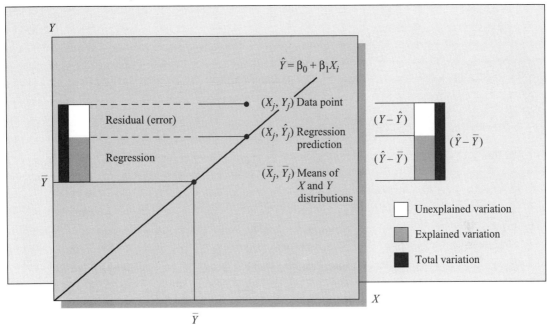

ance into component parts. For regression, it comprises explained deviations, $\hat{Y} - \bar{Y}$, and unexplained deviations, $Y - \hat{Y}$. Together they constitute the total deviation, $Y - \bar{Y}$. This is shown graphically in Figure 17–14. These sources of deviation are squared for all observations and summed across the data points.

In Table 17–6, we develop this concept sequentially concluding with the F test of the regression model for the wine data. Based on the results presented in that table, we find statistical evidence of a linear relationship between variables. The alternative hypothesis, $r^2 \neq 0$, is accepted with $F = 32.02$, d.f., (1,8), $p < .005$. The null hypothesis for the F test had the same effect as $\beta_1 = 0$ since we could select either test.

Coefficient of Determination   In predicting the values of Y without any knowledge of X, our best estimate would be $\bar{Y}$, its mean. Each predicted value that does not fall on $\bar{Y}$ contributes to an error of estimate, ($Y - \bar{Y}$). The total squared error for several predictions would be $\Sigma(Y_i - \bar{Y})^2$. By introducing known values of X into a regression equation, we attempt to reduce this error even further. Naturally, this is an improvement over using $\bar{Y}$, and the result is ($\hat{Y} - \bar{Y}$). The total improvement based on several estimates is $\Sigma(\hat{Y}_i - \bar{Y})^2$, the amount of variation explained by the relationship between X and Y in the regression. Based on the formula, the *coefficient of determination* is the ratio of the line of best fit's error over that incurred *by using* $\bar{Y}$. One

TABLE 17–6   Progressive Application of Partitioned Variance Concept

General Concept

$(\hat{Y} - \bar{Y})$	$+$	$(Y - \hat{Y})$	$=$	$(Y - \bar{Y})$
Explained Variation (the regression relationship between X and Y)		Unexplained Variation (cannot be explained by the regression relationship)		Total Variation

ANOVA Application

$\sum\limits_{i=1}^{n} (\hat{Y} - \bar{Y})^2$	$\sum\limits_{i=1}^{n} (Y - \hat{Y})^2$	$\sum\limits_{i=1}^{n} (Y - \bar{Y})^2$
SSr Sum of Squares Regression	SSe Sum of Squares Error	SSt Sum of Squares Total

Contents of Summary Table

Source	Degrees of Freedom	Sum of Squares	Mean Square	F ratio
Regression	1	SSr	$MSr = \dfrac{SSr}{1}$	$\dfrac{MSr}{MSe}$
Error	$n - 2$	SSe	$MSe = \dfrac{SSe}{n - 2}$	
Total		SSt		

ANOVA Summary Table: Test of Regression Model

Source	Degrees of Freedom	Sum of Squares	Mean Square	F ratio
Regression	1	9,287,143.11	9,287,143.11	32.02
Residual (error)	8	2,320368.49	290,046.06	
Total		11,607,511.60		

Significance of $F = .0005$

purpose of testing, then, is to discover whether the regression equation is a more effective predictive device than the mean of the dependent variable.

As in correlation, the coefficient of determination is symbolized by r^2.[13] It has several purposes. As an index of fit, it is interpreted as the total proportion of variance in Y explained by X. As a measure of linear relationship, it tells us how well the regression line fits the data. It is also an important indicator of the predictive accuracy of the equation. Typically, we would like to have an r^2 that explains 80 percent or more of the variation. Lower than that, predictive accuracy begins to fall off. The coefficient of determination, r^2, is calculated like this:

$$r^2 = \frac{\sum_{i=1}^{n}\left(\hat{Y} - \overline{Y}\right)^2}{\sum_{i=1}^{n}\left(Y - \overline{Y}\right)^2} = \frac{SS_r}{SS_e} = 1 - \frac{SS_e}{SS_t}$$

For the wine price study, r^2 was found by using the data from the bottom of Table 17–6.

$$r^2 = 1 - \frac{2320368.49}{11607511.61} = .80$$

Eighty percent of the variance in price may be explained by growing-season temperatures. With actual data and multiple predictors, our results would improve.

NONPARAMETRIC MEASURES OF ASSOCIATION[14]

Measures for Nominal Data

Nominal measures are used to assess the strength of relationships in cross-classification tables. They are often used with chi-square or may be used separately. In this section, we provide examples of three statistics based on chi-square and two that follow the proportional reduction in error approach.

There is no fully satisfactory all-purpose measure for categorical data. Some are adversely affected by table shape and number of cells; others are sensitive to sample size or marginals. It is perturbing to find similar statistics reporting different coefficients for the same data. This occurs because of a statistic's particular sensitivity or the way it was devised.

Technically, we would like to find two characteristics with nominal measures: (1) When there is no relationship at all, the coefficient should be 0. (2) When there is a complete dependency, the coefficient should display unity or 1. This does not always happen. In addition to the sensitivity problem, analysts should be alerted to the need for careful selection of tests.

TABLE 17–7   Chi-Square-Based Measures of Association

		On-the-Job Accident		
	Count	Yes	No	Row Total
Smoker	Yes	21	10	31
	No	13	22	35
	Column Total	34	32	66

Chi-Square	Value	d.f.	Significance
Pearson	6.16257	1	.01305
Continuity correction	4.99836	1	.02537

Minimal expected frequency 15.030

Statistic	Value	Approximate Significance
Phi	.30557	.01305*
Cramer's *V*	.30557	.01305*
Contigency coefficient	.29223	.01305*

*Pearson chi-square probability.

Chi-Square-Based Measures   Table 17–7 reports a 2×2 variation of the data on smoking and job-related accidents. In this example, the observed significance level is less than the testing level ($\alpha = .05$), and the null hypothesis is rejected. A correction to chi-square is provided. We now turn to measures of association to detect the strength of the relationship. Notice that the table also provides an approximate significance of the coefficient based on the chi-square distribution. This is a test of the null hypothesis: no relationship between the variables of accidents and smoking.

The first **chi-square-based measure** is applied to smoking and on-the-job accidents. It is called **phi.** Phi ranges from 0 to +1.0 and attempts to correct χ^2 proportionately to *N*. Phi is best employed with 2×2 tables like this one since its coefficient can exceed +1.0 when applied to larger tables. Phi is calculated:

$$\phi = \sqrt{\frac{\chi^2}{N}} = \sqrt{\frac{6.616257}{66}} = .3056$$

Phi's coefficient shows a moderate relationship between smoking and job-related accidents. There is no suggestion in this interpretation that one variable causes the other, nor is there an indication of the direction of the relationship.

Cramer's *V* is a modification of phi for larger tables and has a range up to 1.0 for tables of any shape. It is calculated like this:

$$V = \sqrt{\frac{\chi^2}{N(k-1)}} = \sqrt{\frac{6.616257}{66(1)}} = .3056$$

where

k = the lesser number of rows or columns.

In Table 17–7, the coefficient is the same as phi.

The **contingency coefficient** C is reported last. It is not comparable to other measures and has a different upper limit for various table sizes. The upper limits are determined as

$$\sqrt{\frac{k-1}{k}}$$

where

k = the number of columns.

For a 2×2 table, the upper limit is .71; for a 3×3, .82; and for a 4×4, .87. Although this statistic operates well with tables having the same number of rows as columns, its upper-limit restriction is not consistent with a criterion of good association measurement. C is calculated as

$$C = \sqrt{\frac{\chi^2}{\chi^2 + N}} = \sqrt{\frac{6.616257}{6.61625 + 66}} = .2922$$

The chief advantage of C is its ability to accommodate data in almost every form: skewed or normal, discrete or continuous, and nominal or ordinal.

Proportional Reduction in Error   **Proportional reduction in error (PRE)** statistics are the second type used with contingency tables. Lambda and tau are the examples discussed here. The coefficient **lambda** (λ) is based on how well the frequencies of one nominal variable offer predictive evidence about the frequencies of another. Lambda is asymmetrical—allowing calculation for the direction of prediction—and symmetrical, predicting row and column variables equally.

The computation of lambda is straightforward. In Table 17–8, we have results from an opinion survey with a sample of 400 shareholders. Only 180 out of 400 (45 percent) favor capping executives' salaries; 220 (55 percent) do not favor it. With this information alone, if asked to predict the opinions of an individual in the sample, we would achieve the best prediction record by always choosing the modal category. Here it is "do not favor." By doing so, however, we would be wrong 180 out of 400 times. The probability estimate for an incorrect classification is .45, $P(1) = (1 - .55)$.

Now suppose we have prior information about the respondents' occupational status and are asked to predict opinion. Would it improve predictive ability? Yes, we would make the predictions by summing the probabilities of all cells that are not the modal value for their rows (for example, cell (2, 1) is 20/400 or .05):

$$P(2) = \text{cell } (1, 2) \ .05 + \text{cell } (2, 1) \ .15 + \text{cell } (3, 1) \ .075 = .275$$

TABLE 17–8   Proportional Reduction in Error Measures

What is your opinion about capping executives' salaries?

Count Col. Pct.		Favor	Do not Favor	Row Total
	Managerial	90 22.5	20 5.0	110
Occupational Class	White collar	60 15.0	80 20.0	140
	Blue collar	30 7.5	120 30.0	150
	Column Total	180 45.0%	220 55.0%	400 100.0%

Chi-Square	Value	d.f.	Significance
Pearson	98.38646	2	.00000
Likelihood ratio	104.96542	2	.00000

Minimum expected frequency 49.500

Statistic	Value	ASE1	T Value	Approximate Significance
Lambda:				
symmetric	.30233	.03955	6.77902	
with occupation dependent	.24000	.03820	5.69495	
with opinion dependent	.38889	.04555	7.08010	
Goodman & Kruskal tau:				
with occupation dependent	.11669	.02076		.00000*
with opinion dependent	.24597	.03979		.00000*

*Based on chi-square approximation.

Lambda is then calculated:

$$\lambda = \frac{P(1) - P(2)}{P(1)} = \frac{.45 - .275}{.45} = .3889$$

Note that the asymmetric lambda in Table 17–8, where opinion is the dependent variable, reflects this computation. As a result of knowing the respondents' occupational classification, we improve our prediction by 39 percent. If we wish to predict occupational classification from opinion instead of the opposite, a λ of .24 would be secured. This means that 24 percent of the error in predicting occupational class is eliminated by knowledge of opinion on the executives' salary question. Lambda varies between 0 and 1, corresponding with no ability to eliminate errors to elimination of all errors of prediction.

Goodman and Kruskal's **tau** uses table marginals to reduce prediction errors. In predicting opinion on executives' salaries without any knowledge of occupational class, we would expect a 50.5 percent correct classification and a 49.5 percent probability of error. These are based on the column marginal percentages in Table 17–8.

Column Marginal		*Column Percent*		*Correct Cases*
180	*	45	=	81
220	*	55	=	121
Total correct classification				202

Correct classification of the opinion variable = .505 = $\dfrac{202}{400}$

Probability of error, $P(1) = (1 - .505) = .495$

When additional knowledge of occupational class is used, information for correct classification of the opinion variable is improved to 62.7 percent with a 37.3 percent probability of error. This is obtained by using the cell counts and marginals for occupational class (refer to Table 17–8), as shown below:

Row 1	$\left(\dfrac{90}{110}\right)90 + \left(\dfrac{20}{110}\right)20$	=	$73.6364 + 3.6364$	=	77.2727
Row 2	$\left(\dfrac{60}{140}\right)60 + \left(\dfrac{80}{140}\right)80$	=	$25.7143 + 45.7142$	=	71.4286
Row 3	$\left(\dfrac{30}{150}\right)30 + \left(\dfrac{120}{150}\right)120$	=	$6.0 + 96.0$	=	102.0000

Total correct classification (with additional information on occupational class)   250.7013

Correct classification of opinion variable = .627 = $\dfrac{250.7}{400}$

Probability of error, $P(2) = (1 - .627) = .373$

Tau is then computed like this:

$$\tau \frac{P(1) - P(2)}{P(1)} = \frac{.495 - .373}{.495} = .246$$

Table 17–8 shows that the information about occupational class has reduced error in predicting opinion to approximately 25 percent. The table also contains information on the test of the null hypothesis that tau = 0 with an approximate observed significance level and asymptotic error (for developing confidence intervals). Based on the small observed significance level, we would conclude that tau is significantly different from a coefficient of 0 and that there is an association between opinion on executives' salaries and occupational class in the population from which the sample was selected. We can also establish the confidence level for the coefficient at the 95 percent level as approximately $.25 \pm .04$.

TABLE   17–9   Tabled Ranks for Management and Fitness Levels

Management Level

Count		Lower	Middle	Upper	
Fitness	High	14	4	2	20
	Moderate	18	6	2	26
	Low	2	6	16	24
		34	16	20	70

Statistic	*Value**
Gamma	−.70242
Kendall's tau *b*	−.51279
Kendall's tau *c*	−.49714
Somers's *d*	
Symmetric	−.51263
With fitness dependent	−.52591
With management-level dependent	−.50000

*The *t* value for each coefficiant is −5.86451.

Measures for Ordinal Data

When data require **ordinal measures,** there are several statistical alternatives. We will illustrate gamma, Kendall's tau *b* and tau *c*, Somers's *d*, and Spearman's rho. All but Spearman's rank-order correlation are based on the concept of concordant and discordant pairs. None of these statistics requires the assumption of a bivariate normal distribution, yet by incorporating order, most produce a range from −1.0 (a perfect negative relationship) to +1.0 (a perfect positive one). Within this range, a coefficient with a larger magnitude (absolute value of the measure) is interpreted as having a stronger relationship. These characteristics allow the analyst to interpret both the direction and the strength of the relationship.

Table 17–9 presents data for 70 managerial employees of a large industrial design firm who have been evaluated for coronary risk by the firm's health insurer. The management levels are ranked, as are the fitness assessments by the physicians. If we were to use a nominal measure of association with this data (such as Cramer's *V*), the computed value of the statistic would be positive since order is not present in nominal data. But using ordinal measures of association reveals the actual nature of the relationship. In this example, all coefficients have negative signs.

The information in the table has been arranged so the number of concordant and discordant pairs of individual observations may be calculated. When a subject that ranks higher on one variable also ranks higher on the other variable, the pairs of observations are said to be **concordant.** If a higher ranking on one variable is accompanied by a lower ranking on the other variable, the pairs of observations are **discordant.** Let *P* stand for concordant pairs and *Q* stand for discordant. When concordant pairs exceed discordant pairs in a $P - Q$ relationship, the statistic reports a positive association between the variables under study. As discordant pairs increase over concordant pairs, the association becomes negative. A balance indicates no relationship between the variables. Table 17–10 summarizes the procedure for calculating the summary terms needed in all the statistics we are about to discuss.[15]

Goodman and Kruskal's **gamma** (γ) is a statistic that compares concordant and discordant pairs and then standardizes the outcome by maximizing the value of the denominator. It has a proportional reduction of error (PRE) interpretation that connects nicely with what we already know about PRE nominal measures. Gamma is defined as

$$\gamma = \frac{P - Q}{P + Q} = \frac{172 - 984}{172 + 984} = \frac{-812}{1156} = -.7024$$

For the fitness data, we conclude that as management level increases, fitness decreases. This is immediately apparent from the larger number of discordant pairs. A more precise explanation for gamma takes its absolute value (ignoring the sign) and relates it to PRE. Hypothetically, if one was trying to predict whether the pairs were concordant or discordant, one might flip a coin and classify the outcome. A better way is to make the prediction based on the preponderance of concordance or discordance; the absolute value of gamma is the proportional reduction in error when prediction is done the second way. For example, you would get a 50 percent hit ratio using the coin. A PRE of .70 improves your hit ratio to 85 percent $(.50 \times 70) + (.50) = .85$.

With a γ of $-.70$, 85 percent of the pairs are discordant and .15 percent are concordant.[16] There are almost six times as many discordant pairs as concordant pairs. In situations where the data call for a 2×2 table, the appropriate modification of gamma is Yule's Q.[17]

Kendall's **tau b** (τ_b) is a refinement of gamma that considers tied pairs. A tied pair occurs when subjects have the same value on the X variable, on the Y variable, or on both. For a given sample size, there are $n(n - 1)/2$ pairs of observations.[18] After concordant pairs and discordant pairs are removed, the remainder are tied. Tau b does not have a PRE interpretation but does provide a range of -1.0 to $+1.0$ for square tables. Its compensation for ties uses the information found in Table 17–10. It may be calculated as

$$\tau_b = \frac{P - Q}{\sqrt{\left(\frac{n(n-1)}{2} - T_x\right)\left(\frac{n(n-1)}{2} - T_y\right)}}$$

$$= \frac{172 - 984}{\sqrt{(2415 - 871)(2415 - 791)}} = -.5128$$

Kendall's **tau c** (τ_c) is another adjustment to the basic $P - Q$ relationship of gamma. This approach to ordinal association is suitable for tables of any size. Although we illustrate tau c, we would select tau b since the cross-classification table for the fitness data is square. The adjustment for table shape is seen in the formula.

TABLE   17–10   Calculation of Concordant (*P*), Discordant (*Q*), Tied (*T_x*,*T_y*), and Total Paired Observations

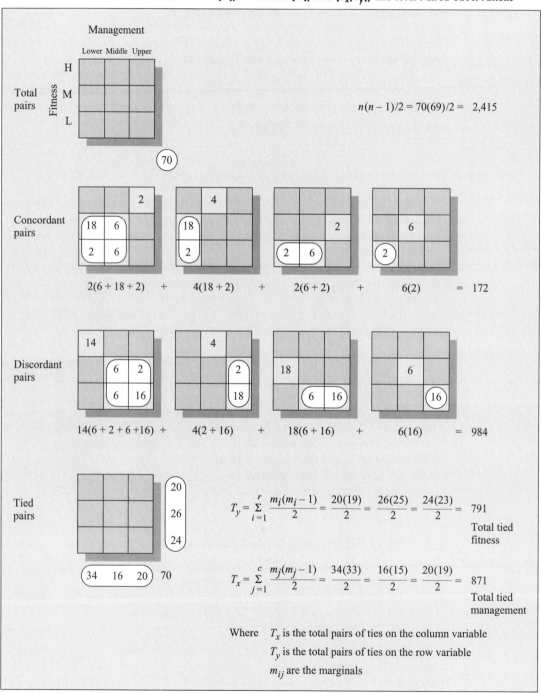

Management

Lower Middle Upper

Total pairs   Fitness   H   M   L

$$n(n-1)/2 = 70(69)/2 = 2,415$$

⑦⓪

Concordant pairs

$$2(6 + 18 + 2) \quad + \quad 4(18 + 2) \quad + \quad 2(6 + 2) \quad + \quad 6(2) \quad = \quad 172$$

Discordant pairs

$$14(6 + 2 + 6 + 16) \quad + \quad 4(2 + 16) \quad + \quad 18(6 + 16) \quad + \quad 6(16) \quad = \quad 984$$

Tied pairs

$$T_y = \sum_{i=1}^{r} \frac{m_i(m_i - 1)}{2} = \frac{20(19)}{2} = \frac{26(25)}{2} = \frac{24(23)}{2} = 791$$

Total tied fitness

$$T_x = \sum_{j=1}^{c} \frac{m_j(m_j - 1)}{2} = \frac{34(33)}{2} = \frac{16(15)}{2} = \frac{20(19)}{2} = 871$$

Total tied management

Where T_x is the total pairs of ties on the column variable

T_y is the total pairs of ties on the row variable

m_{ij} are the marginals

$$\tau_c = \frac{2m(P-Q)}{N^2(m-1)} = \frac{2(3)(172-984)}{(70)^2(3-1)} - .4971$$

where m is the smaller number of rows or columns.

Somers's d rounds out our coverage of statistics employing the concept of concordant-discordant pairs. This statistic's utility comes from its ability to compensate for tied ranks and adjust for the direction of the dependent variable. Again, we refer to the preliminary calculations provided in Table 17–10 to compute the symmetric and asymmetric ds. As before, the symmetric coefficient (equation 3) takes the row and column variables into account equally. The second and third calculations show fitness as the dependent and management level as the dependent, respectively.

$$d_{sym} = \frac{(P-Q)}{n(n-1)-T_xT_y/2} = \frac{-812}{1584} = -.5126 \tag{3}$$

$$d_{y-x} = \frac{(P-Q)}{\dfrac{n(n-1)}{2} - T_x} = \frac{-812}{2415-871} = -.5259 \tag{4}$$

$$d_{x-y} = \frac{(P-Q)}{\dfrac{n(n-1)}{2} - T_y} = \frac{-812}{2415-791} = -.5000 \tag{5}$$

The **Spearman's rho** (ρ) correlation is a popular ordinal measure. Along with Kendall's tau, it is among the most widely used of ordinal techniques. Rho correlates ranks between two ordered variables. Occasionally, researchers find continuous variables with too many abnormalities to correct. Then scores may be reduced to ranks and calculated with Spearman's rho.

As a special form of Pearson's product moment correlation, rho's strengths outweigh its weaknesses. When data are transformed by logs or squaring, rho remains unaffected. Second, outliers or extreme scores that were troublesome before ranking no longer pose a threat since the largest number in the distribution is equal to the sample size. Third, it is an easy statistic to compute. The major deficiency is its sensitivity to tied ranks. Too many ties distort the coefficient's size. However, there are rarely too many ties to justify the correction formulas available.

To illustrate the use of rho, consider a situation where a brokerage firm is recruiting account executive trainees. Assume the field has been narrowed to 10 applicants for final evaluation. They arrive at the company headquarters, go through a battery of tests, and are interviewed by a panel of three executives. The test results are evaluated by an industrial psychologist who then ranks the 10 candidates. The executives produce a composite ranking based on the interviews. Your task is to decide how well these two sets of ranking agree. Table 17–11 contains the data and preliminary calculations. Substituting into the equation, we get

TABLE 17–11 Data for Spearman's rho

	Rank by			
Applicant	Panel x	Psychologist y	d	d^2
1	3.5	6	−2.5	6.25
2	10	5	5	25.00
3	6.5	8	−1.5	2.25
4	2	1.5	0.5	0.25
5	1	3	−2	4.00
6	9	7	2	4.00
7	3.5	1.5	2	4.00
8	6.5	9	−2.5	6.25
9	8	10	−2	4.00
10	5	4	1	1.00
				57.00

NOTE: Tied ranks were assigned the average (of ranks) as if no ties had occurred.

$$r_s = 1 - \frac{6\Sigma d^2}{n^3 - n} = \frac{6(57)}{(10)^3 - 10} = .654$$

where n is the number of subjects being ranked.

The relationship between the panel's and the psychologist's ranking is moderately high, suggesting agreement between the two measures. The test of the null hypothesis that there is no relationship between the measures ($r_s = 0$) is rejected at the .05 level with $n - 2$ degrees of freedom.

$$t = r_s \sqrt{\frac{n-2}{1-r_s^2}} = \sqrt{\frac{8}{1-.4277}} = 2.45$$

Summary

Management research questions frequently involve relationships between two or more variables. Correlation analysis may be applied to study such relationships. Parametric correlation requires two continuous variables measured on an interval or ratio scale. The product moment correlation coefficient represents an index of the magnitude of the relationship, its sign governs the direction, and its square explains the common variance. Bivariate correlation treats X and Y variables symmetrically and is intended for use with variables that are linearly related.

Scatterplots allow the researcher to visually inspect relationship data for appropriateness of the selected statistic. Direction, magnitude, and shape of a relationship are conveyed in a plot. The shape of linear relationships is characterized by a straight line, whereas nonlinear relationships are curvilinear or parabolic or have other curvature. The assumptions of linearity and bivariate normal distribution may be checked through plots and diagnostic tests.

A correlation matrix is a table used to display coefficients for more than two variables. Matrices form the basis for computation and understanding of the nature of relationships in multiple regression, discriminant analysis, factor analysis, and many multivariate techniques.

A correlation coefficient of any magnitude or sign, regardless of statistical significance, does not imply causation. Similarly, a coefficient is not remarkable simply because it is statistically significant. Practical significance should be considered in interpreting and reporting findings.

Regression analysis is used to further our insight about the relationship of Y with X. When we take the observed values of X to estimate or predict corresponding Y values, the process is called simple prediction. When more than one X variable is used, the outcome is a function of multiple predictors. Simple and multiple predictions are made with regression analysis.

A straight line is fundamentally the best way to model the relationship between two continuous variables. The method of least squares allows us to find a regression line, or line of best fit, that minimizes errors in drawing the line. It uses the criterion of minimizing the total squared errors of estimate. Point predictions made from well-fitted data are subject to error. Prediction and confidence bands may be used to find a range of probable values for Y based on the chosen predictor. The bands are shaped in such a way that predictors farther from the mean have larger band widths.

We test regression models for linearity and to discover whether the equation is effective in fitting the data. An important test in bivariate linear regression is whether the slope is equal to zero. In bivariate regression, t and F tests of the regression produce the same result since t^2 is equal to F.

Often the assumptions or the required measurement level for parametric techniques cannot be met. Nonparametric measure of association offer alternatives. Nominal measures of association are used to assess the strength of relationships in cross-classification tables. They are often used in conjunction with chi-square or may be based in the proportional reduction in error (PRE) approach.

Phi ranges from 0 to +1.0 and attempts to correct chi-square proportionately to N. Phi is best employed with 2×2 tables. Cramer's V is a modification of phi for larger tables and has a range up to 1.0 for tables of any configuration. Lambda, a PRE statistic, is based on how well the frequencies of one nominal variable offer predictive evidence about the frequencies of another. Goodman and Kruskal's tau uses table marginals to reduce prediction errors.

Measures for ordinal data include gamma, Kendall's tau b and tau c, Somers's d, and Spearman's rho. All but Spearman's rank-order correlation are based on the concept of concordant and discordant pairs. None of these statistics requires the assumption of a bivariate normal distribution, yet by incorporating order, most produce a range from −1 to +1.

Key Terms

artifact correlations
bivariate correlation analysis
bivariate normal distribution
chi-square-based measures
  contingency coefficient C
  Cramer's V
  phi (ϕ)
coefficient of determination
concordant/discordant
correlation matrix
error term
goodness of fit
linearity
method of least squares

ordinal measures
  gamma (γ)
  Somers's d
  Spearman's rho (ρ)
  tau b (τ_b)
  tau c (τ_c)
Pearson correlation coefficient
prediction and confidence bands
proportional reduction in error
  lambda (λ)
  tau (τ)
regression analysis
regression coefficients
  intercept
  slope
  residual
  scatterplots

Cases

Workload Ratings
Overdue Bills
The Brazing Operation
Performance Evaluations
(These are cases found in the optional casebook available with the text.)

Discussion Questions

1. Distinguish between the following:
   a. Regression coefficient and correlation coefficient
   b. $r = 0$ and $\rho = 0$
   c. The test of the true slope, the test of the intercept, and $r^2 = 0$
   d. r^2 and r
   e. A slope of 0
   f. F and t_2

2. In this data,

X	Y
3	6
6	10
9	15
12	24
15	21
18	20

    a. Create a scatterplot of the data.

    b. Find the least-squares line.

    c. Plot the line on the diagram.

    d. Predict: Y if X is 10

              Y if X is 17

3. Describe the relationship between the two variables in the four plots.

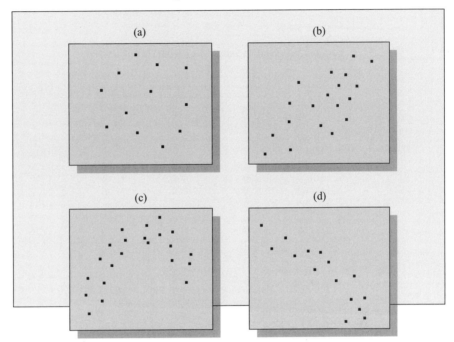

4. For the X and Y pairs below,

X	Y
2	1
3	3
5	5
6	6
8	5
10	3

    a. Create a scatter plot of the data.

    b. Which measure of association is appropriate for this data?

5. Fill in the missing blocks for the ANOVA summary table on net profits and market value used with regression analysis.

    a. What does the F tell you? ($\alpha.05$).

    b. What is the t value? Explain its meaning.

ANOVA Summary Table

	DF	Sum of Squares	Mean Square	F
Regression	1	11116995.47		
Error			116104.63	
Total	9	12045832.50		

6. Using a computer program, produce a correlation matrix for the following data:

Forbes 500 Random Subsample (dollars in millions)

Assets	Sales	Market Value	Net Profit	Cash Flow	Number of Employees (thousands)
1034.00	1510.00	697.00	82.60	126.50	16.60
956.00	785.00	1271.00	89.00	191.20	5.00
1890.00	2533.00	1783.00	176.00	267.00	44.00
1133.00	532.00	752.00	82.30	137.10	2.10
11682.00	3790.00	4149.00	413.50	806.80	11.90
6080.00	635.00	291.00	18.10	35.20	3.70
31044.00	3296.00	2705.00	337.30	425.50	20.10
5878.00	3204.00	2100.00	145.80	380.00	10.80
1721.00	981.00	1573.00	172.60	326.60	1.90
2135.00	2268.00	2634.00	247.20	355.50	21.20

7. Secure Spearman rank-order correlations for the largest Pearson coefficient in the matrix from question 6. Explain the differences between the two findings.

8. A tax on the market value of stock and bond transactions has been proposed as one remedy for the budget deficit. The following data were collected on a sample of 60 registered voters by a polling organization.

		Education	
Opinion About Market Tax	H.S.	College Grad.	MBA
Favorable	15	5	0
Undecided	10	8	2
Unfavorable	0	2	18

a. Compute gamma for the table.

b. Compute tau b or tau c for the same data.

c. What accounts for the differences?

d. Which is more suitable for this data?

9. Using the table data in question 8, compute Somers's d symmetric; and then use opinion as the dependent variable. Interpret your results.

10. For the data below,

X	Y
25	5
19	7
17	12
14	23
12	20
9	25
8	26
7	28
3	20

a. Calculate the correlation between X and Y.

b. Interpret the sign of the correlation.

c. Interpret the square of the correlation.

d. Plot the least-squares line.

e. Test for a linear relationship:

(1) $\beta_1 = 0$

(2) $r = 0$

(3) An F test

11. A research team conducted a study of voting preferences among 130 registered Democrats and 130 registered Republicans before an election on a specific tax proposal. They secured the following results:

	Favor	*Against*
Democrats	50	80
Republicans	90	40

Calculate an appropriate measure of association.

12. Using the matrix data in question 6, select a pair of variables and run a simple regression. Then investigate the appropriateness of the model for the data using diagnostic tools for evaluating assumptions.

Reference Notes   1. Typically, we plot the X (independent) variable on the horizontal axis and the Y (dependent) variable on the vertical axis. Although correlation does not distinguish between independent and dependent variables, the convention is useful for consistency in plotting and will be used later with regression.

2. F. J. Anscombe, "Graphs in Statistical Analysis," *American Statistician* 27 (1973), pp. 17-21. Cited in Samprit Chaterjee and Bertram Price, *Regression Analysis by Example* (New York: Wiley, 1977), pp. 7–9.

3. Amir D. Aczel, *Complete Business Statistics,* 2nd ed. (Homewood, IL: Irwin, 1993), p. 433.

4. The coefficient for net profits and cash flow in the example calculation used a subsample ($n = 10$) and was found to be .93. The matrix shows the coefficient as .95. The matrix calculation was based on the larger sample (n = 100).

5. This section is partially based on the concepts developed by Emanuel J. Mason and William J. Bramble, *Understanding and Conducting Research* (New York: McGraw-Hill, 1989), pp. 172–82; and elaborated in greater detail by Aczel, *Complete Business Statistics,* pp. 414–29.

6. Technically, estimation uses a concurrent criterion variable where prediction uses a future criterion. The statistical procedure is the same in either case.

7. Peter Passell, "Can Math Predict a Wine? An Economist Takes a Swipe at Some Noses," *International Herald Tribune,* March 5, 1990, p. 1; Jacques Neher, "Top Quality Bordeaux Cellar Is an Excellent Buy," *International Herald Tribune,* July 9, 1990, p. 8.

8. See Alan Agresti and Barbara Finlay, *Statistical Methods for the Social Sciences* (San Francisco: Dellen Publishing, 1986), pp. 248–49. Also see the discussion of basic regression models in John Neter, William Wasserman, and Michael H. Kutner, *Applied Linear Statistical Models* (Homewood, IL: Irwin, 1990), pp. 23–49.

9. We distinguish between the error terms $\varepsilon_1 = Y_i - E[Y_i]$ and the residual $e_i = (Y_i - \hat{Y}_i)$. The first is based on the vertical deviation of Y_i from the true regression line. It is unknown and estimated. The second is the vertical deviation of Y_i from the fitted $\hat{Y}$ on the estimated line. See Neter et al., *Applied Linear Statistical Models,* p. 47.

10. For further information on software-generated regression diagnostics, see Marija J. Norusis/SPSS, Inc., *SPSS for Windows Base System User's Guide, Release 6.0* (Chicago: SPSS, Inc., 1993); Marija J. Norusis/SPSS, Inc., *SPSS Advanced Statistics User's Guide* (Chicago: SPSS, Inc., 1990); *MINITAB Reference Manual, Release 7* (State College, PA: Minitab, Inc., 1989); W. J. Dixon, ed., *BMDP Statistical Software Manual,* vols. 1 and 2 (Berkeley: University of California Press, 1988); *SAS User's Guide: Statistics,* Version 6 ed. (Cary, NC: SAS Institute, 1987).

11. Aczel, *Complete Business Statistics,* p. 434.

12. This calculation is normally listed as the standard error of the slope (SE B) on computer printouts. It is further defined as for this data:

$$s(b_1) = \frac{8}{\sqrt{SS_x}} = \frac{538.559}{\sqrt{198.249}} = 38.249$$

where
   s = The standard error of estimate (and the square root of the mean square error of the regression)
   SS_x = The sum of squares for the X variable

13. Computer printouts use uppercase (R^2) because most procedures are written to accept multiple and bivariate regression.

14. The table output for this section is modified from SPSS and described in Norusis/SPSS, Inc., *SPSS Base System User's Guide.* For further discussion and examples of nonparametric measures of association, see S. Siegel and N. J. Castellan, Jr., *Nonparametric Statistics for the Behavioral Sciences,* 2nd ed. (New York: McGraw-Hill, 1988).

15. Calculation of concordant and discordant pairs is adapted from Agresti and Finlay, *Statistical Methods for the Social Sciences,* pp. 221–23.

16. We know that the percentage of concordant plus the percentage of discordant pairs sums to 1.0. We also know their difference is –.70. The only numbers satisfying these two conditions are .85 and .15 (.85 + .15 = 1.0, .15 – .85 = –.70).

17. G. U. Yule and M. G. Kendall, *An Introduction to the Theory of Statistics* (New York: Hafner, 1950).

18. M. G. Kendall, *Rank Correlation Methods,* 4th ed. (London: Charles W. Griffin, 1970).

Suggested Readings

1 Aczel, Amir D. *Complete Business Statistics,* 3rd ed. Burr Ridge, IL: Irwin, 1996. Chapter 10 covers simple regression/correlation with impeccable exposition and examples. Highly recommended.

2. Agresti, Alan, and Barbara Finlay. *Statistical Methods for the Social Sciences.* San Francisco: Dellen Publishing, 1986. Highly readable coverage of nonparametric measures of association.

3. Chatterjee, Samprit, and Bertram Price. *Regression Analysis by Example,* 2nd ed. New York: Wiley, 1991.

4. Draper, N. R., and H. Smith. *Applied Regression Analysis;.* 2nd ed. New York: Wiley, 1981. An advanced text that requires familiarity with matrix algebra.

5. Neter, John, Michael H. Kutner, Christopher J. Nachtsheim, and William Wasserman. *Applied Linear Statistical Models,* 4th ed. Burr Ridge, IL: Irwin, 1996. Chapters 1 through 10 and 15 provide an excellent introduction to regression and correlation analysis.

6. Siegel, S., and N. J. Castellan, Jr. *Nonparametric Statistics for the Behavioral Sciences,* 2nd ed. New York: McGraw-Hill, 1988.

MULTIVARIATE ANALYSIS: AN OVERVIEW

 CHAPTER NAVIGATION

BRINGING RESEARCH TO LIFE

Dorrie Henry would have tolerated Henry Parker's habit of dropping in unexpectedly if he were not a bore and a grabbing bore at that, one who had to seize you by the lapel or grasp your elbow while he shared his every vagrant thought. He was displaying his annoying habits at this very moment.

"I was driving by and saw two cars in your driveway and said, 'Henry, if Cousin Dorrie and her Jason are home on a Wednesday, then you had better stop in for a lemonade and a chat.'" This was supposed to be the day she caught up on her medical record keeping and Jason did tax reports for both of them. But here she was with Henry's arm draped on her shoulder and him waving his iced lemonade wildly to and fro.

She extricated herself by leveling with him. "Henry, I am not at all comfortable with you holding me so tightly." When she saw she had hurt his feelings, she softened her assertiveness with a little lie. "There is a strain of flu running around the clinic, you know, and though I am certainly immune, I would hate to pass it you."

"Oh, sure, no problem, *doctor.* Anyway, *doctor,* I mostly want to fill your husband in on some late-breaking developments." In a single smooth motion he spun loose from his grip on Dorrie and surprised Jason with a lock on Jason's left forearm. Dorrie saw Jason's pupils first dilate and then contract, in a sure sign of annoyance, and she feared he would deal with Henry not as diplomatically as she had.

Jason had a name for Henry, "Ceteribus Parker," an allusion to *ceteribus paribus,* the Latin words for "all things being equal." It was Henry's annoying practice, while holding you in his firm grip (if you let him do so), to make amazingly improbable comparisons between people, groups, institutions, products, services, practices—anything and everything—by declaring the likes of, "All things being equal, Mercury would seem to be a more congenial planet on which life might emerge than Earth." Meaning, if

you allowed for its atmosphere being nonexistent, and its temperature being 1,380 degrees Fahrenheit, there was presumably *something* about its gravitational fields or length of day that fitted Henry's preferred cosmology. "*Ceteribus paribus,*" he once said, "my electric bill would be cheaper if I lived in Antarctica than in Death Valley." You cannot argue against that kind of pseudoscientific blather.

Now he was lecturing Jason about an appointment Henry had taken as the business's representative to the governing board of the public housing authority. "The best tenants are the Pantamarians," he declared. "All things being equal, they are the most law abiding and hard working tenants."

"You mean Panamanians," Jason stated indifferently. It wasn't even a question, just a flat accusation of error.

"No, no, not Panamanians. These folks are *Pantamarians*. They are English-speakers from little islands south of Florida. Never heard of Pantamarie before I was put on the Authority, but, I tell you, they are the most law-abiding tenants. . . ."

". . . *ceteribus paribus,*" echoed Jason ironically, as the very same words slipped from Henry's mouth. Dorrie saw signs of Jason's increasing impatience, as the color flushed his neck and he struggled to free himself from her cousin's grip. She was seriously worried what he would do to Henry. An honest request to loosen the grip would not be sufficiently treacherous for her husband, if he was in his ten-year-old phase.

"Do be more specific," urged Jason. "Are you telling me that the Pantamarians—have I got that right? Pantamarians?—have the lowest crime rate in the Authority? You must have data—you take federal funds, don't you? So you must have data."

"Well," said Henry, evasively, "you have got to allow for these Pantamarians having very large families. And they did not get much schooling, on the plantations back home."

"So what is not equal is their family size and education. Right? What else? What else is not equal?" Jason had leaned forward into Henry's grip and *(continued)* was now staring icily into Dorrie's cousin's eyes. Henry let loose his grip, set down his beverage, and reached for a handful of cocktail napkins, which he began to dab at his brow, mouth, and neck.

"Oh, well, you know. They are young. And there are other things. You know. Other things." Henry's voice had trailed off to a mere whisper as Jason bore in conversationally.

"No, I don't know. But I have good news for you, Henry. You can be sure that the Authority staff have been keeping really good records. We can go down there right now—wonderful of you to drop in on a working day—and ask staff to roll out their records. Family size, education, age, everything. You can bet you have all that and more in your computers down there at the Authority. The Federal Housing and Urban Development people won't give you a penny without it."

Henry stumbled into a chair. He was trembling. Dorrie felt for a pulse. Okay, so far. With his history, he must not be pushed too far.

"Be right back," said Jason. He reappeared almost at once, carrying his laptop. "Good news, Henry. There are statistical techniques called *multi-variate analysis*, that in fact make all other things equal. Look here: This is a data cable. Let's hop in the car and run down to the Authority. You flash your identification, and I suck the data out of their computer into mine along this cable. Then we apply a technique called *analysis of covariance*—ANCOVA. We set crime rate as the dependent variable—you know what that means, don't you?—and country of origin as the independent variable. Then we use ANCOVA to correct for the effects of years of school, education, household size, whatever, and *voilà!!!* your Pantamarians are the most law-abiding tenants, or they aren't. *Ceteribus paribus!!!!*"

Henry grabbed at his chest. "In my pocket," he croaked. "My pill box." Dorrie moved fast and had placed a nitro pill under Henry's tongue before Jason realized what was happening.

After she'd stabilized Henry and called for Cousin Anita to take him to his family doctor for a long-delayed checkup, Jason remained remorse-free. "That's the beautiful part of having a portable computer," he asserted. "In ten minutes I would have shown Henry up for the old blowhard he is."

Following this inexcusable thrust, Jason slept for three nights on the sofa.

INTRODUCTION

In recent years, multivariate statistical tools have been applied with increasing frequency to research problems. This is a recognition that many problems we encounter are more complex than the problems bivariate models can explain. Simultaneously, computer programs have taken advantage of the complex mathematics needed to manage multiple variable relationships. Today, desktop computers and versatile software bring these powerful techniques to researchers.

Throughout the functional areas of management, more and more problems are being addressed by considering multiple independent and/or multiple dependent variables. Sales managers base forecasts on various product history variables; marketers consider the complex set of buyer preferences and preferred product options; financial analysts classify levels of credit risk based on a set of predictors; and human resource managers devise future wage and salary compensation plans with multivariate techniques.

Many of the examples presented in this text could be considered multivariate problems. The revenue improvements for a physicians' group that decided to join a different insurance program were based on multiple factors. In another example, the aviation industry was attempting to control radiation risks for passengers and crew by altering the proximity of air routes to the poles, aircraft shielding, altitude, and other variables. The price of investment-grade wine was forecast based on spring and harvest rainfall and growing-season temperatures.

One author defines **multivariate analysis** as "those statistical techniques which focus upon, and bring out in bold relief, the structure of simultaneous relationships among three or more phenomena."[1] Our overview of multivariate analysis seeks to illustrate the meaning of this definition while building on your understanding of bivariate statistics from the last few chapters. Several common multivariate techniques and examples will be discussed.

Because a complete treatment of this subject would require a thorough consideration of the mathematics, assumptions, and diagnostic tools appropriate for each technique, our coverage is necessarily limited. Readers needing greater detail are referred to the suggested readings at the end of the chapter.

SELECTING A MULTIVARIATE TECHNIQUE

Multivariate techniques may be classified as **dependency** and **interdependency techniques.** Selecting an appropriate technique starts with an understanding of this distinction. If criterion and predictor variables exist in the research question, then we will have an assumption of dependence. Multiple regression, MANOVA, and discriminant analysis are techniques where criterion or dependent variables and predictor or independent variables are present. Alternatively, if the variables are interrelated without designating some dependent and others independent, then interdependence of the variables is assumed. Factor analysis, cluster analysis, and multidimensional scaling are examples of interdepedency techniques.

Figure 18–1 provides a diagram to guide in the selection of techniques. Let's take an example to show how you might make a decision. Every other year since 1978, the Roper organization has tracked public opinion toward business by providing a list of items that are said to be the responsibility of business. The respondents are asked whether business fulfills these responsibilities "fully, fairly well, not too well, or not at all well." The following issues make up the list:[2]

- Developing new products and services
- Producing good-quality products and services
- Making products that are safe to use
- Hiring minorities
- Providing jobs for people
- Being good citizens of the communities in which they operate
- Paying good salaries and benefits to employees
- Charging reasonable prices for goods and services
- Keeping profits at reasonable levels
- Advertising honestly
- Paying their fair share
- Cleaning up their own air and water pollution

You have access to data on these items and wish to know if they could be reduced to a smaller set of variables that would account for most of the variation among respondents. In response to the first question in Figure 18–1, you correctly determine there are no dependent variables in the data set. You then check to see if the variables are **metric** or **nonmetric measures.** In the figure, *metric* refers to ratio and interval measurements, and *nonmetric* refers to data that are nominal and ordinal. Based on the measurement scale, which appears to have equal intervals, and preliminary findings that show a linear relationship between several variables, you decide the data are metric. This decision leads you to three options: multidimensional scaling, cluster analysis, or factor analysis. *Multidimensional scaling* develops a geometric picture or map of the locations of some objects relative to others. This map specifies how the objects differ. *Cluster analysis* identifies homogeneous subgroups or clusters. *Factor analysis* looks for patterns among the variables to discover if an underlying combination of the original variables (a factor) can summarize the original set. Based on your research objective, you select factor analysis.

Suppose you are interested in predicting family food expenditures from family income, family size, and whether the family's location is rural or urban. Returning to Figure 18–1, you conclude there is a singular dependent variable, family food expenditures. You decide this variable is metric since dollars are measured on a ratio scale. The independent variables, income and family size, also meet the criteria for metric data. However, you are not sure about the location variable since it appears to be a dichotomous nominal variable. According to the figure, your choices are automatic interaction detection (AID), multiple classification analysis (MCA), and multiple regression. You recall from Chapter 15 that AID was designed to locate the most

FIGURE 18–1 **Selecting from the Most Common Multivariate Techniques**

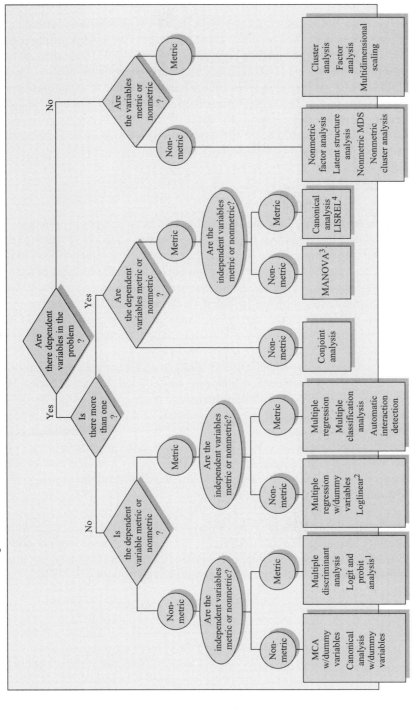

NOTES:

[1]The independent variable is metric only in the sense that a transformed proportion is used.

[2]The independent variable is metric only when we consider that the number of cases in the crosstabulation cell are used to calculate the logs.

[3]Factors may be considered nonmetric independent variables in that they organize the data into groups. We do not classify MANOVA and other multivariate analysis of variance models.

[4]LISREL refers to a linear structural equations model for latent variables. It is a family of models appropriate for confirmatory factor analysis, path analysis, time series analysis, recursive and nonrecursive models, and covariance struture models. Because it may handle dependence and interdependence, metric and nonmetric, it is arbitrarily placed in this diagram.

SOURCE: Partially adapted from T. C. Kinnear and J. R. Taylor, "Multivariate Methods in Marketing: A Further Attempt at Classification," *Journal of Marketing,* October 1971, p. 57; and J. F. Hair, Jr., Rolph E. Anderson, Ronald L. Tatham, and Bernie J. Grablowsky, *Multivariate Data Analysis* (Tulsa, OK: Petroleum Publishing Co., 1979), pp. 10–14.

important interaction effects and typically uses numerous independent variables in its sequential partitioning procedure. MCA handles weak predictors (including nominal variables), correlated predictors, and nonlinear relationships. Multiple regression is the extension of bivariate regression. You believe that your data exceed the assumptions for the first two techniques, and that by treating the nominal variable's values as 0 or 1, you could use it as an independent variable in a multiple regression model. You prefer this to losing information from the other two variables—a certainty if you reduce them to nonmetric data.

In the next two sections, we will extend this discussion as we illustrate dependency and interdependency techniques.

DEPENDENCY TECHNIQUES

Multiple Regression

Multiple regression is used as a descriptive tool in three types of situations. First, it is used often to develop a self-weighting estimating equation by which to predict values for a criterion variable (DV) from the values for several predictor variables (IVs). Thus, we might try to predict company sales on the basis of new housing starts, new marriage rates, annual disposable income, and a time factor. Another prediction study might be one in which we estimate a student's academic performance in college from the variables of rank in high school class, SAT verbal scores, SAT quantitative scores, and a rating scale reflecting impressions from an interview.

Second, a descriptive application of multiple regression calls for controlling for confounding variables to better evaluate the contribution of other variables. For example, one might wish to control the brand of a product and the store in which it is bought to study the effects of price as an indicator of product quality.[3] A third use of multiple regression is to test and explain causal theories. In this approach, often referred to as **path analysis,** regression is used to describe an entire structure of linkages that have been advanced from a causal theory.[4] In addition to being a descriptive tool, a multiple regression is also used as an inference tool to test hypotheses and to estimate population values.

Method   Multiple regression is an extension of the bivariate linear regression presented in Chapter 17. The terms defined in that chapter will not be repeated here. Although **dummy variables** (nominal variables coded 0, 1) may be used, all other variables must be interval or ratio. The generalized equation is

$$Y = \beta_0 + \beta_1 X_1 + \beta_2 X_2 + \cdots + \beta_n X_n + \epsilon$$

where

β_0 = A constant, the value of Y when all X values are zero.

β_i = The slope of the regression surface or the response surface. The β represents the regression coefficient associated with each X_i.

ϵ = An error term, normally distributed about a mean of 0. For purposes of computation, the ϵ is assumed to be 0.

The regression coefficients are stated either in raw score units (the actual X values) or as **standardized coefficients** (X values restated in terms of their standard deviations). In either case, the value of the regression coefficient states the amount that Y varies with each unit change of the associated X variable when the effects of all other X variables are being held constant. When the regression coefficients are standardized, they are called **beta weights** (β), and their values indicate the relative importance of the associated X values, particularly when the predictors are unrelated. For example, in an equation where $\beta_1 = .60$ and $\beta_2 = .20$, one concludes that X_1 has three times the influence on Y as does X_2.

Example   We will use a food expenditure problem to illustrate multiple regression. The equation includes the following variables:

Y = Annual family food expenditures
X_1 = Annual family income
X_2 = Family size
X_3 = Family location (0 = rural, 1 = urban)

A computer program is used to compute the correlation values and the regression coefficients. The standard elements in a printout are shown in Figure 18–2. The inclusion of the three independent variables correlates well with family food

FIGURE   18–2   Multiple Regression Analysis of Family Income, Family Size, and Location, on Family Food Expenditures

```
MULTIPLE REGRESSION

------------------------- MULTIPLE REGRESSION ------------------------- VARIABLE LIST 1
                                                                        REGRESSION LIST 1

DEPENDENT VARIABLE . .      V2     FOOD

VARIABLE(S) ENTERED ON STEP NUMBER 1 . .    X3    LOCATION
                                            X1      HOUSEHOLD INCOME
                                            X2      HOUSEHOLD SIZE

MULTIPLE R         0.87804    ANALYSIS OF VARIANCE   DF   SUM OF SQUARES   MEAN SQUARE      F
R SQUARE           0.77095    REGRESSION             3.        66.19259      22.06420   29.17050
ADJUSTED R SQUARE  0.74452    RESIDUAL              26.        19.66607       0.75639
STANDARD ERROR     0.86971

-------------VARIABLES IN THE EQUATION-------------      ---VARIABLES NOT IN THE EQUATION---
VARIABLE        B            BETA    STD ERROR B     F    VARIABLE BETA IN PARTIAL TOLERANCE F

X3        1.102366        0.27560      0.38594    8.159
X1        0.758286D-01    0.61723      0.01189   40.659
X2         .6076182       0.44860      0.12890   22.221
(CONSTANT) -.1899372

ALL VARIABLES ARE IN THE EQUATION

STATISTICS WHICH CANNOT BE COMPUTED ARE PRINTED AS ALL NINES.
```

Source: Data are hypothetical.

expenditures ($R = .878$). The R^2 of .771 indicates that about 77 percent of the variation in family food expenditures for this sample of 30 families is explained by family income, family size, and whether families live in urban or rural areas.

The other reported statistics have the following interpretations.

1. Adjusted R square = .7445. R^2 is adjusted to reflect the model's goodness of fit for the population. The net effect of this adjustment is to reduce the R^2 slightly but to make it comparable to other R^2s from equations with a different number of independent variables.

2. Standard error = .8697. This is the standard deviation of actual values of Y about the regression line of estimated Y values.

3. Analysis of variance measures whether or not the equation represents a set of regression coefficients that, in total, are statistically significant from zero. The critical value for F is found in Appendix Table F–9, with degrees of freedom for the numerator equaling k, the number of independent variables, and for the denominator, $n - k - 1$, where n for this problem is 30 observations. Thus, d.f. = (3, 26). Appendix Table F–9 indicates a critical value of 2.98 for an $\alpha = .05$. The equation is statistically significant.

4. The column headed "B" indicates the regression coefficients for the equation

$$Y = -.1899 + .0758X_1 + .6076X_2 + 1.1024X_3$$

5. The column headed "Beta" gives the regression coefficients expressed in standardized form. When these are used, the regression Y intercept is zero. The beta weights also show the relative contribution of the three independent variables to the explanatory power of this equation. Household income explains more than either of the other two variables.

6. Standard error of B is a measure of the sampling variability of each regression coefficient—that is, .01189 is the standard deviation of the sampling variability of .0758, the regression coefficient for family income.

7. The column headed "F" measures the statistical significance of each of the regression coefficients. Again compare these to the table of F values in Appendix Table F–9, using degrees of freedom for one independent variable, d.f. = (1, 26). All three regression coefficients are judged to be significantly different from zero. Therefore, the regression equation in 4 above shows the relationship between the dependent variable, food expenditures, and three independent variables: income, family size, and location. The regression coefficients are both individually and jointly statistically significant. The independent variable location influences food expenditures the most, followed by family size and then income.

One difficulty with multiple regression is **multicollinearity**—the situation where some or all of the independent variables are highly correlated. When this condition exists, the estimated regression coefficients can fluctuate widely from sample to sample, making it risky to use the coefficients as an indicator of the relative importance of predictor variables. Just how high can acceptable correlations be between independent variables? There is no definitive answer, but correlations at a .80 or greater level should be dealt with in one of two ways: (1) Choose one of the variables and delete the other, or (2) create a new variable that is a composite of the highly intercorrelated variables and use this new variable in place of its components. In the example just presented, the correlation matrix of simple correlations shows there is no correlation between any two independent variables greater than .20, indicating that multicollinearity is not a problem.

Another difficulty with regression occurs when researchers fail to evaluate the equation with data beyond those used originally to calculate it. A practical solution is to set aside a portion of the data (from a fourth to a third) and use only the remainder to compute the estimating equation. This is called a **holdout sample.** One then uses the equation on the holdout data to calculate an R^2. This can then be compared to the original R^2 to determine how well the equation predicts beyond its database.

Discriminant Analysis

Researchers often wish to classify people or objects into two or more groups. One might need to classify persons as either buyers or nonbuyers, good or bad credit risks, or superior, average, or poor performers in some activity. The objective is to establish a procedure to find the predictors that best classify subjects.

Method   **Discriminant analysis** joins a nominally scaled criterion or dependent variable with one or more independent variables that are interval or ratio scaled. Once the discriminant equation is found, it can be used to predict the classification of a new observation. This is done by calculating a linear function of the form

$$D_i = d_0 + d_1X_1 + d_2X_2 + \cdots + d_pX_p$$

where

D_i is the score on discriminant function i
The d_is are weighting coefficients; d_0 is a constant
The Xs are the values of the discriminating variables used in the analysis

A single discriminant equation is required if the categorization calls for two groups. If three groups are involved in the classification, it requires two discriminant equations. If more categories are called for in the dependent variable, it is necessary to calculate a separate discriminant function for each pair of classifications in the criterion group.

While the most common use for discriminant analysis is to classify persons or objects into various groups, it can also be used to analyze known groups to determine the relative influence of specific factors for deciding into which group various cases fall. Assume we have supervisory ratings that enable us to classify administrators as successful or unsuccessful on administrative performance. We might also be able to secure test results on three measures: ability to work with others (X_1), motivation for administrative work (X_2), and general professional skill (X_3). Suppose the discriminant equation is:

$$D = .06X_1 + .45X_2 + .30X_3$$

Since discriminant analysis uses standardized values for the discriminant variables, we conclude from the coefficients that ability to work with others is less important than the other two in classifying administrators.[5]

Example   An illustration of the method takes us back to the problem in the last chapter where a brokerage firm was hiring MBAs for its account executive program. Over the years the firm had indifferent success with the selection process. You are asked to develop a procedure to improve this. It appears that discriminant analysis is a perfect technique. You begin by gathering data on 30 MBAs who were hired in recent years. Fifteen of these have been successful employees while the other 15 were unsatisfactory. The personnel files provide the following information that can be used to conduct the analysis:

X_1 = Years of prior work experience
X_2 = GPA in graduate program
X_3 = Employment test scores

An algorithm determines how well these three independent variables will correctly classify those who are judged successful from those judged unsuccessful. The classification results are shown in Table 18–1. This indicates that 25 of the 30 cases were correctly classified using these three variables.

The standardized and unstandardized discriminant function coefficients are as follows:

	Unstandardized	Standardized
X_1	.36084	.65927
X_2	2.61192	.57958
X_3	.53028	.97505
(constant)	12.89685	

These results indicate that X_3 (the employment test) has the greatest discriminating power. Several significance tests are also computed. One, Wilk's lambda, has a chi-square transformation for testing the significance of the discriminant function. It indicates the equation is statistically significant at the α = .0004 level. Using the discriminant equation,

$$D = .659X_1 + .580X_2 + .975X_3$$

you can now predict whether future candidates will likely be successful account executives.

TABLE   18–1   Discriminant Analysis Classification Results

Actual Group		Number of Cases	Predicted Group Membership	
			0	*1*
Unsuccessful	0	15	13	2
			86.7%	13.3%
Successful	1	15	3	12
			20.0%	80.0%

Percent of "grouped" cases correctly classified: 83.33%

MANOVA

Multivariate analysis of variance, or **MANOVA,** is a commonly used multivariate technique. MANOVA assesses the relationship between two or more dependent variables and classificatory variables or factors. In business research, MANOVA can be used to test differences among samples of employees, customers, manufactured items, production parts, and so forth.

Method   MANOVA is similar to the univariate ANOVA described earlier, with the added ability to handle several dependent variables. If ANOVA is applied consecutively to a set of interrelated dependent variables, erroneous conclusions may result. MANOVA can correct this by simultaneously testing all the variables and their interrelationships. MANOVA employs sums-of-squares and cross-products (SSCP) matrices to test for differences among groups. The variance between groups is determined by partitioning the total SSCP matrix and testing for significance. The F ratio, generalized to a ratio of the within-group variance and total-group variance matrices, tests for equality among treatment groups.

MANOVA examines similarities and differences among the multivariate mean scores of several populations. The null hypothesis for MANOVA is that all of the **centroids** (multivariate means) are equal, $H_0 : \mu_1 = \mu_2 = \mu_3 = \ldots \mu_n$. The alternative hypothesis is that the vectors of centroids are unequal, $H_A : \mu_1 \neq \mu_2 \neq \mu_3 \neq \ldots \mu_n$. Figure 18–3

FIGURE   18–3   MANOVA Techniques Show These Three Centroids to Be Unequal

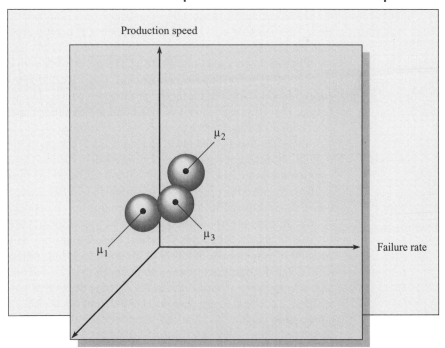

Adherence
to specifications

shows graphically three populations whose centroids are unequal, allowing the researcher to reject the null hypothesis. When the null hypothesis is rejected, additional tests are done to better understand the data. Several alternatives may be considered:

1. Univariate *F* tests can be run on the dependent variables.
2. Simultaneous confidence intervals can be produced for each variable.
3. Step-down analysis, like stepwise regression, can be run by computing *F* values successively. Each value is computed after the effects of the previous dependent variable are eliminated.
4. Multiple discriminant analysis can be used on the SSCP matrices. This aids in the discovery of which variables contribute to the MANOVA's significance.[6]

Example To illustrate, let's look at a firm that manufactures compact disc (CD) players. The plant manager is concerned about the quality of CD players coming off the manufacturing line. Two measures are used to assess quality in this example: adherence to product specifications and time before failure. Measured on a 0–100 scale with 100 meeting all product specifications, the specification variable is averaging approximately 90. The mean time before failure is calculated in weeks; it is approximately 159 weeks, or three years.

The plant manager asks the industrial engineering department to devise a modified manufacturing procedure that will improve the quality measures but not change the production rate significantly. A new method is designed that includes more efficient parts handling and "burn-in" time where CD players are powered up and run at high temperatures.

Engineering takes a sample of 15 CD players made with the old manufacturing method and 15 made with the new method. The players are measured for their adherence to product specifications and are stress-tested to determine their time before failure. The stress test uses accelerated running conditions and adverse environmental conditions to simulate years of use in a short time.

Table 18–2 shows the mean and standard deviation of the dependent variables (failure, specifications, and manufacturing speed) for each level of method.[7] Level 1 represents the current manufacturing process, and level 2 is the new process. The new method extended the time before failure to 181 weeks, compared to 159 weeks for the existing method. The adherence to specifications is also improved, up to 95 from 90. But the manufacturing speed is slower by approximately 30 minutes (.473 hour).

We have used diagnostics to check the assumptions of MANOVA except for equality of variance. Both levels of the manufacturing method variable produce a matrix, and the equality of these two matrices must be determined. Table 18–3 contains homogeneity of variance tests for separate dependent variables and a multivariate test. The former are known as univariate tests. The multivariate test is a comparable version that tests the variables simultaneously to determine whether MANOVA should proceed.

The significance levels of Cochran's *C* and Bartlett-Box *F* do not allow us to reject any of the tests for the dependent variables considered separately. This means

TABLE   18–2   MANOVA Cell Means and Standard Deviations

VARIABLE	FACTOR	LEVEL	MEAN	STD. DEV.
FAILURE				
	METHOD	1	158.867	4.998
	METHOD	2	181.067	5.994
	For entire sample		169.967	12.524
SPECIFICATIONS				
	METHOD	1	89.800	2.077
	METHOD	2	94.800	2.178
	For entire sample		92.300	3.292
SPEED				
	METHOD	1	2.126	.061
	METHOD	2	2.599	.068
	For entire sample		2.362	.249

the two methods have equal variances in each dependent variable. This fulfills the univariate assumptions for homogeneity of variance. We then consider the variances and covariances simultaneously with Box's *M*, also found in Table 18–3. Again, we are unable to reject the homogeneity of variance assumption regarding the matrices. This satisfies the multivariate assumptions.

TABLE   18–3   MANOVA Homegeneity of Variance Tests

VARIABLE	TEST	RESULTS
FAILURE		
	Cochran's C (14,2) =	.58954, P = .506 (approx.)
	Bartlett-Box F (1,2352) =	.44347, P = .506
SPECIFICATIONS		
	Cochran's C (14,2) =	.52366, P = .862 (approx.)
	Bartlett-Box F (1,2352) =	.03029, P = .862
SPEED		
	Cochran's C (14,2) =	.55526, P = .684 (approx.)
	Bartlett-Box F (1,2352) =	.16608, P = .684

Multivariate Test for Homogeneity of Dispersion Matrices

Box's M =		6.07877
F with (6,5680) DF =		.89446, P = .498 (approx.)
Chi-Square with 6 DF =		5.37320, P = .497 (approx.)

When MANOVA is applied properly, the dependent variables are correlated. If the dependent variables are unrelated, there would be no necessity for a multivariate test, and we could use separate F tests for failure, specifications, and speed much like the ANOVAs in Chapter 16. Bartlett's test of sphericity helps us decide if we should continue analyzing MANOVA results or return to separate univariate tests. In Table 18–4, we will look for a determinant value that is close to 0. This implies that one or more dependent variables is a linear function of another. The determinant has a chi-square transformation that simplifies testing for statistical significance. Since the observed significance is below that set for the model ($\alpha = .05$), we are able to reject the null hypothesis and conclude there are dependencies among the failure, specifications, and speed variables.

We now move to the test of equality of means that considers the three dependent variables for the two levels of manufacturing method. This test is analogous to a t or F test for multivariate data. The sums-of-squares and cross-products (SSCP) matrices are used. Table 18–5 shows three tests, including the Hotelling T^2. All the tests provided are compared to the F distribution for interpretation. Since the observed significance level is less than $\alpha = .05$ for the T^2 test, we reject the null hypothesis that said methods 1 and 2 provide equal results with respect to failure, specifications, and speed. Similar results are obtained from the Pillai trace and Wilks' statistic.

Finally, to detect where the differences lie, we can examine the results of univariate F tests in Table 18–6. Since there are only two methods, the F is equivalent to t^2 for a two-sample t test. The significance levels for these tests do not reflect that several comparisons are being made, and we should use them principally for diag-

TABLE 18–4   Bartlett's Test of Sphericity

```
Statistics for WITHIN CELLS correlations

Log (Determinant) =                    -3.92663
Bartlett's test of sphericity =     102.74687 with 3 D.F.
Significance =                           .000

F(max) criterion =                  7354.80161 with (3,28) D.F.
```

TABLE 18–5   Multivariate Tests of Significance

```
Multivariate Tests of Significance (S = 1, M = 1/2, N = 12)

Test Name      Value       Exact F   Hypoth. DF   Error DF   Sig. of F

Hotelling    51.33492    444.90268      3.00        26.00      .000
Pillai         .98089    444.90268      3.00        26.00      .000
Wilks          .01911    444.90268      3.00        26.00      .000
```

NOTE: F statistics are exact.

TABLE 18–6   Univariate Tests of Significance

```
Univariate F-tests with (1,28) D.F.

Variable  Hypoth. SS    Error SS    Hypoth. MS    Error MS         F    Sig. of F

FAILURE   3696.30000   852.66667   3696.30000   30.45238   121.37967      .000
SPECS      187.50000   126.80000    187.50000    4.52857    41.40379      .000
SPEED        1.67560      .11593      1.67560      .00414   404.68856      .000
```

NOTE: *F* statistics are exact.

nostic purposes. This is similar to problems that require the use of multiple comparison tests in univariate analysis of variance. Note, however, that there are statistically significant differences in all three dependent variables resulting from the new manufacturing method. Techniques for further analysis of MANOVA results were listed at the beginning of this section.

LISREL[8]

LISREL, an acronym for *linear structural relationships,* was introduced by Karl Jöreskog in 1973. It is a complicated technique, well beyond the scope of this text, but is extremely useful in explaining causality among constructs that cannot be directly measured. It is used in various ways in the social and behavioral sciences; its application to business issues can be seen in macroeconomic policy formation, racial discrimination in employment, and consumer behavior, among others.

LISREL analyzes covariance structures. It has two parts, one is a *measurement model.* Since hypothetical constructs cannot be measured directly, the measurement model is used to relate the observed, recorded, or measured variables to the latent variables (constructs). For example, to understand an employee's performance, several variables may be used, including (1) the manager's observations, (2) recorded measures of work output, and (3) the number of requests for peer assistance from the employee. These variables can be combined to give the researcher an understanding of the employee's performance. Measurement models are important for modeling constructs such as attitude, feelings, and motivation that cannot be directly observed.

The second part of the LISREL is the *structural equation model.* This model shows the causal relationships among the latent variables. In addition, it describes the causal effects and the variance that are unexplained. The structural equation model is often diagrammed for better understanding. This is a form of path analysis, and the resulting figure is a path diagram. Translated into mathematics, the model is described by a set of linear structural equations. A causal structure among the variables is assumed.

Figure 18–4 shows a path diagram of employee performance. In this example, the latent factors are training, motivation, and performance, shown within circles. The observable or measurable variables are shown within rectangles. Arrows signify influence. Since the latent factors affect the measurable variables (motivation affects the motivation test results, not vice versa), the arrows point from the construct to the measured variables. The figure also shows an interrelationship between motivation

FIGURE   18–4   Path Diagram for Employee Performance

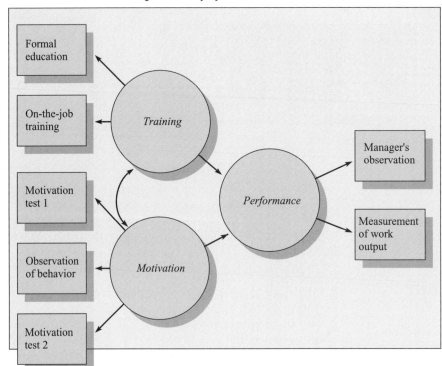

and training. The researchers believe motivation enhances the effectiveness of training and training reciprocally influences motivation. Each of these independent variables has a causal effect on the employee's performance. A more complex representation of this model would show error variances influencing each of the measurable variables and the dependent factor.

Although it is a complicated technique, LISREL allows researchers to analyze complex covariance structures. Latent, interdependent, and reciprocally causal variables are easily handled within the measurement and structural equation models.

Conjoint Analysis

In management research, the most common applications for conjoint analysis are market research and product development. Consumers buying a home computer, for example, may evaluate a set of attributes to choose the product that best meets their needs. They may consider brand, speed, price, educational values, games, or capacity for work-related tasks. The attributes and their features require the buyer to make trade-offs in the final decision making.

Method   **Conjoint analysis** typically uses input from nonmetric independent variables. Normally, we would use cross-classification tables to handle such data, but even multiway tables become quickly overwhelmed by the complexity. If there were three prices, three brands, three speeds, two levels of educational values, two categories for games, and two categories for work assistance, the model would have 216 decision levels ($3 \times 3 \times 3 \times 2 \times 2 \times 2$). A choice structure this size poses enormous difficulties for respondents and analysts. Conjoint analysis solves this problem with various optimal scaling approaches, often with loglinear models, to provide researchers with reliable answers that could not be obtained otherwise.

The objective of conjoint analysis is to secure *part-worths,* or **utility scores** that represent the importance of each aspect of a product or service in the subjects' overall preference ratings. Utility scores are computed from the subjects' rankings or ratings of a set of cards. Each card in the deck describes one possible configuration of combined product attributes.

The first step in a conjoint study is to select the attributes most pertinent to the purchase decision. This may require an exploratory study such as a focus group, or it could be done by an expert with thorough market knowledge. The attributes selected are the independent variables and are called *factors.* The possible values for an attribute are called *factor levels.* In the home computer example, the speed factor may have levels of 200 megahertz (MHz), 233MHz, and 266MHz. Speed, like price, approaches linear measurement characteristics since consumers typically choose higher speeds and lower prices. Other factors like brand are measured as discrete variables.

After selecting the factors and their levels, a computer program determines the number of product descriptions necessary to estimate the utilities. SPSS procedures ORTHOPLAN, PLANCARDS, and CONJOINT build a file structure for all possible combinations, generate the subset required for testing, produce the card descriptions, and analyze results. The command structure within these procedures provides for holdout sampling, simulations, and other requirements frequently used in commercial applications.[9]

Example Water sports enthusiasts know the dangers of ultraviolet (UV) light. It fades paint and clothing; yellows surfboards, skis, and sailboards; and destroys sails. More important, UV damages the eye's retina and cornea. At the beginning of the 1990s, Americans were spending $1.3 billion on 189 million pairs of sunglasses, most of which failed to provide adequate UV protection. Manufacturers of sunglasses for specialty markets have improved their products to where all of the companies in our example advertised 100 percent UV protection. Many other features influence trends in this market. We chose four factors from information contained in a review of sun protection products.[10]

Brand		Style	Flotation	Price
Bolle	A	Multiple color choices for	Yes	$100
Hobbies		frames, lenses, and temples	No	72
Oakley	B	Multiple color choices for		60
Ski Optiks		frames, lenses, and straps		40
		(no hard temples)		
	C	Limited colors for frames,		
		lenses, and temples		

This is a $4 \times 4 \times 3 \times 2$ design or a 96-option full-concept study. The algorithm selected 16 cards to estimate the utilities for the full concept. Combinations of interest that were not selected can be estimated later from the utilities. In addition, four holdout cards were administered to subjects but evaluated separately. The cards shown in Figure 18–5 were administered to a small sample ($n = 10$). Subjects were asked to

FIGURE   18–5   Concept Cards for Conjoint Example

Card 2

Watersport Eyewear Comparison

Style and design: C
Brand name: Bolle
Flotation?   No
Price: $72

Card 1

Watersport Eyewear Comparison

Style and Design: A
Brand Name: Oakley Eyeshade
Flotation?   Yes
Price: $60

Style and Design

Multiple color choice: frames, lenses, temples

order their cards from most to least desirable. The data produced the results presented in Figures 18–6 and 18–7.

Figure 18–6 contains the results of the eighth subject's preferences. This individual was an avid boardsailor, and flotation was the most important attribute for her, followed by style and price and then brand. From her preferences, we can compute her total utility score:

$$(Style B) 3.46 + (Oakley brand) 1.31 + (flotation) 20.75$$
$$+ (price @ \$40) 5.90 + (constant) - 8.21 = 23.21$$

FIGURE   18–6   Conjoint Results for Subject 8

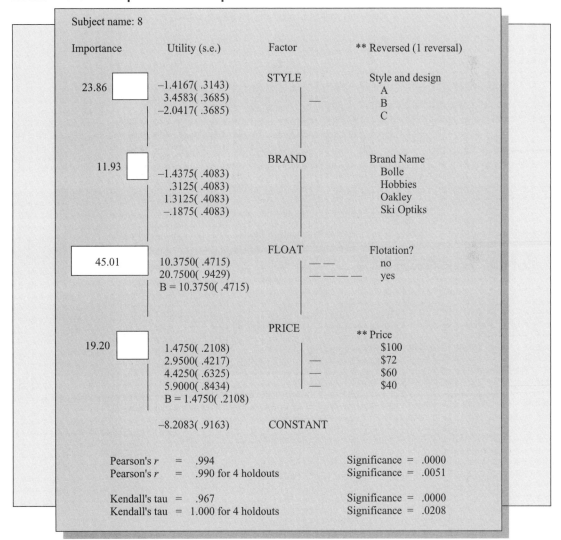

Subject name: 8

Importance	Utility (s.e.)	Factor	** Reversed (1 reversal)
		STYLE	Style and design
23.86	−1.4167(.3143)		A
	3.4583(.3685)		B
	−2.0417(.3685)		C
		BRAND	Brand Name
11.93	−1.4375(.4083)		Bolle
	.3125(.4083)		Hobbies
	1.3125(.4083)		Oakley
	−.1875(.4083)		Ski Optiks
		FLOAT	Flotation?
45.01	10.3750(.4715)		no
	20.7500(.9429)		yes
	B = 10.3750(.4715)		
		PRICE	** Price
19.20	1.4750(.2108)		$100
	2.9500(.4217)		$72
	4.4250(.6325)		$60
	5.9000(.8434)		$40
	B = 1.4750(.2108)		
	−8.2083(.9163)	CONSTANT	

Pearson's r = .994   Significance = .0000
Pearson's r = .990 for 4 holdouts   Significance = .0051

Kendall's tau = .967   Significance = .0000
Kendall's tau = 1.000 for 4 holdouts   Significance = .0208

If brand and price remain unchanged, a design that uses a hard temple with limited color choices (Style C) and no flotation would produce a considerably lower total utility score for this respondent. For example:

$$\text{(Style C)} - 2.04 + \text{(Oakley brand)}\ 1.31 + \text{(no float)}\ 10.38$$
$$+ \text{(price @ \$40)}\ 5.90 + \text{(constant)} - 8.21 = 7.34$$

We could also calculate other combinations that would reveal the range of this individual's preferences. Our prediction that respondents would prefer less expensive prices did not hold for the eighth respondent as revealed by two asterisks next to the

FIGURE 18–7 **Conjoint Results for Sample (*n* = 10)**

Importance	Utility	Factor	
		STYLE	Style and design
18.31	1.1583		A
	−1.9667	—	B
	.8083		C
		BRAND	Brand Name
7.62	.1938		Bolle
	−.7813		Hobbies
	.5187		Oakley
	.0688		Ski Optiks
		FLOAT	Flotation?
31.57	5.3875	— —	no
	10.7750	— — — —	yes
	B = 5.3875		
		PRICE	Price
42.50	2.4175	—	$100
	4.8350	— —	$72
	7.2525	— — —	$60
	9.6700	— — — —	$40
	B = 2.4175		
	−3.4583	CONSTANT	

Pearson's *r* = .995		Significance = .0000	
Pearson's *r* = .976 for 4 holdouts		Significance = .0120	
Kendall's tau = .950		Significance = .0000	
Kendall's tau = 1.000 for 4 holdouts		Significance = .0208	

price factor in Figure 18–6. She reversed herself once on price to get flotation. Other subjects also reversed once on price to trade off for other factors.

The results for the sample are presented in Figure 18–7. In contrast to individuals, the sample placed price first in importance, followed by flotation, style, and brand. Group utilities may be calculated just as we did for the individual. At the bottom of the printout we find Pearson's *r* and Kendall's tau. Each was discussed in Chapter 11. In this application, they measure the relationship between observed and estimated preferences. Since holdout samples (in conjoint, regression, discriminant, and other methods) are not used to construct the estimating equation, the coefficients for the holdouts are often a more realistic index of the model's fit.

Conjoint analysis is an effective tool for researchers to match preferences to known characteristics of market segments and design or target the product accordingly.

INTERDEPENDENCY TECHNIQUES

Factor Analysis

Factor analysis is a general term for several specific computational techniques. All have the objective of reducing to a manageable number many variables that belong together and have overlapping measurement characteristics. The predictor-criterion relationship that was found in the dependence situation is replaced by a matrix of intercorrelations among several variables, none of which is viewed as being dependent on another. For example, one may have data on 100 employees with scores on six attitude scale items.

Method Factor analysis begins with construction of a new set of variables based on the relationships in the correlation matrix. While this can be done in a number of ways, the most frequently used approach is **principal components analysis.** This method transforms a set of variables into a new set of composite variables or principal components that are not correlated with each other. These linear combinations of variables, called **factors**, account for the variance in the data as a whole. The best combination makes up the first principal component and is the first factor. The second principal component is defined as the best linear combination of variables for explaining the variance *not* accounted for by the first factor. In turn, there may be a third, fourth, and *k*th component, each being the best linear combination of variables not accounted for by the previous factors.

The process continues until all the variance is accounted for, but as a practical matter it is usually stopped after a small number of factors have been extracted. The output of a principal components analysis might look like the hypothetical data shown in Figure 18–8.

Numerical results from a factor study are shown in Table 18–7. The values in this table are correlation coefficients between the factor and the variables (.70 is the *r* between variable A and factor I.) These correlation coefficients are called **loadings.** Two other elements in Table 18–7 need explanation. Eigenvalues are the sum of the variances of the factor values (for factor I the eigenvalue is $.70^2 + .60^2 + .50^2 + .60^2 + .60^2$). When divided by the number of variables, an eigenvalue yields an estimate of the

FIGURE 18–8   Principal Components Analysis from a Three-Variable Data Set

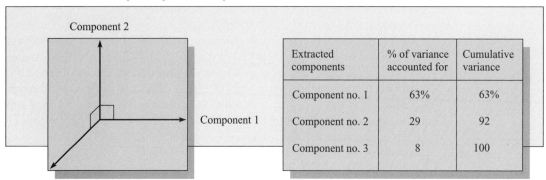

Extracted components	% of variance accounted for	Cumulative variance
Component no. 1	63%	63%
Component no. 2	29	92
Component no. 3	8	100

amount of total variance explained by the factor. For example, factor I accounts for 36 percent of the total variance. The column headed h^2 gives the **communalities** or estimates of the variance in each variable that is explained by the two factors. With variable A, for example, the communality is $.70^2 + (-.40)^2 = .65$, indicating that 65 percent of the variance in variable A is statistically explained in terms of factors I and II.

In this case, the unrotated factor loadings are not enlightening. What one would like to find is some pattern in which factor I would be heavily loaded (have a high r) on some variables and factor II on others. Such a condition would suggest rather "pure" constructs underlying each factor. You attempt to secure this less ambiguous condition between factors and variables by **rotation.** This procedure can be carried out by either orthogonal or oblique methods, but only the former will be illustrated here.

To understand the rotation concept, consider that you are dealing only with simple two-dimensional rather than multidimensional space. The variables in Table 18–7 can be plotted in two- dimensional space as shown in Figure 18–9. Two axes divide this space, and the points are positioned relative to these axes. The location of these axes is arbitrary, and they represent only one of an infinite number of reference

TABLE 18–7   Factor Matrices

Variable	A Unrotated Factors			B Rotated Factors	
	I	II	h^2	I	II
A	.70	−.40	.65	**.79**	.15
B	.60	−.50	.61	**.75**	.03
C	.60	−.35	.48	**.68**	.10
D	.50	.50	.50	.06	**.70**
E	.60	.50	.61	.13	**.77**
F	.60	.60	.72	.07	**.85**
Eigenvalue	2.18	1.39			
Percent of variance	36.30	23.20			
Cumulative percent	36.30	59.50			

FIGURE 18–9   Orthogonal Factor Rotations

frames that could be used to reproduce the matrix. As long as you do not change the intersection points and keep the axes at right angles, when an orthogonal method is used you can rotate the axes to find a better solution or position for the reference axes. "Better" in this case means a matrix that makes the factors as pure as possible (each variable loads onto as few factors as possible). From the rotation shown in Figure 18–9, it can be seen that the solution is improved substantially. Using the rotated solution suggests that the measurements from six scales may be summarized by two underlying factors (see the rotated factors section of Table 18–7).

The interpretation of factor loadings is largely subjective. There is no way to calculate the meanings of factors; they are what one sees in them. For this reason, factor analysis is largely used for exploration. One can detect patterns in latent variables, discover new concepts, and reduce data. Factor analysis is also used to test hypotheses, although the confirmatory models are beyond the scope of this discussion.

Example   Student grades make for an interesting example. The director of an MBA program has been reviewing grades for the first-year students and is struck by the patterns in the data. His hunch is that distinct types of people are involved in the study of management, and he decides to gather evidence for this idea.

Suppose a sample of 21 grade reports is chosen for students in the middle of the GPA range. Three steps are followed:

1. Calculate a correlation matrix between the grades for all pairs of the 10 courses for which data exist.
2. Factor-analyze the matrix by the principal components method.
3. Select a rotation procedure to clarify the factors and aid in interpretation.

Table 18–8 shows a portion of the correlation matrix. These data represent correlation coefficients between the 10 courses. For example, grades secured in V1 (Financial Accounting) correlated rather well (0.56) with grades received in course V2 (Managerial Accounting). The next best correlation with V1 grades is an inverse correlation (−.44) with grades in V7 (Production).

After the correlation matrix, the extraction of components is shown in Table 18–9. While the program will produce a table with as many as 10 factors, you choose, in this case, to stop the process after three factors have been extracted. Sev-

TABLE 18–8 Correlation Coefficients, Student Grade Data

Variable	Course	V1	V2	V3	V10
V1	Financial Accounting	1.00	.56	.17	−.01
V2	Managerial Accounting	.56	1.00	−.22	.06
V3	Finance	.17	−.22	1.00	.42
V4	Marketing	−.14	.05	−.48	−.10
V5	Human Behavior	−.19	−.26	−.05	−.23
V6	Organization Design	−.21	−.00	−.56	−.05
V7	Production	−.44	−.11	−.04	−.08
V8	Probability	.30	.06	.07	−.10
V9	Statistical Inference	−.05	.06	−.32	.06
V10	Quantitative Analysis	−.01	.06	.42	1.00

TABLE 18–9 Factor Matrix Using Principal Factor with Iterations, Student Grade Data

Variable	Course	Factor 1	Factor 2	Factor 3	Communality
V1	Financial Accounting	.41	.71	.23	.73
V2	Managerial Accounting	.01	.53	−.16	.31
V3	Finance	.89	−.17	.37	.95
V4	Marketing	−.60	.21	.30	.49
V5	Human Behavior	.02	−.24	−.22	.11
V6	Organization Design	−.43	−.09	−.36	.32
V7	Production	−.11	−.58	−.03	.35
V8	Probability	.25	.25	−.31	.22
V9	Statistical Inference	−.43	.43	.50	.62
V10	Quantitative Analysis	.25	.04	.35	.19
Eigenvalue		1.83	1.52	.95	
Percent of variance		18.30	15.20	9.50	
Cumulative percent		18.30	33.50	43.00	

eral features in this table are worth noting. Recall that the communalities indicated the amount of variance in each variable that is being "explained" by the factors. Thus, these three factors accounted for about 73 percent of the variance in grades in the Financial Accounting course. It should be apparent from these communality figures that some of the courses are not explained well by the factors selected.

The eigenvalue row in Table 18–9 is a measure of the explanatory power of each factor. For example, the eigenvalue for factor 1 is 1.83 and is computed as follows:

$$1.83 = (.41)^2 + (.01)^2 + \cdots + (.25)^2$$

The percent of variance accounted for by each factor in Table 18–9 is computed by dividing eigenvalues by the number of variables. When this is done, one sees that the three factors accounted for about 43 percent of the total variance in course grades.

In an effort to further clarify the factors, a varimax (orthogonal) rotation is used to secure the matrix shown in Table 18–10. The heavy factor loadings for the three factors are as follows:

Factor 1		*Factor 2*		*Factor 3*	
Financial Accounting	.84	Finance	.90	Marketing	.65
Managerial Accounting	.53	Organization Design	−.56	Statistical Inference	.79
Production	−.54				

Interpretation   The varimax rotation appears to clarify the relationship among course grades, but as pointed out earlier, the interpretation of the results is largely subjective. We might interpret the above results as showing three kinds of students, classified as the accounting, finance, and marketing types. Other interpretations could be made.

A number of problems affect the interpretation of these results. Among the major ones are these:

1. The sample is small and any attempt at replication might produce a different pattern of factor loadings.
2. From the same data, another number of factors rather than three can result in different patterns.

TABLE   18–10   Varimax Rotated Factor Matrix, Student Grade Data

Variable	*Course*	*Factor 1*	*Factor 2*	*Factor 3*
V1	Financial Accounting	.84	.16	−.06
V2	Managerial Accounting	.53	−.10	.14
V3	Finance	−.01	.90	−.37
V4	Marketing	−.11	−.24	.65
V5	Human Behavior	−.13	−.14	−.27
V6	Organization Design	−.08	−.56	−.02
V7	Production	−.54	−.11	−.22
V8	Probability	.41	−.02	−.24
V9	Statistical Inference	.07	.02	.79
V10	Quantitative Analysis	−.02	.42	.09

3. Even if the findings are replicated, the differences may be due to the varying influence of professors or the way they teach the courses rather than to the subject content.

4. The labels may not truly reflect the latent construct that underlies any factors we extract.

This suggests that factor analysis can be a demanding tool to use. It is powerful, but the results must be interpreted with great care.

Cluster Analysis

Unlike techniques for analyzing the relationships between variables, **cluster analysis** is a set of techniques for grouping similar objects or people. Originally developed as a classification device for taxonomy, its use has spread because of classification work in medicine, biology, and other sciences. Its visibility in those fields and the availability of high-speed computers to carry out the extensive calculations have sped its adoption in engineering, economics, marketing, and a host of other areas.

Cluster shares some similarities with factor analysis, especially when factor is applied to people (*Q*-analysis) instead of to variables. It differs from discriminant analysis in that discriminant begins with a well-defined group composed of two or more distinct sets of characteristics in search of a set of variables to separate them. Cluster starts with an undifferentiated group of people, events, or objects and attempts to reorganize them into homogeneous subgroups.

Method   Five steps are basic to the application of most cluster studies:

1. Selection of the sample to be clustered (e.g., buyers, medical patients, inventory, products, employees)

2. Definition of the variables on which to measure the objects, events, or people (e.g., financial status, political affiliation, market segment characteristics, symptom classes, product competition definitions, productivity attributes)

3. Computation of similarities among the entities through correlation, Euclidean distances, and other techniques

4. Selection of mutually exclusive clusters (maximization of within-cluster similarity and between-cluster differences) or hierarchically arranged clusters

5. Cluster comparison and validation

Different clustering methods can and do produce different solutions. It is important to have enough information about the data to know when the derived groups are real and not merely imposed on the data by the method.

The example shown in Figure 18–10 shows cluster analysis of individuals based on three dimensions: age, income, and family size. Cluster analysis could be used to segment the car-buying population into distinct markets. For example, cluster A may be targeted as potential minivan or sport-utility vehicle buyers. The market segment represented by cluster B would be a sports and performance car segment. Clusters C and D would both be targeted as buyers of sedans, but the C cluster would be the luxury buyer. This form of clustering or a hierarchical arrangement of the clusters may be used to plan marketing campaigns and develop strategies.

Example   Serious movie fans find that Paris offers one of the world's best selections of films. Residents of New York and Los Angeles are often surprised to discover their cities are eclipsed by Paris's average of 300 films per week shown in over 100 locations.

We selected ratings from 12 cinema reviewers using sources ranging from *Le Monde* to international publications sold in Paris. The reviews reputedly influence box-office receipts, and the entertainment business takes them seriously.

The object of this cluster example was to classify 19 films into homogeneous subgroups. The production companies were American, Canadian, French, Italian, Spanish, Finnish, Egyptian, and Japanese. Three genres of film were represented: comedy, dramatic comedy, and psychological drama. Table 18–11 shows the data by film name, country of origin, and genre. The table also lists the clusters for each film using the *average linkage method.* This approach considers distances between all possible pairs rather than just the nearest or farthest neighbor.

The sequential development of the clusters and their relative distances are displayed in a diagram called a *dendogram.* Figure 18–11 shows that the clustering procedure begins with 19 films and continues until all the films are again an undifferentiated group. The solid vertical line shows the point at which the clustering solution best represents the data. This determination was guided by coefficients provided by the SPSS program for each stage of the procedure. Five clusters explain this data set.

The first cluster shown in Figure 18–11 has four French-language films, all of which are dramatic comedies. Cluster two consists of comedy films. Two French and

FIGURE   18–10   Cluster Analysis on Three Dimensions

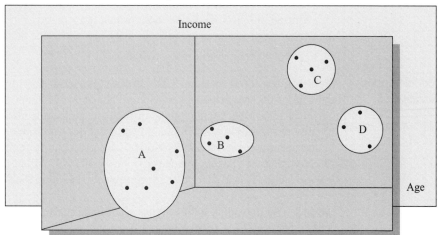

Family size

TABLE   18–11   Film, Country, Genre, and Cluster Membership

				Number of Clusters			
Film	*Country*	*Genre*	*Case*	*5*	*4*	*3*	*2*
Cyrano de Bergerac	France	DramaCom	1	1	1	1	1
Il y a des Jours	France	DramaCom	4	1	1	1	1
Nikita	France	DramaCom	5	1	1	1	1
Les Noces de Papier	Canada	DramaCom	6	1	1	1	1
Leningrad Cowboys . . .	Finland	Comedy	19	2	2	2	2
Storia de Ragazzi . . .	Italy	Comedy	13	2	2	2	2
Conte de Printemps	France	Comedy	2	2	2	2	2
Tatie Danielle	France	Comedy	3	2	2	2	2
Crimes and Misdem . . .	USA	DramaCom	7	3	3	3	2
Driving Miss Daisy	USA	DramaCom	9	3	3	3	2
la Voce della Luna	Italy	DramaCom	12	3	3	3	2
Che Hora e	Italy	DramaCom	14	3	3	3	2
Attache-Moi	Spain	DramaCom	15	3	3	3	2
White Hunter Black . . .	USA	PsyDrama	10	4	4	3	2
Music Box	USA	PsyDrama	8	4	4	3	2
Dead Poets Society	USA	PsyDrama	11	4	4	3	2
La Fille aux All . . .	Finland	PsyDrama	18	4	4	3	2
Alexandrie, Encore . . .	Egypt	DramaCom	16	5	3	3	2
Dreams	Japan	DramaCom	17	5	3	3	2

two other European films joined at the first stage, and then these two groups came together at the second stage. Cluster three, composed of dramatic comedies, is otherwise diverse. It is made up of two American films with two Italian films adding to the group at the fourth stage. Late in the clustering process, cluster three is completed when a Spanish film is appended. In cluster four, we find three American psychological dramas combined with a Finnish film at the second stage. In cluster five, two very different dramatic comedies are joined in the third stage.

Cluster analysis classified these productions based on reviewers' ratings. The similarities and distances are influenced by film genre and culture (as defined by the translated language).

Multidimensional Scaling

Multidimensional scaling (MDS) creates a spacial description of a respondent's perception about a product, service, or other object of interest. This often helps the business researcher to understand difficult-to-measure constructs such as product quality or desirability. In contrast to variables that can be measured directly, many constructs are perceived and cognitively mapped in different ways by individuals. With MDS, items that are perceived to be similar will fall close together in multidimensional space, and items that are perceived to be dissimilar will be farther apart.

Method   We may think of three types of attribute space, each representing a multidimensional map. First, there is objective space in which an object can be positioned in terms of its measurable attributes: its flavor, weight, and nutritional value. Second, there is subjective space where perceptions of the object's flavor, weight, and nutri-

FIGURE   18–11   Dendogram Using Average Linkage

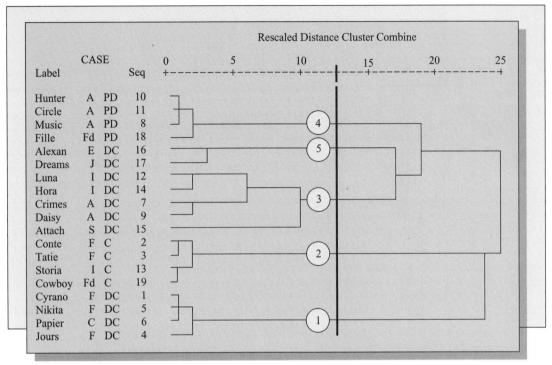

With a third map we can describe respondents' preferences using the object's attributes. This represents their ideal; all objects close to this ideal point are interpreted as preferred by respondents to those that are more distant. Ideal points from many people can be positioned in this preference space to reveal the pattern and size of preference clusters. These can be compared to the subjective space to assess how well the preferences correspond to perception clusters. In this way, cluster analysis and MDS can be combined to map market segments and then examine products designed for those segments.

tional value may be positioned. Objective and subjective attribute assessments may coincide, but often they do not. A comparison of the two allows us to judge how accurately an object is being perceived. Individuals may hold different perceptions of an object simultaneously, and these may be averaged to present a summary measure of perceptions. In addition, a person's perceptions may vary over time and in different circumstances; such measurements are valuable to gauge the impact of various perception-affecting actions, such as advertising programs.

Example   We illustrate multidimensional scaling with a study of 16 companies from *Business Week*'s "Executive Compensation Scoreboard."[11] The companies chosen are from the natural resources (fuel) segment of the scoreboard. *Business Week* reported data from 1989 including executive total compensation (salary, bonus, and long-term compensation for 1987–1989), shareholders' return (the 1989 year-end value based on $100 invested in corporate stock in 1987), and the company's return on common equity (ROE) for the three-year period, 1987–1989. We created a metric algorithm measuring the similarities among the 16 companies based on total executive compensation and the ROE. The matrix of similarities is shown in Table 18–12. Higher numbers reflect the items that are more dissimilar.

If we were using respondents and producing a matrix of similarities among the perception of objects, we might obtain ordinal data. Then the matrix would contain ranks with 1 representing the most similar pair and *n* indicating the most dissimilar pair.

A computer program is used to analyze the data matrix and generate a spatial map.[12] The objective is to find a multidimensional spatial pattern that best reproduces the original order of the data. For example, the most similar pair (companies 3, 6) must be located in this multidimensional space closer together than any other pair. The least similar pair (companies 14, 15) must be the farthest apart. The computer program presents these relationships as a geometric configuration so all distances between pairs of points closely correspond to the original matrix.

Determining how many dimensions to use is complex. The more dimensions of space we use, the more likely the results will closely match the input data. Any set of *n* points can be satisfied by a configuration of $n - 1$ dimensions. Our aim, however, is to secure a structure that provides a good fit for the data and has the fewest dimensions. MDS is best understood using two or at most three dimensions.

Most algorithms include the calculation of a **stress index** (*S*-stress or Kruskal's stress) that ranges from the worst fit (1) to the perfect fit (0). This study, for example, had a stress of .001. Another index, R^2, is interpreted as the proportion of variance of transformed data accounted for by distances in the model. A result close to 1.0 is desirable.

TABLE   18–12   Similarities Matrix of 16 Companies

	1	2	3	4	5	6	7	8	9	10	11	12	13	14	15	16
1	0															
2	3.9	0														
3	4.7	6.7	0													
4	4.4	2.8	4.7	0												
5	14.0	12.4	18.5	15.2	0											
6	4.9	6.9	0.2	4.9	18.7	0										
7	0.8	3.7	4.1	3.7	14.5	4.3	0									
8	6.0	2.1	8.5	4.0	11.8	8.7	5.8	0								
9	4.3	6.9	1.1	5.3	18.3	1.2	3.8	8.9	0							
10	8.2	4.9	8.5	4.1	15.3	8.6	7.6	3.9	9.3	0						
11	8.6	8.7	4.7	5.9	21.1	4.5	7.8	9.7	5.7	7.7	0					
12	2.2	3.7	6.9	5.5	11.8	7.1	2.8	5.5	6.5	8.5	10.5	0				
13	8.4	9.8	3.7	7.2	22.0	3.5	7.8	11.2	4.5	10.0	2.9	10.6	0			
14	12.8	13.4	8.2	10.6	25.8	8.1	12.1	14.4	9.1	12.0	4.7	14.9	4.6	0		
15	19.1	18.2	23.8	21.0	6.2	24.0	19.7	17.8	23.4	21.5	26.9	16.9	27.4	31.5	0	
16	2.6	5.2	2.1	4.0	16.5	2.3	2.0	7.2	1.9	8.0	6.3	4.8	5.8	10.3	21.7	0

SOURCE: Similarities matrix based on data from "Executive Compensation Scoreboard," *International Business Week,* May 7, 1990, pp. 74–75.

FIGURE   18–12   Multidimensional Scaling Plot of Natural Resource Companies' Return on Equity and Executive Compensation

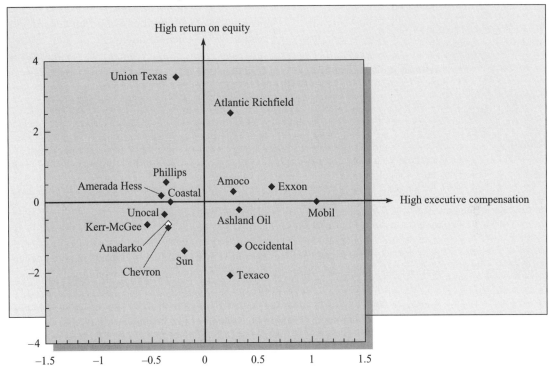

SOURCE: Input data from *International Business Week,* May 7, 1990, pp. 74–75.

In the executive compensation example, we conclude that two dimensions represent an acceptable geometric configuration as shown in Figure 18–12. The distance between Anadarko and Chevron (3, 6) is the shortest, while that between Texaco and Union Texas Petro Holdings (14, 15) is the longest. As with factor analysis, there is no statistical solution to the definition of the dimensions represented by the X and Y axes. The labeling is judgmental and depends on the insight of the researcher, analysis of information collected from respondents, or another basis. Respondents sometimes are asked to state the criteria they used for judging the similarities, or they are asked to judge a specific set of criteria. In this example, the horizontal dimension approximates the total executive compensation while the vertical dimension represents return on equity.

Consistent with raw data, Union Texas and Atlantic Richfield have high ROE but compensate their executives close to the sample mean. In contrast, Exxon and Mobil generated an ROE close to the sample's average while providing higher compensation for their executives. We could hypothesize that the latter two companies may be more difficult to run—are larger and more complex—but that would need to be confirmed with another study. The clustering of companies in attribute space shows that they are perceived to be similar along the dimensions measured.

MDS is most often used to assess perceived similarities and differences among objects. Using MDS allows the researcher to understand constructs that are not directly measurable. The process provides a spatial map that shows similarities in terms of relative distances. It is best understood when limited to two or three dimensions that can be graphically displayed.

Summary

The application of multivariate statistical tools to research problems has multiplied in recent years. Recognition of the complexities of problems coupled with the computer revolution has been largely responsible.

Multivariate techniques are classified into two categories: dependency and interdependency. When the problem reveals the presence of criterion and predictor variables, we have an assumption of dependence. If the variables are interrelated without designating some dependent and others independent, then interdependence of the variables is assumed. The choice of techniques is guided by the number of dependent and independent variables involved and whether they are measured on metric or nonmetric scales.

Multiple regression is an extension of bivariate linear regression. When a researcher is interested in explaining or predicting a metric dependent variable from a set of metric independent variables (although dummy variables may also be used), multiple regression is often selected. Regression results provide information on the statistical significance of the independent variables, the strength of association between one or more of the predictors and the criterion, and a predictive equation for future use.

Discriminant analysis is used to classify people or objects into groups based on several predictor variables. The groups are defined by a categorical variable with two or more values whereas the predictors are metric. The effectiveness of the discriminant equation is based not only on its statistical significance but also on its success in correctly classifying cases to groups.

Multivariate analysis of variance, or MANOVA, is one of the more adaptive techniques for multivariate data. MANOVA assesses the relationship between two or more metric dependent variables and classificatory variables or factors. MANOVA is most commonly used to test differences among samples of people or objects. In contrast to ANOVA, MANOVA handles multiple dependent variables, thereby simultaneously testing all the variables and their interrelationships.

The LISREL technique is extremely useful in explaining causality among constructs that cannot be directly measured. LISREL has two parts, a measurement model and a structural equation model. The measurement model is used to relate the observed, recorded, or measured variables to the latent variables (constructs). The structural equation model specifies causal relationships, causal effects, and unexplained variance among the constructs.

Conjoint analysis is a technique that typically handles nonmetric independent variables. Conjoint analysis allows the researcher to determine the importance of product or service attributes and the levels or features that are most desirable. Respondents provide preference data by ranking or rating cards that describe products. These data became utility weights of product characteristics by means of optimal scaling and loglinear algorithms.

Interdependence techniques are used when there is no assumption of asymmetry, influence, or causality. Principal components analysis extracts uncorrelated factors that account for the largest portion of variance from an initial set of variables. Factor analysis goes one step farther by attempting to reduce the number of variables and discover the underlying constructs that explain the variance. A correlation matrix is used to derive a factor matrix from which the best linear combination of variables may be extracted. In many applications, the factor matrix will be rotated to simplify the factor structure.

Unlike techniques for analyzing the relationships between variables, cluster analysis is a set of techniques for grouping similar objects or people. The cluster procedure starts with an undifferentiated group of people, events, or objects and attempts to reorganize them into homogeneous subgroups.

Multidimensional scaling (MDS) is often used in conjunction with cluster analysis or conjoint analysis. It allows a respondent's perception about a product, service, or other object of attitude to be described in a spatial manner. MDS assists the business researcher to understand difficult-to-measure constructs such as product quality or desirability, which are perceived and cognitively mapped in different ways by individuals. Items judged to be similar will fall close together in multidimensional space and are revealed numerically and geometrically by spatial "maps."

Key Terms

beta weights
centroids
cluster analysis
communalities
conjoint analysis
dependency techniques
discriminant analysis
dummy variables
factor analysis
factors
holdout sample
interdependency techniques
LISREL
loadings

metric/nonmetric measures
multicollinearity
multidimensional scaling
multiple regression
multivariate analysis
multivariate analysis of variance
 (MANOVA)
path analysis
principal components analysis
rotation
standardized coefficients
stress index
utility scores (part-worths)

Cases

Medical Laboratories
Waste Paper
Performance Evaluations
(These are cases found in the optional casebook available with the text.)

Discussion Questions

1. Distinguish among multidimensional scaling, cluster analysis, and factor analysis.

2. Describe the differences between dependency techniques and interdependency techniques. When would you choose a dependency technique?

3. How could discriminant analysis be used to provide insight to MANOVA results where the MANOVA has one independent variable (a factor with two levels)?

4. Describe how you would create a conjoint analysis study of off-road vehicles. Restrict your brands to three, and suggest possible factors and levels. The full-concept description should not exceed 256 decision options.

5. An analyst sought to predict the annual sales for a home-furnishing manufacturer using the following predictor variables:

   X_1 = Marriages during the year
   X_2 = Housing starts during the year
   X_3 = Annual disposable personal income
   X_4 = Time trend (first year = 1, second year = 2, and so forth)

   Using data for 24 years, the analyst calculated the following estimating equation:

   $$Y = 49.85 - .068X_1 + .036X_2 + 1.22X_3 - 19.54X_4$$

   The analyst also calculated an R^2 = .92 and a standard error of estimate of 11.9. Interpret the above equation and statistics.

6. What type of multivariate methods do you recommend in each of the following and why?

   a. You want to develop an estimating equation that will be used to predict which applicants will come to your university as students.

   b. You would like to predict family income using such variables as education and stage in family life cycle.

   c. You wish to estimate standard labor costs for manufacturing a new dress design.

   d. You have been studying a group of successful salespeople. You have given them a number of psychological tests. You want to bring meaning out of these test results.

7. A researcher was given the assignment of predicting which of three actions would be taken by the 280 employees in the Desota plant that was going to be sold to its employees. The alternatives were to:

    a. Take severance pay and leave the company

    b. Stay with the new company and give up severance pay

    c. Take a transfer to the plant in Chicago

    The researcher gathered data on employee opinions, inspected personal files, and the like, and then did a discriminant analysis. Later, when the results were in, she found the results listed below. How successful was the researcher's analysis?

	Predicted Decision		
Actual Decision	*A*	*B*	*C*
A	80	5	12
B	14	60	14
C	10	15	70

8. Referring to the example in this chapter concerning student grades, answer the following questions:

    a. How are the factor loadings interpreted?

    b. What is the meaning of a communality of .11 found in Table 18–9?

    c. Give another interpretation of the three factors extracted in Table 18–10.

9. Sales of a product are influenced by the salesperson's level of education and gender, as well as consumer income, ethnicity, and wealth.

    a. Formulate this statement as a multiple regression model (form only, without parameter estimation).

    b. Specify dummy variables.

    c. If the effects of consumer income and wealth are not additive alone, and an interaction is expected, specify a new variable to test for the interaction.

10. What multivariate technique would you use to analyze each of these problems? Explain your choice.

    a. Employee job satisfaction (high, normal, low) and employee success (0–2 promotions, 3–5 promotions, 5+ promotions) are to be studied in three different departments of a company.

    b. Consumers making a brand choice decision between three brands of coffee are influenced by their own income levels and the extent of advertising of the brands.

    c. Consumer choice of color in fabrics is largely dependent on ethnicity, income levels, and the temperature of the geographical area. There is detailed areawide demographic data on income levels, ethnicity, and population, as well as the weather bureau's historical data on temperature. How would you identify geographical areas for selling dark colored fabric? You have sample data for 200 randomly selected consumers: their fabric color choice, income, ethnicity, and the average temperature of the area where they live.

Reference Notes

1. Jagdish N. Sheth, ed., *Multivariate Methods for Market and Survey Research* (Chicago: American Marketing Association, 1977), p. 3.
2. William Schneider, "Opinion Outlook," *National Journal* (July 1985).
3. Benson Shapiro, "Price Reliance: Existence and Sources," *Journal of Marketing Research* (August 1973), pp. 286–89.
4. For a discussion of path analysis, see Elazar J. Pedhazur, *Regression in Behavioral Research: Explanation and Prediction,* 2nd ed. (New York: Holt, Rinehart & Winston, 1982), chap. 15.
5. Fred Kerlinger, *Foundations of Behavioral Research,* 3rd ed. (New York: Holt, Rinehart & Winston, 1986), p. 562.
6. Joseph F. Hair, Jr., Rolph E. Anderson, Ronald L. Tatham, and William C. Black, *Multivariate Data Analysis with Readings* (New York: Macmillan, 1992), pp. 153–81.
7. This section is based on the SPSS procedure, MANOVA, described in Marija J. Norusis/SPSS, Inc., *SPSS Advanced Statistics Users Guide* (Chicago: SPSS, Inc., 1990), pp. 71–104.
8. This section is based on Karl G. Jörgeskog, Dag Sorbom/SPSS, Inc., *LISREL 7: A Guide to the Program and Applications,* 2nd ed. (Chicago: SPSS, Inc., 1989).
9. SPSS, Inc., *SPSS Categories* (Chicago: SPSS, Inc., 1990).
10. Product specifications adapted from Lewis Rothlein, "A Guide to Sun Protection Essentials," *Wind Rider* (June 1990), pp. 95–103.
11. "Executive Compensation Scoreboard," *International Business Week,* May 7, 1990, pp. 74–75.
12. See the ALSCAL procedure in Marija J. Norusis/SPSS, Inc., *SPSS Base System User's Guide* (Chicago: SPSS, Inc., 1990), pp. 397-416.

Suggested Readings

1. Hair, Joseph F., Jr., Rolph E. Anderson, Ronald L. Tatham, and William C. Black. *Multivariate Data Analysis with Readings,* 4th ed. Englewood Cliffs, NJ: Prentice-Hall, 1995. A very readable book covering most multivariate statistics.
2. Myers, R. *Classical and Modern Regression with Applications,* 2nd ed. Boston: Duxbury Press, 1990. Excellent coverage of regression analysis.
3. Norusis, Marija J.,SPSS, Inc. *SPSS for Windows Base Systems User's Guide, Release 6.0* Chicago: SPSS, Inc., 1993; and Norusis, Marija J.,SPSS, Inc. *SPSS Advanced Statistics User's Guide.* Chicago: SPSS, Inc., 1990. These two texts link computer program usage, sample problems, and coverage of most multivariate techniques in an understandable style.

4. Pedhazur, Elazar J., and L. Pedhazur-Schmelkin. *Measurement, Design, and Analysis.* Hillsdale, NJ: Lawrence Erlbaum Associates, 1991. An excellent introduction to multivariate with LISREL and EQS examples.

5. Sage Series in Quantitative Applications in the Social Sciences. Thousand Oaks, CA: Sage Publishing. This monograph series includes papers on most multivariate methods.

6. Stevens, James P. *Applied Multivariate Statistics for the Social Sciences,* 3rd ed. Hillsdale, NJ: Lawrence Erlbaum Associates, 1996. Comprehensive coverage with excellent computer examples.

CHAPTER

19

PRESENTING RESULTS: WRITTEN AND ORAL REPORTS

CHAPTER NAVIGATION

BRINGING
RESEARCH TO LIFE

"Has it occurred to you that your draft of the MindWriter report has not been touched in the last two days? The stack of marked-up pages is right there on your desk, and you have been working all around it."

Jason frowned and momentarily flicked his eyes to the papers and immediately glanced away at his shoe tops.

But Myra plunged ahead with her complaint. "It's no big deal, you know. You promised to chop out three pages of methodology that nobody will care about but your fellow statistics jocks. . . ." Jason shot her an aggrieved look. ". . . And to remove your recommendations and provide them in a separate, informal letter so that Gracie or I can distribute them under our name and claim credit for your 'brilliance.'"

"I think I have writer's block."

"No. Writer's block is when you can't write. You have already written. You can't unwrite; that's the problem. You have unwriter's block."

"Well, it isn't funny, Myra. That report might as well be a 15,000-volt power line. I know that if I touch it, I'll never be able to let go."

"OK, Jason. You are right. It isn't funny to have an emotional block against writing . . . or unwriting, but as your client, you do not want to see me fretting over your delay."

"It's not an emotional problem, Myra."

"Well, of course it is. It always is. Your brain has not deteriorated, has it? In the last week?

"Some people do great research and then panic when they have to decide what goes in the report and what doesn't. Or they can't take all the great ideas running around in their heads and express their abstractions in words. Or they don't believe they are smart enough to communicate with their clients, or vice versa. So they freeze up. There is some sort of emotional problem around this Mind-Writer report, Jason, and you have got to face it."

"But I love the MindWriter project."

"Ah, *there's* the problem," she said.

"What? That I love it? Loving it is a problem?"

"Jason, I have heard you say that you hated projects for other clients, and I have heard you say that you *liked* projects. But this is the first time I have heard you say you *loved* a project."

"I still don't see the problem."

"Then let me tell you a story. My son-in-law has been assigned to a submarine tender in Iceland. My daughter wants to bring the kids and move in with me. I think I am going to have to tell her no, and the decision is killing me."

"The decision."

"She is my only child. After Harry was gone I raised her alone. I would have been a network anchor, Jason, if I hadn't made it my number one priority to raise Janice. I had to be her father and mother. The week she married I stayed awake for three days and nights, just crying. Not because she married a bad person, but because I had to let go. There comes a time when, after you have nurtured something, you have to let go. Then it isn't yours. It is someone else's, or it is its own thing, but it is not yours."

"When something is not yours anymore . . . when someone is their own person . . . or some work is passed to someone else . . . you don't own it. You do not get to go back and change it. It is out of your hands."

She paused. "Take Janice. She is a delight. I love to have her and the kids for a visit. But she can't come back. I have my life. She has hers. I don't own her anymore. She is not mine the way she was, and it is very important that I accept that unconditionally."

"I think I know what you mean. This MindWriter project was my baby—well, yours and mine. If I chop five pages out of the report, it is finished. Then it belongs to you—and I guess, Gracie. I don't own it anymore. I can't fix it. I can't change anything. I can't have second thoughts."

"Fix it, then. Send us an invoice. Write a proposal for follow-up work. Do *something,* Jason. Find another project you love just as much. Finish it. Let go and move on."

THE WRITTEN RESEARCH REPORT

It may seem unscientific and even unfair, but a poor final report or presentation can destroy a study. Research technicians may appreciate the brilliance of badly reported content, but most readers will be influenced by the quality of the reporting. This fact should prompt researchers to make special efforts to communicate clearly and fully.

The research report contains findings, analysis of findings, interpretations, conclusions, and sometimes recommendations. The researcher is the expert on the topic and knows the specifics in a way no one else can. Because a research report is an authoritative one-way communication, it imposes a special obligation for maintaining objectivity. Even if your findings seem to point to an action, you should demonstrate restraint and caution when proposing that course.

Reports may be defined by their degree of formality and design. The formal report follows a well-delineated and relatively long format. This contrasts to the informal or short report.

Short Reports

Short reports are appropriate when the problem is well defined, is of limited scope, and has a simple and straightforward methodology. Most informational, progress, and interim reports are of this kind: a report of cost-of-living changes for upcoming labor negotiations or an exploration of filing "dumping" charges against a foreign competitor.

Short reports are about five pages. At the beginning, there should be a brief statement about the authorization for the study, the problem examined, and its breadth and depth. Next come the conclusions and recommendations, followed by the findings that support them. Section headings should be used.

A letter of transmittal is a vehicle to convey short reports. A five-page report may be produced to track sales on a quarterly basis. The report should be direct, make ample use of graphics to show trends, and refer the reader to the research department for further information. Detailed information on the research method would be omitted, although an overview could appear in an appendix. The purpose of this type of report is to distribute information quickly in an easy-to-use format. Short reports are also produced for clients with small, relatively inexpensive research projects.

The letter is a form of a short report. Its tone should be informal. The format follows that of any good business letter and should not exceed a few pages. A letter report is often written in personal style (*we, you*), although this depends on the situation.

Memorandum reports are another variety and follow the *To, From, Subject* format.

These suggestions may be helpful for writing short reports:

- Tell the reader why you are writing (it may be in response to a request).
- If the memo is in response to a request for information, remind the reader of the exact point raised, answer it, and follow with any necessary details.

- Write in an expository style with brevity and directness.
- If time permits, write the report today and leave it for review tomorrow before sending it.
- Attach detailed materials as appendices when needed.

Long Reports

Long reports are of two types, the technical or base report and the management report. The choice depends on the audience and the researcher's objectives.

Many projects will require both types of reports: a **technical report,** written for an audience of researchers, and a **management report,** written for the nontechnically oriented manager or client. While some researchers try to write a single report that satisfies both needs, this complicates the task and is seldom satisfactory. The two types of audiences have different technical training, interests, and goals.

The Technical Report   This report should include full documentation and detail. It will normally survive all working papers and original data files and so will become the major source document. It is the report that other researchers will want to see because it has the full story of what was done and how it was done.

While completeness is a goal, you must guard against including nonessential material. A good guide is that sufficient procedural information should be included to enable others to replicate the study. This includes sources of data, research procedures, sampling design, data-gathering instruments, index construction, and data analysis methods. Most information should be attached in an appendix.

A technical report should also include a full presentation and analysis of significant data. Conclusions and recommendations should be clearly related to specific findings. Technical jargon should be minimized but defined when used. There can be brief references to other research, theories, and techniques. While you expect the reader to be familiar with these references, it is useful to include some short explanations, perhaps as footnotes or endnotes.

The Management Report   Sometimes the client has no research background and is interested in results rather than in methodology. The major communication medium in this case is the management report. It is still helpful to have a technical report if the client later wishes to have a technical appraisal of the study.

Because the management report is designed for a nontechnical audience, the researcher faces some special problems. Readers are less concerned with methodological details but more interested in learning quickly the major findings and conclusions. They want help in making decisions. Often the report is developed for a single person and needs to be written with that person's characteristics and needs in mind.

The style of the report should encourage rapid reading, quick comprehension of major findings, and prompt understanding of the implication and conclusions. The report tone is journalistic and must be accurate. Headlines and underlining for emphasis are helpful; pictures and graphs often replace tables. Sentences and paragraphs should be short and direct. Consider liberal use of white space and wide margins. It may be desirable to put a single finding on each page. It also helps to have a theme running through the report and even graphic or animated characters designed to vary the presentation.

RESEARCH REPORT COMPONENTS

Research reports, long and short, have a set of identifiable components. Usually headings and subheadings divide the sections. Each report is individual; sections may be dropped or added, condensed or expanded to meet the needs of the audience. Figure 19–1 lists four types of reports, the sections that are typically included, and the general order of presentation. Each of these formats can be modified to meet the needs of the audience.

The technical report follows the flow of the research. The prefatory materials, such as a letter of authorization and a table of contents, are first. An introduction cov-

FIGURE   19–1   Research Report Sections and Their Order of Inclusion

	Short Report		Long Report	
Report Modules	*Memo or Letter*	*Short Technical*	*Management*	*Technical*
Prefatory information		1	1	1
Letter of transmittal		✔	✔	✔
Title page		✔	✔	✔
Authorization statement		✔	✔	✔
Executive summary		✔	✔	✔
Table of contents			✔	✔
Introduction	1	2	2	2
Problem statement	✔	✔	✔	✔
Research objectives	✔	✔	✔	✔
Background	✔	✔	✔	✔
Methodology		✔ (briefly)	✔ (briefly)	3
Sampling design				✔
Research design				✔
Data collection				✔
Data analysis				✔
Limitations		✔	✔	✔
Findings		3	4	4
Conclusions	2	4	3	5
Summary and conclusion	✔	✔	✔	✔
Recommendations	✔	✔	✔	✔
Appendices		5	5	6
Bibliography				7

ers the purpose of the study and is followed by a section on methodology. The findings are presented next, including tables and other graphics. The conclusions section includes recommendations. Finally, the appendices contain technical information, instruments, glossaries, and references.

In contrast to the technical report, the management report is for the nontechnical client. The reader has little time to absorb details and needs a prompt exposure to the most critical findings; thus the report's sections are in an inverted order. After the prefatory and introductory sections, the conclusions with accompanying recommendations are presented. Individual findings are presented next, supporting the conclusions already made. The appendices present any required methodological details. The order of the management report allows clients to grasp the conclusions and recommendations quickly, without much reading. Then, if they wish to go further, they may read on into the findings. The management report should make liberal use of visual displays.

The short technical report covers the same items as the long technical report but in an abbreviated form. The methodology is included as part of the introduction and takes no more than a few paragraphs. Most of the emphasis is placed on the findings and conclusions. A memo or letter format covers only the minimum: what the problem is and what the research conclusions are.

Prefatory Items

Prefatory materials do not have direct bearing on the research itself. Instead, they assist the reader in using the research report.

Letter of Transmittal   When the relationship between the researcher and the client is formal, a **letter of transmittal** should be included. This is appropriate when a report is for a specific client (e.g., the company president) and when it is generated for an outside organization. The letter should refer to the authorization for the project and any specific instructions or limitations placed on the study. It should also state the purpose and the scope of the study. For many internal projects, it is not necessary to include a letter of transmittal.

Title Page   The title page should include four items: the title of the report, the date, and for whom and by whom it was prepared. The title should be brief but include the following three elements: (1) the variables included in the study, (2) the type of relationship among the variables, and (3) the population to which the results may be applied.[1] Redundancies such as "A Report of" and " A Discussion of" add length to the title but little else. Single-word titles are also of little value. Here are three acceptable ways to word report titles:

Descriptive study:	The Five-Year Demand Outlook for Plastic Pipe in the United States
Correlation study:	The Relationship Between the Value of the Dollar in World Markets and Relative National Inflation Rates
Causal study:	The Effect of Various Motivation Methods on Worker Attitudes among Textile Workers

Authorization Letter   When the report is sent to a public organization, it is common to include a letter of authorization showing the authority for undertaking the research. This is especially true for reports to federal and state governments and nonprofit organizations. The letter not only shows who sponsored the research but also delineates the original request.

Executive Summary   An **executive summary** can serve two purposes. It may be a report in miniature—covering all the aspects in the body of the report, but in abbreviated form. Or it may be a concise summary of the major findings and conclusions, including recommendations. Two pages are generally sufficient for executive summaries. Write this section after the rest of the report is finished. It should not include new information but may require graphics to present a particular conclusion. Expect the summary to contain a high density of significant terms since it is repeating the highlights of the report.

Table of Contents   As a rough guide, any report of several sections that totals more than 6 to 10 pages should have a table of contents. If there are many tables, charts, or other exhibits, they should also be listed after the table of contents in a separate table of illustrations.

Introduction

The introduction prepares the reader for the report by describing the parts of the project: the problem statement, research objectives, and background material.[2] In most projects, the introduction can be taken from the research proposal with minor editing.

Problem Statement   The problem statement contains the need for the research project. The problem is usually represented by a management question. It is followed by a more detailed set of objectives.

Research Objectives   The research objectives address the purpose of the project. These may be research question(s) and associated investigative questions. In correlational or causal studies, the hypothesis statements are included. As we discussed in Chapter 2, hypotheses are declarative statements describing the relationship between two or more variables. They state clearly the variables of concern, the relationships among them, and the target group being studied. Operational definitions of critical variables should be included.

Background   Background material may be of two types. It may be the preliminary results of exploration from an experience survey, focus group, or another source. Alternatively, it could be secondary data from the literature review. A traditional organizational scheme is to think of the concentric circles of a target. Starting with the outside ring, the writer works toward the center. The bull's-eye contains the material directly related to the problem. Sources and means for securing this information are presented in Chapter 10 and in Appendix A.

Previous research, theory, or situations that led to the management question are also discussed in this section. The literature should be organized, integrated, and presented in a way that connects it logically to the problem. The background includes definitions, qualifications, and assumptions. It gives the reader the information needed to understand the remainder of the research report.[3]

Background material may be placed before the problem statement or after the research objectives. If it is composed primarily of literature review and related research, it should follow the objectives. If it contains information pertinent to the management problem or the situation that led to the study, it can be placed before the problem statement (where it is found in many applied studies).

Methodology

In short reports and management reports, the methodology should not have a separate section; it should be mentioned in the introduction, and details should be placed in an appendix. However, for a technical report, the methodology is an important section, containing at least five parts.

Sampling Design   The researcher explicitly defines the target population being studied and the sampling methods used. For example, was this a probability or nonprobability sample? If probability, was it simple random or complex random? How were the elements selected? How was the size determined? How much confidence do we have, and how much error was allowed?

Explanations of the sampling methods, uniqueness of the chosen parameters, or other points that need explanation should be covered with brevity. Calculations should be placed in an appendix instead of in the body of the report.

Research Design   The coverage of the design must be adapted to the purpose. In an experimental study, the materials, tests, equipment, control conditions, and other devices should be described. In descriptive or ex post facto designs, it may be sufficient to cover the rationale for using one design instead of competing alternatives. Even with a sophisticated design, the strengths and weaknesses should be identified and the instrumentation and materials discussed. Copies of materials are placed in an appendix.

Data Collection   This part of the report describes the specifics of gathering the data. Its contents depend on the selected design. Survey work generally uses a team with field and central supervision. How many were involved? What was their training? How were they managed? When were the data collected? How much time did it take? What were the conditions in the field? How were irregularities handled? In an experiment, we would want to know about subject assignment to groups, the use of standardized procedures and protocols, the administration of tests or observational forms, manipulation of the variables, and so forth.

Typically, you would include a discussion on the relevance of secondary data that guided these decisions. Again, detailed materials such as field instructions should be included in an appendix.

Data Analysis   This section summarizes the methods used to analyze the data. Describe data handling, preliminary analysis, statistical tests, computer programs, and other technical information. The rationale for the choice of analysis approaches should be clear. A brief commentary on assumptions and appropriateness of use should be presented.

Limitations   This topic is often handled with ambivalence. Some people wish to ignore the matter, feeling that mentioning limitations detracts from the impact of the study. This attitude is unprofessional and possibly unethical. Others seem to adopt a masochistic approach of detailing everything. The section should be a thoughtful presentation of significant methodology or implementation problems. An even-handed approach is one of the hallmarks of an honest and competent investigator. All research studies have their limitations, and the sincere investigator recognizes that readers need aid in judging the study's validity.

Findings

This is generally the longest section of the report. The objective is to explain the data rather than draw interpretations or conclusions. When quantitative data can be presented, this should be done as simply as possible with charts, graphics, and tables.

The data need not include everything you have collected. The criterion for inclusion is, "Is this material important to the reader's understanding of the problem and the findings?" However, make sure to show findings unfavorable to your hypotheses and those that support them.

It is useful to present findings in numbered paragraphs or to present one finding per page with the quantitative data supporting the findings presented in a small table or chart on the same page (see Figure 19–2). While this arrangement adds to the bulk of the report, it is convenient for the reader.

Conclusions

Summary and Conclusions   The summary is a brief statement of the essential findings. Sectional summaries may be used if there are many specific findings. These may be combined into an overall summary. In simple descriptive research, a summary may complete the report, because conclusions and recommendations may not be required.

Findings state facts; conclusions represent inferences drawn from the findings. A writer is sometimes reluctant to make conclusions and leaves the task to the reader. Avoid this temptation when possible. As the researcher, you are the one best informed on the factors that critically influence the findings and conclusions.

Conclusions may be presented in a tabular form for easy reading and reference. Summary findings may be subordinated under the related conclusion statement. These may be numbered to refer the reader to pages or tables in the findings sections.

Recommendations   There are usually a few ideas about corrective actions. In academic research, the recommendations are often further study suggestions that broaden or test understanding of the subject area. In applied research the recommendations

FIGURE   19–2   Example of a Findings Page in a Commercial Bank Market Study

Findings: 1. In this city, *commercial banks are not the preferred savings medium*. Banks are in a weak
                third place behind money market accounts.
            2. Customers of the Central City Bank have a *somewhat more favorable attitude toward bank
               savings* and less of a preference for government bonds.

Question: Suppose that you have just received an extra $1,000 and have decided to save it. Which of the
            savings methods listed would be your preferred way to save it?

Savings Method	*Total Replies*	*Central City Customers*	*Other Bank Customers*
Government bonds	24%	20%	29%
Savings and loan	43	45	42
Bank	13	18	8
Credit union	9	7	11
Stock	7	8	5
Other	4	2	5
Total	100%	100%	100%
	$n = 216$	105	111

will usually be for managerial action rather than research action. The writer may
offer several alternatives with justifications.

Appendices

The appendices are the place for complex tables, statistical tests, supporting documents, copies of forms and questionnaires, detailed descriptions of the methodology,
instructions to field workers, and other evidence important for later support. The
reader who wishes to learn about the technical aspects of the study and to look at statistical breakdowns will want a complete appendix.

Bibliography

The use of secondary data requires a bibliography. Proper citation, style, and formats
are unique to the purpose of the report. The instructor, program, institution, or client
often specifies style requirements. The uniqueness of varying requirements makes
detailed examples in this chapter impractical although the endnotes and references in
this book provide an example. As in Chapter 4, on the research proposal, we recommend the *Publication Manual of the American Psychological Association;* Kate L.
Turabian, *A Manual for Writers of Term Papers, Theses, and Dissertations;* and
Joseph Gibaldi, *MLA Handbook for Writers of Research Papers.*

WRITING THE REPORT

Students often give inadequate attention to reporting their findings and conclusions.
This is unfortunate. A well-presented study will often impress the reader more than
a study with greater scientific quality but a weaker presentation. Report-writing
skills are especially valuable to the junior executive or management trainee who as-
pires to rise in an organization. A well-written study frequently enhances career
prospects.

**Prewriting
Concerns**

Before writing, one should ask again, "What is the purpose of this report?" Writing a reply to this question is one way to crystallize the problem.

The second prewriting question is, "Who will read the report?" Thought should be given to the needs, temperament, and biases of the audience. You should not distort facts to meet these needs and biases but should consider them while developing the presentation. Knowing who reads the report may suggest its appropriate length. Generally, the higher the report goes in an organization, the shorter it should be.

Another consideration is technical background—the gap in subject knowledge between the reader and the writer. The greater the gap, the more difficult it is to convey the full findings meaningfully and concisely.

The third prewriting question is, "What are the circumstances and limitations under which you are writing?" Is the nature of the subject highly technical? Do you need statistics? Charts? What is the importance of the topic? A crucial subject justifies more effort than a minor one. What should be the scope of the report? How much time is available? Deadlines often impose limitations on the report.

Finally, "How will the report be used?" Try to visualize the reader using the report. How can the information be made more convenient? How much effort must be given to getting the attention and interest of the reader? Will the report be read by more than one person? If so, how many copies should be made? What will be the distribution of the report?

The Outline   Once the researcher has made the first analysis of the data, drawn tentative conclusions, and completed statistical significance tests, it is time to develop an outline. A useful system employs the following organization structure:

    I. *Major Topic Heading*
        A. Major subtopic heading
            1. Subtopic
                a. Minor subtopic
                    (1) Further detail
                       (a) Even further detail

Software for developing outlines and visually connecting ideas simplifies this once-onerous task. Two styles of outlining are widely used—the **topic outline** and the **sentence outline.** In the topic outline, a key word or two is used. The assumption is that the writer knows its significance and will later remember the nature of the argument represented by that word or phrase or, alternatively, the outliner knows that a point should be made but is not yet sure how to make it.

The sentence outline expresses the essential thoughts associated with the specific topic. This approach leaves less development work for later writing, other than elaboration and explanation to improve readability. It has the obvious advantages of pushing the writer to make decisions on what to include and how to say it. It is probably the best outlining style for the inexperienced researcher because it divides the writing job into its two major components—what to say and how to say it.

Here is an example of the type of detail found with each of these outlining formats:

Topic Outline	Sentence Outline

I. Demand
  A. How measured
    1. Voluntary error
    2. Shipping error
      a. Monthly variance
	I. Demand for refrigerators
	  A. Measured in terms of factory shipments as reported to the U.S. Department of Commerce
	    1. Error is introduced into year-to-year comparisons because reporting is voluntary
	    2. A second factor is variations from month to month because of shipping and invoicing patterns
	      a. Variations up to 30 percent this year depending on whether shipments were measured by actual shipment date or invoice date

The Bibliography   Long reports, particularly technical ones, require a bibliography. A bibliography documents the sources used by the writer. Although bibliographies may contain work used as background or for further study, it is preferable to include only sources used for preparing the report.

Bibliographic retrieval software allows researchers to locate and save references from online services and translate them into database records. Entries can be further searched, sorted, indexed, and formatted into bibliographies of any style. Many retrieval programs are network compatible and connect to popular word processors. Chapter 10 also mentions a recording system for converting source notes to footnotes and bibliographies.

Style manuals such as the *Publication Manual of the American Psychological Association, MLA Handbook for Writers of Research Papers,* and Turabian's *A Manual for Writers* provide guidelines on form, section and alphabetical arrangement, and annotation. Projects using many electronic sources may benefit from the comparison of APA and MLA citations in Table 19–1.

Writing the Draft   Once the outline is complete, decisions can be made on the placement of graphics, tables, and charts. Each should be matched to a particular section in the outline. It is helpful to make these decisions before your first draft. While graphics might be added later or tables changed into charts, it is helpful to make a first approximation of the graphics before beginning to write. Choices for reporting statistics will be reviewed later in this chapter.

Each writer uses different mechanisms for getting thoughts into written form. Some will write in longhand, relying on someone else to transcribe their prose into typewritten or word-processed format. Others are happiest in front of a word processor, able to add, delete, and move sections at will. Whichever works for you is the best approach to use.

TABLE   19–1   Citing Electronic Sources

Type	APA	MLA
Full-text sources from library resources (online and CD-ROM)	Last name of author, first initial. (Year, month day). Title. *Journal* [Type of medium], volume (issue), paging if given or other indicator of length. Available: supplier/database name and number/identifier number, item, or accession number [access date].	Last name of author, first initial. (Year, month day). "Title." Journal [Type of medium], volume (issue) paging if given or other indicator of length. Available: supplier/database name and number/identifier number, item or accession number [access date].* *Access date not needed if CD-ROM.
	Crow, P. (1994). GATT shows progress in Congress. *The Oil and Gas Journal* [Online], 92(49), 32 (1p.). Available: Information Access/Expanded Academic Index ASAP/A15955498 [1996, March 13].	Crow, P. (1994). "GATT shows progress in Congress." *The Oil and Gas Journal* [Online]. 92.49 (1994): 32–33. Online. Available: Information Access Company. *Expanded Academic Index ASAP.* 13 Mar. 1996.
WWW sites: individual works with print equivalent	Last name of author/editor, first initial. (Year, month day). *Title* (Edition). [Type of medium]. Producer. Available: address or source/path/file [access date].	Last name of author/editor, first name. *Title of print version of work.* Edition statement. Place of publication: publisher, date. *Title of electronic work.* Medium[Online]. Information supplier. Available protocol: http://www.address.goes.here. Access date [dy mo yr].
	Bartlett, J. (1995, March). *Familiar quotations: Passages, phrases & proverbs traced to their sources* (9th ed.).[Online]. Columbia University. Available: http//www.columbia.edu/acis/bartleby/bartlett/ [1996, March 19].	Bartlett, J. *Familiar Quotations: Passages, Phrases & Proverbs Traced to Their Sources in Ancient & Modern Literature,* 9th ed. Boston: Little, Brown & Co., 1901. *Familiar Quotations: Passages, Phrases & Proverbs Traced to their Sources.* Online. Columbia University. Available HTTP: http://www.columbia.edu/acis/bartleby/bartlett/ 19 Mar. 1996.
WWW sites: parts of works	Last name of author/editor, first initial. (Year, month day). Title of article or document. In Title of Source (edition), [Online]. Paging or indicator of length. Available: address or source/path/file [access date].	Last name of author, first name. "Title of article or document." Title of journal, newsletter, or conference. Volume. Issue number (year) or date of publication: number of pages or pars. Medium [online]. Available protocol: http://www.address.goes.here. Access date [dy mo yr].
	Steinfield, C., Kraut, R., & Plummer, A. (1995). The impact of interorganizational networks on buyer-seller relationships. *Journal of Computer-Mediated Communication* [Online], 1(3) 56 paragraphs. Available: http://shum.juji.ac.il/jcmc/vol1/issue3/steinfld.html [1996, April 22].	Steinfield, C., Kraut, R., & Plummer, A. "The impact of interorganizational networks on buyer-seller relationships." *Journal of Computer-Mediated Communication* 1.3 (1995): 56 pars. Online. Available HTTP: http://shum.juji.ac.il/jcmc/vol1/issue3/steinfld.html. 22 Apr. 1996.
WWW sites: e-mail, listserv, and discussion list messages	Last name of author, first initial (if known). (Year, month day). Subject of message. Discussion List [Online]. Available E-mail: LISTSERV@e-mail address [Access date].	Last name of author, first name (if known). "Subject line from posting." Date. Medium [online]. Discussion List. Available E-mail: LISTSERV@e-mail address. Access date.
	Wagner, K. (1996, February 6). Re: Citing/evaluating web resources. NETLIBS [Online]. Available E-mail netlibs@qut.edu.au [1996, February 7].	Wagner, Kurt W. "Re: Citing/evaluating web resources." Online. NETLIBS. Available E-mail: netlibs@qut.edu.au 7 Feb. 1996.

TABLE   19–1   (continued)

Type	APA	MLA
WWW sites: home page	Last name of author/editor, first initial (if known). (Last update or copyright date). Home Page Title [Home page of . . .]. Available: http//www.address.goes.here [Access date].	
	House, P. (1997, March 26—last update). The Smithsonian: America's treasure house for learning [Home Page of the Smithsonian Institution], [Online].Available: http://www.si.edu/newstart.htm [1997, March 27].	

SOURCE: Adapted from *APA Guides for Citing Electronic Sources* and *Guidelines for Citing Electronic Sources—MLA*, Cedarville College Centennial Library, Cedarville, OH 45314.

Computer software packages check for spelling errors and provide a thesaurus for looking up alternative ways of expressing a thought. Writers with CD-ROM equipment can call up the 20-volume *Oxford English Dictionary,* believed to be the greatest dictionary in any language. Common word confusion (*there* for *their, to* for *too,* or *effect* for *affect*) will not be found by standard spelling checkers. Advanced programs will scrutinize your report for grammar, punctuation, capitalization, doubled words, transposed letters, homonyms, style problems, and readability level. The style checker will reveal misused words and indicate awkward phrasing. Figure 19–3 shows sample output from a commercial package used on one of this text's vignettes. The program shown writes comments to a text file, prepares a backup copy of the original, and generates a statistics report. The statistics summarize the program's evaluation of readability, grade level, and sentence structure. Comparisons to "reference" documents, or documents that you submit for comparisons, may be made. The software cannot guarantee an error-free report but will greatly reduce your time in proofreading and enhance the style of the completed product.[4]

Readability   Sensitive writers consider the reading ability of their audience to achieve high readership. You can obtain high readership more easily if the topic interests the readers and is in their field of expertise. In addition, you can show the usefulness of the report by pointing out how it will help the readers. Finally, you can write at a level that is appropriate to the readers' reading abilities. To test writing for difficulty level, there are standard **readability indices.** The Flesch Reading Ease Score gives a score between 0 and 100. The lower the score, the harder the material is to read. The Flesch Kincaid Grade Level and Gunning's Fog Index both provide a score that corresponds with the grade level needed to easily read and understand the document. Although it is possible to calculate these indices by hand, some software packages will do it automatically. The most sophisticated packages allow you to specify the preferred reading level. Words that are above that level are highlighted to allow you to choose an alternative.

FIGURE   19–3   Grammar and Style Proofreader Results

Statistics

Statistics for: Chapter 3 Vignette   Problems marked/detected: 8/8

Readability Statistics

Flesch Reading Ease: 66   Flesch-Kincaid Grade Level: 8

Gunning's Fog Index: 11

Paragraph Statistics

Number of paragraphs: 25   Average length: 2.2 sentences

Sentence Statistics

Number of sentences: 55	Passive voice:	4
Average length:	13.8 words	Short (< 12 words) :	39
End with "?" :	2	Long (> 28 words) :	7
End with "!" :	0		

Word Statistics

Number of words: 759   Average length: 4.58 letters

Document Summary for: Chapter 3 Vignette   Problems detected: 8

	Interpretation
Readability Statistics	
Grade level:	Preferred level for most readers.
8 (Flesch-Kincaid)	
Reading ease score:	This represents 6 to 10 years
66 (Flesch)	of schooling.
Passive voice:	Writing may be difficult to read or
331	ambiguous for this writing style.
Average sentence length:	Most readers could easily understand
13.8 words	sentences of this length.
Average word length:	Vocabulary used in this document
1.50 syl.	is understandable for most readers.
Average paragraph length:	Most readers could easily follow
2.2 sentences	paragraphs of this length.

Comparisons

Readability Comparison Chart

Flesch Reading Ease Score

Chapter 3 Vignette	66
Gettysburg Address	64
Hemingway short story	86
Life insurance policy	45

Flesch-Kincaid Grade Level

Chapter 3 Vignette	8
Gettysburg Address	11
Hemingway short story	5
Life insurance policy	13

Sentence Statistics Comparison Chart

Average Sentence per Paragraph

Chapter 3 Vignette	2.2
Gettysburg Address	4.1
Hemingway short story	2.8
Life insurance policy	3.2

Average Words per Sentence

Chapter 3 Vignette	13.8
Gettysburg Address	26.8
Hemingway short story	13.5
Life insurance policy	23.9

Word Statistics Comparison Chart

Average Letters per Word

Chapter 3 Vignette	4.5
Gettysburg Address	4.2
Hemingway short story	4.0
Life insurance policy	4.7

Advocates of readability measurement do not claim that all written material should be at the simplest level possible. They argue only that the level should be appropriate for the audience. They point out that comic books score about 6 on the Gunning scale (that is, a person with a sixth-grade education should be able to read that material). *Time* usually scores about 10, while *The Atlantic* is reported to have a score of 11 or 12. Material that scores much above 12 becomes difficult for the public to read comfortably. Such measures obviously give only a rough idea of the true readability of a report. Good writing calls for a variety of other skills to enhance reading comprehension.

Comprehensibility   Good writing varies with the writing objective. Research writing is designed to convey information of a precise nature. Avoid ambiguity, multiple meanings, and allusions. Take care to choose the right words—words that convey thoughts accurately, clearly, and efficiently. When concepts and constructs are used, they must be defined, either operationally or descriptively.

Words and sentences should be carefully organized and edited. Misplaced modifiers run rampant in carelessly written reports. Subordinate ideas mixed with major ideas make the report confusing to readers, forcing them to sort out what is important and what is secondary when this should have been done for them.

Finally, there is the matter of pace. **Pace** is defined as

> The rate at which the printed page presents information to the reader. . . . The proper pace in technical writing is one that enables the reader to keep his mind working just a fraction of a second behind his eye as he reads along. It logically would be slow when the information is complex or difficult to understand; fast when the information is straightforward and familiar. If the reader's mind lags behind his eye, the pace is too rapid; if his mind wanders ahead of his eye (or wants to) the pace is too slow.[5]

If the text is overcrowded with concepts, there is too much information per sentence. By contrast, sparse writing has too few significant ideas per sentence. Writers use a variety of methods to adjust the pace of their writing:

- Use ample white space and wide margins to create a positive psychological effect on the reader.
- Break large units of text into smaller units with headings to show organization of the topics.
- Relieve difficult text with visual aids when possible.
- Emphasize important material and deemphasize secondary material through sentence construction and judicious use of italicizing, underlining, capitalization, and parentheses.
- Choose words carefully, opting for the known and short rather than the unknown and long. Graduate students, in particular, seem to revel in using jargon, pompous constructions, and long or arcane words. Naturally, there are times when technical terms are appropriate. Scientists communicate

efficiently with jargon, but the audiences for most applied research are not scientifically trained and need more help than many writers supply.

- Repeat and summarize critical and difficult ideas so readers have time to absorb them.
- Make strategic use of service words. These are words that "do not represent objects or ideas, but show relationship. Transitional words, such as the conjunctions, are service words. So are phrases such as 'on the other hand,' 'in summary,' and 'in contrast.' "[6]

Tone   Review the writing to ensure the tone is appropriate. The reader can, and should, be referred to, but researchers should avoid referring to themselves. One author notes that the "application of the 'you' attitude . . . makes the message sound like it is written to the reader, not sent by the author. A message prepared for the reader conveys sincerity, personalization, warmth, and involvement on the part of the author."[7] To accomplish this, remove negative phrasing and rewrite the thought positively. Do not change your recommendations or your findings to make them positive. Instead, review the phrasing. Which of the following sounds better?

> End users do not want the Information Systems Department telling them what software to buy.

> End users want more autonomy over their computer software choices.

The messages convey the same information, but the positive tone of the second message does not put readers from the Information Systems Department on the defensive.

Final Proof   It is helpful to put the draft away for a day before doing the final editing. Go to the beach, ride a bicycle in the park, or see a movie—do anything that is unrelated to the research project. Then return to the report and read it with a critical eye. Does the writing flow smoothly? Are there transitions where they are needed? Is the organization apparent to the reader? Do the findings and conclusions adequately meet the problem statement and the research objectives? Are the tables and graphics displaying the proper information in an easy-to-read format? After assuring yourself that the draft is complete, write the executive summary.

Presentation Considerations

The final consideration in the report-writing process is production. Reports can be typed; printed on an ink-jet, laser, color, or other printer; or sent out for typesetting. Most student and small research reports are typed or produced on a computer printer. The presentation of the report conveys to the readers the professional approach used throughout the project. Care should be taken to use compatible fonts throughout the entire report. The printer should produce consistent, easy-to-read letters on quality paper. When reports are photocopied for more than one reader, make sure the copies are clean and have no black streaks or gray areas.

Overcrowding of text creates an appearance problem. Readers need the visual relief provided by ample white space. We define "ample" as one inch of white space at the top, bottom, and right-hand margins. On the left side, the margin should be at least one and one-fourth inches to provide room for binding or punched holes. Even greater margins will often improve report appearance and highlight key points or sections. Overcrowding also occurs when the report contains page after page of large blocks of unbroken text. This produces an unpleasant psychological effect on readers because of its formidable appearance. Overcrowded text, however, may be avoided:

- Use shorter paragraphs. As a rough guide, any paragraph longer than half a page is suspect. Remember that each paragraph should represent a distinct thought.
- Indent parts of text that represent listings, long quotations, or examples.
- Use headings and subheadings to divide the report and its major sections into homogeneous topical parts.
- Use vertical listings of points (such as this list).

Inadequate labeling creates another physical problem. Each graph or table should contain enough information to be self-explanatory. Text headings and subheadings also help with labeling. They function as signs for the audience, describing the organization of the report and indicating the progress of discussion. They also help readers to skim the material and to return easily to particular sections of the report.

CLOSE-UP

A written report is the culmination of the Mind-Writer project, which has illustrated the research process throughout the book. Jason's contract for the CompleteCare project requires a report about the size of a student term project. Although repetitive portions have been omitted to conserve space, it should give the reader some ideas of how an applied project of this size is summa-rized. Descriptive statistics and simple graphics are used to analyze and present most of the data. References to chapters where specific details may be reviewed are shown in the marginal comments.

The presentation of findings follows the content specifications of Figure 19–1 for short reports. It falls between a memo/letter and a short technical report. The objective was to make it available quickly for feedback to the CompleteCare team. It was therefore set up as a facsimile document.

(continued)

FAX Transmittal Memo

To:	Ms. Gracie Uhura	**From:**	Jason Henry
Company:	MindWriter Corp.	**Company:**	Henry Associates
Location:	Austin, TX Bldg 5	**Location:**	Palm Beach, FL
Telephone:	512.555.1234	**Telephone:**	407.555.4321
Fax:	512.555.1250	**Fax:**	407.555.4357

Total number of pages including this one: 10

The fax cover sheet acts as a temporary transmittal letter until the plain paper copies are sent.

It provides all necessary identification and contact information. The writer's and recipient's relationship makes using first names appropriate.

January 5, 1998

Dear Gracie,

This fax contains the CompleteCare December report requested by Mr. Malraison through Myra Wines. You may expect the plain paper copies tomorrow morning for distribution.

We hope that the Call Center will complete the nonrespondent survey so that we can discover the extent to which these results represent all CompleteCare customers.

This month's findings show improvements in the areas we discussed last week by telephone. The response rate is also up. You will be delighted to know that our preliminary analysis shows improvements in the courier's ratings.

Best regards,

Jason

Authorization for the study. Scope of findings (month). Specific instructions for process issues.

Request for follow-up by the client to reduce the study's limitations.

Progress update and feedback on improvements.

CompleteCare Customer Survey Results for December

Title contains reference to a known survey and program. Descriptions of variables, relationships, and population are unnecessary.

Prepared for Ms. Gracie Uhura
MindWriter Corporation
January 1998

The recipient of the report, corporation, and date appear next.

Henry Associates
Research Services
200 ShellPoint Tower
Palm Beach, Florida 33480

407.555.4321

The report's preparer, location, and telephone number facilitate contact for additional information.

MindWriter CONFIDENTIAL

The information level identifies this as a restricted circulation document for in-house use only.

MINDWRITER COMPLETECARE DECEMBER RESULTS

Title repeated.

Introduction

This report is based on the December data collected from the MindWriter CompleteCare Survey. The survey asks customers about their satisfaction with the CompleteCare repair and service system. Its secondary purpose is to identify monthly improvement targets for management.

The findings are organized into the following sections: (1) an executive summary, (2) the methods used, (3) the Service Improvement Grid, (4) detailed findings for each question, and (5) patterns in the open-ended questions.

Executive Summary

The highest degrees of satisfaction with CompleteCare were found in the categories of "delivery speed" and "pickup speed." Average scores on these items were between 4.2 and 4.4 on a 5-point scale. "Speed of repair," "condition on arrival," and "overall impression of CompleteCare's effectiveness" also scored relatively well. They were above the *met all expectations* level (see appropriate charts).

Several questions were below the *met all expectations* level. From the lowest, "Call Center's responsiveness," to "Call Center's technical competence," and "courier service's arrangements," the average scores ranged from 2.0 to 3.9. In general, ratings have improved since November with the exception of "condition on arrival."

The three items generating the most negative comments are (1) problems with the courier's arrangements, (2) long telephone waits, and (3) transfer among many people at the Call Center. These same comments carry over for the last two months.

CompleteCare's criteria for Dissatisfied Customers consist of negative comments in the Comments/Suggestions section or ratings of less than three (3.0) on questions one through eight. Forty-three percent of the sample met these criteria, down from 56% last month. By counting only customer's comments (positive/negative or +/–), the percentage of Dissatisfied Customers would be 32%.

The ratio of negative to positive comments was 1.7 to 1, an improvement over November's ratio (2.3 to 1).

Section headings are used.

Introduction contains period of coverage for report, management question, and secondary research objective.

An overview of the report's contents allows readers to turn to specific sections of interest.

The executive summary provides a synopsis of essential finding. It is the report in miniature— six paragraphs.

Both positive and negative results are capsulized.

Criteria for indices are provided as reminders.

When the expectation-based satisfaction scores are adjusted for perceived importance, "Call Center responsiveness," "Call Center technical competence," and "courier's arrangements" are identified as action items. "Repair speed" and "problem resolution" maintained high importance scores and are also rated above average.

Methodology

The data collection instrument is a postage-paid postcard that is packed with the repaired product at the time the unit is shipped back to the customer.

The survey consists of twelve satisfaction questions measured on five-point scales. The questions record the degree to which the components of the CompleteCare process (arrangements for receiving the customer's computer through return of the repaired product) meet customer's *expectations*. A final categorical question asks whether customers will use CompleteCare again. Space for suggestions is provided.

Sample

The sample consisted of 175 customers who provided impressions of CompleteCare's effectiveness. For the four-week period, the response rate was 35% with no incentive given. Nothing is yet known about the differences between respondents and nonrespondents.

Service Improvement Grid

The grid on page three compares the degree to which expectations were met along with the *derived importance* of those expectations. The average scores for both axes determine the dividing lines for the four quadrants. The quadrants are labeled to identify actionable items to highlight those that bear watching for improvement or deterioration.

The **Concentrate Efforts** quadrant is the area where customers are marginally satisfied with service but consider service issues important. Question 1a, "Call Center's responsiveness," Question 1b, "Call Center's technical competence," and Question 2a, "Courier arrangements" are found here. "Technical competence" was similarly rated last month. Its perceived importance was rated higher in previous months. "Courier arrangements" has increased in perceived importance over previous reports.

The methodology, reported in brief, reminds the reader of the data collection method, nature and format of the questionnaire, scales used, and target measurement issues.

The sample, a self-selecting nonprobability sample, and the response rate are shown. With respondents' data from the postcards and the Call Center's files on nonrespondents, a future study on nonresponse bias is planned.

This section begins the Findings section. Findings consist of the action planning grid and detailed results sections. The headings were specified by the client.

The method for creating the planning grid and the grid's contents are highlighted.

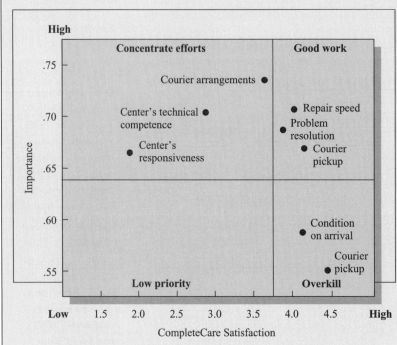

NOTE: Satisfaction scores are in the range of 1.0 to 5.0 and importance is in the range of 0 to 1.0.

The statistical technique for producing the grid is correlation. A modification of scatterplots was used to create a plot with reference lines (see Chapter 17).

In the **Good Work** quadrant, CompleteCare has, on average, *met all expectations* with the "repair speed" and "courier pickup" questions. Their mean scores are greater than 4.0 and considered important by respondents. "Problem resolution" has improved but remains a borderline concern.

There are no items in the **Low Priority** quadrant.

Overkill, the last quadrant, contains two questions. Question 5, "condition on arrival," has improved its ratings over last month but has dropped slightly on the importance scale because the average of importance scores (horizontal line) moved upward. Question 2c, "courier delivery speed," has a high satisfaction rating, but respondents considered this item to have lower importance than most issues in CompleteCare.

The contents of each quadrant are described. Comparisons and connections to the next section are previewed.

Detailed Findings

The figures that follow provide (1) a comparison of the mean scores for each of the questions for the last three months and (2) individual question results. The latter contains frequencies for the scale values, percentages for each category, mean scores, standard deviations, and valid cases for each question. (See Appendix for question wording and placement.)

The three-month comparison (October, November, December) shows results for all scaled questions. December data bars (in black) reveal improvements on all average scores (vertical axis) except Question 5, "condition on arrival." Most aspects of the service/repair process have shown improvement over the three-month period.

Detailed findings show the results of individual questions. This section announces the two-part content and presents, briefly and in a direct style, the most pertinent outcomes.

This graphic gives the reader a three-month view and all questions at a glance. Vertical bars are the simplest and easiest to read for the amount of space allocated. Horizontal grid lines guide the eye from the bar tops to the closest value on the mean score axis.

Charts similar to these may be produced by the same spreadsheet that handles data entry. Charting programs offer other options and will import the data from spreadsheets.

Question 1a. Call Center's Responsiveness.   This question has the lowest mean score of the survey. Using a top-box method of reporting (combining the top two categories), 11% of the respondents felt that the Call Center met or exceeded their expectations for service responsiveness. This has improved only marginally since November and has significant implications for program targets. Based on our visit and recent results, we recommend that you begin immediately the contingency programs we discussed: additional training for Call Center operators and implementation of the proposed staffing plan.

The first individual item is reported with means scores, percentages, and recommendations for improvement.

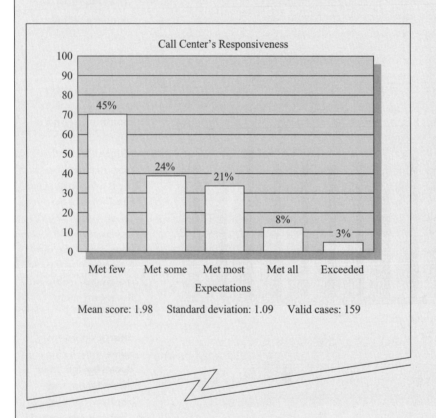

This chart conveys the message of low responsiveness rather well but does not have a label for the vertical axis. It is easy to confuse percentages with the number of respondents (which it is supposed to represent).

Similar reporting formats are skipped.

Question 6. Overall Impression of CompleteCare's Effectiveness. CompleteCare has increased the number of truly satisfied respondents with 46% (versus 43% in November) in the *exceeded* expectations category. The top-box score has increased to 75% of respondents (against 70% in November).

Question 6 shows the respondents' overall impression of CompleteCare. It would be an ideal dependent variable for a regression study in which questions 1 through 5 were the independent variables (see Chapters 17 and 18).

Overall Impression of CompleteCare's Effectiveness

Expectations

Mean score: 4.14   Standard deviation: 0.98   Valid cases: 169

Question 8a. Likelihood of Repurchasing MindWriter Based on Service/Repair Experience. Respondents' average scores (4.02) for this likelihood scale are the highest this month since measurement began. Improvement of the courier service's arrangements with customers and the resolution of the problem that prompted service appear to be the best predictors of repurchase at this time.

Question 8a is another question for more detailed research. It allows the researcher to connect the variables that describe the service/repair experience with repurchase intentions.

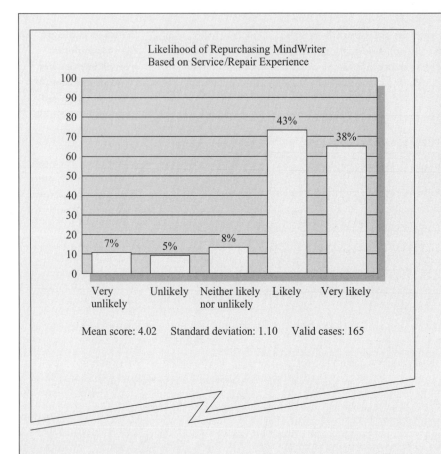

Likelihood of Repurchasing MindWriter
Based on Service/Repair Experience

Mean score: 4.02   Standard deviation: 1.10   Valid cases: 165

Using regression, it was possible to identify two key influences for this question.

Question 8b (not shown) is similar, asking about the relation of product performance with repurchase intention.

Patterns in the Open-Ended Questions

The following categories were found when the comments and suggestions were analyzed. The ratio of negative to positive comments was 1.7 to 1. Pick-up problems continue to be "courier only" problems and coordination between MindWriter's telephone support and the courier. Customers complain of holding on the phone for long periods and transfer between support people. Problems with service are split between large problems that have not been fixed and small, nuisance problems that customers are prepared to live with. Positive comments commend turnaround and service and also praise specific technical operators.

The questionnaire has one open-ended question that encourages respondents to make comments or suggestions.

Content analysis is used to distill the reponses (see Chapter 15).

Negative Comments	Count
Shipping	19
Pick-up problems (15)	
Delivery problems (2)	
Box damage (1)	
The courier charged customer (1)	
Call Center	19
Too long on hold (9)	
Transferred call too frequently / confusion (8)	
Untrained / Hard to understand (2)	
Service	13
Problem continues (5)	
Small things not fixed / damaged (6)	
Took too long (2–7 weeks) (2)	
Product	6
Multiple repairs needed (3)	
Paint wears off (2)	
General dislike of product (1)	

Positive Comments	
General positive comment about the process	13
Quick response	12
Great service	7
Helpful phone personnel	6

Other Comments	
MindWriter shouldn't need to be repaired	4
Provide more information on what was done	2
Offer extended warranty	1
Won't use MindWriter Call Center again	1

Although content analysis produces more than frequency counts of recurring themes, it is a labor-intensive process. The project's restrictive budget and the needs of the audience made this section of the report adequate for its purpose.

Appendix Contents: Sample Questionnaire

The report's appendix contains a copy of the questionnaire (see Chapter 12).

MindWriter personal computers offer you ease of use and maintenance. When you need service, we want you to rely on *CompleteCare,* wherever you may be. That's why we're asking you to take a moment to tell us how well we've served you.

	Met **few** expectations 1	Met **some** expectations 2	Met **most** expectations 3	Met **all** expectations 4	**Exceeded** expectations 5

1. Telephone assistance with your problem: 1   2   3   4   5
   - a. Responsiveness   1   2   3   4   5
   - b. Technical competence   1   2   3   4   5
2. The courier service's effectiveness:
   - a. Arrangements   1   2   3   4   5
   - b. Pickup speed   1   2   3   4   5
   - c. Delivery speed   1   2   3   4   5
3. Speed of the overall repair process.   1   2   3   4   5
4. Resolution of the problem that prompted service/repair.   1   2   3   4   5
5. Condition of your MindWriter on arrival.   1   2   3   4   5
6. Overall impression of CompleteCare's effectiveness.   1   2   3   4   5
7. Likelihood of using CompleteCare on another occasion.
   (1 = very unlikely 3 = neither likely nor unlikely 5 = very likely)   1   2   3   4   5
8. Likelihood of repurchasing a MindWriter based on:
   (1 = very unlikely 3 = neither likely nor unlikely 5 = very likely)
   - a. Service/repair experience   1   2   3   4   5
   - b. Product performance   1   2   3   4   5

Comments/Suggestions: _____

_____

How may we contact you to follow up on any problems you have experienced?

_____   (_____) _____

Last Name   First Name   Phone

_____

City   State   Zip

Service Code

PRESENTATION OF STATISTICS[8]

The presentation of statistics in research reports is a special challenge for writers. Four basic ways to present such data are in (1) a text paragraph, (2) semitabular form, (3) tables, or (4) graphics.

Text Presentation

This is probably the most common when there are only a few statistics. The writer can direct the reader's attention to certain numbers or comparisons and emphasize specific points. The drawback is that the statistics are submerged in the text, requiring the reader to scan the entire paragraph to extract the meaning. The following material has a few simple comparisons but becomes more complicated when text and statistics are combined.

> A comparison of the three aerospace and defense companies from the high-tech stratum of the Forbes 500 sample show that Sundstrand had the best sales growth record over the years 1988–1989. Its growth was 8.0 percent—with sales significantly lower than the other two firms in the sample. This compares to sales growth for Rockwell International of 3.3 percent, and Allied-Signal was third at only 0.8 percent sales increase. Rockwell International generated the most profits in 1989 among the three companies. Rockwell's net profits were $720.7 million as compared to $528 million for Allied-Signal and $120.8 million for Sundstrand.

Semitabular Presentation

When there are just a few figures, they may be taken from the text and listed. Lists of quantitative comparisons are much easier to read and understand than embedded statistics. An example of semitabular presentation is shown below.

> A comparison of the three aerospace-defense companies in the Forbes 500 sample shows that Sundstrand showed the best sales growth between 1988 and 1989. Rockwell International generated the highest net profits for the year 1989.

	Annual Sales Growth	*1989 Net Profits ($ millions)*
Sundstrand	8.0%	$120.8
Rockwell	3.3	720.7
Allied-Signal	0.8	528.0

Tabular Presentation

Tables are generally superior to text for presenting statistics, although they should be accompanied by comments directing the reader's attention to important figures. Tables facilitate quantitative comparisons and provide a concise, efficient way to present numerical data.

Tables are either general or summary in nature. General tables tend to be large, complex, and detailed. They serve as the repository for the statistical findings of the study and are usually in the appendix of a research report.

TABLE   19–2   **U.S. Production of Shoes and Slippers, by Class, 1965 and 1975 } Title**
(millions of pairs)*

Class	1965	1975 } Column heads
Total	626.7	433.7
Footwear, except slippers	536.0	365.2
Men	118.2	104.8
Youth and boys	25.6	17.7
Women	280.0	173.5
Stub { Misses	36.5	15.2 } **Body**
Children	33.5	17.2
Infants and babies	32.5	21.9
Athletic shoes	7.0	11.4
Other footwear	2.5	3.5
Slippers	90.7	68.5

Footnote { *Excludes Alaska and excludes rubber footwear.
Source note { SOURCE: U.S. Bureau of Census, Current Industrial Reports, M31A.

Summary tables contain only a few key pieces of data closely related to a specific finding. To make them inviting to the reader (who often skips them), the table designer should omit unimportant details and collapse multiple classifications into composite measures that may be substituted for the original data.

Any table should contain enough information for the reader to understand its contents. The title should explain the subject of the table, how the data are classified, the time period, or other related matters. A subtitle is sometimes included under the title to explain something about the table; most often this is a statement of the measurement units in which the data are expressed. The contents of the columns should be clearly identified by the column heads, and the contents of the stub should do the same for the rows. The body of the table contains the data, while the footnotes contain any needed explanations. Footnotes should be identified by letters or symbols such as asterisks, rather than by numbers, to avoid confusion with data values. Finally, there should be a source note if the data do not come from your original research. Table 19–2 illustrates the various parts of a table.

Graphics

Compared with tables, graphs show less information and often only approximate values. However, they are more often read and remembered than tables. Their great advantage is that they convey quantitative values and comparisons more readily than tables. With personal computer charting programs, you can easily turn a set of numbers into a chart or graph.

There are many different graphic forms. Figure 19–4 shows the most common ones and how they should be used. Statistical explanation charts such as boxplots, stem-and-leaf displays, and histograms were discussed in Chapter 15. Line graphs, area, pie, and bar charts, and pictographs and 3-D graphics receive additional attention here.

FIGURE 19–4   **Guide to Graphs**

Column Compares sizes and amounts of categories usually for the same time. Places categories on X axis and values on Y axis.

Bar Same as the column but positions categories on Y axis and values on X axis. Deviations, when used, distinguish positive from negative values.

Stacked Bar In either bar or column, shows how components contribute to the total of the category.

Pie Shows relationship of parts to the whole. Wedges are row values of data.

Stacked Pie Same as pie but displays two or more data series.

Multiple Pie Uses same data as stacked pie but plots separate pies for each column of data without stacking.

Line Compares values over time to show changes in trends.

Filled Line Similar to line chart, but uses fill to highlight series.

Area (surface) Like line chart, compares changing values but emphasizes relative value of each series.

Step Compares discrete points on the value axis with vertical lines showing difference between points. Not for showing a trend.

Scatter Shows if relationship between variables follows a pattern. May be used with one variable at different times.

Bubble Used to introduce third variable (dots of different sizes). Axes could be sales, profits; bubbles are assets.

Spider (and Radar) Radiating lines are categories; values are distances from center (shows multiple variables, e.g. performance, ratings, progress).

Polar Shows relationship between a variable and angle measured in degrees (cyclical trends, pollution source vs. wind direction, etc.).

Open Hi Lo Close Shows fluctuating values in a given period (hour, day). Often used for investments.

Boxplots Displays distribution(s) and compares characteristics of shape (Ch. 15).

Pictographic Special chart that uses pictures or graphic elements in lieu of bars.

Line Graphs   Line graphs are used chiefly for time series and frequency distribution. There are several guidelines for designing a **line graph:**

- Put the time units or the independent variable on the horizontal axis.
- When showing more than one line, use different line types (solid, dashed, dotted, dash-dot) to enable the reader to easily distinguish among them.
- Try not to put more than four lines on one chart.
- Use a solid line for the primary data.

It is important to be aware of perceptual problems with line diagrams. The first is the use of a zero baseline. Since the length of the bar or distance above the baseline indicates the statistic, it is important that graphs give accurate visual impressions of values. A good way to achieve this is to include a zero baseline on the scale on which the curves are plotted. To set the base at some other value is to introduce a visual bias. This can be seen by comparing the visual impressions in Parts A and B of Figure 19–5. Both are accurate plots of the gross national product of the United States from 1972 through 1977. In Part A, however, using the baseline of zero places the curve well up on the chart and gives a better perception of the relation between the absolute size of GNP and the changes from year to year. The graph in Part B, with a baseline at $1,000 billion, can easily give the impression that the growth was at a more rapid rate. When space or other reasons dictate using shortened scales, the zero base point should still be used but with a break in the scale as shown in Part C of Figure 19–5. This will warn the reader that the scale has been reduced.

The balance of size between vertical and horizontal scales also affects the reader's impression of the data. There is no single solution to this problem, but the results can be seen by comparing Parts B and C in Figure 19–5. In Part C, the horizontal scale is twice that in Part B. This changes the slope of curve, creating a different perception of growth rate.

A third distortion with line diagrams occurs when relative and absolute changes among two or more sets of data are shown. In most charts, we use arithmetic scales where each space unit has identical value. This shows the absolute differences between variables, as in Part A of Figure 19–6, which presents the total U.S. population and that of the three Pacific states. This is an arithmetically correct way to present these data; but if we are interested in rates of growth, the visual impressions from a semilogarithmic scale are more accurate. A comparison of the line diagrams in Parts A and B of Figure 19–6 shows how much difference a semilogarithmic scale makes. Each is valuable and each can be misleading. In Part A, notice that both areas have been growing in population and that the population of the Pacific states is only a small portion of total U.S. population. One can even estimate what this proportion is. Part B gives insight into growth rates that are not clear from the arithmetic scale. Part B shows that the Pacific states' population has grown at a much faster rate than the U.S. population as a whole.

Area (Stratum or Surface) Charts   An **area chart** is also used for a time series. Consisting of a line that has been divided into component parts, it is best used to show

FIGURE   19–5   U.S. Gross National Product, 1972–1977 (dollars in billions)

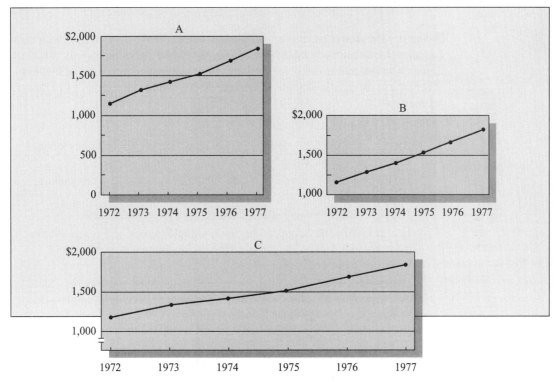

FIGURE   19–6   Population of the United States and Pacific States Area, 1920–1970 (millions)

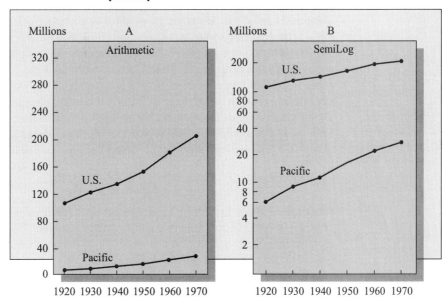

SOURCE: U.S. Department of Commerce.

changes in patterns over time. The same rules apply to stratum charts as to line charts (see Figure 19–4).

Pie Charts   **Pie charts** are another form of area chart. They are often used with business data. However, they can easily mislead the reader or be improperly prepared. Research shows that readers' perceptions of the percentages represented by the pie slices are consistently inaccurate.[9] Consider the following suggestions when designing pie charts:

- Show 100 percent of the subject being graphed.
- Always label the slices with "call-outs" and with the percentage or amount that is represented. This allows you to dispense with a legend.
- Put the largest slice at twelve o'clock and move clockwise in descending order.
- Use light colors for large slices, darker colors for smaller slices.
- In a pie chart of black and white slices, a single red one will command the most attention and be memorable. Use it to communicate your most important message.[10]
- Do not show evolution over time with pie charts as the only medium. Since pie charts always represent 100 percent, growth of the overall whole will not be recognized. If you must use a series of pie charts, complement them with an area chart.

As shown in Figure 19–7, pie charts portray frequency data in interesting ways. In addition, they can be stacked to show relationships between two sets of data.

Bar Charts   **Bar charts** can be very effective if properly constructed. Use the horizontal axis to represent time and the vertical axis to represent units or growth-related variables. Vertical bars are generally used for time series and for quantitative classifications. Horizontal bars are less often used. If neither variable is time related, either format can be used. A computer-charting program easily generates charts. If you are preparing a bar chart by hand, leave space between the bars equal to at least half the width of the bar. An exception to this is the specialized chart—the histogram—where continuous data are grouped into intervals for a frequency distribution (see Chapter 15). A second exception is the multiple variable chart, where more than one bar is located at a particular time segment. In this case, the space between the groups of bars is at least half the width of the group. Bar charts come in a variety of patterns. In Chapter 15, Figure 15–9 shows a standard vertical bar graph. Variations are illustrated in Figure 19–4.

Pictographs and Geo-Graphics   These graphics are used in popular magazines and newspapers because they are eye-catching and imaginative. *USA Today* and a host of imitators are often guilty of taking this to the extreme, creating graphs that are incomprehensible. A **pictograph** uses pictorial symbols (an oil drum for barrels of oil, a stick figure for numbers of employees, or a pine tree for amount of wood). The symbols represent data volume and are used instead of a bar in a bar-type chart. It is

FIGURE   19–7   Examples of Area Charts: A Stratum Chart and Two Pie Charts

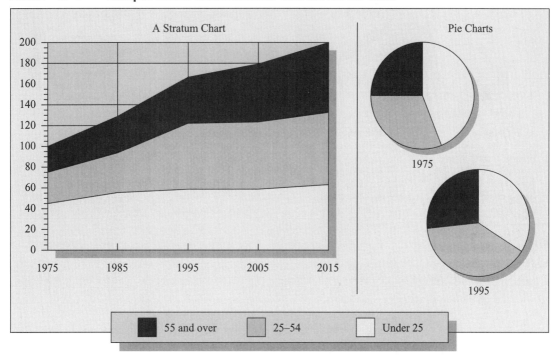

Notice the two pie charts seem to indicate a dramatic decrease in the number of "under 25" category. Now look at the stratum chart. The number of "under 25" never decreased; it only changed relative to the entire population. It is important not to use pie charts alone in a time series, to avoid giving erroneous impressions.

proper to stack same-size images to express more of a quantity and to show fractions of an image to show less. But altering the scale of the symbol produces problems. Since the pictures represent actual objects, doubling the size will increase the area of the symbol by four (and the volume by more). This misleads the reader into believing the increase is larger than it really is. The exception is a graphic that is easily substituted for a bar such as the pencils in Figure 19–4.

Geo-graphic charts use a portion of the world's map, in pictorial form, to show differences in regions. They can be used for product production, per capita rates, demographics, or any of a number of other geographically specific variables.

3-D Graphics   With current charting techniques, virtually all charts can now be made three dimensional. Although **3-D graphics** add interest, they can also obscure data. Care must be used in selecting 3-D chart candidates (see Figure 19–8). Pie and bar charts achieve dimensionality simply by adding depth to the graphics; this is not 3-D. A 3-D column chart allows you to compare three or more variables from the sample in one bar chart–type graph. If you want to display several quarters of sales results for Hertz, Avis, Budget, and National, you have 3-D data. But be careful about converting line charts to ribbon charts, and area charts to 3-D area charts.

FIGURE   19–8   3-D Charts

3-D Column
A variation on column charts, they compare variables to each other or over time. Axes: X = categories, Y = series, Z = values. Other variations include 3-D area charts and connect-the-dots scatter charts.

3-D Ribbon This example is a one-wall plot showing columns of data (series) as ribbons. One or more columns are used. Axes: X = categories, Y = series, Z = values.

3-D Wireframe
A variation of a contour or response surface; suitable for changes in time and multivariate data. Axes: X = values, Y = series, Z = values.

3-D Surface Line
Handles three columns of data and plots XYZ coordinates to show a response surface. Helpful for multivariate applications.

Surface charts and 3-D scatter charts are helpful for displaying complex data patterns if the underlying distributions are multivariate. Otherwise, do not enter the third dimension unless your data are there.

Improvement and Control Charts

We have previously discussed tools of the quality movement that provide graphic visualization of data. These included histograms and exploratory data techniques (in Chapter 15) and scatter diagrams (in Chapter 17). In this section we will add control charts and Pareto diagrams because of their unique ability to simplify results for the reader.

Statistical process control (SPC) uses statistical tools to analyze, monitor, and improve process performance. A process is any business system that transforms inputs to outputs. Production of automobiles, manufacturing plastic pipe, preparing restaurant meals, and service and administrative business activities are all made up of processes. Processes that operate within control limits are stable, predictable, and responsive to improvement. Walter Shewhart at Bell Laboratories defined this concept for production processes during the 1920s; it was later expanded by W. Edwards Deming to become an integral part of **Total Quality Management (TQM).**

The element of the process control system that pertains to the presentation of results is its charting system. SPC charts provide easily understood and reliable visuals for evaluating point values and trends and can graphically depict variation. Control charts help managers focus on special causes of variation in a process by revealing whether a system is under control (as an early warning of change) and substantiate results from improvements (confirming results).

A **control chart** displays sequential measurements of a process together with a center line and control limits. Limit lines provide guides for evaluating performance. These lines show the dispersion of data within a statistical boundary (generally three standard deviations above and below the average or centerline). If an observation falls beyond the area marked by the **upper control limit (UCL)** or the **lower control limit (LCL),** there is evidence that the process is out of control or special causes are adversely affecting it. However, even if all data points are within the boundaries, the time plot (the sequence of points along the *X*-axis) can reveal that the process has sudden jumps, drifts, cycles, or the beginning of a trend. The elements that make up a control chart are shown in Figure 19–9.

Types of Control Charts   The selection of a control chart depends on the level of data you are measuring. Figure 19–10 provides a diagram for selecting an appropriate chart. In this figure, *variables data* are ratio or interval measurements (such as the diameter of a bearing, units/ hour, the thickness of a plastic film, temperature, or blood pressure). Variables data are typically presented in *X-bar* and *R-charts* and *X-bar* and *s-charts.* *Attributes data* are nominal or categorical data that can be counted. Examples include the number of defects/part, abnormals/1,000 processed, and scratches per item. Attributes data are usually nonconforming units shown in control charts called *c, u, p, np* charts. Variables data have the advantage because they reveal how close we are to a specification—just as interval data provides more information on attitudes than does nominal data.

R-charts and X-bar are often displayed together as illustrated in Figure 19–11. The measurements describe an outboard motor manufacturer whose motors for

FIGURE   19–9   Control Chart Characteristics

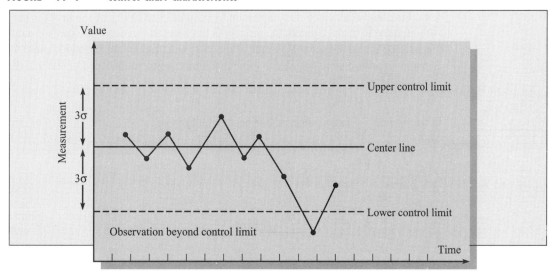

FIGURE   19–10   Control Chart Selection

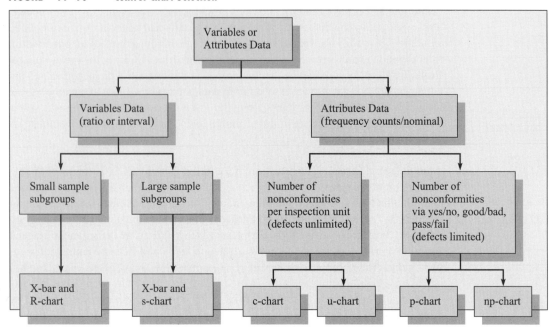

small fishing boats require control to deliver a constant ten horsepower. The process characteristics are reported in Table 19–3 showing small subgroups of three observations per subgroup. (This type of control chart usually has constant size samples of two to five measurements per subgroup.) We first evaluate the variance, as represented by the range, since it is important to keep the variability of the process low. Although the R-chart suggests the process is technically in control, we can see a potential problem in the second sample and erratic fluctuations throughout the range. There are no assignable causes for these discrepancies so we proceed to analyze the

TABLE   19–3   Sample Data for Outboard Motor Example

Subgroup	Horsepower Output		
1	10.22	10.31	9.79
2	10.25	10.33	10.12
3	10.37	9.92	10.80
4	10.46	9.94	10.26
5	10.06	9.39	10.31
6	10.59	10.15	10.23
7	10.82	10.85	10.20
8	10.52	10.14	10.07
9	10.13	10.69	10.15
10	9.88	10.32	10.31

X-bar chart. Here it is apparent that subgroup 4 is above the upper control limit—overproducing horsepower. One inference is that we should monitor production carefully and secure further samples. Another is that like cars, a really good outboard motor comes off the line with no explanation other than the random but perfect optimization of components.

X-bar and s-charts (sample standard deviation) are also used jointly. The sample standard deviation is a more efficient indicator of process variability, especially with larger sample sizes. However, it is less sensitive in detecting special causes of variation when a single value in a subgroup is found to be unusual.

Other varieties of control charts have a layout similar to the charts in Figure 19–11 but differ as to purpose. The c-chart and p-chart are used primarily for attributes data. P-charts ("proportion" charts) show the percentage of production that is defective: The light bulb illuminates or it doesn't; the aspirin bottle cap is sealed or it isn't; the diskette is preformatted or it isn't. C-charts (occasionally called "count" charts) add up defects per unit over consecutive periods of time: The stapler has two defects per unit, or the television has one defect per submodule.

Managers should look for the following visual characteristics in reports containing control charts: (1) *Outliers* are observations that fall outside the control lines. (2) *Runs* are data points in a series over or below the central line. A "run" of 7 consecutive points or 10 out of 11 points indicates an anomaly. Other methods reveal runs, such as finding two of the last three data points beyond two standard deviations and cumulative sum procedures, which involve adding up standardized deviations

FIGURE   19–11   R-Chart and X-Bar Chart for Outboard Motor Data

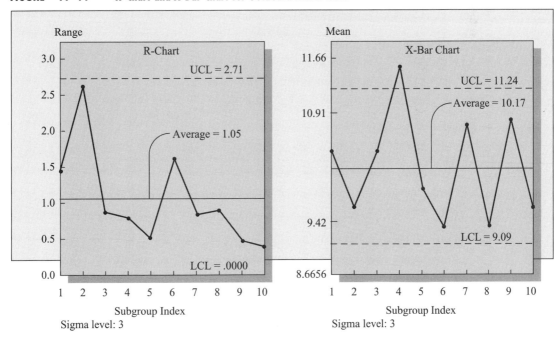

from the calculated mean. (3) The continual rise or fall of data points announces *trends*. (4) Data that show the same pattern of change over time, creating a cycle, describe *periodicity*.

Pareto Diagrams   Pareto diagrams derive their name from a nineteenth-century Italian economist. J. M. Juran, of quality management, first applied this concept to the industrial environment. He noted that only a *vital few* defects account for most problems evaluated for quality, and that the *trivial many* explain the rest. Historically, this has come to be known as the 80/20 rule—that is, an 80 percent improvement in quality or performance can be expected by eliminating 20 percent of the causes of unacceptable quality or performance.

The **Pareto diagram** is a bar chart whose percentages sum to 100 percent. The causes of the problem under investigation are sorted in decreasing importance with bar height descending from left to right. The pictorial array that results reveals the highest concentration of quality improvement potential in the fewest number of remedies. A content analysis of MindWriter customer complaints is depicted as a Pareto diagram in Figure 19–12. The cumulative frequency line in this figure shows that the top two problems (the repair did not resolve the customers' problem, and the product was returned multiple times for repair) accounted for 80 percent of the perceptions of inadequate repair service.

FIGURE   19–12   Pareto Diagram of MindWriter Repair Complaints

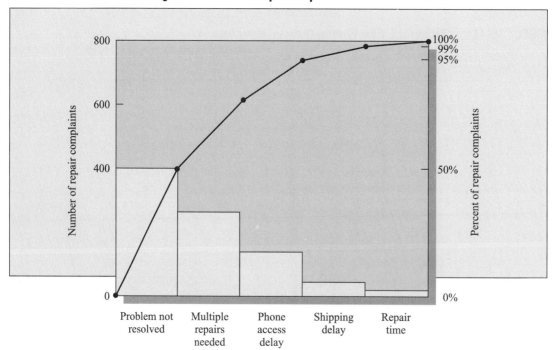

ORAL PRESENTATIONS

Researchers often present their findings orally. These presentations, sometimes called **briefings,** have some unique characteristics that distinguish them from most other kinds of public speaking: Only a small group of people is involved; statistics normally constitute an important portion of the topic; the audience members are usually managers with an interest in the topic, but they want to hear only the critical elements; speaking time will often be as short as 20 minutes but may run longer than an hour; and the presentation is normally followed by questions and discussion.

Preparation A successful briefing typically requires condensing a lengthy and complex body of information. Since speaking rates should not exceed 100 to 150 words per minute, a 20-minute presentation limits you to about 2,000 to 2,500 words. If you are to communicate effectively under such conditions, you must plan carefully. Begin by asking two questions. First, how long should you plan to talk? Usually there is an indication of the acceptable presentation length. It may be the custom in an organization to take a given allotted time for a briefing. If the time is severely limited, then the need for topical priorities is obvious. This leads to the second question: What are the purposes of the briefing? Is it to raise concern about problems that have been uncovered? Is it to add to the knowledge of audience members? Is it to give them conclusions and recommendations for their decision making? Questions such as these illustrate the general objectives of the report. After answering these questions, you should develop a detailed outline of what you are going to say. Such an outline should contain the following major parts.

1. *Opening.* A brief statement, probably not more than 10 percent of the allotted time, sets the stage for the body of the report. The opening should be direct, get attention, and introduce the nature of the discussion that follows. It should explain the nature of the project, how it came about, and what it attempted to do.
2. *Findings and conclusions.* The conclusions may be stated immediately after the opening remarks, with each conclusion followed by the findings that support it.
3. *Recommendations.* Where appropriate, these are stated in the third stage; each recommendation may be followed by references to the conclusions leading to it. Presented in this manner, they provide a natural climax to the report. At the end of the presentation, it may be appropriate to call for questions from the audience.

Early in the planning stage you need to make two further decisions. The first concerns the type of audiovisuals (AV) that will be used and the role they will play in the presentation. AV decisions are important enough that they are often made *before* the briefing outline and text are developed. More will be said about AV later.

Then you must decide on the type of presentation. Will you give a memorized speech, read from your manuscript, or give an extemporaneous presentation? We rule out the impromptu briefing as an option because impromptu speaking does not involve preparation. Your reputation and the research effort should not be jeopardized by "winging it."

Memorization is a risky and time-consuming course to follow. Any memory slip during the presentation can be a catastrophe, and the delivery sounds stilted and distant. Memorization virtually precludes establishing rapport with the audience and adapting to their reactions while you speak. It produces a self- or speaker-centered approach and is not recommended.

Reading a manuscript is also not advisable even though many professors seem to reward students who do so (perhaps because they themselves get away with it at professional meetings). The delivery sounds dull and lifeless because most people are not trained to read aloud and therefore do it badly. They become focused on the manuscript to the exclusion of the audience. This head-down preoccupation with the text is clearly inappropriate for management presentations.

The **extemporaneous presentation** is audience centered and made from minimal notes or an outline. This mode permits the speaker to be natural, conversational, and flexible. Clearly, it is the best choice for an organizational setting. Preparation consists of writing a draft along with a complete sentence outline and converting the main points to notes. In this way, you can try lines of argument, experiment with various ways of expressing thoughts, and develop phraseology. Along the way, the main points are fixed sequentially in your mind, and supporting connections are made.

Audiences accept notes, and their presence does wonders in allaying speaker fears. Even if you never use them, they are there for psychological support. Many prefer to use 5-by-8-inch cards for their briefing notes because they hold more information and so require less shuffling than the smaller 3-by-5 size. Card contents vary widely, but here are some general guidelines for their design:

- Place title and preliminary remarks on the first card.
- Use each of the remaining cards to carry a major section of the presentation. The amount of detail depends on the need for precision and the speaker's desire for supporting information.
- Include key phrases, illustrations, statistics, dates, and pronunciation guides for difficult words. Include also quotations and ideas that bear repeating.
- Along the margin, place instructions and cues, such as SLOW, FAST, EMPHASIZE, TRANSPARENCY A, TURN CHART, and GO BACK TO CHART 3.

After the outline and the AV aids comes the final stage of preparation—the rehearsal. Rehearsal, a prerequisite to effective briefing, *is too often slighted,* especially by inexperienced speakers. Giving a briefing is an artistic performance, and nothing improves it more than for the speaker to demonstrate mastery of the art. First rehearsal efforts should concentrate on those parts of the presentation that are awkward or poorly developed. After the problem areas have been worked out, there should be at least a few full-scale practices under simulated presentation conditions. All parts should be timed and edited until the time target is met. A videotape recorder is an excellent diagnostic tool.

Delivery

While the content of a report is the chief concern, the speaker's delivery is also important. A polished presentation adds to the receptiveness of the audience, but there is some danger that the presentation may overpower the message. Fortunately, the typical research audience knows why it is assembled, has a high level of interest, and does not need to be entertained. Even so, the speaker faces a real challenge in communicating effectively. The delivery should be restrained. Demeanor, posture, dress, and total appearance should be appropriate for the occasion. Speed of speech, clarity of enunciation, pauses, and gestures all play their part. Voice pitch, tone quality, and inflections are proper subjects for concern. There is little time for anecdotes and other rapport-developing techniques, yet the speaker must get and hold audience attention.

Speaker Problems   Inexperienced speakers have many difficulties in making presentations. They often are nervous at the start of a presentation and may even find breathing difficult. This is natural and should not be of undue concern. It may help to take a deep breath or two, holding each for a brief time before exhaling as fully as possible. This can be done inconspicuously on the way to the podium.

Several characteristics of inexperienced speakers may be summarized as questions. Even if you are an accomplished speaker, it is helpful to review them as you watch videotape of your presentation.

1. Vocal characteristics
   a. Do you speak so softly that someone cannot hear you well? It is helpful to have someone in the back of the room who can signal if your voice is not carrying far enough.
   b. Do you speak too rapidly? Remind yourself to slow down. Make deliberate pauses before sentences. Speak words with precision without exaggerating. However, some people talk too slowly, and this can make the audience restive.
   c. Do you vary volume, tone quality, and rate of speaking? Any of these can be used successfully to add interest to the message and engage audience attention. Speakers should not let their words trail off as they complete a sentence.
   d. Do you use overworked pet phrases, repeated "uhs," "you know," and "in other words"?
2. Physical characteristics
   a. Do you rock back and forth or roll or twist from side to side or lean too much on the lectern?
   b. Do you hitch or tug on clothing, scratch, or fiddle with pocket change, keys, pencils, or other devices?
   c. Do you stare into space? Lack of eye contact is particularly bothersome to listeners and is common with inexperienced speakers. Many seem to choose a spot above the heads of the audience and continue to stare at this spot except when looking at notes. *Eye contact is important.* Audience members need to feel that you are looking at them. It may be helpful to

pick out three people in the audience (left, right, and center) and practice looking at them successively as you talk.

  d. Do you misuse visuals by fumbling, putting them on in incorrect order or upside down? Do you turn your back to the audience to read from visuals?

Audiovisuals

Researchers can use a variety of AV media with good results. While there is some need for computer-assisted media in many business applications, they will be mentioned only briefly. Our emphasis is on **visual aids** that are relatively simple and inexpensive to make.

1. *Chalkboards and whiteboards.* Chalkboards are flexible, inexpensive, and require little specific preparation. On the other hand, they are not novel and do not project a polished appearance. Whiteboards, both portable and installed, provide visual relief, particularly when color markers are used. Both varieties reduce speaking time while the speaker is writing. If you use either, write legibly or print, leave space between lines, and do not talk to the board with the audience to your back. If you are in an unfamiliar room, it is best to arrive prepared with erasable markers (or chalk) and erasure materials.

2. *Handout materials.* These are inexpensive but can have a professional look if done carefully. Handouts can include pictures and graphic materials that might be difficult to display otherwise. The disadvantages include the time needed to produce them and their distracting impact if not properly used. You may distribute them when the audience leaves, but a better use is to refer to them during your talk. If you use them this way, *do not hand them out until you are ready to refer to them.*

3. *Flip charts.* You can show color, pictures, and large letters with these. They are easy and inexpensive to make; they can focus listener attention on a specific idea. If not well made, they can be distracting. Unless they are large, they should be restricted to small groups and to types of material that can be summarized in a few words.

4. *Overhead transparencies.* These may be of different sizes, but the most common is about the same as an 8 1/2-by-11-inch page. They are easily made with color markers or with a copy machine. Computer graphics can be plotted or printed directly to transparencies for a more accurate and professional look. Multiple-color and single-color renditions are available. You can also show overlays and buildups. In using transparencies, be sure they are in correct order and right side up when you place them on the projector.

5. *Slides.* Most slides are 35mm, but larger sizes are sometimes used. They are relatively inexpensive and colorful and present a professional-looking image if done well. They are somewhat more difficult to make but can be prepared with a personal computer and slide-construction software.

6. *Computer-drawn visuals.* For transparencies and slides, the draw and paint programs for personal computers provide the presenter with limitless options for illustrating the message. Stored visuals can be teamed with a device for projecting the computer output to a screen, or the briefer can use the software to create the image at the moment a question is asked or a demonstration is appropriate. Be careful that the technology does not distract from the purpose of the message.

7. *Computer animation.* The development of larger and faster processors, memory chips, and disks has made it possible to store voice and image data in quantity in personal computers. Technology permits multimedia presentations using videotape, videodisc, and CD-ROM elements that are integrated for the ultimate in image reproduction. For proposals, large contracts, or other business applications, the preparation and expense may be justifiable.

The choice of visual aids is determined by your intended purpose, the size of the audience, meeting room conditions, time and budget constraints, and available equipment.

Visual aids serve the presenter of a research presentation in several ways. They present materials that cannot otherwise be communicated effectively. Statistical relationships are difficult to describe verbally, but a picture or graph communicates well. How better to describe some object or material than to show it or picture it?

Visual aids help the speaker to clarify major points. With visual reinforcement of a verbal statement, the speaker can stress the importance of points. In addition, the use of two channels of communication (hearing and sight) enhances the probability that the listener will understand and remember the message.

The continuity and memorability of the speaker's message are also improved with visual aids. Verbal information is so transient that any slight lapse of listener attention results in losing the information thread. The failure to fully comprehend a given point cannot be remedied by going back to hear it again, for the speaker has gone on. With a visual aid, however, there is more opportunity to review this point, relate it to earlier comments by the speaker, and improve retention.

Summary

A quality presentation of research findings can have an inordinate effect on a reader's or a listener's perceptions of a study's quality. Recognition of this fact should prompt a researcher to make a special effort to communicate skillfully and clearly.

Research reports contain findings, analysis, interpretation, conclusions, and sometimes recommendations. They may follow the short, informal format typical of memoranda and letters, or they may be longer and more complex. Long reports are of either a technical or a management type. In the former, the problem is presented and followed by the findings, conclusions, and recommendations. In the management report, the conclusions and recommendations precede the findings. The technical report is targeted at the technically trained reader; the management report is intended for the manager-client.

The writer of research reports should be guided by four questions: (1) What is the purpose of this report? (2) Who will read it? (3) What are the circumstances and limitations under which it is written? (4) How will the report be used? Reports should be clearly organized, physically inviting, and easy to read. Writers can achieve these goals if they are careful with mechanical details, writing style, and comprehensibility. There is a special challenge to presenting statistical data. While some may be incorporated in the text, most statistics should be placed in tables, charts, or graphs. The choice of a table, chart, or graph depends on the specific data and presentation purpose.

Oral presentations of research findings are common and should be developed with concern for the communication problems that are unique to such settings. Briefings are usually under time constraints; good briefings require careful organization and preparation. Visual aids are a particularly important aspect of briefings but are too often ignored or treated inadequately.

Whether written or oral, poor presentations do a grave injustice to what might otherwise be excellent research. Good presentations, on the other hand, add luster to both the research and the reputation of the researcher.

Key Terms

area charts
bar charts
briefings
control chart
executive summary
extemporaneous presentation
letter of transmittal
line graphs
lower control limit
management report
pace
Pareto diagram

pictographs (geo-graphics)
pie charts
readability indices
sentence outline
statistical process control
technical report
3-D graphics
topic outline
Total Quality Management
upper control limit
visual aids

Discussion Questions

1. Distinguish between the following:
   a. Speaker-centered presentation and extemporaneous presentation
   b. Technical report and management report
   c. Topic outline and sentence outline
2. What should you do about each of these?
   a. Putting information in a research report concerning the study's limitations
   b. The size and complexity of tables in a research report
   c. The physical presentation of a report
   d. Pace in your writing

3. What type of report would you suggest be written in each of the following cases?

   a. The president of the company has asked for a study of the company's pension plan and its comparison to the plans of other firms in the industry.

   b. You have been asked to write up a marketing experiment, which you recently completed, for submission to the *Journal of Marketing Research.*

   c. Your division manager has asked you to prepare a forecast of cash requirements for the division for the next three months.

   d. The National Institutes of Health has given you a grant to study the relation between industrial accidents and departmental employee morale.

4. Research reports often contain statistical materials of great importance that are presented poorly. Discuss ways to improve statistical presentation.

5. The typical student research report has many deficiencies in presentation in addition to its limitations in project design and content. Make a list of what you believe to be the major presentation problems of student written research reports and student oral research reports.

6. What major problems do you personally have with writing good reports? What can you do about these problems?

7. Outline a set of visual aids that you might use in an oral briefing on these topics:

   a. How to write a research report

   b. The outlook for the economy over the next year

   c. The major analytical article in the latest issue of *Business Week*

8. There are a number of graphic presentation forms. Which would you recommend to show each of the following? Why?

   a. A comparison of changes in average annual per capita income for the United States and Japan from 1990 to 2000.

   b. The percentage composition of average family expenditure patterns, by the major types of expenditures, for families whose heads are under age 35 compared with families whose heads are 55 or older.

   c. A comparison of the change between December 31, 1997, and December 31, 1996, in the value of the common stock of six major electronics firms.

Reference Notes

1. Paul E. Resta, *The Research Report* (New York: American Book Company, 1972), p. 5.
2. John M. Penrose, Jr., Robert W. Rasberry, and Robert J. Myers, *Advanced Business Communication* (Boston: PWS–Kent Publishing, 1989), p. 185.
3. Ibid., p. 185.
4. Most word processors contain dictionaries. All-purpose word processors such as MS Word, WordPerfect, WriteNow, AmiPro, or MacWritePro contain a spelling checker, table and graphing generators, and a thesaurus. For style and grammar checkers, programs such as Grammatik, RightWriter, Spelling Coach, Thunder, and Punctuation + Style are

available. New programs are reviewed periodically in the business communication literature and in magazines devoted to personal computing. Figure 19–3 was prepared from
GrammatikMac™ output.

5. Robert R. Rathbone, *Communicating Technical Information* (Reading, MA: Addison-
Wesley Publishing Company, 1966), p. 64. Reprinted with permission.

6. Ibid., p. 72.

7. Penrose, Rasberry, and Myers, *Advanced Business Communication,* p. 89.

8. The material in this section draws on Stephen M. Kosslyn, *Elements of Graph Design*
(San Francisco: W. H. Freeman, 1993); DeltaPoint, Inc., *DeltaGraph User's Guide 4.0*
(Monterey, CA: DeltaPoint, Inc., 1996); Gene Zelazny, *Say It with Charts* (Homewood,
IL: Business One Irwin, 1991); Jim Heid, "Graphs that Work," *MacWorld* (February
1994), pp. 155–56; and Penrose, Rasberry, and Myers, *Advanced Business Communica-
tion,* chap. 3.

9. Marilyn Stoll, "Charts Other than Pie Are Appealing to the Eye," *PC Week,* March 25,
1986, p. 138–39.

10. Stephen M. Kosslyn and Christopher Chabris, "The Mind Is Not a Camera, the Brain Is
Not a VCR," *Aldus Magazine* (September/October 1993), p. 34.

**Suggested
Readings**

1. Kosslyn, Stephen M. *Elements of Graph Design.* San Francisco: W. H. Freeman, 1993.

2. Lesikar, Raymond. *Basic Business Communication,* 6th ed. Burr Ridge, IL: Irwin, 1993.
Practical guidance for writing and presenting reports.

3. Moyer, Ruth, Eleanor Stevens, and Ralph Switzer. *The Research Handbook for Managers
and Executives in Business, Industry, and Government.* New York: Wiley, 1981. A comprehensive source on the preparation of reports, their documentation, sources of information,
and writing style.

4. Penrose, John M., Robert W. Rasberry, and Robert J. Myers. *Advanced Business Communication,* 3rd ed. Cincinnati, OH: South-Western Publishing, 1996. A presentation of all
aspects of business communications from organization through final writing and oral presentation.

5. Strunk, William, Jr., and E. B. White. *The Elements of Style.* New York: Macmillan, 1959.
A classic on the problems of writing style.

6. Tufte, Edward R. *The Visual Display of Quantitative Information.* New Haven, CT: Graphics Press, 1983. The book that started the revolution against gaudy, infographics.

APPENDICES

A GUIDE TO REFERENCE AND SEARCHING

In this appendix we develop in some detail ideas discussed briefly in Chapter 10, and we make recommendations on reference, database, and nondatabase materials for business research.

We assume you will be using an Internet connection to explore resources on the World Wide Web, documents that explain important points that would be difficult to keep up-to-date in a textbook or would fill many pages. It is characteristic of the Internet that even high-quality documents are rapidly replaced by better ones, that documents are relocated or disappear, and that there is an overall atmosphere of transience. Therefore, to keep us up-to-date, this appendix will be maintained on an independent Web site, linked to the McGraw-Hill home page (http://www.mhhe.com/irwin/). At that location we will frequently insert the best documents with accurate URLs (accurate addresses) so that you may proceed with confidence.

We will deal with two types of reference sources: the commercial database and the Internet document. The author or reseller/marketer of a commercial database, using a standard search language/syntax, almost always indexes the commercial database, so these databases may be searched more or less systematically and quickly. The reseller/marketer is also responsible for making the database accessible by Internet, modem, or CD/DVD-ROM, and for handling billing and other marketing services.

On the Internet, however, documents and their indexes are separately published. Internet documents maybe be the work of professionals who take a good deal of care and pride in the work, or they may be the hastily thrown together work of amateurs. Searching the Internet is an adventure with very unpredictable rates of success and satisfaction or productivity.

COMMERCIAL DATABASES

Commercial databases are authored and maintained by various profit-making and not-for-profit organizations and are generally marketed/resold by large vendors, notably Dialog (http://www.dialog.com), a subsidiary of Knight-Ridder Information (http://www.krinfo.com).

Here are World Wide Web links to two Knight-Ridder databases, one containing mostly numeric data, one a collection of abstracts and a collection of full-text. Using these links, you will be able to learn about the databases but not gain access to them. Access is for subscribers to various K-R services.

Econbase: Time Series and Forecasts (http://www.krinfo.com/dialog/databases/netscape1.1/bl0565.html)	A data file index principally. Time series used in short-term and long-term economic forecasting.	Assembled from various sources, such as Bureau of Economic Analysis, Bureau of Labor Statistics, Bureau of Census, Federal Reserve Bank. Authored by the WEFA Group of Eddystone, PA. Marketed by Dialog.
Business and Industry (http://www.krinfo.com/dialog/databases/netscape1.1/bl0009.html)	An abstracting index principally. Abstracts (some full-text) of leading trade magazines, newsletters, general business press, regional newspapers, and international business dailies.	Originated by Responsive Database Services of Beachwood, Ohio. Marketed by Dialog.

So that you will better understand commercial database searching, let's explore the Internet site of one of the largest database resellers/marketers, Knight-Ridder Information (http://www.krinfo.com).

A first step to understanding the Dialog collection is to examine a list of the databases that are available by Internet. (The number that is available on CD/DVD-ROM is a smaller set. More about this below.) For each of its databases, Dialog publishes a Bluesheet, a detailed description of the database's contents and internal organization, plus special advice on how to use the generic Dialog search language for most effective use with the particular database. We suggest you examine the Bluesheet list and then examine one or more individual Bluesheets.

For a list of Bluesheets organized by subject area—Business Statistics, Chemistry, etc	(http://www.krinfo.com/dialog/databases/ netscape1.1/bls.html)
For an alphabetical list of Bluesheets	(http://www.krinfo.com/dialog/databases/ netscape1.1/blf.html)

Having achieved an appreciation of the variety of databases available through one reseller/marketer, Knight-Ridder Information, examine the search language/syntax employed by Knight-Ridder Information. Making searches more accessible is a high priority of the profession of library and information science. We can expect rapid advances to occur in natural language searching and in meta-syntaxes that will accommodate not only Knight-Ridder Information but also other resellers/marketers, plus individual library systems' indexes of holdings. For the time being, we suggest you visit the tutorials on the Knight-Ridder Information/Knight-Ridder pages and study the information there.

Item	Where We Found the Guides
A guide to search language/syntax used by Knight-Ridder Information databases	(http://www.krinfo.com/frames/frames_ subjects.html)
An example of the use of search language/ syntax to pursue federal contracts and procurement in the Commerce Business Daily	(http://www.krinfo.com/dialog/train/quick/ solutions/4903.html)
Download HOTCOPY, an interactive tutorial you can run on your Windows-compatible computers, for syntax practice. Or try your hand at an online interactive tutorial.	(http://www.krinfo.com/dialog/train/quick/ quick.html)

Though all of the Knight-Ridder Information databases are available by wide-area online, a subset has been made available on CD/DVD-ROM for use in personal computers and local-area online. The Dialog/Knight-Ridder main page contains a listing of these.

Item	Where We Found the Guides
Listing of KR Ondisc Products	On the Knight-Ridder main page, we followed a link to "Products and Services," where there was a link to KR Ondisc Products (http://www.krinfo.com/frames/frames_ products.html).

If you intend to search the database by Internet, you have several choices.

Choice #1	Choice #2	
Ask the reference department of your cardholder library to give you a quotation on the library's doing the search, and make arrangement for payment.	Buy an annual membership in Knight-Ridder Information, to gain access to all databases or a subset of databases, and make arrangements to pay on a per use basis. Reach the sales department (which for Knight-Ridder Information is http://www.krinfo.com/frames/ frames_sales.html).	The latter choice involves a substantial annual fee but gives you greater control over the time and money you spend online.

Having studied the materials above, you should have a good idea of how online databases may be searched. In practice, what must you do? When you know you need to do a search in a particular topic, go to the listing of Knight-Ridder Information Bluesheets, arranged by topic (http://www.krinfo. com/dialog/databases/-netscape1.1/bls.html), and browse through the Bluesheets to determine which is most suitable. Or consult with a reference librarian about databases which are not in the Knight-Ridder Information collection.

When you are ready to settle on one or more databases, look for a convenient, relatively inexpensive way to access the database. Probably the least expensive way is to see if the library of which you are a cardholder has the database on CD/DVD-ROM. Here you have two ways to proceed.

Method #1	Method #2	
Call the reference department of your cardholder library and ask if the database is available on CD/DVD-ROM, or . . .	. . . find your library's Online Public Access Catalog (OPAC) on the Internet by searching in the Yahoo virtual library. (http://www.yahoo.com/ Reference/Libraries).Explore your OPAC's main page for links to local online engines (CD/DVD).	The former method is faster, but the latter builds intellectual muscle.

ABOUT USING LIBRARY INDEXES FOR LIBRARY MATERIALS

The terminals of your local library are database search engines. Unfortunately, different libraries, even libraries in the same geographic area that happen to belong to different systems (a university library and a public library in the same city that do not share a common computer system), may use search languages/syntax that differ in details. This means that for each library you use, you will have to learn a different search language/syntax.

Visit your cardholder library's OPAC on the Internet and examine its online search engine. It will very likely contain instructions for the search language/syntax of the library's terminals.

Here is an example of a large research library in a technical university, with its own search language/syntax.

Here is the OPAC at Rennselaer Polytechnic Institute (RPI): (http://www. lib.rpi.edu/dept/library/html/ LibInfo.html).

Here is the RPI search index: (http://opac.lib.rpi.edu/).

Here are the instructions for the search engine at RPI: (http://opac.lib.rpi.edu/search/w).

Now find your cardholder library, locate its search engine, and identify its search language/syntax screens.

Here are links to university libraries: (http://www.yahoo.com/Reference/Libraries/University_Libraries/). Here are links to public libraries: (http://www.yahoo.com/Reference/Libraries/Public_Libraries). Here, for the brave infonauts, are links to online libraries that do not exist in hardcopy: (http://www.yahoo.com/Reference/Libraries/On_Line_Libraries/).

If a database is not available on local-area online by CD/DVD, you will have to access it by wide-area online, by Internet or modem connection, or you will have to license the CD/DVD for use on your personal computer. Since annual license fees run in the hundreds of dollars, you had better want the database badly.

SEARCHING THE INTERNET

As we explained earlier, the Internet is shapeless and disorganized— there are essentially no obstructions to anyone posting practically anything. Although there are carefully organized databases on the World Wide Web, the Web is full of amateurish attempts at electronic publishing. Therefore, we suggest the following strategy:

- Use a virtual library if you are looking for more or less authoritative, carefully organized documents. Such a search site is organized hierarchically by topic, and each of the links has been visited and evaluated by a human being.

- We use a robot search engine or Web crawler to search for rare items which may have escaped the attention of the humans who organize the virtual libraries. A robot search engine visits and indexes as many sites as possible, and does so without discriminative human evaluations of worth.

Here are some of the effective virtual libraries that index the World WideWeb.

Infomine is organized by the University of California library system (http://lib-www.ucr.edu/).

Suitable for scholars and researchers. There is no top level in the hierarchy devoted to business and economics.

Excite is a commercially sponsored site (http://www.excite.com/).

For business and investing, start here (http://my.excite.com/channel/business/?a-chb-t).

Yahoo is the old dependable, the first of the successful virtual libraries. Unfortunately, it contains too many links to advertising sites (http://www.yahoo.com/).

For business, start here (http://www.yahoo.com/Business/).

Argus Clearinghouse is very selective (http://www.clearinghouse.net/).

Disinformation is an index of selected muckraking articles (http://www.disinfo.com/).

For business, start here (http://www.clearinghouse.net/cgi=bin/chadmin/viewcat/Business___Employment?kywd++).

The Web robots are not topically organized and are indiscriminate in indexing every site visited. Each robot/crawler has its own search language/syntax, which you have to learn for best results. Each site responds differently to the same key words, because of differences in syntax. For an interesting tutorial on robot syntax, visit Internet Sleuth (http://www.isleuth.com/search-techniques.html).

AltaVista advanced search (http://altavista.digital.com/cgi-bin/query?pg=aq&what=web). Allows considerable precision in searching, if you are willing to use its complicated syntax.

Lycos is one of the oldest robot searchers (http://lycos.com/).

Many searchers respect Hotbot (http://www.hotbot.com/).

Here is the search language/syntax for the advanced searching features of AltaVista: (http://altavista.digital.com/cgi-bin/query?pg=ah).

Here is the syntax for Lycos: (http://www.lycos.com/help/search-help.html).

Here is the syntax for Hotbot: (http://www.hotbot.com/Help/).

Meta-search engines accept search terms and feed them into several search engines at once, then collate the results. Here are several meta-search engines, which we highly recommend if you have not already bonded with a favorite robot searcher.

Cyber 411 (http://www.cyber411.com/)

Dogpile (http://www.dogpile.com/)

Internet Sleuth (http://www.isleuth.com/)

Syntax for Cyber 411: (http://www.cyber411.com/help.html)

Syntax for Dogpile: (http://www.dogpile.com/notes.html)

Syntax for Internet Sleuth: (http://www.isleuth.com/search-techniques.html)

On its Infomine site, the University of California library system maintains a site that explains how World Wide Web search engines work (http://lib-www.ucr.edu/infomine/exp/finding.html). The site also contains links to recommended search engines.

LINKS TO MATERIAL CITED IN CHAPTER 10

This section contain quotations from Chapter 10 that are referenced to specific links. When this appendix is used at our website, online, the links are active and you may navigate by clicking on the highlighted URL.

- "The Electric Library, for an additional $9.95 a month, gives access to an encyclopedia (*Colliers*), a library of reference books, hundreds of magazines, hundreds of radio-TV transcripts, and a huge collection of local and nationally known newspapers, all very neatly indexed for rapid search and retrieval." Here is the Electric Library (http://www.elibrary.com/), a full-text collection of newspaper, journal, and magazine articles; radio-TV transcripts; maps; photos; and reference books, including an encyclopedia. Apply for a trial period (http://www.elibrary.com/s-default/info/trial.html); then decide if you want to subscribe.

- "In its online public access catalog, the University of Florida library (http://nervm.nerdc.ufl.edu/) suggests a six-step process for secondary data collection and analysis."

- "For the very latest books as they reach the bookstores, visit one of the mega-bookstores on the Internet's World Wide Web, such as amazon.com or Barnes and Noble." Here is a link to the amazon.com online bookstore (http://www.amazon.com/). And here is Barnes and Noble online (http://www.barnesandnoble.com/).

- "Many newspapers are now available on the Internet a few days after they appear. These include *New York Times* (http://www.nytimes.com/) and *Wall Street Journal* (http://www.yahoo.com/Business_and_Economy/Companies/ Financial_Services/Investment_Services/Market_Information_and_Research/ Dow_Jones___Company_Inc_/Products_and_Services/Wall_Street_Journal/). Also on the Internet are the Reuters News Service and UP News Service. Generally, the fastest way to locate the news services is by accessing Lycos, Yahoo, or one of the other super-search engines. To check the availability of your local newspaper on the Internet, visit one of the World Wide Web sites listed in Appendix A."

- Also on the Internet are Lycos (http://www.lycos.com/news/), Associated Press (http://www.washingtonpost.com/wp-srv/searches/mainsrch.htm), and Yahoo News (http://www.yahoo.com/headlines/).

- For a top-notch collection of newspapers, visit (http://www.isleuth.com/ news.html). To check the availability of your local newspaper on the Internet, visit (http://www.newspapers.com). If you are looking for an Internet version of a favorite magazine, try here (http://www.yahoo.com/News/Magazines/).

- "It would be wrong to think that the local-area online and Internet services are 'merely' replacing hard-copy services. Many of the search engines have virtual reference rooms that go far beyond their hard-copy versions in traditional libraries and include services that are impossible to render in hard copy. In the traditional vein, there are conventional online dictionaries (http://www.m-w.com/netdict.htm), such as *Bartlett's Familiar Quotations* (http://www.columbia.edu/acis/bartleby/bartlett/)." Here is the reference rooms of Yahoo (http://www.yahoo.com/Reference/).

- "A Web site called FedWorld (http://www.yahoo.com/Government/Agencies/ FedWorld/) is organized by the federal government as a gateway into the federal departments. State government is not nearly so accessible, perhaps because no state has nearly so large a user base as the federal government. Several World Wide Web documents attempt to organize state and local government sites (county and city, for instance) that are quite difficult to find. Some state sites attempt to provide links down to the local sites." See if this helps you to find what you need for state government: (http://search. yahoo.com/bin/search?p=state+government).

- "Wally decided to use the Excite Web engine, using a single key word, 'homeless.' He was presented with a number of possibilities and, on a hunch, chose the Web page of the National Coalition for the Homeless. This document proved to be well suited to his task, since it contained a number of what appeared to be authoritative essays on the extent and causes of homelessness, as well as prospects for relieving it and possible sources of grant money. A phone call to his county's local coalition for the homeless verified his belief that the National Coalition was a reliable source." Here is what you get when you ask the Excite search engine to locate "Homeless": (http://www.excite.com/search.gw?trace=a&search=Homeless). And here is the page of the National Coalition: (http://nch.ari.net/).

- "Also, she (Martina G.) used the Business Newswire (http://www.businesswire.com/) to search for news releases on 'reinventing.'"

- "Jeff wanted a bibliography for his work. He used the Alta Vista search engine with the search terms ["real estate investment" AND (bibliographies and bibliography)], and found a bibliography on "real estate investment" at the pages of the Evanston, Illinois, Public Library (http://www.evanston.lib. il.us/library/bibliographies/) and a "Futures and Options Bibliography" by a professor of finance at Florida International University (http://www.fiu.edu/~daiglerr/bib.htm)."

B DECISION THEORY PROBLEM

The value of research information can be assessed by several means, one of which is decision theory. The example considered here concerns the case of a manager who is deciding on a change in production equipment. Research information will play a major role in this decision. The new equipment can be leased for five years and will replace several old machines that require constant attention to operate. The problem facing the manager is, "Shall I lease the new machines with the attendant efficiencies, reduced labor, and higher lease charges, or shall I continue to use the old equipment?"

The decision situation has been prompted by news that the firm might secure several large orders from companies that have not been previous customers. With added volume, departmental profit contributions will increase substantially with the new equipment. For this decision, the manager adopts the decision variable "average annual departmental profit contribution."[1] The decision rule is, "Choose that course of action that will provide the highest average annual contribution to departmental profits."

Exhibit B–1 indicates the results of the evaluation of the two available actions. Under the conditions cited, it is obvious that course A_1 is preferred.

CONDITIONS OF CERTAINTY

Exhibit B–1 presents the case with the assumption that the anticipated new business will materialize. It therefore represents, in decision theory terminology, *decision making under conditions of certainty*. It is assumed the payoffs are certain to occur if the particular action is chosen and the probability of the additional business being secured is 1.0.[2] The decision to choose action A_1 is obvious under these conditions with the given payoff data and decision rule.

CONDITIONS OF UNCERTAINTY

In a more realistic situation, the outcome is less than certain. The new business may not materialize, and then the department might be left with costly excess capacity. The union may resist introduction of the new equipment because it replaces workers. The new equipment may not perform as anticipated. For these or other reasons, the decision maker may be uncertain about the consequences (for instance, that course A_1 will result in a \$20,000 contribution).

Suppose the manager considers these other possible outcomes and concludes the one serious uncertainty is that the new business may not be forthcoming. For purposes of simplicity, one of two conditions will exist in the future—either the new business will be secured as expected (O_1), or the new business will not materialize (O_2). In the first case, the expected payoffs would be the same as in Exhibit B–1; but if the new business is not secured, then the addition of the new equipment would give

EXHIBIT B–1   Payoff Under Conditions of Certainty

Course of Action	Average Annual Departmental Profit Contribution
A_1—Lease new equipment	\$20,000
A_2—Retain old equipment	12,000

EXHIBIT   B–2   Payoff Under Conditions of Uncertainty

	Average Annual Departmental Profit Contribution		
Course of Action	New Business (O_1)	No New Business (O_2)	Expected Monetary Value
A_1—Lease new equipment	$20,000	$5,000	$14,000
A_2—Retain old equipment	12,000	9,000	10,800

the department costly excess capacity, with fixed lease changes. The payoff table may now be revised as Exhibit B–2.

Under these conditions, the original decision rule does not apply. That rule said, "Choose that course of action which will provide the highest average annual contribution to departmental profit." Under the conditions in Exhibit B–2, action A_1 would be better if the new business is secured, but A_2 would be the better choice if the new business is not secured. If the decision can be delayed until the new order question is resolved, the dilemma is escapable. However, because of lead times, the equipment decision may need to be made first.

When faced with two or more possible outcomes for each alternative, the manager can adopt one of two approaches. First, the likelihood that the company will receive the new business cannot be judged. Even so, a rational decision can be made by adopting an appropriate decision rule. For example, "Choose that course of action for which the minimum payoff is the highest." This is known as the *maximum criterion* because it calls for maximizing the minimum payoff. In Exhibit B–2, the minimum payoff for alternative A_1 is shown as $5,000, and the minimum payoff for A_2 is $9,000. According to the *maximum* rule, the choice would be A_2 because it is the best of the worst outcomes. This decision is a "cut your losses" strategy.

The second approach is to use subjective judgment to estimate the probability that either O_1 or O_2 will occur.[3] When the assumption was decision under certainty, only one event was possible (had a probability of 1.0). Now, however, with experience and information from other sources, there is a less-than-certain chance of the new business materializing, and this doubt should be part of the decision.

One might estimate that there is a 0.6 chance the new business will be secured and a 0.4 chance it will not. With this or any other set of similar probabilities, an overall evaluation of the two courses of action is possible. One approach is to calculate an *expected monetary value (EMV)* for each alternative.[4]

THE DECISION FLOW DIAGRAM

The decision problem already has been summarized in a payoff table, but further illustration in the form of a decision flow diagram (or decision tree) may be helpful. The decision tree for the equipment problem is shown in Exhibit B–3. The diagram may be seen as a sequential decision flow. At the square node on the left, the manager must choose between A_1 and A_2. After one of these actions, a chance event will occur—either the new business will be received by the company (O_1), or it will not be received (O_2). At the right extremity of the branches are listed the conditional

EXHIBIT   B–3   Decision Tree for the Equipment Problem

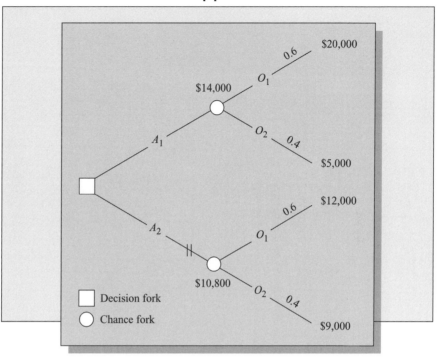

payoffs that will occur for each combination of decision and chance event. On each chance branch is placed the expected probability of that chance event occurring. Keep in mind that these are subjective probability estimates by the manager that express a degree of belief that such a chance event will occur.

Having set up this series of relationships, one calculates back from right to left on the diagram by an *averaging out and folding back* process. At each decision juncture, the path that yields the best alternative for the decision rule is selected. Here the EMV for A_1 averages out to $14,000, while the EMV for A_2 is $10,800. The double slash line on the A_2 branch indicates it is the inferior alternative and should be dropped in favor of A_1.

THE CONTRIBUTION OF RESEARCH

Now, the contribution of research can be assessed. Recall that the value of research may be judged as "the difference between the results of decisions made with the information and the results that would be made without it." In this example, the research need is to decide whether the new business will be secured. This is the uncertainty that, if known, would make a perfect forecast possible. Just how much is a perfect forecast worth in this case?

Consider Exhibit B–3 once again. What would happen if the manager had information to accurately predict whether the new business orders would be secured? The choice would be A_1 if the research indicated the orders would be received, and A_2 if

EXHIBIT   B–4   The Value of Perfect Information

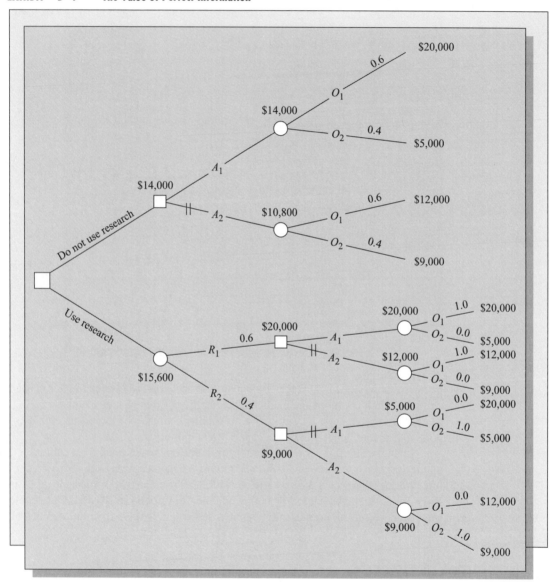

the research indicated the orders would not be received. However, at the decision point (before the research is undertaken), the best estimate is that there is a 0.6 chance that the research will indicate the O_1 condition and 0.4 that the condition will be O_2. The decision flow implications of the use of research are illustrated in Exhibit B–4.

The decision sequence begins with the decision fork at the left. If the manager chooses to do research (R), the first chance fork is reached where one of two things will occur. Research indicates either that the orders will be received (R_1) or the orders will not be received (R_2). Before doing the research, the best estimate of the probability of R_1 taking place is the same as the estimate that O_1 will occur (0.6). Similarly, the best estimate that R_2 will occur is 0.4.

After the manager learns R_1 or R_2, there is a second decision fork: A_1 or A_2. After the A_1–A_2 decision, there is a second chance fork (O_1 or O_2) that indicates whether the orders were received. Note that the probabilities at O_1 and O_2 have now changed from 0.6 and 0.4, respectively, to 1.0 and 0.0, or to 0.0 and 1.0, depending on what was learned from the research. This change occurs because we have evaluated the effect of the research information on our original O_1 and O_2 probability estimates by calculating *posterior probabilities*. These are revisions of our prior probabilities that result from the assumed research findings. The posterior probabilities (for example, $P(O_1|R_i)$ and $P(O_2|R_i)$ are calculated by using Bayes's theorem.[5]

| | **States of Nature** | | | **Posterior Probabilities** | |
| | | | *Marginal* | | |
Research Outcomes	O_1	O_2	*Probabilities*	$P(O_1|R_i)$	$P(O_2|R_i)$
R_1	0.6	0.0	0.6	1.0	0.0
R_2	0.0	0.4	0.4	0.0	1.0
Marginal probabilities	0.6	0.4			

The manager is now ready to average out and fold back the analysis from right to left to evaluate the research alternative. Clearly, if R_1 is found, A_1 is chosen with its EMV of $20,000 over the A_2 alternative of $12,000. If R_2 is reported, then A_2 is more attractive. However, before the research, the probabilities of R_1 and R_2 being secured must be incorporated by a second averaging out. The result is an EMV of $15,600 for the research alternative versus an EMV of $14,000 for the no-research path. The conclusion then is this: Research that would enable the manager to make a perfect forecast regarding the potential new orders would be worth up to $1,600. If the research costs more than $1,600, decline to buy it because the net EMV of the research alternative would be less than the EMV of $14,000 of the no-research alternative.

IMPERFECT INFORMATION

The analysis up to this point assumes that research on decision options will give a perfect prediction of the future states of nature, O_1 and O_2. Perfect prediction seldom occurs in practice. Sometimes research reveals one condition when later evidence shows something else to be true. Thus, we need to consider that the research in the machinery decision will provide less-than-perfect information and is, therefore, worth less than the $1,600 calculated in Exhibit B–4.

Suppose the research in that example involves interviews with the customers' key personnel and some customers' executives. They might all answer our questions to the best of their ability but still predict imperfectly what will happen. Consequently, we might judge that the chances of their predictions being correct are no better than 3 to 1, or 0.75. If we accept that our research results may provide imperfect information in this manner, we need to factor this into our evaluation decision. We do this by averaging out and folding back again. The results are shown in Exhibit B–5. The revised

EXHIBIT   B–5   The Value of Imperfect Information

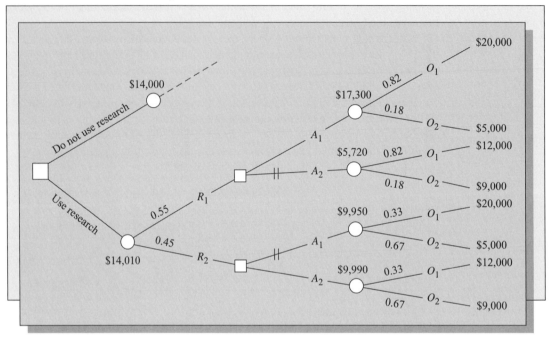

EMV, given research judged to be 75 percent reliable, is $14,010. This revised EMV is only $10 higher than the $14,000 EMV using no research and would seem to be hardly worth consideration.

PRAGMATIC COMPLICATIONS

This discussion, while simplified, contains the basic concepts for finding the value of research. Practical difficulties complicate the use of these concepts. First, the situation with two events and two alternatives is artificial. Problems with more choices and events are common, and the chief complication is the increased number of calculations.

	States of Nature			Posterior Probabilities	
Research Outcomes	O_1	O_2	*Marginal Probabilities*	$P(O_1|R_i)$	$P(O_2|R_i)$
R_1	0.45	0.10	0.55	0.82	0.18
R_2	0.15	0.30	0.45	0.33	0.67
Marginal probabilities	0.60	0.40			

A more serious problem is posed by the measurement of outcomes. We have assumed we could assess the various actions in terms of an unambiguous dollar value, but often we cannot. It is difficult to place a dollar value on outcomes related to morale or public image, for example.

An allied problem lies in the exclusive use of EMV as the criterion for decision. This is correct in an actuarial sense and implies that each decision maker has a linear system of evaluation. In truth, we often use another evaluation system. The person who accepts EMV as a criterion sees that an even bet of $20 between two people on the toss of a fair coin is a fair bet. Many people, however, may not be willing to make such a bet because they fear the loss of $20 more than they value the gain of $20. They may need to be offered a chance, say, to win $20 but to lose only $10 before they would be willing to bet. These persons have a nonlinear decision scale. The "utility" concept is more relevant here.

The development of more precise methods of evaluating the contribution of research continues. In the meantime, continued emphasis on improvement of our understanding of the researcher's task and the research process will make research more valuable when it is conducted.

Reference Notes

1. Recall that the decision variable is the unit of measurement used in the analysis. At this point, we need not be concerned with how this measure is calculated or whether it is the appropriate decision variable. Assume for purposes of this illustration that it is appropriate.

2. A probability is a measure between 1.0 and 0.0 that expresses the likelihood of an event occurring. For example, the probability of a "head" on a toss of a coin is 0.5. Under conditions of certainty, the forecasted outcome is assumed to have a probability of 1.0 even though we might agree that we normally cannot know the future with certainty. In most forecasting where a specific amount is named, there is an implicit assumption of certainty.

3. Concepts of probability enter into three types of situations. In the classical situation, each possible outcome has a known chance of occurrence. For example, a coin tossed in the air has a 0.5 chance of landing heads up; a spade card has a 0.25 chance of being drawn from a well-mixed deck.

    In the same type of situation, probabilities are thought of as "relative frequencies." Even if the probability is not known from the structure of the problem (as it is in the classical case), it can still be estimated if there is a body of empirical evidence. For example, experience may show that about 1 in 50 products produced is defective. From this statistic, one can estimate there is a 0.02 chance that any given product will be defective.

    If there is no direct empirical evidence, one can still assess probability on the basis of opinion, intuition, and/or general experience. In such cases, uncertainty is expressed as a subjectively felt "degree of confidence" or "degree of belief" that a given event will occur. The discussions in this appendix are cases in point. For more information on probability concepts, see any modern statistics text.

4. One calculates an EMV for an alternative by weighting each conditional value (for example, $20,000 and $5,000 for A_1) by the estimated probability of the occurrence of the associated event (0.6 probability of the $20,000 being made).

$$EMV = P_1(\$20,000) + P_2(\$5,000)$$
$$= 0.6(\$20,000) + 0.4(\$5,000)$$
$$= \$14,000$$

5. Bayes's theorem with two states of nature is

$$P(O_1 \mid R_i) = \frac{P(R_i \mid O_1) \times P(O_1)}{P(R_i \mid O_1) \times P(O_1) + P(R_i \mid O_2) \times P(O_2)}$$
$$= \frac{1.0 \times 0.6}{(1.0 \times 0.6) + (0.0 \times 0.4)}$$
$$= 1.0$$

C REQUEST FOR PROPOSAL (RFP): ASSESSMENT AND CONTENTS

Chapter 4 identified the request for proposal (RFP) as a means to formalize the process of documenting, justifying, and authorizing a procurement of research. RFPs provide the opportunity to evaluate different solutions and offer a mechanism to establish, monitor, and control the performance of the winning supplier of research services.

SUMMARY OF RFP EFFECTIVENESS

In the literature (the *ABI/Inform* database), over 100 journal articles discussed the role of RFPs, ranging from the reasons to use them to specific industry applications. The emerging consensus is that, except for government contracts and highly specialized industrial applications (e.g., engineering, manufacturing, construction, hospital systems), *traditional RFPs are not time and cost effective.* Commonly, the cost of preparing the RFP exceeds fifteen percent of the final bid, the preparation can take as long as two years, and the document may run between several hundred and a thousand pages. An article in the *Journal of Business Communication* said this device has become virtually worthless for the procurement of services.

Several modifications or alternatives to RFPs are currently being considered:

- Send shorter RFPs by investing time up front to decide specific, desirable outcomes.
- Use site visits and demonstrations to be certain the suppliers' designs or systems can meet their claims.
- Automate the process to reduce time and cost of preparation (Strategic Systems Solutions International offers software called Product Analyzer to simplify objective supplier evaluation through various scoring algorithms).
- Replace the RFP with a request for application (RFA). The RFA would consist of the following:
  —An overview of the requesting firm's organizational structure
  —Business objectives
  —Basic operational procedures
  —Problems that the supplier's bid should address
- Replace the RFP with a request for recommendation (RFR). The RFR would contain a clear statement of the problem and be sent to a small number of credible suppliers. The suppliers' responses would
  —Be limited to a ten-page reply
  —Contain ballpark prices for the information to be provided
  —Include supplier recommendations with brief descriptions of solutions and support that can be offered
  —Be due in three to four weeks (saving the cost of a consultant to prepare an RFP and leaving the firm with the flexibility to maintain control of the project's ultimate direction)

Suppliers (usually no more than six) would be invited to visit the firm and make a two-hour presentation. The firm's statement of work would then be refined and the supplier list narrowed.

- Similar to RFAs and RFRs, the request for information (RFI) is often the first step in overall RFP development. The RFI lets a supplier know you are gathering information but are not prepared to purchase a good or service. It provides the company with an opportunity to more carefully define its requirements and alerts suppliers to the opportunity to respond to its requirements. There are several advantages to RFIs. An RFI

  —Is an accepted method for determining if the techniques and methods are available, if cost estimates are reasonable, and if solutions exist

  —Requires in-house people to agree on the requirements and set minimal expectations

  —Eliminates supplier surprise, thereby helping suppliers to build a better response

  —Requires a formal written response that may later be incorporated into the contract

  —Provides a qualified list of suppliers and eliminates those who could not have responded to the RFP

THE ORGANIZATION AND CONTENT OF AN RFP

The RFP process, properly modified, allows an organization to analyze its current operations, problems, and future challenges. Communications with potential suppliers can be clear and based on a mutual understanding of the problems being addressed and the proposed solutions. Proper planning and management commitment to the project are essential.

The first step in developing an RFP is to fully understand and define the problem being addressed. In a formal RFP process, an internal set of experts defines the problem. (One can hire an expert or a group of experts who specialize in the problem area to help in defining the problem and writing the RFP.) Once the problem is defined, the technical section of the RFP can be written.

Besides defining the technical requirements, critical components of the RFP include project management, pricing, and contract administration. These sections allow the supplier to understand and meet expectations of the management team for carrying out the contracted services. Also, a section on the proposal administration, including important dates, is included.

The components of an RFP are

- Proposal administration information
- Summary statement of the problem
- Technical section
- Management section

- Pricing section
- Contracts and license section

Proposal Administration

This section is an overview with important information on the administration of the proposal itself. It establishes the dates of the RFP process—when the RFP is released, the time when the RFP team is available for questions, the date the proposals are expected, and the dates of the evaluation and supplier selections. It includes all requirements for preparing the proposal and describes how the proposals will be evaluated. Contact names, addresses, and relevant telephone and fax information are listed.

Summary Statement of the Problem

This section can be an abstract of the technical section, or it can be included as the first page of the technical section.

Technical Section

Technical information needed for the supplier to create the proposal is presented in this section. It begins by describing the problems to be addressed and the technical detail of each requirement. It loosely describes the services to be performed and the equipment, software, and documentation required. This section should be neither too specific nor too general to allow the suppliers flexibility in design creativity but restrict them to meeting the needs of the corporation. Typically, the following would be included:

- Problem statement
- Description of functional requirements
- Identification of constraints

Management Section

Each project requires some level of management. The extent to which the corporation expects schedules, plans, and reports is included in this section. The management section should include requirements for implementation schedules, training and reporting schedules, and other documentation. If specific supplier qualifications are needed, they should be shown here. References from the supplier's customer should also be requested.

Pricing Section

To cost the proposal, all information needed by the supplier is contained in this section. By using a rigid format, proposals with different approaches can be compared on costs. The following list shows examples of items that should be included:

- Services
- Data collection
- Data analysis
- Meetings with client

- Travel
- Respondent survey incentives
- Mail and telephone costs
- Design meetings
- Facilities and equipment
- Extensions to work agreements
- Pilot tests
- Report preparations
- Computer models
- Project management
- Deliverables
  —Training
  —Brochures/literature
  —Videotapes
  —Reports
- Questionnaire and reproduction costs
- Manpower costs

Contracts and License Section

This section includes the types of contracts the supplier is expected to sign and any nondisclosure agreements. The safeguarding of intellectual property and the use of copyright are discussed. Terms of payment and required benchmarks are set forth. Typically a sample purchase contract would be included.

CONCLUSION

A well-written RFP allows an organization to request state-of-the-art proposals for dealing with complex problems. When not done properly, the process will take longer, cost more, and not provide a complete long-term solution. Therefore, it is essential when an organization decides to put a project to bid using an RFP-type mechanism that time and effort are invested at the beginning of the process. Modifications to traditional RFP methods would also be beneficial. Clear communications with suppliers through a coherent RFP will result in a well-managed project with long-term benefits.

SAMPLE STUDENT
TERM PROJECT

Four members of a graduate research methods course formed a team to investigate career prospects in product management. Their stated research objectives were (1) to provide an inventory of major U.S. manufacturers that use the product management system, (2) to gather descriptive data on the nature and degree of product management, and (3) to collect information on how product managers are recruited, selected, and prepared for their responsibilities.

The research question was: "What is the role and scope of product management in U.S. manufacturing companies?" Since financial support from the student research fund was limited to *Fortune*'s top 1,000 manufacturing companies, the students further defined manufacturers according to this criterion. Their investigative questions were:

1. What is the incidence of use of the product manager system?
    a. To what degree is it presently in use?
    b. Has it been used in the past and discontinued?
    c. Was it considered and not adopted?
    d. What are future expectations regarding its use?
2. How are product managers recruited and selected?
3. What are the qualifications for employment as a product manager?
4. How does the product manager function in the company?
5. How can we classify the characteristics of individuals and companies to discern trends and differences?

They selected a mail survey as their data collection method. Their initial plan was to use a screening or qualifying question to establish which companies use product management.

The team members developed the following procedure for constructing their questionnaire. Having agreed on the investigative questions, each member attempted to write measurement questions aimed at tapping the essence of each investigative question. Each measurement question was written on a 5-by-8-inch card to facilitate comparisons, revisions, additions, and deletions. At a meeting of the team, all questions were reviewed, duplicates were eliminated, and a general winnowing occurred. The remaining 31 questions were included in questionnaire draft 1, shown in Exhibit D–1. In this first draft, there was no effort to place questions in sequence or to present them graphically as they would eventually be seen by respondents.

After discussion, the team members concluded the questionnaire would probably need to be three pages long. In addition, the cover letter would require a page. They decided to use a printed cover letter and to incorporate it as the first page of the questionnaire. The combination would be printed on both sides of an 11-by-17-inch sheet of paper, folded in booklet form to $8^1/_2$-by-11 inches.

Each team member was assigned the task of translating draft 1 into draft 2. In the new draft, the questions were in planned sequence, had response formats chosen, and had graphic arrangements selected. Individual drafts were submitted to a subcommittee of the team who used them as the basis for developing questionnaire draft 2. This is shown in Exhibit D–2.

EXHIBIT D–1   Preliminary Questionnaire, Product Manager Study—Draft 1

1. What is your position in the company?
2. Is your company engaged primarily in industrial products, consumer products, or both?
3. Does your company use product managers?
4. How many product managers does the company have?
5. How many products are assigned to one PM?
6. Would you please give or include a job description of your company's PM position?
7. How many brands does your company have?
8. Approximately what percentage of your company's brands have product managers?
9. What percentage of sales volume do the brands in question 8 account for as a whole?
10. How long have product managers been used in your company?
11. Has a PM system been used and dropped in your company? If yes, why was it dropped?
12. Has a PM system ever been considered but never adopted in your company? If yes, why was it not adopted?
13. Are there any plans for the adoption of a PM system in the future?
14. What percentage of your product managers come *directly* from each of the following sources? Campuses, within the company, other companies, other (list).
15. If PMs come from within the company, what department or departments do they come from? Sales, marketing, production, advertising, other (list).
16. If PMs come from outside the company (other than campuses), what department or departments do they come from? Product manager, sales, marketing, production, advertising, other (list).
17. If PMs are recruited directly from campuses, what, if any, are typical degrees required?
18. Rank on a scale from 1 to 5 the relative importance of each of the following qualifications for a PM (1 denotes the greatest importance). Education, age, work experience, personality, creativity.
19. If PMs are recruited from within the company, what is the average age, length of work experience (with the company), and educational background?
20. If PMs are recruited from outside the company (not including campuses), what is the average age, length of work experience, and educational background?
21. What functions (advertising, pricing, etc.) does the PM actually perform in day-to-day activities, and what percentage of time is spent on each?
22. Of those functions listed in 21, which, if any, does the PM have *final* authority over?
23. To whom does the PM report?
24. Does your company have a structured training program for product management? If yes, please explain.
25. On the basis of which of the following is the PM evaluated? Market share, ROI, sales volume, profits, other (list).
26. What were the objectives of the company in instituting the PM concept?
27. How successful has the PM concept been in fulfilling the objectives set for it?
28. What were the characteristics of the PM concept that contributed to the fulfillment of these objectives?
29. What elements, if any, of the PM system did not adequately contribute to the fulfillment of the objectives?
30. What specific actions, if any, have been taken to deal with the inadequacies listed in 29?
31. If your company is currently planning any broad revisions in the present PM program, please describe.

Draft 2 was reproduced and submitted to other members of the research class for critique. Comments and challenges were sought on (1) sources of confusion and vagueness; (2) question value (What useful information does the question provide? Not provide?); (3) appropriateness of the proposed response formats and suggestions for improvement; and (4) gaps in question coverage.

After this critique, a second subcommittee revised the questionnaire. This resulted in questionnaire draft 3 (not presented here). The draft was again reviewed by the full team, and modest changes were made to produce draft 4.

By this time, the team members were eager to test the questionnaire with respondents. Arrangements were made to have several local corporate executives complete the questionnaire. Team members picked up the completed questionnaires,

EXHIBIT   D–2   Product Manager Questionnaire—Draft 2

1. Does your company now use product managers? yes _____ no _____ (If no, please go to question 17).
2. Would you please send a copy of your job description?
3. How many product managers does your company have? _____
4. What percentage of your total sales is accounted for by product managers? _____ %
5. How long have product managers been used by your company? _____ years
6. What percentage of your personnel enters the product management program from the following sources?

    Campuses _____ %

    Within the company _____ %

    From elsewhere _____ %
7. If product managers come from within the company or elsewhere, what department(s) do they come from?

    Sales _____ %

    Marketing _____ %

    Production _____ %

    Advertising _____ %

    Other product management programs _____ %

    Advertising agencies _____ %

    Elsewhere _____ %
8. If product managers are recruited directly from campuses, please rank the following degrees from 1 to 6, with 1 being the most desirable, 2 the next most desirable, and so forth.

    BS _____ areas _____

    AB _____ areas _____

    BSBA (BBA)_____ areas _____

    MA _____ areas _____

    MBA _____ areas _____

    PhD _____ areas _____

9. Briefly state what you consider to be an appropriate profile of a product manager recruited directly from the campus.
    Age

    Work experience (length and type)

    Personal traits (personality, creativity, aggressiveness, etc.)

    Education

---

interviewed the executives about their answers, and secured comments they had about the questions and the study. These experiences led to a revised draft 5. This was repeated twice more with other executives, finally ending with draft 7 shown here as Exhibit D–3. The limitations of time and money led the team to depend on local product managers for testing rather than on a full-scale dress rehearsal by mail. This decision limited the value of the pretesting but was accepted as a limitation of a student project.

EXHIBIT   D–2   *(concluded)*

10. What do you consider to be an appropriate profile for a product manager recruited from within or from another company?
    Age

    Work experience (length and type)

    Personal traits (personality, creativity, aggressiveness, etc.)

    Education

11. To whom does the product manager report? _____
12. What percentage of his or her time does the product manager spend in various functionary areas, such as production, advertising, pricing, etc.? Please list.
13. Please rank on a scale of 1 to 5 (1 is most important) the following criteria used in evaluating a product manager.
    _____ Market share
    _____ Return on investment
    _____ Sales volume
    _____ Profits
    _____ Other (please explain)   _____
14. Does the company have a structured training program?
    yes _____ no _____ If yes, please describe. _____
15. What prompted your firm to initiate the product manager system?
16. Is your company currently planning any future revisions in the product manager system?
    yes _____ no _____ If yes, please explain. _____
17. Is your company primarily engaged in
    Industrial goods _____ %
    Food products _____ %
    Consumer package goods _____ %
    Consumer durable goods _____ %
    Automotive products _____ %
    Other (list)
    _____   _____ %
    _____   _____ %
18. What is your company's total sales volume? $ _____
    If you answered question 1 yes, you have completed the questionnaire. If your answer was no, please answer question 19.
    Thank you for your cooperation.
19. Please check which of the following best describes your company's use of product managers.
    _____ Have never considered product managers
    _____ Have considered, but never adopted product management
    _____ Have used previously and discontinued
    _____ Presently considering adoption of the system in the future

The survey was sent to the top 1,000 manufacturing companies in the form described. Only one mailing was made because of time and money limitations. Usable returns numbered 492 at the cutoff point. Approximately 50 companies sent job descriptions of their product management positions.

EXHIBIT   D–3   Product Manager Questionnaire—Final Draft

METRO UNIVERSITY
GRADUATE SCHOOL OF BUSINESS ADMINISTRATION
DES MOINES, IA 50301

Inside Address

Dear Sir:

We at the Metro University Business School are interested in learning more about the actual recruitment and use of product or brand managers. Our objective is to help expand the body of knowledge about this important area of marketing.

To do this, of course, means going to someone such as yourself who *knows*. Your help with the few questions on the attached pages will take only a few minutes and will make a real contribution to the accuracy and success of this study.

Your reply will be treated in strict confidence and will be available only to my research staff and me. Any publication will be only of statistical totals for groups of companies.

Your assistance will be greatly appreciated and will help us to know more about product management and to teach about it in a more relevant and effective manner.

Sincerely,

William Urbandale
Professor of Marketing

We define a *product manager* (also called a *brand manager*) as one who is responsible for the integration and planning of a broad range of marketing functions (pricing, distribution, and so forth) for a specific product, brand, or homogeneous group of products. The position usually has limited or no line authority, especially over the sales force.

1. Please indicate which of the following best describes your company/division's use of product managers.

    _____ We are currently using product managers.

    _____ We have previously used product managers, but discontinued.

    _____ We have considered the system, but never implemented it.

    _____ Presently considering adoption of the system in the future.

    _____ We have never considered product managers.

    If you are currently using product managers, please continue. If *you are not* currently using product managers, you have completed the questionnaire. Thank you for your cooperation.

                                                         (please check)
2. Will you be answering the following for: _____   your company
                                                _____   your division
3. How many product managers (include all levels such as group PM, PM, assoc. PM, and assistant PM) does your company/division employ?   _____
4. How long have product managers been used by your company/division?   _____ years
5. What percentage of your company/division total sales are accounted for by products controlled by product managers? _____ %
6. From the following, please indicate whether the position exists in your company/division. Then indicate the source from which the personnel at the various levels were obtained to fill that position. If you have a similar position but with a different name, please indicate that position in the blank.

EXHIBIT D–3   *(continued)*

	Do You Have?		(please check) Major Sources			
			Within Company			
	Yes	*No*	*Campuses*	*Other PM Jobs*	*Other Jobs*	*Other Companies*
Group PMs	____	____	____	____	____	____
PMs	____	____	____	____	____	____
Assoc. PMs	____	____	____	____	____	____
Asst. PMs	____	____	____	____	____	____
Other (specify)	____	____	____	____	____	____

7. What is the typical age of your

    Group product managers   _____ years

    Product managers   _____ years

    Associate PMs   _____ years

    Assistant PMs   _____ years

8. Of the following personal traits, would you please indicate the degree of importance in the evaluation of a candidate for a product management position.

	(please check)			
	Not Important	*Desirable*	*Very Desirable*	*Essential*
Leadership	____	____	____	____
Creativity	____	____	____	____
Aggressiveness	____	____	____	____
Analytical ability	____	____	____	____
Communications skill	____	____	____	____
Ability to work with others	____	____	____	____
Other _____	____	____	____	____

9. *(If you recruit directly from campus)* Please indicate the importance of the following traits of a product manager candidate.

	(please check)			
	Not Important	*Desirable*	*Very Desirable*	*Essential*
Business experience	____	____	____	____
High grade-point avg.	____	____	____	____
Extracurricular activities	____	____	____	____
MBA	____	____	____	____
Master's, technical	____	____	____	____
Bachelor's, technical	____	____	____	____
Bachelor's, business	____	____	____	____
Other (specify) _____	____	____	____	____

10. If you recruit into your PM group from other jobs (either from your company or other companies), please indicate the importance of the following experiences.

Experience	(please check)			
	Not Important	*Desirable*	*Very Desirable*	*Essential*
Sales	____	____	____	____
Other product manager programs	____	____	____	____
Other marketing positions	____	____	____	____
Production	____	____	____	____

Exhibit   D–3   *(concluded)*

Ad agencies   ____   ____   ____   ____
Undergraduate degree   ____   ____   ____   ____
Graduate degree   ____   ____   ____   ____
Other (specify)   ____   ____   ____   ____

11. Please indicate the percentage of time a typical product manager spends in the following activities:

Advertising   _____ %
Pricing   _____
Distribution   _____
Packaging   _____
Product Development   _____
Marketing Research   _____
Production Liaison   _____
Finance and Budgeting   _____
Other (specify) _____ _____
Other (specify) _____ _____
        Total _____   100%

12. Please indicate which of the following criteria are used in evaluating product managers in your company/division.

a. _____ Market share

    _____ Return on investment

    _____ Sales volume

    _____ Dollar profits

    _____ Other (please specify) _____

b. Which one is most important? _____

13. Does your company/division have a structured training program for product managers?
yes _____   no _____ (If yes, please describe.)

    _____
    _____
    _____

14. Is your company/division currently planning any revision in its product manager system?
yes _____   no _____ (If yes, please describe.)

    _____
    _____
    _____

15. Judging from your company's experience, what do you feel is the major problem facing the product management system?

    _____
    _____
    _____

16. It would be most valuable to our studies if you could supply a sample job description of your product manager positions.
Are such available?
_____ Yes, examples enclosed
_____ Yes, examples sent under separate cover
_____ Not available

Thank you for your assistance.

17. If you would like a summary of the results of this survey, please check here. _____

NONPARAMETRIC SIGNIFICANCE TESTS

This appendix contains additional nonparametric tests of hypotheses to augment those described in Chapter 16 (see Figure 16–5).

ONE-SAMPLE CASE

Kolmogorov-Smirnov Test

This test is appropriate when the data are at least ordinal and the research situation calls for a comparison of an observed sample distribution with a theoretical distribution. Under these conditions, the Kolmogorov-Smirnov (KS) one-sample test is more powerful than the χ^2 test and can be used for small samples when the χ^2 test cannot. The KS is a test of goodness of fit in which we specify the *cumulative* frequency distribution that would occur under the theoretical distribution and compare that with the observed cumulative frequency distribution. The theoretical distribution represents our expectations under H_0. We determine the point of greatest divergence between the observed and theoretical distributions and identify this value as D (maximum deviation). From a table of critical values for D, we determine whether such a large divergence is likely on the basis of random sampling variations from the theoretical distribution. The value for D is calculated as follows:

$$D = \text{maximum} \, | F_O(X) - F_T(X)|$$

in which

$F_O(X)$ = The observed cumulative frequency distribution of a random sample of n observations. Where X is any possible score, $F_O(X) = k/n$, where k = the number of observations equal to or less than X.

$F_T(X)$ = The theoretical frequency distribution under H_0.

We illustrate the KS test, with an analysis of the results of the dining club study, in terms of various class levels. Take an equal number of interviews from each class, but secure unequal numbers of people interested in joining. Assume class levels are ordinal measurements. The testing process is as follows (see accompanying table):

1. *Null hypothesis.* H_0: There is no difference among student classes as to their intention of joining the dining club.

   H_A: There is a difference among students in various classes as to their intention of joining the dining club.

2. *Statistical test.* Choose the KS one-sample test because the data are ordinal measures and we are interested in comparing an observed distribution with a theoretical one.

3. *Significance level.* $\alpha = .05$, $n = 60$.

4. *Calculated value.* $D = \text{maximum} \, |F_O(X) - F_T(X)|$.

	Freshman	Sophomore	Junior	Senior	Graduate
Number in each class	5	9	11	16	19
$F_O(X)$	5/60	14/60	25/60	41/60	60/60
$F_T(X)$	12/60	24/60	36/60	48/60	60/60
$|F_O(X) - F_T(X)|$	7/60	10/60	11/60	7/60	0

$D = 11/60 = .183$;
$n = 60$

5. *Critical test value.* We enter the table of critical values of *D* in the KS one-sample test (see Appendix Table F–5) and learn that with $\alpha = .05$ the critical value for *D* is

$$D = \frac{1.36}{\sqrt{60}} = .175$$

6. *Decision.* The calculated value is greater than the critical value, indicating we should reject the null hypothesis.

TWO-SAMPLES CASE

Sign Test

The sign test is used with matched pairs when the only information is the identification of the pair member that is larger or smaller or has more or less of some characteristic. Under H_0, one would expect the number of cases in which $X_A > X_B$ to equal the number of pairs in which $X_B > X_A$. All ties are dropped from the analysis, and *n* is adjusted to allow for these eliminated pairs. This test is based on the binomial expansion and has a good power efficiency for small samples.

Wilcoxon Matched-Pairs Test

When you can determine both *direction* and *magnitude* of difference between carefully matched pairs, use the Wilcoxon matched-pairs test. This test has excellent efficiency and can be more powerful than the *t* test in cases where the latter is not particularly appropriate. The mechanics of calculation are also quite simple. Find the difference score (d_i) between each pair of values, and rank-order the differences from smallest to largest without regard to sign. The actual signs of each difference are then added to the rank values, and the test statistic *T* is calculated. *T* is the sum of the ranks with the less frequent sign. Typical of such research situations might be a study where husband and wife are matched, where twins are used, where a given subject is used in a before-after study, or where the outputs of two similar machines are compared.

Two types of ties may occur with this test. When two observations are equal, the *d* score becomes zero, and we drop this pair of observations from the calculation. When two or more pairs have the same *d* value, we average their rank positions. For example, if two pairs have a rank score of 1, we assign the rank of 1.5 to each and rank the next largest difference as third. When $n < 25$, use the table of critical values (see Appendix Table F–4). When $n > 25$, the sampling distribution of *T* is approximately normal with

$$\text{Mean} = \mu_T = \frac{n(n+1)}{4}$$

$$\text{Standard deviation} = \sigma_T = \sqrt{\frac{n(n+1)(2n+1)}{24}}$$

The formula for the test is

$$z = \frac{T - \mu_T}{\sigma_T}$$

Suppose you conduct an experiment on the effect of brand name on quality perception. Ten subjects are recruited and asked to taste and compare two samples of product, one identified as a well-known drink and the other as a new product being tested. In truth, however, the samples are identical. The subjects are then asked to rate the two samples on a set of scale items judged to be ordinal. Test these results for significance by the usual procedure.

1. *Null hypothesis.* H_0: There is no difference between the perceived qualities of the two samples.

    H_A: There is a difference in the perceived quality of the two samples.

2. *Statistical test.* The Wilcoxon matched-pairs test is used because the study is of related samples in which the differences can be ranked in magnitude.

3. *Significance level.* $\alpha = .05$, with $n = 10$ pairs of comparisons minus any pairs with a d of zero.

4. *Calculated value. T* equals the sum of the ranks with the less frequent sign. Assume we secure the following results:

Pair	Branded	Unbranded	d_i	Rank of d_i	Rank with Less Frequent Sign
1	52	48	4	4	
2	37	32	5	5.5*	
3	50	52	−2	−2	2
4	45	32	13	9	
5	56	59	−3	−3	3
6	51	50	1	1	
7	40	29	11	8	
8	59	54	5	5.5*	
9	38	38	0	*	
10	40	32	8	7	$T = 5$

*There are two types of tie situations. We drop out the pair with the type of tie shown by pair 9. Pairs 2 and 8 have a tie in rank of difference. In this case, we average the ranks and assign the average value to each.

5. *Critical test value.* Enter the table of critical values of *T* with $n = 9$ (see Appendix Table F–4) and find that the critical value with $\alpha = .05$ is 6. Note that with this test, the calculated value must be smaller than the critical value to reject the null hypothesis.

6. *Decision.* Since the calculated value is less than the critical value, reject the null hypothesis.

Kolmogorov-Smirnov Two-Samples Test

When a researcher has two independent samples of ordinal data, the Kolmogorov-Smirnov (KS) two-samples test is useful. Like the one-sample test, this two-samples test is concerned with the agreement between two cumulative distributions, but both represent sample values. If the two samples have been drawn from the same population, the cumulative distributions of the samples should be fairly close to each other, showing only random deviations from the population distribution. If the cumulative distributions show a large enough maximum deviation D, it is evidence for rejecting the H_0. To secure the maximum deviation, one should use as many intervals as are available so as not to obscure the maximum cumulative difference.

The two-samples KS formula is

$$D = \text{maximum } |F_{N1}(X) - F_{N2}(X)| \text{ (two-tailed test)}$$

$$D = \text{maximum } |F_{N1}(X) - F_{N2}(X)| \text{ (one-tailed test)}$$

D is calculated in the same manner as before, but the table for critical values for the numerator of D, K_D (two-samples case) is presented in Appendix Table F–6 when $n_1 = n_2$ and is less than 40 observations. When n_1 and/or n_2 are larger than 40, D from Appendix Table F–7 should be used. With this larger sample, it is not necessary that $n_1 = n_2$.

Here we use a different sample from the smoking-accident study. (To make $n_1 = n_2$, we increased the sample size of no accidents to 34. Nonsmokers with no accidents is 24.) Suppose the smoking classifications represent an ordinal scale, and you test these data with the KS two-samples test. Proceed as follows:

1. *Null hypothesis. H_0:* There is no difference in on-the-job accident occurrences between smokers and nonsmokers.

   H_A: The more a person smokes, the more likely that person is to have an on-the-job accident.

2. *Statistical test.* The KS two-samples test is used because it is assumed the data are ordinal.

3. *Significance level.* $\alpha = .05$. $n_1 = n_2 = 34$.

4. *Calculated value.* See One-Sample calculation and compare with table below.

5. *Critical test value.* We enter Appendix Table F–6 with $n = 34$ to find that $K_D = 11$ when $p \leq .05$ for a one-tailed distribution.

	Heavy Smoker	Moderate Smoker	Nonsmoker
$F_{n1}(X)$	12/34	21/34	34/34
$F_{n2}(X)$	4/34	10/34	34/34
$d_i = K_{D/n}$	8/34	11/34	0

6. *Decision.* Since the critical value equals the largest calculated value, we reject the null hypothesis.

Mann-Whitney U Test

This test is also used with two independent samples if the data are at least ordinal; it is an alternative to the t test without the latter's limiting assumptions. When the larger of the two samples is twenty or less, there are special tables for interpreting U; when the larger sample exceeds twenty, a normal curve approximation is used.

In calculating the U test, treat all observations in a combined fashion and rank them, algebraically, from smallest to largest. The largest negative score receives the lowest rank. In case of ties, assign the average rank as in other tests. With this test, you can also test samples that are unequal. After the ranking, the rank values for each sample are totaled. Compute the U statistic as follows:

$$U = n_1 n_2 + \frac{n_1(n_1 + 1)}{2} - R_1$$

or

$$U = n_1 n_2 + \frac{n_2(n_2 - 1)}{2} - R_2$$

in which

n_1 = Number in sample 1
n_2 = Number in sample 2
R_1 = Sum of ranks in sample 1

With this equation, you can secure two U values, one using R_1 and the second using R_2. For testing purposes, use the smaller U.

An example may help to clarify the U statistic calculation procedure. Let's consider the sales training example with the t distribution discussion. Recall that salespeople with training method A averaged higher sales than salespeople with training method B. While these data are ratio measures, one still might not want to accept the other assumptions that underlie the t test. What kind of a result could be secured with the U test? While the U test is designed for ordinal data, it can be used with interval and ratio measurements.

1. *Null hypothesis. H_0:* There is no difference in sales results produced by the two training methods.

   H_A: Training method A produces sales results superior to the results of method B.

2. *Statistical test.* The Mann-Whitney U test is chosen because the measurement is at least ordinal, and the assumptions under the parametric t test are rejected.

3. *Significance level.* $\alpha = .05$ (one-tailed test).

4. *Calculated value.*

Sales Per Week per Salesperson

Training Method A	Rank	Training Method B	Rank
1,500	15	1,340	10
1,540	16	1,300	8.5
1,860	22	1,620	18
1,230	6	1,070	3
1,370	12	1,210	5
1,550	17	1,170	4
1,840	21	1,770	20
1,250	7	950	1
1,300	8.5	1,380	13
1,350	11	1,460	14
1,710	19	1,030	2
	$R_1 = 154.5$		$R_2 = 98.5$

$$U = (11)(11) + \frac{11(11+1)}{2} - 154.5 = 32.5 \qquad U = (11)(11) + \frac{11(11+1)}{2} - 98.5 = 88.5$$

5. *Critical test value.* Enter Appendix Table F–8 with $n_1 = n_2 = 11$, and find a critical value of 34 for $\alpha = 0.5$, one-tailed test. Note that with this test, the calculated value must be smaller than the critical value to reject the null hypothesis.

6. *Decision.* Since the calculated value is smaller than the critical value $(34 > 32.5)$, reject the null hypothesis and conclude that training method A is probably superior.

Thus, one would reject the null hypothesis at $\alpha = .05$ in a one-tailed test using either the t or the U test. In this example, the U test has approximately the same power as the parametric test.

When $n > 20$ in one of the samples, the sampling distribution of U approaches the normal distribution with

$$\text{Mean} = \mu_U = \frac{n_1 n_2}{2}$$

$$\text{Standard deviation } \sigma_U = \sqrt{\frac{(n_1)(n_2)(n_1 + n_2 + 1)}{12}}$$

and

$$z = \frac{U - \mu_U}{\sigma_U}$$

Other Nonparametric Tests

Other tests are appropriate under certain conditions when testing two independent samples. When the measurement is only nominal, the Fisher exact probability test may be used. When the data are at least ordinal, use the median and Wald-Wolfowitz runs tests.

k-SAMPLES CASE

You can use tests more powerful than χ^2 with data that are at least ordinal in nature. One such test is an extension of the median test mentioned earlier. We illustrate here the application of a second ordinal measurement test known as the Kruskal-Wallis one-way analysis of variance.

Kruskal-Wallis Test

This is a generalized version of the Mann-Whitney test. With it we rank all scores in the entire pool of observations from smallest to largest. The rank sum of each sample is then calculated, with ties being distributed as in other examples. We then compute the value of H as follows:

$$H = \frac{12}{N(N-1)} \sum_{j=1}^{k} \frac{T_j^2}{n_j} - 3(N+1)$$

where

T_j = Sum of ranks in column j
n_j = Number of cases in jth sample
N = Σw_j = Total number of cases
k = Number of samples

When there are a number of ties, it is recommended that a correct factor *(C)* be calculated and used to correct the *H* value as follows:

$$C = 1 - \left\{ \dfrac{\displaystyle\sum_i^G \left(t_i^3 - t_i\right)}{N^2 - N} \right\}$$

where

> G = Number of sets of tied observations
> t_I = Number tied in any set i
> $H' = H/C$

To secure the critical value for *H'*, use the table for the distribution of χ^2 (see Appendix Table F–3), and enter it with the value of *H'* and d.f. = *k* – 1.

To illustrate the application of this test, use the price discount experiment problem. The data and calculations are shown in Exhibit E–1 and indicate that, by the Kruskal-Wallis test, one again barely fails to reject the null hypothesis with $\alpha = .05$.

EXHIBIT   E–1   **Kruskal-Wallis One-Way Analysis of Variance (price differentials)**

One Cent		Three Cents		Five Cents	
X_A	*Rank*	X_B	*Rank*	X_C	*Rank*
6	1	8	5	9	8.5
7	2.5	9	8.5	9	8.5
8	5	8	5	11	14
7	2.5	10	11.5	10	11.5
9	8.5	11	14	14	18
11	14	13	16.5	13	16.5
	$T_j = 33.5$		60.5		77.0

$T = 33.5 + 60.5 + 77$

    $= 171$

$$H = \frac{12}{18(18-1)} \left[\frac{33.5^2 + 60.5^2 + 77^2}{6} \right] - 3(18+1)$$

$$= \frac{12}{342} \left[\frac{1,122.25 + 3,660.25 + 5,929}{6} \right] - 57$$

$$= 0.0351 \left[\frac{10,711.5}{6} \right] - 57$$

$H = 5.66$

$$C = 1 - \left(\frac{3\left[(2)^3 - 2\right] + 2\left[(3)^3 - 3\right] + 4\left[(4)^3 - 4\right]}{18^3 + 18} \right)$$

$$= 1 - \frac{18 + 48 + 60}{5814}$$

$$= .978$$

$H' = \dfrac{H}{C} = \dfrac{5.66}{.978} = 5.79$

d.f. $= k - 1 = 2$

   $p > .05$

SELECTED STATISTICAL TABLES

 NAVIGATION

TABLE F–1 **Areas of the Standard Normal Distribution**

Second Decimal Place in z

z	0.00	0.01	0.02	0.03	0.04	0.05	0.06	0.07	0.08	0.09
0.0	0.0000	0.0040	0.0080	0.0120	0.0160	0.0199	0.0239	0.0279	0.0319	0.0359
0.1	0.0398	0.0438	0.0478	0.0517	0.0557	0.0596	0.0636	0.0675	0.0714	0.0753
0.2	0.0793	0.0832	0.0871	0.0910	0.0948	0.0987	0.1026	0.1064	0.1103	0.1141
0.3	0.1179	0.1217	0.1255	0.1293	0.1331	0.1368	0.1406	0.1443	0.1480	0.1517
0.4	0.1554	0.1591	0.1628	0.1664	0.1700	0.1736	0.1772	0.1808	0.1844	0.1879
0.5	0.1915	0.1950	0.1985	0.2019	0.2054	0.2088	0.2123	0.2157	0.2190	0.2224
0.6	0.2257	0.2291	0.2324	0.2357	0.2389	0.2422	0.2454	0.2486	0.2517	0.2549
0.7	0.2580	0.2611	0.2642	0.2673	0.2704	0.2734	0.2764	0.2794	0.2823	0.2852
0.8	0.2881	0.2910	0.2939	0.2967	0.2995	0.3023	0.3051	0.3078	0.3106	0.3133
0.9	0.3159	0.3186	0.3212	0.3238	0.3264	0.3289	0.3315	0.3340	0.3365	0.3389
1.0	0.3413	0.3438	0.3461	0.3485	0.3508	0.3531	0.3554	0.3577	0.3599	0.3621
1.1	0.3643	0.3665	0.3686	0.3708	0.3729	0.3749	0.3770	0.3790	0.3810	0.3830
1.2	0.3849	0.3869	0.3888	0.3907	0.3925	0.3944	0.3962	0.3980	0.3997	0.4015
1.3	0.4032	0.4049	0.4066	0.4082	0.4099	0.4115	0.4131	0.4147	0.4162	0.4177
1.4	0.4192	0.4207	0.4222	0.4236	0.4251	0.4265	0.4279	0.4292	0.4306	0.4319
1.5	0.4332	0.4345	0.4357	0.4370	0.4382	0.4394	0.4406	0.4418	0.4429	0.4441
1.6	0.4452	0.4463	0.4474	0.4484	0.4495	0.4505	0.4515	0.4525	0.4535	0.4545
1.7	0.4554	0.4564	0.4573	0.4582	0.4591	0.4599	0.4608	0.4616	0.4625	0.4633
1.8	0.4641	0.4649	0.4656	0.4664	0.4671	0.4678	0.4686	0.4693	0.4699	0.4706
1.9	0.4713	0.4719	0.4726	0.4732	0.4738	0.4744	0.4750	0.4756	0.4761	0.4767
2.0	0.4772	0.4778	0.4783	0.4788	0.4793	0.4798	0.4803	0.4808	0.4812	0.4817
2.1	0.4821	0.4826	0.4830	0.4834	0.4838	0.4842	0.4846	0.4850	0.4854	0.4857
2.2	0.4861	0.4864	0.4868	0.4871	0.4875	0.4878	0.4881	0.4884	0.4887	0.4890
2.3	0.4893	0.4896	0.4898	0.4901	0.4904	0.4906	0.4909	0.4911	0.4913	0.4916
2.4	0.4918	0.4920	0.4922	0.4925	0.4927	0.4929	0.4931	0.4932	0.4934	0.4936
2.5	0.4938	0.4940	0.4941	0.4943	0.4945	0.4946	0.4948	0.4949	0.4951	0.4952
2.6	0.4953	0.4955	0.4956	0.4957	0.4959	0.4960	0.4961	0.4962	0.4963	0.4964
2.7	0.4965	0.4966	0.4967	0.4968	0.4969	0.4970	0.4971	0.4972	0.4973	0.4974
2.8	0.4974	0.4975	0.4976	0.4977	0.4977	0.4978	0.4979	0.4979	0.4980	0.4981
2.9	0.4981	0.4982	0.4982	0.4983	0.4984	0.4984	0.4985	0.4985	0.4986	0.4986
3.0	0.4987	0.4987	0.4987	0.4988	0.4988	0.4989	0.4989	0.4989	0.4990	0.4990
3.1	0.4990	0.4991	0.4991	0.4991	0.4992	0.4992	0.4992	0.4992	0.4993	0.4993
3.2	0.4993	0.4993	0.4994	0.4994	0.4994	0.4994	0.4994	0.4995	0.4995	0.4995
3.3	0.4995	0.4995	0.4995	0.4996	0.4996	0.4996	0.4996	0.4996	0.4996	0.4997
3.4	0.4997	0.4997	0.4997	0.4997	0.4997	0.4997	0.4997	0.4997	0.4997	0.4998
3.5	0.4998									
4.0	0.49997									
4.5	0.499997									
5.0	0.4999997									
6.0	0.499999999									

TABLE F–2 Critical Values of *t* for Given Probability Levels

	Level of Significance for One-Tailed Test					
	.10	.05	.025	.01	.005	.0005
	Level of Significance for Two-Tailed Test					
d.f.	.20	.10	.05	.02	.01	.001
1	3.078	6.314	12.706	31.821	63.657	636.619
2	1.886	2.920	4.303	6.965	9.925	31.598
3	1.638	2.353	3.182	4.541	5.841	12.941
4	1.533	2.132	2.776	3.747	4.604	8.610
5	1.476	2.015	2.571	3.365	4.032	6.859
6	1.440	1.943	2.447	3.143	3.707	5.959
7	1.415	1.895	2.365	2.998	3.499	5.405
8	1.397	1.860	2.306	2.896	3.355	5.041
9	1.383	1.833	2.262	2.821	3.250	4.781
10	1.372	1.812	2.228	2.764	3.169	4.587
11	1.363	1.796	2.201	2.718	3.106	4.437
12	1.356	1.782	2.179	2.681	3.055	4.318
13	1.350	1.771	2.160	2.650	3.012	4.221
14	1.345	1.761	2.145	2.624	2.977	4.140
15	1.341	1.753	2.131	2.602	2.947	4.073
16	1.337	1.746	2.120	2.583	2.921	4.015
17	1.333	1.740	2.110	2.567	2.898	3.965
18	1.330	1.734	2.101	2.552	2.878	3.922
19	1.328	1.729	2.093	2.539	2.861	3.883
20	1.325	1.725	2.086	2.528	2.845	3.850
21	1.323	1.721	2.080	2.518	2.831	3.819
22	1.321	1.717	2.074	2.508	2.819	3.792
23	1.319	1.714	2.069	2.500	2.807	3.767
24	1.318	1.711	2.064	2.492	2.797	3.745
25	1.316	1.708	2.060	2.485	2.787	3.725
26	1.315	1.706	2.056	2.479	2.779	3.707
27	1.314	1.703	2.052	2.473	2.771	3.690
28	1.313	1.701	2.048	2.467	2.763	3.674
29	1.311	1.699	2.045	2.462	2.756	3.659
30	1.310	1.697	2.042	2.457	2.750	3.646
40	1.303	1.684	2.021	2.423	2.704	3.551
60	1.296	1.671	2.000	2.390	2.660	3.460
120	1.289	1.658	1.980	2.358	2.617	3.373
∞	1.282	1.645	1.960	2.326	2.576	3.291

SOURCE: Abridged from Table III of Fisher and Yates. *Statistical Tables for Biological, Agricultural, and Medical Research,* 6th ed., published by Oliver and Boyd Ltd., Edinburgh, 1963. By permission of the publishers.

TABLE   F–3   **Critical Values of the Chi-Square Distribution**

0   Critical
                                            value

Probability Under H_0 that $\chi^2 \geq$ Chi Square

d.f.	*.10*	*.05*	*.02*	*.01*	*.001*
1	2.71	3.84	5.41	6.64	10.83
2	4.60	5.99	7.82	9.21	13.82
3	6.25	7.82	9.84	11.34	16.27
4	7.78	9.49	11.67	13.28	18.46
5	9.24	11.07	13.39	15.09	20.52
6	10.64	12.59	15.03	16.81	22.46
7	12.02	14.07	16.62	18.48	24.32
8	13.36	15.51	18.17	20.09	26.12
9	14.68	16.92	19.68	21.67	27.88
10	15.99	18.31	21.16	23.21	29.59
11	17.28	19.68	22.62	24.72	31.26
12	18.55	21.03	24.05	26.22	32.91
13	19.81	22.36	25.47	27.69	34.53
14	21.06	23.68	26.87	29.14	36.12
15	22.31	25.00	28.26	30.58	37.70
16	23.54	26.30	29.63	32.00	39.29
17	24.77	27.59	31.00	33.41	40.75
18	25.99	28.87	32.35	34.80	42.31
19	27.20	30.14	33.69	36.19	43.82
20	28.41	31.41	35.02	37.57	45.32
21	29.62	32.67	36.34	38.93	46.80
22	30.81	33.92	37.66	40.29	48.27
23	32.01	35.17	38.97	41.64	49.73
24	33.20	36.42	40.27	42.98	51.18
25	34.38	37.65	41.57	44.31	52.62
26	35.56	38.88	42.86	45.64	54.05
27	36.74	40.11	44.14	46.96	55.48
28	37.92	41.34	45.42	48.28	56.89
29	39.09	42.56	46.69	49.59	58.30
30	40.26	43.77	47.96	50.89	59.70

SOURCE: Abridged from Table IV of Fisher and Yates, *Statistical Tables for Biological, Agricultural, and Medical Research,* 6th ed., published by Oliver and Boyd Ltd., Edinburgh, 1963. By permission of the publishers.

TABLE F—4   Critical Values of *T* in the Wilcoxon Matched-Pairs Test

	Level of Significance for One-Tailed Test		
	.025	.01	.005
N	Level of Significance for Two-Tailed Test		
	.05	.02	.01
6	0	—	—
7	2	0	—
8	4	2	0
9	6	3	2
10	8	5	3
11	11	7	5
12	14	10	7
13	17	13	10
14	21	16	13
15	25	20	16
16	30	24	20
17	35	28	23
18	40	33	28
19	46	38	32
20	52	43	38
21	59	49	43
22	66	56	49
23	73	62	55
24	81	69	61
25	89	77	68

SOURCE: Adapted from Table 1 of F. Wilcoxon, *Some Rapid Approximate Statistical Procedures* (New York: American Cyanamid Company, 1949), p. 13, with the kind permission of the publisher.

TABLE F–5 **Critical Values of *D* in the Kolmogorov-Smirnov One-Sample Test**

Sample Size *N*	Level of Significance for D = Maximum $|F_0(X) - S_N(X)|$				
	.20	*.15*	*.10*	*.05*	*.01*
1	.900	.925	.950	.975	.995
2	.684	.726	.776	.842	.929
3	.565	.597	.642	.708	.828
4	.494	.525	.564	.624	.733
5	.446	.474	.510	.565	.669
6	.410	.436	.470	.521	.618
7	.381	.405	.438	.486	.577
8	.358	.381	.411	.457	.543
9	.339	.360	.388	.432	.514
10	.322	.342	.368	.410	.490
11	.307	.326	.352	.391	.468
12	.295	.313	.338	.375	.450
13	.284	.302	.325	.361	.433
14	.274	.292	.314	.349	.418
15	.266	.283	.304	.338	.404
16	.258	.274	.295	.328	.392
17	.250	.266	.286	.318	.381
18	.244	.259	.278	.309	.371
19	.237	.252	.272	.301	.363
20	.231	.246	.264	.294	.356
25	.21	.22	.24	.27	.32
30	.19	.20	.22	.24	.29
35	.18	.19	.21	.23	.27
Over 35	$\dfrac{1.07}{\sqrt{N}}$	$\dfrac{1.14}{\sqrt{N}}$	$\dfrac{1.22}{\sqrt{N}}$	$\dfrac{1.36}{\sqrt{N}}$	$\dfrac{1.63}{\sqrt{N}}$

SOURCE: F. J. Massey, Jr., "The Kolmogorov-Smirnov Test for Goodness of Fit," *Journal of the American Statistical Association* 46, p. 70. Adapted with the kind permission of the publisher.

TABLE F–6 Critical Values of K_D in the Kolmogorov-Smirnov Two-Samples Test (small samples)

	One-Tailed Test*		Two-Tailed Test[†]	
N	$\alpha = .05$	$\alpha = .01$	$\alpha = .05$	$\alpha = .01$
3	3	—	—	—
4	4	—	4	—
5	4	5	5	5
6	5	6	5	6
7	5	6	6	6
8	5	6	6	7
9	6	7	6	7
10	6	7	7	8
11	6	8	7	8
12	6	8	7	8
13	7	8	7	9
14	7	8	8	9
15	7	9	8	9
16	7	9	8	10
17	8	9	8	10
18	8	10	9	10
19	8	10	9	10
20	8	10	9	11
21	8	10	9	11
22	9	11	9	11
23	9	11	10	11
24	9	11	10	12
25	9	11	10	12
26	9	11	10	12
27	9	12	10	12
28	10	12	11	13
29	10	12	11	13
30	10	12	11	13
35	11	13	12	
40	11	14	13	

*SOURCE: Abridged from I. A. Goodman, "Kolmogorov-Smirnov Tests for Psychological Research," *Psychological Bulletin* 51 (1951), p. 167, copyright (1951) by the American Psychological Association. Reprinted by permission.

†SOURCE: Derived from Table 1 of F. J. Massey, Jr., "The Distribution of the Maximum Deviation Between Two Sample Cumulative Step Functions," *Annals of Mathematical Statistics* 23 (1951), pp. 126–27, with the kind permission of the publisher.

TABLE   F–7   Critical Values of *D* in the Kolmogorov-Smirnov Two-Samples Test for Large Samples (two-tailed)

Level of Significance	Value of D So Large as to Call for Rejection of H_0 at the Indicated Level of Significance, Where $D = Maximum \ |S_{n_1}(X) - S_2(X)|$
.10	$1.22\sqrt{\dfrac{n_1 + n_2}{n_1 n_2}}$
.05	$1.36\sqrt{\dfrac{n_1 + n_2}{n_1 n_2}}$
.025	$1.48\sqrt{\dfrac{n_1 + n_2}{n_1 n_2}}$
.01	$1.63\sqrt{\dfrac{n_1 + n_2}{n_1 n_2}}$
.005	$1.73\sqrt{\dfrac{n_1 + n_2}{n_1 n_2}}$
.001	$1.95\sqrt{\dfrac{n_1 + n_2}{n_1 n_2}}$

SOURCE: Adapted from N. Smirnov, "Table for Estimating the Goodness of Fit of Empirical Distribution," *Annals of Mathematical Statistics* 18 (1948), pp. 280–81, with the kind permission of the publisher.

TABLE F–8 Partial Table of Critical Values of *U* in the Mann-Whitney Test

Critical Values for One-Tailed Test at α = .025 or a Two-Tailed Test at α = .05

n_1\n_2	9	10	11	12	13	14	15	16	17	18	19	20
1												
2	0	0	0	1	1	1	1	1	2	2	2	2
3	2	3	3	4	4	5	5	6	6	7	7	8
4	4	5	6	7	8	9	10	11	11	12	13	13
5	7	8	9	11	12	13	14	15	17	18	19	20
6	10	11	13	14	16	17	19	21	22	24	25	27
7	12	14	16	18	20	22	24	26	28	30	32	34
8	15	17	19	22	24	26	29	31	34	36	38	41
9	17	20	23	26	28	31	34	37	39	42	45	48
10	20	23	26	29	33	36	39	42	45	48	52	55
11	23	26	30	33	37	40	44	47	51	55	58	62
12	26	29	33	37	41	45	49	53	57	61	66	69
13	28	33	37	41	45	50	54	59	63	67	72	76
14	31	36	40	45	50	55	59	64	67	74	78	83
15	34	39	44	49	54	59	64	70	75	80	85	90
16	37	42	47	53	59	64	70	75	81	86	92	98
17	39	45	51	57	63	67	75	81	87	93	99	105
18	42	48	55	61	67	74	80	86	93	99	106	112
19	45	52	58	65	72	78	85	92	99	106	113	119
20	48	55	62	69	76	83	90	98	105	112	119	127

Critical Values for One-Tailed Test at α = .05 or a Two-Tailed Test at α = .10

n_2\n_1	9	10	11	12	13	14	15	16	17	18	19	20
1											0	0
2	1	1	1	2	2	2	3	3	3	4	4	4
3	3	4	5	5	6	7	7	8	9	9	10	11
4	6	7	8	9	10	11	12	14	15	16	17	18
5	9	11	12	13	15	16	18	19	20	22	23	25
6	12	14	16	17	19	21	23	25	26	28	30	32
7	15	17	19	21	24	26	28	30	33	35	37	39
8	18	20	23	26	28	31	33	36	39	41	44	47
9	21	24	27	30	33	36	39	42	45	48	51	54
10	24	27	31	34	37	41	44	48	51	55	58	62
11	27	31	34	38	42	46	50	54	57	61	65	69
12	30	34	38	42	47	51	55	60	64	68	72	77
13	33	37	42	47	51	56	61	65	70	75	80	84
14	36	41	46	51	56	61	66	71	77	82	87	92
15	39	44	50	55	61	66	72	77	83	88	94	100
16	42	48	54	60	65	71	77	83	89	95	101	107
17	45	51	57	64	70	77	83	89	96	102	109	115
18	48	55	61	68	75	82	88	95	102	109	116	123
19	51	58	65	72	80	87	94	101	109	116	123	130
20	54	62	69	77	84	92	100	107	115	123	130	138

SOURCE: Abridged from D. Auble, "Extended Tables from the Mann-Whitney Statistic," *Bulletin of the Institute of Educational Research at Indiana University 1, no. 2,* reprinted with permission. For tables for other size samples consult this source.

TABLE   F–9   Critical Values of the *F* Distribution for $\alpha = .05$

Degrees of Freedom for Numerator

n_2	1	2	3	4	5	6	7	8	9	10	12	15	20	24	30	40	60	120	∞
1	161.4	199.5	215.7	224.6	230.2	234.0	236.8	238.9	240.5	241.9	243.9	245.9	248.0	249.1	250.1	251.1	252.2	253.3	243.3
2	18.51	19.00	19.16	19.25	19.30	19.33	19.35	19.37	19.38	19.40	19.41	19.43	19.45	19.45	19.46	19.47	19.48	19.49	19.50
3	10.13	9.55	9.28	9.12	9.01	8.94	8.89	8.85	8.81	8.79	8.74	8.70	8.66	8.64	8.62	8.59	8.57	8.55	8.53
4	7.71	6.94	6.59	6.39	6.26	6.16	6.09	6.04	6.00	5.96	5.91	5.86	5.80	5.77	5.75	5.72	5.69	5.66	5.63
5	6.61	5.79	5.41	5.19	5.05	4.95	4.88	4.82	4.77	4.74	4.68	4.62	4.56	4.53	4.50	4.46	4.43	4.40	4.36
6	5.99	5.14	4.76	4.53	4.39	4.28	4.21	4.15	4.10	4.06	4.00	3.94	3.87	3.84	3.81	3.77	3.74	3.70	3.67
7	5.59	4.74	4.35	4.12	3.97	3.87	3.79	3.73	3.68	3.64	3.57	3.51	3.44	3.41	3.38	3.34	3.30	3.27	3.23
8	5.32	4.46	4.07	3.84	3.69	3.58	3.50	3.44	3.39	3.35	3.28	3.22	3.15	3.12	3.08	3.04	3.01	2.97	2.93
9	5.12	4.26	3.86	3.63	3.48	3.37	3.29	3.23	3.18	3.14	3.07	3.01	2.94	2.90	2.86	2.83	2.79	2.75	2.71
10	4.96	4.10	3.71	3.48	3.33	3.22	3.14	3.07	3.02	2.98	2.91	2.85	2.77	2.74	2.70	2.66	2.62	2.58	2.54
11	4.84	3.98	3.59	3.36	3.20	3.09	3.01	2.95	2.90	2.85	2.79	2.72	2.65	2.61	2.57	2.53	2.49	2.45	2.40
12	4.75	3.89	3.49	3.26	3.11	3.00	2.91	2.85	2.80	2.75	2.69	2.62	2.54	2.51	2.47	2.43	2.38	2.34	2.30
13	4.67	3.81	3.41	3.18	3.03	2.92	2.83	2.77	2.71	2.67	2.60	2.53	2.46	2.42	2.38	2.34	2.30	2.25	2.21
14	4.60	3.74	3.34	3.11	2.96	2.85	2.76	2.70	2.65	2.60	2.53	2.46	2.39	2.35	2.31	2.27	2.22	2.18	2.13
15	4.54	3.68	3.29	3.06	2.90	2.79	2.71	2.64	2.59	2.54	2.48	2.40	2.33	2.29	2.25	2.20	2.16	2.11	2.07
16	4.49	3.63	3.24	3.01	2.85	2.74	2.66	2.59	2.54	2.49	2.42	2.35	2.28	2.24	2.19	2.15	2.11	2.06	2.01
17	4.45	3.59	3.20	2.96	2.81	2.70	2.61	2.55	2.49	2.45	2.38	2.31	2.23	2.19	2.15	2.10	2.06	2.01	1.96
18	4.41	3.55	3.16	2.93	2.77	2.66	2.58	2.51	2.46	2.41	2.34	2.27	2.19	2.15	2.11	2.06	2.02	1.97	1.92
19	4.38	3.52	3.13	2.90	2.74	2.63	2.54	2.48	2.42	2.38	2.31	2.23	2.16	2.11	2.07	2.03	1.98	1.93	1.88
20	4.35	3.49	3.10	2.87	2.71	2.60	2.51	2.45	2.39	2.35	2.28	2.20	2.12	2.08	2.04	1.99	1.95	1.90	1.84
21	4.32	3.47	3.07	2.84	2.68	2.57	2.49	2.42	2.37	2.32	2.25	2.18	2.10	2.05	2.01	1.96	1.92	1.87	1.81
22	4.30	3.44	3.05	2.82	2.66	2.55	2.46	2.40	2.34	2.30	2.23	2.15	2.07	2.03	1.98	1.94	1.89	1.84	1.78
23	4.28	3.42	3.03	2.80	2.64	2.53	2.44	2.37	2.32	2.27	2.20	2.13	2.05	2.01	1.96	1.91	1.86	1.81	1.76
24	4.26	3.40	3.01	2.78	2.62	2.51	2.42	2.36	2.30	2.25	2.18	2.11	2.03	1.98	1.94	1.89	1.84	1.79	1.73
25	4.24	3.39	2.99	2.76	2.60	2.49	2.40	2.34	2.28	2.24	2.16	2.09	2.01	1.96	1.92	1.87	1.82	1.77	1.71
26	4.23	3.37	2.98	2.74	2.59	2.47	2.39	2.32	2.27	2.22	2.15	2.07	1.99	1.95	1.90	1.85	1.80	1.75	1.69
27	4.21	3.35	2.96	2.73	2.57	2.46	2.37	2.31	2.25	2.20	2.13	2.06	1.97	1.93	1.88	1.84	1.79	1.73	1.67
28	4.20	3.34	2.95	2.71	2.56	2.45	2.36	2.29	2.24	2.19	2.12	2.04	1.96	1.91	1.87	1.82	1.77	1.71	1.65
29	4.18	3.33	2.93	2.70	2.55	2.43	2.35	2.28	2.22	2.18	2.10	2.03	1.94	1.90	1.85	1.81	1.75	1.70	1.64
30	4.17	3.32	2.92	2.69	2.53	2.42	2.33	2.27	2.21	2.16	2.09	2.01	1.93	1.89	1.84	1.79	1.74	1.68	1.62
40	4.08	3.23	2.84	2.61	2.45	2.34	2.25	2.18	2.12	2.08	2.00	1.92	1.84	1.79	1.74	1.69	1.64	1.58	1.51
60	4.00	3.15	2.76	2.53	2.37	2.25	2.17	2.10	2.04	1.99	1.92	1.84	1.75	1.70	1.65	1.59	1.53	1.47	1.39
120	3.92	3.07	2.68	2.45	2.29	2.17	2.09	2.02	1.96	1.91	1.83	1.75	1.66	1.61	1.55	1.50	1.43	1.35	1.25
∞	3.84	3.00	2.60	2.37	2.21	2.10	2.01	1.94	1.88	1.83	1.75	1.67	1.57	1.52	1.46	1.39	1.32	1.22	1.00

Degrees of Freedom for Denominator

SOURCE: Reprinted by permission from *Statistical Methods* by George W. Snedecor and William G. Cochran, 6th edition, © 1967 by Iowa State University Press, Ames, Iowa.

TABLE F–10   Random Numbers

97446	30328	05262	77371	13523	62057	44349	85884	94555	23288
15453	75591	60540	77137	09485	27632	05477	99154	78720	10323
69995	77086	55217	53721	85713	27854	41981	88981	90041	20878
69726	58696	27272	38148	52521	73807	29685	49152	20309	58734
23604	31948	16926	26360	76957	99925	86045	11617	32777	38670
13640	17233	58650	47819	24935	28670	33415	77202	92492	40290
90779	09199	51169	94892	34271	22068	13923	53535	56358	50258
71068	19459	32339	10124	13012	79706	07611	52600	83088	26829
55019	79001	34442	16335	06428	52873	65316	01480	72204	39494
20879	50235	17389	25260	34039	99967	48044	05067	69284	53867
00380	11595	49372	95214	98529	46593	77046	27176	39668	20566
68142	40800	20527	79212	14166	84948	11748	69540	84288	37211
42667	89566	20440	57230	35356	01884	79921	94772	29882	24695
07756	78430	45576	86596	56720	65529	44211	18447	53921	92722
45221	31130	44312	63534	47741	02465	50629	94983	05984	88375
20140	77481	61686	82836	41058	41331	04290	61212	60294	95954
54922	25436	33804	51907	73223	66423	68706	36589	45267	35327
48340	30832	72209	07644	52747	40751	06808	85349	18005	52323
23603	84387	20416	88084	33103	41511	59391	71600	35091	52722
12548	01033	22974	59596	92087	02116	63524	00627	41778	24392
15251	87584	12942	03771	91413	75652	19468	83889	98531	91529
65548	59670	57355	18874	63601	55111	07278	32560	40028	36079
48488	76170	46282	76427	41693	04506	80979	26654	62159	83017
02862	15665	62159	15159	69576	20328	68873	28152	66087	39405
67929	06754	45842	66365	80848	15262	55144	37816	08421	30071
73237	07607	31615	04892	50989	87347	14393	21165	68169	70788
13788	20327	07960	95917	75112	01398	26381	41377	33549	19754
43877	66485	40825	45923	74410	69693	76959	70973	26343	63781
14047	08369	56414	78533	76378	44204	71493	68861	31042	81873
88383	46755	51342	13505	55324	52950	22244	28028	73486	98797
29567	16379	41994	65947	58926	50953	09388	00405	29874	44954
20508	60995	41539	26396	99825	25652	28089	57224	35222	58922
64178	76768	75747	32854	32893	61152	58565	33128	33354	16056
26373	51147	90362	93309	13175	66385	57822	31138	12893	68607
10083	47656	59241	73630	99200	94672	59785	95449	99279	25488
11683	14347	04369	98719	75005	43633	24125	30532	54830	95387
56548	76293	50904	88579	24621	94291	56881	35062	48765	22078
35292	47291	82610	27777	43965	31802	98444	88929	54383	93141
51329	87645	51623	08971	50704	82395	33916	95859	99788	97885
51860	19180	39324	68483	78650	74750	64893	58042	82878	20619
23886	01257	07945	71175	31243	87167	42829	44601	08769	26417
80028	82310	43989	09242	15056	48250	04529	96941	48190	69644
83946	46858	09164	18858	12672	55190	02820	45861	29104	75386
00000	41586	25972	25356	54260	95691	99431	89903	22306	43863
90615	12848	23376	29458	48239	37628	59265	50152	30340	40713
42003	10738	55835	48218	23204	19188	13556	06610	77667	88068
86135	26174	07834	17007	97938	96728	15689	77544	89186	41252
54436	10828	41212	19836	89476	53685	28085	22878	71868	35048
14545	72034	32131	38783	58588	47499	50945	97045	42357	53536
43925	49879	13339	78773	95626	67119	93023	96832	09757	98545

SOURCE: The Rand Corporation, *A Million Random Digits with 100,000 Normal Deviates* (Glencoe, IL: Free Press, 1955), p. 225.

Index